Distributed Computing Innovations for Business, Engineering, and Science

Alfred Waising Loo
Lingnan University, Hong Kong

A volume in the Advances in Systems
Analysis, Software Engineering, and High
Performance Computing (ASASEHPC)
Book Series

Information Science
REFERENCE
An Imprint of IGI Global

Managing Director:	Lindsay Johnston
Editorial Director:	Joel Gamon
Book Production Manager:	Jennifer Romanchak
Publishing Systems Analyst:	Adrienne Freeland
Development Editor:	Austin DeMarco
Assistant Acquisitions Editor:	Kayla Wolfe
Typesetter:	Deanna Jo Zombro
Cover Design:	Nick Newcomer

Published in the United States of America by
Information Science Reference (an imprint of IGI Global)
701 E. Chocolate Avenue
Hershey PA 17033
Tel: 717-533-8845
Fax: 717-533-8661
E-mail: cust@igi-global.com
Web site: http://www.igi-global.com

Library of Congress Cataloging-in-Publication Data

Distributed computing innovations for business, engineering, and science / Alfred Waising Loo, editor.
     pages cm
  Summary: "This book is a collection of widespread research providing relevant theoretical frameworks and research findings on the applications of distributed computing innovations to the business, engineering and science fields"-- Provided by publisher.
  Includes bibliographical references and index. ISBN 978-1-4666-2533-4 (hardcover) -- ISBN 978-1-4666-2534-1 (ebook) -- ISBN 978-1-4666-2535-8 (print & perpetual access) 1. Electronic data processing--Distributed processing. I. Loo, Alfred Wai-Sing, 1951- editor of compilation.
  QA76.9.D5D516 2013
  004'.36--dc23
                                     2012023339

This book is published in the IGI Global book series Advances in Systems Analysis, Software Engineering, and High Performance Computing (ASASEHPC) Book Series (ISSN: 2327-3453; eISSN: 2327-3461)

British Cataloguing in Publication Data
A Cataloguing in Publication record for this book is available from the British Library.

All work contributed to this book is new, previously-unpublished material. The views expressed in this book are those of the authors, but not necessarily of the publisher.

Advances in Systems Analysis, Software Engineering, and High Performance Computing (ASASEHPC) Book Series

Vijayan Sugumaran
Oakland University, USA

ISSN: 2327-3453
EISSN: 2327-3461

MISSION

The theory and practice of computing applications and distributed systems has emerged as one of the key areas of research driving innovations in business, engineering, and science. The fields of software engineering, systems analysis, and high performance computing offer a wide range of applications and solutions in solving computational problems for any modern organization.

The **Advances in Systems Analysis, Software Engineering, and High Performance Computing (ASASEHPC) Book Series** brings together research in the areas of distributed computing, systems and software engineering, high performance computing, and service science. This collection of publications is useful for academics, researchers, and practitioners seeking the latest practices and knowledge in this field.

COVERAGE

- Computer Graphics
- Computer Networking
- Computer System Analysis
- Distributed Cloud Computing
- Enterprise Information Systems
- Metadata and Semantic Web
- Parallel Architectures
- Performance Modeling
- Software Engineering
- Virtual Data Systems

IGI Global is currently accepting manuscripts for publication within this series. To submit a proposal for a volume in this series, please contact our Acquisition Editors at Acquisitions@igi-global.com or visit: http://www.igi-global.com/publish/.

Titles in this Series

For a list of additional titles in this series, please visit: www.igi-global.com

Service-Driven Approaches to Architecture and Enterprise Integration
Raja Ramanathan (Independent Researcher, USA) and Kirtana Raja (Independent Researcher, USA)
Information Science Reference • copyright 2013 • 367pp • H/C (ISBN: 9781466641938) • US $195.00 (our price)

Progressions and Innovations in Model-Driven Software Engineering
Vicente García Díaz (Universidad de Oviedo, Spain) Juan Manuel Cueva Lovelle (University of Oviedo, Spain) B. Cristina Pelayo García-Bustelo (University of Oviedo, Spain) and Oscar Sanjuan Martinez (University of Oviedo, Spain)
Engineering Science Reference • copyright 2013 • 352pp • H/C (ISBN: 9781466642171) • US $195.00 (our price)

Knowledge-Based Processes in Software Development
Saqib Saeed (Bahria University Islamabad, Pakistan) and Izzat Alsmadi (Yarmouk University, Jordan)
Information Science Reference • copyright 2013 • 318pp • H/C (ISBN: 9781466642294) • US $195.00 (our price)

Distributed Computing Innovations for Business, Engineering, and Science
Alfred Waising Loo (Lingnan University, Hong Kong)
Information Science Reference • copyright 2013 • 369pp • H/C (ISBN: 9781466625334) • US $195.00 (our price)

Data Intensive Distributed Computing Challenges and Solutions for Large-scale Information Management
Tevfik Kosar (University at Buffalo, USA)
Information Science Reference • copyright 2012 • 352pp • H/C (ISBN: 9781615209712) • US $180.00 (our price)

Achieving Real-Time in Distributed Computing From Grids to Clouds
Dimosthenis Kyriazis (National Technical University of Athens, Greece) Theodora Varvarigou (National Technical University of Athens, Greece) and Kleopatra G. Konstanteli (National Technical University of Athens, Greece)
Information Science Reference • copyright 2012 • 330pp • H/C (ISBN: 9781609608279) • US $195.00 (our price)

Principles and Applications of Distributed Event-Based Systems
Annika M. Hinze (University of Waikato, New Zealand) and Alejandro Buchmann (University of Waikato, New Zealand)
Information Science Reference • copyright 2010 • 538pp • H/C (ISBN: 9781605666976) • US $180.00 (our price)

DISSEMINATOR OF KNOWLEDGE

www.igi-global.com

701 E. Chocolate Ave., Hershey, PA 17033
Order online at www.igi-global.com or call 717-533-8845 x100
To place a standing order for titles released in this series, contact: cust@igi-global.com
Mon-Fri 8:00 am - 5:00 pm (est) or fax 24 hours a day 717-533-8661

Table of Contents

Detailed Table of Contents

Section 1
Algorithms and Infrastructures

Current advances in computer architectures have transformed clusters, traditional high performance distributed platforms, into hierarchical environments, where each node has multiple heterogeneous processing units including accelerators such as GPUs. Although parallel heterogeneous environments are becoming common, their efficient use is still an open problem. Current tools for development of parallel applications are mainly concerning with the exclusive use of accelerators, while it is argued that the adequate coordination of heterogeneous computing cores can significantly improve performance. The approach taken in this chapter to efficiently use such environments, which is experimented in the context of replicated dataflow applications, consists of scheduling processing tasks according to their characteristics and to the processors specificities. Thus, we can better utilize the available hardware as we try to execute each task into the best-suited processor for it. The proposed approach has been evaluated using two applications, for which there were previously available CPU-only and GPU-only implementations. The experimental results show that using both devices simultaneously can improve the performance significantly; moreover, the proposed method doubled the performance of a demand driven approach that utilizes both CPU and GPU, on the two applications in several scenarios.

The use of relay nodes to improve the performance of broadband wireless access (BWA) networks has been the subject of intense research activities in recent years. Relay enhanced BWA networks are anticipated to support diverse multimedia traffic (i.e., voice, video, and data traffic). In order to guarantee service to users, efficient network resource distribution is imperative. Wireless multihop networks are distinguished primarily from their wired counterparts through the presence of interference. Wireless interference greatly influences the ability of users to obtain the necessary resources for service. This chapter provides a comprehensive study on the topic of interference aware resource allocation by investigating the impact of interference on various aspects of resource allocation, ranging from fairness to spectrum utilization. In this regard, the focus of this chapter is to investigate the problem of traffic flow routing and fair bandwidth allocation under interference constraints for multihop BWA networks.

Lev Levitin, Boston University, USA

Mark Karpovsky, Boston University, USA

Mehmet Mustafa, Boston University, USA

The problem of preventing deadlocks and livelocks in computer communication networks with wormhole routing is considered. The method to prevent deadlocks is to prohibit certain turns (i.e., the use of certain pairs of connected edges) in the routing process, in such a way that eliminates all cycles in the graph. A new algorithm that constructs a minimal (irreducible) set of turns that breaks all cycles and preserves connectivity of the graph is proposed and analyzed. The algorithm is tree-free and is considerably simpler than earlier cycle-breaking algorithms. The properties of the algorithm are proven, and lower and upper bounds for minimum cardinalities of cycle-breaking connectivity preserving sets for graphs of general topology, as well as for planar graphs, are presented. In particular, the algorithm guarantees that not more than 1/3 of all turns in the network become prohibited. Experimental results are presented on the fraction of prohibited turns, the distance dilation, as well as on the message delivery times and saturation loads for the proposed algorithm in comparison with known tree-based algorithms. The proposed algorithm outperforms the tree-based algorithms in all characteristics that were considered.

Mark Karpovsky, Boston University, USA

Lev Levitin, Boston University, USA

Mehmet Mustafa, Boston University, USA

In this chapter, the problem of constructing minimal cycle-breaking connectivity preserving sets of turns for graphs that model regular or near regular multiprocessor systems, as a method to prevent deadlocks is investigated. Cycle-breaking provides for deadlock-free wormhole routing defined by turns prohibited at some nodes. The lower and upper bounds for minimal cardinalities of cycle-breaking connectivity preserving sets for several classes of graphs such as homogeneous meshes, p-ary n-cubes, cube-connected cycles, hexagonal and honeycomb meshes and tori, Hamiltonian graphs and others are obtained and presented along with some preliminary experimental results.

Shing-Tsaan Huang, National Central University, Taiwan

Chi-Hung Tzeng, National Tsing Hua University, Taiwan

Jehn-Ruey Jiang, National Central University, Taiwan

The concept of self-stabilization in distributed systems was introduced by Dijkstra in 1974. A system is said to be self-stabilizing if (1) it can converge in finite time to a legitimate state from any initial state, and (2) when it is in a legitimate state, it remains so henceforth. That is, a self-stabilizing system guarantees to converge to a legitimate state in finite time no matter what initial state it may start with; or, it can recover from transient faults automatically without any outside intervention. This chapter first introduces the self-stabilization concept in distributed computing. Next, it discusses the coloring problem on graphs and its applications in distributed computing. Then, it introduces three self-stabilizing algorithms. The first two are for vertex coloring and edge coloring on planar graphs, respectively. The last one is for edge coloring on bipartite graphs.

Chapter 6

The Web started as a means to navigate in hypermedia documents but has evolved to a pervasive Web of Services, raising distribution and interoperability problems. Web Services appeared as a solution but have grown to become a complex technology, leading many web application providers to adopt a much simpler architectural style, REST. Each style has advantages and disadvantages. As always, the trick is to learn from both sides and to use a flexible technology that can adapt and support both styles. This chapter establishes a model, based on resources, services, and processes, and discusses the various possible combinations, putting the current architectural styles into perspective. Based on this, this chapter proposes one single language to support several levels that are currently implemented in separate technologies: data (including schema, usually described in XML or JSON), interface (WSDL for Web Services and HTTP verbs for Restful applications), and behavior (usually done in BPEL or in a general programming language).

Chapter 7

Business collaboration is increasingly conducted over the Internet. Trading parties require business-level protocols for enabling their collaborative processes and a number of standardised languages, and approaches have been proposed for specifying business-level protocols. To illustrate the specification of web services based collaborative processes, three inter-related specification languages, namely, the ebXML Business Process Specification Schema (BPSS), the Web Service Business Process Execution Language (WSBPEL), and the Web Services Conversations Language (WSCL) are discussed in this chapter. A contract negotiation protocol is used as an example to illustrate the concepts involved in the specification. The chapter also discusses different strategies for deploying these specification languages.

Section 2
Cloud Computing

Chapter 8

Cloud Computing is a prevalent issue for organizations nowadays. Different service providers are starting to roll out their Cloud services to organizations in both commercial and industrial sectors. As for an enterprise, the basic value proposition of Cloud Computing includes but not limit to the outsourcing of the in-house computing infrastructure without capitalizing their investment to build and maintain these infrastructures. Challenges have never been ceased for striking a balance between Cloud deployment and the need to meet the continual rise in demand for computing resources. It becomes a strategic tool to increase the competitive advantage and to survival in the market for an enterprise. To reconcile this conflict, IT leaders must find a new IT operating model which can enhance business agility, scalability, and shifts away from traditional capital-intensive IT investments.

Chapter 9

This chapter explores the interface between virtualization and cloud computing for global enterprise mobility. It also investigates the potential both virtualization and cloud computing hold for global enterprises. In this context, it argues that the virtualization of computing operations, applications, and services and the consumerization of digital technologies serve as one of the key drivers of cloud computing. Against this backdrop, the chapter first provides an overview of virtualization, consumerization, and cloud computing. Second, it showcases real life instances in which five enterprises leverage virtualization and cloud computing as part of their cloud business solutions. Third, it outlines some of the hollows and pain points characterizing cloud computing. Fourth and last, the chapter briefly presents possible future trends likely to typify cloud computing.

Chapter 10

In recent years, so-called Infrastructure as a Service (IaaS) clouds have become increasingly popular as a flexible and inexpensive platform for ad-hoc parallel data processing. Major players in the cloud computing space like Amazon EC2 have already recognized this trend and started to create special offers which bundle their compute platform with existing software frameworks for these kinds of applications. However, the data processing frameworks which are currently used in these offers have been designed for static, homogeneous cluster systems and do not support the new features which distinguish the cloud platform. This chapter examines the characteristics of IaaS clouds with special regard to massively-parallel data processing. The author highlights use cases which are currently poorly supported by existing parallel data processing frameworks and explains how a tighter integration between the processing framework and the underlying cloud system can help to lower the monetary processing cost for the cloud customer. As a proof of concept, the author presents the parallel data processing framework Nephele, and compares its cost efficiency against the one of the well-known software Hadoop.

Section 3
Applications of Distributed Computing

There is a growing interest in the research and industry communities to examine the possible weaving of social elements into Web services-based applications. This interest is backed by the widespread adoption of Web 2.0 technologies and tools developed using various online means such as social networks and blogs. Social Web services incorporate the result of this weaving and are concerned with establishing relationships with their peers like people do daily. This chapter reviews the recent developments in this new topic and identifies new research opportunities and directions that are still unexplored such as security, engineering, reputation, trust, and argumentation.

IEEE 802.11p is a technology used for communication among vehicles, related to security issues, warning of incidents, or mere exchange of different types of information. Future cars will have the ability to communicate among them and with roadside data systems to spread information about congestion, road conditions, and accidents. They will also have access to travel-related Internet services, publicity from business nearby, tourist information, or even to exchange user files. In this chapter, the authors base their work on an ad-hoc highly configurable agent-based simulator that models communication among cars in a distributed vehicular urban network. Using this model, they provide different measurements concerning coverage and dissemination times to describe the behavior of the standard protocol for disseminating warning messages. Based on the results obtained, the chapter presents proposals to enhance the behavior of the protocol, some of them changing the specification, and others with the use of location-based information.

The proliferation of location-aware mobile devices, together with the advent of Web 2.0 services, promotes the creation of hybrid applications which can provide innovative personalized context-aware services. Personalized recommendation services aim at suggesting products and services to meet users' preferences and needs, while location-based services focus on providing information based on users' current positions. Due to the fast growing of users' needs in the mobile tourism domain, the provision of personalized location-based recommendation services becomes a critical research and practical issue. In this proposal, the authors present GiveMeAPlan, a mobile service which supplies tourist recommendations taking into account both the user preferences (personalization) and context information (time, location, weather, etc.) enriched with social features and targeted advertisements to support its business model. An application prototype is also being implemented to illustrate and test the system feasibility and effectiveness.

Social Question Answering (SQA) services are emerging as a valuable information resource that is rich not only in the expertise of the user community but also their interactions and insights. The next generation SQA services are challenged in many fronts, including but not limited to: massive, heterogeneous, and streaming collections, diverse and challenging users, and the need to be sensitive to context and ambiguity. However, scholarly inquiries have yet to dovetail into a composite research stream where techniques gleaned from various research domains could be used for harnessing the information richness in SQA services to address these challenges. This chapter first explores the SQA domain by understanding the service and its modules, and then investigating previous studies that were conducted in this domain. This chapter then compares SQA services with traditional question answering systems to identify possible research challenges. Finally, new directions in SQA are proposed.

Chapter 15

    Wikan Danar Sunindyo, CDL-Flex, ISIS, Vienna University of Technology, Austria
        & STEI-ITB, Indonesia
    Thomas Moser, CDL-Flex, ISIS, Vienna University of Technology, Austria
    Dietmar Winkler, CDL-Flex, ISIS, Vienna University of Technology, Austria
    Richard Mordinyi, CDL-Flex, ISIS, Vienna University of Technology, Austria
    Stefan Biffl, CDL-Flex, ISIS, Vienna University of Technology, Austria

Automation systems like power plants or industrial production plants usually involve heterogeneous engineering domains, e.g., mechanical, electrical, and software engineering, which are required to work together to deliver good products and/or services to the customers. However, the heterogeneity of workflows used in different engineering domains makes it hard for project managers to integrate and validate such workflows. A workflow modification language can be used to define the workflows and their modifications; however, further formalization is needed to integrate the workflows. The authors of this chapter propose to extend the Engineering Service Bus (EngSB) framework with a mechanism to integrate and validate heterogeneous workflows from different engineering fields and to link connections between different types of signals in broader sense, including process interfaces, electrical signals, and software I/O variables. For evaluation, they perform a feasibility study on a signal change management use case of an industry partner in the hydro power plant engineering domain. Major results show that the framework can support workflow validation and improve the observability of heterogeneous workflows in collaborative engineering environments.

Chapter 16

    Salahdine Hachimi, Université Lyon 1, France
    Noura Faci, Université Lyon 1, France
    Zakaria Maamar, Zayed University, UAE

Web services substitution is a promising solution that enables process continuity of SOA-based applications associated with composite Web services (WSs). This chapter proposes an approach that assesses the impact of substitution on the composition and selects the best substitute, from a pool of substitutes, in order to reduce potential conflicts due to different ontologies with other peers in this composition, for example. Two types of impact along with their assessment metrics are defined: local (semantic/policy compatibility matching degree) and global (QoS satisfaction degree). This chapter addresses the selection issue as an optimization problem whose main objective is to minimize the efforts to put into resuming the ongoing composition under some temporal constraints. A set of experiments are conducted as a proof of concept and the findings show that our approach provides the necessary means for achieving Web services substitution with minimal disruption time.

Preface

The number of distributed systems has been increasing dramatically in the past few years. Many people are using distributed technologies every day, and their lives depend on various distributed systems. However, end users might not be aware of these distributed systems, because these computers and devices are connected and working together in a seamless and transparent way.

New distributed systems and related applications are being enabled by recent advancements in different areas of development and research. The first is the proliferation of mobile devices such as smart phones and tablets. In the latest Cisco Visual Networking Index: Global Mobile Data traffic Forecast Update report (Cisco, 2012), "last year's mobile data traffic was three times the size of the entire global internet in 2000." It also predicts that number of mobile devices in year 2015 will be increased to 7.1 billion which approximately equals to the world's population in that year. Instead of being a client in traditional distributed systems, mobile device can be a server as well because its processing capacity improves significantly in the past few years. Coupled with plummeting prices and higher speed of wireless communication (e.g. wifi, 3G, and 4G), these mobile devices can be connected with traditional computer systems efficiently in a distributed environment. Advances in sensors also have dramatic effects. Sensors are smaller and less expensive nowadays. They can be embedded to distributed systems easily. These changes provide a lot of opportunities for designers to design new applications with new types of distributed systems.

Another important improvement is the advancements in cloud computing. Due to large investment of big computer companies (e.g. IBM, Microsoft, Google, Apple, etc.), cloud computing became more mature, and a lot of problems have been solved. Many companies are now considering cloud adoption. Distributed Systems Designers will discover that they can get the distributed computing power at a lower price and in more flexible ways.

On the other hand, the above new developments also provide new challenges to designers, implementers, and researchers. In order to compute efficiently and smoothly in distributed systems, one must understand the fundamental principles, costs and benefits, related algorithms, possible limitations, and available tools. This book collects the latest development and research results in distributed computing. There are three sections and 16 chapters. Each chapter covers one topic, and they are independent. The book will be useful for graduate students and senior level undergraduate in related fields. It will be a good reference for systems designers, practitioners, and researchers in distributed computing.

Alfred Waising Loo
Lingnan University, Hong Kong

REFERENCES

Cisco Systems. (2012, February 14). *Cisco visual networking index: Global mobile data traffic forecast update: 2011-2016.* Cisco White Paper. Retrieved from http://www.cisco.com/en/US/solutions/collateral/ns341/ns525/ns537/ns705/ns827/white_paper_c11-520862.html

Section 1
Algorithms and Infrastructures

Chapter 1
Efficient Execution of Dataflows on Parallel and Heterogeneous Environments

George Teodoro
Emory University, USA

ABSTRACT

Current advances in computer architectures have transformed clusters, traditional high performance distributed platforms, into hierarchical environments, where each node has multiple heterogeneous processing units including accelerators such as GPUs. Although parallel heterogeneous environments are becoming common, their efficient use is still an open problem. Current tools for development of parallel applications are mainly concerning with the exclusive use of accelerators, while it is argued that the adequate coordination of heterogeneous computing cores can significantly improve performance. The approach taken in this chapter to efficiently use such environments, which is experimented in the context of replicated dataflow applications, consists of scheduling processing tasks according to their characteristics and to the processors specificities. Thus, we can better utilize the available hardware as we try to execute each task into the best-suited processor for it. The proposed approach has been evaluated using two applications, for which there were previously available CPU-only and GPU-only implementations. The experimental results show that using both devices simultaneously can improve the performance significantly; moreover, the proposed method doubled the performance of a demand driven approach that utilizes both CPU and GPU, on the two applications in several scenarios.

INTRODUCTION

With the current advances in computer architectures, traditional distributed platforms are fast transforming into hierarchical environments, where each computing node may have multiple

processors that are, further, multi-core systems. Moreover, the same advances have brought forth the development of new highly parallel architectures, as is the case of GPUs, which have been systematically used as co-processors capable of significantly improving the performance of applications under certain conditions. The end result

DOI: 10.4018/978-1-4666-2533-4.ch001

is that we now see the availability of clusters of computers, each having several heterogeneous computing devices available for processing.

The problem discussed in this chapter is that of efficiently executing component-based applications on heterogeneous clusters of GPU-equipped multi-core computers. The proposed techniques are evaluated in the context of the filter-stream programming model, a type of dataflow system where applications are decomposed into components, called filters, which can be replicated on multiple nodes of a distributed system. These filters communicate using logical streams that are capable of delivering data from an instance of the source filter to an instance of the destination filter. Filters, in our run-time framework, are multi-threaded and may have different versions of their codes so they can execute on heterogeneous processors.

An important facet of our work is that the performance of accelerators, such as GPUs, are data-dependent, meaning that the speedup achieved over the CPU varies according to the type of computation and the input data. Moreover, the variation in performance may occur in two different levels: (i) on the component (filter) level, when there is a performance variation among the processors as different filters' internal computations are carried out, and (ii) on the application level, which is observed as multiple executions of the same application, using CPU or GPU exclusively, have different relative performance according to the application input data and parameters used.

Therefore, our approach to execute dataflow computations on heterogeneous environments consists into assign the execution of each task to the device in which it yields the best relative performance, while all devices are kept busy with different tasks. The proposed solution is extensible to both levels of scheduling, while on the component level the concept of task is related to each event ready to be executed on the application filters, in the application level it is an entire execution of the application.

The proposed solution is materialized by a hierarchical scheduler, which is performed at the level where the performance variations are observed. The approach at the filter level aims to optimize each execution of the application, coordinating the assignment of its internal tasks (data buffers) to the appropriate devices. While at the application level scheduling we focus on optimizing the execution of a workload containing executions of the same application (jobs), by triggering multiple of them in parallel on the available hardware. Thus, at the application level, each execution of the application is performed using only one type of processor, which is chosen according to the estimated relative performance.

The problem of assigning tasks in heterogeneous environments has been the target of research for a long time. Recently, with the increasing ubiquity of GPUs in mainstream computers, the scientific community has examined the use of nodes with CPUs and GPUs in more detail. In Mars (He, 2008), an implementation of the MapReduce programming model for CPU- and GPU-equipped nodes, it was evaluated the collaborative use of CPUs and GPUs to process Map and Reduce tasks that are divided among processor using a fixed relative performance between devices. The Qilin system (Luk, 2009), on the other hand, argues that the processing rates of system processors dependent on the data size. By generating a model of the processing rates for each of the processors in the system in a training phase, Qilin determines how best to split the work among the processors for successive executions of the application. However, these works do not consider that some tasks have different characteristics, making them suitable to different processors. Thus, Qilin and Mars proposed schedulers are not capable to maximize the hardware exploitation when there is inter-task performance variability.

The scheduler proposed in this work, on the other hand, deals with performance variations among the application internal tasks, and among executions of the same application. If the internal tasks are heterogeneous, and, consequently, more adequate for different types of processors, then multiple processors are allocated to the each execution of the application, while at run-time as tasks are created inside filters their performances are estimated and used to decided what processor should be used to each of them. When the application internal tasks have the same relative performance on the available processors, scheduling at the component may not be adequate because the internal are known prior to execution to be more suited to a given processor. Thus, instead using multiple processors to each execution of the application and make the assignment at the component level, a single processor type is assigned to each execution of the application according to its estimated performance on the existing devices. Moreover, multiple executions of the application, each one on the most adequate processor, are triggered in parallel to fully exploit the available hardware in the case of application level scheduling.

Extending previous works (Teodoro, 2009; Teodoro, 2010), this chapter leverages a performance estimator for component level and application level scheduling. We note that the accurate performance estimation is a core premise to the proposed task assignment, and if it is left to the application programmer an undesirable overhead could be created. Thus, a performance estimation module was developed to automate the relative performance estimation based on the applications input parameters. Also, we propose a novel hierarchical scheduler that is able to efficiently deal with a larger number of applications, when compared the cited past works.

It is also important to highlight that although an important active research topic, generating code for the GPU is beyond the scope of this paper. We assume that the necessary code to run the application on both the CPU and the GPU are provided by the programmer, and we focus on the efficient coordination of the execution on heterogeneous environments, as most of the related work relegates this problem to the programmer and either focuses only on the accelerator performance or assumes the speedup of the device is constant for all tasks. For GPU programming we refer to the CUDA (NVIDIA, 2007) toolkit and mention other GPU programming research based on compiler techniques (Ramanujam, 2008), specialized libraries (Buck, 2004; Sundaram, 2009. Also, though we focus on GPUs and CPUs and replicated dataflow applications, the scheduling techniques proposed in this work can be easily applied to more than two types of processors, as well as to other distributed dynamic load balancing systems, such as work stealing systems (Frigo, 1998).

The rest of this chapter is organized as follows. Section II describes the two motivating applications, discusses how the variations in speedups are observed. Section III presents an overview of Anthill framework, as it is the basis for our implementation. Then, in Section IV, the performance estimation approach is presented. Section V describes the proposed hierarchical scheduling to filter-stream applications on heterogeneous environments. Sections VI and VII present and evaluate the proposed schedulers. We conclude and present directions for future work in Section VIII.

MOTIVATING APPLICATIONS AND PROBLEM DISCUSSION

This section presents the motivating applications, briefly describe their dataflow parallelization, and discuss how the variation in relative performance is observed in both application, and component level. The two motivating applications described below are relevant and representative as they exercise different real world problems with different computation demands. The first one is from data mining, with irregular memory access patterns. The second one is an image analysis algorithm used for classification of Neuroblastoma cancer that contains stencil-like computations, which are commonly found in image analysis applications, as well as many scientific computing applications.

Eclat (Zaki, 1997): is an algorithm used to identify causal relationships between frequent co-occurring items in a database. Such relations are named association rules, and the first step to compute them is to determine all co-occurring sets that appear in the database more frequently than a given threshold. The Eclat algorithm has been implemented in Anthill using three filters: Counter, Verifier, and Candidate Generator. The input database is originally partitioned among the copies of the Counter filter that are responsible for counting the local frequency of each candidate itemset (a set of co-occurring items). The Verifier filters then reduce the local counts received from the Counter filters and check whether or not the overall frequency of a particular itemset is above the given threshold. The Candidate Generator filter creates new candidates based on previously discovered frequent itemsets. In the implementation of Eclat, the Counter filter was identified as the most compute intensive stage; therefore, its handler function was implemented for CPU and GPU. Thus, it can process events using CPU, GPU, or both collaboratively.

NBIA: The multi-resolution Neuroblastoma image analysis (NBIA) is an automated system to classify digitized tissue samples into different subtypes that have prognostic significance, which concentrate on the classification of the stromal development as either stroma-rich or stroma-poor. As the slides can have very high resolution, they are first decomposed into smaller image tiles and each image tile is processed independently. NBIA, then, employs a multi-resolution approach (Sertel, 2009), which mimics the way pathologists examine the tissue slides under the microscope. The image analysis starts from the lowest resolution, which corresponds to the lower magnification levels in a microscope and uses the higher resolution representations in regions where the decision for the classification requires more detailed information. The images are, thus, decomposed, from the original image, into multiple resolutions: for example, a three-layered multi-resolution could be constructed by tiles of (64x64), (256x256), and (1Kx1K) pixels.

The basic classification strategy starts using the lowest resolution images, and stop at the resolution level where a pre-determined criteria of the classification is satisfied (Sertel, 2009). The result of the image analysis is a classification label assigned to each image tile indicating the underlying tissue subtype, e.g., stroma-rich or stroma-poor, or background. NBIA has been implemented in Anthill using four filters (Teodoro, 2009): (i)~Image Reader, responsible for reading the tiles in the RGB color space and send to the next step; (ii)~Image Processor that applies an color conversion, and extracts statistical features from each tile, and (iii) Classifier, which receives the feature vector and applies the classification and the hypothesis testing to decide whether or not the classification is satisfactory, and, finally, (iv) the Start/Output filter, that controls the processing flow. It starts at the lowest resolution tiles, switching to higher-resolution until the classification is satisfactory, or they are computed at highest resolution. The Image Processor filter is the most compute intensive part of the application hence we have implementations for both CPU and GPU.

PERFORMANCE VARIATIONS DISCUSSION

This section presents how the relative performance (speedup) variations are observed in our three motivating applications. Figure 1 presents the speedups for each application, according to their sequential CPU-only versions, using a single node as we vary one of its input parameters. Although there is other impacting parameters they remain fixed on these experiments. As shown for our three use case applications, the performance can be strongly affected by the input parameters. This variation is evidence that the assignment of these applications to heterogeneous environments should be carefully done, in order to assign computations to processors where they have good performance.

Figure 1. Applications performance: speedup as we varied the input parameters

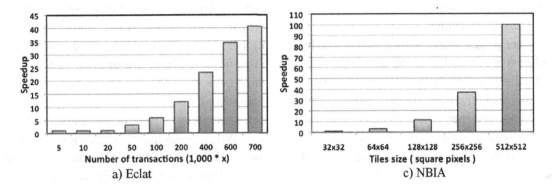

a) Eclat

c) NBIA

Furthermore, although the variations are observed in the two applications, they are dependent of the input parameters, and occurred in different levels. The first of them appears when multiple executions of the same application on different processors have different relative performance as the input data and parameters are modified. This variation, which occurred in Eclat, is called application level heterogeneity. For NBIA it is not possible to accurately estimate the relative performance among the device to an entire execution of the application, because it depends of the number of tiles processed in each resolution that is only known at the end of the execution. On the other hand, the NBIA internal tasks exhibit relative performance variability that depends on the input tile size that is only know at run-time, when events are triggered to execute inside the filters. Moreover, variations in the performance of applications' internal tasks are also observed in various research areas as computer vision, image processing, medicine, and signal processing (Hoppe, 1997; Iverson, 1995; Maes, 1999; Rosenfeld, 1984; Sharp, 2006).

Therefore, we proposed a scheduler to exploit the performance variability at the level where it occurs, while the decision is based on the relative performance of the tasks to the available devices in both levels. Thus, it can coordinate the execution on the available processors, assigning to each of them the task that maximizes its performance. In the application level, as the applications internal tasks have similar homogeneous performance, each execution of the application is assigned to the type of processor where it achieves the best performance. Thus, there is nothing to be done at the component level scheduler during the execution, because the filters can only execute their events using the device assigned at the application level. The component level scheduler, on the other hand, is useful to scenarios where the internal tasks of the applications have different performance on the available devices. In this case, our approach it to assign multiple devices to each execution of the application, and postpone the decision of the appropriate device to each task to be taken at run-time as tasks are created and devices become available.

ANTHILL

Anthill (Teodoro, 2008) is a run-time support system based on the filter-stream (Beynon, 2000) programming model and, as such, applications are decomposed into processing stages named filters which communicate with each other using unidirectional streams. The application is then described as a graph representing the logical interconnection of the filters. At run-time, Anthill spawns instances of each filter on multiple nodes of the cluster, which are called transparent copies.

Anthill includes several features about handling run-time communications and state partition among transparent copies.

The filter programming abstraction provided by Anthill is event-oriented. The programmer provides event handler functions that process events created as data arrives in the input streams and specified dependencies are met. These dependencies are solved by matching functions also provided by the programmer. The events are asynchronous in the dataflow model, meaning that if resources are available, multiple handlers can be dispatched concurrently. This feature is essential in exploiting the full capability of current multi-core architectures and can also be taken advantage of, in heterogeneous platforms, to execute tasks in multiple devices. To accomplish that, Anthill allows the user to provide different event handlers each associated to a specific device and the system decides, at run-time, which handler to invoke for each task.

Considering a distributed memory machine with GPUs, Anthill is capable of scheduling events to GPUs on any node, for any filter that has an event handler for GPU. If a filter has both implementations, it can also schedule events concurrently to both CPU and GPU transparently. Anthill also provides some wrapper functions to abstract from the programmer some of the device particularities (e.g., memory management).

Figure 2 illustrates the architecture of a typical filter. It receives data from multiple input streams (*In1, In2, and In3*), each generating its own event queue, and there are handler functions associated with each of them. As shown, these functions are implemented targeting different types of processors for each event queue. The Component level Scheduler, depicted in the picture is responsible for consuming events from the queues invoking appropriate handlers according to the availability of compute resources. As events are consumed, eventually some data is generated on the filter that needs to be forwarded to the next filter. This is done by the run-time system though it is not depicted in the figure.

The assignment of events to processors is demand-driven. Thus, when events are queued, they are not immediately assigned to a processor. Rather, this occurs on-demand as devices become idle and new events are queued. In the current implementation, the demand-driven, first-come, first-served task assignment policy is used as default strategy of the Component Level Scheduler. When launching an application, Anthill has the flexibility of spawning the transparent copies of the filters anywhere. There is a module within Anthill that is responsible for this filter placement. Once the filters are spawned everywhere, the computation is initiated by assigning one or more jobs to the entry filters of the application. Each job triggers events in the initial filters that will in turn trigger new events in the downstream filters as the computation progresses. It is important to notice that events triggered and queued within the filters are independent of each other. Data dependencies are handled within the user matching functions, which will not trigger events for which there are unresolved dependencies. Therefore, the events that are queued within the filters can be scheduled in any order.

Figure 2. Filters architecture

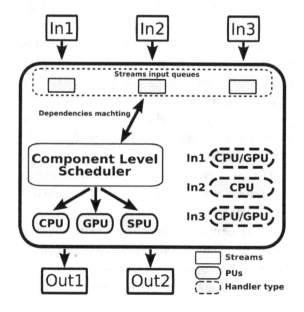

PERFORMANCE ESTIMATOR

As highlighted earlier, at the core of the techniques proposed in this work is the fact that the relative performance of GPUs is data dependent. With that in mind, the decision about where to assign each task has to be taken by the run-time into the adequate scheduling level and determining the relative performance is central to our approach. Although modeling the performance of applications has been an open challenge for decades (Mesnier, 2006), we believe the use of relative performance of the same algorithm running on heterogeneous devices is easier to predict than execution times, and is accurate enough to the proposed schedulers. However, this task should not be left to the application programmer, but rather, should be part of the system and so we propose the Performance Estimator.

The proposed solution (Teodoro, 2010), depicted in Figure 3, uses a two-phase strategy. In the first phase, when a new application is implemented, it is benchmarked for a representative workload and the execution times are stored. The profile generated in this phase consists of the application input parameters, targeted devices and execution times, and construes a training dataset that is used during the actual performance prediction.

The second stage implements a model-learning algorithm, and can employ different strategies to estimate the targeting relative performance. However, it is important to notice that modeling the

behavior of applications based on their inputs is beyond any basic regression models. Also, it is beyond the scope of this chapter to study this specific problem and propose a final solution. Rather, we propose an algorithm that has been validated experimentally and shown to yield sufficient accuracy for the decision-making in study. The algorithm used as the model learning is kNN (Fix, 1951). When a new application task is created, the k nearest executions in our profile are retrieved based on a distance metric on the input parameters and their execution times are averaged, and used to computed the relative speedup of the task on the different processors.

For the purpose of evaluating the effectiveness of the Performance Estimator, we evaluated six representative applications (see Table 1) with the technique described above. The evaluation has two main purposes: (i) understand whether the proposed technique performs an acceptable estimation; and, (ii) discuss our insights that relative performance (speedup) is easier to predict accurately than execution times. The results shown were obtained by performing a first-phase benchmark using a workload containing 30 jobs, which are executed on both the CPU and the GPU. The estimator errors are calculated using a 10-fold cross-validation, and $k=2$ were utilized as it achieved near-optimal estimations for all configurations.

The average speedup error for each application is shown in Table 1. First of all, the proposed

Figure 3. Anthill relative's performance estimator

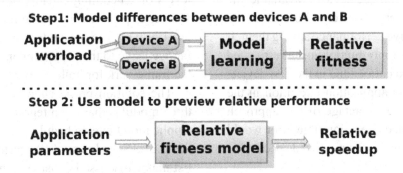

Table 1. Evaluating the performance estimator prediction

Benchmark	Speedup avg. error (%)	CPU Time avg. error (%)	Description	App. source
Black-Scholes	2.5	70.5	European option price	CUDA SDK
N-body	7.3	11.6	Simulate N-body interactions	CUDA SDK
SEAH	13.8	41.9	Simulate electrical heart activity	(Rocha, 2009)
kNN	8.7	21.2	Find k-nearest neighbors	Anthill
Eclat	11.2	102.6	Calculate frequent itemsets	Anthill
NBIA	7.4	30.3	Neuroblastoma classification	(Sertel, 2009)

methodology's accuracy was high, since the worst-case error is not higher than 14%, while the average error among all the applications is as low as 8.52%. For the use case applications, whose accuracy was about the average, this error level does not impact the performance, because it is sufficient to maintain the optimal order of the tasks. We also used the same approach to estimate task execution times for the CPU, using the same workload as before. During this second evaluation, we simply computed the predicted execution times as the average of the k nearest samples' execution times. The CPU execution time error is also shown in the same table; those errors are much higher than the speedup errors for all applications, although the same prediction methodology is employed.

This empirical evaluation is interesting for two different reasons: (i) as our task assignment relies on relative performance estimation, it should perform better for this requirement than for time-based strategies; (ii) the speedup can also be used to predict execution times of an application in different run-time environments. For instance, if the execution time in one device is available, the time in a second processor could be calculated utilizing the relative performance among them. It could be done by simply multiplying the estimated speedup by the execution time in the first device, resulting so in the application execution in the second device. The advantage of this approach is that the estimated execution time error would be equal to the error of the predicted speedup.

We believe that relative performance is easier to predict, because it abstracts effects like conditional statements or loop breaks that highly affect the execution times modeling. Moreover, the relative performance does no try to model the application itself, but the differences between devices when running the same program and input data.

MULTI-LEVEL SCHEDULING INTEGRATION

This section describes the hierarchical approach to coordinate the use of multiple heterogeneous devices for filter-stream applications. As seen in the previous sections, the relative performance of different devices may vary significantly according to the task characteristic. Based on this observation, our approach is to allocate the execution of each task to the device in which it yields the best performance, while maintaining all available devices busy. Because the performance heterogeneity happens in two levels, we propose two levels of scheduling capable of exploiting both sources of performance variability. Selecting the level in which to schedule each application, so far, we leave to the programmer, but we provide the framework for both.

The solution proposed was built based into three modules that are integrated to Anthill: the Application Level Scheduler (ALS), the Component Level Scheduler (CLS), and the Performance Estimator, discussed in last section. The overview

Figure 4. Overview of the system architecture

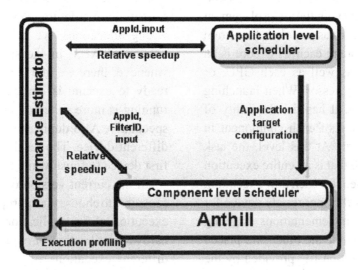

of the system is shown in Figure 4. For both scheduling levels, when new tasks are received the Performance Estimator is executed to perform a run-time estimation of the relative speedup, which is later used to decide the appropriate device to each of them.

The overall algorithm behind both schedulers is to maintain a priority queue for each device with all the tasks sorted by the speedup of the task in that device. The tasks are initially allocated from the highest speedup downwards, and once the task is allocated to a device, it is removed from all priority queues. Once all devices are busy, new tasks are inserted into priority queues and when a device becomes idle, it takes the task with the highest speedup on that device. Note that, as discussed before, the tasks at the schedulers have different definitions: while for the ALS it is the execution of an entire application, for the CLS it is an event processed by a filter of the application. Although they have different granularity, the input parameters still impacting to the performance of both.

It is also important to notice that, in practice, we never have the whole set of tasks/data buffers to be scheduled in advance for both schedulers, but we may still apply the presented approach considering the set of known tasks at run-time time. It is intuitive to see that the larger the set of known tasks, the better the schedule is. On the other hand, it does not seem to be worth having processors idle just because, in a given moment, there is only a small set of tasks. Again, we choose to keep the processors busy, as a strategy to maximize the computational efficiency of the platform. In the next two sections, we describe each level of scheduling and their experimental results.

APPLICATION LEVEL SCHEDULING

The Application Level Scheduler (ALS) targets applications for which there are variations in the speedup among different executions of the application (jobs), and such variation can be estimated based on the job parameters. When there is no performance heterogeneity across jobs, or it depends on the data itself, and not just on the parameters, scheduling at this level will not be so efficient as the case where the variation exists. Moreover, in such a case, the gains will be similar to those achieved by an efficient demand driven policy, as the relative performance is the same among the jobs, and no matter the processor used by each of them.

ALS works as a front-end to run-time environment that integrates with the filter placement subsystem in Anthill. It has a global, fine-grain view of the entire system: each CPU core is an independent device, as well as each GPU, or any other available processor. When launching an Anthill application, it has the flexibility of choosing the placement of each component in the distributed platform. At this level, the task corresponds to the job that is an entire execution of the application. Then, for each new execution, ALS chooses what is the appropriate device for the filters that have implementations targeting multiple processors, while the others are placed based on the configuration file provided by the programmer. Thus, in order to exploit all the available devices, ALS triggers the execution of multiples jobs concurrently, assigning each of them to one specific processor.

The algorithm employed by ALS is the same that was outlined earlier. It obtains the relative speedups for all the available jobs from the Performance Estimator, as shown in Figure 4, and assigns those with the best speedups to the appropriate devices. It continues until all devices are busy, thus the run-time platform is exploited by making multiple executions of the same application in parallel, with each of them on the most appropriate device. Then, when a job finishes its execution and a device becomes available, the best-queued job for that processor is scheduled there. Notice that ALS may be receiving jobs as it runs, thus the performance estimation occurs on the fly and these jobs are added to the queues when they become available.

As noticed, in order to fully utilize the processors, the proposed heuristic algorithm allocates jobs to devices until all them are occupied or there are no more available jobs. Although interesting, this approach may suffers from bad allocation, for example, at the end of the execution, when the number of processors is higher than the number of available jobs. Thus, in some cases, a job already assigned to a processor where it performs poorly can become the bottleneck to the entire workload execution. In order to reduce the impact of these wrong allocations, we proposed a speculative version of ALS. In the speculative approach, whenever there are idle devices; the list of jobs ready to execute is empty; and a job already running is more suited to an idle processor; the speculative ALS duplicates the running job in a different device. The result is the output of the first device to finish while the second is killed.

In the current version of Anthill, ALS is responsible to choose the appropriate device to each execution of the application, optimizing so the hardware utilization through its sharing among different executions of the same application. The scheduling done by ALS, on the other hand, assumes that the number of machines used by the application is given by the programmer, as is the case of real world cluster and grid resource manager systems as Sun Grid Engine (Gentzsch, 2001) and TORQUE (Staples, 2006). However, we intend to study the problem of automatically make the application placement for each submitted job, choosing, for example, the best number of copies of each filter according to its input parameters.

EXPERIMENTAL SETUP

The experiments were performed using a cluster of 5 PCs connected using a Gigabit Ethernet. Each node has a dual quad-core AMD Opteron 2.00GHz processor, 16GB of main memory, an NVidia GeForce GTX260 GPU, and Linux operating system. Each result shown in this paper is the average of four executions. During the evaluations with GPU, one CPU core is kept occupied as it is managing the GPU. The experiments presented in this section have been executed using 5 PCs, and, for simplicity, when we say that the application is using X CPU cores, the application is using X CPU core per machine. The speedups are calculated according to the CPU-only versions of the applications.

In this section we experimented ALS for Eclat as it has heterogeneity at the application level, and compared ALS to traditional scheduling policies such as First-Come First-Served (FCFS), and Shortest Job First (SJF). For the experiments with SJF we created two queues of jobs, one for each device, containing all jobs of the workload sorted by the execution time in each particular device. Thus, when a device is idle the scheduler selects the job with smallest execution time to that specific processor, while the same job is removed from the second queue. The execution times used as input to SJF were measured in previous executions. The evaluation was mainly conducted with 3 performance metrics: total workload execution time, which is the total time to execute all the jobs in our workload; the mean job wait time, the average of jobs queuing times; and the mean job response time, the average time that jobs spent until their assigned processors finished their execution.

The workloads used as input to Eclat were generated based on the characterization of data mining jobs executed by users of the Anteater (Guedes, 2006) platform. Anteater is a service-oriented data mining platform executing on different clusters, where its scalable algorithms are used for processing large databases. The workload characterization was done from clusters where Anteater is being used to mine government databases (one on public expenditures, another on public safety - 911

calls), using algorithms as Eclat, kNN, and ID3. Finally, the generated workloads have 100 jobs each. During the Eclat placement we allocate one instance of Counter filter per machines, and one copy of Merger and Generate candidates filters. The Merger and Generate candidates filters of all running jobs never occupied more than one CPU-core.

Experimental Evaluation

The evaluation starts with a comparison among the GPU-only version of Eclat to its CPU and GPU version, using ALS and FCFS scheduling policies, and 5 different workloads. During these experiments we assumed, for readability reasons, that there is only one CPU core available in addition to the GPU, thus we could run only two jobs in parallel: the first one using the GPU, while the second utilizes the CPU. The results, presented in Figure 5(a), show that the collaborative use of CPU and GPU improved significantly the performance of Eclat when compared to the GPU-only version in all scenarios, achieving an gains of up to 41% for ALS. Moreover, the comparison of ALS to FCFS shows that the first policy is always faster, and, in the best case, ALS is near to 33% faster than FCFS.

Further, the impact of increasing the number of CPU cores used in addition to the GPU is in-

Figure 5. Eclat: performance evaluation for multiple workloads - a) Performance evaluation for multiple workloads; b) Workload exec. times for different scheduling strategies and number of CPU-cores

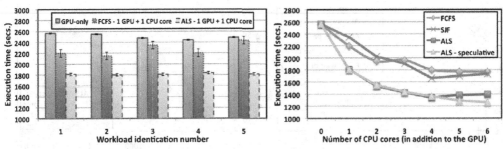

a) Performance evaluation for multiple workloads.

b) Workload exec. times for different scheduling strategies and number of CPU-cores.

vestigated, for four configurations: (i) FCFS, (ii) SJF, (iii) ALS, and (iv) ALS with speculation. Although these experiments were executed for the 5 workloads used before, just one is present as there were no significant differences in the results. The results, presented in Figure 5(b), show that ALS performs better than FCFS and SJF for all number of CPU cores, near to doubling the performance of the GPU-only version of Eclat for the configuration with 4 additional CPU cores.

The best ALS results were achieved for the configuration with 4 CPU cores in addition to the GPU, and the use of more CPU cores degrades the performance. This performance slowdown occurred because, when using more than 4 CPU cores, some jobs that are inefficiently executed by CPU, are assigned to it near to the end of the execution. Thus, instead of contribute to improving the performance; these extra cores became a bottleneck to the overall workload execution.

In order to reduce the impacts of these bad allocations, a speculative version of ALS was proposed as discussed on the beginning of this section. This approach duplicates jobs already running on idle processors where their relative performance are better, then ALS with speculation alleviates the impacts of these allocations to non-appropriate devices in the end of the workloads. As shown in Figure 5(b), it improved the best performance of ALS without speculation in

6%, and the execution times are reduced as the number of utilized CPU cores increase up to 6.

The mean job wait and response time metrics have been evaluated for two schedulers: FCFS and ALS (see Figure 6(a)). As presented, although ALS execution times are smaller than FCFS times, FCFS has better results for both metrics up to the configuration with 4 CPU cores. To understand these results, we used the FCFS and ALS cumulative throughput for two different configurations: (i) GPU + 1 CPU core, for which FCFS has better results, and (ii) GPU + 6 CPU cores, when ALS metrics are superior.

The throughput for these configurations is then presented in Figure 6(b). As shown, when using 1 CPU core in addition to the GPU, FCFS cumulative throughput is higher than ALS at the beginning of the execution, until 75% of the execution, which implies ALS had more jobs queued during this time interval and hence worse wait and response times. This situation occurred because, at the beginning of the execution, ALS utilizes the GPU to process the most time-consuming jobs. However, as ALS utilizes the CPU cores to the shortest jobs, and, consequently, in the configuration with GPU and 6 CPU cores, ALS has higher cumulative throughput than FCFS.

Finally, we compared ALS speculative scheduling to a hypothetical optimum scheduling. The optimum scheduling was created using a brute force

Figure 6. Eclat performance evaluation: a) Mean wait and response times; b) Throughput of ALS and FCFS

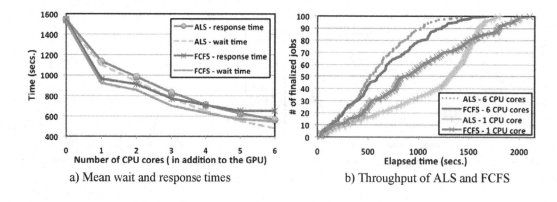

a) Mean wait and response times

b) Throughput of ALS and FCFS

algorithm that verifies the scheduling with smallest execution time, using execution times from previous runs of the workload on each device. For these experiments we used 5 workloads with 25 jobs and the configuration with GPU and 1 CPU core. The original workloads with 100 jobs were not used in this experiment, because it was too expensive to compute their optimum scheduling. For instance, the time to generate the optimum scheduling with 25 jobs is comparable to the end-to-end workload execution using only the GPU. These experiments shown that ALS performs only 1.8% worse than the optimum scheduling on average, and the maximum difference between them was not higher than 3%.

COMPONENT LEVEL SCHEDULING

Some applications have data dependent heterogeneity among its internal tasks. However, it may be possible to exploit such variation at a lower level. The Component Level Scheduler (CLS) considers each component (filter) of the application independently, and the tasks are the events arriving in the event queue. If the variation, at this level, can be estimated, it can effectively schedule them to appropriate devices.

The global placement for CLS is done by allocating multiple devices to the filters with multiple handler codes, while maintaining the original Anthill placement for the other filters. CLS itself is integrated into Anthill run-time, and runs when events are produced. As events are created in each filter, the speedups are estimated on-line for each device, and they are scheduled using the same algorithm described earlier. Multiple events can be dispatched concurrently into a filter, and multiple filters may be using CLS independently.

In this scheduling level, the focus is optimization present at each filter's input streams that have multiple handler implementations (Teodoro, 2009). This optimization is made by triggering the execution of multiple events in parallel, using the appropriate device for each of them. The algorithm used by this scheduling strategy is almost identical to ALS described in last section. But, differently from ALS, it only runs one application execution at time, allocating the available GPU and CPU cores to its internal tasks. In other words, when events are created due the arrival of messages at input streams, they are then ordered according to their relative speedups, retrieved from the Performance Estimator, and assigned to the appropriate devices.

In our experience with the filter-stream programming model, most applications are bottleneck free, and the number of active internal tasks is higher than the available processing cores. Thus, the proposed approach to exploit heterogeneous resources consists of allocating multiple tasks concurrently to processors where they will perform the best. Also, the computation time of applications' tasks dominates the overall application execution times; so overlapping communication with computation can easily hide the cost of the communication latency. Although these premises are valid for a broad range of applications, there is also interesting work on linear algebra computation for multi-core processors (Song, 2009), for instance, including heterogeneous computing with GPUs (Augonnet, 2009), where the amount of application's concurrent tasks are smaller than the number of processing cores. The authors improve application performance by creating algorithms to solve task dependencies, in order to increase the number of concurrent active tasks, allowing them to take advantage of multi-core systems.

Experimental Evaluation

This evaluation used NBIA with input images that are divided into 27,742 tiles, represented in two resolutions: (*32* x *32*) and (*512* x *512*). The experiments were executed using one copy of each filter per machine. The evaluation was conducted using 5 machines, and when we mention that X CPU cores or the GPUs are used, for example, this number of CPU cores and GPUs are used on each machine of the distributed environment.

Figure 7(a) shows NBIA speedups for FCFS and CLS as we increased the number of CPU cores for a workload with 100 jobs/images. The performance of the application using FCFS increased slightly with the number of CPU cores, while CLS almost doubled it for several recalculation rates. The results presented in Figure 7(b) also show degradation when using more than 5 CPU cores for processing, which occurred because after this configuration there is a high competition for the available CPU cores. When the application is using 5 additional CPU cores as processing units, the other 3 CPU cores are already being used by the Reader filter, for managing the GPU, and the third is occupied by an Anthill's process that is responsible for the communication.

The analysis of wait and response times, presented in Figure 7(b), shows better values for both metrics when using CLS. This result is plausible as CLS runs one job at time, which uses the whole computing platform and accelerates each execution by the appropriate assignment of the application internal tasks to the available devices. In order to understand the performance gains due to the use of CLS for each single job, we studied the scheduling impacts for single executions of the application as the input characteristics are modified. Thus, we varied the tile recalculation rate, that is, the rate in which tiles have to be reprocessed at higher resolution, for each scheduling: CLS and FCFS, as presented in Figure 8.

Figure 7. NBIA performance evaluation: a) Speedup; b) Metrics

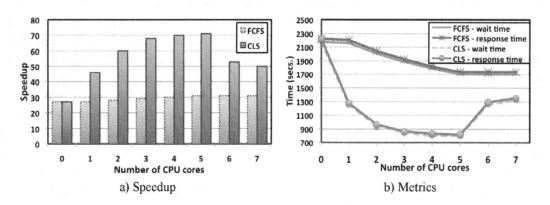

a) Speedup

b) Metrics

Figure 8. NBIA: scheduling strategies evaluation

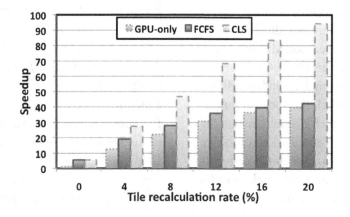

These results show that FCFS significantly improves the application performance only for a 0% tile recalculation rate. When no tiles are recalculated, and both the CPU and the GPU process tiles of the smallest size, for which they have the same performance. CLS, on the other hand, have a better performance for all other recalculation rates, achieving an improvement of 123% over FCFS for 20% of tile recalculation rate.

CONCLUSION AND FUTURE DIRECTIONS

In this work, we presented an approach for efficiently executing replicated dataflow applications on distributed heterogeneous environments. Our solution, which has been implemented as an extension to Anthill, is based on a multi-level scheduler that considers the tasks relative performance variations to better utilize the available resources, e.g., CPU and GPU, according to their specificities and the characteristics of the tasks.

We proposed to use kNN based performance estimator for estimating relative performance of the components on different devices. We tested our performance estimator on six different applications, and empirically showed that estimating relative speedup is less error-prone than estimating execution times. The experimental results for three representative application: Eclat, SEAH, and NBIA, shown that the proposed scheduling technique, which utilizes the tasks speedup heterogeneity in multiple levels to assign work, almost doubled the performance of scheduling policies which do not consider variations in performance for several scenarios.

As future work, we intend to evaluate the impact of our techniques on scheduling applications in environments with heterogeneity between the cluster nodes, as for example a cluster with different processors as Cell blades, CPU, and GPU. We also want to extend the performance estimator module, evaluating other algorithms for building the application's performance model.

REFERENCES

Augonnet, C., Thibault, S., Namyst, R., & Wacrenier, P. A. (2009). Starpu: A unified platform for task scheduling on heterogeneous multicore architectures. In *Euro-Par '09: Proceedings of the 15th International Euro-Par Conference on Parallel Processing* (pp. 863–874).

Beynon, M., Ferreira, R., Kurc, T. M., Sussman, A., & Saltz, J. H. (2000). DataCutter: Middleware for filtering very large scientific datasets on archival storage systems. In *IEEE Symposium on Mass Storage Systems* (pp.119–134).

Buck, I., Foley, T., Horn, D., Sugerman, J., Fatahalian, K., Houston, M., & Hanrahan, P. (2004). Brook for GPUs: Stream computing on graphics hardware. *ACM Transactions on Graphics, 32*(3).

Fix, E., & Hodges, J. (1951). *Discriminatory analysis, non-parametric discrimination, consistency properties.* School of Aviation Medicine, Randolph Field, Texas, Computer Science Technical Report.

Frigo, M., Leiserson, C. E., & Randall, K. H. (1998). *The implementation of the cilk-5 multithreaded language* (pp. 212–223). PLDI.

Gentzsch, W. (2001). *Sun grid engine: Towards creating a compute power grid.* Retrieved September 1, 2011, from http://ieeexplore.ieee.org/xpls/abs all.jsp?arnumber=923173

Guedes, D. W. M. Jr, & Ferreira, R. (2006). Anteater: A service-oriented architecture for high-performance data mining. *IEEE Internet Computing, 36*–43. doi:10.1109/MIC.2006.69

He, B., Fang, W., Luo, Q., Govindaraju, N. K., & Wang, T. (2008). Mars: A mapreduce framework on graphics processors. In *Proceedings of the 17th International Conference on Parallel Architectures and Compilation Techniques,* (pp. 260-269).

Hoppe, H. (1997). View-dependent refinement of progressive meshes. In *SIGGRAPH 97 Proceedings* (pp. 189–198).

Iverson, M., Ozguner, F., & Follen, G. (1995). Parallelizing existing applications in a distributed heterogeneous environment. In *4th Heterogeneous Computing Workshop* (pp. 93–100).

Lee, S., Min, S.-J., & Eigenmann, R. (2009). OpenMP to GPGPU: A compiler framework for automatic translation and optimization. In *PPoPP'09: Proceedings of the 14th ACM SIGPLAN Symposium on Principles and Practice of Parallel Programming* (pp. 101–110).

Luk, C.-K., Hong, S., & Kim, H. (2009). *Qilin: Exploiting parallelism on heterogeneous multiprocessors with adaptive mapping*. In 42nd International Symposium on Microarchitecture (MICRO).

Maes, F., Vandermeulen, D., & Suetens, P. (1999). Comparative evaluation of multiresolution optimization strategies for multimodality image registration by maximization of mutual information. *Medical Image Analysis, 3*, 373–386. doi:10.1016/S1361-8415(99)80030-9

Mesnier, M., Wachs, M., Salmon, B., & Ganger, G. R. (2006). *Relative fitness models for storage* (pp. 23–28). SIGMETRICS Performance Evaluation Review.

NVIDIA. (2007). *NVIDIA CUDA SDK*. Retrieved in September, 10, 2011 from http:// nvidia.com/ cuda

Ramanujam, J. (2008). *Toward automatic parallelization and auto-tuning of affine kernels for GPUs*. In Workshop on Automatic Tuning for Petascale Systems.

Rocha, B. M., Campos, F. O., Plank, G., dos Santos, R. W., Liebmann, M., & Haase, G. (2009). *Simulations of the electrical activity in the heart with graphic processing units*. In Eighth International Conference on Parallel Processing and Applied Mathematics.

Rosenfeld, A. (1984). *Multiresolution image processing and analysis*. Berlin, Germany: Springer. doi:10.1007/978-3-642-51590-3

Sertel, O., Kong, J., Shimada, H., Catalyurek, U. V., Saltz, J. H., & Gurcan, M. N. (2009). *Computer-aided prognosis of neuroblastoma on whole-slide images: Classification of stromal development* (pp. 1093–1103). Pattern Recognition, Special Issue on Digital Image Processing and Pattern Recognition Techniques for the Detection of Cancer.

Sharp, R., Ridgway, R., Iyengar, S., Gulacy, A., Wenzel, P., & de Bruin, A. … Saltz, J. H. (2006). Registration and 3D visualization of large microscopy images. In *Proceedings of the SPIE Annual Medical Imaging Meetings* (pp. 923–934).

Song, F. YarKhan, A., & Dongarra, J. (2009). Dynamic task scheduling for linear algebra algorithms on distributed-memory multicore systems. In *SC '09: Proceedings of the Conference on High Performance Computing Networking, Storage and Analysis.*

Staples, G. (2006). Torque resource manager. In *SC '06: Proceedings of the 2006 ACM/IEEE Conference on Supercomputing.*

Sundaram, N., Raghunathan, A., & Chakradhar, S. T. (2009). A framework for efficient and scalable execution of domain-specific templates on GPUs. In *IPDPS '09: Proceedings of the 2009 IEEE International Symposium on Parallel & Distributed Processing* (pp. 1–12).

Teodoro, G., Fireman, D., Guedes, D., Jr, W. M., & Ferreira, R. (2008). *Achieving multi-level parallelism in filter-labeled stream programming model*. In The 37th International Conference on Parallel Processing (ICPP).

Teodoro, G., Hartley, T. D. R., Catalyurek, U. V., & Ferreira, R. (2010). Run-time optimizations for replicated dataflows on heterogeneous environments. In *Proceedings of the 19th ACM International Symposium on High Performance Distributed Computing* (HPDC).

Teodoro, G., Sachetto, R., Sertel, O., Gurcan, M., & Jr, W. M. Catalyurek, U., & Ferreira, R. (2009). *Coordinating the use of GPU and CPU for improving performance of compute intensive applications*. In IEEE Cluster.

Zaki, M. J., Parthasarathy, S., Ogihara, M., & Li, W. (1997). New algorithms for fast discovery of association rules. In *3rd International Conference on Knowledge Discovery and Data Mining* (pp. 283– 296).

Chapter 2
Interference Aware Resource Allocation in Relay Enhanced Broadband Wireless Access Networks

Preetha Thulasiraman
Naval Postgraduate School, USA

ABSTRACT

The use of relay nodes to improve the performance of broadband wireless access (BWA) networks has been the subject of intense research activities in recent years. Relay enhanced BWA networks are anticipated to support diverse multimedia traffic (i.e., voice, video, and data traffic). In order to guarantee service to users, efficient network resource distribution is imperative. Wireless multihop networks are distinguished primarily from their wired counterparts through the presence of interference. Wireless interference greatly influences the ability of users to obtain the necessary resources for service. This chapter provides a comprehensive study on the topic of interference aware resource allocation by investigating the impact of interference on various aspects of resource allocation, ranging from fairness to spectrum utilization. In this regard, the focus of this chapter is to investigate the problem of traffic flow routing and fair bandwidth allocation under interference constraints for multihop BWA networks.

First, a novel interference aware routing metric for multipath routing considering both interflow and intraflow interference will be discussed. Second, in order to ensure quality of service (QoS), an interference aware max-min fair bandwidth allocation algorithm is addressed using lexicographic ordering and optimization. A comparison among various interference based routing metrics and interference aware bandwidth allocation algorithms established in the literature is shown through simulation results derived from NS-2 and CPLEX. It is shown that the proposed interference aware resource allocation framework improves network performance in terms of delay, packet loss ratio, and bandwidth usage. Lastly, future challenges and emerging research topics and opportunities are outlined.

DOI: 10.4018/978-1-4666-2533-4.ch002

INTRODUCTION

The communications landscape has been changing dramatically in recent years under the increasing pressure of rapid technological development and intense competition. Thus, wireless networks are becoming more pervasive, accelerated by new wireless communication technologies, inexpensive wireless equipment and broader Internet access availability. Broadband wireless access (BWA) networks are one such technology that is fast becoming a viable solution to provide ubiquitous communications.

BWA networks are designed to support fixed and mobile users with heterogeneous and high traffic rate requirements. In such networks, a single base station is deployed to cover a cellular area. In such a large area, users at the cell edge often experience bad channel conditions. Moreover, in urban regions, shadowing by various obstacles can degrade the signal quality in some areas. Emerging broadband wireless applications require increasingly high throughput and more stringent quality of service (QoS) requirements. As real-time applications (i.e., voice over IP and video streaming) rapidly grow, BWA networks are expected to achieve efficient communications. Increasing capacity along with coverage in conventional networks dictates the dense deployment of base stations. Increasing the number of base stations is an expensive solution and increasing the base station power only increases the intercell interference. To meet the goal of low cost network deployment for both short range and long range coverage, the use of relay nodes has been shown to be a promising solution (Pabst et al., 2004; Soldani & Dixit, 2008). Broadband cellular multihop networks consist of fixed infrastructure relay nodes whose sole priority is to forward data to and from the users to the base station. Deploying relays is a feasible solution since typical relays are cheaper than base stations and they do not need their own wired backhaul.

The use of relays to improve the performance of BWA networks has been the subject of intense research in recent years because of their several performance benefits. First, a relay works on behalf of the base station to increase the network coverage. While conventional cellular systems normally cover a diameter of 2-5km, a relay normally covers a region (subcell) with diameter 200-500m. If the density of relay stations is somewhat high, most user-terminals will be close to one or more relays than to a base station. This has two primary advantages: the radio propagation paths are shortened so that the pathloss is lowered, and the path essentially can be routed around obstacles to mitigate effects of shadowing (Pabst et al., 2004). This results in higher data rates on the links between relays and users, thereby increasing throughput. Also, from the point of view of the user, the relay acts like a base station and so by having intermediate points of traffic aggregation, the capacity per area element can be balanced (Walke, Mangold, & Berlemann, 2006). Second, because relay stations are closer to the individual user terminals, the transmit power required for a relay to transmit to a user and vice versa is significantly lower than for a base station, thereby allowing for energy saving. Thus, the practical rationale for the deployment of relay enhanced BWA networks is to ensure that the QoS of a user, in terms of data rate, delay, outage probability, etc. does not wholly depend on its location and distance from the base station.

Resource Allocation in the Presence of Interference

Interference is the major limiting factor in the performance of wireless multihop networks. Sources of interference include simultaneous transmissions within a certain range as well as concurrent use of the same frequency channel for transmission. Interference is severe in urban areas due to the large number of base stations and mobile users. Interference has been recognized as a major bottleneck in increasing network capacity and throughput and is often responsible for dropped transmissions (Rappaport, 2002). Interference experienced at individual nodes (relays and users) is impacted by variations in network size (number of nodes), network density (relative positions of nodes) and traffic per node. There are two widely used models to characterize interference in a wireless network, namely, the protocol model and the physical model (Gupta & Kumar, 2000). The protocol model, also known as the unified disk graph model, has been widely used by researchers in the wireless networking community as a way to simplify the mathematical characterization of the physical layer. Under the protocol model, a successful transmission occurs when a node falls inside the transmission range of its intended transmitter and falls outside the interference ranges of other non-intended transmitters. The setting of the transmission range is based on a signal-to-noise-ratio (SNR) threshold. The setting of the interference range is a heuristic approximation and remains an open problem (Shi, Hou, Liu, & Kompella, 2009). Under the protocol model, the impact of interference from a transmitting node is binary and is solely determined by whether or not a receiver falls within the interference range of this transmitting node. That is, if a node falls in the interference range of a non-intended transmitter, then this node is considered to be interfered and thus cannot receive correctly from its intended transmitter; otherwise, the interference is assumed to be negligible (Iyer, Rosenberg, & Karnik, 2009). Various graph based approaches have been developed for modeling interference using the protocol model. The most common and widely used model is the conflict graph model (Jain, Padhye, & Padmanabhan, 2003). The nodes in the conflict graph, G_c, represent edges in the original connectivity graph G. An edge is placed between two nodes in the conflict graph if the corresponding links in the connectivity graph interfere. Due to such simplification, the protocol model has been widely used in developing algorithms and protocols in wireless networks

(Alicherry, Bhatia, & Li, 2006; Ramachandran, Belding, Almeroth, & Buddhikot, 2006; Tang, Xue, Chandler, & Zhang, 2005).

The physical model, also known as the SINR model, is based on considerations arising from practical transceiver designs of communication systems that treat interference as noise. Under the physical model, a transmission is successful if and only if signal-to-interference-and-noise-ratio (SINR) at the intended receiver exceeds a threshold so that the transmitted signal can be decoded with an acceptable bit error probability. Furthermore, capacity calculation is based on SINR (via Shannon's formula), which takes into account interference due to simultaneous transmissions by other nodes. This model is less restrictive than the protocol interference model as it may occur that a message from node u to node v is correctly received even if there is a simultaneous transmitting node w close to v (for instance, because node u is using a much larger transmit power than node w). As a result, higher network capacity can be achieved by applying the physical interference model. However, the use of the SINR model is computationally more complex and requires various optimization and heuristic techniques to be used to obtain a solution. Nonetheless, it has been shown that despite the computational complexity, the SINR model provides a more practical and realistic assessment of wireless interference (Iyer et al., 2009; Brar, Blough, & Santi, 2006).

In wireless communications, resource management is vital in controlling how scarce resources can be allocated, distributed, and utilized among all nodes in a system. Unlike wired links which have a constant link capacity, wireless links are relatively vulnerable due to fading over frequency and interference over time. Interference aware resource allocation involves striking a good balance between fair and efficient distribution of spectral resources throughout the network while concurrently mitigating the resulting interference. One of the major difficulties associated with interference mitigation is the lack of predictability of interference coming from other links that have simultaneous transmissions combined with channel variability.

In order to develop efficient resource allocation algorithms that are cognizant of interference, certain potential issues must be addressed, outlined as follows:

1. Interference and Fairness in Routing and Bandwidth Allocation: Efficient routing between pairs of nodes in communication networks is a basic problem of network optimization. Achieving high throughput and fair allocation of resources among competing users (or flows) in wireless networks is one of the most important problems in data communications and is directly coupled with routing between nodes. Throughput enhancement and fairness can not be simultaneously achieved, but rather must be balanced (Cheng & Zhuang, 2008). Max-min fairness (MMF) is considered to be an efficient approach that balances these two conflicting objectives by preventing starvation of any flow, and at the same time, increases the bandwidth of a flow as much as possible. In the wireless environment, allocation of bandwidth to paths sharing a set of links is further complicated by the inherent interference that is generated by simultaneous transmissions. Interference can be divided into two categories: interflow and intraflow. Interflow interference is generated when two links belonging to different flows are active on the same channel at the same time. Intraflow interference is when two links belonging to the same flow are active on the same channel at the same time. The effects of interference using the MMF approach have been quantified using graph theoretic approaches (i.e., conflict/contention graph) which ultimately exploits the protocol interference model (i.e., transmissions interfere

only within a specific range) (Tang et al., 2005; Wang, Jiang, Zhuang, & Poor, 2008). Although, (Tang et al., 2005; Wang et al., 2008) have provided a theoretical foundation for fairness in wireless networks, the reliance on such graph based models induces binary conflicts which means any two links either interfere with each other or they are active simultaneously regardless of other ongoing transmissions, which is not true in practice (Brar et al., 2006). The use of the SINR model in determining MMF bandwidth allocation and fair routing would provide a less restrictive and more realistic allocation of bandwidth to the various network paths. Therefore, a SINR based MMF routing and bandwidth allocation optimization formulation would serve to fairly distribute resources and reduce competition between simultaneous flows.

2. Multipath Routing Using SINR Constraints: Discovering available relaying paths (routes) between a source and base station is a critical prerequisite for the success of multihop wireless networks. Multipath routing (MPR) has long been recognized as an effective strategy to achieve load balancing and increase reliability (Huang & Fang, 2008). To improve the transmission reliability and avoid shared-link (or node) failures, the multiple paths can be selected to be link or node disjoint. In this case, the MPR approach is referred to as disjoint multipath routing (DMPR). DMPR provides better robustness and a greater degree of fault tolerance than compared to the generic MPR. Due to these advantages, DMPR schemes have been researched in the context of wireless networks in order to enhance network survivability (Thulasiraman, Ramasubramanian, & Krunz, 2006; Thulasiraman, Ramasubramanian, & Krunz, 2007). Several routing metrics to capture interference on routing paths have been introduced in the literature. However,

the metrics developed have either 1) been based on extending existing routing metrics (i.e., expected transmission count (ETX)) or existing routing algorithms (Subramanian, Buddhikot, & Miller, 2006; Langar, Bouabdallah, & Boutaba, 2009) or 2) have integrated interference into variations of the shortest path routing scheme (Kar, Kodialam, & Lakshman, 2000; Qi, Biaz, Wu, & Ji, 2007). In the above mentioned works, the interference that is quantified does not refer to the interference received from the physical layer (i.e., signal strength). Rather, there has been a consistent focus on the level of interference in terms of distance using the protocol interference model because of ease of implementation. Limited research on SINR based routing schemes exist. Furthermore, in terms of interference based multipath routing, research has focused on the use of straightforward methods to quantify interference. Specifically, in (Teo, Ha, & Tham, 2008), the authors use an extension of the correlation factor (correlation factor is defined as the number of links connecting two paths) which captures interpath interference but provides little information about the level of interference between simultaneous transmissions. In addition to interference based routing, guaranteeing QoS provisions has also been investigated within this context (Wen & Lin, 2007; Xu, Huang, & Cheng, 2008). Providing fault tolerance and QoS provisioning in the presence of interference are major issues that must be studied jointly in wireless systems in order to gauge a realistic sense of network performance, particularly in terms of throughput.

Chapter Objectives

The purpose of this chapter is to provide a framework for interference aware resource allocation by studying multipath routing and fairness as discussed above. The objectives of this chapter are twofold and can be summarized as flows: First, an isotonic loop free routing metric is designed which is cognizant of interference and provides reliable multipath routing. The routing metric is used to quantify the interference on the network links such that least interfering paths can be obtained. The Routing with Interflow and Intraflow Interference Metric (RI^3M) captures both interflow and intraflow interference while balancing link loads. The isotonicity of the RI^3M routing metric is proven through virtual network decomposition and is used to find disjoint paths from each user to the base station. Second, an MMF optimization formulation to find the largest (lexicographically largest) bandwidth allocation vector for user traffic demands is discussed. This algorithm is referred to as the Lexicographic MMF Multipath Flow ($LMX:M^3F$) algorithm and explicitly considers the constraints of the wireless interference on the individual flows.

This chapter will show that the proposed routing metric and bandwidth allocation formulation improves bandwidth usage, throughput, and delay in comparison to existing interference aware fair bandwidth allocation algorithms[1].

BACKGROUND

Interference and Fairness in Routing

With the use of multihop relaying, increasing number of users, and limited spectrum, wireless multihop BWA networks are limited by two main resources: bandwidth and network capacity. While bandwidth refers to the achievable data rate, capacity refers to the data transport capacity available for each link in the network. Achieving high throughput and fair allocation of resources among competing users (or flows) in wireless networks is one of the most important problems in data communications. However, these two objectives may conflict with each other (Cheng

& Zhuang, 2008). In resource allocation, two situations must be avoided: 1) a flow must not be starved because of inefficient resources for transmission (i.e., bandwidth); and 2) a flow must not be provided more resources than necessary since only some of the resources may be used and the remaining will be wasted. Resources can be utilized efficiently if only the terminal with the best channel condition transmits, whereby the maximum throughput can be acquired. Such an opportunistic transmission, however, gives rise to unfairness and possibly violates the QoS requirements of some wireless nodes. The concept of fairness in wireless networks is a QoS policy and can be applied to various design issues such as scheduling and routing (Tassiulas & Sarkar, 2005; Maatta & Braysy, 2009).

The classic MMF problem was originally defined for wired networks in order to allocate bandwidth to a set of given routes (Bertsekas & Gallagher, 1992). Research on MMF routing in the wired environment can be split into two categories: nonsplittable and splittable (multipath). In the nonsplittable case (Bertsekas & Gallagher, 1992; Kleinberg, Rabani, & Tardos, 2001), a MMF distribution of resources (bandwidth) to connections is done for fixed single path routing. In the splittable (multipath) MMF routing case, the traffic demands are allowed to be split among multiple flows (paths) (Nace, 2002; Nace, Doan, Gourdin, & Liau, 2006; Allalouf & Shavitt, 2008; Nace, Doan, Klopfenstein, & Bashlari, 2008). It has been shown in (Nace & Pioro, 2008) that multipath (splittable) demand routing is a linear relaxation of the nonsplittable case, thus rendering the problem computationally tractable. To improve the transmission reliability and increase the probability of network survivability, the multiple paths can be selected to be link or node disjoint.

An important feature of multipath routing is the ability to provide QoS in terms of fair bandwidth allocation. Fairness based routing protocols that use the max-min model have been recently proposed in the literature (Pal, 2008; Huang,

Feng, & Zhuang, 2009; Mansouri, Mohsenian-Rad, & Wong; Tang, Hincapie, Xue, Zhang, & Bustamente, 2010; Chou & Lin, 2009). All these works focus on the lexicographic (node ordering) optimization of routing for fair bandwidth allocation. These solutions can lead to high throughput solutions with guaranteed max-min bandwidth allocation value. However, they are formulated for ideal scenarios. Specifically, the inherent influence of interference has not been taken into account.

Interference Based Routing Metrics

Providing fault tolerance and QoS provisioning in the presence of interference are major issues that must be studied jointly in wireless networks in order to get a realistic sense of network performance. Developing routing metrics has long been the central focus of network layer protocol design. To compute paths using an interference aware routing metric is essentially equivalent to computing minimum weight (shortest) paths where the link weight is generated by the routing metric. In order to efficiently compute minimum weight paths using algorithms such as Dijkstra's shortest path or Bellman-Ford, the routing metric must be isotonic. The isotonic property essentially means that a routing metric should ensure that the order of the weights of two paths are preserved if they are appended by a common third path. In addition, isotonicity ensures loop free routing. If a routing metric is not isotonic, only algorithms with exponential complexity can calculate minimum weight paths, which is not tractable for networks of even moderate size (Yang, Wang & Kravets, 2005). The two most prominent metrics are Expected Transmission Count (ETX) (De Couto, Aguaya, Bicket, & Morris, 2003) and Expected Transmission Time (ETT) (Draves, Padhye & Zill, 2004). ETX is defined as the expected number of MAC layer transmissions needed to successfully deliver a packet through a wireless link. ETT improves upon ETX by considering the differences in transmission rates. Although both metrics are isotonic, neither considers interference. The earliest metric to consider interference is Weighted Cumulative ETT (WCETT) (Draves et al., 2004). This metric essentially captures intra-flow interference by reducing the number of nodes on a path of a flow that transmit on the same channel; it gives low weight to paths that have more diversified channel assignments. However, WCETT does not capture interflow interference and is not isotonic which prevents the use of an efficient loop free routing algorithm to compute minimum weight paths. The Metric for Interference and Channel switching (MIC) (Yang et al., 2005) improves WCETT by capturing interflow interference and overcomes the non-isotonicity problem. However, MIC does not measure interference dynamically, meaning that changes to interference level over time due to signal strength and traffic load may not be captured accurately. The Interference AWARE (iAWARE) routing metric (Subramanian et al., 2006) computes paths with lower interflow and intraflow interference than MIC and WCETT. It uses SNR and SINR to continuously monitor neighboring interference variations. Yet, iAWARE is not isotonic. Recently, improvements to the ETX and ETT metrics such as Interferer Neighbor Count (INX) were proposed in (Langar et al., 2009). Similar to MIC, INX takes into account interference through the number of links that can interfere on a link *l*. This metric performs better only in low traffic load conditions, and therefore load balancing is not completely resolved.

According to the main requirements of interference, load awareness and isotonicity, existing routing metrics address only some specific requirements. For this reason, in this chapter, a new routing metric is proposed in order to simultaneously address all of these aspects.

SYSTEM MODEL

The work presented in this chapter considers a multihop cellular network (MCN) consisting of a base station, R fixed relay stations and N users. The network topology is based on the MCN model used in emerging BWA networks (Park & Bakh, 2009). As shown in Figure 1, the proposed network architecture is based on three tiers of wireless devices: 1) set N of user nodes which are the lowest tier have limited functionality (i.e., do not communicate with one another and have no routing capability); 2) set R of relay nodes that route packets between the user and the base station is the second tier. They also communicate with one another; and 3) the base station is the highest tier and is connected to the wired infrastructure. In order to avoid single points of failure (i.e., failure of a relay node which will disrupt traffic flow), the relays are connected in a mesh manner so that multiple paths are available between the user and the base station, thereby increasing service availability and fault tolerance. Mesh networking is a promising technology for numerous applications (i.e., broadband networking) and has garnered significant attention as a cost effective way of deploying wireless broadband networks (Thulasiraman, Chen, & Shen, 2010). The combination of wireless mesh networks and relay networks has been discussed in the literature where the general structure of a mesh network has been incorporated with relaying aspects (Thulasiraman & Shen, 2010). The defined network architecture uses a wireless relay network structure that is enhanced with mesh networking capabilities.

This topology setup ensures that the network is at least 2-link connected (i.e., each node has at least two link connections to other nodes). In DMPR schemes, the disjointedness property ensures that when k multiple paths are constructed, no set of $k-1$ link failures can disconnect all the paths. Through Menger's Theorem (Bagchi, Chaudhary, & Kolman, 2005), it has been shown that for two distinct nodes x and y, the minimum number of edges whose removal disconnects x and y is equal to the maximum number of pairwise link disjoint paths from x to y. Thus, in this case, 2-connectivity is a necessary and sufficient con-

Figure 1. Network architecture

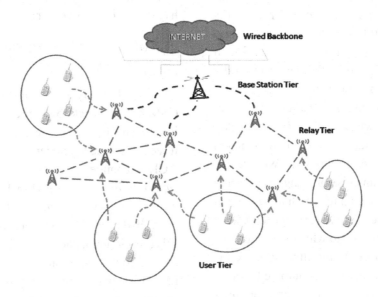

dition to find a solution for two disjoint paths for each user node to the base station. Two-connectivity in wireless networks has been studied in (Thulasiraman et al., 2006; Thulasiraman et al., 2007)[2].

It is assumed that each relay node is equipped with omnidirectional transceivers and that relays are used purely for packet forwarding (i.e., relays do not inject traffic into the network). It is also assumed that each user and relay node has a maximum power level, P_{max}, where the P_{max} value is different for the user and relay node. It is also assumed that channels have been assigned to the links in the network using a generic link coloring approach. In addition, each node knows the geographic location of all the other nodes in the cell via location discovery schemes (Mauve, Widmer, & Hartenstein, 2001). This information is necessary for the receivers to feedback SINR measurements to their respective transmitters.

Interference Model

The network architecture is represented by a communication graph, $G = (V, E)$, where V is the set of nodes (relays, users and base station) and E is the set of edges. The physical interference model states that a communication between nodes u and v is successful if the SINR at v (the receiver) is above a certain threshold. The SINR for transmission between u and v is given as follows

$$SINR_{uv} = \frac{P_v(u)}{N + \sum_{w \in V'} P_v(w)} \geq \beta \qquad (1)$$

where $P_v(u)$ is the received power at node v due to node u, N is the noise power, V' is the subset of nodes in the network that are transmitting simultaneously and β is the SINR threshold.

In this chapter, both the protocol and physical interference models are considered, similar to the approach given in (Brar et al., 2006). To be specific, the following variation of the protocol model is used to accurately mimic the behavior of carrier sense multiple access/collision avoidance (CSMA/CA) relay based cellular networks (Park & Bakh, 2009). Let R_T^{max} (r_T^{max}) and $R_I^{max}(r_I^{max})$ represent the maximum transmission and interference ranges of each relay (user) node, respectively. All relay nodes use the same maximum transmission range (R_T^{max}) as do all the user nodes (r_T^{max}). Each wireless node i (either relay or user node) has a transmission range which is a circle in a 2D plane, centered at i with radius R_T^{max} (r_T^{max}). The transmission range represents the maximum distance up to which a packet can be received, while the interference range represents the maximum distance up to which simultaneous transmissions interfere. In the literature, the interference range is usually chosen to be twice as large as the transmission range which is not necessarily a practical assumption (Iyer et al., 2009). The actual values of the transmission and interference ranges depend on the transmission power used by the nodes. To provide realistic limits for R_T^{max} (r_T^{max}) and $R_I^{max}(r_I^{max})$, a method called a "reality check" is used. The reality check method, introduced in (Shi et al., 2009), essentially sets a realistic interference range in which links are assumed to interfere. For the protocol model, R_T^{max} (r_T^{max}) and $R_I^{max}(r_I^{max})$ are the only two parameters used. Since the underlying physical layer is the same, the parameter R_T^{max} (r_T^{max}) should be consistent with the β parameter in the physical model, as shown in Equation (1). Two nodes with distance R_T^{max} (r_T^{max}) should be able to communicate with each other under the maximum transmission power P_{max} and the SINR should be β. As a result, according to (Shi et al., 2009), R_T^{max} (r_T^{max}) is $\dfrac{P_{max}}{\beta}$.

Note that the maximum interference range, R_I^{max} (r_I^{max}), is a parameter introduced by the protocol model and there is no corresponding parameter in the physical model. The only requirement on $R_I^{max}(r_I^{max})$ is $R_I^{max}(r_I^{max}) > R_T^{max}$ (r_T^{max}) i.e., a lower bound for $R_I^{max}(r_I^{max})$ is R_T^{max} (r_T^{max}). Thus,

if the interference range is set to be slightly higher than the transmission range, $R_T^{max}(r_T^{max}) = \dfrac{P_{max}}{\beta}$, then the solution is more realistic.

Since link layer availability is required for CSMA/CA, an acknowledgement (ACK) packet is generated by each receiver for every data packet it receives. Due to carrier sensing and RTS/CTS/ACK exchanges, a transmission along link $e = (u, v)$ (in either direction) blocks all simultaneous transmissions within the interference ranges of u and v. In the physical interference model, successful reception of a packet sent by node u to node v depends on the SINR at v. To be coherent with the link-layer availability, the physical interference model is extended as follows. It is assumed that a packet sent by node u is correctly received by node v if and only if the packet is successfully received by v, and the ACK sent by node v is correctly received by node u. Furthermore, for a transmission from node x to node y that is concurrent with the packet on (u,v), the interference from both node x's data packet and from node y's ACK is accounted for. Although only one of x and y transmits at a time, their data and ACK packets could both overlap with either the data packet or the ACK along (u, v). Thus, the maximum of the interferences from x and y is chosen when calculating the total interferences at u and v. Note that which of the two (x or y) contributes the maximum interference could be different at u and v. Thus, a packet sent along link (u, v) (in either direction) is correctly received if and only if:

$$SINR_{uv} = \frac{P_v(u)}{N + \sum_{(x,y) \in E'} \max(P_v(x), P_v(y))} \geq \beta$$

(2)

and

$$SINR_{vu} = \frac{P_u(v)}{N + \sum\limits_{(x,y)\in E'} \max(P_u(x), P_u(y))} \geq \beta$$

$$(3)$$

where E' contains all the links that have simultaneous transmissions concurrent with the one on (u, v).

It must be noted that optimization techniques to find an efficient algorithm that determines the collision domain and backoff times for each node based on the interference range have been studied in (Zhou & Mitchell, 2010). The authors propose closed-form expressions for the mean backoff time in terms of path flow variables, making it possible to optimize the network based on multipath routing. However, their approach is analytically complex. In addition, since the focus of this chapter is to incorporate the physical-layer interference into the protocol model, determining the optimal collision domain and wait periods is not relevant.

Isotonocity

As mentioned earlier, isotonicity reflects the ability of a routing metric to compute minimum weight and loop-free paths. Assume that for any path a, its weight is defined by a routing metric, which is a function of a, denoted as $W(a)$. Denoting the concatenation of two paths a and b by $a \oplus b$, isotonicity can be defined as follows:

Definition 3.1: isotonicity: A routing metric, $W(\cdot)$, is isotonic if $W(a) \leq W(b)$ implies that both

$$W(a \oplus c) \leq W(b \oplus c)$$

and

$$W(c' \oplus a) \leq W(c' \oplus b),$$

for all *a, b, c, and c'*.

In (Yang et al., 2005) it was shown that isotonicity is a sufficient and necessary condition for both the Bellman-Ford and Dijkstra's algorithms to find minimum weight paths that are loop free. Therefore if a routing metric can be proven to be isotonic, any variation of a shortest path algorithm can be used to route packets in a wireless network.

ROUTING WITH INTERFLOW AND INTRAFLOW INTERFERENCE METRIC (RI^3M)

Problem Formulation

The RI^3M interference routing metric takes into consideration the following three factors: interflow interference, intraflow interference, and traffic load. Interflow interference generally results in bandwidth starvation for some nodes since a flow contends for bandwidth along its own path and its neighboring area. To prevent such starvation, the routing metric must balance the traffic load along the path of the flow and reduce the interflow interference imposed in the neighboring area. RI^3M consists of two components. The first component, IL, deals with interflow interference and load awareness. The second component, channel switching cost CSC, captures intraflow interference. The interference aware routing metric can be formalized as follows. Let $G(V,E)$ be an undirected, two-connected network, where V is the set of nodes and E is the set of links. Let p be a path from a user node to the base station. RI^3M is defined as follows:

$$\sum_{\forall (i,j)\in p} IL_{ij} + \sum_{\forall i\in p} CSC_i \qquad (4)$$

where node i represents a node on path p and link (i,j) represents a link on the path p.

IL_{ij} Component

The IL_{ij} component is intended to depict information about the interflow interference and traffic load simultaneously. It consists of two separate subcomponents. To capture the interflow interference, the concept of the interference ratio (*IR*) (Subramanian et al., 2006), which is based on the physical interference model, is used. The *IR* depicts the interference based on the ratio between SNR and SINR. The *IR* captures interference by monitoring the signal strength values. When there is no interference (i.e., no interfering neighbors or no traffic generated by interfering neighbors), the SINR of link *(i,j)* is independent of the interflow interference and the quality of the link is determined by the intraflow interference component. Equation (5) shows the *IR* ratio:

$$IR_{ij} = \frac{SINR_{ij} + SINR_{ji}}{SINR_{ij}} \qquad (5)$$

where SNR is given by $\dfrac{P_j(i)}{N}$ and the SINR in the numerator is the sum of the SINR values given in Equations (2) and (3).

To estimate the traffic load on a wireless relay node, a typical approach is to measure the traffic volume going through the corresponding node in terms of byte rate or packet rate. Unfortunately, this approach is unable to give an accurate estimate of the usage of the radio channel at which the node operates because the total capacity of the network is not fixed and depends on many factors, such as the physical transmission rate of each relay node, frame size, number of retransmissions, interference, etc. Simply counting the bytes or even packets going through a relay node fails to take into account these factors. In light of these limitations, the authors of (Athanasiou, Korakis, Ercetin, & Tassiulas, 2009) adopt an alternative approach to estimate the traffic load, which is based on the percentage of channel time of the relay node that is consumed for frame transmission.

To measure the traffic load, the concept of Channel Busy Time (*CBT*) is used. A radio channel's time consists of a series of interleaved busy periods and idle periods. A busy period is a time period in which one node attempts to transmit frames, while other nodes hold off their transmission. An idle period is a time period in which every node considers the radio medium available for access. Using the *CBT*, it is possible to estimate the traffic load (channel utilization) on each link. The *CBT* calculation is the percentage of time that a channel is busy (transmitting). In order to compute this time, the different states that a node can be assigned must be defined first:

- **Success:** This state refers to the case where a node has successfully received the acknowledgment of the packet it has sent.
- **Backoff:** Even though a node has some data to transmit and the medium is free, there is a random waiting period (during which the wireless medium has to remain idle) before it starts sending its data.
- **Wait:** If there are ongoing transmissions within the interference range of the node which causes the SINR threshold to drop below β, it has to wait until the ongoing communications are completed before starting its own.
- **Collision:** In this state, a node which has sent a packet never receives an acknowledgment for this packet.

Let $T_{success}$, $T_{backoff}$, T_{wait}, and $T_{collision}$ be the time spent in the states Success, Backoff, Wait, and Collision, respectively. The idle time (i.e., time where there is no data to keep the channel busy), T_{idle}, considers backoff times, collision times, and the waiting times. Thus, the percentage of time the channel spends idle is defined as

$$T_{idle} = \frac{T_{backoff} + T_{collision} + T_{wait}}{T_{backoff} + T_{collision} + T_{wait} + T_{success}}$$

$$(6)$$

Let us denote the denominator of Equation (6) as the total time T_{total}. Then, the CBT for a link (i,j) is defined as

$$CBT_{ij} = \frac{T_{total} - T_{idle}}{T_{total}} \qquad (7)$$

The CBT is used as a smoothing function, weighted over IR_{ij}. Using the IR_{ij} and CBT_{ij} sub-components, IL_{ij} is defined as follows:

$$IL_{ij} = (1 - IR_{ij}) * CBT_{ij} \qquad (8)$$

where $0 \leq IR \leq 1$ and $0 \leq CBT \leq 1$.

CSC Component

To reduce the intraflow interference, the RI^3M routing metric uses the CSC component. CSC, originally defined in (Yang et al., 2005), designates paths with consecutive links using the same channel with higher weight than paths that alternate their channel assignments. This allows paths with more diversified channel assignments to be favored in the routing process. Intraflow interference can occur between successive nodes on a path, however, depending on the interference range, it can also occur between nodes further away along the path. In this case, it is necessary to consider the channel assignments at more hops in order to choose an effective path that reduces intraflow interference. To eliminate the intraflow interference between node i and its previous hop,

$prev(i)$, node i must transmit to the next hop, $next(i)$, using a different channel from the one it uses to receive from $prev(i)$. CSC denotes $CH(i)$ as the channel that node i transmits on to $next(i)$. The CSC of node i for intraflow interference reduction of successive nodes is given as

$$CSC_i = \begin{cases} w_1, & \text{if } CH(prev(i)) \neq CH(i) \\ w_2, & \text{if } CH(prev(i)) = CH(i) \end{cases} \qquad (9)$$

where $w_2 \geq w_1 \geq 0$ to ensure that a higher cost is imposed for those nodes that transmit on the same channel consecutively. In order to capture intraflow interference between two nodes that are two hops away, node i interferes with both nodes $prev(i)$ and $prev^2(i)$, where $prev^2(i)$ is the node that is the two hop precedent of i. According to (Yang et al., 2005), the multihop extension of the CSC equation of Equation (9) is Equation (10) where w_3 captures the intraflow interference between nodes $prev^2(i)$ and i and w_2 captures the intraflow interference between nodes $prev(i)$ and i. The weight w_3 must be strictly less than the weight w_2 because since the further away that two nodes are, the less interference exists between them. The intraflow interference is considered to be up to the limit of a node's interference range which is typically within a three hop range.

Equation 10.

$$CSC_i = \begin{cases} w_2, & \text{if } CH(prev^2(i)) \neq CH(i) = CH(prev(i)) \\ w_3, & \text{if } CH(prev^2(i)) = CH(i) \neq Ch(prev(i)) \\ w_2 + w_3, & \text{if } CH(prev^2(i)) = CH(i) = CH(prev(i)) \\ w_1, & \text{otherwise} \end{cases}$$

Figure 2. (a) Example to illustrate the non-isotonocity of the RI³M routing metric; (b) Decomposition of the network in (a) into a virtual network to show that RI³M is isotonic

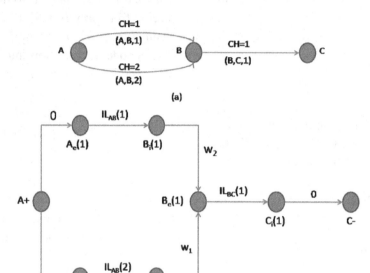

Virtual Network Decomposition to Illustrate Isotonicity

The RI^3M routing metric is not isotonic if used directly. This can be seen in the example network given in Figure 2a. In the example, a link is represented by three parameters: starting node of the link, ending node of the link, and the channel the link transmits on. If it is assumed that link $(A, B, 1)$ has a smaller RI3M value than link $(A, B, 2)$, the weights of paths $(A, B, 1)$ and $(A, B, 2)$ satisfy: $RI^3M(A, B, 1) < RI^3M(A, B, 2)$. However, adding path $(B, C, 1)$ to path $(A, B, 1)$ introduces a higher cost than adding $(B, C, 1)$ to $(A, B, 2)$ because of the reuse of channel 1 on path $(A, B, 1) \oplus (B, C, 1)$. Thus

$$RI^3M((A, B, 1) \oplus (B, C, 1)) \\ > RI^3M((A, B, 2) \oplus (B, C, 1)),$$

which does not satisfy the definition of isotonicity.

To make RI^3M into an isotonic routing metric, a decomposition technique is used that creates a virtual network from the real network and decomposes RI^3M into isotonic link weight assignments on the virtual network. First introduced in (Yang et al., 2005) to prove the isotonicity of the MIC routing metric, the decomposition of RI^3M is based on the fact that the non-isotonic behavior of RI^3M is caused by the different increments of path weights due to the addition of a link on a path. Whether a cost increment will be different by adding a link is only related to the channel assignment of the previous link on the path. Since the possible assignments of channels for the precedent link are limited, several virtual nodes are introduced to represent these possible channel assignments. Namely, for every channel c that a node X's radios are configured to, two virtual nodes $X_i(c)$ and $X_e(c)$ are introduced. $X_i(c)$ indicates that node $prev(X)$ transmits to X on channel c. $X_e(c)$ indicates that node X transmits to its next hop, $next(X)$, on channel c. The subscript i stands for ingress and the subscript e stands for egress. In addition, two additional virtual nodes are introduced, *X-* and *X+*, which represent the start and end nodes of a flow (i.e., *X-* is used as the virtual destination node for flows destined to node *X* and *X+* is used as the virtual source node for flows starting at node *X*. Hence, *X+* has a link weight with 0 pointing to each egress virtual node and *X-* has a link weight 0 pointing away from each ingress virtual node of *X*.

Links from the ingress virtual nodes to the egress virtual nodes at node *X* are added and the weights of these links are assigned to capture different *CSC* costs. Link $(X_i(c), X_e(c))$ represents that node *X* does not change channels while forwarding packets, and hence, weight w_2 is assigned to this link. Similarly, weight w_1 is assigned to link, $(X_i(c), X_e(c1))$ where $c \neq c1$, to represent the low cost of changing channels while forwarding packets. Links between the virtual nodes belonging to different real nodes are used to capture the *IL* weight. Figure 2b shows the virtual decomposition of Figure 2a.

By building the virtual network from a real network, *RI³M* is essentially decomposed in the real network into weight assignments to the links between virtual nodes. This is because the *RI³M* weight of a real path in a real network can be reconstructed by aggregating all of the weights of the virtual links on the corresponding virtual path. The *IL* part of *RI³M* is reflected in the weight of the links between virtual nodes in different real nodes. The *CSC* costs are captured by routing through different virtual links inside real nodes.

Multipath Routing Using *RI³M*

Now that *RI³M* has been shown to be isotonic using a virtual network decomposition, it can be used with any shortest path algorithm to find least interfering (minimum weight) paths. The problem of finding two link disjoint paths (primary and backup) of minimum total weight across a network has been dealt with efficiently

by Suurballe's algorithm (Bhandari, 1999). The algorithm developed by Suurballe has become the reference algorithm for finding link disjoint paths in wireless networks. Suurballe's algorithm always finds two link disjoint paths from a source node to the destination, as long as the paths exist in the network, assuring the total weight of both paths is the minimum among all pairs of paths in the network. Suurballe's algorithm is run on the virtual network $G_v(V_v, E_v)$, where V_v and E_v are the nodes and links of the virtual network, respectively. The link weights are determined by the values of the *RI³M* routing metric. Due to space constraints, the steps of Suurballe's routing algorithm are omitted in this chapter. For further details of Suurballe's algorithm, refer to (Bhandari, 1999).

LEXICOGRAPHIC MMF MULTIPATH FLOW (*LMX:M³F*) ROUTING ALGORITHM WITH INTERFERENCE CONSTRAINTS

Problem Formulation

In this chapter, the MMF bandwidth allocation problem is modeled as a multicommodity flow (MCF) problem. The MCF problem is a network flow problem where multiple commodities (demands) flow through the network (Shahrokhi & Matula, 1990). It is assumed that each demand has two candidate paths (where the paths are determined by using *RI³M*). Thus, the flows realizing each demand volume are split among the allowable paths. In the remainder of this chapter, vectors will be denoted with an arrow overhead. Optimal vectors will be denoted as regular vectors except with an additional star (*).

Definition: multicommodity flow: Given *D* demands, let $\delta_{edp} x_{dp} \geq 0$ be the flow allocated to path *p* of commodity (demand) *d*, $d \in D$ in link $e \in E$, where δ_{edp} is a binary variable that denotes whether link *e* belongs to path *p* or not. Also, consider a vector $\vec{X}_d = (x_{dp} : \forall p, d \in D)$ as a single commodity flow of commodity d. A multicommodity flow is the union of flows for each commodity. Specifically, $\vec{X} = (\vec{X}_d : d \in D)$ is a feasible multicommodity flow if

$$\sum_{d \in D} \sum_{p \in P_d} \delta_{edp} x_{dp} \leq C_e, \forall e \in E.$$

The capacity of link $e \in E$ is denoted C_e and is mathematically expressed as

$$C_e = \log_2(1 + SINR_e) \geq \beta \qquad (11)$$

where $SINR_e$ is given in Equation (1).

In this chapter, the objective is to attain the MMF bandwidth allocation vector under interference constraints where the allocation vector is lexicographically the largest possible.

Definition: An n-vector $\vec{x} = (x_1, x_2, ..., x_n)$ sorted in non-decreasing order $(x_1 \leq x_2 \leq ... \leq x_n)$ is *lexicographically greater* than another n-vector $\vec{y} = (y_1, y_2, ..., y_n)$ sorted in non-decreasing order $(y_1 \leq y_2 \leq ... \leq y_n)$ if an index k, $0 \leq k \leq n$ exists, such that $x_i = y_i$ for $i = 1, 2, ..., k$ and $x_k > y_k$.

In the following section, the formulation of the lexicographic bandwidth allocation algorithm will be discussed using the interference-aware routing metric, RI^3M, that was developed earlier in the chapter.

LMX:M³F Algorithm

Given the network G, paths for routing the traffic flow are found by using the routing metric, RI^3M, and running Suurballe's multipath routing algorithm. Given these paths, the formulation of the lexicographically largest allocation vector using MMF considering interference constraints and the subsequent methodology used to solve it is provided. The *LMX:M³F* formulation is given in Equations (12)-(15) (referred to as Problem A in the remainder of the chapter) and follows a multicommodity flow approach.

LMX:M³F

Problem A

Objective: Find the total bandwidth allocation vector such that it is lexicographically maximal among all total bandwidth allocation vectors.

$$\text{lexicographically maximize } \vec{X} \qquad (12)$$

subject to

$$\sum_{p \in P_d} x_{dp} = X_d, \qquad \forall d \in D \qquad (13)$$

$$\sum_{d \in D} \sum_{p \in P_d} \delta_{edp} x_{dp} \leq C_e, \qquad \forall e \in E \qquad (14)$$

$$x_{dp} \geq 0 \qquad (15)$$

where P_d are the paths for demand d, x_{dp} is the flow (bandwidth) allocated to demand path p of demand d, and X_d is the total flow (bandwidth) allocated to demand d, $\vec{X} = (X_1, X_2, ..., X_D)$.

In order to find the MMF allocation vector for the corresponding paths, the quantity known as the *demand satisfaction vector* $\vec{t}$ is defined. Let $\gamma_d \geq 0$ be the flow value of x_{dp}, and $\zeta^+(v)$ and $\zeta^-(v)$ be the outgoing and incoming links to node v, respectively. The law of flow conservation states that

$$\sum_{e \in \zeta^+(v)} x_{dp} - \sum_{e \in \zeta^-(v)} x_{dp} = \begin{cases} \gamma_d, & \text{if } v = \text{base station} \\ -\gamma_d, & \text{if } v = \text{source} \\ 0, & \text{otherwise} \end{cases} \qquad (16)$$

A feasible multicommodity flow $\vec{X}$, with $\gamma_d \geq h_d$, $d \in D$ defines an admissible flow (bandwidth), where h_d is the amount of demand to be routed. Assume that $\vec{X}$ is feasible and also consider a vector $\vec{t} = (t_d \geq 0 : d \in D)$ such that $\gamma_d = t_d h_d$ in Equation (16). If $t_d \geq 1$ for all $d \in D$, then the flow is admissible (i.e., it fulfills the demand requirement $h_d, d \in D$). Thus, $\vec{t}$ is denoted as the demand satisfaction vector for routing vector $\vec{X}$. Specifically, the physical meaning of the value t is the amount that is added to saturate/satisfy x_{dp}. The optimization formulation given in Equations (17)-(21) (referred as Problem B in the remainder of the chapter) is used to solve for t.

Problem B

maximize t $\hspace{3cm}$ (17)

subject to

$$X_d = \sum_{p \in P_d} x_{dp}, \qquad \forall d \in D \qquad (18)$$

$$t - X_d \leq 0, \quad \forall d \in D \qquad (19)$$

$$\sum_{d \in D} \sum_{p \in P_d} \delta_{edp} x_{dp} \leq C_e, \qquad \forall e \in E \qquad (20)$$

$$x_{dp} \geq 0 \qquad (21)$$

The objective function in Equation (17) and the constraint in Equation (19) are equivalent to the ultimate objective to be achieved given in Equation (22):

$$\max \min \ X_d : d \in D \qquad (22)$$

Problem A can be solved by computing consecutively the value of the demand satisfaction vector of Problem B. Primarily, the idea is that first, the lowest value among the components of $\vec{t}$ has to be maximized before the second lowest value is maximized. In order to ensure that the demands are satisfied, it is necessary to check which total demand allocations, X_d, can be further increased. A demand d whose satisfaction value t_d cannot be further increased is called blocking (Nace & Pioro, 2008). To check the satisfaction of a demand, the following linear program (LP) (Equations (23)-(27)), referred to as Problem C, is solved for each demand d.

Problem C

maximize X_d $\hspace{3cm}$ (23)

subject to

$$X'_d = \sum_{p \in P_{d'}} x_{d'p}, \qquad \forall d' \in D \qquad (24)$$

$$t_{d'} - X_{d'} \leq 0, \qquad \forall d' \in D \qquad (25)$$

$$\sum_{d' \in D} \sum_{p \in P_{d'}} \delta_{ed'p} x_{d'p} \leq C_e, \qquad \forall e \in E \qquad (26)$$

$$x_{d'p} \geq 0 \qquad (27)$$

where $t_{d'}$ are constants. To put Problem C in perspective, let t^* be the optimal solution of the LP. A demand is nonblocking (can be further increased) if the optimal X_d value, X^*_d, is strictly greater than t^* (i.e., $X^*_d > t^*$).

The components of Problem B and Problem C are used in conjunction to solve the original $LMX{:}M^\beta F$ (Problem A) problem. The algorithm for solving $LMX{:}M^\beta F$ is given as follows:

Step1: Solve Problem B. Let $(t^*, \vec{x}^*, \vec{X}^*)$ be the optimal solution of Problem A. Initialize: $k := 0$ (number of iterations), $Z_0 := \varnothing$ (set of demands that are blocking/saturated), $Z_1 = \{1, 2, ..., D\}$, and $t_d := t^*$ for each $d \in Z_1$.

Step2: $k := k + 1$. Consider each demand, $d \in Z_1$, one by one to check whether the total allocated bandwidth X_d^* can be increased more than t^* without decreasing the already found maximal allocations t_d' for all other demands, d'. To check the demands, solve Problem C. If there are no blocking demands in Z_1, go to Step3. Otherwise for blocking demand d, add d to set Z_0 and delete it from set

$$Z_1, Z_0 := Z_0 \cup \{d\}, Z_1 := Z_1 \setminus \{d\}.$$

If $Z_1 = \varnothing$ STOP. Then,

$$\vec{X}^* = (X_1^*, X_2^*, ..., X_D^*) = (t_1, t_2, ..., t_d)$$

is the solution of Problem A.

Step3: To improve the current best bandwidth allocation, solve the following LP (Problem D).

maximize t

subject to

$$X_d = \sum_{p \in P_d} x_{dp}, \qquad \forall d \in Z_1$$

$$t - X_d \leq 0, \qquad \forall d \in Z_0$$

$$\sum_{d \in D} \sum_{p \in P_d} \delta_{edp} x_{dp} \leq C_e, \qquad \forall e \in E$$

$$x_{dp} \geq 0$$

Let $(t^*, \vec{x}^*, \vec{X}^*)$ be the optimal solution of Problem D. Put $t_d := t^*$ for each $d \in Z_1$. Go to Step2.

PERFORMANCE EVALUATION

Simulation Model and Performance Metrics

For the simulations, a two-connected cellular network G in a 900 x 900 m² region where all nodes are stationary is considered. Each user generates traffic and the flows are routed to and from the base station. NS-2 is used to simulate the networks and CPLEX is used to solve the optimization formulation for *LMX:M³F*. The base station is located in the center of the network. Locations for the set of relay nodes that form the mesh network and the users are randomly generated. It is assumed that the base station and relays have an infinite buffer, thus eliminating complications due to buffer overflow. The simulation parameters used are as follows: system bandwidth (W) = 1MHz, additive white Gaussian noise (AWGN) = -90 dBW/Hz; transmission power: relay (35 dBm), user (24 dBm) (note that the power levels of the nodes are such that it is sufficient to allow nodes to connect to at least two of its neighbors, ensuring two-connectivity); physical layer specification: 802.11; number of channels per radio: 12; and antenna: omnidirectional. To evaluate the performance of *RI³M*, the following performance metrics are studied: 1) end-to-end delay (amount of time it takes to deliver packets from the client node to the base station) and 2) flow throughput. Twenty simulations are run for each set of data and the average results are shown. To evaluate the performance of *LMX:M³F*, the following performance metrics are adopted: 1) bandwidth blocking ratio (BBR): BBR represents the percentage of the amount of blocked traffic over the amount of bandwidth requirements of all traffic requests (connection requests) during the entire simulation period; 2) total bandwidth usage: this measurement helps examine whether the $LMX{:}M^3F$ algorithm can save more network resources (use less) than other established MMF routing algorithms that incorporate interference; and 3) link load: measurement that indicates the traffic load on each link due to different routing approaches. Note that the performance evaluation of $LMX{:}M^3F$ is based upon the paths determined from using the RI^3M routing metric.

As benchmarks for evaluating the effectiveness of the proposed routing metric, five other routing metrics in the literature are used for comparison. Specifically, ETX (De Couto et al., 2003), ETT (Draves et al., 2004), MIC (Yang et al., 2005), iAWARE (Subramanian et al., 2006), and INX (Langar et al., 2009). Each metric is used with Suurballe's disjoint multipath routing algorithm. The proposed routing metric is also used with two disjoint multipath routing algorithms. First, the algorithm developed in (Kortebi, Gourhant, & Agoulmine, 2007) introduces a routing metric where a node calculates the SINR to its neighboring links based on a 2-Hop interference estimation algorithm (2-HEAR). Second, the algorithm developed in (Teo et al., 2008) provides an interference minimized multipath routing (I2MR) algorithm that increases throughput by discovering zone disjoint paths using the concept of path correlation. As benchmarks for evaluating the effectiveness of the bandwidth allocation algorithm, $LMX{:}M^3F$ is compared to two MMF bandwidth allocation algorithms that consider interference when allocating bandwidth. First, the algorithm developed in (Tang et al., 2005) is an interference-based routing and bandwidth algorithm, known as MICB. The protocol model is used to create an auxiliary graph such that the maximum interference level within the network does not exceed a maximum value. Second, the algorithm described in (Wang et al., 2008) quantifies interference through the creation of contention graphs where interfering

flows are captured in multihop wireless networks. The implementations of these algorithms are modified so that multiple paths are considered.

Simulation Results and Discussion

RI^3M is evaluated first in terms of end-to-end delay. The end-to-end user demand delivery delay is used as a metric to evaluate the impact of the interference quantification method of RI^3M in comparison to the existing routing metrics and the two established disjoint multipath routing algorithms. To measure the end-to-end delay, the transmitting rate of the user and relay nodes are set to 4.5 Mbps. All routing flows are CBR flows with 512 byte packets. To model the packet dropping error, for a given SINR value, the packet error ratio (PER) (Takai, Martin, & Bragodia, 2001) is used, which is readily available in NS-2.

Performance Evaluation of RI³M

RI^3M is first compared with the existing routing metrics. Networks with 100 nodes (1 base station, 6 relays, and 93 user nodes) are simulated. Figure 3 shows the average end-to-end delay values of RI^3M versus the other routing metrics, measured against varying demands (traffic load). It can be seen that the proposed RI^3M routing metric achieves the lowest delay in comparison to the other metrics, particularly as demands increase. It can be said that RI^3M quantifies interference more accurately because it considers the influence of interflow and intraflow interference which thereby allows us to avoid paths with high interference, and reduce the time taken to deliver a packet. The remaining metrics behave somewhat similarly because most of them are derived from one another. Therefore, despite small implementation differences, there is no overarching performance improvement among the remaining metrics (i.e., ETT, ETX, MIC, and iAWARE). As can be seen from Figure 3, the delay values for all the metrics

Figure 3. Average end-to-end delay values for RI³M compared to prominent routing metrics in the literature

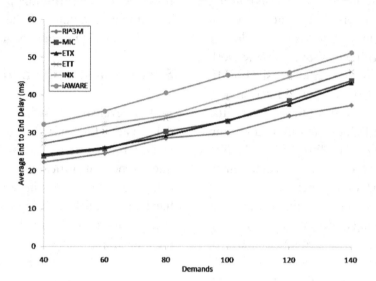

(including *RI³M*) increase as demands increase, which intuitively is true.

In Figure 4, the average end-to-end delay values for *RI³M* with Suurballe's algorithm, referred to as SRA-*RI³M* in the simulation graphs, is compared to the two aforementioned disjoint multipath routing algorithms. They are referred to as 2-HEAR and I2MR in the simulation graphs. The SRA-*RI³M* achieves the lowest end-to-end delay compared to the other algorithms. The better performance of the SRA-*RI³M* can be justified as follows: In both 2-HEAR and I2MR, the paths are formed using incomplete interference information. In 2-HEAR, the SINR calculated by each

Figure 4. Comparison of average end-to-end delay for Suurballe's disjoint multipath routing algorithm using RI³M (SRA-RI³M) and two established disjoint multipath routing algorithms: I2MR and 2-HEAR

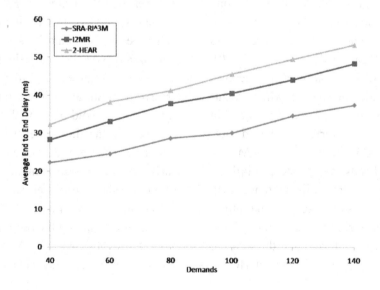

Figure 5. Average flow throughput generated by RI³M versus prominent routing metrics in the literature

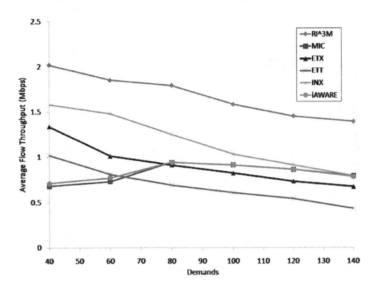

node only includes those nodes within a 2-hop range which means that even if interference beyond this range occurs, it is not captured in the routing metric (interflow and intraflow interference not fully accounted for). If the interference level is high beyond the 2-hop range, then any paths built may not be successful as interference may cause a drop in packets and a retransmission is required. This obviously incurs delay. A similar argument can be used with the I2MR algorithm. In this case, RI^3M quantifies the interference from both within flows and in the neighboring area.

Next, the average flow throughput that results from the use of the various routing metrics is discussed. Figure 5 shows the average flow throughput using RI^3M and prominent routing metrics in the literature. It can be seen that MIC and iAWARE have the lowest throughput at low traffic demands in comparison to the other metrics. ETX and INX have better throughput with low loads, but their performance decreases with high traffic demands. In Figure 5, the ETT metric exhibits unstable behavior primarily because it overestimates link quality by inaccurately probing the channel. Moreover, ETT does not depend on the traffic load. Although MIC and iAWARE

partially rely on ETT, these metrics employ normalization functions to smoothen ETT values, and therefore, become more stable. This indicates the unpredictability of the results for the three metrics: ETT, MIC, and iAWARE. The remaining metrics behave intuitively, i.e., lower throughput as demands increase. Overall, RI^3M is able to achieve higher throughput than the remaining metrics over the varying traffic demands shown.

Performance Evaluation of LMX:M³F

For the $LMX:M^3F$ algorithm, it is first evaluated in terms of BBR. It is compared with MICB (Tang et al., 2005) and MMFContGr (Wang et al., 2008), respectively, as shown in the simulation graphs. All three algorithms are run on networks with different densities. Figure 6 shows the BBR results from the simulated networks with 46 (6 relays and 40 users). The networks have only one base station each. It can be seen that the $LMX:M^3F$ algorithm performs the best in most cases. The blocking ratio increases no matter which algorithm is used because of heavier traffic load. The average blocking ratio difference between the proposed solution of $LMX:M^3F$ and that of MICB and

Figure 6. BBR comparison for networks with 46 nodes (6 relays and 40 users)

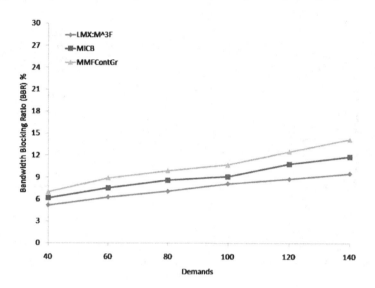

MMFContGr is 16 and 13 percent, respectively for the network of size 46 nodes. Essentially, the BBR indicates if a connection request for traffic is blocked. If traffic is blocked, it means that there is less bandwidth on a link than there should be to accommodate the offered traffic. For the best performance, the BBR should be kept as low as possible. Given the BBR results in Figure 6, the BBR of *LMX:M³F* is lower than that of the MICB and MMFContGr algorithms. Therefore, it can be claimed that the network performance improves under the proposed algorithm. Similar results were observed with varying sizes of networks.

Next, the real-time network resource usage for all three algorithms is shown. Figure 7 shows the results of the bandwidth usage for the three algorithms. As expected, *LMX:M³F* uses the least amount of bandwidth for varying demands. In the case of 46 nodes, on average, the bandwidth usage of *LMX:M³F* compared to MICB and MMFContGr is 11 and 14 percent less, respectively. Similar simulations were conducted on networks with less density (i.e., less number of nodes) and it was observed that there was less clarity in the total bandwidth usage for such networks. In other words, there was little variation in bandwidth usage be-

tween the three algorithms. The conclusion is that the proposed algorithm is more effective in network resource usage in higher density networks. Given that BWA networks are generally used in dense urban settings, the *LMX:M³F* fits the application. However, the *LMX:M³F* algorithm is time consuming to solve for very large networks with thousands of demands because each demand must be checked for bandwidth satisfaction (see Problem C). Thus, the algorithm is limited to a certain extent because of scalability.

Lastly, the impact that the *LMX:M³F* algorithm has on the load balancing of the network across various links is discussed. The *LMX:M³F* algorithm is compared with that of an unbalanced routing scheme (no fairness incorporated) and a traditional max-min fair routing approach, which minimizes the load of only the maximally loaded link in the network (does not look for the lexicographically highest). Networks with 10 (2 relays and 8 users) nodes (each network has one base station) are simulated. Figure 8 shows the link load on various links for networks of 10 nodes. The link number represents each individually numbered link in the network. It can be seen that the unbalanced routing scheme has some links

Figure 7. Comparison of total bandwidth usage for networks with 46 nodes (6 relays and 40 users)

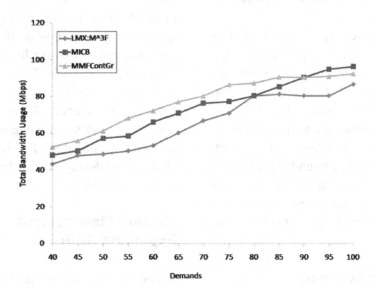

Figure 8. Link loads on various links for network with 10 nodes

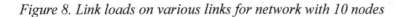

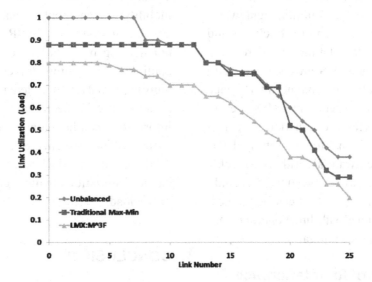

with 100 percent utilization. When the traditional max-min routing approach is used, the link load utilization is better, but there are still some links that are nearly 90 percent loaded. The lexicographic bandwidth allocation algorithm performs an optimization of all the links and presents a better load balance of the traffic load, as can be seen in the results. It can be observed that the

$LMX:M^3F$ algorithm generally results in approximately 75 percent of the links having the same load. It can also be seen that the maximum load of any link is less than 1. This allows for spare capacity to exist on the link so that a proportionate increase in demands can be tolerated.

FUTURE RESEARCH DIRECTIONS

In this chapter, key research issues related to interference aware resource allocation have been presented. The results demonstrate the effectiveness of the proposed routing metric and the bandwidth allocation algorithm. From this research, important future research directions to improve system performance have been revealed. This chapter is the first step to understanding the impact of interference on resource management in broadband wireless access networks. Further research directions should address the following important issues.

Relay Node Displacement

Employing various relay nodes alleviates the problem of traffic congestion and single points of failure. In the presence of multiple gateways, traffic load can be balanced more effectively and efficiently, thereby facilitating traffic routing, packet scheduling, and QoS provisioning. With better traffic distribution, co-channel interference can be reduced to a greater extent. However, to achieve optimal interference reduction, the placement of the relay nodes has to be carefully determined. Interference aware algorithms for relay node placement need to be investigated to study the potential capacity gains that can be derived. Frequency reuse coupled with directional antennas can achieve interference mitigation.

Topology Control for Interference

Topology control is a technique used mainly in wireless ad hoc and sensor networks in order to reduce the initial topology of the network to save energy and extend the lifetime of the network. The main goal is to reduce the number of active nodes and active links, preserving the saved resources for future maintenance. Much of the research in the literature deals with topology control for energy consumption. The natural question that arises is what are the best topologies from the radio interference point of view? Answering this question can be simplified if all the nodes use the same transmit power level, however, that is not a practical scenario. Thus, setting an accurate transmitting range is critical for connectivity and reducing interference. The issue of determining interference-optimal topologies has not been addressed in the literature. This study would further enhance the deployment of broadband wireless access networks.

Handoff Management Exploiting SINR

Related to the relay placement problem, mobility plays a role in achieving interference limited performance. Handoff to base stations across a multi-cell network is an important aspect of mobility management. A handoff management architecture using the SINR of the present and neighboring base stations can improve service continuity. Maintaining this continuity is increasingly important for multimedia applications. Using a mobile user's speed, handoff signaling delay information can be maintained while enhancing the handoff performance. Specifically, integrating SINR into the handoff scheme can reduce false handoff initiations which create unnecessary traffic loads.

CONCLUSION

The success of achieving ubiquitous wireless connectivity in broadband wireless access networks is contingent upon how resources are allocated to ensure that each user has service availability. With increasing number of users demanding multimedia services (i.e., video and voice data), the limited spectrum of wireless networks make resource allocation techniques indispensable. In addition to spectrum limitations, wireless networks are inhibited by other inherent characteristics.

Specifically, wireless interference has been shown to be the most critical factors in hindering performance. Therefore, new and realistic paradigms for resource allocation considering the impact of interference and mobility are necessary to support high throughput and provide QoS guarantees. In this chapter, a framework for interference aware resource allocation has been introduced. A novel routing metric, RF^3M, is proposed by considering both interflow and intraflow interference to enhance the selection of good quality paths. Using virtual network decomposition, it is shown that RF^3M is an isotonic routing metric that outperforms the most prominent and relevant routing metrics used in the literature in terms of end-to-end delay and throughput. In addition, an MMF bandwidth allocation algorithm for multipath flow routing in multihop wireless networks is developed. To ensure QoS, the $LMX:M^3F$ optimization formulation has been shown to provide better utilization of bandwidth resources in comparison to well-respected MMF algorithms established in the literature particularly in terms of blocking ratio, bandwidth usage and link load.

REFERENCES

Alicherry, M., Bhatia, R., & Li, E. (2006). Joint channel assignment and routing for throughput optimization in multiradio wireless mesh networks. *IEEE Journal on Selected Areas in Communications*, *24*(11), 1960–1971. doi:10.1109/JSAC.2006.881641

Allalouf, M., & Shavitt, Y. (2008). Centralized and distributed algorithms for routing and weighted max-min fair bandwidth allocation. *IEEE/ACM Transactions on Networking*, *16*(5), 1015–1024. doi:10.1109/TNET.2007.905605

Athanasiou, G., Korakis, T., Ercetin, O., & Tassiulas, L. (2009). Cross-layer framework for association control in wireless mesh networks. *IEEE Transactions on Mobile Computing*, *8*(1), 65–80. doi:10.1109/TMC.2008.75

Bagchi, A., Chaudhary, A., & Kolman, P. (2005). Short length Menger's theorem and reliable optical routing. *Theoretical Computer Science*, *339*(2), 315–332. doi:10.1016/j.tcs.2005.03.009

Bertsekas, D., & Gallagher, R. (1992). *Data networks*. Englewood Cliffs, NJ: Prentice- Hall.

Bhandari, R. (1999). *Survivable networks: Algorithms for diverse routing*. Boston, MA: Kluwer Academic Publishers.

Brar, G., Blough, D. M., & Santi, P. (2006). Computationally efficient scheduling with the physical interference model for throughput improvement in wireless mesh networks. In *Proceedings of ACM International Conference on Mobile Computing and Networking (MobiCom)*, (pp. 2-13). Los Angeles, CA.

Cheng, H., & Zhuang, W. (2008). An optimization framework for balancing throughput and fairness in wireless networks with QoS support. *IEEE Transactions on Wireless Communications*, *7*(2), 584–593. doi:10.1109/TWC.2008.060507

Chou, J., & Lin, B. (2009). Optimal multi-path routing and bandwidth allocation under utility max-min fairness. In *Proceedings of ACM/IEEE International Workshop on Quality of Service (IWQoS)*, (pp. 1-9). Charleston, SC.

De Couto, D. S. J., Aguayo, D., Bicket, J., & Morris, R. (2003). A high throughput path metric for multihop wireless routing. In *Proceedings of ACM International Conference on Mobile Computing and Networking (MobiCom)*, (pp. 134-146). San Diego, CA.

Draves, R., Padhye, J., & Zill, B. (2004). Routing in multi-radio, multi-hop wireless mesh networks. In *Proceedings of ACM MobiCom*, (pp. 114-128). Philadelphia, PA.

Gupta, P., & Kumar, P. R. (2000). The capacity of wireless networks. *IEEE Transactions on Information Theory*, *46*(2), 388–404. doi:10.1109/18.825799

Huang, X., & Fang, Y. (2008). Multiconstrained QoS multipath routing in wireless sensor networks. *Wireless Networks*, *14*(4), 465–478. doi:10.1007/s11276-006-0731-9

Huang, X., Feng, S., & Zhuang, H. (2009). Cross-layer fair resource allocation for multi-radio multi-channel wireless mesh networks. In *Proceedings of 5th International Conference on Wireless Communications, Networking and Mobile Computing (WiCom)*, (pp. 2639-2643). Beijing, China.

Iyer, A., Rosenberg, C., & Karnik, A. (2009). What is the right model for wireless channel interference. *IEEE Transactions on Wireless Communications*, *8*(5), 2662–2671. doi:10.1109/TWC.2009.080720

Jain, K., Padhye, J., Padmanabhan, V., & Qiu, L. (2003). Impact of interference on multihop wireless network performance. In *Proceedings of ACM MobiCom*, (pp. 66-80). San Diego, CA.

Kar, K., Kodialam, M., & Lakshman, T. V. (2000). Minimum interference routing of bandwidth guaranteed tunnels with MPLS traffic engineering applications. *IEEE Journal on Selected Areas in Communications*, *18*(12), 2566–2579. doi:10.1109/49.898737

Kleinberg, J., Rabani, Y., & Tardos, E. (2001). Fairness in routing and load balancing. *Journal of Computer and System Sciences*, *63*(1), 568–578. doi:10.1006/jcss.2001.1752

Kortebi, R., Gourhant, Y., & Agoulmine, N. (2007). On the user of SINR for interference-aware routing in wireless multi-hop networks. In *Proceedings of ACM International Workshop Modeling, Analysis, and Simulation of Wireless and Mobile Systems (MSWiM)*, (pp. 395-399). Crete Island, Greece.

Langar, R., Bouabdallah, N., & Boutaba, R. (2009). Mobility-aware clustering algorithms with interference constraints. *Computer Networks*, *53*(1), 25–44. doi:10.1016/j.comnet.2008.09.012

Maatta, J., & Braysy, T. (2009). A novel approach to fair routing in wireless mesh networks. *EURASIP Journal on Wireless Communications and Networking, Special Issue on Fairness in radio Resource Magement for Wireless Networks*, 1-13.

Mansouri, V. S., Mohsenian-Rad, A. H., & Wong, V. W. S. (2009). Lexicographically optimal routing for wireless sensor networks with multiple sinks. *IEEE Transactions on Vehicular Technology*, *58*(3), 1490–1500. doi:10.1109/TVT.2008.928898

Mauve, M., Widmer, J., & Hartenstein, H. (2001). A survey on position based routing in mobile ad hoc networks. *IEEE Network*, *15*(6), 30–39. doi:10.1109/65.967595

Nace, D. (2002). A linear programming based approach for computing optimal fair splittable routing. In *Proceedings of IEEE Symposium on Computers and Communication (ISCC)*, (pp. 468-474). Taormina, Italy.

Nace, D., Doan, L., Klopfenstein, O., & Bashllari, A. (2008). Max-min fairness in multicommodity flows. *Computers & Operations Research*, *35*(2), 557–573. doi:10.1016/j.cor.2006.03.020

Nace, D., Doan, N., Gourdin, E., & Liau, B. (2006). Computing optimal max-min fair resource allocation for elastic flows. *IEEE/ACM Transactions on Networking*, *14*(6), 1272–1281. doi:10.1109/TNET.2006.886331

Nace, D., & Pioro, M. (2008). Max-min fairness and its applications to routing and load balancing in communications networks: A tutorial. *IEEE Communications Surveys and Tutorials, 10*(4), 5–17. doi:10.1109/SURV.2008.080403

Pabst, R., Walke, B. H., Schultz, D., Herhold, P., Yanikomeroglu, H., & Mukherjee, S. (2004). Relay-based deployment concepts for wireless and mobile broadband radio. *IEEE Communications Magazine, 42*(9), 80–89. doi:10.1109/MCOM.2004.1336724

Pal, R. (2008). A lexicographically optimal load balanced routing scheme for wireless mesh networks. In *Proceedings of IEEE International Conference on Communications (ICC)*, (pp. 2393-2397). Beijing, China.

Park, W., & Bakh, S. (2009). Resource management policies for fixed relays in cellular networks. *Computer Networks, 32*(4), 703–711.

Qi, B., Biaz, S., Wu, S., & Ji, Y. (2007). An interference-aware routing metric in multi-radio multihop networks. In *Proceedings of the ACM 45th Annual Southeast Regional Conference*, (pp. 549-500). Salem, MA, USA.

Ramachandran, K., Belding, E. M., Almeroth, K. C., & Buddhikot, M. M. (2006). Interference aware channel assignment in multiradio wireless mesh networks. In *Proceedings of IEEE International Conference on Computer Communications (INFOCOM)*, (pp. 1-12). Barcelona, Spain.

Rappaport, T. (2002). *Wireless communications: Principles and practice* (2nd ed.). Prentice Hall.

Shahrokhi, F., & Matula, D. W. (1990). The maximum concurrent flow problem. *Journal of the ACM, 37*(2), 318–334. doi:10.1145/77600.77620

Shi, Y., Hou, Y. T., Liu, J., & Kompella, S. (2009). How to correctly use the protocol interference model for multihop wireless networks. In *Proceedings of ACM International Symposium on Mobile Ad Hoc Networking and Computing (MobiHoc)*, (pp. 239-248). New Orleans, LA.

Soldani, D., & Dixit, S. (2008). Wireless relays for broadband access. *IEEE Communications Magazine, 46*(3), 58–66. doi:10.1109/MCOM.2008.4463772

Subramanian, A. P., Buddhikot, M. M., & Miller, S. (2006). Interference aware routing in multi-radio wireless mesh networks. In *Proceedings of IEEE Workshop in Wireless Mesh Networks (WiMesh)*, (pp. 55-63). Reston, VA.

Takai, M., Martin, J., & Bragodia, R. (2001). Effects of wireless physical layer modeling in mobile ad hoc networks. In *Proceedings of ACM International Symposium on Mobile Ad Hoc Networking and Computing (MobiHoc)*, (pp. 87-94). Long Beach, CA.

Tang, J., Hincapie, R., Xue, G., Zhang, W., & Bustamente, R. (2010). Fair bandwidth allocation in wireless mesh networks with cognitive radios. *IEEE Transactions on Vehicular Technology, 59*(3), 1487–1496. doi:10.1109/TVT.2009.2038478

Tang, J., Xue, G., Chandler, C., & Zhang, W. (2005). Interference-aware routing in multihop wireless networks using directional antennas. *Proceedings of IEEE International Conference on Computer Communications (INFOCOM)*, (pp. 751-760). Miami, FL.

Tassiulas, L., & Sarkar, S. (2005). Maxmin fair scheduling in wireless ad hoc networks. *IEEE Journal on Selected Areas in Communications, 23*(1), 163–173. doi:10.1109/JSAC.2004.837365

Teo, J.-Y., Ha, Y., & Tham, C.-K. (2008). Interference minimized multipath routing with congestion control in wireless sensor network with high rate streaming. *IEEE Transactions on Mobile Computing*, 7(9), 1124–1137. doi:10.1109/TMC.2008.24

Thulasiraman, P., Chen, J., & Shen, X. (2010). Max-min fair multipath routing with physical interference constraints for multihop wireless networks. In *Proceedings of IEEE International Conference on Communications (ICC)*, (pp. 1-6). Cape Town, South Africa.

Thulasiraman, P., Chen, J., & Shen, X. (2011). Multipath routing and max-min fair QoS provisioning under interference constraints in wireless multihop networks. *IEEE Transactions on Parallel and Distributed Systems*, 22(5), 716–728. doi:10.1109/TPDS.2010.145

Thulasiraman, P., Ramasubramanian, S., & Krunz, M. (2006). Disjoint multipath routing in dual homing networks using colored trees. In *Proceedings of IEEE Global Communications Conference (GLOBECOM)*, (pp. 1-5). San Francisco, CA.

Thulasiraman, P., Ramasubramanian, S., & Krunz, M. (2007). Disjoint multipath routing to two distinct drains in a multi-drain sensor network. In *Proceedings of IEEE International Conference on Computer Communications (INFOCOM)*, (pp. 643-651). Anchorage, AK.

Thulasiraman, P., & Shen, X. (2010). Disjoint multipath routing and QoS provisioning under physical interference constraints. In *Proceedings of IEEE Wireless Communications and Networking Conference (WCNC)*, (pp. 1-6). Sydney, Australia.

Walke, B. H., Mangold, S., & Berlemann, L. (2006). *IEEE 802 Wireless systems: Protocols, multihop mesh/relaying, performance and spectrum coexistence*. West Sussex, UK: John Wiley. doi:10.1002/9780470058800

Wang, P., Jiang, H., Zhuang, W., & Poor, H. V. (2008). Redefinition of max-min fairness in multi-hop wireless networks. *IEEE Transactions on Wireless Communications*, 7(12), 4786–4791. doi:10.1109/T-WC.2008.070804

Wen, Y.-F., & Lin, Y.-S. (2007). Fair bandwidth allocation and end to end delay routing algorithms for wireless mesh networks. *IEICE Transactions on Communications*, 90-B(5), 1042–1051. doi:10.1093/ietcom/e90-b.5.1042

Xu, Z., Huang, C., & Cheng, Y. (2008). Interference-aware QoS routing in wireless mesh networks. In *Proceedings of 4th International Conference on Mobile Ad-Hoc and Sensor Networks*, (pp. 95-98). Wuhan, China.

Yang, Y., Wang, J., & Kravets, R. (2005). Designing routing metrics for mesh networks. In *Proceedings of IEEE Workshop in Wireless Mesh Networks (WiMesh)*. Santa Clara, CA.

Zhou, J., & Mitchell, K. (2010). A scalable delay based analytical framework for CSMA/CA wireless mesh networks. *Computer Networks*, 54(2), 304–318. doi:10.1016/j.comnet.2009.05.013

ADDITIONAL READING

Fleischer, L. (2000). Approximating fractional multicommodity flows independent of the number of commodities. *SIAM Journal on Discrete Mathematics*, 13(4), 505–520. doi:10.1137/S0895480199355754

Frederikos, V., & Papadaki, K. (2008). Interference aware routing for minimum frame length schedules in wireless mesh networks. *EURASIP Journal on Wireless Communications and Networking*, 1–13. doi:10.1155/2008/817876

Genc, V., Murphy, S., Yang, Y., & Murphy, J. (2008). IEEE 802.16j relay-based wireless access networks: an overview. *IEEE Wireless Communications*, *15*(5), 56–63. doi:10.1109/MWC.2008.4653133

Huang, L., Rong, M., Wang, L., Xue, Y., & Schulz, E. (2008). Resource scheduling for OFDMA/TDD based relay enhanced cellular networks. In *Proceedings of IEEE Wireless Communications and Networking Conference (WCNC)*, (pp. 1544-1548). Las Vegas, NV.

Kwon, S., & Shroff, N. B. (2009). Energy-efficient SINR based routing for multihop wireless networks. *IEEE Transactions on Mobile Computing*, *8*(5), 668–681. doi:10.1109/TMC.2008.165

Lee, K. D., & Leung, V. C. M. (2006). Fair allocation of subcarrier and power in an OFDMA wireless mesh network. *IEEE Journal on Selected Areas in Communications*, *24*(11), 2051–2060. doi:10.1109/JSAC.2006.881628

Li, G., & Liu, H. (2006). Resource allocation for OFDMA relay networks with fairness constraints. *IEEE Journal on Selected Areas in Communications*, *24*(11), 2061–2069. doi:10.1109/JSAC.2006.881627

Pareek, D. (2006). *WiMax: Taking wireless to the max*. Boca Raton, FL: Auerbach Publications. doi:10.1201/9781420013436

Peters, S. W., & Heather, R. W. (2009). The future of WiMax: Multihop relaying with IEEE 802.16j. *IEEE Communications Magazine*, *47*(1), 104–111. doi:10.1109/MCOM.2009.4752686

Prasad, P. S., & Agarwal, P. (2010). A generic framework for mobility prediction and resource utilization in wireless networks. In *Proceedings of IEEE International Conference on Communications Networks and Systems (COMSNETS)*, (pp. 1-10). Bangalore, India.

Salem, M., Adinoyi, A., Rahman, M., Yanikomeroglu, H., Falconer, D., & Kim, Y. (2010). Opportunities and challenges in OFDMA based cellular relay networks: A radio resource management perspective. *IEEE Transactions on Vehicular Technology*, *59*(5), 2497–2510. doi:10.1109/TVT.2010.2042736

Shen, Z., Andrews, J. G., & Evans, B. L. (2005). Adaptive resource allocation in multiuser OFDM systems with proportional fairness. *IEEE Transactions on Wireless Communications*, *4*(6), 2726–2737. doi:10.1109/TWC.2005.858010

Shin, J., Kumarand, R., Shing, Y., & La Porta, T. F. (2008). Multihop wireless relay networks of mesh clients. In *Proceedings of IEEE Wireless Communications and Networking Conference (WCNC)*, (pp. 2717-2722). Las Vegas, NV.

Tam, Y. H., Benkoczi, H. S., Hassanein, H. S., & Akl, S. G. (2010). Channel assignment in multihop cellular networks: minimum delay. *IEEE Transactions on Mobile Computing*, *9*(7), 1022–1034. doi:10.1109/TMC.2010.41

Yang, Y., Hu, H., Xu, J., & Mao, G. (2009). Relay technologies for WiMax and LTE advanced mobile systems. *IEEE Communications Magazine*, *47*(10), 100–105. doi:10.1109/MCOM.2009.5273815

Yang, Y., Murphy, S., & Murphy, L. (2009). Interference aware relay station location planning for IEEE 802.16j mobile multihop relay network. In *Proceedings of 4th ACM Workshop on Performance Monitoring and Measurement of Heterogeneous Wireless and Wired Networks (PM2HW2N)*, (pp. 201-208). Canary Islands, Spain.

Zhang, W., Bai, S., Xue, G., Tang, J., & Wang, C. (2011). DARP: Distance aware relay placement in WiMax mesh networks. *Proceedings of IEEE Conference on Computer Communications (INFOCOM)*, (pp. 2060-2069). Shanghai, China.

KEY TERMS AND DEFINITIONS

Broadband Wireless Access: A specific wireless technology that provides ubiquitous high speed internet services over a wide geographic area.

Fairness: the ability to distribute resources to users based on need and in a manner that does not unnecessarily starve or over allocate the end users.

Multicommodity Flow: Illustrates a network flow problem in which there are multiple traffic demands by multiple users that each flow through the network to different destinations.

Multipath Routing: The ability to use multiple paths for routing of traffic flows from source to destination such that the paths do not form loops and so as to increase load balancing, fault tolerance, and energy efficiency.

Quality of Service: Ability to provide different priority levels to different applications, users, or data traffic flow, or to guarantee a certain level of performance to a data flow given specific network characteristics and conditions.

Resource Allocation: The assignment of available resources and the scheduling of transmissions in computer networks in an efficient and fair manner.

Wireless Interference: The interference between simultaneous transmissions within a certain proximity due to inherent wireless characteristics that causes performance degradation in terms of packet loss, throughput, and latency.

ENDNOTES

[1] This chapter is based on work presented in (Thulasiraman, Chen, & Shen, 2011).

[2] It must be noted that maintaining two-connectivity is a necessary condition for finding two disjoint paths from each user to the base station. Guaranteeing two-connectivity is feasible in a static wireless environment as considered in this chapter. However, in the presence of mobility, two-connectivity of the network cannot be ensured due to time varying changes in the topology. Thus, this constraint and the solutions obtained in this chapter are pertinent for static wireless networks.

Chapter 3
Deadlock Prevention with Wormhole Routing:
Irregular Topology

Lev Levitin
Boston University, USA

Mark Karpovsky
Boston University, USA

Mehmet Mustafa
Boston University, USA

ABSTRACT

The problem of preventing deadlocks and livelocks in computer communication networks with wormhole routing is considered. The method to prevent deadlocks is to prohibit certain turns (i.e., the use of certain pairs of connected edges) in the routing process, in such a way that eliminates all cycles in the graph. A new algorithm that constructs a minimal (irreducible) set of turns that breaks all cycles and preserves connectivity of the graph is proposed and analyzed. The algorithm is tree-free and is considerably simpler than earlier cycle-breaking algorithms. The properties of the algorithm are proven, and lower and upper bounds for minimum cardinalities of cycle-breaking connectivity preserving sets for graphs of general topology, as well as for planar graphs, are presented. In particular, the algorithm guarantees that not more than 1/3 of all turns in the network become prohibited. Experimental results are presented on the fraction of prohibited turns, the distance dilation, as well as on the message delivery times and saturation loads for the proposed algorithm in comparison with known tree-based algorithms. The proposed algorithm outperforms the tree-based algorithms in all characteristics that were considered.

DOI: 10.4018/978-1-4666-2533-4.ch003

1. INTRODUCTION AND RELATED WORK

With its simplicity, low channel setup times, and its high performance in delivering messages, wormhole routing has been widely investigated (Dally & Seitz, 1987; Boppana & Chalasani, 1993; Chalasani & Boppana, 1995; Duato, Yalamancili, & Ni, 1997; Ni & McKinley, 1993), and recently is being revisited for Networks-on-Chips technologies (Mello, Ost, Moraes, & Calazans, 2004; Hu & Marculescu, 2004). Wormhole routing and its variants, (Gaughan & Yalamanchili, 1995) virtual cut-through and pipelined circuit switching, PCS, have been used in regular topologies from chip-scale networks (Mello et al., 2004; Hu & Marculescu, 2004), to rack-packed Blue Gene (Klepacki, 2003), to irregular topologies formed by interconnecting low-cost workstations in an ad hoc manner, forming what is referred to as Network of Workstations (NOWs) (Libeskind-Hadas, Mazzoni, & Rajagopalan, 1998; Silla, Duato, Sivasubramaniam, & Das, 1998; Silla & Duato, 2000). Nodes in such networks consist of processing element connected to a router or switching element via a channel with full duplex links. Messages originate and are consumed in the processing elements. Messages that are flowing from a router towards a processing element use what is known as the consumption channel and those that are flowing away from the processing element towards the router use the injection channel. The consumption and the injection channels together form the full duplex communication link between the processor and the router. Routers are connected to other routers in the network using full duplex links as well. Messages, also known as 'worms', are made up of flits that are transmitted atomicly, one flit at a time, from node to node in the network. In contrast to this technique which is known as the wormhole routing, in the store and forward routing technique, the message in its entirety is received by each and every intermediate node, and only then it is transmitted to the next node. Therefore, wormhole routing provides for much faster message delivery. The header flit, containing the destination address is immediately followed by the payload or data flits (Ni & McKinley, 1993). Another aspect that makes wormhole routing and routers attractive is that each channel requires only a few flits deep buffer space (Dally & Seitz, 1986; Glass & Ni, 1992). In wormhole routed networks, messages traverse the network in a pipelined fashion, such that parts of the message occupy different network resources, while the header flit requests yet other resources. Under this policy, when there is no contention, as in lightly loaded networks, the latency of message (average delivery time) varies very slowly with the distance (Ni & McKinley, 1993). However, when a message is blocked, the header and the rest of the message wait until the blockage is removed. As a result, messages could hold up potentially large number of network resources while attempting to reserve others.

In congested networks with high injected traffic, improperly designed routing protocols can lead to a network state, in which no progress can be made in delivering, not only of the current messages but all subsequent messages in the network. This network state, in which worms are in a cyclic dependency of each other's held-up resources, is known as deadlock. Figure 1 depicts a section of a network in which no measures were taken to prevent deadlock. (The rest of the network where four deadlocked messages have originated is not shown.) The figure shows four-port routers with their local processors presented as circles. Assume that each message M_i is destined for node i. In the figure communication channels have been occupied by the messages shown juxtaposed next to them. The rest of the messages occupy a number of other channels in the network. It can be seen that four messages, M_1, M_2, M_3, and M_4 are blocking each other, so that none of the messages can move forward. For example, message M_2 has acquired ownership of the vertical com-

Figure 1. Deadlock formation in a section of network in which all turns are permitted where message M_i isdestinedforprocessor P_i, $i = 1, 2, 3,$ and 4

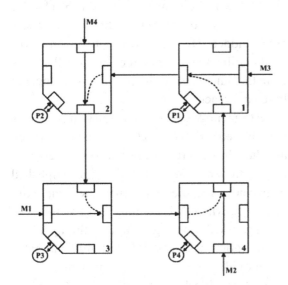

munication channel south of node 4, within node 4, and north of node 4 but is waiting for the channel between nodes 1 and 2 which has already been committed to M_3.

When a message from a source is intended to be sent to a single destination, the delivery mechanism of such a message is known as unicast. Network resources that are being held by competing unicast messages are the communication channels in the network. Cycles in channel dependency graphs (CDG), have been identified as the root cause of deadlocks in wormhole networks for unicast messaging. In (Duato, 1993, 1994), it has been shown that necessary and sufficient condition for eliminating deadlocks is the elimination of cycles in the corresponding CDG. Given a graph, constructing the CDG for it is at best tedious. However, cycles of nodes in the CDG graph correspond to"cycles of edges", as defined below, in the original network graph. A similar problem caused by presence of cycles, the so

called"livelocks", appears in Ethernet type networks.

Because of its susceptibility to deadlocks, considerable body of work has been dedicated to designing wormhole routing algorithms that prevent deadlocks from occurring (Dally & Seitz, 1986, 1987; Dally & Aoki, 1997; Duato, 1993), (Glass & Ni, 1994; Ni & McKinley, 1993; Zakrevski, Jaiswal, Levitin, & Karpovsky, 1999), (Zakrevski, Jaiswal, & Karpovsky, 1999; Zakrevski, Mustafa, & Karpovsky, 2000; Lysne, Skeie, Reinemo, & Theiss, 2006; Sancho, Robles, Lopez, Flich, & Duato, 2003). In these proactive deadlock prevention schemes, either virtual channels were added (Dally & Seitz, 1986; Lysne et al., 2006), or some resources were prevented from being used.

Virtual channels have been introduced and considered as a tool to avoid deadlocks in a number of papers (Duato et al., 1997; Duato, 1991; Pifarré, Gravano, Denicolay, & Sanz, 1994), often in combination with the dimension-ordered routing (DOR) technique (Min, Ould-Khaoua, Kouvatsos, & Awan, 2004). However, as pointed out in (Duato, 1991), the use of virtual channels may have a negative effect on the message latency.

To provide deadlock-free adaptive routing, Glass and Ni (Glass & Ni, 1994), presented a method that requires neither additional physical nor virtual channels. The turn model is based on analyzing the directions in which packets can turn in regular networks and the cycles that the turns can form. By prohibiting just sufficient number of turns to break all of the cycles, produces a routing algorithm that is deadlock free and livelock free. It was determined that in an n-dimensional mesh only one quarter of the turns must be prohibited to prevent deadlocks. Only 90 degree turns in regular topologies were considered.

The motivation for seeking the minimal fraction of prohibited turns is originally due to Glass and Ni (Glass & Ni, 1994). They have found that reduction in the number of prohibited turns results in a decrease of average path length and the average message delivery time, thereby increasing the throughput. After Glass and Ni showed it for regular topologies such as meshes and tori, this conclusion was confirmed by other authors (Mustafa, Karpovsky, & Levitin, 2005; Levitin, Karpovsky, Mustafa, & Zakrevski, 2006) for irregular topologies as well. Experimental data show that there is a considerable gain of approximately 7-8% in the maximum sustainable throughput in the network, for each percentage point reduction in the fraction of prohibited turns. Similar to spanning tree approaches, prohibiting a carefully selected set of the turns in the network, provides deadlock freedom. However, unlike the spanning tree based approaches, the cycle-breaking approach allows all communication links in the network to be used. The only restriction is that some pairs of communication links, namely, those that form the prohibited turns, are prevented from being used sequentially.

The simplest deadlock prevention approach utilizes spanning tree based routing for message delivery. Since messages propagate along the tree edges deadlocks are prevented from occurring. However, in this approach a large number of network communication channels are not being used as they are not part of the spanning tree. This is not only inefficient and ineffective use of the available resources but can also lead to hot spots in the network close to the root of the spanning tree. Identification of the root node also could have a significant adverse effect on fraction of prohibited turns. In short, construction of the best spanning tree is not a trivial undertaking.

The Up/Down approach, first introduced in Autonet (Schroeder et al., 1990) routing algorithm improves this shortcoming of the spanning tree approach by using the cross links, non-tree links, under certain conditions. The rooted spanning tree is labeled in partial order determined by the spanning tree. With this labeling the root node has the smallest label and the leaf nodes have the largest labels. Because of the partial order, all edges are given either up or down directional attributes. From routing perspective, a message is permitted to traverse zero or more up links followed by zero or more down links. Once a message has made a transition to a down directed edge, then it is on the down virtual network and it will remain in the down virtual network until it reaches its destination; all down then up directed traversals are forbidden. The Up/Down approach improves on the utilization of resources but it still suffers from the other shortcomings of the spanning tree based approach.

In (Sancho & Robles, 2000) all spanning trees are explored with every node acting as the root node and then the best tree is selected. The selection of the best tree and root combination is accomplished by two heuristic rules with a run-time complexity of $O(N^3)$, where N is the number of switches in the network. According to authors, this approach allows more messages to follow minimal paths and provide better traffic load balancing.

In (Starobinski, Karpovsky, & Zakrevski, 2003) a version of the turn prohibition algorithm was used that enabled generalizing the application of Network Calculus to arbitrary topologies. By prohibiting turns, cycles of independent packet flows were eliminated. Central issue that is tackled in Network calculus is determining conditions which lead to network stability. Because network stability establishment is easier in feed forward topologies, network calculus had been applied only to such topologies in which packets do not create cyclic dependencies. Application of turn prohibition to arbitrary topologies rendered them acyclic, which facilitated the use network calculus successfully in these arbitrary topologies. In their article, authors also demonstrated that the set of prohibited turns generated by the earlier version of the turn prohibition algorithm is not irreducible.

In (Skeie, Lysne, & Theiss, 2002) and (Lysne et al., 2006) a technique called LAyered SHortest, LASH, path algorithm was used that guarantees shortest path routing, in-order message delivery, and that avoids deadlocks by using virtual channels. In this approach a number of source and destination pairs, sd-pairs, are assigned to a virtual channel, or layer. Each sd-pair is assigned to exactly one virtual channel in a way that channel dependencies do not generate cycles in each layer. As an sd-pair is assigned to a layer, if deadlock freedom cannot be assured, another virtual channel is created and the sd-pair is assigned to that layer. It should be noted that virtual channels are not free and there is a cost, hardware and control complexity associated with virtual channels.

With a goal to reduce the restrictions imposed by the current Up/Down routing algorithm, an alternative methodology has been investigated in constructing the routing tables for NOWs. The new methodology is based on computing a depth-first search (DFS) spanning tree of the network graph which decreases the number of routing restrictions. In this approach, first a DFS spanning tree is constructed. Then nodes at the same level are labeled in a way to reduce the number of prohibited turns. Then links are given either Up or Down directionality which is different than what had been defined in (Schroeder et al., 1990). Authors in (Sancho, Robles, & Duato, 2004) defined the Up end of an edge as the edge having the larger label. Using the new methodology prevents the root from being the "natural path" to other nodes along the DFS spanning tree and thus the hot links at or near the root node are alleviated and throughput have increased by a factor of up to 2.48.

In (Pellegrini, Starobinski, Karpovsky, & Levitin, 2004), a variant of turn prohibition called Tree-Based Turn-Prohibition, TBTP, has been investigated, in which authors show that the TBTP algorithm is of polynomial-time complexity, that it is backward compatible with the IEEE 802.1d standard. This algorithm selects a node and prohibits all turns at the selected node excluding those that involve the spanning tree links, and permits all turns that start with the selected node. A greedy criterion is used that selects a node that maximizes the difference between the number of permitted turns and the number of prohibited turns. All cross-edges at the selected node are

then deleted and process is repeated on the remaining graph until there no cross-edges are left in the graph. A distributed version of the TBTP algorithm (Pellegrini, Starobinski, Karpovsky, & Levitin, 2006) is reported by using localized neighborhood concept where only information about two-hop neighborhood is maintained by nodes. The centralized version of the TBTP algorithm (Pellegrini et al., 2004) has reportedly an order of magnitude better message delivery latency performance than the spanning tree approach. The distributed approach is reported to cause some minor performance penalty. With an upper bound of 1/2 for the fraction of prohibited turns, the shortcoming of the TBTP approach is that it could potentially restrict the use of a large number of turns.

In (Shevtekar & Zakrevski, 2004) a hybrid methodology using both proactive and reactive approaches was proposed, in which, routing restrictions are adjusted dynamically based on network congestion. In this hybrid approach for routing some prohibition is imposed on routing together with a type of deadlock recovery. The main idea of the proposed method consists of selecting some of the sequential turns and prohibiting them during routing. A cost formula is proposed to estimate cost of implementing both strategies in a network. The main concern about the deadlock recovery is that identification of the deadlock condition is not a reliable process and current techniques require all messages to be short (Duato et al., 1997).

Another class of deadlock-preventing algorithms, the so-called, tree-free cycle-breaking algorithms, were developed in (Zakrevski, Jaiswal, Levitin, & Karpovsky, 1999; Zakrevski, Jaiswal, & Karpovsky, 1999; Zakrevski et al., 2000), (L. B. Levitin et al., 2006; Mustafa et al., 2005; L. Levitin, Karpovsky, & Mustafa, May, 2009, 2010). These algorithms (TP and SCB algorithms) have been proved to create a minimal (irreducible) set of prohibited turns the size of which never exceeds 1/3 of the total number of turns in any graph. They have been shown to outperform the tree-based algorithms with respect to three basic characteristics: fraction of prohibited turns, distance dilation, latency and the saturation load. For some broad classes of network topologies, those algorithms provide an optimum solution of the turn prohibition problem (Levitin et al., 2010). The computational complexity of the tree-free algorithms is $O(N^2\Delta)$, where Δ is the maximum node degree (number of neighbors) in the graph. The algorithms are topology agnostic. However, the application of those general algorithms may be still unnecessarily complex in the case of graphs with certain regularities in their structure (see next chapter).

In this chapter a simplified and improved tree-free turn prohibition algorithm is proposed referred to as the Simple Cycle-Breaking (SCB) algorithm. The algorithm provides a minimal (irreducible) set of prohibited turns which breaks all cycles and preserves connectivity of the network. The number of prohibited turns is shown to satisfy an upper bound that does not exceed 1/3 of the total number of turns in the network. A better upper bound, which is tight for certain types of graphs, is also established. For certain classes of network topologies, the algorithm yields an optimal solution.

Section 2 of this chapter contains definitions, formulation of the Turn Prohibition (TP) problem and lower bounds on the number of prohibited turns. The SCB algorithm is presented in Section 3. The properties of the SCB algorithm are analyzed in Section 4. It is conjectured that the SCB algorithm is an approximation algorithm for the TP problem with a constant approximation ratio bound. An investigation of planar graphs follows in Section 5. Experimental results and comparisons with other turn prohibition algorithms are presented in Section 6. Conclusions are given in Section 7.

2. DEFINITIONS, FORMULATION OF PROBLEM, AND LOWER BOUNDS

Consider an undirected connected graph $G(V, E)$, with $N = |V|$ vertices (nodes), denoted by $a, b, ...,$ and $M = |E|$ edges, denoted by (a, b), etc. that represents a communication network. A cut node (articulation point) in G is a node whose removal results in a disconnected graph ((Cormen, Leiserson, & Rivest, 1989), Ch. 23). A turn in G is a triplet of nodes (a, b, c) if (a, b) and (b, c) are edges in G and $a \neq c$. Assume that turns are bidirectional: turns (a, b, c) and (c, b, a) are considered to be the same turn. If the degree (the number of neighbors) of node j is d_j, the total number of turns $T(G)$ in G is given by $T(G) = \sum_{j=1}^{N} \binom{d_j}{2}$. A path $P = (v_0, v_1, ..., v_{L1}, v_L)$ of length L, $L \geq 1$ from node a to node b in G is a sequence of nodes $v_i \in V$ such that, $v_0 = a$ and $v_L = b$, and every two consecutive nodes are connected by an edge. Subsequences of the form (v_i, v_k, v_i) are not permitted in a path. Nodes and edges in the path are not necessarily all different. A turn (a, b, c) belongs to path $P = (v_0, v_1, ..., v_L)$ and P is covered by (a, b, c), if $(a, b, c) = (v_i, v_{i+1}, v_{i+2})$, for certain $i = 0, 1, ..., L-2$. Path $P = (v_0, v_1, v_2, ..., v_k, v_0, v_1)$ in G is called a cycle. Note that, by this definition, a directed edge (v_0, v_1) rather than a node must be repeated in the same direction to make a cycle. Thus, this chapter considers "cycles of edges", instead of the more common definition of a cycle as a "cycle of nodes".

Consider a set $W(G)$ of turns in G. Any path in G includes at least one turn from $W(G)$ that is prohibited from being used for routing. Therefore, $W(G)$ is called the set of prohibited turns. The set $W(G)$ is called cycle-breaking if every cycle in G includes at least one turn from $W(G)$. $W(G)$ is called connectivity-preserving if for any $a, b \in V$ there exists a path $P(a, ..., b)$ in G, such that does not include any turn from $W(G)$. The *minimum* cardinality of cycle-breaking and connectivity-preserving set $W(G)$ for a given graph G is denoted by $Z(G)$ and the fraction of prohibited turns is denoted by $z(G) = Z(G) / T(G)$.

Since turn prohibition imposes restrictions on the paths, between nodes, obviously, the smaller $W(G)$ the better. Thus, the Turn Prohibition (TP) problem can be formulated as follows.

Given: An undirected graph $G(V, E)$.

Find: A connectivity-preserving cycle-breaking (CPCB) set of turns $W(G)$ with the minimum (smallest) number of prohibited turns $Z(G)$.

Conjecture 1: The Turn Prohibition problem is NP-hard.

Though the Turn Prohibition problem is not yet proven to be NP-hard, it looks at least as hard as similar NP-hard graph problems. At the first glance, it is closely related to the well-known Feedback Arc Set (FAS) problem for directed graphs (Ausiello et al., 2003, p 374), which is to find the minimum set of arcs whose removal makes a directed graph acyclic. But in fact these two problems are quite different. The Turn Prohibition problem for a network graph is equivalent to the FAS problem for the corresponding directed channel dependency graph *under the condition that the network graph remains connected*. This additional condition changes radically the nature of the problem. It is easy to construct examples (the simplest is the bipartite graph $K_{2,3}$) where the optimal solution of the FAS problem for the channel dependency graph violates the connectivity of the network graph. Therefore, the known approximation algorithms for the FAS problem (and the related Feedback Vertex Set problem) are not applicable to the TP problem. Thus, one has to look for specific (low complexity) algorithms that would provide suboptimal solutions of the

TP problem. This goal is pursued in Section 3 of this chapter.

Let G be a connected graph with minimum degree δ. Consider a set of R cycles in G such that no more than r cycles are covered by the same turn. Then (Levitin et al., 2006), the number of prohibited turns $Z(G)$ and fraction of prohibited turns $z(G)$ satisfy the following inequalities:

$$Z(G) \geq M - N + 1, \tag{1}$$

$$z(G) \geq \frac{R}{rT(G)}, \tag{2}$$

and

$$Z(G) \geq M - N + \binom{\delta - 1}{2} + 1, \quad \delta > 2. \tag{3}$$

Bound (3) is tight for some values of M, N, and δ. For example, for all planar graphs without cut nodes and with degrees 2 and 3, for planar graphs with girth g 6, for the bipartite graph $K_{3,3}$, for the Petersen graph and for all two-dimensional rectangular and honeycomb meshes (see (Zakrevski, 2000) and Section 5 below).

3. A GENERAL ALGORITHM FOR CONSTRUCTION OF MINIMAL CYCLE-BREAKING SETS OF TURNS

In this section, an algorithm, called the Simple Cycle-Breaking (SCB) algorithm, is presented that is much simpler than and at least as efficient as those in (Zakrevski, Jaiswal, & Karpovsky, 1999; Levitin et al., 2006; Mustafa et al., 2005).

Lemma 1: If a connected graph G has cut nodes, then there exists a connected subgraph H which consists of non-cut nodes only of the original graph G and is connected to the rest of G via only one cut node $c \in G \setminus H$ (i.e., if $a \in H$, $b \in G \setminus H$, and $P(a,b)$ is a path from node a to node b, then $c \in P(a,b)$).

Proof: Suppose G has cut nodes. Let S_i be the set of connected components of G obtained by deleting cut node $c_i (i = 1, 2, \ldots)$ from G. Consider the union $\bigcup_i S_i$. Let $H_i S_i$ be the connected component with the smallest number of nodes. This component does not include any cut nodes from the original graph (otherwise it would not be the smallest component). Thus, if H is obtained by deleting cut node c from graph G, then H is a connected subgraph which is connected to $G \setminus H$ via one cut node c only.

Lemma 2: In any connected graph G, there exists a non-cut node a of degree d, such that

$$2\binom{d}{2} \leq \sum_{i=1}^{d}(d_i - 1), \qquad (4)$$

where d_i $(i = 1, 2, \ldots, d)$ are the degrees of the neighbors of a (nodes adjacent to a).

Proof: Using Lemma 1, consider a subgraph that consists of non-cut nodes and at most one cut node, connecting this subgraph to the remaining part of the graph. Select a non-cut node a of the minimum degree d among all non-cut nodes in this subgraph. If a is not adjacent to the cut node, then inequality (4) is obviously satisfied. Suppose now that all nodes with minimum degree d are adjacent to the cut node with degree $d' < d$. Then the selected node a has at most $d' - 1$ neighbors of degree d, while at least $(d - 1) - (d' - 1) = d - d'$ of its neighbors have degrees at least $d + 1$. Thus

$$\sum_{i=1}^{d}(d_i - 1) \geq (d' - 1)(d - 1) + (d - d')d + (d' - 1)$$

$$\geq d(d - 1) = 2\binom{d}{2}.$$

Lemma 2 will be used below to prove properties of a new algorithm for obtaining a minimal cycle-breaking set of turns.

Given a connected graph $G(V, E)$, the SCB algorithm creates two sets: the set $W(G)$ of prohibited turns and the set $A(G)$ of permitted turns. It also labels all nodes by natural numbers starting with 1, in the order they are selected by the algorithm. In the beginning, $W(G) = \varnothing$, $A(G) = \varnothing$, and all nodes are unlabeled. If $|V| = N$, the algorithm consists of $N - 1$ stages. Each stage consists of 3 steps described below.

1. If $|V| = 2$, label the nodes by the smallest unused natural numbers, select and delete the node with label $\ell = N - 1$ and return sets $W(G)$ and $A(G)$. Otherwise, go to Step 2.

2. Select a non-cut node a of the minimum degree d, such that inequality (4) is satisfied. Prohibit all turns of the form (b, a, c) and include them in $W(G)$. Permit all turns of the form (a, b, c) and include them in $A(G)$. Label a by the smallest unused natural number $\ell(a)$.

3. Delete node a to obtain a graph $G' = G \setminus a$ and go to Step 1 for G'.

Note that at the stage of the algorithm when node a is selected, all other undeleted nodes are unlabeled. In fact, they will be labeled later. As a result, turn (b, a, c) is prohibited *iff* $\ell(a) < \ell(b)$ and $\ell(a) < \ell(c)$. The prohibition rule for the SCB algorithm can be expressed in different terms.

Let us call an edge (a,b) positive, if $\ell(a) < \ell(b)$, and negative otherwise. Then the path P is prohibited *iff* it includes a pair of consecutive edges such that the first edge is negative and the second edge is positive. Then the connectivity means that SCB algorithm labels nodes in such a way that for any two nodes there exists a path between them in which all positive edges (if any) precede all negative ones (if any).

Example 1. Figure 2 demonstrates the operation of the SCB algorithm. The original graph is shown in Figure 2(A). Since there are 11 nodes the completion of the algorithm would involve 10 stages. Before the algorithm begins to execute, the two sets $W(G)$ and $A(G)$ are initialized to be empty and the label is initialized to be 1. At the first stage, Step 1 determines that the number of remaining nodes in the graph is not equal to 2 and immediately transitions to Step 2. At this step, the minimum degree non-cut node is selected. Since node f is a cut node, it cannot be selected. The minimum degree non cut nodes are nodes a, b, c, d, h, k, m, and n. The criterion in (4) is applied and all of the candidate nodes satisfy the inequality. For example, for node a, both the left and right hand side of (4) evaluate to 6, hence, node a is selected. As shown in Figure 2(B), three turns are prohibited, denoted by three arcs, i.e., (b, a, c), (b, a, e), (c, a, e). The node is assigned the label 1, and transition is made to Step 3. In Step 3, the selected node a is deleted to obtain the subgraph with 10 nodes as shown in Figure 2(D). The SCB algorithm begins executing the stage 2. In this stage, node c is selected, one turn (b, c, d) prohibited, node c is labeled with 2, and deleted to obtain the 9-node subgraph shown in Figure 2(D), and stage 3 of the algorithm begins. Since node b is of the minimum degree 1, and a non-cut node, it is selected,

no turns are prohibited, node b is labeled 3 and deleted. In stages 4, 5, and 6, nodes d, e, and f are selected and labeled as shown. In stage 7, node g is selected, one turn, namely (h, g, n), is prohibited, node g is labeled 7, deleted, and stage 8 begins executing. The stages 8 and 9 select nodes h and m in that order, and prohibit the indicated turns. During stage 10, Step 1 of the algorithm labels nodes k and n and the algorithm terminates. In Figure 2(E) the graph is shown with all of the prohibited turns and the node labels. It is clear that in all prohibited turns (x, y, z) the labels satisfy $\ell(y) < \ell(x)$ and $\ell(y) < \ell(z)$. The stage-by-stage operation of the algorithm is also shown in Table 1 in which each row corresponds to a stage.

4. PROPERTIES OF THE SCB ALGORITHM

Theorem 1: *The SCB algorithm has the following four properties.*

  ***Property 1:** Any cycle in G contains at least one turn from W (G).*

  ***Property 2:** SCB preserves connectivity; for any two nodes $a, b \in V$, there exists a path between a and b that does not include turns from W (G).*

  ***Property 3:** The set W (G) of prohibited turns generated by SCB algorithm is minimal (irreducible).*

  ***Property 4:** For any graph G, $W(G) \leq T(G) / 3$, where T (G) is the total number of turns in G.*

Proof of Property 1. Consider the node a with the minimum label $\ell(a)$ in any cycle C in G. Then in the turn (b, a, c) $(b, a, c \in C)$, $\ell(a) < \ell(b)$ and $\ell(a) < \ell(c)$. Thus, turn (b, a, c) is prohibited and cycle C is broken.

Figure 2. Example demonstrating the operation of the SCB algorithm resulting in a fraction of prohibited turns of $z(G) = 7 \,/\, 31$

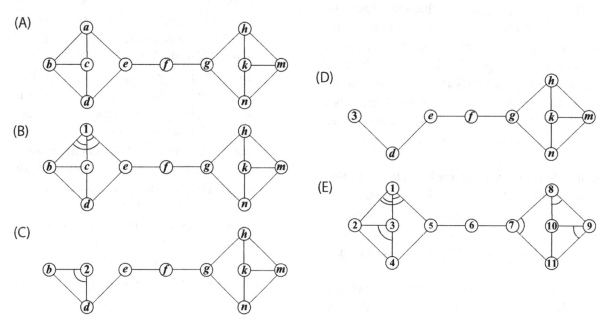

Table 1. Stage-by-stage operation of the SCB algorithm

Selected Node	Node Label	Set of Prohibited Turns
a	1	$\{(b,a,c),(b,a,e),(c,a,e)\}$
c	2	$\{(b,c,d)\}$
b	3	$\varnothing$
d	4	$\varnothing$
e	5	$\varnothing$
f	6	$\varnothing$
g	7	$\{(h,g,n)\}$
h	8	$\{(k,h,m)\}$
m	9	$\{(k,m,n)\}$
k	10	$\varnothing$
h	11	$\varnothing$

Proof of Property 2. The proof is by induction. Consider the first selected node a, $\ell(a) = 1$. Since a is a non-cut node, after all turns of the form (b, a, c) are prohibited and node a is deleted, there still exists a path from any node x to any node y, where $x, y \in G \setminus a$. Also, since all turns of the form (a, b, c) are permitted, there exists a path from a to any node $x \in G$. Now assume that connectivity is preserved after the first n stages of the algorithm, so that the next selected node a has label $\ell(a) = n + 1$. Node a is a non-cut node in the graph that remains after deletion of the first n selected nodes. Therefore, after prohibition of all turns (b, a, c) there still exits a path between any two unlabeled nodes x and y. Consider now paths from a labeled node u, $\ell(u) \le \ell(a)$ to another previously labeled node v, $\ell(v) < \ell(a)$, or to an unlabeled node y. If such a path P does not include a turn of the form (b, a, c), where b and c are unlabeled, it remains permitted. Now suppose P in-

Figure 3. Figure depicting the state of the graph at stage $n + 1$ of the SCB algorithm

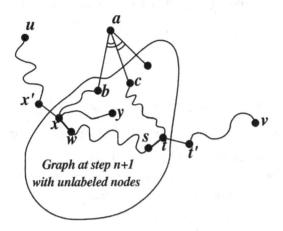

Graph at step n+1 with unlabeled nodes

cludes such a turn (Figure 3). Then, let x be the first unlabeled node in the path from u to v or from u to y, and z be the last unlabeled node in the path from u to v. The part of P from x to y, or from x to z, can be replaced respectively, by a path that does not include a (such a path exists, since a is a non-cut node) and obtain a path P^*. Let x' be the node already labeled that immediately precedes x in P and in P^*, and z' be the labeled node that immediately follows z in P and P^* (in the case when such a node exists). Since all turns (x', x, w) and (w, z, z') are permitted, path P^* does not contain prohibited turns, and connectivity is preserved at the $(n + 1)^{th}$ stage of the algorithm. Thus, Property 2 is proved by induction. Path

$$P = (u, \ldots, x', x, \ldots, b, a, c, \ldots, t, t', \ldots, v)$$

is prohibited due to the prohibited turn at node a. Path

$$P^* = (u, \ldots, x', x, w, \ldots, s, t, t', \ldots, v)$$

is permitted since it does not involve any prohibited turns.

Proof of Property 3. Consider a prohibited turn (b, a, c). Since connectivity is preserved and a is a non-cut node, there exists a permitted path (b, P, c) from b to c that does not include a. Adding edges (a, b) and (c, a) to this path, a cycle $C = (a, b, P, c, a, b)$ is obtained. Since turns of the form (a, b, x) and (a, c, y) are permitted, the only prohibited turn in C is (b, a, c). By removing this turn from $W(G)$, a cycle would be created in G and violate the cycle-breaking Property 1. Thus, set $W(G)$ is minimal.

Proof of Property 4. At the stage of the algorithm when node a is selected (stage $\ell(a)$, all turns (b, a, c) become prohibited, and all turns (a, b, c) become permitted, where $\ell(a) < \ell(b)$ and $\ell(a) < \ell(c)$ The number of prohibited turns is $\binom{d}{2}$ where d is the degree of node a (in the subgraph that remains at stage $\ell(a)$); the number of permitted turns is $\sum_{i=1}^{d}(d_i - 1)$, where d_i, $(i = 1, \ldots, d)$ are degrees of all neighbors of a. By Lemma 2, it is always possible to select a non-cut node such that inequality (4) is satisfied. This means that the number of permitted turns is larger than the number of prohibited turns by at least a factor of two. Since this is true for each stage of the algorithm, it follows that $W(G) \leq T(G) / 3$.

In general, the fraction of prohibited turns yielded by the SCB algorithm is considerably smaller than the upper bound of 1/3. The only class of graphs where the fraction is exactly 1/3 is the complete graphs K_n with $|V| = n$ and $|E| = n(n-1) / 2$. Indeed, the closer is a graph to a complete one, the larger is the fraction of prohibited turns, as shown by the following theorem which provides a better upper bound on the ratio $|W(G)|/T(G)$.

Theorem 2: *Let $G = (V, E)$ be a connected graph with N nodes and M edges. The fraction of prohibited turns $z_{SCB}(G)$ yielded by the SCB algorithm satisfies the upper bound:*

$$z_{SCB}(G) = \frac{|W(G)|}{T(G)} \le \frac{1}{3} - \frac{2N - 3 - \sqrt{8\beta + 1}}{3[2N + (\beta - 1)(\sqrt{8\beta + 1} + 3)]}, \tag{5}$$

where $\beta = M - N + 1$ is the cyclomatic number.

Proof. When a node is selected in the course of the SCB algorithm, all its edges are deleted. Thus, if d_ℓ is the degree of node with label ℓ at the stage when it is selected, then

$$\sum_{\ell=1}^{N} d_\ell = M. \tag{6}$$

The total number of prohibited turns is

$$|W(G)| = \sum_{\ell=1}^{N} \frac{d_\ell(d_\ell - 1)}{2}. \tag{7}$$

Note that, for the SCB algorithm,

$$d_{\ell+1} \ge d_\ell - 1. \tag{8}$$

(Otherwise, the nodes would be selected in the opposite order). Obviously, $d_N = 0$ $d_{N-1} = 1$. The quadratic sum (7) under the constraint (6) achieves maximum if the values of d_ℓ are maximally unequal, so that some of them are as large as possible. Looking at the sequence (d_ℓ) in the backward direction, from $\ell = N$ to $\ell = 1$, one can see that, because of (8), the sequence can increase only by 1 from one term to the another:

$$d_N = 0, d_{N-1} = 1, d_{N-2} \le 2, \dots, d_{N-i} \le i.$$

Hence, there exists a subsequence (d_{ℓ_j}) such $d_{\ell_j} = j$, where j takes on all integer values from 0 to a certain k. The value of $|W(G)|$ achieves its maximum, if k is the largest integer that satisfies two conditions. On one hand,

$$M \ge \sum_{j=0}^{k} j = \frac{k(k + 1)}{2}. \tag{9}$$

On the other hand, since the graph remains connected through the course of the algorithm, the number of remaining edges should be no smaller than the number of remaining nodes:

$$M - \frac{k(k + 1)}{2} \ge N - (k + 1). \tag{10}$$

The number of prohibited turns in the nodes of the subsequence (d_{ℓ_j}) is

$$\sum_{j=1}^{k} \frac{j(j - 1)}{2} = \frac{(k + 1)k(k - 1)}{6}. \tag{11}$$

The upper bound on $|W(G)|$ is obtained for the value of k (not necessarily an integer) that turns (10) into equality, i.e. for the root of the equation:

$$M - N = \frac{(k - 2)(k + 1)}{2}. \tag{12}$$

Hence,

$$k = \frac{1 + \sqrt{8(M - N + 1) + 1}}{2} = \frac{1 + \sqrt{8\beta + 1}}{2}.$$

$$(13)$$

Then, by (11),

$$|W(G)| \leq \frac{(M - N + 1)\left(\sqrt{8(M - N + 1) + 1} + 3\right)}{6}$$

$$= \frac{\beta(\sqrt{8\beta + 1} + 3)}{6}.$$

$$(14)$$

Now let us estimate the total number of turns. According to the proof of Property 4 in Theorem 1, if the degree of the selected nodes is k, then there exist at least k other nodes with the sum of degrees at least k^2. The total number of turns at these $k + 1$ nodes is minimal, if all degrees are equal to $d = k$. Since the graph is connected, the remaining $N - k - 1$ nodes add at least $N - k - 1$ turns. Thus the total number of turns $T(G)$ satisfies the inequality

$$T(G) \geq \frac{(k + 1)k(k - 1)}{2} + N - k + 1, \qquad (15)$$

where k is given by (13).

It follows that the fraction of prohibited turns $z(G)$ is upperbounded by

$$z(G) \leq \frac{|W(G)|}{T(G)}$$

$$\leq \frac{1}{3}\left[1 - \frac{2N - 3 - \sqrt{8\beta + 1}}{2N + (\beta - 1)(\sqrt{8\beta + 1} + 3)}\right].$$

$$(16)$$

Bound (14) and (16) are tight for all values of M and N such that $M - N = \dfrac{(k - 2)(k + 1)}{2}$, where k is a natural number and $k < N$, in particular, for a tree $(M = N - 1)$, for a ring

$(M = N)$, and for a complete graph $K_N\left(M = \dfrac{N(N - 1)}{2}\right)$.

Note that bound (16) converges to 1/3 iff the cyclomatic number $\beta = M - N + 1 = \Omega(N^{2/3})$. It will be shown below (see Section 3) that for some classes of graphs, the SCB algorithm guarantees that the fraction of prohibited turns is substantially smaller than that given by bound (16).

Theorem 3: *The fraction of prohibited turns is* $z\left(G\right) = 1 / 3$ *iff* $G = K_N$.

Proof. It is seen from (16) that if $M < \begin{pmatrix} N \\ 2 \end{pmatrix}$ then $z(G) < 1/3$. For a K_N, $M = \begin{pmatrix} N \\ 2 \end{pmatrix}$, and then $z(G) \leq 1/3$. On the other hand, there are $\begin{pmatrix} N \\ 3 \end{pmatrix}$ turn-disjoint triangles and $N\begin{pmatrix} N - 1 \\ 2 \end{pmatrix}$ turn in the complete graph K_N. Hence, by use of bound (2), $z(K_N) \geq 1/3$ is obtained. It follows that $z(G) = 1/3$ iff G is a complete graph K_N.

Though in general, the SCB algorithm is suboptimal, it can be readily shown by the use of the lower bounds (1)-(3) that the algorithm provides optimal solutions, for several broad classes of network topologies, in particular, for the following:

- All n-dimensional p-ary meshes and tori (including hypercubes $\mathbf{Z}_2^n$);
- All hexagonal and honeycomb meshes and tori;
- All homogeneous meshes;
- All fractahedrons;

- All graphs for which the bound (14) is achieved (including all complete graphs);
- All planar graphs without cut-nodes and with degrees not larger than 3;
- All planar graphs of girths $g \geq 6$;
- Certain special graphs, e.g. all Plato's polyhedra, the Petersen graph, the bipartite graph $K_{3,3}$, etc.

Earlier versions of a tree-free turn prohibition algorithms (the TP and CB algorithms) were presented in (Zakrevski, Jaiswal, & Karpovsky, 1999; Mustafa et al., 2005; Levitin et al., 2006). They have been shown to outperform the Up*/Down* algorithm in terms of the fraction of prohibited turns, average distance between nodes, and saturation load (see (Mustafa et al., 2005; Levitin et al., 2006)). However the earlier algorithms were more complicated than the SCB algorithm. Indeed, every recursive call in TP and CB algorithms involved as many as ten steps. In particular, at every stage all connected components that appear after a node removal had to be identified, special edges had to be determined, nodes had to be examined in order to be characterized as forcing or delayed, a *"halfloop"* flag had to be examined and set, etc (for detail, see (Levitin et al., 2006)). In contrast, the SCB algorithm does not use recursive calls, but only iterations, and it has only three steps in each iteration, which is easier for implementation and reduces the memory requirements. The simplification is achieved by elimination of complexities of dealing with cut nodes and is based on theoretical results described in Lemma 1 and Lemma 2. Though the order of the worst-case asymptotic time complexity of SCB algorithm remains the same as in previous works ((Mustafa et al., 2005; Levitin et al., 2006)), the practical implementation is substantially simpler.

A straightforward evaluation of the SCB worst-case time complexity is $O(NM)$. This follows from the fact that it takes $O(M)$ time to determine all cut nodes ((Cormen et al., 1989), Ch. 23, Problem 23-2).

Conjecture 2: The SCB algorithm is a polynomial-time approximation algorithm for the turn prohibition problem with a constant approximation ratio bound:

$$\frac{Z_{SCB}(G)}{Z(G)} \leq \rho = const.$$

Here $Z_{SCB}(G)$ and $Z(G)$ are the numbers of prohibited turns in the solution of the TP problem obtained by the SCB algorithm and in the optimal (minimum) solution, respectively.

5. TURN PROHIBITIONS FOR PLANAR GRAPHS

Planar graphs defined as those which can be embedded in a plane without any crossing edges form an important class of graphs. A large number of physical problems such as transportation highways (without underpasses), telecommunication networks, and physical circuit (or component) layout problems are modeled by planar graphs. For example, for proper operation, all physical layout problems in a printed circuit board as well as VLSI designs involve constructing conductive (metallic) signal pathways that must be prevented from crossing each other; therefore, these problems naturally map into planar graphs. In VLSI chips, either the entire chip or large sections of the chip are modeled by planar graphs (Agarwal, Mustafa, & Pandya, 2006). In (Agarwal et al., 2006; Agarwal, Mustafa, Shankar, Pandya, & Lho, 2007) authors introduced turn prohibition in Network-On-Chips (NOC) architectures where multiple processing elements are networked on one VLSI chip, in which the layout is planar. In this section constructive upper bounds on the minimum fraction of turns, $z(G)$ to be prohibited to break all cycles in any planar graph G are presented.

An important characteristic of a planar graph is the number of edges in the shortest cycle known as its girth.

Lemma 3: The average degree $\bar{d}$ in a planar graph with N nodes and girth g obeys inequality

$$\bar{d} \le \frac{2g}{g-2} - \frac{4g}{N(g-2)}. \tag{17}$$

Proof. Let G be a planar graph with F faces and girth $g(G) = g$. Since each edge belongs to either one or two faces, it follows that $2M \ge \sum_{j=1}^{F} g_j \ge Fg$ where g_j is the number of edges of face j. Hence

$$F \le \frac{2M}{g}. \tag{18}$$

Substituting (18) into the Euler equation $F = M - N + 2$, one obtains

$$M \le \frac{g(N-2)}{g-2}. \tag{19}$$

Thus, the average node degree is

$$\bar{d} = \frac{2M}{N} \le \frac{2g}{g-2} - \frac{4g}{N(g-2)}.$$

It is seen that the upper bound on d given by (17) decreases monotonically with girth.

Since the probability of a deadlock in a network with a uniform traffic and without turn prohibitions decreases with increasing girth, it may be conjectured that the cost of deadlock prevention in terms of the fraction of turns required to be prohibited decreases as well as the girth increases. The following theorem proves this idea.

Theorem 4: *If G is a planar graph without triangles, then*

$$z(G) \le \frac{1}{4}. \tag{20}$$

Proof. With no triangles in a planar graph, the girth of the graph is $g(G) = g \ge 4$. Then the average degree $\bar{d}$ in (17) becomes $\bar{d} \le 4 - 8/N$, which means that a planar graph without triangles contains at least two nodes of degree less than four. Note that any subgraph of G is also a planar graph with girth at least four and an average degree $\bar{d} \le 4 - 8/n$, where n is the number of nodes in the subgraph. By Lemma 1, there exists a subgraph H of G that consists of non-cut nodes only and connected to the rest of the graph by at most one cut node. Consider a subgraph of G formed by subgraph H and this cut node. It follows that this graph contains a non-cut node of degree at most 3.

At every step of the execution of the SCB algorithm (see Section 3), a minimum degree node is selected according to the rule (4). Let $A_i (i = 1, 2, 3)$ be the number of nodes of degree i that were selected during the execution of the algorithm. Since the last node left is a node of degree zero and all edges are deleted in the course of the algorithm,

$$A_1 + A_2 + A_3 = N - 1, \tag{21}$$

$$A_1 + 2A_2 + 3A_3 = M. \tag{22}$$

Hence,

$$A_2 + 2A_3 = M - N + 1 = F - 1. \tag{23}$$

Note that the number of prohibited turns in the SCB procedure is given by

$$Z = A_2 + 3A_3. \tag{24}$$

Hence, an upper bound for Z would correspond to a maximal A_3 and a minimal A_2. Obviously, the deletion of a degree 2 node decreases the number of faces by 1, and the deletion of a degree 3 node decreases this number by 2. The algorithm terminates when the number of faces is reduced to 1. It is easy to show, using (17), (18), and the Euler equation, that for girth $g \geq 4$,

$$\bar{d} \leq \frac{4(F-2)}{F(g-2)+4} + 2 \leq \frac{4(F-2)}{2(F+2)} + 2 = 4 - \frac{8}{F+2}.$$

Hence, for any graph with girth $g \geq 4$ $(F \leq 5)$, $\bar{d} = 3 - \frac{1}{7} < 3$.

Thus any such graph has non-cut nodes of degree 2 or 1. Therefore, $A_3 \leq (F-4)/2$ and $A_2 \geq 3$ (provided $F \geq 4$). Then, using (23) and (24):

$$Z = \frac{3}{2}(A_2 + 2A_3) - \frac{A_2}{2} = \frac{3}{2}(M - N + 1) - \frac{A_2}{2}.$$

Finally, since $A_2 \geq 3$, it follows that

$$Z(G) \leq Z \leq \frac{3}{2}(M - N). \tag{25}$$

Here, $Z(G)$ is the minimum number of prohibited turns for G. To estimate the total number of turns $T(G)$, we note that there are two cases; first, when the average degree $\bar{d} = 2M / N$ is $3 \leq \bar{d} \leq 4 - 8 / N$ and second, when $\bar{d} < 3$. In the first case, $T(G)$ is minimal if nodes are of degree 3 and degree 4 only and in the second case if nodes are of degree 2 and degree 3 only. As-

suming first that nodes are of degree 3 and 4 only, we determine that $N_3 = 4N - 2M$ and $N_4 = 2M - 3N$, where N_3 and N_4 designate the number of nodes of degree 3 and degree 4, respectively, in the graph. It follows that $T(G) = 6(M - N)$, and the fraction of prohibited turns $z(G) = Z(G)/T(G)$ is

$$z(G) \leq \frac{1}{4}. \tag{26}$$

For the case when $2 \leq \bar{d} < 3$, $T(G)$ is minimal if there are N_2 nodes of degree 2 and $N_3 = N - N_2$ nodes of degree 3. Then $N_2 = 3N - 2M$, and $N_3 = 2(M - N)$, and

$$T(G) = 4M - 3N$$
$$= 6(M - N) + (3N - 2M) \geq 6(M - N)$$

(since $\bar{d} = 2M / 3 < 3$). Hence in both cases the upper bound for the fraction of prohibited turns is

$$z(G) \leq \frac{1}{4}. \tag{27}$$

Theorem 5: *If G is a planar graph with N nodes and girth $g \geq 6$, then*

$$z(G) \leq \frac{2}{g+6} - \frac{(g-2)(g-6)}{(g+6)\big[g(N-8)+6N\big]}, \tag{28}$$

and

$$z(G) \leq \frac{2}{g+6}. \tag{29}$$

Proof. Note that, by (17), for girth $g = 6$ the average degree becomes

Figure 4. Planar graph with girth g = 8, N = 32, M = 40, and T = 64. Prohibited turns are shown as arcs

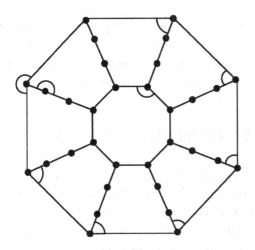

$\bar{d} \le 3 - 6 / N < 3$.

For the case of $g \ge 6$, if there are only N_2 nodes of degree 2 and N_3 nodes of degree 3, we get $N_2 = 3N - 2M$,

$N_3 - 2(M - N)$,

and the total number of turns, $T(G) = N_2 + 3N_3 = 4M - 3N$. Since $T(G)$ achieves minimum if the degrees take values closest to the given average degree, it follows that $T(G) \ge 4M - 3N$. By the same argument that is given in the first paragraph of the proof of Theorem 4, there will always be non-cut nodes of degree at most 2 available for selection at every step of the algorithm; and therefore $A_3 = 0$. From $A_1 + A_2 = N - 1$ and

$A_1 + 2A_2 = M$, we obtain that $Z = A_2 = M - N + 1 = F - 1$ and the upper bound for the fraction of prohibited turns will be

$$z(G) \le \frac{M - N + 1}{4M - 3N}.$$

Substituting $x = M / N$, we get

$$z(G) \le \frac{1}{4} - \frac{1/4 - 1/N}{4x - 3}. \tag{30}$$

The right-hand side of (30) is a monotonically increasing function of x. Note that from $\bar{d} = 2M / N = 2x$ we get

$$x \le \frac{g}{g - 2} - \frac{2g}{N(g - 2)}.$$

Substituting the maximum value of x into (30) we obtain

$$z(G) \le \frac{2}{g + 6} - \frac{(g - 2)(g - 6)}{(g + 6)[g(N - 8) + 6N]},$$

and

$$z(G) \le \frac{2}{g + 6}.$$

The bound (28) is tight as shown by the following example.

Example 2. Consider the planar graph G of girth $g = 8$ shown in Figure 4, with $N = 32$, $M = 40$, and $T = 64$. For this graph, $Z = M - N + 1$ and $z(G) = 9 / 64$ is equal to the right-hand part of inequality (28).

To avoid misunderstanding, let us point out that it is planarity and girth constraints that result in (20) and (28), but not the limits on the average degree alone. It is easy to construct graphs with average degree $\bar{d}$ arbitrarily close to 2, for which $z(G)$ is arbitrarily close to 1/3.

For girth $g(G) = 5$ planar graphs, the average degree in (17) becomes

Figure 5. An infinite planar graph with average degree $\bar{d} = 10 / 3$

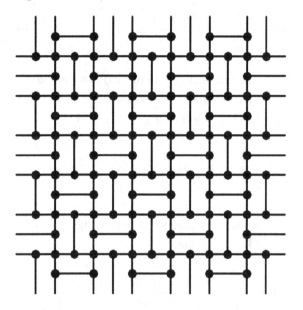

$$\bar{d} \leq \frac{10}{3} - \frac{20}{3N}. \tag{31}$$

This bound is tight and is achieved for example for the infinite graph of Figure 5.

For $N < 20$ ($F < 12$) the average degree $\bar{d} < 3$ and it follows that such graphs would always have a node of degree 2.

Conjecture 3. If G is a planar graph with girth $g(G) = 5$, then $z(G) \leq 1/5$. Note that Theorems 4 and 5 do not apply to non-planar graphs. For example, for bipartite graph $K_{4,4}$ with $N = 8$ nodes, we have

$$z(K_{4,4}) = 14 / 48 > 1 / 4.$$

The proofs of Theorem 4 and Theorem 5 suggest a somewhat more general result.

Theorem 6: *If in the course of the SCB algorithm, all selected nodes are of degree 2 or less, then the solution given by SCB is optimal, and,*

$$| W(G) | = M - N + 1. \tag{32}$$

Proof. The result follows immediately from the expressions (23) and (24), and lower bound (1).

In particular, the SCB algorithm provides an optimal solution for 2-dimensional rectangular meshes and honeycomb meshes (Parhami, 1998) – two popular network topologies.

6. EXPERIMENTAL RESULTS

In this section the results of simulation experiments are presented with turn prohibition for the SCB, Up*/Down*-DFS (where the spanning tree is constructed by depth-first search), Up*/Down*-BFS (where the spanning tree is constructed by breadth-first search), and L-turn algorithms. Simulation experiments involving message delivery simulations were performed using the Modeler from OPNET Technologies. Modeler provides a powerful discrete event simulation environment where flits are tracked and timed from their creation at the source processor to their consumption at the destination processor. In all of the experiments and simulations, network topologies were first generated using tools that were developed for this purpose. All of the topologies used in our work are represented by 64-node undirected graphs. Seven hundred different connected irregular graphs of various average degrees were generated, 100 graphs each for average degrees 4, …, 10. In each graph, a node could have a degree from 1 to 16. Four algorithms that were investigated are then used to prohibit turns in each graph. When determining the prohibited turns, the algorithms as defined in (Koibuchi et al., 2001) for the L-turn, in (Schroeder et al., 1990) for the Up*/Down*-BFS, and in (J. Sancho & Robles, 2000; J. Sancho et al., 2000; J. C. Sancho et al., 2004) for the Up*/Down*-DFS were used. Exactly the same spanning trees have been used for both the L-turn and Up*/Down*-BFS algorithms. In the case of the Up*/Down*-DFS, following (Sancho et

Figure 6. Fraction of prohibited turns as a function of the average degree. Each point is the average of the results of 100 different random graphs.

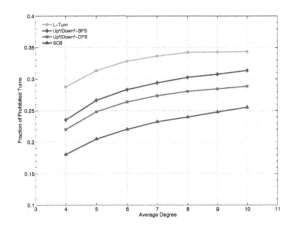

al., 2004), we used the heuristic to select the next node to be added to the already constructed depth first spanning tree. The set of prohibited turns, the fraction of prohibited turns, the average distance and dilation calculations are then performed to obtain the results presented next.

In Figure 6 the results for the fraction of prohibited turns are shown. It can be noted that the SCB algorithm consistently performs better than the three other algorithms.

Consider now the notion of dilation in a network topology due to turn prohibitions. Paths that involve prohibited turns are prohibited and are not used for communication. Thus, one side effect of turn prohibitions is that, prohibiting certain paths from being used for message routing, may increase distances between some nodes. The net result of this is that the average distance of the network graph will be increased. To facilitate the investigation of this phenomenon, we introduced the notion of distance dilation which we define as the ratio of the average distance after turn prohibitions to the average distance with no turn prohibition. When the dilation is 1 it would imply that the turn prohibitions have not caused any lengthening of the average distance. For example, in complete graphs, the fraction of prohibited turns achieves the upper bound, but the dilation is 1.

In Figure 7 we show the results of the dilation calculations for the four algorithms for random graphs. One can see that the SCB algorithm yields dilation in the range between 3.2%-9.6%.

Calculations for *planar* graphs follow a similar approach. We first generated 6 families of planar graphs with girths from 3,..., 8, each family of 100 graphs. In all of our constructions, all faces (including the infinite one) are all regular and have the same number of edges equal to the girth g. After the planar graphs are generated, we then applied the SCB algorithm to break all cycles as before. Results of these calculations are shown below. In Figure 8, the fractions of prohibited turns are shown for families of planar graphs with girths 3 through 8 together with the theoretical upper bounds (20) and (28). In this figure we also show the fraction of prohibited turns for an icosahedron ($g = 3$, $z(G) = 4 / 15$) and the dodecahedron ($g = 5$, $z(G) = 1 / 5$).

Results of dilation calculations for planar graphs are shown in Figure 9, where we see that as the girth increases the average dilation increases, predicting a better performance for message delivery times for planar graphs with smaller girths. In particular, for girths 3 and 4 topologies, the dilations are very small (1.0002 and 1.0009 respectively).

Figure 7. Average distance dilation for 64 node graphs as a function of the average degree. Each point is the average of the results of 100 different random graphs.

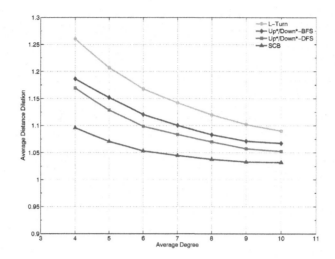

Figure 8. Fraction of prohibited turns for SCB in 64 node planar graphs as a function of girth

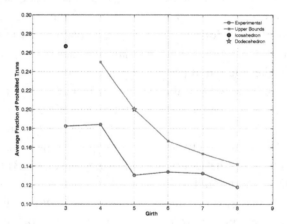

For message delivery experiments, we implemented wormhole node models (Mustafa et al., 2005; Levitin et al., 2006; Mustafa, Levitin, & Karpovsky, August 2006) with 16 bidirectional full-duplex ports and a local port. Messages, also known as "worms", are generated at a module attached to the local port of each node. All messages in our simulations, 200 flits long, were generated using uniform traffic model with exponential inter-arrival times. As worms are injected into the network via the local channel, the router at the node determines, using a routing table, which output port to use to route the message. If the output port is free, it is immediately committed to the incoming message port for the duration of the message, otherwise the message is blocked until the output port is freed up. A routing table at each node is generated using the all-pairs shortest path algorithm with an additional criterion that the selected shortest paths do not include any prohibited turns. With this approach both deadlock and live-lock conditions are proactively prevented from occurring during the actual routing of messages. We believe that

Figure 9. Average distance dilation in planar topologies with 64 nodes after the SCB generated turn prohibitions as a function of girth

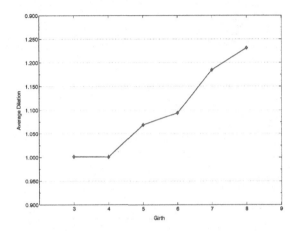

Figure 10. End-to-end message latency as a function of average message generation rate for 64-node degree 4 random graphs

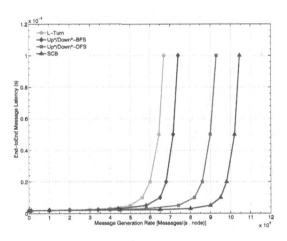

using the same underlying wormhole routing models and changing only the routing tables generated identically using the prohibited turns generated by the various algorithms is the fairest way of comparing the performances of the algorithms. (Of course, it must be taken into account that turn prohibitions in the L-turn algorithm are unidirectional). The simulations are repeated with message generation rate increasing step by step until the latency becomes at least two orders of magnitude larger than for the smallest generation

rate. The same experiment is repeated with all of the graphs and for all algorithms.

Figure 10 shows the dependence between the latency (message delivery time) and the average load (message generation rate). The load has been averaged over all 100 graphs of average degree 4 for each fixed latency value. For low offered loads all algorithms perform equally well. As the offered load is increased we note that the SCB algorithm maintains lower latency values for larger offered loads.

Figure 11. Saturation points (maximum sustainable message generation rates per second per node) as a function of average node degree for 64 node random graphs

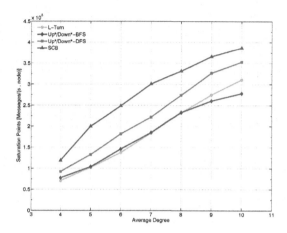

Figure 12. Saturation points (maximum sustainable message generation rates per second per node) as a function of the girth of 64-node planar graphs

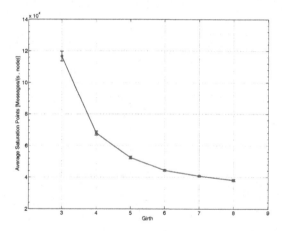

The average saturation points for all 100 graphs of each average degree have been calculated and plotted in Figure 11.

The results of the SCB algorithm applied to planar graphs are presented in Figure 12. These results are in agreement with the anticipated behavior. In particular, since the average distance increases with girth in planar networks with a given number of nodes, one would expect better performance in networks of smaller girths. Indeed as seen at Figure 12, the saturation load increases for smaller girths.

Our experiments clearly demonstrate the superior performance of the SCB algorithm as compared to the tree-based algorithms. When the SCB algorithm is used, the fraction of prohibited turns is smaller by up to 17.9%, 23.2%, and 37.2% than when Up*/Down*-DFS, Up*/Down*-BFS, and L-turn algorithms are used, respectively. The distance dilation for the SCB algorithm is smaller than for the tree-based algorithms by a factor between 1.64 and 2.72. The SCB algorithm provides for the increase in the maximum sustainable message generation rate of up to 95% over L-turn, up to 92% over Up*/Down*-BFS and up to 51% over Up*/Down*-DFS.

Perhaps, what is even more significant is the difference in the network performance in the "working range" of loads. With the SCB algorithm, when the message generation rate increases from 0 to 90,000 messages per second per node, the latency increases only by a factor of 2.7, while with other algorithms the network becomes practically saturated. Among the tree-based algorithms, the Up*/Down*-DFS algorithm seems to be the best, but the application of heuristic rules for constructing the spanning tree involves a substantial computational cost of $O(N^3)$. Remarkably, though the fraction of prohibited turns is considerably larger for the L-turn algorithm than for the Up*/Down*-BFS algorithm, the difference between them in terms of the saturation load is not large (actually, L-turn algorithm looks better for dense networks). A possible explanation of this observation is that L-turn algorithm provides for a more even distribution of the traffic, while the Up*/Down*-BFS algorithm suffers from congestion at and near the root.

7. CONCLUSION

This chapter considers the problem of constructing minimal connectivity-preserving cycle-breaking (CPCB) set of turns for graphs that model communication networks. This problem is important for deadlock-free and livelock-free message routing in computer communication networks. We formulate the general Turn Prohibition (TP) problem of finding such a set with minimum number of prohibited turns and conjectured that the problem is NP-hard. We prove lower bounds on the minimum number of prohibited turns. We present a new algorithm called the Simple Cycle-Breaking (SCB) algorithm and conjectured that this algorithm satisfies a constant approximation ratio bound for the TP problem. In contrast with a number of other turn prohibition algorithms (e.g.,

Up*/Down*-BFS, Up*/Down*-DFS, and L-turn algorithms), the SCB algorithm is tree-free, i.e., it does not use a spanning tree for construction of the CPCB set of prohibited turns. Therefore, it is free of problems stemming from the choice of the spanning tree and its root. The SCB algorithm implements a procedure to label all nodes and to prohibit or permit turns according to this labeling.

The SCB algorithm guarantees that the fraction of prohibited turns does not exceed an upper bound that is less than or equal to 1/3, as given by (5), and that the set of prohibited turns is minimal (irreducible). Comparison with lower bounds shows that the SCB algorithm yields optimal solutions for broad classes of network topologies. An important class of network topologies, namely, planar graphs, has been investigated, and stricter upper bounds on the number of prohibited turns produced by the SCB algorithm have been obtained. In particular, for a graph without triangles, the fraction of prohibited turns does not exceed 1/4.

Experimental results show that the SCB algorithm dramatically outperforms the tree-based algorithms in terms of all four basic characteristics: the fraction of prohibited turns, the distance dilation, the message delivery time, and the saturation load.

REFERENCES

Agarwal, A., Mustafa, M., & Pandya, A. S. (2006, May). *QOS driven network-on-chip design for real time systems* (pp. 1291-1295). Ottawa, Canada: IEEE CCECE/CCGEI.

Agarwal, A., Mustafa, M., Shankar, R., Pandya, A. S., & Lho, Y. (2007, April). A deadlock free Router design for network on chip architecture. *Journal of Korea Institute of Maritime Information and Communication Sciences, 11*(4), 696–706.

Ausiello, G., Crescenzi, P., Gambosi, G., Kann, V., Marchetti-Spaccamela, A., & Protasi, M. (2003). *Complexity and approximation*. Berlin, Germany: Springer-Verlag.

Boden, N. J., Cohen, D., Felderman, R. E., Seitz, C. L., Seizovic, J. N., & Su, W.-K. (1995). Myrinet: A gigabit per second local area network. *IEEE Micro, 15*(1), 29–35. doi:10.1109/40.342015

Boppana, R., & Chalasani, S. (1993). A comparison of adaptive wormhole routing algorithms. *Computer Architecture News, 21*(2), 351–360. doi:10.1145/173682.165177

Boppana, R. V., Chalasani, S., & Raghavendra, C. (1998). Resource deadlocks and performance of wormhole multicast routing algorithms. *IEEE Transactions on Parallel and Distributed Systems, 9*(6), 535–549. doi:10.1109/71.689441

Chalasani, S., & Boppana, R. V. (1995). Fault-tolerant wormhole routing algorithms in mesh networks. *IEEE Transactions on Computers, 44*(7), 848–864. doi:10.1109/12.392844

Cormen, T. H., Leiserson, E. C., & Rivest, R. L. (1989). *Introduction to algorithms*. The MIT Press.

Dally, W., & Aoki, H. (1997). Deadlock-free adaptive routing in multicomputer networks using virtual channels. *IEEE Transactions on Parallel and Distributed Systems, 4*(4), 466–475. doi:10.1109/71.219761

Dally, W. J., & Seitz, C. L. (1986). The torus routing chip. *Journal of Distributed Computing, 1*(3), 187–196. doi:10.1007/BF01660031

Dally, W. J., & Seitz, C. L. (1987). Deadlock-free message routing in multiprocessor interconnection networks. *IEEE Transactions on Computers, 36*, 547–553. doi:10.1109/TC.1987.1676939

de Mello, A. V., Ost, L. C., Moraes, F. G., & Calazans, N. L. V. (2004, May). *Evaluation of routing algorithms on mesh based NoCs (Tech. Rep. No. 040)*. Rio Grande, Brazil: Faculdade de Informatica PUCRS-Brazil.

Duato, J. (December 1991). Deadlock-free adaptive routing algorithms for multicomputers: Evaluation of a new algorithm. In *Proceedings of the Third IEEE Symposium Parallel and Distributed Processing* (pp. 840-847). Dallas, TX: IEEE Computer Society.

Duato, J. (1993). A new theory of deadlock-free adaptive routing in wormhole networks. *IEEE Transactions on Parallel and Distributed Systems, 4*, 1320–1331. doi:10.1109/71.250114

Duato, J. (1994). A necessary and sufficient condition for deadlock-free adaptive routing in wormhole networks. *Proceedings of International Conference on Parallel Processing*, (pp. 142-149).

Duato, J. (1995, October). A necessary and sufficient condition for deadlock-free adaptive routing in wormhole networks. *IEEE Transactions on Parallel and Distributed Systems, 6*(10), 1055–1067. doi:10.1109/71.473515

Duato, J., Yalamancili, S., & Ni, L. (1997). *Interconnection networks: An engineering approach*. Silver Spring, MD: IEEE Computer Society Press.

Einhoff, G., & Fidler, M. (June 2004). The turn-net concept: Routing in feed-forward networks with prohibited turns. In *2004 IEEE International Conference on Communications*, (Vol. 4, pp. 2009-2013).

Fleury, E., & Fraigniaud, P. (1998). A general theory for deadlock avoidance in wormhole-routed networks. *IEEE Transactions on Parallel and Distributed Systems, 9*(7), 626–638. doi:10.1109/71.707539

Gaughan, P., & Yalamanchili, S. (1995). A family of fault tolerant routing protocols for direct multiprocessor networks. *IEEE Transactions on Parallel and Distributed Systems*, 6(5), 482–497. doi:10.1109/71.382317

Glass, C., & Ni, L. (1992). The turn model for adaptive routing. *Proceedings of the 19th Annual International Symposium on Computer Architecture*, (pp. 278-286).

Glass, C., & Ni, L. (1994). The turn model for adaptive routing. *Journal of the ACM, 5*, 874–902. doi:10.1145/185675.185682

Horst, R. (1996). ServerNet(TM) deadlock avoidance and fractahedral topologies. *Proceedings of IEEE International Parallel Processing Symposium*, (pp. 274-280).

Hu, J., & Marculescu, R. (2004). DyAD - Smart routing for networks-on-chip. *Proceedings of the 41st annual conference on Design Automation*, (pp. 260-263).

Jayasimha, D. N., Schwiebert, L., Manivannan, D., & May, J. A. (2003). A foundation for designing deadlock-free routing algorithms in wormhole networks. *Journal of the ACM, 50*(2), 250–275. doi:10.1145/636865.636869

Jouraku, A. (2007). An effective design of deadlock-free routing algorithms based on 2d turn model for irregular networks. *IEEE Transactions on Parallel and Distributed Systems, 18*(3), 320–333. doi:10.1109/TPDS.2007.36

Klepacki, D. (2003). *Blue gene*. Retrieved from http://lobster.bu.edu/SCV/Archive/IBM/BGL-BU.pdf

Koibuchi, M., Funahashi, A., Jouraku, A., & Amano, H. (2001, September). L-turn routing: An adaptive routing in irregular networks. In *Proceedings of IEEE International Conference on Parallel Processing* (pp. 383-392).

Levitin, L., Karpovsky, M., & Mustafa, M. (May, 2009). Deadlock prevention by turn prohibitions in interconnection networks. In *2009 IEEE International Symposium on Parallel & Distributed Processing* (pp. 1-7). Rome, Italy: IEEE Computer Society.

Levitin, L. B., Karpovsky, M. G., Mustafa, M., & Zakrevski, L. (2006). New algorithm for finding cycle-breaking sets of turns in a graph. *Journal of Graph Algorithms and Applications, 10*(2), 387–420. doi:10.7155/jgaa.00134

Libeskind-Hadas, R., Mazzoni, D., & Rajagopalan, R. (1998). Tree-based multicasting in wormhole-routed irregular topologies. *Proceedings of the Merged 12th International Parallel Processing Symposium and the 9th Symposium on Parallel and Distributed Processing*, (pp. 244-249).

Lysne, O., Skeie, T., Reinemo, S. A., & Theiss, I. (2006). Layered routing in irregular networks. *IEEE Transactions on Parallel and Distributed Systems, 17*(1), 51–56. doi:10.1109/TPDS.2006.12

Mejia, A., Flitch, J., Duato, J., Reinemo, S. A., & Skeie, T. (2006). *Segment-based routing: An efficient fault-tolerant routing algorithm for meshes and tori*. In 20th international Parallel and distributed processing symposium, IPDPS 2006. IEEE.

Min, G., Ould-Khaoua, M., Kouvatsos, D., & Awan, I. (2004, May). A queuing model of dimension-ordered routing under self-similar traffic loads. In *Proceedings of the 18th International Parallel and distributed processing symposium, 2004* (pp. 601-613). Washington, DC: IEEE Computer Society.

Mustafa, M., Karpovsky, M., & Levitin, L. (2005, August). *Cycle breaking in wormhole routed computer communication networks*. OPNET Technologies.

Mustafa, M., Levitin, L., & Karpovsky, M. (August 2006). *Weighted turn prohibition in computer communication networks.* Washington, DC: OPNET Technologies, Inc.

Ni, L. M., & McKinley, P. K. (1993). A survey of wormhole routing techniques in directed networks. *Computer, 26,* 62–76. doi:10.1109/2.191995

Parhami, B. (1998). *Introduction to parallel processing: Algorithms and architectures.* Plenum Press.

Pellegrini, F. D., Starobinski, D., Karpovsky, M., & Levitin, L. (2004). Scalable cycle-breaking algorithms for gigabit Ethernet backbones. *Proceedings - IEEE INFOCOM,* 2004.

Pellegrini, F. D., Starobinski, D., Karpovsky, M. G., & Levitin, L. B. (2006, February). Scalable, distributed cycle-breaking algorithms for gigabit Ethernet backbones. *Journal of Optical Networks, 5*(2), 122–144. doi:10.1364/JON.5.000122

Pifarré, G. D., Gravano, L., Denicolay, G., & Sanz, J. L. C. (1994). Adaptive deadlock-and livelock-free routing in the hypercube network. *IEEE Transactions on Parallel and Distributed Systems, 5*(11), 1121–1139. doi:10.1109/71.329674

Sancho, J., & Robles, A. (2000, August). Improving the up*/down* routing scheme for networks of workstations. In *Proceedings Euro-Par 2000.*

Sancho, J., Robles, A., & Duato, J. (2000). *A flexible routing scheme for networks of workstations* (pp. 260–267). ISHPC. doi:10.1007/3-540-39999-2_23

Sancho, J. C., Robles, A., & Duato, J. (2004, August). An effective methodology to improve the performance of the up*/down* routing algorithm. *IEEE Transactions on Parallel and Distributed Systems, 15*(8), 740–754. doi:10.1109/TPDS.2004.28

Sancho, J. C., Robles, A., Lopez, P., Flich, J., & Duato, J. (2003). Routing in infiniband™ torus network topologies. *International Conference on Parallel Processing,* (p. 509).

Schroeder, M. D., Birrell, A. D., Burrows, M., Murray, H., Needham, R. M., Rodeheer, T. L., et al. (1990, April). *AutoNet: A high-speed self configuring local area network using point-to-point links* (Tech. Rep. No. SRC Research Report 59). Digital Equipment Corporation, SRC.

Schwiebert, L. (2001). Deadlock-free oblivious wormhole routing with cyclic dependencies. *IEEE Transactions on Computers, 50*(9), 865–876. doi:10.1109/12.954503

Schwiebert, L., & Jayasimha, D. N. (1996). A necessary and sufficient condition for deadlock-free wormhole routing. *Journal of Parallel and Distributed Computing, 32*(1), 103–117. doi:10.1006/jpdc.1996.0008

Seitz, C. L. (1985, March). *The hypercube communication chip* (Display File 5182:DF:85). California Institute of Technology.

Shevtekar, A., & Zakrevski, L. (2004). *Hybrid turn-prohibition routing algorithm for the networks of workstations* (pp. 1383–1389). Parallel and Distributed Processing Techniques and Applications.

Silla, F., & Duato, J. (2000). High-performance routing in networks of workstations with irregular topology. *IEEE Transactions on Parallel and Distributed Systems, 11*(7), 699–719. doi:10.1109/71.877816

Silla, F., Duato, J., Sivasubramaniam, A., & Das, C. R. (1998). Virtual channel multiplexing in networks of workstations with irregular topology. *Proceedings of the International Conference on High Performance Computing,* (pp. 147-154).

Skeie, T., Lysne, O., & Theiss, I. (2002). Layered shortest path (LASH) routing in irregular system area networks. In *International Parallel and Distributed Processing Symposium: IPDPS 2002 Workshops* (pp. 162-170). Fort Lauderdale, FL.

Starobinski, D., Karpovsky, M., & Zakrevski, L. (2003). Application of network calculus to general topologies using turn prohibition. *IEEE/ACM Transactions on Networking, 11*(3), 411–421. doi:10.1109/TNET.2003.813040

Sun, Y.-M., Yang, C.-H., Chung, Y.-C., & Huang, T.-Y. (2004). An efficient deadlock-free tree-based routing algorithm for irregular wormhole-routed networks based on the turn model. In *ICPP '04: Proceedings of the 2004 International Conference on Parallel Processing* (pp. 343–352). Washington, DC: IEEE Computer Society.

Zakrevski, L. (2000). *Fault-tolerant wormhole message routing in computer communication networks*. Doctoral dissertation, Boston University, College of Electrical Engineering.

Zakrevski, L., Jaiswal, S., & Karpovsky, M. (1999). Unicast message routing in communication networks with irregular topologies. *Proceeding of Computer Aided Design* (CAD-99).

Zakrevski, L., Jaiswal, S., Levitin, L., & Karpovsky, M. (1999). A new method for deadlock elimination in computer networks with irregular topologies. *Proceedings of the International Association of Science and Technology for Development (IASTED) Conference, Parallel and Distributed Computing Systems* (PDCS-99), Vol. 1, (pp. 396-402).

Zakrevski, L., Mustafa, M., & Karpovsky, M. (2000). Turn prohibition based routing in irregular computer networks. *Proceedings of the IASTED International Conference on Parallel and Distributed Computing and Systems*, (pp. 175-179).

Zhou, J., Lin, X.-Y., & Chung, Y.-C. (2006). A tree-turn model for irregular networks. In *NCA '06: Proceedings of the Fifth IEEE International Symposium on Network Computing and Applications* (pp. 11–18). Washington, DC: IEEE Computer Society.

KEY TERMS AND DEFINITIONS

Cycle of Edges: A path in which the last edge is the same as the first one and is traversed in the same direction.

Deadlock: A situation in a communication network, when several messages block one another around a cycle, so that no one can move ahead.

Degree of a Node: The number of edges ending in the node.

Path in a Graph: A sequence of nodes in which each node is connected to the next node by an edge.

Turn Prohibition: A set of restrictions in routing that prohibits messages from using certain turns, in order to prevent deadlocks.

Turn: A pair of edges having the same node as their endpoint.

Wormhole Routing: A method of routing in communication networks in which all parts of a message (flits) follow the same path, at any moment of time occupying a number of nodes and edges (links) along the path.

Chapter 4
Deadlock Prevention with Wormhole Routing:
Regular Topology

Mark Karpovsky
Boston University, USA

Lev Levitin
Boston University, USA

Mehmet Mustafa
Boston University, USA

ABSTRACT

In this chapter, the problem of constructing minimal cycle-breaking connectivity preserving sets of turns for graphs that model regular or near regular multiprocessor systems, as a method to prevent deadlocks is investigated. Cycle-breaking provides for deadlock-free wormhole routing defined by turns prohibited at some nodes. The lower and upper bounds for minimal cardinalities of cycle-breaking connectivity preserving sets for several classes of graphs such as homogeneous meshes, p-ary n-cubes, cube-connected cycles, hexagonal and honeycomb meshes and tori, Hamiltonian graphs and others are obtained and presented along with some preliminary experimental results.

1. INTRODUCTION

In previous chapter, we analyzed communication networks that are irregular, where nodes have arbitrary number of adjacent neighbor nodes. Because of the way they evolve in an ad hoc manner, networks of workstations (NOWS) are as a rule irregular. This chapter is devoted to

DOI: 10.4018/978-1-4666-2533-4.ch004

procedures that guarantee deadlock-free wormhole routing in multiprocessor systems with regular or almost regular interconnection topologies. The approach is based on minimizing the number of turns that are prohibited and therefore are not available for routing. The regularities in the structure of networks make it possible to derive simple and efficient solutions for the turn prohibition problem. Thus, the general algorithms developed previously for arbitrary topologies, e.g., (Dally

& Seitz, 1987; Boppana & Chalasani, 1993; Chalasani & Boppana, 1995; Duato, Yalamancili, & Ni, 1997; Ni & McKinley, 1993), (Dally & Seitz, 1986), (Duato, 1993), (Dally & Aoki, 1997), (Zakrevski, Jaiswal, Levitin, & Karpovsky, 1999; Zakrevski, Jaiswal, & Karpovsky, 1999; Zakrevski, Mustafa, & Karpovsky, 2000; Lysne, Skeie, Reinemo, & Theiss, 2006; Schroeder, Birrel, Burrows, Murray, Needham, Rodeheer, et al., 1990; Sancho & Robles, 2000), (Skeie, Lysne, & Theiss, 2002; Sancho et al., 2004; Pellegrini et al., 2004, 2006), (Mustafa et al., 2005; Levitin et al., 2006; Levitin et al., May, 2009, 2010) are not used here. Instead, optimal or asymptotically optimal solutions of the turn prohibition problem for general classes of special topologies, prevalent in multiprocessor systems are presented. These solutions are obtained by application of simple rules, run-time complexities of which do not exceed $O\left(N\right)$ (i.e., linear in the number of nodes N), and, in many cases, is $O\left(1\right)$ (i.e., constant). The memory requirements for computing the solutions do not exceed $O\left(\log N\right)$. The proposed turn prohibition rules can be easily implemented for execution in a distributed way.

It should be pointed out that turn prohibition algorithms are, in fact, pre-routing procedures; they do no prescribe any specific routing policy, but just restrict the set of turns permitted for use in routing tables. Therefore, they are compatible with any routing algorithm, in particular, with the fully adaptive minimal routing (of course, paths that include prohibited turns are excluded from consideration during the construction of the routing tables).

A few particular regular topologies have been considered in several papers (Glass & Ni, 1994; Horst, 1996; Decayeux & Seme, 2005; Nocetti, Stojmenovic, & Zhang, 2002; Parhami & Kwai, 2001; Stojmenovic, 1997; Dolter, Ramanathan, & Shin, 1991), (Dally & Seitz, 1986). This chapter presents methods applicable to a number of classes of popular regular graphs, such as homogeneous

meshes, p-ary n-cubes, cube connected cycles, hexagonal and honeycomb meshes and tori and Hamiltonian graphs.

The dimension-ordered routing (DOR) (Min et al., 2004) has been popular for meshes. However, as shown in Section 3, the use of DOR algorithm results in prohibition of much larger fraction of turns in the network than the approach developed in the present chapter. For multi-dimensional meshes, the fraction of turns prohibited by DOR tends to 1/2. Methods developed in this chapter guarantee that the fraction of prohibited turns never exceeds 1/4.

Section 2 introduces and studies embedded graphs and homogeneous meshes. A number of well known regular topologies are analyzed in Section 3. Section 4 discusses the dilation of the average distances as a result of turn prohibitions. Conclusions are presented in Section 5.

Certain notations, definitions, lower bounds, and other basic graph theoretic concepts used in this chapter are presented in Section 2 of the previous chapter

2. EMBEDDED GRAPHS AND HOMOGENEOUS MESHES

Consider a graph $G = (V, E)$ which is embedded in the n-dimensional real space $\mathbb{R}^n$, so that each node $\mathbf{x}$ is a point in $\mathbb{R}^n$.

Definition 1: *An embedded graph G is a homogeneous mesh, if each node $\mathbf{x}$ has a degree $d = 2t$, and if $\mathbf{x} \in V$, then its neighbors are nodes $\mathbf{x} \pm \mathbf{a}_i, i = 1, 2, \ldots, t,$ where $\mathbf{a}_i$ are vectors in $\mathbb{R}^n$ and elements of a set $D = \{\pm\mathbf{a}_i, i = 1, \ldots, t\}$.*

Several important topologies, such as multi-dimensional meshes and tori, can be embedded into n-dimensional real spaces and can be considered as homogeneous meshes.

We call $\mathbf{a} \in D$ positive, $\mathbf{a} > 0$, if the first non-zero component of $\mathbf{a}$ is positive, otherwise $\mathbf{a}$ is negative, $\mathbf{a} < 0$. For example, in a two dimensional space, $(0,1) > 0$, and $(-1,1) < 0$.

Consider the following turn prohibition rule for homogeneous meshes. Turn $(\mathbf{x}_1, \mathbf{x}_2, \mathbf{x}_3) = (\mathbf{x}_2 - \mathbf{x}_1, \mathbf{x}_3 - \mathbf{x}_2)$ is prohibited *iff* $\mathbf{x}_2 - \mathbf{x}_1 < 0$ and $\mathbf{x}_3 - \mathbf{x}_2 < 0$. Let $W(M_D)$ be a set of prohibited turns for a homogeneous mesh M_D.

Theorem 1: *As described, the turn prohibition rule has the following properties.*

1. For any mesh M_D and any $\mathbf{x}, \mathbf{y} \in V$ there exists a path from $\mathbf{x}$ to $\mathbf{y}$ not containing any turns from $W(M_D)$.

2. For any cycle in M_D there exists a turn which belongs to the cycle and also belongs to $(W(M_D))$, the set of prohibited turns.

3. The set of prohibited turns is minimum

4. The minimum fraction of prohibited turns for a homogeneous mesh M_D with size of D equal to d is

$$z(G) = \frac{1}{4}\left(1 - \frac{1}{d-1}\right). \qquad (4)$$

Proof:

1. Consider a path $P = (\mathbf{x}_0, \mathbf{x}_1, \ldots, \mathbf{x}_k)$ from node $\mathbf{x}_0$ to $\mathbf{x}_k$, where $\mathbf{x}_{i+1} = \mathbf{x}_i + \mathbf{b}_i$; $i = 0, \ldots, k-1$, $\mathbf{b}_i \in D$. The corresponding sequence of edges is $S = (\mathbf{x}_0, \mathbf{x}_1, \ldots, \mathbf{b}_{k-1})$. Note that path P is prohibited *iff* there exists a pair of consecutive edges $(\mathbf{b}_{i-1}, \mathbf{b}_i)$ in S such that $\mathbf{b}_{i-1} > 0$ and $\mathbf{b}_i < 0$. It follows from Definition 1 that if S forms a path from $\mathbf{x}_0$ to $\mathbf{x}_k$, then any permutation of $\mathbf{b}_0, \mathbf{b}_1, \ldots, \mathbf{b}_{k-1}$ also corresponds to a path from $\mathbf{x}_0$ to $\mathbf{x}_k$, since the mesh is homogeneous and $\mathbf{x}_k = \mathbf{x}_0 + \sum_{i=0}^{k-1} \mathbf{b}_i$. Then there exists a permutation $S' = (\mathbf{b}'_0, \mathbf{b}'_1, \ldots, \mathbf{b}'_{k-1})$ of S in which all negative vectors (if any) precede all positive ones (if any). The corresponding path

$$P' = (\mathbf{x}_0, \mathbf{x}'_1 = \mathbf{x}_0 + \mathbf{b}'_0, \ldots, \mathbf{x}_k = \mathbf{x}'_{k-1} + \mathbf{b}'_{k-1})$$

has no prohibited turns and thus, nodes $\mathbf{x}_0$ and $\mathbf{x}_k$ are connected.

2. Consider a cycle $C = (\mathbf{x}_0, \mathbf{x}_1, \ldots, \mathbf{x}_k, \mathbf{x}_0, \mathbf{x}_1)$ and the corresponding cycle of edges $S = (\mathbf{b}_0, \mathbf{b}_1, \ldots, \mathbf{b}_k, \mathbf{b}_0)$, where $\mathbf{b}_i = \mathbf{x}_{i+1} - \mathbf{x}_i$, $i = 0, 1, \ldots, k-1$; $\mathbf{b}_k = \mathbf{x}_0 - \mathbf{x}_k$. Note that $\sum_{i=0}^{k} \mathbf{b}_i = 0$. Therefore, among vectors $\mathbf{b}_0, \mathbf{b}_1, \ldots, \mathbf{b}_k$ must be both positive and negative ones. Since sequence S starts and ends with the same vector (either positive or negative), it must include at least one pair $\mathbf{b}_{i-1}, \mathbf{b}_i$, where $\mathbf{b}_{i-1}$ is positive and $\mathbf{b}_i$ is negative. Thus, the corresponding cycle is prohibited.

3. Let us consider cycles of length four, $C = (\mathbf{x}_0, \mathbf{x}_1, \mathbf{x}_2, \mathbf{x}_3, \mathbf{x}_0, \mathbf{x}_1)$, where $\mathbf{x}_1 = \mathbf{x}_0 + \mathbf{b}_0$, $\mathbf{x}_2 = \mathbf{x}_1 + \mathbf{b}_1$, $\mathbf{x}_3 = \mathbf{x}_2 - \mathbf{b}_0 = \mathbf{x}_3 + \mathbf{b}_1$. All sets of turns corresponding to different choices of nodes $\mathbf{x}_0, \mathbf{x}_1, \mathbf{x}_2$ are disjoint. Hence, in order to break all cycles, it is necessary to prohibit at least one turn in each of such cycles. Indeed, according to our prohibition rule, in the sequence of edges $(\mathbf{b}_0, \mathbf{b}_1, -\mathbf{b}_0, -\mathbf{b}_1, \mathbf{b}_0)$ exactly one turn is prohibited (e.g., if $\mathbf{b}_0, \mathbf{b}_1 > 0$, then turn $(\mathbf{b}_1, \mathbf{b}_0)$ is prohibited). Thus, the set of prohibited turns is the smallest possible.

4. Obviously, in the set $D = \{\pm \mathbf{a}_i, i = 1, \ldots, t\}$ exactly $t = \frac{d}{2}$ vectors are positive, and the other half are negative. Therefore

$$z(G) = \frac{\binom{d/2}{2}}{\binom{d}{2}} = \frac{1}{4}\left(1 - \frac{1}{d-1}\right).$$

Remarkably, result 4 does not depend on the choice of the coordinate system and on the particular topology of the mesh. For example, Figure 1 shows two different topologies which have the same node degree d and, thus, the same $z(G)$.

It is interesting to compare (4) with the fraction of prohibited turns when one uses the popular DOR algorithm [28]. For the case of an n-dimensional mesh the fraction of prohibited turns given by (4) is $\frac{n-1}{2(2n-1)}$. The DOR algorithm prohibits a portion of the turns equal to $\frac{n-1}{2n-1}$, i.e., twice as large as our approach.

A more general situation can be described as follows. Consider an embedded graph $G = (V, E)$ that consists of m different types of nodes, $V = \bigcup_{k=1}^{m} V_k$ such that all nodes of type k have the same degree d_k, and if $\mathbf{x} \in V_k$, then its neighbors are $\mathbf{x} + \mathbf{a}_{ki}$, $i = 1, 2, \ldots, d_k$. Let $d_k = d_k^{(+)} + d_k^{(-)}$, where $d_k^{(+)}$ and $d_k^{(-)}$ are the numbers of positive and negative vectors, respectively, in the set $A_k = \{\mathbf{a}_{ki}\}$. We call such embedded graphs *multicomponent meshes*.

Suppose we prohibit all turns $(\mathbf{x}_1, \mathbf{x}_2, \mathbf{x}_3)$, such that $\mathbf{x}_1 - \mathbf{x}_2 < 0$ and $\mathbf{x}_3 - \mathbf{x}_2 < 0$, or, alternatively, such that $\mathbf{x}_1 - \mathbf{x}_2 > 0$ and $\mathbf{x}_3 - \mathbf{x}_2 > 0$. Let us call such turns "negative" or, respectively, "positive". Assuming that the connectivity is preserved and following the same reasoning, as in the proof of Theorem 1, we obtain Corollary 1.

Corollary 1: *Prohibition of all negative or of all positive turns in graph G described above breaks all the cycles in G. The fraction of prohibited turns $z(G)$ obeys an upper bound*

$$z(G) \leq \frac{\min\left\{\sum_{k=1}^{m} \rho_k \binom{d_k^{(-)}}{2}, \sum_{k=1}^{m} \rho_k \binom{d_k^{(+)}}{2}\right\}}{\sum_{k=1}^{m} \rho_k \binom{d_k}{2}}, \quad (5)$$

where ρ_k is the density of nodes of type k.

Here, as usual (Honkala, Karpovsky, & Levitin, 2006) the density ρ_k of a subset V_k of nodes in an infinite embedded graph $G(V, E)$ is defined as follows. Consider a ball $B(R)$ of radius R in $\mathbb{R}^n$. Then

$$\rho_k = \limsup_{R \to \infty} \frac{|V_k \bigcap B(R)|}{|V \bigcap B(R)|}.$$

Figure 1. Different topologies with the same degree $d = 6$ have the same fraction $z(G)$

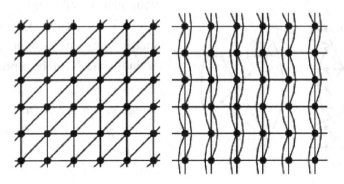

Note that if $\mathbf{y} = \mathbf{x} + \mathbf{a}$, where $\mathbf{a} > 0$, then $\mathbf{x} = \mathbf{y} + \mathbf{b}$, where $\mathbf{b} = -\mathbf{a} < 0$. Therefore, $\sum_{k=1}^{m} \rho_k d_k^{(-)}$. However, for some structures prohibition of positive vs. negative turns can give rather different results, as shown by Example 1.

Example 1: The embedded graph in Figure 2 has three different types of nodes with degrees 2, 3, and 5, each with a density of $\rho = 1/3$. As shown in the enlarged view, all positive turns prohibited at the node of degree 5, and all negative turns prohibited at nodes of degree 2 and degree 3. Prohibition of negative and positive turns yields different fractions of prohibited turns equal to 3/7 and 1/7, respectively.

Example 2: The embedded graph called the "*Brick Mesh*" is shown in Figure 3. There are five types of nodes in this mesh; type 1 nodes are of degree 4, and type 2, type 3, type 4, and type 5 nodes are of degree 3, as shown in the insert. Considering the building block of this mesh, shown as the darker rectangular region in the figure, one determines that the density of each of the degree 3 node types is 1/6 and the density of the degree 4

Figure 2. A multicomponent mesh with three different types of nodes of degrees 2, 3, and 5. In the enlarged view we show all positive turns prohibited at the node of degree 5, and all negative turns prohibited at nodes of degree 2 and degree 3.

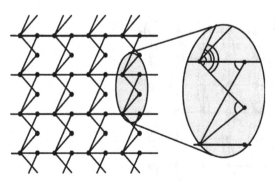

node type is 1/3. If we consider the prohibition of the negative turns as shown in the enlarged view in Figure 3, we determine that the fraction of prohibited turns is $z \leq 1/6$.

Another interesting topology is the honeycomb mesh (see Section 3, Figure 7 (B)).

In general, the bounds in (5) depend on the choice of the coordinate system, in particular, on the order of the coordinates.

Note also that the prohibition rule given above for a multicomponent mesh does not guarantee, in general, the preservation of connectivity. However, it can be shown that for a two-component mesh $(m = 2)$ connectivity is always preserved, provided that $d_k^{(+)} > 0$ and $d_k^{(-)} > 0$ for $k = 1, 2$. For example, for the honeycomb mesh (Figure 7 (B)), $m = 2$, $d_1^{(+)} = 2$, $d_1^{(-)} = 1$, $d_2^{(+)} = 1$, $d_2^{(-)} = 2$, $\rho_1 = \rho_2 = 1/2$ and $z(G) = 1/6$ (see Section 3).

Homogeneous meshes considered so far in this section are of infinite extent with infinite number of nodes. Now finite D-Meshes $M_D(p_1, \ldots, p_n)$ and finite wraparound D-meshes $M_D^W(p_1, \ldots, p_n)$ will be defined.

Let $D = \{\pm \mathbf{a}_1, \pm \mathbf{a}_2, \ldots, \pm \mathbf{a}_t\}$, $\mathbf{a}_i \in \mathbb{R}^n$, $i = 1, 2, \ldots, t$ and $d = 2t$ be the degree of every node. Then $n \leq t$, (otherwise the mesh is embedded in a space of a smaller dimensionality), and there are n linearly independent vectors in D. Henceforth we will assume that there exists a basis $B = \{\mathbf{a}_1, \ldots, \mathbf{a}_n\}$, $B \subseteq D$ such that any point in the mesh can be represented as a linear combination of vectors from B with integer coefficients. Denote $\mathbf{C} = \mathbf{A}^{-1}$ where $\mathbf{A}$ is the matrix with columns $\mathbf{a}_1, \mathbf{a}_2, \ldots, \mathbf{a}_n$. Then any node $\mathbf{x}$ in the mesh can be represented in basis B as $\tilde{\mathbf{x}} = \mathbf{C}\mathbf{x} = (\tilde{x}^{(1)}, \tilde{x}^{(2)}, \ldots, \tilde{x}^{(n)})$, where all $\tilde{x}^{(i)}$ are integers, $i = 1, 2, \ldots, n$.

Let $p_1, p_2, \ldots, p_n$ be positive integers, $p_i \geq 2$, $i = 1, 2, \ldots, n$.

Figure 3. Multicomponent "Brick Mesh" in which degree 3 and degree 4 nodes have densities of 1/6 and of 1/3 respectively. Five different node types are identified in the enlarged view by the numbers adjacent to the nodes.

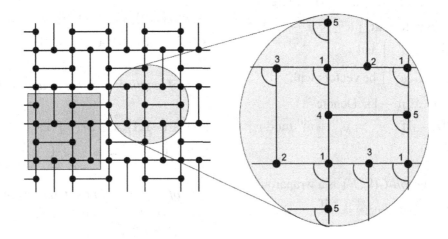

Definition 2: *A graph $G(V, E)$ is a finite D-mesh $M_D(p_1, p_2, \ldots, p_n)$ if*

$$V = \{ \mathbf{x} \mid \tilde{x}^{(i)} \in \{0, 1, \ldots, p_i - 1\}, i = 1, \ldots, n \}.$$

Then $(\mathbf{x}, \mathbf{y}) \in E$ if $\mathbf{C}(\mathbf{x} - \mathbf{y}) \in D_C$ or $\mathbf{C}(\mathbf{y} - \mathbf{x}) \in D_C$, where

$$D_C = \{ \pm \mathbf{Ca}_i \mid i = 1, \ldots, t \}$$
$$= \{ \pm(1, 0, 0, \ldots, 0), \pm(0, 1, 0, \ldots, 0), \ldots,$$
$$\pm(0, 0, 0, \ldots, 1) \pm \mathbf{Ca}_{n+1}, \ldots, \pm \mathbf{Ca}_t \}$$

Example 3: *Let $n = 2$ and*

$$D = \{ \pm \mathbf{a}_1, \pm \mathbf{a}_2, \pm \mathbf{a}_3 \}$$
$$= \left\{ \pm \left(\tfrac{1}{2}, \tfrac{\sqrt{3}}{2} \right), \pm \left(-\tfrac{1}{2}, \tfrac{\sqrt{3}}{2} \right), \pm (1, 0) \right\}.$$

Note that $\mathbf{a}_3 = \mathbf{a}_1 - \mathbf{a}_2$, and

$$\mathbf{A} = \begin{bmatrix} \tfrac{1}{2} & -\tfrac{1}{2} \\ \tfrac{\sqrt{3}}{2} & \tfrac{\sqrt{3}}{2} \end{bmatrix}, \quad \mathbf{C} = \begin{bmatrix} 1 & \tfrac{\sqrt{3}}{3} \\ -1 & \tfrac{\sqrt{3}}{3} \end{bmatrix},$$

and $D_C = \{ \pm(1, 0), \pm(0, 1), \pm(1, -1) \}$. The finite mesh $M_D(4, 3)$ is shown in Figure 4.

Next finite wraparound meshes $M_D^W(p_1, p_2, \ldots, p_n)$ are defined. Let p_i be positive integers larger than 2. We will also assume that for the set $D = \{ \pm \mathbf{a}_1, \pm \mathbf{a}_2, \ldots, \pm \mathbf{a}_t \}$,

Figure 4. Finite D-Mesh $M_D(4, 3)$ with $D = \left\{ \pm \left(\tfrac{1}{2}, \tfrac{\sqrt{3}}{2} \right), \pm \left(-\tfrac{1}{2}, \tfrac{\sqrt{3}}{2} \right), \pm (1, 0) \right\}$ and $D_C = \{ \pm(1, 0), \pm(0, 1), \pm(1, -1) \}$

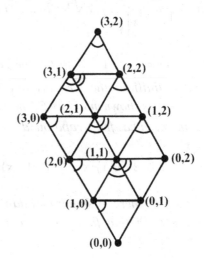

$(\mathbf{a}_i \in \mathbb{R}^n, n \leq t)$, vectors $\mathbf{a}_1, \mathbf{a}_2, \ldots, \mathbf{a}_n\}$ are linearly independent and each

$\mathbf{a}_{n+j} = \sum_{i=1}^n u^{(i)} \mathbf{a}_j \, (j = 1, \ldots, t - n)$, where $c^{(i)}$ are integers, such that $|u^{(i)}| \leq p_i - 1$. Let $\mathbf{U}_1 = \left(u_1^{(1)}, u_1^{(2)}, \ldots, u_1^{(n)}\right)$ and $\mathbf{U}_2 = \left(u_2^{(1)}, u_2^{(2)}, \ldots, u_2^{(n)}\right)$ be vectors with $u_1^{(i)}, u_2^{(i)} \in \{0, 1, \ldots, p_i - 1\}$. Denote $\mathbf{U}_3 = \mathbf{U}_1 \oplus \mathbf{U}_2$, if $u_3^{(i)} = u_1^{(i)} + u_2^{(i)} \bmod p_i$, $i = 1, 2, \ldots, n$.

Definition 3: *A graph* $G(V, E)$ *is a wraparound D-Mesh* $M_D^W(p_1, p_2, \ldots, p_n)$ *if*

$$V = \{\mathbf{x} \mid \tilde{x}^{(i)} \in \{0, 1, \ldots, p_i - 1\}, i = 1, 2, \ldots, n\}$$

and the edge $(\mathbf{x}, \mathbf{y}) \in E$ *if there exists a vector* $\mathbf{h}$ *such that* $\tilde{\mathbf{x}} \oplus \tilde{\mathbf{h}} = \tilde{\mathbf{y}}$, *and* $\tilde{h} = \tilde{b}$ *for some* $b \in D$. *(Here,* $\tilde{\mathbf{x}} = \mathbf{C}\mathbf{x}$, $\tilde{\mathbf{h}} = \mathbf{C}\mathbf{h}$, $\tilde{\mathbf{y}} = \mathbf{C}\mathbf{y}$, *and* $\tilde{\mathbf{b}} = \mathbf{C}\mathbf{b}$.)

Example 4: *Let* $n = 2$ *and*

$$D = \{\pm\mathbf{a}_1, \pm\mathbf{a}_2, \pm\mathbf{a}_3\}$$
$$= \left\{\pm\left(\frac{1}{2}, \frac{\sqrt{3}}{2}\right), \pm\left(-\frac{1}{2}, \frac{\sqrt{3}}{2}\right), \pm(1, 0)\right\}.$$

As in Example 3, select $\mathbf{a}_1 = (1/2, \sqrt{3}/2)$ *and* $\mathbf{a}_2 = (-1/2, \sqrt{3}/2)$. *Then* $\mathbf{C} = \begin{bmatrix} 1 & \frac{\sqrt{3}}{3} \\ -1 & \frac{\sqrt{3}}{3} \end{bmatrix}$, $\mathbf{a}_3 = \mathbf{a}_1 - \mathbf{a}_2$, *and* $\mathbf{C}\mathbf{a}_3 = \tilde{\mathbf{a}}_3 = (1, -1)$. *With this neighborhood definition, the wraparound mesh* $M_D^W(5, 4)$ *is shown in Figure 5. This wraparound mesh has five wraparound cycles*

$$\left(\tilde{\mathbf{x}}, \tilde{\mathbf{x}} \oplus (0, 1), \tilde{\mathbf{x}} \oplus 2 \cdot (0, 1), \tilde{\mathbf{x}} \oplus 3 \cdot (0, 1), \tilde{\mathbf{x}}\right)$$

of length 4, where $\oplus$ *stands for addition of vectors such that first components are*

added modulo 5 and the second components are added modulo 4, four wraparound cycles

$$\left(\tilde{\mathbf{x}}, \tilde{\mathbf{x}} \oplus (1, 0), \tilde{\mathbf{x}} \oplus 2 \cdot (1, 0), \right.$$
$$\left. \tilde{\mathbf{x}} \oplus 3 \cdot (1, 0), \tilde{\mathbf{x}} \oplus 4 \cdot (1, 0), \tilde{\mathbf{x}}\right)$$

of length 5, and one wraparound cycle

$$\left(\tilde{\mathbf{x}}, \tilde{\mathbf{x}} \oplus (-1, 1), \tilde{\mathbf{x}} \oplus 2 \cdot (-1, 1), \right.$$
$$\left. \tilde{\mathbf{x}} \oplus 3 \cdot (-1, 1), \ldots, \tilde{\mathbf{x}} \oplus 19 \cdot (-1, 1), \tilde{\mathbf{x}}\right)$$

of length 20. In the figure a path from node $\mathbf{x} = (3, 1)$ *to node* $\tilde{\mathbf{y}} = (1, 2)$, $P = ((3, 1), (2, 1), (1, 1), (1, 2))$ *is shown using thick lines. Note that all turns along this path are permitted.*

To construct sets of prohibited turns for $M_D(p_1, P_2, \ldots, p_n)$ or $M_D^W(p_{1'2}, \ldots, p_n)$ we will

Figure 5. Wraparound D-Mesh $M_D^W(5, 4)$ *with* $D = \left\{\pm\left(-1/2, \sqrt{3}/2\right), \pm(1, 0)\right\}$, $D_C = \{\pm(1, 0), \pm(0, 1), \pm(1, -1)\}$ *and a permitted path from node (3,1) to (1,2)*

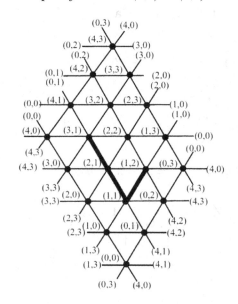

introduce a total ordering of nodes in these meshes.

Definition 4: *If* $\tilde{\mathbf{x}}, \tilde{\mathbf{y}} \in V$ *where* V *is the set of nodes in* $M_D(p_1, p_2, \ldots, p_n)$ *or* $M_{D_{(i)}}^W(p_1, p_2, \ldots, p_n)$, *we will say that* $\tilde{\mathbf{x}} > \tilde{\mathbf{y}}$ *if* $\tilde{\mathbf{x}}^{(i)} > \tilde{\mathbf{y}}^{(i)}$ *where* i *is the smallest integer such that* $\tilde{\mathbf{x}}^{(i)} \neq \tilde{\mathbf{y}}^{(i)}$ ($\tilde{\mathbf{x}} = \mathbf{Cx}, \tilde{\mathbf{y}} = \mathbf{Cy}$).

Theorem 2: *For a finite mesh* $M_D(p_1, p_2, \ldots, p_n)$ *or a wraparound mesh* $M_D^W(p_1, \ldots, p_n)$, *let the set of prohibited turns*

$$F = \{(\tilde{\mathbf{x}}, \tilde{\mathbf{y}}, \tilde{\mathbf{z}}) \mid \tilde{\mathbf{x}}, \tilde{\mathbf{y}}, \tilde{\mathbf{z}} \in V \text{ and } \tilde{\mathbf{y}} > \tilde{\mathbf{x}}, \tilde{\mathbf{y}} > \tilde{\mathbf{z}}\}.$$

Then

1. *For any* $\tilde{\mathbf{x}}, \tilde{\mathbf{y}} \in V$ *there exists a path from* $\mathbf{x}$ *to* $\mathbf{y}$ *containing no turns from* F.
2. *For any cycle there exists a turn in the cycle that belongs to* F.
3. *The set* F *is asymptotically optimal if* $p_i \to \infty$ ($i = 1, \ldots, n$), *and the minimum fraction* z *of prohibited turns for* $M_D(p_1, p_2, \ldots, p_n)$ *or a* $M_D^W(p_1, p_2, \ldots, p_n)$ *with* $\mid D \mid = d$ *is, asymptotically,*

$$\lim_{\substack{p_i \to \infty \\ i=1,\ldots,n}} z = \frac{1}{4}\left(1 - \frac{1}{d-1}\right).$$

Proof:

1. First we will prove that if $\tilde{\mathbf{x}} = \mathbf{Cx} = (\tilde{\mathbf{x}}^{(1)}, \tilde{\mathbf{x}}^{(2)}, \ldots, \tilde{\mathbf{x}}^{(n)})$ and $\tilde{\mathbf{y}} = \mathbf{Cy} = (\tilde{\mathbf{y}}^{(1)}, \tilde{\mathbf{y}}^{(2)}, \ldots, \tilde{\mathbf{y}}^{(n)})$, there exists a path from $\tilde{\mathbf{x}}$ to $\tilde{\mathbf{y}}$ in $M_D(p_1, p_2, \ldots, p_n)$ or in $M_D^W(p_1, p_2, \ldots, p_n)$ containing no turns from F. Let $S_+(\tilde{\mathbf{x}}, \tilde{\mathbf{y}}) = \{i \mid \tilde{\mathbf{x}} \geq \tilde{\mathbf{y}}\}$ and $S_-(\tilde{\mathbf{x}}, \tilde{\mathbf{y}}) = \{i \mid \tilde{\mathbf{x}} < \tilde{\mathbf{y}}\}$. Consider now a node

$\tilde{\mathbf{z}}$ such that $\tilde{\mathbf{z}}^{(i)} = \min(\tilde{\mathbf{x}}^{(i)}, \tilde{\mathbf{y}}^{(i)})$. Obviously, there exists a path from $\tilde{\mathbf{x}}$ to $\tilde{\mathbf{z}}$, such that any next node in the path is smaller than the previous one. Similarly, there exists a path from $\tilde{\mathbf{z}}$ to $\tilde{\mathbf{y}}$ such that any next node is larger than the previous one. Now take the concatenation of these two paths. The turn at node $\tilde{\mathbf{z}}$ is permitted, since $\tilde{\mathbf{z}}$ is smaller than the two neighboring nodes in the path. Thus, there exists a permitted path from $\tilde{\mathbf{x}}$ to $\tilde{\mathbf{y}}$.

2. In every cycle $(\tilde{\mathbf{x}}_1, \tilde{\mathbf{x}}_2, \ldots, \tilde{\mathbf{x}}_{(\ell-1)}, \tilde{\mathbf{x}}_\ell)$ where $\tilde{\mathbf{x}}_{(\ell-1)} = \tilde{\mathbf{x}}_1$ and $\tilde{\mathbf{x}}_\ell = \tilde{\mathbf{x}}_2$ there exists $i \in \{1, 2, \ldots, \ell\}$ such that $\tilde{\mathbf{x}}_i > \tilde{\mathbf{x}}_{(i-1)}$, $\tilde{\mathbf{x}}_i > \tilde{\mathbf{x}}_{(i+1)}$, and turn $(\tilde{\mathbf{x}}_{(i-1)}, \tilde{\mathbf{x}}_i, \tilde{\mathbf{x}}_{(i+1)}) \in F$.

3. We will say that the node $\mathbf{x} \in V$ is internal in $M_D(p_1, p_2, \ldots, p_n)$ or in $M_D^W(p_1, p_2, \ldots, p_n)$ if $0 < \tilde{\mathbf{x}}^{(i)} < p_i - 1$ for all $i = 1, \ldots, n$. If $\mathbf{x}$ is an internal node, then in each pair of its neighbors, $\mathbf{x} \pm \mathbf{a}_i$ ($i = 1, \ldots, t$) one neighbor is larger than $\mathbf{x}$ and the other is smaller than $\mathbf{x}$. Thus for any internal node $\mathbf{x}$ exactly t neighbors are larger than $\mathbf{x}$, and exactly t neighbors are smaller than $\mathbf{x}$. Hence, for every internal node $\mathbf{x}$ there are $\binom{t}{2}$ turns $(\mathbf{y}, \mathbf{x}, \mathbf{z})$ which belong to F. Thus,

$$\lim_{\substack{p_i \to \infty \\ i=1,\ldots,n}} z \leq \frac{\binom{t}{2}}{\binom{2t}{2}} = \frac{1}{4}\left(1 - \frac{1}{d-1}\right).$$

On the other hand, similar to the proof of Theorem 1, for any internal node $\mathbf{x}$ there are $\binom{t}{2}$ cycles in $M_D(p_1, p_2, \ldots, p_n)$ or in $M_D^W(p_1, p_2, \ldots, p_n)$ which contain 4 nodes each that do not have common turns. In the union of these sets for all internal nodes any two cycles do not have common turns. Since ate most $\left\lceil \frac{d}{2} \right\rceil$ turns are prohibited at any non-internal node, the contribution of the non-internal nodes to Z does not exceed their fraction among all nodes, and, therefore, is infinitesimal when $p_i \rightarrow \infty$ $(i = 1, \ldots, n)$. Thus, it follows that

$$\lim_{\substack{p_i \rightarrow \infty \\ i = 1, \ldots, n}} z \geq \frac{1}{4}\left(1 - \frac{1}{d-1}\right).$$

The set $F = W(M_D(4,3))$ of prohibited turns for the $M_D(4,3)$ with

$$D = \{\pm\left(1/2, \sqrt{3}/2\right), \pm\left(-1/2, \sqrt{3}/2\right), \pm\left(1,0\right)\}$$

is shown in Figure 4.

3. SPECIAL TOPOLOGIES

3.1 Finite Meshes and Tori

Meshes and tori have been the most widely used communication network topologies for multiprocessors (Ni & McKinley, 1993; Parhami, 1998). Most recently, "TOFU", a 6-dimensional mesh and torus topologies have been used to provide the extremely high performance and fault tolerant interconnection network, achieving 10 petaflops (Ajima, Sumimoto, & Shimizu, 2009). In this section, square meshes are considered first, with each inner node connected with *2n* nodes, where *n* is the dimension of a mesh. Meshes of this type were investigated in (Glass & Ni, 1994), where only 90-degree turns were taken into account. It was shown, that 1/4 of all such turns has to be prohibited. With the more general turn model, our results are in agreement with authors' conclusion in (Glass & Ni, 1994).

Theorem 3: *For n-dimensional p-ary mesh,* M_p^n

$$z(M_p^n) = \frac{(n-1)(p-1)^2}{2p(p-2) + 4(n-1)(p-1)^2},$$

(6)

and for n-dimensional p-ary tori, Z_p^n, *with* $p > 2$,

$$z(Z_p^n) = \frac{p(n-1) + 2}{2p(2n-1)}.$$

(7)

Proof: To prove the lower bound for meshes we consider the system of all cycles of length 4. There are $R = \binom{n}{2}(p-1)^2 p^{n-2}$ turn disjoint cycles of this type and the total number of turns in M_p^n is equal to

$$T(M_p^n) = n(p-2)p^{n-1} + 4\binom{n}{2}(p-1)^2 p^{n-2}.$$

(8)

The lower bound for $Z(M_p^n)$ follows now by observing that at least as many turns must be prohibited as there are turn disjoint cycles.

The lower bound for tori can be proven in a similar way by considering cycles of length 4 and $np^n - 1$ one-dimensional cycles, containing nodes with fixed $n - 1$ coordinates.

To prove the upper bound of Theorem 3 for p-ary meshes, we prohibit all turns $(\mathbf{a}, \mathbf{b}, \mathbf{c})$, where $l(\mathbf{a}) < l(\mathbf{b})$, $l(\mathbf{b}) > l(\mathbf{c})$ and $l(\mathbf{a}), l(\mathbf{b}), l(\mathbf{c})$ are distances in terms of number of hops from node $(0, 0, \ldots, 0)$ to $\mathbf{a}, \mathbf{b}$ and $\mathbf{c}$. The number of prohibited turns is equal to

$$Z(M_p^n) = \binom{n}{2}(p-1)^2 p^{n-2}.$$

(9)

Then (6) follows from (8) and (9).

For p-ary tori, each node $\mathbf{a} = (a_1, a_2, \ldots, a_n)$ is labeled by $l(\mathbf{a}) = a_1 + a_2 + \ldots, a_n \bmod p$ and the turn $(\mathbf{a}, \mathbf{b}, \mathbf{c})$ is prohibited if $l(\mathbf{a}) = l(\mathbf{c}) = l(\mathbf{b}) - 1 \bmod p$.

The total number of turns in Z_p^n is equal to $T(Z_p^n) = \binom{2n}{2} p^n$, and the number of prohibited turns is equal to $Z(Z_p^n) = \binom{n}{2} p^n + np^n - 1$.

3.2 Hexagonal and Honeycomb Meshes

Next, we consider hexagonal meshes (Parhami, 1998; Decayeux & Seme, 2005; Nocetti et al., 2002) in which each node has up to 6 neighbors and honeycomb meshes (Parhami, 1998; Parhami & Kwai, 2001; Stojmenovic, 1997) where each node has up to 3 neighbors, and their corresponding tori. In a hexagonal mesh of size p denoted by HeM_p, peripheral edges form a regular hexagon where each side has p nodes. A honeycomb mesh of size p, denoted by HoM_p, where each side of the mesh has p hexagonal cells whose centers also form a regular hexagon. The hex-

agonal and honeycomb tori are degree six and degree three regular topologies, respectively.

In a hexagonal mesh HeM_p, there are $N = 3p^2 - 3p + 1$ nodes with labels $0, 1, \ldots, (N-1)$ with the center node having the label 0 (Dolter et al., 1991). Adjacent nodes of any given node a are identified to have labels $a \pm 1$, $a \pm (3p - 1)$, $a \pm (3p - 2)$ where arithmetic operations are $\bmod N$. In the corresponding torus, wrap-around edges are also identified using the same adjacency rules. Labels of adjacent nodes are shown in Figure 6 (A) for the case of a size $p = 3$ torus.

In a honeycomb torus, nodes that are connected by the wrap-around edges are those nodes that are mirror symmetric with respect to the three lines passing through the center and normal to each of three edge orientations (Stojmenovic, 1997). These axes are shown as dashed lines in Figure 6(B).

Theorem 4: *For a hexagonal mesh of size p, HeM_p, with $N - 3p^2 - 3p + 1$ nodes,*

$$z(HeM_p) = \frac{9p^2 - 21p + 13}{45p^2 - 99p + 51}, \qquad (10)$$

Figure 6. Examples hexagonal torus HeT_3 in (A), and honeycomb torus HoT_3 in (B) for $p = 3$, where wraparound links are identified

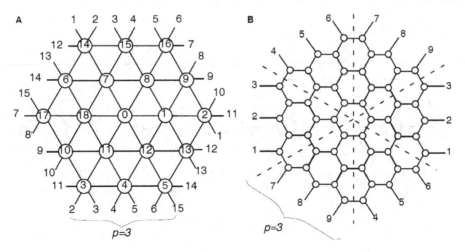

and for a hexagonal tori of size p,

$$z(HeT_p) = \frac{9p^2 - 15p + 10}{45p^2 - 45p + 15}.$$ (11)

Proof: First, note that total number of turns in a HeM_p is equal to:

$$T(HeM_p) = 15(3p^2 - 9p + 7) + 6(6p - 12)$$
$$+ 18 = 45p^2 - 99p + 51$$.

To prove the lower bound, we consider the set of all turn disjoint $6(p-1)$ triangles, and $3p^2 - 9p + 7$ hexagons and observe that we must prohibit at least as many turns as there are turn disjoint cycles, e.g., triangles and hexagons.

Upper bound on $Z(HeM_p)$ can be obtained as shown in Figure 7 (A).

For the case of hexagonal tori with $N(HeT_p) = 3p^2 - 3p + 1$ nodes, $M(HeT_p) = 3N(HeT_p)$ edges, and $T(HeT_p) = 15N(HeT_p)$ turns, additional $6(2p-1)$ turns have to be prohibited to prevent all wrap-around cycles. Therefore, $6(2p-1)$

cycles must be added to the system of turn-disjoint cycles due to triangles and hexagons. Again, observe that we must prohibit at least as many turns as there are turn disjoint cycles. To prove the upper bound, we cut the wrap-around cycles in the hexagonal torus and prohibit all $6(2p-1)$ turns at the nodes on the border of the resulting mesh.

3.3 Locally Complete Tree-Like Topologies

Locally complete tree-like topologies are hybrid topologies incorporating the properties and attributes of its components (Parhami, 1998). Consider a tree $T' = G'(V', E')$ with $M' = |E'|$ undirected edges $\{v_i, v_j\} \in E'$ and $N' = |V'|$ nodes v_i, $i = 0, \ldots, N' - 1$. Assume that each node of the tree is now replaced with a complete graph K_n with $n \geq d_i$ nodes where d_i is the degree of node v_i of the original tree T', to obtain the augmented graph $G(V, E)$ which is locally complete. The locally complete graph has $N = |V| = N'n$ nodes and $|E| = N' - 1 + N'\binom{n}{2}$ edges. Let us denote the nodes of K_n that replaces node v_i of the original tree by

Figure 7. Prohibited turns for Hexagonal (A) and Honeycomb (B) meshes

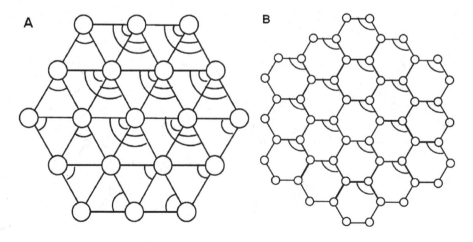

Figure 8. Embedding a complete graph K_4 at tree nodes $v_i = 4$ and $v_i = 5$. Port numbers at nodes $v_i = 4$, $v_i = 5$, and the node numbers of the complete graph K_4 are displayed.

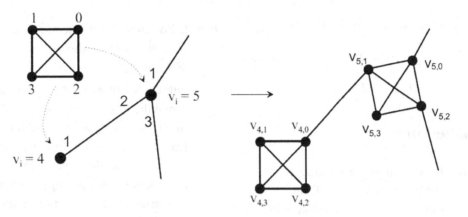

$v_{i,m}$ $(m = 0, 1, \ldots, n - 1)$. Embedding of the complete graph K_n is done in such a way that if the v_i is the parent of nodes v_j and v_k, then in the locally complete graph $v_{j,0}$ is connected to node $v_{i,r}$ and $v_{k,0}$ is connected to node $v_{i,s}$, where $r \neq s$ and $r, s \neq 0$ (Figure 8).

Theorem 5: *For a locally complete tree-like graph obtained as described above, the fraction of prohibited turns is given by*

$$z(G) = \frac{1}{3} \cdot \frac{N'n(n-2)}{N'n(n-2) + 4(N'-1)}. \tag{12}$$

Proof: Since the minimum degree nodes will always be at the leaf node positions of the original tree, the number of prohibited turns in each embedded K_n is given by $Z(K_n) = \binom{n-1}{2} + Z(K_{n-1})$. Solving this recursion equation we obtain $Z(K_n) = \frac{1}{6} n(n-1)(n-2)$. Hence, for the augmented graph G with N' nodes we have

$$Z(G) = N'Z(K_n) = \frac{1}{6} N'n(n-1)(n-2).$$

In embedding a K_n at a tree node of degree d_i, only d_i nodes of the K_n will be connected directly to the original tree. This means that embedding a K_n graph at an original tree node, will create nodes of at most degree n in the locally complete graph. Also, note that when a K_n is embedded at a tree node with degree d_i, there will be $n\binom{n-1}{2}$ turns contributed by the K_n and $(n-1)d_i$ turns contributed by the d_i edges of the original tree. With these observations the total number of turns is

$$T(G) = N'n\binom{n-1}{2} + \sum_{i=1}^{N'} (n-1)d_i$$
$$= N'n\binom{n-1}{2} + (n-1)\sum_{i=1}^{N'} d_i$$

or

$$T(G) = \frac{1}{2} N'n(n-1)(n-2) + 2(n-1)(N'-1).$$

Hence,

$$z(G) = \frac{1}{3} \frac{N'n(n-2)}{N'n(n-2) + 4(N'-1)}.$$

For example, for $n = 3$ and $N' \to \infty$,

$z(G) = \dfrac{3}{3+4} = \dfrac{1}{7}$, and for $n = 4$, and

$N' \to \infty$, $z(G) = \dfrac{1}{3} \dfrac{8}{12} = \dfrac{2}{9}.$

3.4 Fractahedrons

Fractahedrons have been used by Tandem Computers (Horst, 1996) as topology of choice. A fractahedron with ℓ levels is a tree-like graph, where each tree node is replaced by one K_4, a complete graph with four nodes. The tree is balanced with ℓ levels where all non-terminal nodes are of degree four. An example of a 2-level fractahedron is shown in Figure 9. The set of prohibited turns for this fractahedron is also shown in the figure as arcs drawn between the two edges of each prohibited turn.

Theorem 6: *For an ℓ -level fractahedron*

Figure 9. Two-level fractahedron with prohibited turns

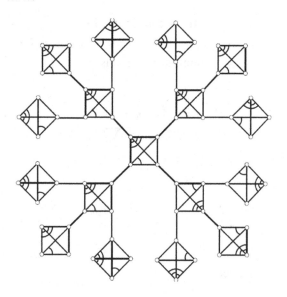

$$z(G) = \frac{2 \cdot 3^{\ell} - 1}{3(3^{\ell+1} - 2)}. \tag{13}$$

Proof: For an ℓ -level fractahedron the number of turns which should be prohibited is $Z(G) = 4B$, where $B = 2 \cdot 3^{\ell} - 1$ is the number of blocks, or K_4 sub-graphs. To prove the lower bound, we consider the set of all different triangles, and observe that at least as many turns must be prohibited as there are triangles, one in each triangle, to break all cycles. The upper bound for $Z(G)$ can be proven by induction on number ℓ of levels, since only 4 turns within each block should be prohibited.

To calculate $T(G)$, we note that all nodes except those at level ℓ are of degree four. Three nodes at each block at level ℓ are of degree three. Number of nodes at level ℓ that are of degree three is $12 \cdot 3^{\ell-1}$, and $T(G) = 12(3^{\ell+1} - 2)$.

Alternatively, since an ℓ -level fractahedron is a tree-like structure with $N' = 2 \cdot 3^{\ell} - 1$ tree nodes, each of which is replaced with $n = 4$ node complete graph K_4, substituting these values for N' and n into (11) we obtain (13) directly.

Note that at first level $\ell = 0$, we have only one K_4, and for $\ell = 3$ -level fractahedron $z(G) = 53 / 237$.

3.5 Cube Connected Cycles

We will consider now a binary n-cube connected cycles, CCC (Parhami, 1998), where each node of an n-dimensional binary cube is replaced by a cycle of n nodes of degree 3 (see Figure 10 for n = 3). These interconnection networks are popular, since they combine the properties of small node degree and small diameter of the network graph (Harary, 1998). First, we will establish upper and

Figure 10. Labeled binary 3-cube connected cycles

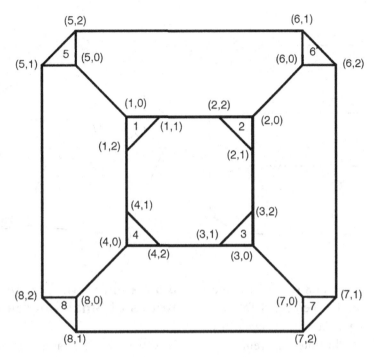

lower bounds with Theorem 7 for a slightly larger class of graphs.

Theorem 7: *If graph G is obtained from d-regular graph $H(d_i = d$ for all i, $d > 2)$ with $N(H)$ nodes by replacing each node by the cycle of d nodes, then*

$$\frac{1}{6} + \frac{2}{3dN(H)} \leq z(G) \leq \frac{1}{6} + \frac{1}{3d}. \tag{14}$$

Proof: The lower bound can be obtained from $Z(G) \geq M - N + 1$, since for G there are $M(G) = 1.5N(H)d$ edges and $T(G) = 3N(H)d$ turns.

To prove the upper bound, we label all nodes in G as (i,j), where i is the number of the cycle containing the node i in G, and j is the number of a node within each cycle of length d, $i \in \{1, \dots, N(H)\}$, $j \in \{0, 1, \dots, (d-1)\}$, as shown in Figure

10. In each cycle, nodes are labeled subsequently. In cycle i we prohibit the turn $((i, d-1), (i, 1), (i, 2))$. There exist $N(H)$ such turns. Also, for each of $N(H)d / 2$ edges between different cycles (edges between cycles in G correspond to edges in H), we prohibit turn (a, b, c), where $a = (i_1, j_1)$, $b = (i_2, j_2)$, $c = (i_2, j_3)$, if $i_1 < i_2$ and $j_3 = (j_2 + 1) \bmod d$. Then it follows that $z(G) \leq \dfrac{|W|}{T(G)} = \dfrac{1}{6} + \dfrac{1}{3d}$.

The following theorem is generalization of Theorem 7.

Theorem 8: *If all nodes of 3-regular graph G with N nodes can be covered by k non-intersecting simple cycles, then*

$$\frac{1}{6} + \frac{2}{3N} \leq z(G) \leq \frac{1}{6} + \frac{k}{3N}. \tag{15}$$

Figure 11. (A) 4-Pancake graph, (B) and Petersen graph

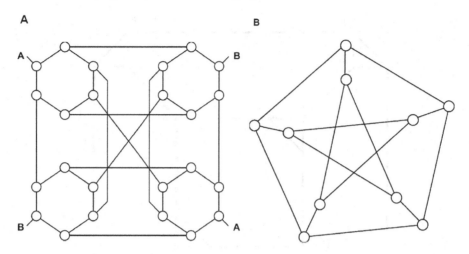

Proof: The proof of Theorem 8 is similar to the proof of Theorem 7 (Theorem 8 follows from Theorem 7 for the case of cycles of equal lengths). To illustrate Theorem 8 let us consider the 4-pancake graph (Parhami, 1998). In a 4-pancake graph, nodes have labels that include all $4! = 24$ orderings of numbers 1, 2, 3, and 4. For the q-pancake, node $(1, 2, \cdots, i-1, i, i+1, \cdots, q)$ is connected to nodes $(i, i-1, \cdots, 2, 1, i+1, \cdots, q)$ for each i, i.e., $1, 2, \cdots, i$ is flipped, like a pancake (Parhami, 1998). In a 4-pancake, nodes that are adjacent to node (1,2,3,4) are (2,1,3,4), (3,2,1,4) and (4,3,2,1) (see Figure 11 (A). For this graph, $N = 24, k = 4$ and according to Theorem 8 and (3), $z(G) = 2/9$.

Another graph, which can be analyzed by Theorem 8, is the Petersen graph (Harary, 1998), which has the smallest diameter (equal to 2) among all regular graphs of degree 3, shown in Figure 11(B). For this graph N = 10, k = 2 and by Theorem 8 and (3) we obtain z(G) = 7/30.

3.6 Hamiltonian Graphs with Nodes of Small Degrees

Now we consider graphs with restricted degrees, for which a Hamiltonian path (a path, containing all nodes exactly once (Harary, 1998)) exists. Since Hamiltonian topologies emulate a linear array algorithm efficiently, existence of a Hamiltonian path in a topology is considered as a desirable property (Parhami, 1998). Many regular graphs (e.g. hypercubes and meshes) belong to this class. (Some current multicast techniques in computer networks are path-based (Sivaram, Panda, & Stunkel, 1997; R. V. Boppana, Chalasani, & Raghavendra, 1998) and use the Hamiltonian path to propagate messages from a source node to all destinations.)

Theorem 9: *If graph G with N nodes is Hamiltonian and degree d regular, then*

$$z(G) \leq \frac{N(d-2)+4}{2Nd}. \tag{16}$$

Proof: A cycle-breaking set of turns can be constructed by labeling all nodes along the Hamiltonian path and prohibiting all turns, with a middle node having the maximal label. Then all turns can be classified into three groups:

1. Turns between edges, belonging to the path. There are $N-1$ such turns, all of them will be permitted;
2. Turns between an edge from the path and an edge not belonging to the path. There are $M_2 = M - N + 1$ such edges not belonging to the path, and each edge generates one prohibited turn;
3. Turns between edges, not belonging to the path. There are not more than

$$T_3 \leq (N-2)\binom{d-2}{2} + 2\binom{d-1}{2}$$
$$= N(d-2)(d-3)/2 + 2(d-2)$$

such turns. Not more than half of them belong to the constructed set of prohibited turns W (otherwise we can construct W, prohibiting all turns, with a middle node having the *minimal* label).

For the number of prohibited turns we then obtain

$$Z(G) \leq M_2 + T_3/2. \tag{17}$$

The total number of turns is upperbounded by $T(G) = Nd(d-1)/2$. Thus, the fraction of prohibited turns will be upperbounded as

$$z(G) \leq \frac{\dfrac{(d-2)N}{2} + 1 + \dfrac{N(d-2)(d-3)}{4} + d - 2}{\dfrac{Nd(d-1)}{2}},$$

$$\leq \frac{N(d-2)+4}{2Nd}.$$

We note that only cases $d=3$, $d=4$, and $d=5$ result in new upper bounds. Taking into account the lower bound given by (3), we obtain for $d=3$

$$z(G) = \frac{N+4}{6N}, \tag{18}$$

and for $d=4$

$$z(G) \leq \frac{N+2}{4N}. \tag{19}$$

For some Hamiltonian graphs we can improve the number of prohibited turns, (17), by dividing T_3 turns between edges, not belonging to the Hamiltonian path, into three groups:

1. Turns (a,b,c), where $a < b$, $b < c$.
2. Turns (a,b,c), where $b < a$, $b < c$.
3. Turns (a,b,c), where $b > a$, $b > c$.

Any one of the two last groups of turns can be selected as a set of prohibited turns, so if there are $F(G)$ turns in the first group, then

$$Z(G) \leq M_2 + (T_3 - F(G))/2. \tag{20}$$

The proposed method can be extended to non-Hamiltonian graphs. Let us consider for the case

Figure 12. Non-Hamiltonian degree-3 regular topology with $t=3$. The spanning tree is shown with edges in thick bold lines.

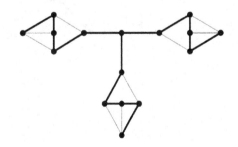

$d = 3$ graph G, which has a spanning tree with t leaves (nodes with degree equal to one). Then we label all nodes preserving the tree order and prohibiting turns with maximal labels for middle nodes and have for the number of prohibited turns

$$Z(G) \le M_2 + T_3 = M - N + t,$$

and

$$z(G) \le \frac{N + 2t}{6N}. \tag{21}$$

As an example consider the degree-3 regular non-Hamiltonian graph in Figure 12, where a spanning tree with $t = 3$ leaves is shown with solid lines. The upper bound for the fraction of prohibited turns for this graph is

$z(G) \le \dfrac{16 + 2(3)}{6(16)} \le \dfrac{11}{48}$, and the lower bound

(3) is $z(G) \ge 10 / 48$.

4. DISTANCE DILATION

Consider now the notion of dilation in a network topology due to turn prohibitions. Paths that involve prohibited turns are prohibited and are not used for communication. Thus, one side effect of turn prohibitions is that, prohibiting certain paths from being used for message routing, may increase distances between some nodes. The net result of this is that the average distance of the network graph will be increased. To facilitate the investigation of this phenomenon, the notion of distance dilation is introduced.

Definition 5: *The dilation in a graph, is the ratio of the average distance after turn prohibition to the average distance without any turn prohibition.*

When the dilation is 1 it implies that the turn prohibitions have not caused any lengthening of the average distance. For example, for complete graphs the fraction of prohibited turns achieves the upper bound, but the dilation is 1. Similarly for homogeneous and D-meshes, for hexagonal

Figure 13. Dilation in p-ary n-dimensional tori due to turn prohibition, in $p = 3, \ldots, 6$ are displayed

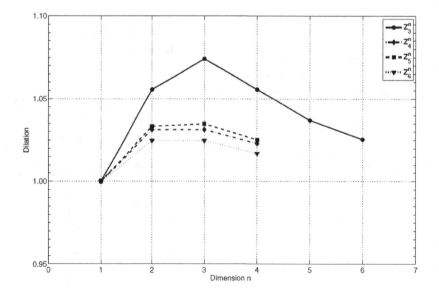

Table 1. Lower and upper bounds on fractions of prohibited turns, $z(G)$, in minimal cycle breaking sets for several regular and semiregular topologies

Topology	Lower bound on $z(G)$	Upper bound on $z(G)$	Asymptotic Limits for $z(G)$
Homogenous meshes - Theorem 1	$\dfrac{1}{4}\left(1 - \dfrac{1}{d-1}\right)$		$\dfrac{1}{4}, d \to \infty$
Complete graph K_n, $n > 2$	$1/3$		$1/3$
n-dimensional p-ary mesh – (6) M_p^n	$\dfrac{(n-1)(p-1)^2}{2p(p-2) + 4(n-1)(p-1)^2}$		$\dfrac{n-1}{4n-2}, p \to \infty,$ $\dfrac{1}{4}, n \to \infty, p \to \infty$
n-dimensional p-ary torus – (7) Z_p^n, $(p > 2)$	$\dfrac{p(n-1)+2}{2p(2n-1)}$		$\dfrac{1}{4}, n \to \infty$
Hypercube Z_2^n - Section 3-5	$1/4$		$1/4, n \to \infty$
Hexagonal mesh of size p - (10)	$\dfrac{9p^2 - 21p + 13}{45p^2 - 99p + 51}$		$\dfrac{1}{5}, p \to \infty$
Hexagonal torus of size p - (11)	$\dfrac{9p^2 - 15p + 10}{45p^2 - 45p + 15}$		$\dfrac{1}{5}, p \to \infty$
Honeycomb mesh of size p - Section 3-2	$\dfrac{3p^2 - 3p + 1}{18p^2 - 12p}$		$\dfrac{1}{6}, p \to \infty$
Honeycomb torus of size p - Section 3-2	$\dfrac{1}{6} + \dfrac{1}{18p^2}$		$\dfrac{1}{6}, p \to \infty$
Fractahedron with ℓ levels - (13)	$\dfrac{2 \cdot 3^\ell - 1}{3\left(3^{\ell+1} - 2\right)}$		$\dfrac{2}{9}, \ell \to \infty$
Cube-connected cycle with $N = 2^n$ *nodes* - (14)	$\dfrac{1}{6} + \dfrac{1}{3N}$	$\dfrac{1}{6} + \dfrac{1}{3d}$	$\dfrac{1}{6}, n \to \infty$
Hamiltonian graph with max degree $\Delta < 5$ - (16)	-	$\dfrac{N(\Delta - 2) + 4}{2N\Delta}$	$\dfrac{1}{2} - \dfrac{1}{\Delta}, N \to \infty$, (upper bound)

cotinued on following page

Table 1. Continued

Topology	Lower bound on $z(G)$	Upper bound on $z(G)$	Asymptotic Limits for $z(G)$
3-regular graph - Section 3-6	$\dfrac{1}{6} + \dfrac{2}{3N}$	$\dfrac{2}{9} + \dfrac{7}{18N}$	$\dfrac{2}{9}$, $N \to \infty$, (upper bound)
4-pancake graph - Section 3-5	2/9		2/9
Petersen graph - Section 3-5	7/30		7/30
Locally Complete graphs - (12) *obtained by replacing each of* N' nodes in a tree by a K_n	$\dfrac{1}{3} - \dfrac{N'n(n-2)}{N'n(n-2) + 4(N'-1)}$		$\dfrac{1}{3} - \dfrac{n(n-2)}{n(n-2) + 4}$, $N' \to \infty$

meshes, p-ary n-dimensional meshes, for locally complete tree-like topologies, and for fractahedrons no dilation is introduced by turn prohibitions. In Figure 13 the distance dilations in p-ary n-dimensional tori are shown. For these calculations, we determined the average distance using the shortest distances between all source destination pairs. For the p=3 torus, the largest dilation is less than 5.5%, whereas for tori with $p = 4$, 5, and 6, the largest dilation is less than 3.5%.

5. CONCLUSION

In this chapter the problem of constructing minimum cycle-breaking sets of turns for graphs that model communication networks in multiprocessor systems with wormhole routing is considered. This problem is important for deadlock-free and livelock-free message routing in these networks. A series of new algorithms were presented that are used to obtain optimal or close to optimal sets of prohibited turns to prevent deadlock formation during routing. Results on minimum fractions of turns that must be prohibited to break all cycles without loss of connectivity for degree-regular connected graphs are presented in Table 1. The results of calculations for dilations as a result of prohibitions in p-ary n-dimensional meshes and tori are also presented. It is noteworthy that meshes

do not suffer from any dilation and the worst case dilation for tori is less than 5.5%.

REFERENCES

Ajima, Y., Sumimoto, S., & Shimizu, T. (2009, November). Tofu: A 6d Mesh/Torus interconnect for exascale computers. *Computer*, *42*(11), 36–40. doi:10.1109/MC.2009.370

Boppana, R., & Chalasani, S. (1993). A comparison of adaptive wormhole routing algorithms. *Computer Architecture News*, *21*(2), 351–360. doi:10.1145/173682.165177

Boppana, R. V., Chalasani, S., & Raghavendra, C. (1998). Resource deadlocks and performance of wormhole multicast routing algorithms. *IEEE Transactions on Parallel and Distributed Systems*, *9*(6), 535–549. doi:10.1109/71.689441

Chalasani, S., & Boppana, R. V. (1995). Fault-tolerant wormhole routing algorithms in mesh networks. *IEEE Transactions on Computers*, *44*(7), 848–864. doi:10.1109/12.392844

Dally, W., & Aoki, H. (1997). Deadlock-free adaptive routing in multiprocessor networks using virtual channels. *IEEE Transactions on Parallel and Distributed Systems*, *4*(4), 466–475. doi:10.1109/71.219761

Dally, W. J., & Seitz, C. L. (1986). The torus routing chip. *Journal of Distributed Computing, 1*(3), 187–196. doi:10.1007/BF01660031

Dally, W. J., & Seitz, C. L. (1987). Deadlock-free message routing in multiprocessor interconnection networks. *IEEE Transactions on Computers, 36,* 547–553. doi:10.1109/TC.1987.1676939

Decayeux, C., & Seme, D. (2005). 9). 3D hexagonal network: Modeling, topological properties, addressing scheme, and optimal routing algorithm. *IEEE Transactions on Parallel and Distributed Systems, 16,* 875–884. doi:10.1109/TPDS.2005.100

Dolter, J. W., Ramanathan, P., & Shin, K. G. (1991). Performance analysis of virtual cut-through switching in HARTS: A hexagonal mesh multicomputer. *IEEE Transactions on Computers, 40*(6), 669–680. doi:10.1109/12.90246

Duato, J. (December 1991). Deadlock-free adaptive routing algorithms for multicomputers: Evaluation of a new algorithm. In *Proceedings of the Third IEEE Symposium Parallel and Distributed Processing* (pp. 840-847). Dallas, TX: IEEE Computer Society.

Duato, J. (1993). A new theory of deadlock-free adaptive routing in wormhole networks. *IEEE Transactions on Parallel and Distributed Systems, 4,* 1320–1331. doi:10.1109/71.250114

Duato, J. (1994). A necessary and sufficient condition for deadlock-free adaptive routing in wormhole networks. *Proceedings of International Conference on Parallel Processing,* (pp. 142-149).

Duato, J., Yalamancili, S., & Ni, L. (1997). *Interconnection networks: An engineering approach.* Silver Spring, MD: IEEE Computer Society Press.

Glass, C., & Ni, L. (1994). The turn model for adaptive routing. *Journal of the ACM, 5,* 874–902. doi:10.1145/185675.185682

Harary, F. (1998). *Graph theory.* Perseus Books.

Honkala, I., Karpovsky, M. G., & Levitin, L. B. (2006, February). On robust and dynamic identifying codes. *IEEE Transactions on Information Theory, 52*(2), 599–613. doi:10.1109/TIT.2005.862097

Horst, R. (1996). ServerNet(TM) deadlock avoidance and fractahedral topologies. *Proceedings of IEEE International Parallel Processing Symposium,* (pp. 274-280).

Levitin, L., Karpovsky, M., & Mustafa, M. (May, 2009). Deadlock prevention by turn prohibitions in interconnection networks. In *2009 IEEE International Symposium on Parallel & Distributed Processing* (pp. 1-7). Rome, Italy: IEEE Computer Society.

Levitin, L., Karpovsky, M., & Mustafa, M. (2010, September). Minimal sets of turns for breaking cycles in graphs modeling networks. *IEEE Transactions on Parallel and Distributed Systems, 21*(9), 1342–1353. doi:10.1109/TPDS.2009.174

Levitin, L. B., Karpovsky, M. G., Mustafa, M., & Zakrevski, L. (2006). A new algorithm for finding cycle-breaking sets of turns in a graph. *Journal of Graph Algorithms and Applications, 10*(2), 387–420. doi:10.7155/jgaa.00134

Lysne, O., Skeie, T., Reinemo, S. A., & Theiss, I. (2006). Layered routing in irregular networks. *IEEE Transactions on Parallel and Distributed Systems, 17*(1), 51–56. doi:10.1109/TPDS.2006.12

Min, G., Ould-Khaoua, M., Kouvatsos, D., & Awan, I. (2004, May). A queuing model of dimension-ordered routing under self-similar traffic loads. In *Proceedings of the 18th International Parallel and Distributed Processing Symposium,* (pp. 601-613). Washington, DC: IEEE Computer Society.

Mustafa, M., Karpovsky, M., & Levitin, L. (2005, August). *Cycle breaking in wormhole routed computer communication networks.* Washington, DC: Opnet Technologies.

Ni, L. M., & McKinley, P. K. (1993). A survey of wormhole routing techniques in direct networks. *Computer, 26*, 62–76. doi:10.1109/2.191995

Nocetti, F. G., Stojmenovic, I., & Zhang, J. (2002). Addressing and routing in hexagonal networks with applications for tracking mobile users and connection rerouting in cellular networks. *IEEE Transactions on Parallel and Distributed Systems, 13*(9), 963–971. doi:10.1109/TPDS.2002.1036069

Parhami, B. (1998). *Introduction to parallel processing: Algorithms and architectures*. New York, NY: Plenum Press.

Parhami, B., & Kwai, D.-M. (2001). A unified formulation of honeycomb and diamond networks. *IEEE Transactions on Parallel and Distributed Systems, 12*(1), 74–80. doi:10.1109/71.899940

Pellegrini, F. D., Starobinski, D., Karpovsky, M., & Levitin, L. (2004). Scalable cycle-breaking algorithms for gigabit Ethernet backbones. *Proceedings - IEEE INFOCOM*, 2004.

Pellegrini, F. D., Starobinski, D., Karpovsky, M. G., & Levitin, L. B. (2006, February). Scalable, distributed cycle-breaking algorithms for gigabit Ethernet backbones. *Journal of Optical Networks, 5*(2), 122–144. doi:10.1364/JON.5.000122

Sancho, J. C., & Robles, A. (2000). *Improving the up*/down* routing scheme for networks of workstations*. European Conference on Parallel Computing (Euro-Par 2000).

Sancho, J. C., Robles, A., & Duato, J. (2004, August). An effective methodology to improve the performance of the up*/down* routing algorithm. *IEEE Transactions on Parallel and Distributed Systems, 15*(8), 740–754. doi:10.1109/TPDS.2004.28

Schroeder, M. D., Birrell, A. D., Burrows, M., Murray, H., Needham, R. M., Rodeheer, T. L., et al. (1990, April). *Autonet: A high-speed self configuring local area network using point-to-point links* (Tech. Rep. No. SRC Research Report 59). Palo Alto, CA: Digital Equipment Corporation, SRC.

Sivaram, R., Panda, D., & Stunkel, C. B. (1997). Multicasting in irregular networks with cut-through switches using tree-based multidestination worms. *Proceedings of the 2nd Parallel Computing, Routing and Communication Workshop,* (pp. 35-48).

Skeie, T., Lysne, O., & Theiss, I. (2002). Layered shortest path (LASH) routing in irregular system area networks. In *International Parallel and Distributed Processing Symposium: IPDPS 2002 Workshops* (pp. 162-170). Fort Lauderdale, FL.

Stojmenovic, I. (1997). Honeycomb networks: Topological properties and communication algorithms. *IEEE Transactions on Parallel and Distributed Systems, 8*(10), 1036–1042. doi:10.1109/71.629486

Zakrevski, L., Jaiswal, S., & Karpovsky, M. (1999). Unicast message routing in communication networks with irregular topologies. *Proceeding of Computer Aided Design* (CAD-99).

Zakrevski, L., Jaiswal, S., Levitin, L., & Karpovsky, M. (1999). A new method for deadlock elimination in computer networks with irregular topologies. *Proceedings of the International Association of Science and Technology for Development (IASTED) Conference, Parallel and Distributed Computing Systems* (PDCS-99), Vol. 1, (pp. 396-402).

Zakrevski, L., Mustafa, M., & Karpovsky, M. (2000). Turn prohibition based routing in irregular computer networks. *Proceedings of the IASTED International Conference on Parallel and Distributed Computing and Systems,* (pp. 175-179).

KEY TERMS AND DEFINITIONS

Cycle of Edges: A path in which the last edge is the same as the first one and is traversed in the same direction.

Deadlock: A situation in a communication network, when several messages block one another around a cycle, so that no one can move ahead.

Degree of a Node: The number of edges ending in the node.

Path in a Graph: A sequence of nodes in which each node is connected to the next node by an edge.

Turn Prohibition: A set of restrictions in routing that prohibits messages from using certain turns, in order to prevent deadlocks.

Turn: A pair of edges having the same node as their endpoint.

Wormhole Routing: A method of routing in communication networks in which all parts of a message (flits) follow the same path, at any moment of time occupying a number of nodes and edges (links) along the path.

Chapter 5
Self–Stabilizing Graph Coloring Algorithms

Shing-Tsaan Huang
National Central University, Taiwan

Chi-Hung Tzeng
National Tsing Hua University, Taiwan

Jehn-Ruey Jiang
National Central University, Taiwan

ABSTRACT

The concept of self-stabilization in distributed systems was introduced by Dijkstra in 1974. A system is said to be self-stabilizing if (1) it can converge in finite time to a legitimate state from any initial state, and (2) when it is in a legitimate state, it remains so henceforth. That is, a self-stabilizing system guarantees to converge to a legitimate state in finite time no matter what initial state it may start with; or, it can recover from transient faults automatically without any outside intervention. This chapter first introduces the self-stabilization concept in distributed computing. Next, it discusses the coloring problem on graphs and its applications in distributed computing. Then, it introduces three self-stabilizing algorithms. The first two are for vertex coloring and edge coloring on planar graphs, respectively. The last one is for edge coloring on bipartite graphs.

INTRODUCTION

A distributed system can be considered as a network of nodes. Each node has program code, constants and variables. Over-heating, electro-magnetic radiation or others may cause faults on a node. A node can easily restore its program code and constants by fetching them from a secondary storage. Or, the program code and constants can be burned in Read-Only-Memory. Therefore, program code and constants can be easily recovered from faults. However, variables which reflect the state of a node must be kept in Random-Access-Memory, and hence are vulnerable to faults. Here in this chapter, we refer faults that only affect the values of variables as *transient faults*. A transient fault on a node may make a variable perturbed to be any possible value. For example, a variable of

DOI: 10.4018/978-1-4666-2533-4.ch005

3 bits may be any value between 0 and 7 after a transient fault.

The system configuration of a distributed system consists of states of all the nodes and hence is reflected by the variables maintained by the nodes. Joining or leaving of nodes from the system changes the system configuration. Therefore, we also model *transient fault*s to include the changes of system configurations, such as joining or leaving of nodes from the system.

The term *self-stabilization* in distributed computing was introduced by Dijkstra (Dijkstra, 1974). The states of a distributed system can be divided into two categories: *legitimate states* and *illegitimate states*. Ideally, the system should remain in legitimate states to work properly, but unexpected transient faults may bring it into an illegitimate state. A system is said to be *self-stabilizing* if (1) it can converge to a legitimate state regardless of any initial (possibly illegitimate) state in finite time, and (2) when it is in a legitimate state, it remains so henceforth. That is, a self-stabilizing system guarantees to converge to a legitimate state in finite time no matter what initial state it may start with; or, it can recover from transient faults automatically without any outside intervention.

As mentioned above, a distributed system can be considered as a network of nodes which can be represented by a graph (V, E), where V is the set of nodes and E is the set of links. Two nodes are said to be each other's neighbor if there is a link between them.

A self-stabilizing algorithm usually consists of several rules for each node. Each rule has the form: *guard* → *move*. The guard is a boolean function depending on the state of the node and the states of its neighbors. And, the move part only changes the state of the node by referencing the state of itself and the states of its neighbors. We say a node has a *privilege* to execute the move part of a rule when the guard of the rule is evaluated to be true. However, to be able to really make a move, the node must be scheduled to execute the move.

There are several execution models (Wuu and Huang, 1995) discussed in the literature for self-stabilization. In this chapter, we only introduce the simplest one, i.e., the central daemon model. This model assumes a centralized scheduler called the *central daemon*. The central daemon *arbitrarily* selects one at a time of the privileged nodes to make a move. After the selected node finishes the move, the daemon again chooses a privileged node, if any, to take another move, and so on. The moves of the nodes are hence serialized. Therefore, it is also called the *serial execution model*. The selection by the central daemon is unpredictable, so the execution sequence can be in any order.

A computation of the system is then a sequence of moves of the nodes. It is usually not an easy task to design a self-stabilizing system because starting from *any arbitrary* initial state or *any possible* state after a transient fault, the system must have the ability to bring itself into a legitimate state in *any possible* execution sequence of finite moves and remains hereafter in legitimate states if no transient fault occurs.

Now, we show a trivial example to see how a self-stabilizing system works. Consider a system with five nodes connected as a ring. Each node x ($0 \leq x \leq 4$) maintains a variable $S.x$ with the range $[0..3]$. The system is said to be in a legitimate state when all $S.x$ have the same value, and in an illegitimate state otherwise. With an arbitrary initialization or after a transient fault, each $S.x$ may have a value of 0, 1, 2, or 3.

There is only one rule for each node.

Rule: $S.x \neq \max(S.x \mid x \in N(x)) \rightarrow S.x = \max(S.x \mid x \in N(x))$,

where $N(x)$ is the set consisting of neighbors of node x and node x itself.

Intuitively, the rule makes each node set the value of its variable S to be equal to the largest one in its neighborhood. Therefore, all nodes will eventually have the same variable S value to reach the legitimate state and remain in there forever if no fault occurs.

With the initial state $(S.0, S.1, S.2, S.3, S.4) = (2, 1, 3, 0, 2)$. The following computation is a possible sequence of moves that bring the system into a legitimate state. The underline indicates the node selected to execute the move by the central daemon.

$(2,\underline{1},3,0,2) \rightarrow (2,3,3,\underline{0},2) \rightarrow (\underline{2},3,3,3,2) \rightarrow (3,3,3,3,\underline{2}) \rightarrow (3,3,3,3,3)$.

At the beginning, nodes 1 and 3 have the privilege; and node 1 is selected to execute the first move and changes its S value from 1 to 3. Then, nodes 0 and 3 have the privilege; and node 3 is selected to execute the second move and changes its S value from 0 to 3.

It is not difficult to see that *any possible* execution sequence will bring the ring into a legitimate state and the ring will remains in legitimate states if no transient fault occurs. For the trivial example, the correctness is obvious. But, it is usually difficult to prove the self-stabilizing property for a system. The readers are referred to the papers (Chen, Yu and Huang, 1991; Huang, 1993) for proving techniques.

As a summary, self-stabilization is an abstraction of fault tolerance with two important characteristics. First, it depends on local detection on faults and independent recovery made by the nodes without having a global view. Second, a self-stabilizing system needs not be initialized to a particular initial state. That is, each node can be started in an arbitrary state. This also allows nodes to join or leave the system freely. Those two characteristics are very desirable for distributed systems because it is usually difficult to have a global view of a distributed system. Also, it is difficult to ask all the nodes to start synchronously with predefined states.

GRAPH COLORING

A *distributed system* can be modeled as a simple connected undirected graph $G = (V, E)$, where V is the set of nodes and E is the set of edges representing intercommunication links between nodes. Graph coloring is an interesting and fundamental problem. Graph vertex coloring colors the nodes of graphs such that no two neighboring nodes have the same color. Whereas, edge coloring assigns each edge a color such that no two adjacent edges (i.e., edges incident to a node) get the same color. Usually, we would want to color the graph with as few colors as possible. The solution can be applied to the fundamental problems in distributed computing such as the scheduling problem, the mutual exclusion problem, the resource-sharing problem, and so on.

Consider a system that no two neighboring nodes can execute a *critical section* at the same time. This is a typical *mutual exclusion* problem. With the nodes being well colored, scheduling the nodes to execute its critical section is a simple job. Only the nodes with the same color can execute its critical section at the same time.

As to edge coloring, consider a network of nodes. Each node may communicate with its neighbors. But, a node can only communicate with one and only one neighbor at a time. For the problem, we may divide the time into slots and assign each slot with a color. With the edges being well colored, two neighboring nodes can safely communicate with each other at a time slot corresponding to the color of the edge connecting them.

In the resource-sharing problem there are a set of nodes and a set of resources. If a node can access certain resource, we then draw an edge between them to construct a bipartite network. The next step is to compute a proper edge coloring for this network. After that, a node is allowed to gain access to the resource when the index of the time slot matches the color of the edge. In this way, resource scheduling is done in advance and thus contention for resources is eliminated.

This chapter introduces three self-stabilizing coloring algorithms. The first algorithm (Huang, Hung, and Tzeng, 2005) uses six colors to color the nodes on planar graphs. A graph is said to be *planar* if it can be drawn in a plane with no crossing edges. The introduced algorithm is deterministic and works on anonymous uniform systems. Nodes in an anonymous uniform system do not need the node identifier. In distributed systems where nodes have unique identifiers, it is often easier to design self-stabilizing algorithms for many problems. Designing algorithms for anonymous uniform networks is thus more challenging.

The second introduced self-stabilizing algorithm (Tzeng, Jiang, and Huang, 2007) colors the edges on planar graphs. It uses $(\Delta + 4)$ colors, where Δ is the maximum degree of the graph. Since each edge has at most $2\Delta - 2$ adjacent edges, we can develop a trivial solution using $2\Delta - 1$ colors. We thus assume $\Delta > 5$ for the algorithm to exclude the trivial solution. The algorithm can be applied to anonymous uniform systems and its time complexity is $O(n^2)$.

It is obvious that at least Δ colors are needed in edge coloring. Given any initially improper edge coloring on a bipartite graph, the last introduced algorithm (Huang and Tzeng, 2009) automatically adjusts that coloring into a proper one. The algorithm is optimal in the sense that it uses exactly Δ colors. The time complexity of the algorithm is $O(n^2k + m)$, where n is the number of nodes, m is the total number of edges and k is the number of edges that are not properly colored in the arbitrary initial configuration.

Self-Stabilizing Vertex Coloring on Planar Graphs

Graph vertex coloring colors the nodes of graphs such that no two neighboring nodes have the same color. It has been proved that any planar graph is 4-colorable (Jensen and Toft, 1995). Some

self-stabilizing coloring algorithms have been proposed in recent years. Please refer to (Huang, Hung, and Tzeng, 2005) for their descriptions.

Here, we introduce a uniform deterministic self-stabilizing coloring algorithm for planar graphs by using six colors. It consists of two layers: the *orientation* layer and the *coloring* layer. First, in the orientation layer, nodes are labeled with the coloring order; then, in the coloring layer, nodes are colored just following the order.

The idea behind the algorithm is closed to the work in (Ghosh and Karaata, 1993), but in comparison with it, the algorithm introduced needs not to construct DAG (direct acyclic graph) in the orientation layer and the orientation only requires a unique n-bounded variable instead of the node identifier and unbounded memory. For coloring planar graphs with six colors, the introduced algorithm is the first deterministic algorithm that does not need the node identifier.

According to the well-known Euler's polyhedron formula, any connected simple and finite planar graph has $n \geq 3$, $m \leq 3n - 6$, where n is the number of nodes and m is the total number of edges. It implies that every planar graph has a node whose degree is at most five. Assume V_0 is the set consisting of the nodes whose degrees are less than six in G, and let $G_1 = (V - V_0, E - E_0)$, where E_0 contains the edges that connect with the nodes in V_0. It is obvious that G_1 is also a planar graph. Similarly, let V_1 be the set consisting of the nodes whose degrees are less than six in G_1, we get $G_2 = (V - V_0 - V_1, E - E_0 - E_1)$. This procedure can be repeated until $V_{k+1} = \psi$, where $k < n$. Finally, we get $V = V_0 \cup V_1 \cup V_2 \cup \ldots \cup V_k$ and for any $0 \leq i$, $j \leq k$, $V_i \cap V_j = \psi$.

The algorithm just follows the above approach and marks the nodes in V_i with number i, which is the coloring order. Then the coloring process stabilizes from the nodes with bigger i after the order is stabilized. That is, the algorithm consists of two layers: the orientation layer decides the coloring order for nodes; the coloring layer colors nodes by following the coloring order. The algorithm is designed as follows:

Each node x maintains two variables: $S.x$ and $C.x$. Variable S is used to order (orient) the nodes in the coloring process; it can be one of the values $0, 1, ..., n-1$. Variable C is the color of the nodes with values $0, 1, ..., 5$.

For the orientation layer, consider any node x and let α be the smallest possible value in $[0..n-1]$ such that $(Deg(x) - |\{y \mid NB(x, y), S.y < \alpha\}|) \leq 5$, where $Deg(x)$ is the degree of x and $NB(x, y)$ means $(x, y) \in E$. For instance, the nodes with less than six degrees get the α values to be zero. In some cases, α value may not exist, such as that a node has more than six degrees and all its neighbors have S value $n - 1$. However, a node always sets S value to α if α exists. For the coloring layer, let β be the smallest possible value in $[0..5]$ such that $\beta \notin \{C.y \mid NB(x,y), S.y \geq S.x\}$. Such β must exist for any node with correct α value, and a node always sets C value to β.

Figure 1 shows an example. The alphabets in the circles denote the nodes for description purpose. In Figure 1(a), node p has eight neighbors, that is $Deg(p) = 8$. The α value of node p is 6 since there are three neighbors (nodes b, e, h) whose S values are less than 6. In Figure 1(b), β value of node p is 3 since there are four neighbors (nodes b, c, d, e) whose S values are greater than $S.p$ and β could not be 0 (same as $C.b$), 1 (same as $C.c$, $C.e$) or 2 (same as $C.d$).

The Algorithm

Let us formally define:

$$\alpha = \min\{k \mid k \in [0.. n - 1], \mid Deg(x) - |\{y \mid NB(x, y), S.y < k\}| \leq 5\}\}$$

for any node x.

$$\beta = \min\{k \mid k \in [0..5], k \notin \{C.y \mid NB(x,y), S.y \geq S.x\}\}$$

for any node x.

Orientation layer:

R0: $\exists \alpha \wedge S.x \neq \alpha \rightarrow$ Let $S.x = \alpha$.
R1: $\exists \alpha \wedge S.x = \alpha \wedge C.x \neq \beta \rightarrow$ Let $C.x = \beta$.

Rule R0 is for orientation layer while Rule R1 is for coloring layer. The coloring layer will stabilize after the orientation layer stabilizes.

Figure 2 shows an example for the orientation layer. The numbers in the figure indicate S values, the underlined nodes have the privilege to execute actions, and the bold circle indicates the

*Figure 1. An example for deriving **s** and **c** values*

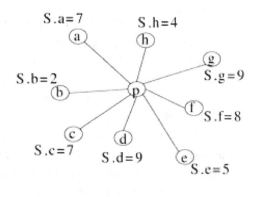

(a)

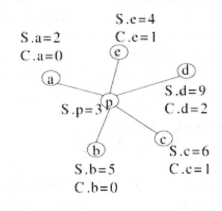

(b)

Figure 2. An example for orientation layer

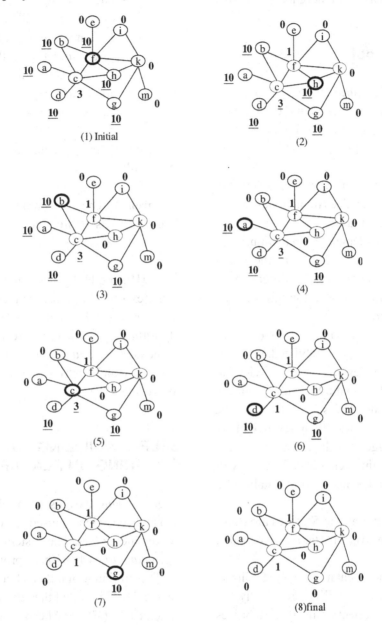

node that is selected to execute in each step. In this example, at state (1), nodes *a, b, d, g, h* have less than five neighbors; they have privilege to set *S* values to 0. Meanwhile all the neighbors of node *c* have *S* values 10, it cannot get the possible *S* value to make the number of neighbors with smaller *S* value less than six. Hence node *c* does not have the privilege until node *h* changes value

at state (2). We also note that there exists properly α value for node f to fine tune at initial state. The orientation layer converges from the nodes with smaller degree and stabilizes at state (8).

A node applies Rule R1 for coloring only when its *S* value meets α value, that is, it has less than six neighbors with bigger *S* values. Hence it can select a proper color from six colors that is different from the colors of the neighbors with bigger S values.

Correctness Proof

According to the described model, all nodes can be decomposed as $V_0, V_1, \ldots, V_k$. $V = V_0 \cup V_1 \cup V_2 \cup \ldots \cup V_k$ and for any $0 \leq i, j \leq k$, $V_i \cap V_j = \psi$. We may refer to this model for proofs.

Lemma 1: The orientation layer stabilizes eventually, that is, the S values of all nodes remain unchanged eventually.

Proof: We prove this lemma by induction:

○ According to the design, the nodes in V_0 set S values to 0 and remain so. Hence the S values of nodes in V_0 are stabilized.

○ Assume the S values of nodes in ($V_0 \cup V_1 \cup \ldots \cup V_j$) are stabilized, $0 \leq j < k$. For the nodes in V_{j+1}, it is obvious to set S values to the S value of nodes in V_j plus one, that is $j + 1$. It makes the nodes have less than six neighbors with bigger S value. Then the value will remain unchanged. So the S values of nodes in V_{j+1} will be stabilized.

By induction, after all the S values are stabilized, the orientation layer will stabilize eventually.

Lemma 2: After the orientation layer stabilizes, the coloring layer stabilizes eventually.

Proof: Assume the orientation layer stabilizes and m is the largest S value. We prove this lemma by induction:

○ Consider these nodes whose S values are m. Since k is the largest S value after the orientation layer stabilizes, these nodes have less than six neighbors whose S values are also k. Hence, it is easy to color these nodes by six colors and remain unchanged.

The coloring for the nodes whose S values are m will be stabilized.

○ Assume the colors of nodes which $S \geq j$ are stabilized, for the nodes which $S = j - 1$, it is easy to find the proper colors for coloring since they have less than six neighbors with $S \geq j$.

By induction, the coloring layer will stabilize eventually.

Theorem 1: The algorithm stabilizes.
Proof: This is a direct consequence of Lemma 1 and 2.

In (Huang, Hung, and Tzeng, 2005), the time complexity of the algorithm is analyzed. It shows that the algorithm takes $O(D)$ rounds for the algorithm to stabilize, where D is the diameter of the network and a *round* is the minimum time period in which each enabled process is scheduled to execute at least once.

SELF-STABILIZING EDGE COLORING ON PLANAR GRAPHS

Edge-coloring assigns each edge a color such that adjacent edges (i.e., edges incident to a node) get distinct colors. The system is said to be in a *legitimate state* when it has a proper edge coloring.

The minimum number of colors sufficient to edge color G is called the *edge chromatic index*, denoted by $\chi'(G)$. Let Δ be the maximum degree of G. It is easy to see that $\chi'(G) \geq \Delta$. Another trivial bound is $\chi'(G) \leq 2\Delta - 1$ because each edge has at most $2\Delta - 2$ adjacent edges.

In the following, we introduce a self-stabilizing edge-coloring algorithm for a planar graph (Tzeng, Jiang, and Huang, 2007). The number of colors used is at most $\Delta + 4$. The algorithm can be applied to anonymous uniform systems since it does not rely on node IDs and each node executes the same code. By labeling nodes, it assigns each edge a priority such that each edge has at most Δ + 3 adjacent edges with equal or higher coloring priorities, where $\Delta \geq 5$ is the maximal degree of the graph. When two adjacent edges are of the same color, the lower-priority one is forced to change its color. The coloring hence settles from the highest-priority edges to the lowest-priority ones. Eventually the graph has a proper edge coloring and no edge can change its color henceforth. And the number of colors used is thus at most $\Delta + 4$. As shown in (Tzeng, Jiang, and Huang, 2007), the time complexity of the algorithm is $O(n^2)$ moves under the central daemon model.

We assume that $\Delta \geq 5$; otherwise the condition $\Delta + 4 > 2\Delta - 1$ holds and we can develop a trivial solution using $2\Delta - 1$ colors. Moreover, we assume that the system is anonymous and uniform; i.e., nodes need no unique identifiers and are all logically equivalent and run the same program.

The Algorithm

To edge color G, our first step is to assign each edge a coloring priority. We give each node a label such that any node has at most five neighbors of equal or larger labels. An edge's coloring priority is then defined to be the sum of its endpoints' labels. As will be shown later, any edge has at most Δ + 3 adjacent edges of equal or higher priorities. The colors are assigned to edges according to their priorities, so $\Delta + 4$ colors are sufficient to edge color G properly.

Below, we explain how to assign labels for nodes. The idea is similar to that in the previous section. G contains at least one node of degree at most 5. We search for such nodes and let them form the set V_0. We then remove from G the nodes in V_0 as well as the edges incident to them to get a planar subgraph $G - V_0$. In a similar manner, we search for the nodes of degree at most 5 in $G - V_0$ and let them form the set V_1. By repeating this procedure, the node set V is partitioned into non-empty, mutually disjoint sets V_0, V_1, ... We define a node's label to be k if and only if it

belongs to V_k. Each node x maintains a variable $L.x$ to denote its label, where $L.x \in \{0, 1 \ldots, n\}$.

The above labeling procedure can be realized in a distributed way. Let $N.x$ denote the set of node u's neighbors and let $N^k.x = \{y \mid y \in N.x, k \leq L.y\}$ denote the subset of x's neighbors whose labels are equal to or larger than k. Node x always sets $L.x$ to be the minimum k such that $|N^k.x| \leq 5$. In this way, any node x in V_0 has $L.x = 0$ because the condition $|N^k.x| \leq 5$ holds for any $k \geq 0$. Based on the similar reason, any node x in V_1 has $L.x = 1, \ldots,$ and so forth. Hence the label-assignment rule R0 for any node x is:

R0: $L.x \neq \min\{k \mid 0 \leq k \leq n, |N^k.x| \leq 5\} \rightarrow L.x = \min\{k \mid 0 \leq k \leq n, |N^k.x| \leq 5\};$

In the design, a node needs to know the labels of all neighbors' neighbors, so each node x maintains a variable $L(y).x$ for each of its neighbors y and sets $L(y).x = L.y$ whenever $L(y).x \neq L.y$. We have the following rule R1:

R1: $\exists y: L(y).x \neq L.y \rightarrow L(y).x = L.y;$

With the help of the labels, we define the coloring priority for an edge (x, y) to be $L.x + L.y$. When the labeling settles, this definition makes (x, y) have at most $\Delta + 3$ adjacent edges with equal or higher priorities for the following reasoning. We first focus on the case $L.x \neq L.y$. Without loss of generality, we further assume that $L.x < L.y$. For node x, it has at most 4 neighbors in $N.x - \{y\}$ having equal or larger labels than $L.x$, so at most 4 edges incident to x have equal or higher coloring priorities than that of (x, y). For node y, it has at most $\Delta - 1$ neighbors in $N.y - \{x\}$ with equal or larger labels than $L.x$, so at most $\Delta - 1$ edges incident to y have equal or higher coloring priority than that of (x, y). On the whole, (x, y) has at most $4 + (\Delta - 1) = \Delta + 3$ adjacent edges with equal or higher coloring priorities than itself. Now, focus on the case $L.x = L.y$. Based on the similar reasoning shown above, at most 4 edges incident to x and at most 4 edges incident to y have equal or higher coloring priorities than that of (x, y). Hence (x, y) has at most 8 (or $\Delta + 3$; this is because $\Delta + 3 \geq 8$ under the assumption of $\Delta \geq 5$) adjacent edges of the same or higher priorities than itself.

Now we begin discussing the coloring. To express an edge (x, y)'s color in a distributed way, node x (resp., node y) maintains a variable $C(y).x$ (resp., $C(x).y$) to be the color associated with this edge. Since each edge has two color variables associated with it, we let the endpoint with the smaller label decide the edge's color and let the other endpoint copy that color. That is, for an edge (x, y) such that $L.x < L.y$, node x selects a proper color for $C(y).x$, and node y just sets $C(x).y – C(y).x$. For the case of $L.x = L.y$, if node x is the first one chosen by the central daemon to make a move, it selects a proper color for $C(y).x$ and then y just copies this color for $C(x).y$, and vice versa. It is noted that the coloring priority of an edge has nothing to do with the order of the endpoints deciding the edge color.

For an edge (x, y) such that $L.x \leq L.y$, let $Z(x^*, y) = \{z \mid z \in N.x, L.x \leq L(z).x\} - \{y\}$ be the set of x's neighbors, except y, whose labels are larger than or equal to x's label. On the other hand, let $Z(x, y^*) = \{z \mid z \in N.y, L.x \leq L(z).y\} - \{x\}$ be the set of y's neighbors, except x, whose labels are larger than or equal to x's label. We also let $Used(x, y) = \{C(z).x \mid z \in Z(x^*, y)\} \cup \{C(z).y \mid z \in Z(x, y^*)\}$ be a set of colors. It contains the colors used by (x, y)'s adjacent edges that have equal or higher priorities than (x, y). By the definition, we have $|Used(x, y)| \leq |Z(x^*, y)| + |Z(x, y^*)| \leq 4 + (\Delta - 1) = \Delta + 3$. If we set $C(y).x$ to be an element not in $Used(x, y)$, we then get a proper edge coloring. Below, we further define two functions $Incorrect(C(y).x)$ and $Decide(C(y).x)$ to help node x decide $C(y).x$. For the sake of presentation, we use $Correct(C(y).x)$ to denote the complement of $Incorrect(C(y).x)$.

$$Incorrect(k) \equiv \begin{cases} true, & if\ k \in Used(x, y) \\ false, & otherwise \end{cases}$$

$Decide(C(y).x) \equiv$ to set $C(y).x = \min(\{0, 1, \ldots, \Delta + 3\} - Used(x, y))$;

With these functions, we have the rules R2 to R4 for a node x to edge color the graph. By the rules, an edge cannot choose the color used by its adjacent edges with equal or higher priorities. On the other hand, an edge may or may not choose the color used by a lower-priority adjacent edge. This is because the set $Used(x, y)$ may contain the colors used by lower-priority adjacent edges when node x decides the color for (x, y). However, since $|Used(x, y)| \leq \Delta + 3$, there is always a color for node x to choose to edge color the graph properly.

R2: $\exists y$: $L.x < L.y \wedge Incorrect(C(y).x) \rightarrow Decide(C(y).x)$;

R3: $\exists y$: $L.x > L.y \wedge C(y).x \neq C(x).y \wedge (Correct(C(x).y)\ by\ y) \rightarrow C(y).x = C(x).y$;

R4: $\exists y$: $L.x = L.y \wedge Incorrect(C(y).x) \wedge Incorrect(C(x).y) \rightarrow Decide(C(y).x)$;

R5: $\exists y$: $L.x = L.y \wedge C(y).x \neq C(x).y \wedge Correct(C(x).y) \rightarrow C(y).x = C(x).y$;

It is noted that in rule R3, "$Correct(C(x).y)$ by y" stands for the result of $Correct(C(x).y)$ evaluated by node y. Since $Used(x, y)$ may be different from $Used(y, x)$ in the case of $L.x \neq L.y$, nodes x and y may get different results of $Correct(C(x).y)$. By reading the variables maintained by both x and y, node x can determine the result of $Correct(C(x).y)$ evaluated by y, so it can evaluate the predicate of R3 correctly.

Proving correctness of the algorithm is rather complicate. Here we omit it. The readers are referred to the paper (Tzeng, Jiang, and Huang, 2007).

SELF-STABILIZING EDGE COLORING ON BIPARTITE GRAPHS

The last self-stabilizing algorithm introduced is to color the edges of a bipartite network such that any two adjacent edges receive distinct colors (Huang and Tzeng, 2009). Edge coloration for bipartite graphs has long been investigated. How to edge color a graph in a distributed or even fault-tolerant way is still an active research topic.

Here, we introduce a self-stabilizing algorithm for finding an optimal edge coloring (i.e., using exactly Δ colors) in a bipartite network. The idea is to keep extending a partial edge coloring to a bigger one. We first maintain a property that adjacent edges, if colored, are of different colors. Then, we systematically move around uncolored edges by a concept called *alternative chain*, an approach similar to path augmentation (Gabow and Kariv, 1982), to places where they can be properly colored — and color them.

The moving-around of the uncolored edges is carried out in a de-centralized way so that there is no leader node responsible for finding a proper coloring from scratch. All the nodes make their decisions based on local information. That gives us an advantage. If there are just a few uncolored edges, a centralized algorithm needs a leader to run a sequential algorithm, compute a new edge coloring, and distribute the result to all the other nodes. The new edge coloring may be completely different from the old one because a slight change of the graph could let the leader make different decisions in the Euler-split procedure, as mentioned in (Gabow and Kariv, 1982). In such a case, a de-centralized algorithm such as the introduced one would be more appropriate since it avoids huge computation performed by the leader. In addition, if there are $O(1)$ edges that are not properly colored, only $O(n)$, rather than $O(m)$, colored edges alter their colors in the introduced algorithm. It is because an uncolored edge moves along a simple path or a simple cycle, as we will show.

As shown in (Huang and Tzeng, 2009), the time complexity of the algorithm is $O(n^2k + m)$ moves, where k is the number of edges that are not properly colored in the arbitrary initial configuration and a move is an execution of a rule. It involves not only the system parameters n and m

but also a parameter k that depends on the initial configuration. If $k = O(1)$, then the stabilization time is $O(n^2)$ moves. On the other hand, if $k = O(m)$, the stabilization time becomes $O(n^2m)$ moves.

The Idea

We first describe a sequential algorithm that edge colors G. Then, we show how to use the idea to design the self-stabilizing algorithm. We assume $n = |V| \geq 4$.

Path augmentation is a well-known approach to coloring a bipartite graph (Gabow and Kariv, 1982). Consider an uncolored edge (x, y). Since there are Δ colors, there is a *missing color* C_1 not appearing on edges incident to x. Similarly, there is another missing color C_2 not appearing on edges incident to y. If $C_1 = C_2$, we just assign C_1 to the edge (x, y). If not, starting from x we find a path of maximal length that is colored by C_2 and C_1 alternately. We then re-color the path by switching C_1 and C_2 and then assign color C_1 to (x, y). Clearly, repeating path augmentation yields a proper edge coloring.

In the following, we show how to use path augmentation to find a proper edge coloring in a self-stabilizing way.

As already known, Δ colors are sufficient to edge color G. Below, we assume the colors are numbered as 0, 1, 2..., and $\Delta - 1$ and all the nodes know the value of Δ.

The color of an edge (x, y) is decided by nodes x and y. Let $C(y).x$ be the color assigned by node x and $C(x).y$ be the color assigned by node y. We say that edge (x, y) is colored if $C(y).x = C(x).y$. That is, a colored edge has a consistent color and an uncolored edge has distinct colors on the two ends. In addition, we say that edge (x, y) is *properly colored* if $C(y).x = C(x).y$ and there are no z_1 and z_2 such that $C(y).x = C(z_1).x$ and $C(x).y = C(z_2).y$.

Let us consider the simplest case first: there is only one uncolored edge while all the others are properly colored. The two colors of the uncolored edge induce a component called *alternative*

Figure 3. An alternative chain

chain, as shown in Figure 3. This alternative chain must be a simple path or a simple cycle; otherwise there exists a node assigning the same color to two edges. In fact, this alternative chain must be a simple path because a cyclic alternative chain with one uncolored edge is of odd size, contradicting to the property that every cycle in a bipartite graph must be of even size. In the rest of the chapter, we simply use the term "chain" instead of "alternative chain".

We can design a simple algorithm for such a case. The idea is to shift the uncolored edge in a *constant* direction until it reaches one end of the chain, and then color it. The algorithm is as follows:

Each node x maintains two variables for each edge (x, y):

$C(y).x$: the color for edge (x, y) decided by node x. Its range is $[0.. \Delta - 1]$.

$T(y).x$: the shifting direction of the uncolored edge. Its value is 0, 1, or 2. All the operations on this variable are under modulo 3. When the equation $T(y).x = T(x).y + 1$ holds, it means that the uncolored edge is shifted in the direction from x to y along the chain.

For the sake of presentation, we define the following functions and notation:

Colored(x, y): returns true if $C(y).x = C(x).y$; false otherwise.

FreeColorSet(x): returns the set of colors that have not been used by x; i.e., $\{0, 1,..., \Delta - 1\} - \{ C(y).x \mid (x, y) \in E\}$.

$x \Leftrightarrow y$: stands for true if $T(y).x = T(x).y$; false otherwise.

$x \Rightarrow y$: stands for the boolean formula $T(y).x = T(x).y + 1$. When it is clear from the context, $x \Rightarrow y$ also stands for the assignment equation $T(y).x = T(x).y + 1$.

The rules for each node x:

S0: $\neg\, Colored(x, y) \wedge (x \Leftrightarrow y) \to x \Rightarrow y$;

S1: $\neg\, Colored(x, y) \wedge (y \Rightarrow x) \wedge (\exists z: Colored(x, z) \wedge C(z).x = C(x).y) \to$ Switch$(C(z).x, C(y).x)$; $x \Rightarrow z$;

S2: $\neg\, Colored(x, y) \wedge C(x).y \in FreeColorSet(x) \to C(y).x = C(x).y$;

Rule S0 determines the shifting direction to be from node x to node y. Rule S1 shifts the uncolored edge from edge (y, x) to edge (x, z). By repeatedly executing S1, the uncolored edge eventually reaches the end of the chain and can be properly colored via rule S2.

In general cases, there might be many uncolored edges contained in many chains, and those chains might interfere with one another. The problem is how to concurrently shift multiple uncolored edges so that they can be properly colored.

The Algorithm

The algorithm needs to deal with the symmetry problem. To break the symmetry, each node is assumed to have a unique ID. For the sake of simplicity, we assume that node ID is in the range $[0.. n - 1]$.

When concurrently shifting multiple uncolored edges, we shall face the problem of endlessly shifting an uncolored edge in a cyclic chain. We may also face the problem of different chains interfering with one another. We give an example in Figure 4. In the illustration, subfigure (a) is a partial edge coloring and subfigures (b), (c) and (d) are the chains of color pairs (0, 1), (0, 2) and (1, 2) respectively. The cyclic chain of color pair (0, 1) contains even number of uncolored edges, which may be shifted in the same direction at the

Figure 4. An example of multiple chains

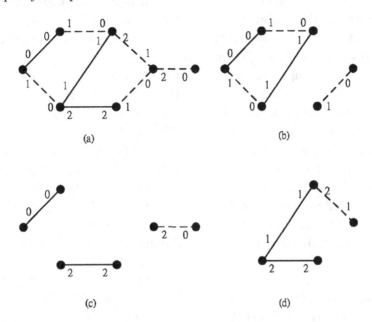

(a)

(b)

(c)

(d)

same speed. Moreover, that chain may interfere with the chain of color pair (1, 2) because they share the edge of color 1.

To solve the interference problem, we use a locking mechanism to prioritize the chains. And, to solve the problem of multiple uncolored edges circulating in a cyclic chain, we let the node with the maximum ID in the chain be a turn-around point. When an uncolored edge is incident to a turn-around point, its shifting direction changes. Thus it has a chance to meet another uncolored edge so that both of them, or one of them, can be colored.

Whenever a node x shifts an uncolored edge from (y, x) to (x, z), it locks both edges. The notation of a lock is LockPair(i, j), where (i, j) is the color pair of that uncolored edge. Locks represent priorities of the chains, and they are totally ordered.

Definition (The Priorities of the Locks)

Let $L_1 = $ LockPair(i_1, j_1) and $L_2 = $ LockPair(i_2, j_2):

- $L_1 > L_2$ if $(\min(i_1, j_1), \max(i_1, j_1)) < (\min(i_2, j_2), \max(i_2, j_2))$
- $L_1 = L_2$ if $(\min(i_1, j_1), \max(i_1, j_1)) = (\min(i_2, j_2), \max(i_2, j_2))$

The above comparison is in lexicographic order: $(i_1, j_1) < (i_2, j_2)$ means $(i_1 < i_2) \lor (i_1 = i_2 \land j_1 < j_2)$; whereas $(i_1, j_1) = (i_2, j_2)$ means $i_1 = i_2 \land j_1 = j_2$. For example, LockPair(2, 5) = LockPair(5, 2); and LockPair(2, 5) > LockPair(6, 2). When two chains interfere with each other, we only allow the higher-priority chain to destroy the locks marked by the lower-priority one. In other words, the lower-priority chain must give way to the higher-priority chain.

It is not easy for a node to determine whether it is the turn-around point in a chain. We use uncolored edges to solve this problem. Each time a node shifts an uncolored edge, it also memorizes the maximum ID which the uncolored edge has encountered so far. However, in an arbitrary initial configuration, this memorized ID might not exist in the cycle so that the uncolored edge is misled and circulates in the chain. Our solution is to use a counter. Whenever a node shifts an uncolored edge, it increments corresponding counters.

The counter is reset to zero in two cases: (1) the counter reaches its upper bound, which is n, the maximum length of all the simple cycles and simple paths, or (2) the uncolored edge reaches a node with ID greater than the memorized ID. When the counter is reset, the uncolored edge also turns around. Therefore, an uncolored edge may turn around several times before it reaches the node with the maximum ID in the chain. Below, we assume that all the nodes know the value of n.

Now, we are going to present the algorithm. Each node x maintains the following variables for each neighbor y:

$C(y).x$: the color assigned by node x, $[0.. \Delta - 1]$.

$L(y).x$: the lock, whose value is $LockPair(i, j)$ or *nil*. We define that any $L(y).x \geq nil$.

$T(y).x$: the trace of the shifting direction. Its value is 0, 1, or 2. All the operations on this variable are under module 3.

$K(y).x$: the counter, $[0.. n]$.

$M(y).x$: the memorized maximum node ID; for the sake of simplicity, we assume $M(y).x \in [0..n]$.

In addition, we also define the following functions:

$ID(x)$: returns the ID of node x.

$FreeColor(x)$: returns an element in $FreeColorSet(x)$ defined in Section 3.1.

$LCP(x, y)$: returns $LockPair(C(y).x, C(x).y)$, a lock identified by the color pair of edge (x, y).

$TurnAround(x, y)$: returns true if $K(y).x = n \lor M(x).y \leq ID(x)$; false otherwise.

$ClearLock(L(y).x)$: removes related locks after coloring an uncolored edge. Its definition is $ClearLock(L(y).x) \equiv L(y).x = nil \land ((x \Rightarrow y \land (L(y).x = L(x).y \lor K(y).x = K(x).y - 1)) \lor (y \Rightarrow x \land \neg(\exists z: x \Rightarrow z \land L(y).x = L(z).x = L(x).y \land K(y).x = K(z).x = K(x).y + 1)) \lor (x \Leftrightarrow y))$

The rules of our edge-coloring algorithm are listed below. If an edge (x, y) satisfies the guard of a rule, then the rule is enabled for the node x.

R0: $\exists z: C(y).x = C(z).x \rightarrow C(y).x = FreeColor(x)$;

R1: $\neg Colored(x, y) \land C(x).y \in FreeColorSet(x) \rightarrow C(y).x = C(x).y$;

R2: $\neg Colored(x, y) \land (\exists z: \neg Colored(x, z) \land C(z).x = C(x).y) \rightarrow Switch(C(z).x, C(y).x)$;

R3: $\neg Colored(x, y) \land (\exists z: Colored(x, z) \land C(z).x = C(x).y \land (x \Leftrightarrow y \lor (x \Rightarrow y \land L(y).x \neq LCP(x, y)))) \rightarrow x \Rightarrow y; L(y).x = LCP(x, y); K(y).x = 0; M(y).x = ID(x)$;

/*Initialize the variables for an uncolored edge (x, y).*/

R4: $\neg Colored(x, y) \land y \Rightarrow x \land L(x).y = LCP(x, y) \land TurnAround(x, y) \land (\exists z: Colored(x, z) \land C(z).x = C(x).y) \rightarrow x \Rightarrow y; L(y).x = LCP(x, y); K(y).x = 0; M(y).x = ID(x)$;

/*Initialize a turn-around point.*/

R5: $\neg Colored(x, y) \land y \Rightarrow x \land L(x).y = LCP(x, y) \land \neg TurnAround(x, y) \land (\exists z: Colored(x, z) \land C(z).x = C(x).y) \land L(x).y \geq L(z).x) \rightarrow Switch(C(z).x, C(y).x); x \Rightarrow z$;

$L(y).x = L(x).y; L(z).x = L(y).x$;
$K(y).x = K(x).y + 1; K(z).x = K(y).x$;
$M(y).x = M(x).y; M(z).x = M(x).y$;

/*Shift an uncolored edge from (x y) to (x z).*/

R6: $Colored(x, y) \land ClearLock(L(y).x) \rightarrow L(y).x = nil$;

Due to arbitrary initialization, a node may assign the same color to two neighboring edges. Rule R0 is used to correct such a situation.

When an uncolored edge reaches the end of a chain, it can be properly colored. Rule R1 is used in that case.

Given two uncolored edges (x, y) and (x, z) satisfying $C(z).x = C(x).y$, edge (x, y) (and possibly (x, z)) can be properly colored. Rule R2 is used in that case.

Rule R3 is used to initialize the shifting direction and the LockPair mark of a chain. It also initializes the variables K and M.

As mentioned before, there are two cases, viz. $K(y).x = n \lor M(x).y \leq ID(x)$, for node x to reset the variables K and M and to change the shifting direction. Rule R4 is used to handle such cases.

Rule R5 is used to shift uncolored edges. When a node executes R5 to do so, it also locks corresponding edges, increments counters and copies the maximum node ID memorized so far. In addition, chains may interfere with one another, and we use rule R5 to allow higher-priority chains to destroy the locks marked by lower-priority ones.

A lock is legal only if we can find an uncolored edge with a consistent trace direction, counter values, and LockPair marks. Rule R6 is used to unlock an illegal lock.

Each rule has its own priority. Rule R0 has the highest priority; R1 and R2 have the second highest priority; R3,..., R6 have the lowest priority. The priority mechanism is not hard to implement since we can use if-then-else statements.

The correctness proving and time complexity analysis of the algorithm is omitted here. The readers are referred to (Huang and Tzeng, 2009) for the details.

There are three main ingredients in the algorithm. In a sequential algorithm, one can easily maintain the color of an edge no matter it is colored or not. However, in a distributed environment, the color of an edge must be agreed by the endpoints. Here, how to maintain and determine the color of an edge is introduced. Locking mechanism is also an important ingredient of the algorithm. Finally, the technique of letting two uncolored edges in a cyclic chain meet is another important idea.

CONCLUSION

In this chapter, at the beginning the term *self-stabilization* in distributed computing is introduced. Self-stabilization is an abstraction of fault tolerance. It detects and recovers faults by the nodes without having a global view; also, each node can be started in an arbitrary state. Those two characteristics are very desirable for distributed systems. A distributed system is usually difficult to have a global view; and, it is also difficult to ask all the nodes to start synchronously with predefined states.

Next, the chapter discusses the *coloring* problem on graphs and its applications in distributed computing. Vertex coloring colors the nodes of a graph in such a way that no two neighboring nodes have the same color. Whereas, edge coloring assigns each edge a color such that no two adjacent edges get the same color. The solution can be applied to the fundamental problems in distributed computing such as scheduling problems and mutual exclusion problems.

Then, the chapter introduces three self-stabilizing algorithms: one for *vertex coloring*, and two for *edge coloring*. The execution model considered in this chapter is the central daemon model, the simplest one discussed in the literature. This model assumes a centralized scheduler called the *central daemon* which *arbitrarily* selects one at a time of the privileged nodes to make a move. The selection made by the central daemon is unpredictable.

As a result, proving correctness of self-stabilizing systems becomes an important and difficult task in this field. This is because starting from *any arbitrary* initial state or *any possible* state after a transient fault, the system must have the ability to bring itself into a legitimate state in *any possible* execution sequence and remains hereafter in legitimate states if no transient fault occurs. The readers are referred to the papers (Chen, Yu, and Huang, 1991; Huang, 1993) for the proving techniques for self-stabilizing systems.

REFERENCES

Chen, N. S., Yu, F. P., & Huang, S. T. (1991). A self-stabilizing algorithm for constructing spanning trees. *Information Processing Letters, 39,* 147–151. doi:10.1016/0020-0190(91)90111-T

Dijkstra, E. W. (1974). Self stabilizing systems in spite of distributed control. *Communications of the ACM, 17,* 643–644. doi:10.1145/361179.361202

Gabow, H. N., & Kariv, O. (1982). Algorithms for edge coloring bipartite graphs and multigraphs. *SIAM Journal on Computing, 11*(1), 117–129. doi:10.1137/0211009

Ghosh, S., & Karaata, M. H. (1993). A self-stabilizing algorithm for coloring planar graph. *Distributed Computing, 7,* 55–59. doi:10.1007/BF02278856

Huang, S. T. (1993). Leader election in uniform rings. *ACM Transactions on Programming Language and Systems, 15*(3), 563–573. doi:10.1145/169683.174161

Huang, S. T., Hung, S. S., & Tzeng, C. H. (2005). Self-stabilizing coloration in anonymous planar networks. *Information Processing Letters, 95,* 307–312. doi:10.1016/j.ipl.2005.03.005

Huang, S. T., & Tzeng, C. H. (2009). Distributed edge coloration for bipartite networks. *Distributed Computing, 22*(1), 3–14. doi:10.1007/s00446-009-0082-8

Jensen, T. R., & Toft, B. (1995). *Graph coloring problems.* New York, NY: John Wiley & Sons.

Tzeng, C. H., Jiang, J. R., & Huang, S. T. (2007). A self-stabilizing ($\Delta+4$)-edge-coloring algorithm for planar graphs in anonymous uniform systems. *Information Processing Letters, 101*(4), 168–173. doi:10.1016/j.ipl.2006.09.004

Wuu, L. C., & Huang, S. T. (1995). Distributed self-stabilizing systems. *Journal of Information Science and Engineering, 11,* 307–319.

Chapter 6
Distributed Service Programming and Interoperability

José C. Delgado
Instituto Superior Técnico, Technical University of Lisbon, Portugal

ABSTRACT

The Web started as a means to navigate in hypermedia documents but has evolved to a pervasive Web of Services, raising distribution and interoperability problems. Web Services appeared as a solution but have grown to become a complex technology, leading many web application providers to adopt a much simpler architectural style, REST. Each style has advantages and disadvantages. As always, the trick is to learn from both sides and to use a flexible technology that can adapt and support both styles. This chapter establishes a model, based on resources, services, and processes, and discusses the various possible combinations, putting the current architectural styles into perspective. Based on this, this chapter proposes one single language to support several levels that are currently implemented in separate technologies: data (including schema, usually described in XML or JSON), interface (WSDL for Web Services and HTTP verbs for Restful applications), and behavior (usually done in BPEL or in a general programming language).

INTRODUCTION

The Web started out as a solution to the problem of browsing remote hypermedia documents (Berners-Lee, 1999). This was essentially an instance of the client-server paradigm geared for global human-to-human interaction, which in fact was the major factor that spurred all subsequent developments.

Up to then, computers could communicate, but this was basically limited to system-to-system or application-to-application data exchange, or human-to-human text messages in e-mail or newsgroups. This was the first time that a human could place a multimedia document in some server

DOI: 10.4018/978-1-4666-2533-4.ch006

and any other human, with a suitable client (the browser), could easily access that document and others accessible from it, with just a few clicks. The world of information had left the realm of specialists and reached the general user.

In those days, text was king. The main inspiration came from the printed document, which essentially was text sprinkled with other artifacts such as pictures and tables. The choice of a text markup document description language (HTML), based on another one coming from the printing world (SGML), seems natural and more than justified (Toshniwal & Agrawal, 2004).

Today, the world is rather different. Text is just one among other formats, with binary information (e.g., pictures, video, voice) taking a great part of the data bandwidth. Humans are no longer satisfied with information browsing and want added value in the form of services. Service providers recognize this value and are moving from face-to-face contact with the customers in physical shops to the virtual presence in sites that allow someone anywhere to instantly access services or buy products. Organizations are also customers of other organizations, in a value-added chain, and began using the same infrastructure to setup their information systems and integrate them with their partners' (enterprise integration), in which web services replaced specific application-to-application protocols.

The human-to-human Web of Documents has evolved into a global Web of Services (Tolk, 2006), in which the interacting parties are both humans and computer applications. Actually, contents are increasingly dynamic, generated on the fly according to some database, and the basic, manual hypermedia document creation (corresponding to the original human-to-human interaction) is decreasing its importance.

What is happening here? Services are replacing static documents and computer applications are filling in the web space once dominated by humans. Human-to-human interaction is now migrating to a higher level, the social network.

However, computer applications were left using the technology once developed to describe data in a user-oriented way (hypermedia document browsing).

Granted, there was a major evolution milestone when HTML evolved into XML, with presentation separated from data description, language extensibility and metadata introduced to self-describe the information. But XML is not really a general data description language, since it has a heavy document-style legacy (text and markup based, weak binary support, element and attribute discrimination, element sequence instead of a composition construct, and so on). Perfectly understandable in terms of evolutionary transition, but still a mismatch towards both humans (verbose and complex, aside trivial cases) and applications (limited regarding binary formats and inefficient due to parsing).

Web Services embodied another major evolution, the transition from the client-server to the service paradigm. But Web Services were built on top of the text document technology (XML) and the actual work must be done by a separate mechanism (either a general programming language or an orchestration language such as BPEL).

Everybody knows that backwards compatibility of a new technology can be both a bonus (things done so far still work) and a curse (many new features become a compromise instead of what they should be). Wrapping a new technology around an older one is just one way to evolve.

This chapter revisits this problem and considers the case of conceiving a Web of Services right from the start, using a service model rather than a document model as a seed, but that can still work with the current XML-based technologies. The main ideas can be summarized as follows:

- The basic web element is the (resource with a) service, not the document;
- The main paradigm is the service, not the process nor the client-server paradigms;

- One language is enough to contemplate several currently separated levels (data, service interface and service behavior, e.g., XML, WSDL and BPEL);
- This language is optimized both for applications and humans (with two formats, automatically synchronized);
- People interface the web not as mere clients but as fully fledged resources with services, which means that they can both invoke and offer services (in other words, humans become first class citizens in the Web of Services). This can be achieved if their web access device is a *browserver* (a browser and a server working together) instead of a mere browser (Delgado, 2012);
- Enterprise information systems should themselves be designed as a tierless Web of Services, not a centralized tier-based system.

The main problems at stake here and that we are trying to solve are:

- Service distribution and interoperability, as a support platform for higher level applications such as user interaction and enterprise integration. Although interoperability can be considered at several levels (Mykkänen & Tuomainen, 2008), this chapter only goes so far as to consider data and service interoperability levels;
- Ease of changeability and maintainability, crucial for the enterprise agility so important in this fast paced world, by using an application driven model while trying to avoid technology imposed features and restrictions.

BACKGROUND

It is interesting to note that it all started with a distributed interoperability problem. The main goal of the Web at its inception was to provide seamless access to hypermedia documents stored at remote servers. In spite of all the solutions found so far, the problem remains a research topic. The difference is that now the envisaged entity is the service, not the document, and interoperability goals have been broadened to include higher levels, namely ontology and behavior.

Service interoperability (Athanasopoulos, Tsalgatidou & Pantazoglou, 2006) implies that interaction occurs according to the assumptions and expectations of the involved services. This involves several levels (Mykkänen & Tuomainen, 2008), such as communication protocol, message structure, data format, service syntax, semantics and composition (Khadka *et al*, 2011) and even non-functional and social aspects (Loutas, Peristeras & Tarabanis, 2011). This is an area of active research, with interoperability levels above interface syntax still largely dependent on manual or semi-automated work from programmers and architects.

Regarding communication and distribution, HTTP-based servers remain the universal workhorses, to maintain compatibility with basic browsing and because firewalls are usually configured to support this protocol. However, HTTP has been designed for a specific context (client-server interaction, namely browsing) and is in fact a layer 7 (application) protocol in the OSI stack, thereby imposing relevant restrictions on the general communication model required by service-oriented systems (Reuther & Henrici, 2008). In particular, it does not support full-duplex, long running sessions required by general services such as those found at the enterprise level. This has spurred workaround technologies such as AJAX (Holdener, 2008) and Comet (Crane & McCarthy, 2008). Web Sockets, now part of the HTML5 world (Lubbers, Albers & Salim, 2010), removes this restriction, adds binary support and increases performance.

Data interoperability has largely followed the XML style, given the HTML momentum and in spite of verbosity and parsing inefficiency. The ability to self-describe data with a schema is one of XML's strongest points, albeit a great source of complexity. JSON is a simpler data format, but very popular in browser-based applications since it is based on a subset of JavaScript, and is a natural format for client-side processing. There is now a proposal for a data schema (Zyp, 2010).

In terms of behavior interoperability, the world is now divided into two main camps: service (Papazoglou, Traverso, Dustdar & Leymann, 2008) and resource (Overdick, 2007) oriented architectures (SOA and ROA).

SOA, which in practice means Web Services, emphasizes behavior (albeit limited to interfaces, with state and structure hidden in the implementation). ROA follows the REST principles (Fielding, 2000) and emphasizes structure and state, by exposing inner URIs (with interaction and application state separated and stored in the client and server, respectively, and behavior hidden in the dynamically changing structure and in the implementation of individual resources). Web Services are technologically more complex, but their model is a closer match to real world resources. REST is simpler and finer grained, but leans towards some restrictions (such as interaction statelessness) and is lower level (higher semantic gap between application concepts and REST resources), which for general, business-like applications means more effort to model, develop and maintain.

SOA and ROA are not really competitors, but complementary, each naturally a better fit to different areas of application domains (Pautasso, Zimmermann & Leymann, 2008). What is lacking is a way to bridge them and to tune up more to one side or another, according to the needs of a particular application.

Another important issue is that neither Web Services nor REST directly support behavior implementation, which must be supplied by components implemented in a generic programming language or by BPEL processes, which can be used both with Web Services (Henkel, Zdravkovic & Johannesson, 2004) and REST (Pautasso, 2009). In any case, another technology is needed. To support the service paradigm in an integrated way, behavior elements (instructions and/or operations) should be integrated with the data elements.

ENVISIONING A WEB OF SERVICES

The Vision

In any case, these are bottom up technologies, in the sense that they started out from the existing Web of Documents and mounted a Web of Services on top of it, maintaining compatibility but enduring the limitations imposed by the previous goals and options taken. For example, in the original Web, documents were passive and the only active entity was the user. Therefore, XML is a data description language and has no behavior elements.

Now let us do the opposite exercise. Imagine for a moment that the Web had not been invented yet and that we had the same goal of providing universal distributed interoperability, but with the capabilities that we know today, in a much more ambitious vision than the original Web. What would this new Web look like?

Figure 1 tries to depict possible scenarios, which include:

Figure 1. Visions of: (a) a Web of Documents and (b) a Web of Services. Arrows denote capability of initiating requests.

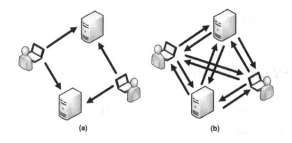

- Users have very dynamic interfaces, which can be automatically updated in real time as a result of remote events, when they occur and as if they have occurred locally;
- Users (through their interfaces) can invoke the functionality of computer applications;
- Users can interact directly, without resorting to remote (server based) computer applications;
- Computer applications can invoke each other's functionality;
- Computer applications can take the initiative of making requests to the users (to ask for some information that has not yet been supplied, for example).

The most striking feature of this vision is that users and computer applications are peers, active on equal terms (both can invoke functionality and be invoked) and first class citizens of a Web in which mutual (not client-server) interaction is the basic tenet. In fact, two users can interact directly, using only their personal computing devices and without resorting to a central server.

Each interacting entity is named a *resource* and its functionality is named a *service*. Documents are modeled as passive resources (their services do not invoke, only get invoked) and hyperlinks are references to other (possibly remote) resources. A click by a user on a link in a document sends a message to the referenced resource, which reacts as it sees fit (probably returning another document, to be displayed). But this is the same general message-based protocol used by all resources, user or computer application, with just transport or session level requirements, and not an application level protocol such as HTTP.

Do we have this vision in place today? Partially yes, but not natively, only as a result of several tricks that simulate a Web of Services on top of the Web of Documents, such as:

- Technologies such as Ajax and Comet need to solve fundamental client-server interac-

tivity issues that were not contemplated by HTTP;
- XML can only describe documents, not services;
- Web Services simulate services with documents that describe them (WSDL), but they have to be implemented in another technology (such as a programming language or a BPEL process);
- SOAP is tunneled on top of HTTP, introducing a layer of complexity;
- The REST architectural style seems to embody a simpler model, at a lower conceptual level, but what it does is to trade behavior complexity for state and resource structure complexity. This can be effective for some applications (typically those in which state diversity is more relevant than behavior diversity, such as user-level web applications), but for others it creates a model mismatch with application entities that needs to be bridged (Laitkorpi, Selonen & Systa, 2009) and that can make system development and maintenance harder.

All these technologies and solutions seem to be more influenced by the assumptions and decisions originally taken by the original Web (and subsequent developments) than by the requirements and semantics of the applications themselves, which naturally do not (should not) depend on the solution adopted.

We need to find a way of implementing this vision of Web of Services in a more general, native and application driven way, without favoring a behavior-first or state-first approach by design, to minimize mismatches and complexity, with the goal of turning modeling, implementation and changeability into easier tasks.

Resources, Services, and Processes

The ontology in this domain is far from being established and universally accepted. The words in the title of this section mean different things to different people. Therefore, in this section we establish our definitions (informal for the sake of brevity and simplicity) and lay out our model, which can be informally and briefly described in the following way:

- A *resource* is anything of any nature (material, virtual, conceptual, noun, action, and so on) that embodies a meaningful, complete and discrete concept (makes sense by itself and can be distinguished from, although interact with, other resources);

- A resource can be atomic (an indivisible whole) or structured (recursively composed of other resources, its *components*, with respect to which it performs the role of *container*). Each component can only have one direct container (yielding a strong composition model, in a tree shaped resource structure);

- The *interior* of a resource is the set of that resource and all its components. The *exterior* is the set of all other existing resources;

- Each resource has at least one property that allows to uniquely identifying it (physical coordinates, name, IP address, URI, etc.) among all existing resources. A *reference* to a resource X is a resource that implements that property, allowing direct interaction with X, without having to follow the tree shaped container hierarchy (in fact, transforming the tree into a directed graph);

- Resources are created in a decentralized way (there is no central resource factory), using some form of replication, and follow a lifecycle that ends by its destruction and is independent of other resources' lifecycle (except its containers). Structured resources have a mechanism to create and destroy its components. Destroying one resource implies destroying all the resources in its interior;

- Resources can *migrate* (move) from one container to another, changing the system's structure. This may involve a change in the resource's lifecycle, evolving to a migration stage, after which is moved and then evolved to an operational stage at the new container;

- Resources can have state, either immutable or changeable. The state of a structured resource is (recursively) the set of the states (if any) of the components in its interior;

- Resources interact exclusively by sending *stimuli* to each other (there can be no direct access to the state of a resource from its exterior, either to read or to change). A resource X can only send stimuli to its direct components and resources accessible by travelling the tree hierarchy upwards from X. A stimulus sent to a reference is automatically forwarded to the referenced resource;

- A stimulus is a resource, created in the interior of one resource (the *sender*) and migrated to the interior of another (the *receiver*), where it generates a *reaction*. Reactions can be of any sort, such as changing the resource's state, creating further resources, deleting existing resources, sending stimuli to other resources (including the sender and the receiver) or just plain ignoring. The concrete reaction does not depend on the sender, only on the stimulus and on the receiver (and its state). However, the sender can also be affected, if the receiver reacts back (sends a stimulus back to the sender);

- If two interacting resources, X and Y, are not in direct contact, they can use an intermediate resource (a *channel*), with which both are in direct contact and through which the stimulus migrates (that is the reaction of the channel when it receives the stimulus). The channel can be a structured resource, to cater for routing;

- A *service* is a set of logically related reactions by a resource. In other words, it is a *facet* of that resource that makes sense in terms of the envisaged system. A service is pure behavior (albeit concrete reactions may depend on implementation and state) that needs a resource (and eventually its components) to be implemented. In most cases, only one service will be defined for each resource, but in other cases, usually more complex, it makes sense to organize the full set of the resource's reactions into several services. Note that a service is defined in terms of reactions to stimuli (an external view) and not in terms of state or state transitions (an internal view);

- A resource *X* that sends a stimulus to a resource *Y* is in fact invoking a service of *Y*, as long as the reaction to that stimulus belongs to that service, in what constitutes a *service transaction* between these two resources and in which the resources *X* and *Y* perform the role of *service consumer* and *service provider*, respectively. A service transaction can entail other service transactions, as part of the (chain) reaction to the stimulus on part of the service provider;

- A *process* is a graph of all service transactions that are allowed to occur, starting with a service transaction initiated at some resource *X* and ending with a final service transaction, which neither reacts back nor initiates new service transactions. This process corresponds to a use case of resource *X* and usually involves other resources as service transactions flow (including loops, eventually).

In summary, resources entail structure, state and behavior. Services refer only to behavior, without implying a specific implementation. Processes are a view on the behavior sequencing and flow along services, which are implemented by resources. This is a model inspired in real life,

applicable not only to computer science but also to humans (themselves resources) and any other type of resources.

For physical resources, the strong composition model is the most adequate. No two resources can share the same physical space and any object is located inside another. Moving an object from one box to the other is actually a migration as described above.

In terms of services, the *society metaphor* is the most familiar to us. Some resource (person or organization) executes an activity as a request of and on behalf of another. Actually, service transactions constitute the foundations of our society. Each resource, from the outside, constitutes a black box which we deal with only by indirect means (by sending it a message). Nobody accesses directly the brain of another person! Each person, organization, and so on, can offer a different service.

This means that the model described above is flexible and natural, constituting a good starting point for distributed system modeling. At this level, there are no restrictions. Stimuli can even be analog and time unbounded. In practical terms and limiting our model to the computer science domain, we discretize and constrain this model in the following way:

- Only digital resources of finite size are considered. Analog resources are discretized and humans are modeled by their roles in the system and other resources they use as interfaces (such as browsers);
- There is a set of predefined resources, atomic and structured. New resources can only be created by replicating an existing resource, predefined or not;
- The lifecycle of a resource is discretized into a finite number of stages, of which Figure 2 represents an example. In each stage, a resource can have a different digital representation, which can only have a finite number of different states. For completeness, Figure 2 also shows that a re-

Figure 2. An example of the lifecycle of resources

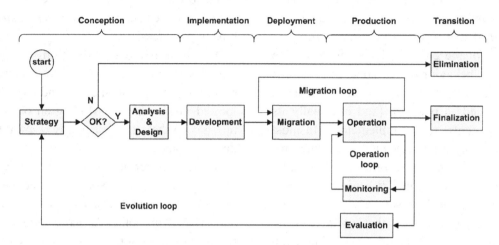

source needs to be monitored (for health checking and management) and evaluated (to check conformance with goals). A resource can have a finite number of versions, which can coexist, or be destroyed;

- Migration of a resource from one container *X* to another *Y* involves changing the representation of the resource to a passive representation (a byte stream), destroying the resource at *X*, sending the byte stream to *Y* and creating a new component in *Y* from that byte stream. This corresponds to the migration loop in Figure 2 (cold start migration, from a permanent store, is called *deployment*);

- Stimuli become *messages* of finite size (time unbounded streams can be modeled as a sequence of messages);

- The number of possible reactions of a resource to messages is discretized and modeled by a finite number of *operations*. Each operation knows only how to react to a limited set of messages;

- Reception of a message by a resource causes the execution of an operation that knows how to react to it. The mechanism that determines this capability is left unspecified at this level. A *policy* needs to be

drawn up on what to do in case a message is received by a resource for which there is no such operation;

- Each operation is modeled by a finite number of *actions* (atomic behavior-only resources);

- Channel transmission time is non-zero, but bounded (if a given time is exceeded, a fault may be assumed). This does not preclude start processing an incoming message before fully receiving it.

Architectural and Applicational Styles

The three main concepts (resources, services and processes) lead to three main architectural styles grasped by the market and industry, according to which is the main concept that guides system modeling:

- Process-oriented architectures (van der Aalst, 1999). This is the classical approach to isolated or loosely integrated information systems, before the advent of XML-based electronic services;

- Service-oriented architectures, or SOA (Earl, 2005). Albeit not necessarily so,

Figure 3. The SRP triangle (S: Service, R: Resource, P: Process)

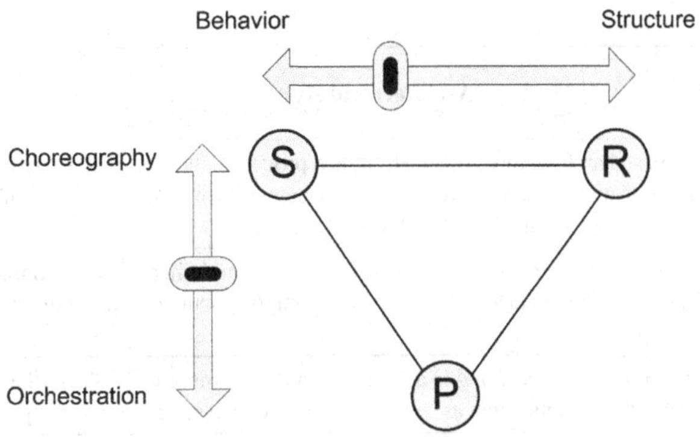

Table 1. Limits of architectural variability

	Pure behavior	Pure structure
Pure choreography	There are only services (with one resource per service, just for implementation). One service starts and invokes others. Each service coordinates the services it invokes, in a decentralized fashion	There are only resources (each implementing the same set of operations). One resource starts by invoking operations on its links. Each resource manages its links, in a decentralized fashion
Pure orchestration	All services are primitive (black box). All the programmable behavior is defined at processes	One resource has links to all others that are relevant and implements the entire functionality

current implementations of SOA usually resort to Web Services and do not follow a pure service-oriented style, since basic functionality is modeled by services but these need to be orchestrated and choreographed by processes (Barros, Dumas & Oaks, 2006), using a language such as BPEL. Nevertheless, services are the innovative factor;

- Resource-oriented architectures, or ROA (Overdick, 2007). In this style, everything is modeled as a resource, including behavior components (operations). Structure (including URIs) and state become the dominant factors and each resource's service is reduced to a CRUD style (create, read, update and delete), following the REST principles enunciated by Fielding (2000). The behavior complexity of SOA is traded for structure and state complexity. Lower level than SOA, has some significant ad-

vantages for client-server web applications with many clients. Services and processes are secondary concepts, used mainly as modeling, intermediate steps (Laitkorpi, Selonen & Systa, 2009).

It is important to acknowledge that any active system (involving some form of activity execution) includes all the concepts defined in the previous section. After all, these are general concepts, stemming from system analysis (problem space) and not from system design (architectural solution space). Which emphasis is given to each of them and to what degree they are combined yields the architectural style of the system. Figure 3 shows the relationship between them and Table 1 describes the limits of the corresponding variability.

Considering again the three main concepts and the relevance given to each in system modeling and design, we can in fact explore the full range

Table 2. Architectural styles and a qualitative assessment of their adequacy to two applicational styles (C-S: client-server and P-P:peer to peer)

Main concepts supported	Architectural style	Applicational style	
		C-S	P-P
P	Pure process-based architectures (everything is a process), stateless. Useful for pipe-line type of applications (such as production processes), in which a process produces an output from an input, without side effects.	− −	+
S	Pure-service oriented (everything is a service), with no implementation (resources missing). Can be useful for abstract system modeling or documentation, but not for execution.	+	+
R	Pure resource-oriented (everything is a resource). One example is REST. In the general case, REST constraints (such as interaction statelessness) need not be imposed.	+ +	− −
P + S	Services serve as functionality primitives and are orchestrated by processes. Typical implementations of SOA fall into this case. Alternatively, a large service's operations can be implemented with processes (a department modeled as a service, for example).	+	+ +
P + R	Classical process-based architectures with state (database), used either to implement a classical stand-alone information system or in enterprise integration.	+	+
S + R	Classical distributed system architecture, in which each resource offers an arbitrary service and is responsible for maintaining its internal data and for choreographing its own behavior. There are no central, orchestrating processes. Resource granularity is medium-low. Historically this corresponds to RPC style architectures, but interoperability today is at the level of a data description language (such as XML).	+	+ +
P + S + R	This architectural style supports all combinations of architectural styles and therefore should be the most flexible and a good fit for most application styles. There are currently no market single solutions at this level, although there are academic efforts towards integrating the service and resource orientations and BPEL has been shown to work under the resource-oriented approach. This chapter makes a proposal for this architectural style.	+ +	+ +

of architectural styles and their adequacy to applicational styles, as depicted in Table 2.

We consider two applicational styles (seemingly the most relevant), which can be identified in Figure 1:

- Client-server, in which many clients are expected for each server. Scalability and performance are the most important issues, given the high number of client requests that a server must support, concurrently. This style is typical of many Web applications;
- Peer to peer. This has nothing to do with file sharing P2P systems and only reflects that interacting parties are peers in similar terms and none has a clear dominance role regarding the others. This style is typical of

enterprise applications, usually in the area of enterprise integration, and the number of parties is usually small. Application interoperability is the main issue.

The classification used is only qualitative and is based essentially on scalability and modeling alignment (ease of expressing the application semantics) between the application styles and the architectural styles used to implement them.

Pure architectural styles are hard to find in practice. Even RESTful applications have frequently several variations and violations of the model. Pure RESTful resources usually implement different services because the semantics of the operations is different. Only the interface (not the semantics) must be uniform. Mixed styles, in

Table 3. Classification of resources by separation of concerns

Kind of resource	Structure	State	Interface	Behavior	Example
Data	Atomic	Immutable	Fixed	Fixed	Atomic constant value (e.g., 3) or a reference (e.g. URI)
		Changeable			Atomic variable
	Structured	Immutable			Structured constant value (e.g., an array initializer)
		Changeable			Structured variable (e.g., a list or an array)
Behavior	Atomic	None	Fixed	Fixed	Simple instruction without result
		Immutable			Simple instruction with result
	Structured	None	Fixed	Changeable	Structured instruction
		None	Changeable	Changeable	Operation without result
		Immutable			Operation with result

which two of the main concepts are combined, is the most common case.

The basic idea is that processes and general services have a good matching to peer style applications, because scalability is not a requirement as important as in the client-server style applications and their flexibility allows a good match between application concepts and architecture entities. Services receive a top grade because service-oriented modeling leads to a better match to real world systems than process-based modeling (for the same reason that object-oriented programming leads to a better modeling match than classic structured programming).

The resource-oriented style (R) shines in client-server style of application, in which it is the best match (good scalability and performance, allied to a small functional variability), but entails a semantic model rather different from the distributed object-oriented view that is typical of applications built out of a set of interacting peers.

The last architectural style (R+S+P) is the most flexible, as long as it supports the various styles, but does not exist as a single implementation and is the subject of active research (Zhang, Li & Chi, 2008; He, 2009), including the work described in this chapter. In simple terms, it can be seen as a SOA with structure and state or as a ROA in which resources can have any type of service, with a process modeled as an operation of a large grained service.

Resources: Composition, Distribution, and Interoperability

Resources are the backbone of any system, as the only entities that we can interact with. Services and processes are just abstractions of that interaction. Therefore, it is important to detail what a resource can be and how it can interoperate with other resources.

Table 3 depicts several kinds of resources, divided into two main categories (data and behavior) and classified according to their structure, state, interface and behavior. A typical resource will be a composition of several resources exhibiting different characteristics.

In practice, however, this complete separation of characteristics does not fully exist. For example, a data component resource has state but must also exhibit a basic getter and setter behavior. But clearly a data component is different from an operation with a behavior that is programmable by composing its internal components.

There must be a set of predefined components, either from the data (data types) and behavior (instructions) categories. Modeling the system is defining new resources be composing predefined and previously defined ones.

Data description languages, such as XML and JSON, cover only the data side of the issue. Web Services specify the data interface of the services, but not behavior components. This must be done by programming languages, such as BPEL, Java, C#, etc., in which a program is a structured resource, built by composing lower level data (variables) and behavior (operations) resources. RESTful applications use data resources (including references, the URIs) that include implicit behavior, in the form of the verbs supported uniformly by all resources. This behavior, however, must also be implemented by a separate language.

Two resources, *X* and *Y*, are said to be *distributed* (relatively to each other) if their lifecycles are not interdependent. This precludes a component and its container from being distributed, since the component depends on what happens to the container. In particular, a component cannot survive the container and migration of a container implies migrating all its components as well. The only way for a resource to interact with another, in a distributed way, is to have a reference (a predefined resource with automatic forwarding behavior) to it. Resource distribution is a concept that has nothing to do with geographical separation.

In this context, the notion of a *server* is that of a top-level resource that has resources (*applications*) as its components and that most likely will also include a *directory* resource (a list of references to these applications). By definition, servers are distributed, in relation to each other, but are connected to a channel (the Internet) and possess references (URIs) to the servers they want to interact with.

In the same way, an application is a structure of resources, implements some service(s) and has a global identifier (URI), formed from the server's URI and the resource path within the server. Applications are distributed in relation to

the others, but not to the server, and can migrate from server to server (albeit changing its URI).

For applications to interact, their identifiers need to have global visibility (which URIs provide), messages must have the concept of addressability and servers must have a dispatch behavior (analyze messages to find the application addressed and forward the message to it).

All this is consistent with today's vision of the Web, including REST and Web Service based applications. Note that we haven't restricted the message protocol to HTTP or some other similar protocol. Only a transport level protocol is needed.

But *connectivity* is not enough. Interacting resources must also have *interoperability*, which essentially means that, if a resource *X* sends a message to *Y*, which answers back, then:

1. The message sent by *X* must *comply* with what *Y* expects and is able to deal with;
2. The corresponding reaction (and eventual side effects) of *Y* must conform to the expectations of *X* (the objective a sending a message to *Y*, in the first place);
3. The answer from *Y* to *X* (also a message) must conform to what *X* expects and is able to deal with.

This three step interaction, which forms a *service transaction*, is a simplified version of a more general transaction pattern (Dietz, 2006), which contemplates other variants, including asynchrony and cancelling the request during step 2. Here, we will only tackle its basic aspects, regarding interoperability and only in what steps 1 and 3 are concerned. Semantic conformance, corresponding to step 2, is much harder to verify and is outside the scope of this chapter.

The notions entailed by interoperability, *compliance* (Kokash & Arbab, 2009) and *conformance* (Black et al., 1987), are fundamental even if only the syntactical interface is verified. Informally, conformance translates to *substitutability*, in the sense that a resource *X* conforms to a resource *Y* if it can replace *Y* wherever *Y* is expected, without breaking the semantics expected from *Y*. In object-oriented programming, conformance is usually achieved by inheritance and constitutes the basis for polymorphism in method invocation. Compliance translates to *usability*, in the sense that the invoker of the method must specify actual arguments that comply with (satisfy) the method's formal arguments, so that it can use that method correctly.

Unfortunately, many languages check interoperability by using the names of the types (classes) of the objects, which means in practice that the lifecycles of the two objects (the one calling the method and the owner of that method) are interdependent and this technique cannot be used in distributed systems.

Instead of using names to identify types at compile time, what we need to check is *structural interoperability* (Läufer, Baumgartner & Russo, 2000; Kim & Shen, 2007; Kokash & Arbab, 2009), in which the structures of two resources are compared, according to some set of rules, to see if one complies in requests and conforms in responses to the other. Predefined resources have predefined interoperability rules and structured resources are recursively checked, component by component, until predefined resources are reached or a mismatch is found. These rules may allow component order to be different, as long as these components have some identifiable designation, such as name or a tag (of the kind found in XML, for example).

XML has some form of structural matching, since unknown or irrelevant tags can be ignored by a XML processor, but there is no notion of compliance or conformance. Note that these are asymmetric by definition (*X* may comply with *Y* without *Y* complying with *X* and *X* may conform to *Y* without *Y* conforming to *X*), as it happens with inheritance, whereas interoperability in XML is achieved by using the same schema in the producer and consumer of a document, in a symmetric arrangement.

This should not be confused with schema matching (Jeong, Lee, Cho & Lee, 2008), which measures similarity among schemas as tool to ease the integration of heterogeneous systems. Interoperability checking is meant for the design and operational stages of a system's lifecycle, to decide whether a resource knows how to cope with an incoming message or to send a correct message to another resource.

IMPLEMENTING DISTRIBUTED SERVICES

We have discussed the two main current architectural styles to implement distributed services, SOA and ROA, and asserted that:

- SOA has a very general model but is complex, embodying a plethora of standards and technologies to simulate a Web of Services on top of a Web of Documents. Tools help, but complexity is there;
- ROA is much simpler, since it maps almost directly onto the basic Web architecture (following the principles of the HTTP design) but are at a much lower level, entailing a relevant semantic gap to applications that do not follow that architecture;
- In either case, behavior needs to be implemented in a separate language (such as BPEL or some general programming language).

What we actually need is:

- A language to describe and implement resources, down from mere structure and content description (document level) up to behavior (service level), in a common, integrated way, with support for distribution and interoperability;
- A platform to execute resources and implement the services.

A Service Language

We have designed such as language, which we named SIL (Service Implementation Language), and implemented its compiler and execution platform, which includes a server. Its main features are:

- It implements the model previously described, with structure, state, behavior, with the asymmetric nature of services and structural interoperability, instead of the symmetric model and data only features, characteristic of languages such as XML;
- A (structured) resource can include all the kinds of components referred to in Table 3;
- Supports asynchronous concurrency and the distributed nature of resources (for instance, assignment has a copy semantics, not reference);
- Interoperability is achieved by structural compliance and conformance, not by schema sharing;
- Two representation formats: text for people and binary for computers, with binary derived from text by compilation, instead of parsing. The advantage is that compilation can be done once at design time and the binary representation used from then onwards, as long as the contract between two resources does not change;
- The binary representation includes a self-description, just like XML Schema, but that is obtained automatically from the text representation by considering only its public part (the language itself includes the schema information), instead of using a separate description. Another distinctive feature is that this self-description describes only the corresponding resource and not a set of similar resources. This allowed by structured interoperability;
- It is communications protocol agnostic (requires only a transport level protocol).

Program 1 gives an idea of what the text representation of SIL looks like, implementing a very simple travel planner, written in service style. By design, its look and feel is similar to an object-oriented language (with data and behavior components), but in which interoperability is made by structural compliance and conformance, not by name, assignment involves copying (no pointers) and there is native support for distributed, asynchronous concurrency. At first look, it bears some resemblance with JSON, given the curly brackets used to define resources and the colon used to define resource components.

Any SIL text file is considered a resource, with implicit curly brackets (the delimiters of structured resources) at the beginning and end. In between, we can specify definitions, data components, instructions and operations. When a resource is created, its body is executed and:

- Its data components are (recursively) created (and executed);
- Instructions are executed but do not create data components;
- Definitions and operations only come into play when executed or invoked.

All statically defined components are created and initialized when their container is created and initialized. Assignment involves copying. There are no pointers, only references to distributed resources, which can be located anywhere. Resources can also dynamically create new components and delete them.

Program 1 starts by specifying four definitions. These are actually the equivalent of WSDL of remote resources, to support compile-time structural conformance checking. date and time have only data and airlineCompany and hotelCompany have only operations, but both could be present. These definitions are called SPID (SIL Public Interface Descriptor) and contain all the information necessary for interoperability. For example, the SPID of the myTrip component is identical to its defini-

Program 1. A simple SIL example

```
define date as { year: integer; month: [1..12]; day: [1..31] };
define time as { hour: [0..23]; minute: [0..59] };
define airlineCompany as {
    bookFlight: operation ({origin: string; destiny: string; onDate: date} ->
            {company: string; flightRef: string; flightTime: time});
    getFlightPrice: operation (string -> number);
};
define hotelCompany as {
    bookroom: operation ({arrival: date; stayNights?: [1..30]} -> number);
};
myTrip: {
    myAirline: airlineCompany:= reference{…some URI…};
myHotel: hotelCompany:= reference{…some URI…};
myDestiny: string;
flightInfo: {
        flightDate: date;
        flightTime: time;
        flightRef: string;
        flightPrice: number;     // integer would not account for cents
    };
    hotelInfo: {
        arrivalDate: date;
        nights: [1..infinity];
        roomRate: number;
    };
    private travelMoney: 500.00;            // my pocket money budget
    bookTrip: operation ({travelDate: date; travelDays: integer;
     whereTo: string}) {
        myDestiny = whereTo;
        flightInfo = myAirline.bookFlight <-| {onDate: travelDate;
origin: "my town";
destiny: whereto};
        hotelInfo =     {roomRate: myHotel.bookRoom <-- {travelDate; travel-
Days-1};
                arrivalDate: travelDate;
             nights: travelDays-1;
            };
    };
    getTripCost: operation (-> number) {     // no parameters, only return
value
        reply flightInfo.flightPrice +
hotelInfo.stayDays * hotelInfo.roomRate +
```

continued on following page

Program 1. Continued

```
travelMoney;
     };
};
myTrip.bookTrip <-- {{2012;8;5}; 3; "Hawaii"};
myExpense: myTrip.getTripCost <--;        // invoke operation without parameters
```

tion, with the exception of the travelMoney and the bodies of the operations, which are private. Any operation declared as private would also not be included. SPIDs are generated automatically by the compiler and made available at a resource directory, much like WSDLs, to include in remote resources.

SPIDS are not mandatory. If, for instance, the myHotel component was declared as myHotel: any;, the invocation my Hotel.bookRoom<-- {travelDate,travelDays-1)} would still work, but the compiler could not check the interface and interoperability checking would have to be done at runtime. A hashcode value, included with the SPID, allows to detect, in each message sent, whether the receiver resource has been changed since the SPID was generated and used by the sender resource.

In terms of data, SIL has a set of predefined resource types (much like any language) and one general composition mechanism, a structured resource, between curly brackets. Components are not defined with a type, which is then instantiated. Resources are created by replication, not instantiation, and have a value and a variability. This means that integer, for example, does not refer to a type, but really to a predefined resource with value 0 and variability from $-\infty$ to $+\infty$. Using it to define the component year of date creates a replica of it (same value, same variability), to which is given the name year. Since date is a definition, this only occurs when it is used to define a component, such as flightDate. Ranges such as [1..12] conform to integer but have limited variability.

The example in Program 1 can be further described as follows:

- The myAirline and myHotel components of myTrip are initialized not with the default values (which in this case would be just replicas of the SPIDs, with default values), but with references to global resources, which basically have a server URI and a path of the resource within it. This could (should) be obtained from a registry (not shown for simplicity). The references automatically forward messages to the referenced resources, using the runtime support platform;

- The structured components flightInfo and hotelInfo are initialized first with default values;

- The component travelMoney is private and constant (no variability);

- Operations are actually behavior components and are declared in a way similar to data components, but with argument and result values declared inside curve parentheses and separated by the -> token. Any of them can be omitted. There can be only one argument, but it can be structured, just like the result;

- When the operation bookFlight is invoked in the body of the bookTrip operation, the three values specified constitute a structured resource that is passed as an argument to the resource referenced by myAirline, using structural compliance. Note that the values are in a different order, but they are assigned to the correct one, since the argument names are specified. These could have been omitted, specifying only the values, but then they would have to be placed in the right order, as it happens in the travelDate argument, which is structured, as shown by the bookFlight operation;

- When the bookFlight operation replies, its result value (the structure of which is specified in the declaration of this operation, following the -> token) is assigned to the flightInfo component. This also requires compliance between the result value and flightInfo. Note that extra components, not defined in flightInfo, are ignored;

- The assignment to hotelInfo illustrates how a structured value can be dynamically constructed and used to assign a new (structured) to a component. Compliance is also used and the components can be in any order;

- Operations are actually resources without state, only behavior, and are invoked by sending them messages, with a message send operator, synchronous (<--) or asynchronous (<-|). In the latter case, illustrated by the invocation of the bookFlight operation,, the runtime support returns a *future* (Schippers, 2009) immediately, upon sending the message. The future is assigned to flightInfo and execution continues, concurrently with the processing of the request by the airline company. When the operation replies, the returned value replaces the future. If the future is accessed in the interim, which is likely to happen due to the invocation of the getTripCost operation (which accesses a component in flightInfo), the process that attempts it is suspended and automatically resumed when the future is replaced, in a dataflow fashion.

SIL also supports REST-style applications, in the following ways:

- Resources exist, with a path (using a dot notation) from the root resource at each SIL platform server, and expose their public components (while hiding the private ones, such as travelMoney). In Program 1, a resource that exists is the one identified by root.myTrip.hotelInfo.arrivalDate. This is a static (program declared) component, but components can be created and deleted dynamically;

- Operations are resources and can be sent messages (as long as they comply with the operation's input argument);

- Since resources can have arbitrary operations defined, nothing prevents from defining the same set of operations for all the resources (namely, CRUD based). Pautasso (2009) suggests extending BPEL to support this type of operations, but there is no need for extensions here;

- Behavior can be implemented in the same language in which the resources are specified. The same happens with results and even with the parameters passed to the operations (SIL is not tied to HTTP);

- While not explored here, parameters passed to operations are normal resources, which means that they can have operations. The structural interoperability supports this. In terms of REST, this means that a resource can be *transferred* from one SIL platform to another (server to server or server to *browserver*, see future research below) and carry its own state and behavior, while maintaining a uniform interface, and be executed in the new platform, *closure* style;

- Stateless interactions can be achieved by storing the result of operations at a client. In fact, myTrip has already been setup that way, albeit not explicitly with REST-style as a goal.

Other aspects, such as reaping the benefits of caching and how to control it, have not been dealt with yet.

A Server Platform

SIL requires a runtime support system, to deal with the message based communication and to implement the behavior. Although SIL is compiled, the generated code is interpreted, much in the line of a Java virtual machine. The instructions generated are binary and are called *silcodes*. The format of a compiled resource is exactly the same for sending it in a message and for storing it in a persistent medium. A silcode is a sequence of bytes with predefined format, in which the first byte determines the meaning of the bytes that follow, using a modified version of the TLV (Tag, Length and Value) scheme used by ASN.1 (Dubuisson, 2000).

According to the generic resource model described previously, a resource can vary its representation, according to the lifecycle stage it is in. To be migrated (the case of a message being sent), a resource must be in the migration stage, as shown in Figure 2. In this stage, the representation of the resource contains all the information necessary to reactivate it to an operation state, at another server. Migration here is to be taken in a broad sense, including storage (which can be thought of as a resource including only components in migration state). A message is a normal resource and follows these rules.

This concept is actually almost universal, and the common representation is the byte stream, which sent through a network is called a message and stored in a persistent medium is usually a file. Libraries of programming languages usually have a means to serialize (as a byte stream) the operational representations of objects.

Therefore, we use the *byte stream* as the common denominator and the unit of processing and migration (including communication). We also want to retain a degree of compatibility with existing technologies, namely those XML, JSON and HTTP based. A stream is merely a sequence of bytes, with no format or endianess (byte order) defined. The *theme* of a stream is the set format and organization rules that define the contents of the stream and allow a (software) processor to interpret its meaning and do something useful with it. A theme may be identified by a specific sequence of bytes (probably using UTF-8 encoding, such as "SIL" or "<?xml") or may require some deeper content inspection.

When a message is received by the SIL server, it checks with each of the defined handlers whether it recognizes it. The first to achieve it gets the message for further processing. In this way, if a message is XML or has some other non-SIL format, the platform is still able to process it, as long as a corresponding handler (an XML parser, for example) is available.

The platform is also able to deal with HTTP and Web Sockets, so that a given URI can be used both for current market technologies and SIL. Although this is far from backwards compatibility, it is a step towards an evolution migration path that we always want as smooth as possible.

DISCUSSION AND RELATED WORK

The current WS-style versus REST-style bears strong similarities with a debate that occurred 30 years ago, in the computer architecture realm. In the beginning of the 80's, in the dawn of the personal computer, complexity was on the rise. The instruction set of computers were growing and architectures were adding more and more features, with the goal of making them more and more powerful and of better supporting the software. Something that today seems to be happening to WS-* technologies.

Unfortunately, instructions more complex meant hardware more complex and longer circuit delays, and even simpler instructions began suffering with this and taking proportionately more time to execute. Researchers started to note not only this but, above all, that the complex instructions were actually seldom used, if at all (Patterson & Ditzel, 1980). Due to complexity and semantic gaps, compilers were not able to benefit from complex instructions and were generating, for the most part, only simpler instructions. It should be stressed that computer architects were not programming and programmers were not designing computers.

A new generation of computers appeared, dubbed RISC (for Reduced Set Instruction Computers), with only a handful of simple instructions, architecture completely open to the compiler and above all designed together with the compilers. These machines were shown to perform better than their CISC (Complex Instruction Set Computers), with emphasis on simplicity and a good match between software and hardware. This bears similarities with REST-style today.

By the early nineties, it became fashionable to have an instruction set as small as possible and RISC manufacturers flourished. However, RISCs didn't win the war and CISCs didn't disappear, far from it. CISCs learned their lesson from RISCs and, without dogmas, asserted that there is nothing wrong in having complexity in the hardware as long as (i) it is truly useful (performance is always a goal) and (ii) does not slow down simple instructions. The secret lies in balancing and matching the capabilities of technology with the requirements of applications.

It is likely that Web Services and RESTful applications will also follow this path. Big companies, with Web scale applications, have moved towards REST-style APIs, in search of simplicity and a better match to the application style. But it is only natural to look as business and other type of applications and try to check how well the REST architectural style can support them (Xu, Zhu, Liu & Staples, 2008; Pautasso, 2009; Li & Chou, 2010; Zou, Mei & Wang, 2010).

REST itself is not at rest and extensions and new perspectives are being proposed, trying to broaden its spectrum of applicability. Inoue, Asakura, Sato and Takahashi (2010) note that session state is needed for authentication and propose an extension to deal with this. Kumaran et al. (2008) propose an information centric process model, centering the resource concept on business entities instead of workflow activity instances.

Others propose to represent and transfer not only data but behavior as well. Xu, Zhu, Kannengiesser and Liu (2010) describe a method to expose process fragments (described declaratively as reusable workflow patterns) as resources and to map business process concepts onto the usual HTTP-style of CRUD operations. Erenkrantz, Gorlick, Suryanarayana and Taylor (2007) go a step further and propose extensions to achieve a Computational REST (CREST), in which the basic entities are computational resources, in the form of continuations (Queinnec, 2003), and provide a base model for code mobility. The client is no longer a mere interface to the user but a computational engine, capable of executing these resources. State transfer is a side effect of this execution.

FUTURE RESEARCH DIRECTIONS

Our view is that all these developments are moving towards the service-oriented vision that we have depicted in Figure 1, in which clients become peers with computational execution capability, with an underlying model that smooths out the mismatches and limitations of current technologies.

Besides continuing the work on SIL, its platform and assessing how well it supports the architectural and applicational styles described previously, we will invest on contributing to make that vision a reality, in two main additional lines of research:

- The *browserver* (Delgado, 2012), a Web access device for users, composed of a browser and a server in tight cooperation.

This corresponds to the client with execution capacity identified by Erenkrantz, Gorlick, Suryanarayana and Taylor (2007), by using true service-oriented technology, not Ajax. It implements the service-oriented vision of Figure 1, in which users can invoke each other's service directly, in a serverless fashion, and receive requests and notifications from a server. We have implemented a first version using an Ajax based implementation (Direct Web Remoting), but the objective is not to produce an implementation with a SIL server and an open-source browser implementation;

- *Tierless enterprise architectures.* Classic information systems are centralized and based on a horizontal segregation of tiers (presentation, business logic and data). This is not a good match for distributed applications. It would be better if these systems were modeled as a set of cooperating services (each implemented by a resource that matches an application level concept), even if they were to reside in the same server and logically separate entities were to be physically mapped onto the same database. Virtual distribution right from the start provides a better support for interoperability and subsequent changes. SIL will be used as the tool to model and implement this approach.

CONCLUSION

We have briefly described a language (SIL) as a solution to the distribution and interoperability problems that are at the heart of the Web, with the goal of implemented a vision of a unified Web of Services, in which both users and applications are first class citizens and both can interact freely as peers. In particular, the direct interaction between users must be possible, without having to resort to servers, and the tools, languages and protocols should be the same to develop applications that interface users or that interact with other applications.

SIL was designed to support this vision by adopting the following goals:

- To implement distributed applications as services with a technology natively conceived for services and not a simulation of services with documents, which is basically what Web Services provide;
- To optimize the representation of resources both for people and for computers (in a synchronized way), instead of using one single representation, text based;
- To use a single language and platform to describe structure, state and behavior, capable of fulfilling the role of several technologies there are needed today, such as XML, WSDL, SOAP and BPEL;
- To base interoperability on structural compliance and conformance, not on the schema sharing mechanism of XML;
- To support resource migration, including data and code;
- To be protocol agnostic, requiring only transport level (such as provided by Web Sockets);
- To provide native support for binary data;
- To be able to deal with current technologies, at the platform level, by invoking the appropriate handlers (such as a XML parser).

We have also discussed the suitability of SIL to support the service and resource-oriented architectural styles. By including structure, state and behavior, it is a complete and integrated solution, able to fulfill the role of several current technologies, in an integrated way. We hope that it constitutes a small contribution to improve the quality of distributed applications and to make their development and maintenance an easier task.

REFERENCES

Athanasopoulos, G., Tsalgatidou, A., & Pantazoglou, M. (2006). Interoperability among heterogeneous services. In *International Conference on Services Computing* (pp. 174-181). IEEE Computer Society Press.

Barros, A., Dumas, M., & Oaks, P. (2006). Standards for web service choreography and orchestration: Status and perspectives. In Bussler, C. (Eds.), *Business Process Management Workshops* (*Vol. 3812*, pp. 61–74). Lecture Notes in Computer Science Berlin, Germany: Springer-Verlag. doi:10.1007/11678564_7

Berners-Lee, T. (1999). *Weaving the web: The original design and ultimate destiny of the World Wide Web by its inventor*. New York, NY: HarperCollins Publishers.

Black, A. (1987). Distribution and abstract types in Emerald. *IEEE Transactions on Software Engineering*, *13*(1), 65–76. doi:10.1109/TSE.1987.232836

Crane, D., & McCarthy, P. (2008). *Comet and reverse Ajax: The next-generation Ajax 2.0*. Berkely, CA: Apress.

Delgado, J. (2012). The user as a service. In Vidyarthi, D. (Ed.), *Technologies and protocols for the future of internet design: Reinventing the web* (pp. 37–59). Hershey, PA: IGI Global. doi:10.4018/978-1-4666-0203-8.ch003

Dietz, J. (2006). *Enterprise ontology: Theory and methodology*. Berlin, Germany: Springer-Verlag. doi:10.1007/3-540-33149-2

Dubuisson, O. (2000). *ASN.1 communication between heterogeneous systems*. San Diego, CA: Academic Press.

Earl, T. (2005). *Service-oriented architecture: Concepts, technology, and design*. Upper Saddle River, NJ: Prentice Hall PTR.

Erenkrantz, J., Gorlick, M., Suryanarayana, G., & Taylor, R. (2007). From representations to computations: The evolution of web architectures. In *6th Joint Meeting of the European Software Engineering Conference and the ACM SIGSOFT Symposium on the Foundations of Software Engineering* (pp. 255-264). ACM Press.

Fielding, R. (2000). *Architectural styles and the design of network-based software architectures*. Unpublished doctoral dissertation, University of California at Irvine, Irvine, California.

He, K. (2009). Integration and orchestration of heterogeneous services. In *Joint Conferences on Pervasive Computing* (pp. 467–470). IEEE Computer Society Press.

Henkel, M., Zdravkovic, J., & Johannesson, P. (2004). Service-based processes– Design for business and technology. In *International Conference on Service Oriented Computing* (pp. 21-29). ACM Press.

Holdener, A. III. (2008). *Ajax: The definitive guide*. Sebastopol, CA: O'Reilly Media, Inc.

Inoue, T., Asakura, H., Sato, H., & Takahashi, N. (2010). Key roles of session state: Not against REST architectural style. In *34th Annual Computer Software and Applications Conference* (pp. 171-178). IEEE Computer Society Press.

Jeong, B., Lee, D., Cho, H., & Lee, J. (2008). A novel method for measuring semantic similarity for XML schema matching. *Expert Systems with Applications*, *34*, 1651–1658. doi:10.1016/j.eswa.2007.01.025

Khadka, R. (2011). Model-driven development of service compositions for enterprise interoperability. In van Sinderen, M., & Johnson, P. (Eds.), *Lecture Notes in Business Information Processing*, *76* (pp. 177–190). Berlin, Germany: Springer. doi:10.1007/978-3-642-19680-5_15

Kim, D., & Shen, W. (2007). An approach to evaluating structural pattern conformance of UML models. In *ACM Symposium on Applied Computing* (pp. 1404-1408). ACM Press.

Kokash, N., & Arbab, F. (2009). Formal behavioral modeling and compliance analysis for service-oriented systems. In Boer, F., Bonsangue, M., & Madelaine, E. (Eds.), *Formal Methods for Components and Objects* (*Vol. 5751*, pp. 21–41). Lecture Notes In Computer Science Berlin, Germany: Springer-Verlag. doi:10.1007/978-3-642-04167-9_2

Kumaran, S., et al. (2008). A RESTful architecture for service-oriented business process execution. In *International Conference on e-Business Engineering* (pp. 197-204). IEEE Computer Society Press.

Laitkorpi, M., Selonen, P., & Systa, T. (2009). Towards a model-driven process for designing ReSTful web services. In *IEEE International Conference on Web Services* (pp. 173-180). IEEE Computer Society Press.

Läufer, K., Baumgartner, G., & Russo, V. (2000). Safe structural conformance for Java. *The Computer Journal*, *43*(6), 469–481. doi:10.1093/comjnl/43.6.469

Li, L., & Chou, W. (2010). Design patterns for RESTful communication. In *International Conference on Web Services* (pp. 512-519). IEEE Computer Society Press.

Loutas, N., Peristeras, V., & Tarabanis, K. (2011). Towards a reference service model for the Web of services. *Data & Knowledge Engineering*, *70*, 753–774. doi:10.1016/j.datak.2011.05.001

Lubbers, P., Albers, B., & Salim, F. (2010). *Pro HTML5 programming: Powerful APIs for richer internet application development*. New York, NY: Apress.

Mykkänen, J., & Tuomainen, M. (2008). An evaluation and selection framework for interoperability standards. *Information and Software Technology*, *50*, 176–197. doi:10.1016/j.infsof.2006.12.001

Overdick, H. (2007). The resource-oriented architecture. In *IEEE Congress on Services* (pp. 340-347). IEEE Computer Society Press.

Papazoglou, P., Traverso, P., Dustdar, S., & Leymann, F. (2008). Service-oriented computing: A research roadmap. *International Journal of Cooperative Information Systems*, *17*(2), 223–255. doi:10.1142/S0218843008001816

Patterson, D., & Ditzel, D. (1980). The case for the reduced instruction set computer. *ACM SIGARCH Computer Architecture News*, *8*(6), 25–33. doi:10.1145/641914.641917

Pautasso, C. (2009). RESTful Web service composition with BPEL for REST. *Data & Knowledge Engineering*, *68*(9), 851–866. doi:10.1016/j.datak.2009.02.016

Pautasso, C., Zimmermann, O., & Leymann, F. (2008). Restful web services vs. "big'" web services: Making the right architectural decision. In *International Conference on World Wide Web* (pp. 805-814). ACM Press.

Queinnec, C. (2003). Inverting back the inversion of control or, continuations versus page-centric programming. *ACM SIGPLAN Notices*, *38*(2), 57–64. doi:10.1145/772970.772977

Reuther, B., & Henrici, D. (2008). A model for service-oriented communication systems. *Journal of Systems Architecture*, *54*, 594–606. doi:10.1016/j.sysarc.2007.12.001

Schippers, H. (2009). Towards an actor-based concurrent machine model. In *4th Workshop on the Implementation, Compilation, Optimization of Object-Oriented Languages and Programming Systems* (pp. 4-9). ACM Press.

Tolk, A. (2006). What comes after the Semantic Web - PADS implications for the dynamic web. In *20th Workshop on Principles of Advanced and Distributed Simulation* (pp. 55-62). IEEE Computer Society Press.

Toshniwal, R., & Agrawal, D. (2004). Tracing the roots of markup languages. *Communications of the ACM, 47*(5), 95–98. doi:10.1145/986213.986218

van der Aalst, W. (1999). Process-oriented architectures for electronic commerce and interorganizational workflow. *Information Systems, 24*(8), 639–671. doi:10.1016/S0306-4379(00)00003-X

Xu, X., Zhu, L., Kannengiesser, U., & Liu, Y. (2010). An architectural style for process-intensive web information systems. In *Web Information Systems Engineering* (*Vol. 6488*, pp. 534–547). Lecture Notes in Computer Science Berlin, Germany: Springer-Verlag. doi:10.1007/978-3-642-17616-6_47

Xu, X., Zhu, L., Liu, Y., & Staples, M. (2008). Resource-oriented architecture for business processes. In *Software Engineering Conference* (pp. 395-402). IEEE Computer Society Press.

Zhang, J., Li, F., & Chi, C. (2008). On web service construction based on representation state transfer. In *International Conference on e-Business Engineering* (pp. 665-668). IEEE Computer Society Press.

Zou, J., Mei, J., & Wang, Y. (2010). From representational state transfer to accountable state transfer architecture. In *International Conference on Web Services* (pp. 299-306). IEEE Computer Society Press.

Zyp, K. (Ed.). (2010). *A JSON media type for describing the structure and meaning of JSON documents*. Internet Engineering Task Force. Retrieved August 26, 2011, from http://tools.ietf.org/html/draft-zyp-json-schema-03

ADDITIONAL READING

Appel, A., & Jim, T. (1989). Continuation-passing, closure-passing style. In *Symposium on Principles of Programming Languages* (pp. 293-302). ACM Press.

Becker, J., Matzner, M., & Müller, O. (2010). Comparing architectural styles for service-oriented architectures - A REST vs. SOAP case study. In Papadopoulos, G. (Eds.), *Information systems development* (pp. 207–215). Springer-Verlag, US. doi:10.1007/b137171_22

Bravetti, M., & Zavattaro, G. (2009). A theory of contracts for strong service compliance. *Journal of Mathematical Structures in Computer Science, 19*(3), 601–638. doi:10.1017/S0960129509007658

Buyya, R., Broberg, J., & Goscinski, A. (2011). *Cloud computing: Principles and paradigms*. Hoboken, NJ: John Wiley & Sons. doi:10.1002/9780470940105

Chen, D., Doumeingts, G., & Vernadat, F. (2008). Architectures for enterprise integration and interoperability: Past, present and future. *Computers in Industry, 59*, 647–659. doi:10.1016/j.compind.2007.12.016

Conrad, M., Dinger, J., Hartenstein, H., Schöller, M., & Zitterbart, M. (2005). Combining service-orientation and peer-to-peer networks. In Müller, P., Gotzhein, R., & Schmitt, J. (Eds.), *Lecture Notes in Informatics* (pp. 181–184). Bonn, Germany: Gesellschaft für Informatik.

Diaz, G., & Rodriguez, I. (2009). Automatically deriving choreography-conforming systems of services. In *IEEE International Conference on Services Computing* (pp. 9-16). IEEE Computer Society Press.

Dillon, T., Wu, C., & Chang, E. (2007). Reference architectural styles for service-oriented computing. In K. Li, et al., (Eds.), *IFIP International Conference on Network and Parallel Computing, Lecture Notes In Computer Science 4672*, (pp. 543–555). Berlin, Germany: Springer-Verlag.

Earl, T. (2007). *SOA: Principles of service design.* Upper Saddle River, NJ: Prentice Hall PTR.

Elgammal, A., Turetken, O., van den Heuvel, W., & Papazoglou, M. (2011). On the formal specification of regulatory compliance: A comparative analysis. In Maximilien, E. (Eds.), *Service-Oriented Computing* (*Vol. 6568*, pp. 27–38). Lecture Notes in Computer Science Berlin, Germany: Springer. doi:10.1007/978-3-642-19394-1_4

Fielding, R., & Taylor, R. (2002). Principled design of the modern web architecture. *ACM Transactions on Internet Technology*, *2*(2), 115–150. doi:10.1145/514183.514185

Formica, A. (2007). Similarity of XML-schema elements: A structural and information content approach. *The Computer Journal*, *51*(2), 240–254. doi:10.1093/comjnl/bxm051

Fricke, E., & Schulz, A. (2005). Design for changeability (DfC): Principles to enable changes in systems throughout their entire lifecycle. *Systems Engineering*, *8*(4), 342–359. doi:10.1002/sys.20039

Ganguly, A., Nilchiani, R., & Farr, J. (2009). Evaluating agility in corporate enterprises. *International Journal of Production Economics*, *118*(2), 410–423. doi:10.1016/j.ijpe.2008.12.009

Grefen, P., Aberer, K., Hoffner, Y., & Ludwig, H. (2000). CrossFlow: Cross-organizational workflow management in dynamic virtual enterprises. *International Journal of Computer Systems. Science & Engineering*, *5*, 277–290.

Havey, M. (2005). *Essential business process modeling.* Sebastopol, CA: O'Reilly.

Heckel, R. (2008). *Architectural transformations: From legacy to three-tier and services* (pp. 139–170). Software Evolution. doi:10.1007/978-3-540-76440-3_7

Iannella, R. (2009). Towards e-society policy interoperability. In Godart, C., Gronau, N., Sharma, S., & Canals, G. (Eds.), *Software Services for e-Business and e-Society, IFIP Advances in Information and Communication Technology* (*Vol. 305*, pp. 369–384). Heidelberg, Germany: Springer-Verlag.

Juric, M., & Pant, K. (2008). *Business process driven SOA using BPMN and BPEL: From business process modeling to orchestration and service oriented architecture.* Birmingham, UK: Packt Publishing.

Kappel, G., Pröll, B., Reich, S., & Retschitzegger, W. (Eds.). (2006). *Web engineering.* Chichester, UK: John Wiley & Sons.

Kruchten, P. (2003). *The rational unified process: An introduction.* New York, NY: Addison Wesley.

Matthijssen, N., et al. (2010). Connecting traces: Understanding client-server interactions in Ajax applications. In *International Conference on Program Comprehension*, (pp. 216–225). IEEE.

Mika, P. (2007). *Social networks and the Semantic Web.* New York, NY: Springer Science.

Mulligan, G., & Gracanin, D. (2009). A comparison of SOAP and REST implementations of a service based interaction independence middleware framework. In M. Rossetti, et al., (Eds.), *Winter Simulation Conference* (pp. 1423-1432). IEEE Computer Society Press.

Papageorgiou, A., et al. (2009). Bridging the gaps towards structured mobile SOA. In *International Conference on Advances in Mobile Computing & Multimedia* (pp. 288-294). ACM Press.

Pautasso, C. (2009). RESTful Web service composition with BPEL for REST. *Data & Knowledge Engineering*, *68*(9), 851–866. doi:10.1016/j. datak.2009.02.016

Pautasso, C., & Wilde, E. (2009). Why is the web loosely coupled? A multi-faceted metric for service design. In *International Conference on World Wide Web* (pp. 911-920). ACM Press.

Peng, Y., Ma, S., & Lee, J. (2009). REST2SOAP: A framework to integrate SOAP services and RESTful services. In *International Conference on Service-Oriented Computing and Applications* (pp. 1-4). IEEE Computer Society Press.

Perepletchikov, M., Ryan, C., Frampton, K., & Tari, Z. (2007). Coupling metrics for predicting maintainability in service-oriented designs. In *Australian Software Engineering Conference* (pp. 329-340). IEEE Computer Society Press.

Petrie, C., & Bussler, C. (2003). Service agents and virtual enterprises: A survey. *IEEE Internet Computing*, *7*(4), 68–78. doi:10.1109/MIC.2003.1215662

Rajesh, A., & Srivatsa, S. (2010). XML schema matching – Using structural information. *International Journal of Computers and Applications*, *8*(2), 34–41. doi:10.5120/1183-1632

Ramakrishnan, R., & Tomkins, A. (2007). Toward a PeopleWeb. *IEEE Computer*, *40*(8), 63–72. doi:10.1109/MC.2007.294

Ross, A., Rhodes, D., & Hastings, D. (2008). Defining changeability: Reconciling flexibility, adaptability, scalability, modifiability, and robustness for maintaining system lifecycle value. *Systems Engineering*, *11*(3), 246–262. doi:10.1002/sys.20098

Schall, D., Dorn, C., Truong, H., & Dustdar, S. (2009). In Feuerlicht, G., & Lamersdorf, W. (Eds.), *On supporting the design of human-provided services in SOA* (Vol. 5472, pp. 91–102). Lecture Notes in Computer Science Heidelberg, Germany: Springer. doi:10.1007/978-3-642-01247-1_9

Spohrer, J., Vargo, S., Caswell, N., & Maglio, P. (2008). The service system is the basic abstraction of service science. In R. Sprague Jr., (Ed.), *41st Hawaii International Conference on System Sciences*. Big Island, Hawaii, (p. 104). Washington, DC: IEEE Computer Society.

Uram, M., & Stephenson, B. (2005). Services are the language and building blocks of an agile enterprise. In Pal, N., & Pantaleo, D. (Eds.), *The agile enterprise*. New York, NY: Springer. doi:10.1007/0-387-25078-6_4

Waldo, J., Wyant, G., Wollrath, A., & Kendall, S. (1994). *A note on distributed computing*. Technical report SMLI TR-94-29, Sun Microsystems, Inc., Mountain View, CA. Retrieved February 1st, 2012, from https://ftp.uwsg.indiana.edu/kde/devel/smli_tr-94-29.pdf

Webber, J., Parastatidis, S., & Robinson, I. (2010). *REST in practice*. Sebastopol, CA: O'Reilly Media.

Wu, L., & Park, D. (2009). Dynamic outsourcing through process modularization. *Business Process Management Journal*, *15*(2), 255–244. doi:10.1108/14637150910949461

Zdun, U., Hentrich, C., & van der Aalst, W. (2006). A survey of patterns for service-oriented architectures. *International Journal of Internet Protocol Technology*, *1*(3), 132–143.

KEY TERMS AND DEFINITIONS

Architectural Style: Set of constraints imposed on a set of resources and on their relationships.

Browserver: A new web access device that extends the browser by adding a local server in close cooperation. The main idea is that the individual user can now become a first class web actor (resource), capable of not only placing requests but also to satisfy requests from other actors, either server applications or other browservers.

This frees the user from many of the limitations of the browser, while maintaining the sandboxing principle.

Compliance: Property between two services, consumer and provider, which expresses that the consumer fulfills all the requirements to invoke the provider. A consumer must comply with the provider, otherwise an error may occur.

Conformance: Property between service A and another B (A conforms to B) that indicates that A implements all the features of B required to allow it to replace B in its role in some process.

Lifecycle: Set of stages which a resource goes through, starting with a motivation to build it and ending with is destruction. Different versions of a resource result from iterations of these stages, in which the resource loops back to an earlier stage so that changes can be made.

Process: A graph of all interactions that are allowed to occur in a set of services, starting with an external request and ending with a service which neither reacts back nor initiates new service interactions.

Resource: An entity of any nature (material, virtual, conceptual, noun, action, and so on) that embodies a meaningful, complete and discrete concept, which makes sense by itself and can be distinguished from, although interact with, other entities;

Service: A set of related functionalities of a resource that define a meaningful concept in a resource interaction context.

Structural Interoperability: Property between two resources, which asserts their service compatibility (conformance and compliance) for interaction, based on their structure and structural interoperability of their components, checked recursively until primitive resources are reached.

Chapter 7

Specifying Business–Level Protocols for Web Services Based Collaborative Processes

W. L. Yeung
Lingnan University, Hong Kong

ABSTRACT

Business collaboration is increasingly conducted over the Internet. Trading parties require business-level protocols for enabling their collaborative processes and a number of standardised languages, and approaches have been proposed for specifying business-level protocols. To illustrate the specification of web services based collaborative processes, three inter-related specification languages, namely, the ebXML Business Process Specification Schema (BPSS), the Web Service Business Process Execution Language (WSBPEL), and the Web Services Conversations Language (WSCL) are discussed in this chapter. A contract negotiation protocol is used as an example to illustrate the concepts involved in the specification. The chapter also discusses different strategies for deploying these specification languages.

1 INTRODUCTION

Business-to-business (B2B) electronic commerce has grown tremendously over the past decade. Alibaba, the biggest Chinese B2B e-commerce company achieved a total revenue of nearly US$1 billion in 2011. The company was valued at nearly US$26 billion when it went public in 2007. Recently, it was valued at US$35-40 bil-

lion in a recent deal between the company and its shareholder Yahoo (The Wall Street Journal, May 22, 2012).

On the technology front, web services are seen as playing a significant role in enabling B2B collaboration (Baek Kim & Segev, 2005; Chen, Zhang, & Zhou, 2007). Web services technology supports business process management (BPM) and enterprise application integration (EAI) within an organization (Lim & Wen, 2003; Zhao & Cheng, 2005; Albrecht, Dean, & Hansen, 2005). Enter-

DOI: 10.4018/978-1-4666-2533-4.ch007

prise applications running at different geographic and functional units of the same company can be implemented as web services and *orchestrated* to run according to graphically defined workflow models. Enterprise applications implemented as web services are loosely coupled and can be dynamically bound together during the execution of a business process. This enables B2B collaborative processes in which partnerships are set up dynamically.

In order to set up partnerships on the Internet, the interacting parties need agreements on the following (Hewlett-Packard Company, 2002):

- **Business payload:** Both parties need to know which information to exchange.
- **Protocol:** Both parties need to know how to exchange business payload.
- **Service location:** To interact with a specific service, both parties need to know which protocols the service supports, which payload it exchanges, and its location, e.g. its HTTP URL.

There are various ways to define the protocol for exchanging business payload among trading parties. While a comprehensive survey of the various languages and approaches for specifying business-level protocols is beyond the scope of this chapter, such a survey can be found in (Ko, Lee, & Lee, 2009; Dorn, Grün, Werthner, & Zapletal, 2009; Mili et al., 2010) which also discuss the strengths and weaknesses of different languages and approaches.

Instead, this chapter focuses on three interrelated approaches to specifying businesslevel protocols and illustrates them using a concrete example. First, the ebXML business process specification schema (BPSS) (OASIS, 2006) supports a *choreographic* approach to representing business-level protocols. Choreography is an explicit built-in concept in ebXML BPSS for B2B protocols. Based on this concept, an independent business-level protocol can be specified based on

the interactions among business partners, rather than the operating procedures of any individual partners.

ebXML is a widely adopted standard for e-commerce with an established record (Kotok, 2007). In U.S., the Centers for Disease Control and Prevention (CDC) has built the Public Health Information Network (PHIN) based on ebXML for exchanging clinical and business messages. In Hong Kong, ebXML messaging is used in the Digital Trade and Transportation Network which connects trading partners in trade, logistics and financial industries.

Given a well defined protocol, business partners need to prepare business payloads and initiate interactions with each other in accordance with the protocol. The web services technology supports the automation of the collaborative process through integration of enterprise applications across the Internet. The Web Services Business Process Execution Language (WS-BPEL) (OASIS, 2007) is a standard means of orchestrating an enterprise's applications. While WS-BPEL is often deployed in the context of business process management within an organisation, it also plays an essential role at the interface with other organisations. Currently, WS-BPEL is the *de facto* standard supported by major vendors for implementing web services systems.

The Web Services Conversation Language (WSCL) (Hewlett-Packard Company, 2002) provides a useful link between ebXML BPSS and WS-BPEL. Since WS-BPEL is executable, it contains all the necessary details for the orchestration of web services in the particular execution environment of a host enterprise. Many of these details are specific to the implementation at the host and are irrelevant from the point of the view of the protocol, ie. the ebXML BPSS specification. A WSCL specification provides an abstract specification of the behaviour of a partner in terms of its business payloads and how it is prepared to interact with its other partners.

The above three specification languages represent three different and yet inter-related approaches to specifying business-level protocols for collaborative processes and it is the purpose of this chapter to illustrate these approaches to the reader. The next section provides some technology background on web services. Section 3 discusses further the motivations and requirements of business-level protocols for collaborative processes. Section 4 introduces the use of ebXML BPSS, WS-BPEL and WSCL in specifying a contract negotiation protocol. Section 5 discusses different strategies for deploying these approaches, taking in account the business environment. Section 6 reviews some related work and Section 7 gives a conclusion.

2 WEB SERVICES ARCHITECTURE

The web services architecture supports the modelling and execution of a business process' workflow with languages and execution engines, respectively, designed for orchestrating web services. The Web Service Business Process Execution Language (WS-BPEL) (OASIS, 2007) has become an industry standard supported by many vendors including IBM, Microsoft and BEA in their software products. Business analysts can use these software products in defining workflow models and automatically translating them into WS-BPEL for execution by an orchestration engine. The orchestration engine executes a workflow model by invoking the web services through SOAP messaging (W3C, 2007). The interface details for invoking a web service (port types, operations, message types, etc.) are described and published in an WSDL document (W3C, 2001). For B2B collaborative processes, potential partners may discover one another's web services by directly exchanging WSD documents or indirectly through UDDI (OASIS, 2005) registries.

Orchestration of web services can be centralized or distributed. An overall workflow model can be defined for the entire collaborative process and one single dominant partner or an independent party can be responsible for orchestrating all the participating web services. Control of the process is thus centralized under the responsible party. With distributed orchestration, partners maintain control of their respective services in the overall process and orchestrate their own web services. Rather than having an overall workflow model, business partners first agree on a protocol for their collaboration. Each partner then defines its own workflow model for orchestrating its own web services accordingly. A partner may also choose not to disclose its executable workflow model but instead only an *abstract* version of it. Such abstract descriptions are not executable but contain sufficient information for others to invoke the corresponding web services.

The Web Services Conversations Language (WSCL) (Hewlett-Packard Company, 2002) and the ebXML BPSS (OASIS, 2006) support the definition of the abstract descriptions/interfaces of web services. Their relationships with WS-BPEL and other standards are illustrated in Figure 1. Note that the ebXML BPSS choreography in Figure 1 lies in between the two parties whereas each party has a WSCL conversation document attached to its interface.

Their positions suggest that the ebXML BPSS choreography is independent and global to the parties involved whereas a WSCL conversation is associated with a particular party. Also notice that neither ebXML BPSS nor WSCL is involved in the actual execution of web services; on the other hand, a WS-BPEL orchestration is responsible for the execution of web services.

3 BUSINESS-LEVEL PROTOCOLS

Workflow systems provide computer-based handling of electronic documents and sequencing of tasks in a business process. A graphical workflow model is required to specify the process flow and

Figure 1. Web services architecture

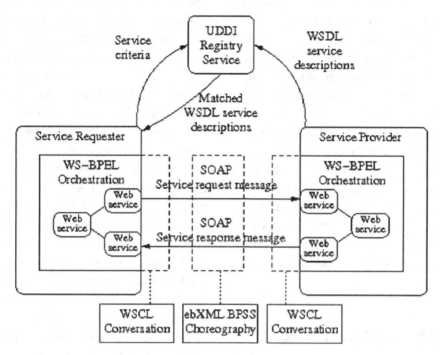

details of document processing. It should be accessible to business analysts without any technical background.

Business process management systems (BPMS) supports a software architecture for modelling entire end-to-end business processes involving multiple software applications. The emergence of web services promises a service-oriented architecture for a new generation of BPMS in which software applications packaged and run as web services are loosely coupled and can be dynamically bound together during the execution of a business process. This supports business-to-business (B2B) collaboration when business partnerships can be set up dynamically with software applications running on diverse platforms, communicating and collaborating through the Internet.

A business can make use of a standard process modelling language such as the Web Services Business Process Execution Language (WS-BPEL) in orchestrating software applications for its internal as well as collaborative processes. While busi-

ness partners can in principle orchestrate their software applications collaboratively according to a model of the overall end-to-end collaborative process, such a comprehensive overall model is in practice unrealistic as business partnerships are set up dynamically. Even in relatively stable partnerships, businesses have chosen not to reveal their internal workflows. Instead, partners prefer to orchestrate their own software applications adhere to a business-level protocol.

In the past, businesses were linked up electronically according to the Electronic Data Interchange (EDI) standards. More recent standards address not only the document formats but also the exchange protocols. For instance, ebXML BPSS and RosettaNet PIPs (Damodaran, 2004) aim to specify document exchange protocols on the level of business transactions such as "request quota" and "query purchase order status" which are some established logical units of processing in a collaborative process.

On the other hand, the external visible behavior of a web service, i.e. its abstract interface, can be specified by the conversations that it supports. This can be done without revealing its application logic or internal (private) processes. This is supported by a W3C standard for specifying web services, namely, the Web Services Conversation Language (WSCL) (Hewlett-Packard Company, 2002).

4 A CONTRACT NEGOTIATION PROTOCOL

A negotiation protocol specifies what deals trading partners can make, and the sequence of offers and counter-offers allowed. It also defines how partners communicate through structured messages (Weigand, Moor, Schoop, & Dignum, 2003). The following subsections describe the specification of a contract negotiation protocol in three complementary specification languages for

web services, namely, ebXML BPSS, WS-BPEL and WSCL. The example protocol is adapted and modified from (Rebstock, Thun, & Tafreschi, 2003; Yeung, 2008).

4.1 Choreographic Protocol in ebXML BPSS

In ebXML BPSS, a *binary collaboration* is defined as a business process involving several business transactions between two partners. A *business transaction* represents a step in the trading arrangement between two business partners. When a business transaction is performed, one partner initiates the transaction by sending a *request* to the other partner; the receiving partner may or may not return a *response*. Figure 2 shows a diagram in UML which illustrates the choreography of transactions between two partners in a contract negotiation process. The

Figure 2. A choreography example

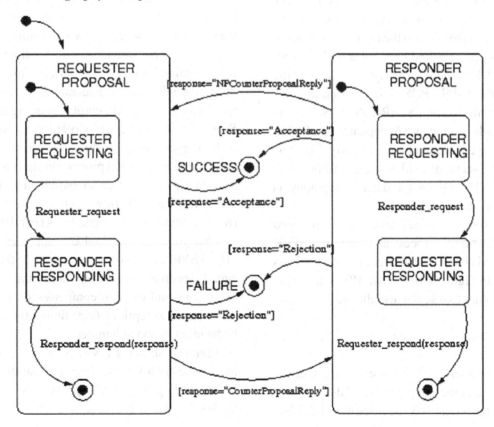

Figure 3. A scenario of interactions between the requester and responder

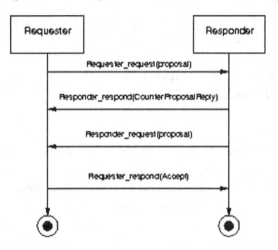

two partners take on specific *roles*, namely, the Requester and the Responder. Figure 3 shows a scenario of the negotiation.

The negotiation process begins with RE-QUESTER-PROPOSAL in which the Requester sends a proposal document to the Responder. The Responder then sends a response back to the Requester. Depending on the response, the negotiation process may end with either a SUCCESS or a FAILURE status, or it may continue with the RESPONDER-PROPOSAL interaction which is similar to the REQUESTER-PROPOSAL. The process ends as soon as a Acceptance or a Rejection response is issued by either party. The corresponding segment (with some details omitted) of the ebXML BPSS for the choreography is shown in Box 1.

The two main business transactions involved in this collaborative process are the REQUESTER PROPOSAL and RESPONDER PROPOSAL, as indicated in Figure 3. In ebXML BPSS, they correspond to the two segments labelled by

```
BusinessTransactionActivity
```

Both transactions involve exchanging documents between the two partners and the sequencing of the transactions is specified by conditional

transitions as shown in the Transition segments above. The initial transaction is the Requester-Proposal transaction, as indicated by the start segment. The Success and Failure segments mark the end of the collaborative process in successful and failed modes, respectively.

4.2 Executable Process in WS-BPEL

An *executable* WS-BPEL process runs on a WS-BPEL engine and delivers the function of a web service through its WSDL-defined interface. Partners execute their respective WSBPEL processes to deliver the necessary web services for their collaborative processes. Web services may interact with each other by exchanging SOAP messages; they only need to know the WSDL interfaces of each other together with an abstract description of each other's behaviour (see below).

A WS-BPEL executable process is defined in terms of activities which can be primitive or structured. Primitive activities include:invoke for calling a Web service's operation; receive for waiting for a message; reply for sending a message; wait for pausing for a period of time; assign for assigning value of one variable to another; throw for initiating an exception; terminate for terminating the service; empty for doing nothing. Structured activities are structuring constructs including sequence, if, while, repeatUntil, which correspond to the usual programming constructs, as well as pick (selection based on timing or incoming triggers), flow (parallel fork), scope (for exception handler), and links (parallel join).

Exception handling is also a supported feature in WS-BPEL. Faults (exceptions) can be thrown to signal exceptional conditions; fault handlers catch exceptions and execute compensation routines. Time-based exceptions (e.g. timeouts) can also be handled by event handlers.

Figure 4 shows a UML activity diagram of the Requester's web service orchestration. The corresponding WS-BPEL process is specified in Box 2.

Box 1.

```
<BinaryColloboration name="ContractNegotiation">
<Role name="Requester"... />
<Role name="Responder"... />
<start toBusinessState="RequesterProposal"... />
<BusinessTransactionActivity name="RequesterProposal" fromRole="Requester"
toRole="Responder"... />
<BusinessTransactionActivity name="ResponderProposal" fromRole="Responder"
toRole="Requester"... />
<Transition fromBusinessState="RequesterProposal
toBusinessState="ReplyState"... />
<Transition fromBusinessState="ResponderProposal"
toBusinessState="ReplyState"... />
<Decision name="ReplyState"... />
<Transition fromBusinessState="RequesterProposal" toBusinessState="ResponderPr
oposal"... >
<ConditionExpression...="CounterProposalReply" />
</Transition>
<Transition fromBusinessState="ResponderProposal" toBusinessState="RequesterPr
oposal"... >
<ConditionExpression...="CounterProposalReply" />
</Transition>
<Success fromBusinessState="ReplyState"... >
<ConditionExpression...="Acceptance" />
</Success>
<Failure fromBusinessState="ReplyState"... >
<ConditionExpression...="Rejection" />
</Failure>
</BinaryCollaboration>
```

In the WS-BPEL specification (Box 2), partnerLink refers to points of web service interactions for the Requester process. There are two process-wide variables involved, namely, proposal and response. The process starts with the receipt of a proposal document from its requester's source and then sending it to the partner through the requesting link. A response is expected from the partner and it is simply passed back to the requester's source. Depending on the response value, the process either expects a counter proposal from the partner, or simply terminates. In the former case, the process will pass the counter proposal to the requester's internal evaluation function and awaits a response, which indicates the acceptance or refusal of the counter proposal or if there is another counter proposal. Based on this response, the process will either conclude or continue for the next cycle.

The orchestration, together with the one dictated by the Responder's WS-BPEL process, are supposed to conform to the ebXML BPSS specification described in the preceding section.

Figure 4. WS-BPEL executable process of the Requester in the contract negotiation process

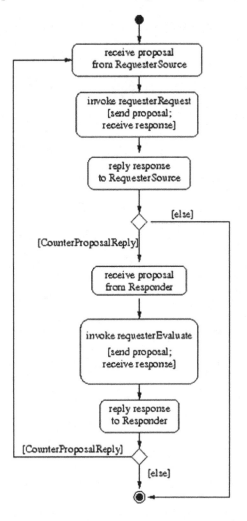

Figure 5 shows a UML activity diagram that formalises the conversations between the Requester and the Responder *from the point of view of the requester*.

Box 3 shows the corresponding WSCL specification for the Requester. The first part of the specification defines interactions between the Requester and Responder. Each interaction has one of the following types: Empty, Send, Send-Receive and ReceiveSend.

The Empty type simply marks the start or end of the process. The Send and Receive types are one-way interactions with documents flowing in one direction only. The SendReceive and ReceiveSend types provide two-way interactions.

The second part of the specification defines how interactions are ordered in the process. The

Figure 5. Abstract behavioural description of the Requester in WSCL

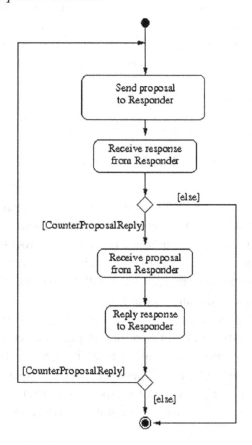

Conformance verification is discussed in the Related Work section (6.2) below.

4.3 Conversational Abstract Service Description in WSCL

WSCL specifies the sequence of messages that a web service can send and receive during a "conversation". The abstract behaviour of the web service is therefore defined in terms of the order of messages exchanged during a conversation. The ordering is expressed in a set of interactions and transitions among them.

Box 2.

```
<process name="requesterProcess"...>
<partnerLinks>
<partnerLink name="requesterProposing"... />
<partnerLink name="requesting"... />
<partnerLink name="responding"... />
<partnerLink name="requesterEvaluating"... />
</partnerLinks>
<variables>
<variable name="proposal" messageType="proposalType"/>
<variable name="response" messageType="responseType"/>
</variables>
<repeatUntil>
<sequence>
<receive partnerLink="requesterProposing"... variable="proposal">
</receive>
<invoke partnerLink="requesting"... inputVariable="proposal"
outputVariable="response"
</invoke>
<reply partnerLink="requesterProposing"... variable="response">
</reply>
<if>
<condition> $response = "CounterProposalReply"
</condition>
<sequence>
<receive partnerLink="responding"... variable="proposal">
</receive>
<invoke partnerLink="requesterEvaluating"... inputVariable="proposal"
outputVariable="response"
</invoke>
<reply partnerLink="requesterProposing"... variable="response">
</reply>
</sequence>
</if>
</sequence>
<condition>
$response != "CounterProposalReply"
</condition>
</repeatUntil>
</process>
```

Box 3. A WSCL specification of the contract negotiation protocol

```
<?xml version="1.0" encoding="UTF-8"?>
<Conversation name="contractNetProtocol" xmlns="http://www.w3.org/2002/02/
wscl10" initialInteraction="Start" finalInteraction="End" >
<ConversationInteractions>
<Interaction interactionType="Send" id="Send proposal to Responder">
<OutboundXMLDocument hrefSchema="http://123.org/Proposal.xsd" id="Proposal"/>
</Interaction>
<Interaction interactionType="Receive" id="Receive response from Responder">
<InboundXMLDocument hrefSchema="http://123.org/Acceptance.xsd"
id="Acceptance"/>
<InboundXMLDocument hrefSchema="http://123.org/Rejection.xsd" id="Rejective"/>
<InboundXMLDocument hrefSchema="http://123.org/CounterProposalAdvice.xsd"
id="CounterProposalAdvice"/>
</Interaction>
<Interaction interactionType="Receive" id="Receive proposal from Responder">
<InboundXMLDocument hrefSchema="http://123.org/Proposal.xsd" id="Proposal"/>
</Interaction>
<Interaction interactionType="Send" id="Reply response to Responder">
<OutboundXMLDocument hrefSchema="http://123.org/Acceptance.xsd"
id="Acceptance"/>
<OutboundXMLDocument hrefSchema="http://123.org/Rejection.xsd" id="Rejective"/>
<OutboundXMLDocument hrefSchema="http://123.org/CounterProposalAdvice.xsd"
id="CounterProposalAdvice"/>
</Interaction>
<Interaction interactionType="Empty" id="Start" />
<Interaction interactionType="Empty" id="End" />
</ConversationInteractions>
<ConversationTransitions>
<Transition>
<SourceInteraction href="Start"/>
<DestinationInteraction href="Send proposal to Responder"/>
</Transition>
<Transition>
<SourceInteraction href="Send proposal to Responder"/>
<DestinationInteraction href="Receive response from Responder"/>
</Transition>
<Transition>
<SourceInteraction href="Receive response from Responder"/>
<DestinationInteraction href="Receive proposal from Responder"/>
<SourceInteractionCondition href="CounterProposalReply"/>
</Transition>
<Transition>
```

continued on following page

Box 3. Continued

```
<SourceInteraction href="Receive response from Responder"/>
<DestinationInteraction href="End"/>
<SourceInteractionCondition href="Acceptance"/>
</Transition>
<Transition>
<SourceInteraction href="Receive response from Responder"/>
<DestinationInteraction href="End"/>
<SourceInteractionCondition href="Rejection"/>
</Transition>
<Transition>
<SourceInteraction href="Receive proposal from Responder"/>
<DestinationInteraction href="Reply response to Responder"/>
</Transition>
<Transition>
<SourceInteraction href="Reply response to Responder"/>
<DestinationInteraction href="Send proposal to Responder"/>
<SourceInteractionCondition href="CounterProposalReply"/>
</Transition>
<Transition>
<SourceInteraction href="Reply response to Responder"/>
<DestinationInteraction href="End"/>
<SourceInteractionCondition href="Acceptance"/>
</Transition>
<Transition>
<SourceInteraction href="Reply response to Responder"/>
<DestinationInteraction href="End"/>
<SourceInteractionCondition href="Rejection"/>
</Transition>
</ConversationTransitions>
</Conversation>
```

process always begins with the Start interaction and ends with the End interaction. It proceeds from one interaction to the next according to the transitions defined among the interactions. A transition may be conditional and form "loops" for repeated interactions.

Comparing the abstract WSCL description with the executable WS-BPEL specification, we can see that the internal activities of the requester are hidden from abstract description and therefore do not appear in the conversation between the requester and the responder. From the responder's point of view, the abstract description provides a template for formulating its conversation with the requester.

Note that a WSCL specification is always expressed from the point of view of one participant. Also, it does not explicitly specify the partner's identity.

5 ALTERNATIVE DEPLOYMENT STRATEGIES FOR EBXML, WSCL, AND WS-BPEL

We have introduced the use of ebXML BPSS, WSCL and WS-BPEL in specifying web services based B2B collaborative processes through a contract negotiation process. Depending on the business context and relationships among trading partners, there are alternative strategies for their deployment. The following subsections consider different scenarios of collaboration and discuss the corresponding deployment strategies for web services integration. For convenience, we call these three different strategies as top-down, bottom-up and peer-to-peer, respectively.

5.1 Top-Down Strategy

With the top-down strategy, the starting point of the collaborative process is an ebXML BPSS protocol specification which serves as a global definition of the interaction among the trading partners in terms of the messages to exchanged. Trading partners may commence their collaboration with a pre-existing protocol specification which has been adopted previously by other parties or has been established as a standard in the business environment. Examples include the FIPA Contract Net Interaction Protocol Specification (Foundation for Intelligent Physical Agents, 2002) and RosettaNet PIPs(Damodaran, 2004).

Alternatively, trading partners may have new or special collaboration needs and work together on a customized protocol for their collaborative process. ebXML supports a Registry Infrastructure that allows partners to register their collaboration requirements in the form of Collaboration Protocol Profiles (CPPs) and Collaboration Protocol Agreements (CPAs) (OASIS, 2006). Once a collaboration protocol has been agreed, partners can proceed to orchestrate their respective web services in accordance with the protocol using

WSBPEL. Partners may also publish the external description of their web services in WSCL which describe the behaviour of individual partners in the conversational style.

The main advantage of the top-down approach is that trading partners have clear and rigorous rules and guidelines on how to implement their respective web services in order to collaborate seamlessly with each other, as long as they adhere to the agreed protocol specification. The assumption is that such a protocol specification exists and is accepted and fully supported by all the parties involved.

5.2 Bottom-Up Strategy

With the bottom-up strategy, one or more dominant partners in the collaborative process have installed their web services and it is for the other partners to access these services according to the rules set by the dominant partners. Such rules of access can be conveniently published by individual partners as WSCL specifications or collectively as a ebXML BPSS protocol specification of the entire collaborative process.

The approach incurs the least overheads as the dominant partner(s) set(s) the standard for the collaborative process for the others to follow. However, this also requires the dominant partner(s) to reveal sufficient information about their web services in order for other partners to orchestrate their web services accordingly.

5.3 Peer-to-Peer Strategy

With the peer-to-peer strategy, there is no pre-existing collaboration protocol available to the trading partners from the start. Each party may have already installed their web services for various trading processes. When needs for collaboration arise, they contact each other for information about their available web services and means of accessing them. Such information can be conveniently made available as WSCL specifications which describe how dialogues can be established between trading parties.

Provided that trading partners can customise their web services for the necessary dialogues, collaboration can proceed without first defining a global interaction protocol in ebXML BPSS. Nevertheless, such a protocol specification would still be useful when the collaborative process evolves as it provides an independent global view of the collaborative process.

6 RELATED WORK

6.1 Choreography Specification Languages/Approaches

Web services choreography is a major approach to defining business-level protocols for global B2B electronic commerce. A web services choreography can serve as a contract for messages to be exchanged among the participants in a collaborative process. While web services orchestration always represents control from one party's perspective, choreography tracks message sequences among multiple parties from a global point of view (Peltz 2003). Apart from ebXML BPSS which has built-in support for choreography, the Web Services Choreography Description Language (WS-CDL) (Kavantzas et al., 2005) is another major standard for web services choreography specification.

Similar to ebXML BPSS, WS-CDL provides explicit support for specifying business-level protocols under the notion of choreography. As another W3C standard language, it has WSDL as one of its foundation. The basic language features of WS-CDL include primitives such as invoke, receive, reply as well as structuring constructs such as sequence, selection and repetition. Advanced features such as exception handling, initialisation/finalisation, parallelization, etc. While closely related to WS-BPEL, WS-CDL is also compat-

ible with as other web service implementation languages such as Java.

A critique of WS-CDL for choreography modelling can be found in (Barros, Dumas, & Oaks, 2005, 2006). In particular, WS-CDL has been criticised for its lack of separation between meta-model and syntax, lack of direct support for certain use cases and lack of formal basis (Barros et al., 2005). Work on formalising WS-CDL is still very much ongoing. For instance, in (Yang, Zhao, Qiu, Pu, & Wang, 2006), a formal model is defined for web services choreography based on WS-CDL and it is based on a small language known as CDL which has a formal (operational) semantics. The main advantage of having a formal semantics is that a choreography can be analysed formally and with the help of automated verification support such as model checking.

In (Motal, Zapletal, & Werthner, 2009), the Business Choreography Language (BCL) is proposed for specifying B2B choreographies for domain-specific applications. BCL is based on UML and therefore can take full advantage of the modelling support associated with UML. In (Barker, Walton, & Robertson, 2009), the Multiagent Protocols (MAP) is proposed for specifying choreographies. Unlike ebXML BPSS and WS-CDL, MAP is directly executable with a formal foundation which facilitate conformance verification in a formal manner (see also the next subsection).

The RosettaNet Partner Interface Processes (PIPs) (Damodaran, 2004) also serve the purpose of specifying business-level protocols. The standard is based on XML and contributes much to the manufacturing and supply chain areas where firms collaborate with each other in their business processes. In specifying business-level protocols, this approach distinguishes itself by its use of a visual flowchart-like notation in specifying interactions between partners. Each PIP corresponds to a typical business transaction such as Request Quote, Query Order Status and defines precisely the messages, interfaces and implementation guidelines for partners to interact smoothly.

6.2 Conformance/ Correctness Verification

Since a business-level protocol serves as the blueprint of a collaborative process, partners must orchestrate their respective web services in such a way that collectively conform to the agreed choreography. While the specification of business-level protocols is the main subject of this paper, the associated subject of conformance verification has been studied elsewhere.

In (Kim & Kim, 2004), a formal approach based on Object Constraint Language (OCL) is proposed for verifying scenarios of business transactions against ebXML BPSS. This helps ensure that a business process satisfies certain constraints imposed by an ebXML BPSS specification.

In (Yeung, 2008), the conformance of a WS-BPEL process against an ebXML BPSS specification is considered based on a process algebra called CSP. Conformance is formulated as a relation between algebraic terms which represent the process and specification, respectively. The relation can then be verified by rules of the process algebra. The main advantage of this approach is that it has a formal basis for carrying out the verification.

Other formalisms have been applied to the problem of choreography conformance verification in general. In (Basu & Bultan, 2011), the authors consider *synchronous* versions of choreography specification and discuss how to represent them in temporal logics which support automatic verification via model checking. In (Bravetti & Zavattaro, 2009), the conformance of a web service against a WS-CDL choreography is verified based on finite labelled transition systems.

In (Pacharoen, Aoki, Surarerks, & Bhattarakosol, 2011), a learning algorithm is proposed to model the behaviour of the black box implementation of a web service. The model (represented by an automaton) can then be checked for conformance against the choreography based on labelled transition systems. In (Rabanal, Mateo, Rodriguez, & Diaz, 2011), a software tool for prototyping

purposes is proposed for automatically deriving choreography-conforming web service orchestrations from a choreography specification based on finite state machines. Finite state machines are also used in representing orchestrations and choreographies for conformance checking in (D´ıaz & Rodr´ıguez, 2009).

Pi-calculus is a formalism for mobile systems (see e.g. (Puhlmann, 2006)) and has also been used in formalizing WS-BPEL (Lucchi & Mazzara, 2007). Petri nets have also been used in modelling web services and verifying their behavioral properties (see (Chi & Lee, 2008; Valero, Cambronero, D´ıaz, & Macia, 2008; Yoo, Jeong, & Cho, 2010)). To specify time constraints in choreographies, timed automata can be used (Cambronero, D´ıaz, Valero, & Mart´ınez, 2008).

(Milanovic & Malek, 2004) provides a survey and comparison of some of the abovementioned formalisms for use in web services composition.

6.3 Visual Modelling

As the choreography approach gains wider adoption, visual modelling languages are needed for supporting the protocol designers. Business analysts who are familiar with visual notations can use their visual modelling tools for specifying choerographies, conversations, orchestrations, etc. for web services implementation.

As an example, BPMN 2.0 (Object Management Group, 2009; Cortes-Cornax, DupuyChessa, Rieu, & Dumas, 2011) supports the choreography view for business process modelling. Apart from choreography, visual modelling notations are also available for web service orchestrations. This allows both the orchestration and choreography of web services to be supported by a single modelling language and thereby facilitating development tasks such as model transformation. For instance, the UML Activity Diagram (Object Management Group, 2010) has often been used for modelling choreographies as well as orchestrations visually (e.g. (Faleh & Bochmann, 2011)).

In (Paurobally & Jennings, 2005), WSCL is extended for specifying complex web service conversations and is coupled with the statecharts notation for modelling protocols visually. Statecharts support many advanced constructs for process behaviour and allow complex conversations to be visualised for analytical purposes.

Care needs to be taken to ensure that these modelling notations support the concepts and features that are essential for expressing web services choreography and orchestration primitives and constructs; and that model transformations (ie. from diagrams to specification languages) preserve the semantics of these notations.

7 CONCLUSION

Standards for defining business protocols are essential for global B2B electronic commerce. We have considered the use of the ebXML Business Process Specification Schema (BPSS), the Web Service Business Process Execution Language (WSBPEL) and the Web Services Conversations Language (WSCL) in specifying business-level protocols for B2B collaborative processes. Their use has been demonstrated with a contract negotiation example. While these specification languages serve different purposes in the development of web services based collaborative processes, they can be selectively deployed depending on the relationships among trading partners.

Business-level protocols and B2B choreographies have been the subjects of much attention in recent years and the field of research is still rapidly developing. While most of the necessary standards are already in place, further developments are expected to be seen in the support of visual modelling and automation of the implementation process. This allows business process modelling and management to be smoothly integrated with B2B processes and also supports business analysts to play an even bigger role in the design and monitoring of collaborative processes.

REFERENCES

Albrecht, C. C., Dean, D. L., & Hansen, J. V. (2005). Marketplace and technology standards for b2b e-commerce: progress, challenges, and the state of the art. *Information & Management*, *42*(6), 865–875. doi:10.1016/j.im.2004.09.003

Baek Kim, J., & Segev, A. (2005). A web services-enabled marketplace architecture for negotiation process management. *Decision Support Systems*, *40*(1), 71–87. doi:10.1016/j.dss.2004.04.005

Barker, A., Walton, C. D., & Robertson, D. (2009). Choreographing web services. *IEEE Transactions on Services Computing*, *2*, 152–166. doi:10.1109/TSC.2009.8

Barros, A., Dumas, M., & Oaks, P. (2005). A critical overview of the web services choreography description language (WS-CDL). *BP Trends*.

Barros, A., Dumas, M., & Oaks, P. (2006). Standards for web services choreography and orchestration: Status and perspectives. In *BPM 2005 International Workshops, BPI, BPD, ENEI, BPRM, WSCOBPM, BPS, Revised Selected Papers*, Nancy, France, September 5, 2005 (Vol. 3812, pp. 61–74). Springer.

Basu, S., & Bultan, T. (2011). Choreography conformance via synchronizability. In *Proceedings of the 20th International Conference on World Wide Web* (pp. 795 804). New York, NY: ACM. Retrieved from http://doi.acm.org/10.1145/1963405.1963516

Bravetti, M., & Zavattaro, G. (2009). Contract compliance and choreography conformance in the presence of message queues. In *Web Services and Formal Methods* (Vol. 5387, pp. 37 54). Springer.

Cambronero, M. E., D'ıaz, G., Valero, V., & Mart'ınez, E. (2008). A tool for the design and verification of composite web services. In G. J. Pace & G. Schneider (Eds.), *Proceedings of the Second Workshop on Formal Languages and Analysis of Contract-Oriented Software,* November 2008, Malta (pp. 9–16).

Chen, M., Zhang, D., & Zhou, L. (2007). Empowering collaborative commerce with Web services enabled business process management systems. *Decision Support Systems*, *43*(2), 530–546. doi:10.1016/j.dss.2005.05.014

Chi, Y., & Lee, H. (2008). A formal modeling platform for composing web services. *Expert Systems with Applications*, *34*(2), 1500–1507. doi:10.1016/j.eswa.2007.01.022

Cortes-Cornax, M., Dupuy-Chessa, S., Rieu, D., & Dumas, M. (2011). Evaluating choreographies in BPMN 2.0 using an extended quality framework. *Business Process Model and Notation*, 103-117.

Damodaran, S. (2004). B2B integration over the Internet with XML — RosettaNet successes and challenges. In *Proceedings of WWW 2004.*

Dıaz, G., & Rodrıguez, I. (2009). Checking the conformance of orchestrations with respect to choreographies in web services: A formal approach. In *Formal techniques for distributed systems* (pp. 231–236). Springer. doi:10.1007/978-3-642-02138-1_17

Dorn, J., Grun, C., Werthner, H., & Zapletal, M. (2009). From business to software: A B2B survey. *Information Systems and e-business Management*, *7*(2), 123 142.

Faleh, M. N. M., & Bochmann, G. V. (2011). Transforming dynamic behavior specifications from activity diagrams to BPEL. In *2011 IEEE 6th International Symposium on Service Oriented System Engineering (SOSE),* (pp. 305 311).

Foundation for Intelligent Physical Agents. (2002, December). *FIPA contract net interaction protocol specification.* Retrieved from http://www.fipa.org/specs/fipa00029/

Hewlett-Packard Company. (2002). *Web services conversation language (WSCL) 1.0.* Retrievedc from http://www.w3.org/TR/wscl10/

Kavantzas, N., et al. (2005). *Web services choreography description language version 1.0.* Retrieved from http://www.w3.org/TR/ws-cdl-10/

Kim, J., & Kim, H. (2004). Semantic constraint specification and verification of ebXML business process specifications. *Expert Systems with Applications*, *27*(4), 571–584. doi:10.1016/j.eswa.2004.06.002

Ko, R. K. L., Lee, S. S. G., & Lee, E. W. (2009). Business process management (BPM) standards: A survey. *Business Process Management Journal*, *15*(5), 744–791. doi:10.1108/14637150910987937

Kotok, A. (2007, Feb). *Adoption of ebXML: Hiding in Plain Sight.* Retrieved from http://www.ebxmlforum.net/articles/Adoption%20of%20ebXML%20Hiding%20in%20Plain%20Sight.html

Lim, B., & Wen, H. J. (2003, Spring). Web services: An analysis of the technology, its benefits, and implementation difficulties. *Information Systems Management*, 49–57. doi:10.1201/1078/43204.20.2.20030301/41470.8

Lucchi, R., & Mazzara, M. (2007, January). A Pi-Calculus based semantics for WS-BPEL. *Journal of Logic and Algebraic Programming*, *70*(1), 96–118. doi:10.1016/j.jlap.2006.05.007

Milanovic, N., & Malek, M. (2004, Nov–Dec). Current solutions for web service composition. *IEEE Internet Computing*, 51–59. doi:10.1109/MIC.2004.58

Mili, H., Tremblay, G., & Jaoude, G. B. Lefebvre, E´., Elabed, L., & Boussaidi, G. E. (2010, December). Business process modeling languages: Sorting through the alphabet soup. *ACM Computer Surveys, 43*(1). Retrieved from http://doi.acm.org/10.1145/1824795.1824799

Motal, T., Zapletal, M., & Werthner, H. (2009). The business choreography language (BCL)-A domain-specific language for global choreographies. In *Proceedings of the 5th 2009 World Congress on Services (SERVICES 2009 PART II),* Bangalore, India.

OASIS. (2005). *UDDI version 3.0.2.* Retrieved from http://uddi.org/pubs/uddi v3.htm

OASIS. (2006, December). *EbXML business process specification schema 4 technical specification V2.0.4.* Retrieved from http://docs.oasis-open.org/ebxml-bp/2.0.4/OS/spec/ebxmlbp-v2.0.4-Spec-os-en.pdf

OASIS. (2007, April). *Web services business process execution language version 2.0.* Retrieved from http://docs.oasis-open.org/wsbpel/2.0/OS/wsbpel-v2.0 OS.html

Object Management Group. (2009, August). *Business process modeling notation (BPMN) version 2 (Beta).* Retrieved from http://www.omg.org/spec/BPMN/2.0

Object Management Group. (2010, May). *OMG unified modeling language (OMG UML), superstructure, V2.3.* Retrieved from http://www.omg.org/spec/UML/2.3/Infrastructure/PDF

Pacharoen, W., Aoki, T., Surarerks, A., & Bhattarakosol, P. (2011). Conformance verification between web service choreography and implementation using learning and model checking. *IEEE International Conference on Web Services,* (pp. 722-723).

Paurobally, S., & Jennings, N. R. (2005). Protocol engineering for web services conversations. *Engineering Applications of Artificial Intelligence, 18*(2), 237–254. doi:10.1016/j.engappai.2004.12.005

Peltz, C. (2003, October). Web services orchestration and choreography. *Computer, 36*(10), 46–52. doi:10.1109/MC.2003.1236471

Puhlmann, F. (2006). Why do we actually need the pi-calculus for business process management? In *Proceedings of the International Conference on Business Information Systems* (pp. 77-89).

Rabanal, P., Mateo, J. A., Rodriguez, I., & Diaz, G. (2011). DIEGO: A tool for deriving choreography-conforming web service systems. *IEEE International Conference on Web Services,* (pp. 187 194).

Rebstock, M., Thun, P., & Tafreschi, O. A. (2003). Supporting interactive multi-attribute electronic negotiations with ebXML. *Group Decision and Negotiation, 12,* 269–286. doi:10.1023/A:1024819904305

Valero, V., Cambronero, M. E., Dıaz, G., & Macia, H. (2008, May-June). A Petri net approach for the design and analysis of Web Services Choreographies. *Journal of Logic and Algebraic Programming, 78*(5), 9–16.

W3C. (2001, March). *Web services description language (WSDL) 1.1.* Retrieved from http://www.w3.org/TR/wsdl

W3C. (2007, April). *SOAP version 1.2 part 1: Messaging framework* (2nd ed.). Retrieved from http://www.w3.org/TR/soap12-part1/

Weigand, H., de Moor, A., Schoop, M., & Dignum, F. (2003). B2B negotiation support: The need for a communication perspective. *Group Decision and Negotiation, 12,* 3–29. doi:10.1023/A:1022294708789

Yang, H., Zhao, X., Qiu, Z., Pu, G., & Wang, S. (2006). A formal model for web service choreography description language (WS-CDL). In *ICWS '06: Proceedings of the IEEE International Conference on Web Services* (pp. 893–894). Washington, DC: IEEE Computer Society.

Yeung, W. L. (2008). A formal basis for cross-checking EbXML BPSS choreography and web service orchestration. In *Proceedings of the Third Asia Pacific Services Computing Conference*, December 2008, Yilan, Taiwan.

Yoo, T., Jeong, B., & Cho, H. (2010). A Petri nets based functional validation for services composition. *Expert Systems with Applications*, *37*(5), 3768–3776. doi:10.1016/j.eswa.2009.11.046

Zhao, J. L., & Cheng, H. K. (2005). Web services and process management: A union of convenience or a new area of research? *Decision Support Systems*, *40*, 1–8. doi:10.1016/j.dss.2004.04.002

KEY TERMS AND DEFINITIONS

Business-to-Business: Electronic commerce is often classified into business-to-consumer (customer) and business-to-business. Other classes include consumer-to-consumer and government-to-consumer (citizen). There are issues specific to different classes of e-commerce.

Collaborative Process: In business-to-business electronic commerce, a collaborative process is a business process which involves two or more business entities and requires their cooperation/collaboration via electronic means. Since individual business entities may have very different technologies and practices, setting up a collaborative process is often more challenging than implementing a business process within a single business.

Electronic Commerce: Electronic commerce, or e-commerce, refers to the conducting of business of all kinds by electronic means. The Internet has played an instrumental role in the proliferation of e-commence. The subject covers a wide range of business, technology and management issues.

Enterprise Application: Enterprise applications running at different geographic and functional units of the same company can be implemented as web services and orchestrated to run according to graphically defined workflow models. Enterprise applications implemented as web services are loosely coupled and can be dynamically bound together during the execution of a business process. This enables B2B collaborative processes in which partnerships are set up dynamically.

Web Services Choreography: Web services choreography is a major approach to defining business-level protocols for global B2B electronic commerce. A web services choreography can serve as a contract for messages to be exchanged among the participants in a collaborative process. While web services orchestration always represents control from one party's perspective, choreography tracks message sequences among multiple parties from a global point of view.

Web Services Conversation: Web services conversation specifies the external visible behavior of a web service, i.e. its abstract interface. This can be done without revealing its application logic or internal (private) processes. This is supported by a W3C standard for specifying web services, namely, the Web Services Conversation Language (WSCL).

Web Services Orchestration: Web services orchestration defines a workflow model for a business process. Control of the process is centralized under the responsible party. The orchestration engine executes a workflow model by invoking the designated web services.

Section 2
Cloud Computing

Chapter 8
Cloud Computing and Enterprise Migration Strategies

Rosiah Ho
Lignan University, Hong Kong

ABSTRACT

Cloud Computing is a prevalent issue for organizations nowadays. Different service providers are starting to roll out their Cloud services to organizations in both commercial and industrial sectors. As for an enterprise, the basic value proposition of Cloud Computing includes but not limit to the outsourcing of the in-house computing infrastructure without capitalizing their investment to build and maintain these infrastructures. Challenges have never been ceased for striking a balance between Cloud deployment and the need to meet the continual rise in demand for computing resources. It becomes a strategic tool to increase the competitive advantage and to survival in the market for an enterprise. To reconcile this conflict, IT leaders must find a new IT operating model which can enhance business agility, scalability, and shifts away from traditional capital-intensive IT investments.

1 INTRODUCTION

Cloud Computing, nowadays has becoming highly visible as the strategic and tactical focus. It provides a definable and predictable model for business and enables technology to be utilized in an on-demand fashion. It promises a service that's infinitely scalable, rapidly provisioned, cost-effective and secure. This new wave has been accelerated by some of the world leading

DOI: 10.4018/978-1-4666-2533-4.ch008

IT companies like Amazon, Apple, Google, Microsoft, Salesforce.com and Yahoo among other international firms. Cloud Computing is a fundamental part of the IT strategic planning for an enterprise. It emphasis around technology, people, process, culture, performance, reliability, security and operability. This chapter separates fact from fiction, reality from myth. It aids to assist those organization decision makers to make decision on the Cloud adoption. This paper also brings up the considerations that are to be insightfully looking into before migrating to Cloud. What are the main issues to consider during transition to the Cloud? What are the security issues that need to be addressed? The scope and terms of the Service Level Agreement (SLA) that need to safeguard the company against any risk due to migration and operation on the Cloud platform. It aims also at filling up the gap of little guidance on Cloud migration and considerations that need to pay specific attention before the actual migration taking place.

Cloud Computing is defined as an Internet-based computing, whereby system's resources, hardware, software and information are provided to end users on demand basis (NIST, 2011). In general, it applies virtualization technology on a larger scale (i.e. one physical server hosts multiple virtual servers). Cloud consists of groups of virtual servers running on a common physical infrastructure platform with access point(s) interfacing with the Cloud users. It can be run in either private, public or hybrid mode. Access to Cloud can be done via client's computer's web browser and the Internet.

Deployment of applications in the Cloud can lower the infrastructure costs of ownership by removing the undifferentiated "heavy lifting" of both software and hardware expenditures of the individual in-house computer and networking systems (Mell & Grance, 2009). It provides opportunities in (i) enabling scalable and resilient services to employees, partners and customers, (ii) increasing the application processing speed, (iii) reducing the administration and maintenance support for licensing issues of software, (iv) removing the time-consuming and costly IT responsibilities from the business line of operation. Hence, (v) increasing in productivity levels; operation efficiency & effectiveness and (vi) reducing the operation cost with higher business agility (TATA, 2011).

Facing with the paradigm shift of organization IT landscape to Cloud Computing, many organizations are worried about the risks of moving to the Cloud. It is anticipated that some legacy applications currently deployed in the business environment might not be technically or practically sensible to move to the Cloud. Before deciding to migrate to Cloud, it is important to understand the potential risks of migration verse the organization requirements towards the new Cloud Computing. Organizations can take incremental steps for the migration. A successful migration relies on: - (i) the application architecture complexity (Sun, 2009); (ii) degree of application coupling with other applications; and (iii) the effort and resources required to be put into migration.

This chapter provides the essential information about the Cloud and will outline the key considerations to be looked into for successful Cloud migration. A phased migration strategy is described with focus on how enterprise to develop his application migration strategy for the organization. A step-by-step, phase-driven approach is described in details. The two major considerations for Cloud migration are:- (i) technical; and (ii) business. The discussion will focus at determining the right approach and the criteria to support Cloud adoption & migration decision (Staten, 2008).

Definition of Cloud Computing

According to National Institute of Standards and Technology (NIST, 2011), Cloud Computing is defined as a model for enabling ubiquitous, convenient, on-demand network access to a shared pool of configurable computing resources (e.g., networks, CPUs, storage, applications, and services) that can be rapidly provisioned and released with minimal management effort or service provider interaction. (Mell & Grance, 2011).

2 CLOUD CHARACTERISTICS AND SERVICE

Cloud Computing can provide organization with predictable and definable model for IT and enables technology to be utilized based on user demand. Cloud providers are promising a technology that can support rapid provisioning, highly scalable and cost-effectiveness in change management.

2.1 Essential Characteristics of Cloud Computing

These characteristics represent utility - delivery of IT services on demand and charge base on usage. Most of the Cloud models exhibit some or all of these characteristics.

a. On-Demand Self-Service

Resources can be provisioned when requested using virtualization techniques. Server, CPU, storage and memory resources can be provisioned and immediately made available via APIs or web interface. There is no need for the support of IT. Cloud service providers include Amazon Web Services (AWS), Microsoft, Google, IBM and Salesforce.com. New York Times and NASDAQ are examples of on-demand self-service.

b. Network Access Support

Cloud capabilities are available via network, ideally anywhere, anytime and access through the Application Programming Interface (APIs) provided by the Cloud provider, mechanisms that accommodate both heterogeneous thin or thick client platforms (e.g., PCs, tablets and mobile devices).

c. Resource Pooling

The provider's computing resources are dynamically grouped to serve different customers in according with their demand as mentioned in the multi-tenant model. In general, the customer has no knowledge about the exact location of the provided resources. These resources include

CPU processing power, storage, memory, network bandwidth and virtual machines. The multi-tenant model of sharing resource can achieve economies of scale, better system utilization and provides instance resources allocation to meet the burst loading requirement of different customers.

d. Rapid Elasticity

Cloud services ideally offer infinite infrastructure resources which can be rapidly and elastically provisioned. It can easily and rapidly scale out and released the infrastructure resource on demand basis to satisfy burst in processing demand.

e. Measured Service

The usage of Cloud Computing resource should be monitored, measured, controlled and reported to stakeholders (i.e. Cloud providers and customers). Metering capability at some specific level of abstraction for the offered services, for instance CPU processing power, storage, bandwidth, and number of active user accounts should be embedded as a feature of Cloud management service. Like the telephone companies selling voice and data services and the utility companies selling electricity to subscribers, Cloud services should be charged based on usage (i.e. Pay per use). The IaaS, PaaS, SaaS and data center hosting services should be readily available on demand and easily billed as a contractual service.

f. Multi Tenancy

A tenant is any application on Cloud that needs its own secure and dedicate virtual operating environment. All Cloud applications have to support multi-user environment and needs to address the tenant issue like user isolation, security and service levels, chargeback & billing mechanism for customers.

2.2 Type of Cloud Services

Cloud service offerings are classified into three service delivery models, namely: - (i) Software as a Service (SaaS); (ii) Platform as a Service (PaaS); and Infrastructure as a Service (IaaS) (Mell & Grance, 2009).

2.2.1 Software-as-a-Service (SaaS)

It offers applications on demand with which a single instance of application software runs on the Cloud can be used to support multiple end users or client organizations. With SaaS, there is no need to install and run the application on the customer's own computer, it minimize the customer's administrative overhead for software maintenance, licensing control, and daily hardware and software support. Some of the well-known SaaS include Google Docs, Gmail, and Facebook. To facilitate the efficient retrieval and update operation for tremendous number of users, the providers use a robust and load balancing application architecture to segregate the loading across a number of servers and locations (CCUG, 2009).

2.2.2 Platform-as-a-Service (PaaS)

It offers hardware and operating system platform on demand for every phase of software development, testing and running. It also provides suites of programming languages to allow users to develop their own applications. Some of the well-known commercial PaaS include Microsoft Windows Azure and Google App Engine. Both allow users to upload their own programs that conform to the service provider's Programming Language and Interface (API). The API acts as the interactive connector for the provider's Cloud infrastructure to communicate with the developed application. Then the program's web interface is deployed in the Cloud to enable it to scale up to support any number of users on the Cloud (CCUG, 2009).

2.2.3 Infrastructure-as-a-Service (IaaS)

It offers direct processing, storage and computing resources to end user on demand over the network. Users are able to access to the Cloud infrastructure by given complete control of it. This can be viewed as renting a physical server in a data center or deployment of a virtual server on a physical machine using virtualization technology. Some of the well-know IaaS include Amazon Web Services. Usually, SaaS Clouds are built on top of PaaS Clouds which in turn runs on IaaS Clouds.

Figure 1 illustrates the Cloud Computing services provisioning and virtualization applications. For SaaS, the service levels, compliance, security & governance are contractually bounded and enforced between the provider and the customer. As for IaaS and PaaS, the consumer's system administrator has the responsibility to effectively manage the applications whereas the provider for securing the underlying platform and infrastructure systems for infrastructure and platform's availability and security. (Miller, 2010).

3 KEY CLOUD COMPUTING MODELS AND PROVIDERS

Cloud Computing can support different types of services (XaaS; where X stands for Infrastructure; Storage; Platform, Software & Application). Different Cloud providers use different access protocols like HTTP, XML, REST, SOAP to access their services using distributed computing, virtualization and hosting as their underlining technologies. Cloud Computing is regarded as a transformative and amalgamated mode of computing of the prior computing models like Server Hosting, Grid Computing, ASP, Virtualization and Utility Computing (Ramakrishnan, 2010).

Figure 1. Cloud computing services, virtualization & application provisioning (Source: CCUG, 2009)

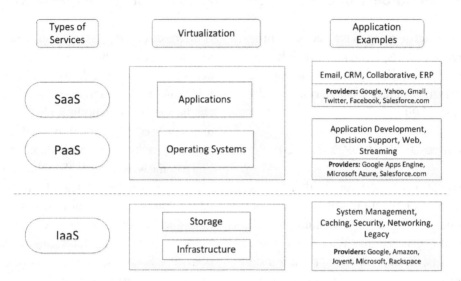

3.1 Cloud Application Deployment Models

Cloud Computing architects should take into consideration the three Cloud application deployment and consumption models, namely; public, private, or hybrid Clouds. Each offers complementary benefits, and has its own trade-offs. There is one another type of Cloud deployment model known as community Cloud which is being used in some instances. See Figure 2.

a.   **Public Clouds:** Public clouds are run by providers; applications from customers are mixed together on the Cloud network and hosted away from customer premises. It provides a way to reduce both cost and customer risk with an extension of the corporate infrastructure. Applications running in the cloud should be transparent to both providers and end users. The public Cloud can shift infrastructure risks from the enterprise to the cloud provider. Some popular cloud vendors include Salesforce.com, Amazon EC2 and Flexi scale.

b.   **Private Clouds**: Private Clouds are built for dedicated and exclusive use of one company, providing stringent control over quality of service, data security and application control. This model renders the highest level of control over the use of cloud resources when compare with the public and hybrid model and is generally adopted by large companies. However, it may negate the benefits of cloud computing as the organizations need to purchase, manage and maintain their own clouds.

c.   **Hybrid Clouds:** Hybrid Clouds combine both private and public Cloud models. It helps to provide on-demand, externally

Figure 2. Cloud application deployment models

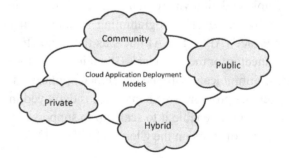

provisioned services. It augments a private Cloud in maintaining service levels during rapid workload fluctuations and to handle planned workload spikes.

d. **Community Clouds:** Community Clouds are customized to share infrastructure between organizations from a specific community with common concerns. (healthcare, compliance, or jurisdiction, etc.). It offers range of services, including IaaS, PaaS, and SaaS.

3.2 Cloud Stakeholders Model

Figure 3 identifies the generic stakeholders for Cloud Computing. Service Consumer uses the services provide by the Cloud and the Service Developer to produce the required services (Ahronovitz, 2010).

a. Service Consumer

It is the organization or end user that consumes the Cloud services (E.g. IaaS, PaaS & Saas). Depending on the type of services and applications, there are different end user consumer interfaces and the back end infrastructure is transparent to consumer. Some interfaces provide Cloud administrative functions like system, backup & storage management and provisioning of virtual

machine and its related resources. Consumers can write application code by using the offered programming interfaces and confine their works with the SLAs which are established between the consumer and the provider.

b. Service Provider

It offers the Cloud service and delivers it to the customer. For IaaS, the provider maintains the hardware infrastructure, processing, network, storage, database, and the hosting services to consumer. The customer cannot physically access the infrastructure that hosts it. For PaaS, the provider manages the infrastructure operating system, the platform, the middleware and the middle tier software for specific application. For SaaS, the provider manages and maintains the application software. The physical infrastructure and the middle tier software and the application software may not be owned by the customer.

In Figure 3, it shows the generic Cloud stakeholder model which shows the role and relationships between the Cloud's Consumer, Service Provider and the Service Developer. The lowest layer which includes the hardware, firmware and the software kernel (OS, VM Manager) represents the IaaS service stack on which everything else is based. Above that, is the virtualized resources and virtual images layer which includes computing,

Figure 3. Stakeholder model for cloud computing

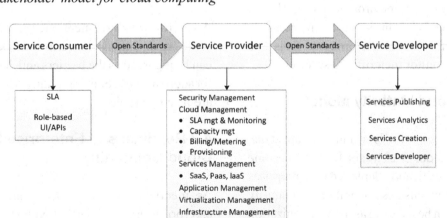

storage, networking system's resource handling and management and the image metadata (the virtualized CPU, memory, storage and middleware) of the Cloud VM manager. It represents the PaaS service stack on which the application is based. As for the system management of the entire Cloud, it requires service metering and auditing to determine: - (i) who uses, and (ii) to what extend the services are being used and (iii) the degree of provisioning of resources that allocated to consumers and (iv) any exceptional report for the offered services.

At a higher level, the SLA management is required for ensuring the terms and conditions of service that offered and delivered to customer are met. Security is essential to all aspects and level of the service provider's operations. Open standards should be adhered and applied to the provider's operations. Compliance of security standards in light of information and data security must be observed to safeguard information integrity, confidentiality and accessibility.

c. Service Developer

It offers cloud solutions and services that are delivered to end users electronically via the SaaS model. Applications developed at the IaaS and PaaS will subsequently be used by developers and the Cloud provider. Unlike the service provider, the developer does not sell or install hardware for customer. Instead, they write codes to suit the customer need and the environment hosted by the Cloud provider. When the service is in operation, the developer provides performance tools and analytics to monitor their offered services.

3.3 The Cloud Maturity Model

With Cloud Computing is still in its infant stage, it may take about 5-10 years for it to become mature and significantly deployed for enterprises to support their business operation. A maturity model will then be useful to assist an organization

in identifying where they are and where to go. Nowadays, the adoption has begun with small scale experimental trials on Cloud services by some departments in some organizations. The next phase will move to a Hybrid model by integrating the Cloud service with the Data Center infrastructure. Upon reaching the final phase, line of business applications will ultimately migrate to the Cloud as a standard service provision.

3.4 Key Cloud Providers

As for Cloud offerings, there are several leading worldwide Cloud service providers that offer different kind of Cloud hosting, storage, platform and application services (Ramakrishnan, 2010). See Table 1.

4 ENTERPRISE ADOPTION AND READINESS FOR CLOUD COMPUTING

4.1 Adoption Drivers

The eight attributes, (Table 2) are regarded as the drivers for the adoption of Cloud Computing. Table 1 describes how these attributes can motivate an organization towards Cloud Computing (Lewis, 2010).

4.2 Adoption Barriers

Apart from the above mentioned drivers, there are some organizational concerns that take place and can be regarded as the barriers and de-motivators for adopting the Cloud Computing. These concerns are listed in Table 3.

4.3 Readiness of Enterprise for Cloud Computing

As mentioned in the Cloud Maturity Model, enterprises are now starting with small and new

Table 1. Cloud Service offerings from large cloud providers

Cloud Provider	Service Offered	Hosting Services	Storage Services	Platform Services	Application Services	Characteristics
Amazon	Amazon Web Services	Y	Y	Y	Y	highly reliable, scalable & low-cost, cover over 190 countries around the world
Google	AppEngine	Y	Y	Y	Y	Web applications on Google's infrastructure. Support dynamic web serving, automatic scaling & load balancing APIs for authenticating users Email using Google Accounts Support scheduled tasks for triggering events at specified times and time intervals.
Microsoft	Azure	Y	Y	Y	Y	provide on-demand services hosted in Microsoft data centers via 3 product brands:- (i) Windows Azure, (ii) SQL Azure and (iii) Windows Azure AppFabric Offers free Ingress for all the Windows Azure customers.
Rackspace	Mosso	Y	Y			Known as Cloud Files hosting services Provides unlimited online storage and Content Delivery Network for media on utility computing basis. Launched as *Mosso CloudFS* Unlimited storage up to 5 GB
Saleforce.com	Force.com	Y	Y	Y	Y	Provide variety of Cloud service categories:- (i)Sales Cloud; (ii) Service Cloud, (iii) Data Cloud; (iv) Collaboration Cloud and (v) Custom Cloud (Force.com).

departmental applications or web applications to become the first mover to Cloud. It includes applications that can:-

1. provide and improve organizational flexibility to respond to unplanned problems, unpredictable workloads as well as ongoing competitive threats and business opportunities.
2. handling and focus on variable workloads which are expensive in cost structures.
3. provide cost-effective disaster recovery functions for mission critical applications and services. With a Cloud solution, disaster recovery systems can be built on a shared, virtualized infrastructure that can reduce costs through increased asset utilization.
4. provide development and testing environments: The IT requirements for a testing environment can be volatile, short-termed & unplanned in nature. Organizations have traditionally been forced to invest in excess capacity. A Cloud solution can reduce or eliminate under-utilized capacity with improvement in responsiveness to requests.
5. provide enterprise storage: With the exponential growth of data and increasing requirements for compliance and data protection, Cloud -based storage solutions can provide a complement to enterprise storage, enabling enterprises to cope with unpredictable growth while reducing costs and cutting infrastructure requirements.
6. provide Virtual Desktop Infrastructure (VDI): As VDI requires significant investment in the central server capacity; variable utilization can limit potential virtualization benefits and reduce ROI. Using Cloud so-

Table 2. Drivers for cloud computing

Drivers	Motivations for Organization Toward Cloud Computing
Availability	Users can access Cloud system resources via a standard API interface and Internet connection.
Collaboration	Users can share some common data, information and work with their other co-worker or partners.
Elasticity	The provider transparently and dynamically manages user's system resource in accordance with their utilization and needs.
Lower Infrastructure Costs	The pay-per-usage model allows an organization to pay as he use. There is no hardware, software maintenance, upgrade and/or software licensing cost to be administered.
Increase in User Mobility	Users can access to Cloud data and applications at any place, any time via a common intelligent portable devices. E.g. Notebook and mobil phone.
Risk Reduction	Organizations can put in their testing environment in the Cloud to test their ideas and concepts without directly affecting their production environment.
Scalability	Users can demand for large extra resources based on their needs and load forecasting.
Virtualization	Allow large number of users to share applications on a common physical platform and device to achieve economy of scale.

lutions to support VDI reduces desktop PC investment, as well as increasing the security for end user computing environments.

7.   provide Data Centre as a Service: Enterprise customers with compute-intensive data center requirements can utilize Data Centre as a Service (DaaS) to provide capacity for processing and storage on the fly. A Cloud -based solution is ready to provide capacity to that level.

5 MIGRATION STRATEGY FOR CLOUD COMPUTING

Changes will be unavoidable when performing transition to the Cloud. Unplanned changes may result in inefficiency or even worse, introduce risks to the organization. Cloud is originally perceived as a solution to achieve operational cost savings, the likelihood of realizing these objectives depend on how well the organization can manage the

Table 3. Barriers for cloud computing

Barriers	De-motivations for Organization Towards Cloud Computing
Interoperability	There still not exist a universal set of Cloud standards and/or interfaces, resulting in a significant risk technical incompatibility between vendors and applications.
Latency	Internet is the media via which end users access to Cloud services. It is a non-deterministic network with high network delay between the service provider and the users.
Platform/Language Constraints	Some Cloud providers only support specific platforms and languages.
Regulations	Strict Law and compliance issues like data protection, fair information practices and international data storage and transfer requirement and jurisdiction have become one of the most significant concerns for adopting of Cloud Computing.
Reliability	Unexpectedly failure in either hardware or software of existing Cloud infrastructures inhibit user's decision on moving to Cloud.
Resource Control	There is always a great difference between Cloud providers in controlling the amount of resources & access to Cloud services.
Security	Data privacy is one of the major concerns for users as they do not have the information where the data are being stored and right to control their own data. Worse still, they cannot know whether their data stored in Cloud is being referenced or accessed by others.

changes that induced due to the Cloud migration. This migration strategy section aims to provide the basic knowledge and a pragmatic picture for organizations which are planned to take up these challenges to migrate to Cloud. It takes a disciplined and insightful approach for Cloud migration, so as to ensure business as usual. The Cloud migration will focus in the following aspects.

5.1 Recent Trend on Cloud Migration

According to the article in InfoSecurity magazine (February, 2010), there were about 60% of business have moved or are planning to move to the Cloud which was confirmed with a recent Gartner report cited in the same source that 40% of firms would have no local IT infrastructure within the next 4 years. There were about 72% of respondents who were concerned about security in the Cloud. A side-effect of the Cloud is that it encourages the use of open-source software which is free from licensing restrictions to run in the Cloud platform (TATA, 2010). Many proprietary software vendors have yet to plan for new licensing models that will suit the new Cloud paradigm (Ronnie, 2012). The stability of using commercially licensed software (more secure & stable) is always the excuse that IT managers shift from using the Cloud (Miller, 2010).

5.2 Benefit of Moving to Cloud

In today's competitive and economically challenged environment, the ability to cut cost while reducing products and services time to marketplace is very compelling. New technologies and service offerings must bring value to the business otherwise they won't be adopted. The essential characteristics that differentiate Cloud from conventional computing (Spinola, 2009) bring both business and technical benefits to the organization. Each organization should assess their needs and benefits before pursuing Cloud initiatives. A summary of the business benefits is described below (Russel, 2010).

- **Reduced IT costs:** Cloud Computing significantly reduces the capital expenditures needed to implement new or extend existing IT services. This is accomplished by either pooling internal IT resources (private Cloud) or subscribing to external IT services (public Cloud) that satisfy the business needs.

- **Faster time to market:** Cloud Computing solutions streamline delivery of technology services needed to support business objectives. Whether it's subscribing to third party application services or leveraging infrastructure automation, Cloud Computing can significantly reduce the time needed to deploy solutions. This enables faster time to market for products and services.

- **Business Agility:** Many businesses are dependent on the Internet to deliver products and services. Cloud Computing affords these businesses the flexibility to scale up and down as needed to meet the demand. During seasonal peaks additional resources can be provisioned on demand. This is a significant departure from the traditional model that required long lead times and significant investment to handle seasonal demand spikes.

- **Quality of service:** Cloud Computing inherently improves the resiliency of IT services and minimizes performance degradation due to system resource constraints (e.g., CPU and memory). The distribute architecture of Cloud Computing reduces service outages caused by single points of failure. Further, customers no longer experience slow performance when unexpected increase in specific resource demand occurs.

- **Improve IT Value:** The automation capability enabled by Cloud Computing reduces routine tasks such as system provisioning and de-provisioning. This will enable IT to focus on more mission critical projects or task that needed to improve the competitiveness of the business. Cloud Computing enables more cost effective delivery of services such as disaster recovery.

5.3 Considerations for Migrating of Legacy Application to Cloud

Cloud Computing is not only a new concept, it is a new way of doing business. Cloud Computing allows separation organization data from IT infrastructure with data replicates in the Cloud (hosted in 'virtual' anywhere). Cloud allows an organization to isolate it's IT infrastructure from its core line of business operation to allow for better, faster, more efficient, greener and less expensive type of computing environment which may free from the burden of ageing IT infrastructure (Russel, 2010). Given the above undeniable benefits of Cloud Computing, organizations are contemplating to shift to the Cloud. The tradeoff is given rise to a new dimension of security, privacy & logistic issues that need to be re-evaluated (Miller, 2010). In addition, organizations are worried about the unintended consequences that may come across (Russel, 2010). This section focuses on the technical and business considerations for migrating to Cloud.

5.3.1 Technical Considerations

A number of technical considerations that need to be think about for an efficient and successful move to Cloud (GTSI, 2011).

a. Applications Characteristics

Some good candidates to move to the Cloud are:

1. **Non-Critical Application:** A non-critical application that has a limited scope and low return on investment (ROI) is good for acting as the pilot for migrating to the Cloud.

2. **Variable Workloads**: Some loading profiles which have low resource requirements in most of the time but occasionally require very high resource requirements. Moving that workload to the Cloud can free the organization to purchase additional system resources to cater for the short period of peak load. Cloud Computing can provide additional resources on demand basis and release those resources when the workload returns to normal.

3. **Non-Essential Tasks**: Some non-mission critical or low-risk applications that could be processed off-site.

4. **Data Mining**: Data mining typically requires substantial hardware to run business intelligent and visualization patterns in processing massive amounts of data. Moving that task to the Cloud can observe substantial hardware savings.

5. **Development and Testing**: It requires substantial resources when done on in-house systems. Moving the testing & development tools to Cloud can ensure that all developers are using the same level of tools for testing and production.

b. Readiness of Legacy Applications to Run in the Cloud

An assessment is needed to determine a legacy application's readiness for the Cloud and the appropriateness to run on private or public Cloud. Most commonly asked questions are: (i) Are the applications which the organization uses already web-based? (ii) Can it be scale up in the Cloud? (Jain & Bhardwa, 2010)(TATA, 2010). Also, traditional & Cloud application are not necessarily compatible and the application migrating may not be necessary effective.

c. Performance

It is important to accurately assess the performance requirements that may require under the Cloud environment. An application with high database inquiry rates, high CPU or RAM requirements may not be appropriate, to move to the Cloud. Adequate performance is crucial for success move to the Cloud. To safeguard the performance requirement, it is necessary to specify the Service Level Objectives (SLOs).

d. Data Security: Accessibility, Location, Ownership and Privacy

Data Security: It is always regarded as the most important issue for migrating data to the Cloud. With a Cloud based application, the data, infrastructure or application are under the total and direct control of the Cloud provider. Strict security controls are deemed necessary for securing any Cloud system (Miller, 2010).

- **Access Control:** To facilitate multiple accesses to different data source on Cloud and to ensure access security, Federated Identity (Single Sign-On) should be in place. Besides, the use of firewalls to prevent unauthorized backdoors from entering into the corporate network other than the application itself is deemed to be essential. Data encrypt between application and external communications will guarantee that only the authorize users can access to the application.
- **Data Storage and Location:** Due to the sensitivity of storing and retending user data, data storage of Cloud should need to pay special attention. For instances, (i) whether the user data is archived off the Cloud to other external resource; (ii) to shared data resources such as network drives to different users, (iii) Centralize the user data in databases or directly copying data between virtual machines are areas that need special attention (Jain & Bhardwa, 2010).

- **Data Privacy & Compliance:** The Cloud provider should protect sensitive data of the organization and to meet the regulatory requirement of the local government. As many data are subject to privacy & copyright laws and/or export restrictions (Miller, 2010). Organizations considering using Cloud services should ensure compliance of these specific requirements stipulated in relevant regulations and Laws with the set of controls provided by the Cloud provider. It requires to setup constant review on the service-level agreements and the compliance requirement, namely are: - PCI, HIPAA, GAAP, SOX, and IFRS.

e. Interoperability and Portability

Moving to the Cloud will lock the organization to a particular Cloud service provider; it means that the organization will be forced to tie to the service level and pricing policies of the selected Cloud provider. Portability and interoperability become crucial for a customer to work with multiple Cloud providers.

f. Data Migration and Application Testing Processes

Data Migration: Vendors must explain to their clients how data migration will be carried out as it not only affects the future operation efficiency but also the data security (Miller, 2010). Vendor should give a detailed plan to customer for approval. *Application Testing*: As Cloud Computing offers rapid elasticity in allocating system resources, it is straightforward and necessary to carry out Stress-testing on multiple instances of an application to verify its performance under heavy loading situation.

5.3.2 Organization and Business Considerations

While the technological issues are undeniably paramount when consider moving to the Cloud, there are also non-technical business considerations that might be significant and have impact on the Cloud's adoption decision (Dirham, 2009). The organization and business considerations which will affect the adoption decision towards Cloud adoption are listed (Pring, 2009)(Rahman, 2010).

a. **Consideration for Information Assets Classification**: The classification will help in understanding the risk, functionality and value proposition that application will make for an organization. Without classification of those assets, it is impossible to make a sound decision of moving to the Cloud (Jain & Bhardwa, 2010).

b. **Requirement, Actual Need and Risks Identification:** Define the real requirements of the organization and identify whether the Cloud provider can capable of delivering those required services with minimum risks to customer. In general, moving to the Cloud does not introduce new risks but may change the nature of existing risk (Miller, 2010).

c. **Cost Benefit & Return on Investment (ROI) Consideration:** It is necessary for an organization to calculate the cost and benefit of moving to the Cloud when compare to the existing costs and benefits. *Cost Benefit Analysis* is essential in deciding whether to move a particular application to the Cloud or not from the Return on Investment (ROI) perspective. Costs are majorly classified as (i) One-off capital investment and (ii) Daily Operational cost.

a. Cost Benefit

The Sunk Costs: Theoretical speaking, sunk costs are costs that have already been invested. They are the cost that often reluctance to be 'throw away". It may be sensible for organizations to look for a gradual migration instead of one-step migration to the Cloud.

The Variability Running Costs: As Cloud Computing resources can be turned off when not used, it implies that with proper management and controls, Cloud computing can save the daily operating cost to certain extend whereas traditional IT investments will continue to be amortized even not being used.

b. Benefit from ROIs

A thorough analysis of the ROI for Cloud Computing should be done to justify:-

*   **Hardware Savings:** To decommission some existing machines by buying less hardware and software.
*   **Staffing Savings:** With the manpower support from the Cloud provider, it may bring substantial staff saving in operating and maintaining the infrastructure.
*   **Power and Cooling:** Having fewer machines to be kept in-house, it will substantially decrease those power and cooling costs.
*   **Application Changes:** For applications that originally hosted and run in the legacy systems, changes might be minimal. Conversely, the applications that run in the proprietary system may require substantial changes for use in the Cloud environment.
*   **Organizational Efficiency:** The ability to automatically provision and de-provision resources can make an organization much more adaptive to change. A more responsive organization will gain higher competitive advantage in the marketplace.

c. Support from Senior Management

Cloud Computing is not just changing the world of IT landscape, it also changing the culture of an organization. An organization will perceive changes in business objectives, authority, operation, staffing and budgeting. Without executive-level support, it would be infeasible to move to the Cloud. It is vital that any new Cloud initiatives & policies should be recommended & supported by senior management to provide directorship and leadership.

d. IT Governance, Policy and Regulatory Concerns

The Cloud provider should ensure to compile:- (i) Government privacy laws that prohibit certain data from being stored on server that located outside their own country; (ii) Trade & industry practitioner's regulations and best practices in deploying, managing, archiving and removing the applications and data. The Cloud provider must always be alerted & keep the organization in compliance.

e. Resistance to Change

There often observe resistance to move to the Cloud for no other reason than just employee's feelings of being threatened. Good management practice should come into place to understand the underlying reasons of objection & negativity. Participative management skills, practices and relevant HR handling procedures can certainly help to gain employee's trust and buy in for migration.

f. Business Partnership Arrangement

Vendor Selection: Organizations should look into a number of different factors for the selection of right Cloud provider/vendor (Miller, 2010):-

- Does the vendor use industry standard APIs or proprietary ones?
- Does the vendor provide data extraction facilities for customer to shift out?
- Does the vendor attach to open standards or proprietary ways of servicing?

- **Billing capabilities:** Does the vendor provide sufficient billing methods to meet the variability of different customers?
- **Fixed costs:** Does the vendor require to charge an initial setup cost for Cloud setup?
- **Transparency:** The vendor should give report to user in relation to Cloud system availability and performance.
- **Support:** A vendor who provides multi-levels of support services is preferable as it would bring benefits and simplicity to organization for moving to Cloud.

g. Service Level Agreements (SLAs)

An SLA governs the rights and liabilities between a Cloud service provider and the consumer. Among other things, an SLA should mentioned: - (i) a set of services that the provider deliver (along with specific definition of each services); (ii) the contractual responsibilities of both service provider and the consumer; (iii) a set of criteria to determine whether the provider is delivering the agreed services and (iv) mechanism of reporting and alerting customers of any problems and outages. Special attention should be paid to some particular situations like vendor collapse, merging, takeover and the provision of disaster recovery plan (IBM, 2010).

h. Maintenance Schedule of Cloud Provider

It is often a norm to update the systems from time-to-time for latest patches and new features. It is necessary to aware these patches will not be adversely affected the applications after the upgrade. The application providers need to ensure service continuity after the patching. To save time and minimize the disturbance to user, it is recommended to coincide both the system patch and the application maintenance schedule to limit the numbers of outages which will affect the Cloud users (IBM, 2010).

i. Technical Support

During migration and daily operation, there always come a time that an organization need some technical support service from the Cloud provider to handle their technical and operation problems. It would be useful for having a service representative to consult in case things going wrong. It is advisable to seek for the provider who provides this service.

j. Availability of Cloud

Business continuity and disaster recovery should be included as one of the essential criteria for availability. An organization should understand what architecture and technology the Cloud provider provides to ensure availability and the recover strategies when system failures, including redundant systems and high availability infrastructures.

5.4 Cloud Paradigm Shift and Migrating Methodology

As more and more enterprises are moving to the Cloud to capitalize their current IT asset to prepare for the future. This section aims to build a migration strategy for organizations (Ronnie, 2012). It highlighted the characteristics, steps, methodologies and the benefits of moving their legacy applications to the Cloud. Amongst the different migration options, a "Phase-Driven Step-by-Step" migration strategy was described. It includes six main stages, namely:- (i) Cloud Assessment, (99) Proof of concept, (iii) data migration, (iv) application migration, (v) leverage the Cloud and (vi) Optimization phases. Figure 4. (GTSI, 2011) (Russel, 2010) (Rackspace, 2011).

5.4.1 Six Major Phases for Cloud Migration

The phase 1 and 2 includes assessments to understand and analyze the issues concerning the migration at the application level, design, and code, architecture, or usage levels (Sun, 2009). This includes assessments of the Cloud onomics, proof of concept, assessing on the migration costs, recurring costs, database data segmentation, database migration, functionalities required, and the non-functional requirements support. The dependencies and solutions to handle them are also included in this stage. The deliverables of this stage are the specified and validated user requirement that leads to the enterprise's Cloud architecture design, thus identifying the desired functionalities that they need (Table 4).

The phase 3, 4 & 5 includes the redesign, re-architect, and re implementation on the Cloud.

Figure 4. A phased migration strategy for cloud computing

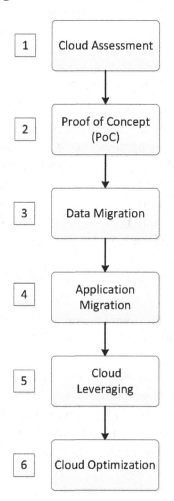

Table 4. A phased migration strategy for cloud computing: step by step guide (Varia, 2010)

Phase	Benefits
Phase-1: Cloud Assessment • Assessment for Total Cost of Ownership • Assessment of Data, Information Security & Compliance • Assessment of Technicality of Applications • Identification of applications for reuse or built • Licensed products migration • Create migration plan and ways to measure outcomes at different phases	Lower TCO, higher flexibility, business agility, faster time to market and scalability Gap identification between traditional legacy IT infrastructure and the next-generation Cloud infrastructure
Phase-2: Proof of Concept (PoC) • Build a pilot Cloud for PoC • Test accuracy, performance, computability & reliability of legacy or new software in the Cloud	Validating the proposed Cloud architecture and ways to mitigate risk
Phase-3: Data Migration • Explore and investigate the different data migration & storage options in the Cloud • Migrate legacy RDBMS to Cloud • Migrate SQL to Cloud	Minimize data redundancy, enhance storage capacity, performance & scalability, automated data backup
Phase-4: Application Migration • Decision on direct, parallel and phased migration • Hybrid migration strategy • Build Cloud-aware layers of code as needed	Future-proof, scaled-out service-oriented elastic architecture
Phase-5: Leveraging the Cloud • Enhance the degree of automate, computing resources elasticity and management of SDLC • Harden both operating system and application security • Create dashboard for easy managing of Cloud resources • Leverage multiple availability zones	• Reduction in capital expenditure • Increase in infrastructure flexibility & agility • improved productivity & degree of automation • Higher Availability (HA)
Phase-6: Cloud Optimization • Optimize usage based on real demand • Improve efficiency and effectiveness • Implement advanced monitoring and telemetry • Re-engineer your application • Making continuous improvements in databases operation	Increased utilization & minimize the transitional impact in Operating expenditure (OpEx) Better visibility through advanced monitoring & telemetry

Functionalities identified in the previous stage are implemented as additional or modifications for the existing or current conventional computing an enterprise is using.

Finally, the phase 6 includes the iterations and optimizations. This includes additional Cloud features, auto scaling, and storage, bandwidth, and security optimizations. This stage also includes compliance with standards and governance enhancement.

Cloud Computing is deployed and consumed. A roadmap for leveraging new Cloud features is also developed at this stage delivering best return of investment (Russel, 2010).

The order of the phases is insignificant. Some organizations may skip the Assessment Phase (1) and drive into the Proof of Concept Phase (2) or directly perform the Application Migration Phase (4) before the Data Migration Phase (3). The deciding of the organization migration strategy needs the overall understanding of the characteristics of different migration options and the balance between the organizational-wide priorities (business model, time-to-market strategy, technical acceptability, competitive landscape & security...etc) and the migration cost (including the opportunity cost) (GTSI, 2011), in particular, cost relates to:- (i) time to move an existing application to the Cloud, (ii) Cloud bandwidth, (iii) the time taken to transfer data from legacy to Cloud platform, (iv) the actual process that involve in the migration (downtime, business continuity & training etc.) (Kundra, 2011).

6 CONCLUSION AND RECOMMENDATIONS

Like most trends and new concepts in the industry, new technology always has a technology diffusion cycle to be overhyped. There often has a time lag between technology innovation and user acceptance. Premature adoption of new technology will lead to unrealistic expectations and disappointments. To solve this problem, it is suggested to set a strategic or business plan for the adoption of Cloud Computing. To assure that the applications being targeted for Cloud running are the ones which best fit for migrating under the current and future business environment with good potential for generating benefits. Whether Cloud Computing is a viable choice for business depends on how well the business ready to define and to setup the organization policy and the governance framework to mitigate the risk and to gain the competitive advantage of adopting Cloud Computing.

To move away from the risk and hype of Cloud Computing, it is advised that both Cloud vendors, developers and the regulatory bodies should work in collaboration on agreeing a common security models, standards & interoperability principles or guidelines for Cloud Computing. The Cloud is believed to reduce the workload for hardware and software administration for an organization in the long run. It is recommended to select the most appropriate model, to decide the type of applications or services that best suit to your business environment; and to ensure the proper implementation of data and information security policies, compliance, and service up-time for specific Cloud provider. Cloud Computing is

all about efficient use of resources specialized in managing capital expenditure and technology support costs. It is not about technology, it's about business processes and models. Cloud Computing is evolving every day, so keep informed and alerted on the weather forecast for the wind and Cloud movement.

Cloud Computing offers on-demand application services over the network for a pool of dynamic, flexibly configured virtualized system resources (i.e., APIs, SAN storage, servers & applications) that can be flexibly & rapidly deployed with minimal administrative effort or support from the service provider. It is considered as a transformative strategy to convert and migrate the legacy way of provisioning the computing resources. A six-step approach to handle the paradigm shift and migrate from conventional computing to Cloud Computing has been discussed (Ronnie, 2012). This includes the steps not only on how to redesign, implement and deliver applications but also the organizational challenges that needs be considered for Cloud migration. An organization, in the first priority, should align with its business goals and objectives for a cheaper, flexible system that minimize the administration support yet can still render high performance, security, privacy and availability to the organization. (Jain & Bhardwa, 2010)

Cloud Computing will remain as a growing theme of investigation and delivery of computing services at present and the near future. It needs insightful analysis on both the technical and business dimensions before it comes up to the final decision (Dargha, 2009). The importance of complete understanding of the nature of the organization data, applications and risks should never been overlook in order to make an objective and sensible business decision for migration. To help with this process, this chapter highlighted both the technical and business key considerations for choosing the right decision and making the right step for migrating to Cloud with successful and confidence (Staten, 2008).

REFERENCES

Ahronovitz, M. (2010). *Cloud computing use cases,* White Paper Version 4.0. Retrieved, June 20, 2011, from http://openCloud manifesto.org/Cloud _Computing_Use_Cases_Whitepaper-4_0.pdf

Caytiles, R. D., Lee, S., & Park, B. (2012). *Cloud computing: The next computing paradigm.* Hannam University. Retrieved May 24, 2012, from http://www.oecd.org/document/31/0,3746 ,en_2649_34223_43912543_1_1_1_1,00.html

Cloud Computing User Group. (2011). *Cloud computing use cases,* White Paper, v.4. Retrieved February 20, 2012, from http://openCloudmani-festo.org/Cloud_Computing_Use_Cases_White-paper-2_0.pdf

Dargha, R. (2009). *Cloud computing key considerations for adoption.* Infosys. Retrieved March 3, 2012, from http://www.infosys.com/Cloud / resource-center/documents/Cloud-computing.pdf

GTSI. (2011). *Cloud computing: Building a framework for successful transition.* GTSI. Retrieved November 3, 2011, from http://www.slideshare. net/jerry0040/Cloud-computing-building-a-framework-for-successful-transition-gtsi

IBM. (2010). *Review and summary of Cloud service level agreements.* Retrieved April 16, 2012, from http://www.ibm.com/developerworks/Cloud /library/cl-rev2sla.html

Jain, L., & Bhardwa, S. (2010). Enterprise cloud computing: Key considerations for adoption. *International Journal of Engineering and IT, 2*(2). Retrieved April 25, 2012, from http://www.techre-public.com/whitepapers/Cloud -computing-key-considerations-for-adoption/1198637

Kundra, V. (2011). *Federal cloud computing strategy.* Washington, DC: White House. Retrieved April 15, 2012, from http://gcn.com/ articles/2011/02/14/federal-Cloud -computing-strategy-released.aspx

Lewis, G. (2010). *Basics about cloud computing.* Carnegie Mellon University.

Mell, G., & Mell, P. (2009). *The NIST definition of cloud computing, version 15.* NIST.

Mell, P., & Grance, T. (2011). *The NIST definition of cloud computing (Draft):- Recommendations of the National Institute of Standards and Technology (NIST).* US Department of Commerce.

Miller, J., Candler, L., & Wald, H. (2010). *Information security governance: Government considerations for the cloud computing environment.* Booz Allen Hamilton. Retrieved April 20, 2011, from www.boozallen.com/insights/insight-detail/42698843

Pring, B., Brown, R. H., Frank, A., Hayward, S., & Leong, L. (2009). *Forecast: Sizing the cloud; Understanding the opportunities in cloud services.* Gartner, Inc. Retrieved November 15, 2010, from http://www.lesechos.fr/me-dias/2009/0519//300350239.pdf

Rackspace Hosting. (2011). *Planning a move to the cloud tips, tricks and pitfalls.* Diversity. Retrieved April 20, 2011, from http://gcn.com/ articles/2011/02/14/federal-Cloud -computing-strategy-released.aspx

Rahman, S. (2010). *The business of cloud computing.* Retrieved November 15, 2010, from http:// www.shibleyrahman.com/business-administra-tion/the-business-of-Cloud -computing.php

Ramakrishnan, R. (2010). *What is cloud computing? What does it mean to enterprises?* Retrieved June 22, 2011, from http://www.cumulux.com/ Cloud %20Computing%20Primer.pdf

Russell, D. (2010). *Weather report: Considerations from migrating to the Cloud.* IBM. Retrieved April 14, 2010, from http://www.ibm.com/developer-works/Cloud /library/cl-wr1migrateappstoCloud /

Scott, K. (2010). *White paper: The basics of cloud computing.* Retrieved, June 16, 2011, from http://www.akilisystems.com/downloads/Basicsof-Cloud Computing.pdf

Spínola, M. (2009). *The five characteristics of cloud computing.* Retrieved October 24, 2010, from http://ornot.files.wordpress.com/2009/08/Cloud -computing-paradigm-chart1.jpg

Staten, J. (2008). *Is cloud computing ready for the enterprise?* Forrester Research, Inc. Retrieved November 27, 2010, from http://ceria.dauphine.fr/cours98/CoursBD/doc/Forrester-Cloud -computing-report080307%5B1%5D.pdf

Sun Microsystems, Inc. (2009). *Introduction to cloud computing architecture*, White Paper, 1st ed.

TATA. (2011). *Moving from legacy systems to cloud computing.* Tata Communication. Retrieved March 23, 2012, from http://www.tatacommunications.com/downloads/whitepapers/Tata_Communications_Cloud Compuing_WhitePaper_v2.0-web.pdf

Varia, J. (2010). *Migrating your existing applications to the AWS cloud: - A phase-driven approach to cloud migration.* Amazon Web Service. Retrieved June 26, 2012, from http://media.amazonwebservices.com/CloudMigration-main.pdf

KEY TERMS AND DEFINITIONS

Application Programming Interface (API): Is a contract that tells a developer how to write code to interact with some kind of system. The API describes the syntax of the operations supported by the system. For each operation, the API specifies the information that should be sent to the system, the information that the system will send back, and any error conditions that might occur.

Broker: It has no Cloud resources of its own, but matches consumers and providers based on the SLA required by the consumer. The consumer has no knowledge that the broker does not control the resources.

Cloud Bursting: Is a technique used by hybrid Cloud s to provide additional resources to private Cloud s on an as-needed basis. If the private Cloud has the processing power to handle its workloads, the hybrid Cloud is not used. When workloads exceed the private Cloud's capacity, the hybrid Cloud automatically allocates additional resources to the private Cloud.

Federation: Is the act of combining data or identities across multiple systems. Federation can be done by a Cloud provider or by a Cloud broker.

Governance: It refers to the controls and processes that make sure policies are enforced.

Integration: Is the process of combining components or systems into an overall system. Integration among Cloud-based components and systems can be complicated by issues such as multi-tenancy, federation and government regulations.

Interoperability: Is concerned with the ability of systems to communicate. It requires that the communicated information is understood by the receiving system. In the world of Cloud Computing, this means the ability to write code that works with more than one Cloud provider simultaneously, regardless of the differences between the providers.

Multi-Tenancy: Is the property of multiple systems, applications or data from different enterprises hosted on the same physical hardware. Multitenancy is common to most Cloud-based systems.

Policy: Is a general term for an operating procedure. For example, a security policy might specify that all requests to a particular Cloud service must be encrypted.

Portability: Is the ability to run components or systems written for one environment in another environment. In the world of Cloud Computing, this includes software and hardware environments (both physical and virtual).

Service Level Agreement (SLA): Is contract between a provider and a consumer that specifies consumer requirements and the provider's commitment to them. Typically an SLA includes items such as uptime, privacy, security and backup procedures.

Virtual Machine (VM): Is a file that when executed, looks to the user like an actual machine. Infrastructure as a Service is often provided as a VM image that can be started or stopped as needed. Changes made to the VM while it is running can be stored to disk to make them persistent.

Chapter 9
Virtualization and Cloud Computing:
Business Models in the Virtual Cloud

Chaka Chaka
Tshwane University of Technology, South Africa

ABSTRACT

This chapter explores the interface between virtualization and cloud computing for global enterprise mobility. It also investigates the potential both virtualization and cloud computing hold for global enterprises. In this context, it argues that the virtualization of computing operations, applications, and services and the consumerization of digital technologies serve as one of the key drivers of cloud computing. Against this backdrop, the chapter first provides an overview of virtualization, consumerization, and cloud computing. Second, it showcases real life instances in which five enterprises leverage virtualization and cloud computing as part of their cloud business solutions. Third, it outlines some of the hollows and pain points characterizing cloud computing. Fourth and last, the chapter briefly presents possible future trends likely to typify cloud computing.

INTRODUCTION

In the ever-evolving and rapidly expanding trajectory of the world of computing, virtualization and cloud computing have become irresistible buzz words attracting the attention of enterprises and consumers alike. Both these twin concepts and processes are at the cusp of revolutionizing the way

conventional enterprise Internet and computing practices operate. By their very nature, these two cognate computing processes are disruptive and transformative, thereby necessitating enterprises to rearchitect and reconfigure themselves as next generation virtual and cloud based organizations. In this way, enterprises that are willing to virtualize their computing architectures, services and activities in the cloud are likely to have a competitive differentiator and value added benefits over their

DOI: 10.4018/978-1-4666-2533-4.ch009

rivals. This is particularly so for global enterprises leveraging mobility as part of their global business strategy. That is, for global enterprises cloud computing serves as a game changing force.

At the core of enterprise cloud computing, especially, is virtualization since the latter is one of the key enablers of cloud computing in general. So, for enterprises to be able to *cloud compute* their services and operations, they also need to virtualize those services and operations including aspects of their technologies (e.g., IT infrastructures, architectures, platforms and applications) from which those services and operations are deployed. Only then, can cloud computing have a requisite disruptive impact expected of it. An essential ingredient into the virtualization and cloud computing mix is consumerization. The latter serves as one of the main drivers for cloud computing and lends itself well as a touchstone that enterprises can use in determining how they can embrace cloud computing.

Based on the foregoing paragraphs, the following areas constitute the main discussion points of this chapter: virtualization, consumerization and cloud computing: an overview; tapping into virtualized clouds: business models in the clouds; hollows and pain points in the clouds; and future trends.

VIRTUALIZATION, CONSUMERIZATION, AND CLOUD COMPUTING: AN OVERVIEW

In the computing and Internet environment, virtualization has at least two related senses. Firstly, it refers to creating an unreal or a simulated replica of something such as a server, an application, an operating system, a storage device, a network resource, a help desk, or a piece of hardware (see *Figure 1*). Secondly, it is a computing technology allowing users to virtually utilize multiple devices, thereby eliminating the need for their physical deployment (see Gondaliya, 2010). In this sense,

it embodies abstract computing platforms and applications (Jäätmaa, 2010) and signifies a shift from traditional siloed IT infrastructures and architectures to virtually distributed and shared ones.

For its part, consumerization is a dual value chain in which consumers or end users utilize digital devices and technologies (e.g., smartphones, iPads, instant messages, social networking sites, microblogs, and virtual storages) in their private lives and end up employing the self-same devices and technologies for enterprise purposes. Put differently, it is a technology trajectory in which technologies with consumer-oriented offerings are embraced and harnessed by businesses for enterprise offerings. Known also as the consumerization of IT, this phenomenon results in the blurring of the classical line between personal and professional lives for employees. Moreover, as more employees *trend* towards adopting consumer technologies for business purposes, their behavioral practice in turn helps facilitate the consumerization of enterprise mobility (see Chaka, 2012; Signorini & Hochmuth, 2010).

Both virtualization and consumerization serve as key enablers of cloud computing in that they provide an enterprise milieu in which the latter can occur. That is, virtualized computing and IT infrastructures, architectures, platforms, applications, services, operations and functions that have a higher degree of consumer and enterprise uptake provide an ideal opportunity for cloud computing. The latter has generated a lot of buzz in the IT world and has also been a subject of myriad defini-

Figure 1. A screenshot of a virtual keyboard and a real keyboard

tions. Hence, as suggested by Cloud Computing World [CCW] (2011a, 2011b), Hagel and Brown (2010), Jäätmaa (2010), Steele (2011) and Winans and Brown (2010), there is a plethora of opinions and theories as to what cloud computing is and is not. In this chapter, cloud computing is viewed as a process, a concept, a model and a metaphor. As a process it has evolved over time in the same way as technologies such as the Internet, the Web, web browsers, distributed computing, grid computing, utility computing, data storage utilities, and web-based applications (e.g., emails) have evolved.

And as a concept, cloud computing entails a technology and mindset shift in relation to deploying IT infrastructures, architectures, platforms, applications, software, operations and functions as services. This shift is embodied in its offerings such as infrastructure as a service (IaaS); hardware as a service (HaaS); platform as a service (PaaS); application as a service (AaaS); software as a service (SaaS); data storage as a service (DaaS) or storage as a service (StaaS); and communication as a service (CaaS). However, concepts like IaaS, HaaS, PaaS and SaaS predate cloud computing as it is presently understood. Cloud computing is also a model in that it is a business approach in which clients source pay-per-use, on-demand, and shared online services (Bo & Rentian, 2009; Business Connexion, 2011; CCW, 2011a, 2011b; Harper, 2011; Jäätmaa, 2010; Solano, 2010; Winans & Brown, 2010). Moreover, as a metaphor it signifies how computers or computing devices within a network are configured vis-à-vis one another such that they operate within a metaphorical cloud environment (Chaka, 2010) as represented in *Figure 2*. Inherent in this view is that all cloud services and operations are hidden and dispersed in an Internet cloud.

Furthermore, cloud computing has other enablers such as service oriented architecture, cluster computing, autonomic computing, and Web 2.0. Service oriented architecture is software architecture for creating and utilizing business processes offered as services. On the one hand,

cluster computing involves pairing several computing devices to perform parallel work so as to configure a single high-performance computing unit. On the other hand, autonomic computing is a form of self-regulating computing system capable of handling progressively complex tasks and running diagnostics and checks to compensate for unexpected glitches or irregularities. And Web 2.0 refers to interoperable and user-driven web applications that are highly interactive and collaborative in nature (CCW, 2011c; Jäätmaa, 2010; Winans & Brown, 2010). Thus, overall, cloud computing is a model offering, on-demand, pay-per-use and self-service computing resources characterized by ubiquitous computing access, location-neutral resource pooling, and rapid elasticity (Hagel & Brown, 2010). In the main, there are four types of cloud computing: public, private, hybrid and community cloud computing (Cloud Security Alliance, 2009; Jäätmaa, 2010).

TAPPING INTO VIRTUALIZED CLOUDS: BUSINESS MODELS IN THE CLOUDS

This section of the chapter investigates the manner in which enterprises – big and small - can leverage cloud computing for their specific needs and tastes

Figure 2. A virtual representation of cloud computing (Source: Virtual Cloud, 2011)

with a view to enhancing both their business value chain and business value streams. In fact, it is vital that when enterprises adopt cloud computing that they do so with the value chain, value streams and business architecture embedded into their business models in mind. In this context, the section also presents five enterprise case studies – VMware, Nimbula, iTricity, IBM and Vodacom - showcasing how cloud computing can be adopted and deployed for enterprise purposes. These enterprises were selected for the agility and innovation they bring to bear to the cloud computing ecosystem in their respective spheres of operation. First, an extensive desktop online engine-powered and database-driven search involving Bing, Google, Google Scholar, Business Technology Solutions (BTS) and Educational Resources Informational Center (ERIC) was mounted to identify these enterprises from their peers. Second, thematic analysis was employed as a technique (Chaka, 2011; Thomas & Harden, 2008) to select the three enterprises from a pool of enterprises.

VMware: Virtualization and Cloud Infrastructure

Among other things, three factors serve as critical differentiators for VMware (VMware, Inc. - a United States based enterprise specializing in virtualization solutions from the desktop to the data center) in the cloud computing arena. These are its industry-firsts – the first hypervisor, the first VMotion™, and the first platform for pooling servers, storage and networking; its VMware vSphere™ 4; and its Cloud Foundry (see *Figure 3*). The last two instances are relevant for the purpose of this section. The former, VMware vSphere™ 4 (both its next generation virtualization platform and its cloud based operating system) was touted as the industry's first when it was launched in 2009 (VMware, 2009). This was a giant step given that a computer operating system (OS) sphere is not even VMware's niche market.

Deployed primarily as an internal cloud OS, VMware vSphere™ 4 enables an efficient, flexible and reliable delivery of IT as a service (ITaaS) to enterprises and service providers. In particular, it is configured to deliver cloud computing to enterprises in an evolutionary, non-disruptive way. Additionally, it aggregates and manages vast quantities of infrastructure (e.g., processors, storage and networks) as a seamless, flexible and dynamic operating whole. Above all, it provisions to clients cloud solutions tailored to their internal cloud infrastructures. In this respect, it intends supporting a dynamic federated synergy between internal and external clouds, thereby creating private cloud environments spanning data centers and cloud providers (VMware, 2009; 2011). Most importantly, VMware vSphere™ 4 positions itself to deliver efficiency, control and choice to enterprises and service providers in relation to their business critical IT for both on-premise and off-premise application hosting. Among the further intended benefits and capabilities it has for clients are the following:

- Zero downtime, zero data loss protection against hardware failures
- Minimized planned downtime owing to storage migration and maintenance

Figure 3. Cloud Foundry as the industry's first open PaaS (Source: VMware, 2011)

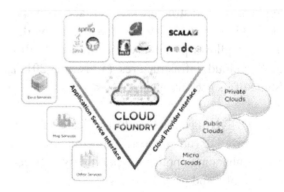

- Quick, simple, integrated and cost effective disk based backup and recovery for all applications
- Easier and stricter security compliance
- Easier application service level management

Moreover, VMware vSphere™ 4 prides itself in aggregating several virtual machines and large quantities of physical infrastructure into a single resource pool on a cloud scale for the purpose of creating a 21st century mainframe. To this effect, it is able to pool together up to:

- 1,280 virtual machines
- 8,000 network ports
- 32 TB of RAM
- 16 petabytes of storage (VMware, 2009; 2011)

The latter, Cloud Foundry (together with its open-source cloud package and its industry's first open platform as a service (PaaS)), is a platform offering developers tools to build applications on public, private, and hybrid cloud environments or anywhere else irrespective of whether the underlying servers run VMware or not (Higginbotham, 2011). In this sense, Cloud Foundry is an instance of a new generation application platform architected purposively for cloud environments and delivered as a service. It qualitatively enhances developers' capability to deploy, run and scale applications while adopting the widest choice of public and private clouds, application infrastructure services, and industry-class, high-productivity developer frameworks. Thus, it allows portability and interoperability across cloud infrastructures (VMware, 2011). Some of its uses for enterprises are:

- Delivering cloud-ready applications optimized to run on virtual infrastructures
- Enhancing application portability between public and private clouds

- Building modern, Web-oriented applications in less than half the time of conventional approaches
- Increasing the reliability, flexibility and scalability of applications
- Overcoming relational database bottlenecks and enabling real-time data

In the main, VMware offers end-user cloud computing solutions as well. For example, its end-user computing solutions enable enterprises to deliver desktop as a service, and to securely provision and deploy customized virtual desktops, applications and data to users across multiple devices, platforms and locations. It also allows end users to: securely access their software as a service (SaaS), Web applications and enterprises; reduce cost and complexity of desktop management; and shift traditional email to next generation email and collaboration software.

Overall, VMware insists that its approach to cloud solutions is not about public versus private versus hybrid cloud models, but about walking enterprises through and provisioning them the cloud model that matches and meets their business needs. However, it concedes that hybrid cloud is more economical than both pure public and pure private cloud models as it tends to maximize enterprise benefits. And with its comprehensive application management solutions, VMware enables enterprises to swiftly, seamlessly and confidently virtualize and migrate applications to the cloud (VMware, 2011). Finally, VMware prides itself in comprehensive cloud computing solutions for enterprise hybrid clouds. In this context, it offers a single comprehensive framework for securing virtual data centers and cloud environments at different levels – network, application, data, host and endpoint. It enables enterprises to centralize security across virtual data centers, protect applications from network related threats, and secure the edges of virtual data centers (VMware, 2011).

Nimbula: Cloud Environment Operating System (OS)

Nimbula is a software startup co-founded by former Amazon executives who developed Amazon's EC2 (Elastic Compute Cloud) public cloud service. It merges public cloud computing (with its scalability and efficiency) with the control and security of the private data center. In this way, it strives to make public and private clouds coexist mutually and seamlessly, thereby challenging and disrupting the perceived dichotomy between the two environments. It thus intends making this synergy hassle-free and liquid and provisioning private data centers that can configure themselves into public clouds like EC2 during peak periods. This is meant to eliminate bottlenecks and siloing characterizing private clouds (Watters, 2010).

Two of Nimbula's critical products are Nimbula Cloud Operating System and Nimbula Director. On the one hand, the former is an automated cloud management system powering EC2-like services behind the firewalls. It offers singularly sophisticated and nuanced solutions for managing clouds of enterprise clients. Its built-in technology enables these clients to easily repurpose their existent infrastructures and build computing clouds in the trusted environments of their own data centers. Leveraging rapid technologies, Nimbula Cloud OS transforms – swimmingly and cost-effectively - under-utilized private data centers into powerful, readily configurable computing capacity. In all, the Nimbula Cloud OS technology is designed with the following value added enterprise cloud offerings in mind:

- **Ease of use:** A highly automated, hands-off install requiring minimal configuration reduces the complexity of deploying on-premise clouds
- **Automated application deployment:** Launch plans allow suites of heterogeneous virtual machines to be launched across multiple sites

- **Scalability:** The Nimbula Cloud OS is specially designed for linear scaling from small clusters up to thousands of computers
- **Flexibility:** The Nimbula technology supports controlled external public and private clouds like Amazon EC2 as required by clients for specific applications or during peak periods
- **Ease of migration:** The Nimbula Cloud OS fosters simple and seamless migration of available applications into the cloud through its support for flexible networking and storage and multi-platform sites
- **Reliability:** Boasting no points of failure, the Nimbula Cloud OS employs sophisticated fail over mechanisms to ensure system resilience and integrity (Nimbula, 2011a).

On the other hand, the latter is a powerful cloud management system configured to deliver utility-grade enterprise cloud offerings. It is differentiated by high levels of flexibility, scalability, automation and security. Some of its key features include:

- **Scalability:** It scales from smaller clusters to thousands of computers.
- **Ease of use:** It quickly installs up to several thousands of servers with a hands-off automated installation; it easily migrates existing applications into the cloud with multi-platform supporting and flexible networking; and it reduces demands on system administrators through low-touch automated cloud management.
- **Flexibility:** It enforces network policy between instances and provides a distributed firewall via network security groups; and it controls utilization of external cloud services with powerful access management via a uniform API.
- **Security:** It controls access to local and external cloud resources with a robust policy based authorization system supporting multi-tenancy (Nimbula, 2011b).

And some of its key benefits for enterprises are:

- Tightly controlling the deployment of services into external clouds via a uniform API with a fine-grained permission management system
- Reducing operational overheads with automation and low friction interfaces
- Quickly turning static private data centers into a flexible pool of compute resources
- Accelerating innovation with a rapid deployment and an increased infrastructural flexibility
- Increasing infrastructure utilization rates with powerful workload distribution
- Facilitating utility-grade cloud features like fine-grained permissions management enabling multi-tenancy (Nimbula, 2011b).

iTricity: Virtualized Data Centers Delivering On-Demand Cloud Computing

The indispensable dependence of 21st century enterprises on IT to power their operations cannot be overstated. The necessity of such enterprises to adopt cloud computing can hardly be overemphasized either. This is where iTricity features in the IT-cloud computing equation. iTricity is a data center service provider (based in the Netherlands) one part of whose vision is to create a computing cloud model - employing virtualized services - that is able to meet clients' needs for on-demand cloud offerings. When it first started as an enterprise, the following were three of its key business challenges:

- Combining five physically separate data centers into a single virtual network
- Greater speed and flexibility of provisioning tailored to specific clients' needs
- Modeling virtual environments and services for clients on a shared infrastructure base

In order to address these challenges and other IT related requirements, iTricity had to rearchitect itself. It positioned itself to provision comprehensive solutions encompassing server, storage and network capacity. It then created a shared infrastructure – *a build once, share many times model* - so as to deliver a tailored mix of services to individual clients while providing regulatory-compliant cloud offerings customized to specific industry conditions. Here its ultimate goal was to establish a multi-tenant, services-on-demand cloud environment. In addition, it set about creating profiles detailing the configurations of resources and services needed by its target clients - both small and large - with a view to contracting from them the burden of developing their own compliant IT infrastructures (Cisco, 2009).

With this in mind, iTricity established its new cloud computing hosting center delivering cloud services (deployed on key technologies from Cisco and IBM) to the Netherlands, Belgium and Luxemburg. This cloud solution is spread across five data centers. The latter are connected together via a Cisco CWDM Multiplexers and Cisco CWDM Gigabit Interface Converters (GBIC)/Small Form-Factor Pluggables (SFP). Furthermore, when the company realized that enterprise clients generated peak bursts of traffic at disparate times, it created a virtualized pool of network capacity with virtualized server and storage capacity. This enabled overcapacity to be shared by multiple users, resulting in a marked improvement in resource utilization (Cisco, 2009).

To cement and consolidate the virtualization of its services, iTricity deployed Cisco technologies to virtualize its underlying network platform and leveraged IBM's Cloud technologies to strengthen its compute and storage resources. This development has yielded the scalability, flexibility and resilience that it so much needs in provisioning its cloud solutions. As a result of this rearchitecting process, iTricity's virtual network has become a platform capable of supporting diverse functions ranging from routing to switching, separating customer networks to load balancing, and deploying firewalls to establishing online security. This means that iTricity is now able to meaningfully share resources among its clients and offer each one of them their own vertical slice of virtualization, configured to meet their specific demands.

Finally, owing to this IT realignment, iTricity has managed to garner the following business benefits:

- **Better use of assets:** Asset utilization at iTricity has improved by 25 to 30 per cent as a result of consolidation and virtualization
- **Pay for what you use model:** iTricity offers capacity on demand (managed or unmanaged) with a customer portal for providing a clear, graphical overview of cloud computing resources deployed
- **Faster response to customer needs:** The time required by iTricity to respond to customer service requests has been correspondingly reduced from two weeks to just one day
- **Supporting customer needs for compliance:** The solution has reduced the time and cost to compliance for iTricity customers
- **Investment model aligned to growth:** Leveraging a Cisco platform has enabled iTricity to better manage its growth and investment (Cisco, 2009).

IBM: Dispensing Clouds to Global Enterprises

For a couple of years now, IBM has been plying its trade in enterprise cloud designs, infrastructures, implementations and solutions, thereby consolidating its position as one of the reputable global bellwethers in these spheres of enterprise computing. While the list of its global enterprise clients is endless, it has over time attracted such clients in areas as diverse as: travel and transportation; telecoms; retail, financial, banking and insurance sectors; media and entertainment; governments; healthcare; education; science and technology; aerospace and defense; computer and IT services; energy and utilities; chemical and petroleum sector; consumer electronics and products; automotive industry; and so on. Three delivery models typify cloud offerings of its global enterprise clients: public, private and hybrid clouds. In the first instance, IT functions or activities are provisioned as a service over the Internet; in the second instance, IT functions or activities are provided as a service over the intranet; and in the third instance, internal and external IT functions are integrated. There are key differences in the provisioning of the first two delivery models as determined by its enterprise clientele. Here public clouds are dominated by SaaS, followed by IaaS whereas private clouds are dominated by IaaS, followed by PaaS (International Business Machines [IBM], 2009, 2010; Kwok, 2009).

IBM has its own private cloud platform for enterprises. Called IBM CloudBurst, this platform provides pre-packaged cloud offerings. Firstly, it integrates service management software system with hardware (e.g., servers, storage, network), and quickstart services as a holistic offering to deliver an internal private cloud. Secondly, it allows for a rapid implementation of a cloud environment and takes the guesswork out of establishing a private cloud by pre-installing and configuring the necessary software on the hardware. In this way, it leverages services for customizing enterprise environments. Thirdly, with IBM CloudBurst enterprise clients can do the following:

- Have rapid provisioning of resources for development and testing
- Deploy private cloud for new enterprise initiatives
- Improve services (e.g., improved time to value services delivered to end users, and reduced human error owing to automation and standardization)

- Reduce operational expenses (e.g., improve asset utilization and return on investment, reclaim capacity and unused compute power, gain productivity through automation, and shift support resources from infrastructure maintenance innovation projects) (IBM, 2009; Kwok, 2009).

Principally, IBM CloudBurst offers value added benefits for enterprise clients since it is:

- Built-for-purpose based on the architectural requirement of specific workloads
- A factory pre-integrated service delivery platform
- Pre-packaged, pre-configured with servers, storage, networking, software and installation that are tailored for private cloud purposes
- Delivered and supported as a single product

In this respect, its quickstart services involve deploying and integrating BladeCenter hardware in customer data centers (e.g., configuring local storage area network, configuring users and security profiles, and configuring and discovering virtualized compute, network and storage resources). They also entail on-site and hands-on platform training, and cover topics such as BladeCenter, local SAN and network switch management, and administrator and user level training, QuicStart Services. Above all, IBM offers cloud consulting and cloud implementation (IBM, 2009; Kwok, 2009).

One real life case study – involving a government as its enterprise client - is the one in which IBM worked with the Shandong Dongying government in China. In this instance, IBM entered into an agreement, called the Yellow River Delta Cloud Computing Strategic Cooperation Agreement, with the Shandong Dongying government. Dongying ranks as China's second largest oil field producing 26 million tons of crude oil per year. So, with this pact, IMB set out to help Dongying develop into a *smarter city*. According to this pact IBM was to:

- Build a cloud providing software development and text resources for software startup companies via the Web involving a self-service user interface
- Expand the cloud into an e-government services platform for the Dongying economic development zone as well as a research and development platform for eco-friendly oil cultivation
- Help Dongying's petroleum industry develop more innovative application services (IBM, 2009)

As part of its cloud solutions intended to translate this agreement into reality, IBM deployed end-to-end IBM Cloud Computing Center based on its cloud offerings; IBM CloudBurst; IBM hardware – System p and BladeCenter; IBM software – Tivoli, Rational, WebSphere and DB2 (IBM, 2009, Kwok, 2009).

In another instance in China, IBM is involved in a China Cloud Center for Software Development and Test project with the Wuxi municipal government. Some of the key goals of the project are:

- Accelerating transformation to a service-led economy
- Promoting software startup company growth
- Provisioning public cloud that can be accessed through the Internet or a secure connection
- Offering secure, network isolated environments
- Delivering backup/Restoring resource capabilities to protect customer assets
- Accelerating development and test cycles through quick resource on-boarding

Lastly, IBM is involved in the IBM China Private Desktop Cloud Deployment project. Based on VMware virtualization technology, this project is one of the largest software development laboratories boasting more than 1,200 vendor software developers and testers. Some of its value added benefits are: operational efficiency; enhanced security management; management simplicity; and green solution (Kwok, 2009).

Vodacom: Partnering to Deliver Cloud Services

Vodacom – majority-owned by a United Kingdom based Vodafone - is one of the leading mobile telecommunications and broadband companies in South Africa. It is currently resolutely making its inroads in the cloud computing market in South Africa. While cloud computing isn't its niche area, it seems to be making a significant investment in this market. For example, in 2008 it opened a \$9.7 million data center in Johannesburg to support its business services division. Recently, (in July 2011) it opened a 16,145 square foot data center in Cape Town so as to meet its growing demands for cloud computing in South Africa. This energy efficient data center is reported to be expandable to 32,291 square feet. This development happens at a time when South African businesses are either migrating or considering migrating to cloud infrastructures amidst concerns about expensive and limited bandwidth. Another development working in Vodacom's favor is the proposed new 8,700 mile fiber-optic submarine cable project that is likely to increase South Africa's broadband capacity by at least 500 gigabytes per second in 2012. This is expected to encourage cloud adoption by many South African enterprises (Henderson, 2011).

Offerings such as virtualization, hosted call centers, telepresence, and convergence are some of the key drivers for this data center. With the establishment of this data center, Vodacom intends positioning itself as a leading cloud-based hosting provider both in South Africa and in the rest of the African continent. Thus, to realize its cloud goals and to provide its enterprise clients with access to flexible, agile and scalable cloud computing, Vodacom has since partnered with both Novell and VMware. In respect of the former, especially, it

intends leveraging four of its solution offerings: Intelligent Workload Management; SUSE® Linux Enterprise Server; Platespin® Virtualization and Workload Management; and Identity and Security. The idea here is to integrate all of these offerings into its cloud hosting solutions. Additionally, the partnership is aimed at enabling enterprises in South Africa and across Africa to securely provision, manage and monitor multi-tenant applications delivered from Vodacom Business's cloud infrastructure (Harper, 2011; PR Newswire, 2011).

In this context, Vodacom Business employs SUSE Linux Enterprise Server to eradicate guesswork from complex server consolidation. It also deploys PlateSpin Recon, PlateSpin Migrate and PlateSpin Protect to effectively respond to increasing business demands, reduce energy consumption, lower costs and improve server workload performance. Moreover, it exploits Novell identity and security management solutions to enable clients to treat their cloud assets as an extended part of their data center. This resonates with Intelligent Workload Management whose core tenet is integrating identity and security management into cloud resources. By so doing, it seeks to ensure that policies and procedures for regulatory compliance and scrupulous business practices are requisitely and ubiquitously enforced. Thus, in the main, Vodacom is set to provide IaaS and SaaS cloud solutions across Africa by deploying Novell technologies (Harper, 2001; PR Newswire, 2011).

HOLLOWS AND PAIN POINTS IN THE CLOUDS

Cloud computing – or *cloud-onomics* (see Solano, 2010) – is touted to offer enterprises many value added benefits. Among such benefits are: virtualization; standardization; automation; modularization; elasticity and scalability; cost-cutting and savings; portability and interoperability; operational agility and efficiency; flexibility; rapid provisioning; asset protection; risk management;

image management; compliance management; built-in security; and better user experience (Blevins, Lounsbury, Kirk & Harding, 2009; Jäätmaa, 2010; Jaekel & Luhn, 2009; Solano, 2010; Winans & Brown, 2010). Despite all these positives, matters of security, privacy, identity protection, and compliance still haunt many enterprises, and as such, serve as key inhibitors to a universal adoption of cloud computing by most enterprises (see Chaka, 2012). Until such matters are satisfactorily and convincingly dealt with, many enterprises are likely to perceive cloud computing as pock-marked with hollows. This is particularly so, if the recent hacking of Amazon's website – in which clients' private information was compromised and, in some instances, stolen – is anything to go by. While this was a one-off occurrence, the fact remains that Amazon is one of the leading cloud pioneers and a reputable cloud provider offering several cloud solutions to many global enterprises and many global individual consumers. So, the hacking incident that dogged it, with the resultant breaching of its data security and the violation of its clients' privacy and identities, points to the many hollows and pain points that still characterize the cloud environment.

Hollows can also manifest themselves at the physical layer, the network and virtualization levels, and at the Internet, server, database, data privacy, and program access points within a cloud ecosystem. In addition to these hollows, there are pain points that can stalk a cloud ecosystem at any given time. These include a disruption of key services; a theft, interception or hacking of critical data/information; a malicious damage of data/information; and a loss of privacy and identity. Alongside these pain points are vulnerabilities within the cloud environment. Among such vulnerabilities are hostile programs; malicious bugs to the virtualized infrastructures; hostile individuals giving wrong instructions to programs; and unscrupulous individuals corrupting programs and data or eavesdropping on critical communication (Saurab, n.d.). Some of the key procedures for dealing with some of these pain points are: sanitization of information/data; instance isolation (Saurab, n.d.); encryption and key management; application security; identity and access management; governance and enterprise risk management; and data security lifecycle (Cloud Security Alliance, 2009; see Chaka, 2012).

FUTURE TRENDS

Four key future trends are likely to typify enterprise cloud computing in the next 5 years. These are: cloud computing as a service (CCaaS); the Semantic Web; autonomic security; and virtual cloud value chain. CCaaS refers to cloud computing being provisioned holistically as a service package to enterprises so as to allow enterprises to choose from the given packaged cloud offerings that meet their business requirements and are tailored to their specific business architectures. Among other things this trend entails virtualization as a service (VaaS) and data centers as a service (DCaaS). For its part the Semantic Web is about cloud computing technologies adopting and leveraging Semantic Web technologies so they can align themselves with Semantic Web based intelligent agents. This is also about delivering Semantic Web driven cloud computing offerings to global enterprises

Closely allied to Semantic Web based cloud computing is autonomic security. The latter refers to cloud computing security that is self-regulating by ensuring that it can service, correct and update itself and the IT infrastructure on which it is deployed instantaneously and swimmingly. Most importantly, this trend is about automated intelligent cloud computing security deployment and management. Finally, virtual cloud value chain involves value added benefits built into cloud offerings, and that infrastructurally and organizationally enhance enterprises' business value streams and business architectures.

CONCLUSION

The chapter has contended that both virtualization and consumerization are some of the necessary preconditions for cloud computing. In this regard, cloud computing offers global enterprises more affordances and benefits than it is expected. In the context of this chapter some of the affordances and benefits identified include: virtualization; ease of use; automated application deployment; elasticity and scalability; flexibility; portability and interoperability; better asset utilization; faster response to customer needs; rapid provisioning of resources; cost-cutting and savings; and operational agility and efficiency. Different cloud service models - e.g., infrastructure as a service (IaaS), hardware as a service (HaaS), platform as a service (PaaS), application as a service (AaaS), software as a service (SaaS), and data storage as a service (DaaS) or storage as a service (StaaS), have been identified. So have four cloud computing deployment models (e.g., private, public, hybrid and community clouds). There are five enterprises – presented as instances of real life applications of cloud computing in five different global regions – that have been shown to be leveraging some of the cloud service and deployment models. In this respect, their concomitant affordances and benefits, in varying degrees have been outlined. Each of these enterprises exhibit different methodologies and different requirements for deploying cloud computing as informed by their given business goals.

In addition, the chapter has highlighted some of the hollows and pain points characterizing cloud computing at any given time. And finally, it has outlined four key trends likely to typify cloud computing in the next five years.

REFERENCES

Blevins, T., Lounsbury, D., Kirk, M., & Harding, C. (2009). *Cloud computing business scenario workshop*. Retrieved August 8, 2011, from https://www.opengroup.org/cloudcomputing/uploads/40/20362/R091.pdf

Bo, Z., & Rentian, C. (2009). *Business model innovations in cloud computing*. Retrieved July 27, 2011, from http://www.huawei.com/en/static/Strategy_New_opportunities--Business_model_innovations_in_cloud_computing-26251-1-087845.pdf

Business Connexion. (2011). *Virtual computing environment*. Retrieved July 27, 2011, from http://www.bcx.co.za/solutions/services/data_centre_solutions/virtual_computing_enviroment/

Chaka, C. (2010). User and enterprise mobility: Mobile social networking and mobile cloud computing. *Cutter IT Journal, 23*(9), 35–39.

Chaka, C. (2011). Social computing: Harnessing enterprise social networking and the relationship economy. In Papadopoulou, P., Kanellis, P., & Martakos, D. (Eds.), *Social computing theory and practice: Interdisciplinary approaches* (pp. 85–100). Hershey, PA: IGI Global.

Chaka, C. (2012). Consumerization of IT, social computing, and mobility as the new desktop. *Cutter IT Journal, 225*(5), 28–33.

Cisco. (2009). *Five virtualised data centres deliver cloud computing*. Retrieved July 27, 2011, from http://www.cisco.com/en/US/solutions/collateral/ns340/ns517/ns224/case_study_itricity.pdf

Cloud Computing World. (2011a). *Defining cloud computing virtualization*. Retrieved July 3, 2011, from http://www.cloudcomputingworld.org/cloud-computing/defining-cloud-computing-virtualization.html

Cloud Computing World. (2011b). *What is cloud computing?* Retrieved July 3, 2011, from http://www.cloudcomputingworld.org/cloud-computing/what-is-cloud-computing.html

Cloud Computing World. (2011c). *Cloud computing vs. autonomic computing.* Retrieved July 3, 2011, from http://www.cloudcomputingworld.org/cloud-computing/cloud-computing-vs-autonomic-computing.html

Cloud Security Alliance. (2009). *Security guidance for critical areas of focus in cloud computing* V2.1. Retrieved August 8, 2011, from https://cloudsecurityalliance.org/csaguide.pdf

Gondaliya, M. (2010). *Virtualization vs cloud computing.* Retrieved July 3, 2011, from http://mayur.gondaliya.com/web-servers/the-difference-between-virtualization-and-cloud-computing-364.html

Hagel, J., & Brown, J. S. (2010). *Cloud computing storms on the horizon.* Retrieved June 6, 2010, from http://www.deloitte.com/assets/Dcom-UnitedStates/Local%20Assets/Documents/TMT_us_tmt/us_tmt_ce_CloudsStormsonHorizon_042010.pdf

Harper, E. (2011). *Vodacom and Novell are changing the rules.* Retrieved July 27, 2011, from http://www.novell.com/connectionmagazine/2011/05/dept2.pdf

Henderson, N. (2011). *Telecom provider Vodacom opens Cape Town data center.* Retrieved August 2, 2011, from http://www.thewhir.com/web-hosting-news/072611_Telecommunications_Provider_Vodacom_Opens_Cape_Town_Data_Center

Higginbotham, S. (2011). *VMware launches open-source cloud.* Retrieved August 3, 2011, from http://gigaom.com/cloud/vmware-open-source-cloud/

IBM. (2009). *Your first step to cloud computing - Building a sustainable future.* Retrieved August 3, 2011, from http://www-07.ibm.com/hk/e-business/events/archives/SCCS/pdf/Your_First_Step_to_Cloud_Computing.pdf

IBM. (2010). *Cloud computing insights from 110 implementation projects.* Retrieved August 3, 2011, from http://public.dhe.ibm.com/common/ssi/ecm/en/ciw03074usen/CIW03074USEN.PDF

Jäätmaa, J. (2010). *Financial aspects of cloud computing business models.* Retrieved July 27, 2011, from http://hsepubl.lib.hse.fi/FI/ethesis/pdf/12435/hse_ethesis_12435.pdf

Jaekel, M., & Luhn, A. (2009). *Cloud computing – Business models, value creation dynamics and advantages for customers.* Retrieved July 27, 2011, from http://cn.siemens.com/cms/cn/English/it-solutions/Documents/WhitePaper_Cloud%20Computing_EN_200911.pdf

Kwok, D. (2009). *Cloud computing - "End user deployment and IBM internal experiences."* Retrieved August 3, 2011, from https://www.opengroup.org/conference-live/uploads/40/20793/Kwok.pdf

Newswire, P. R. (2011). *Vodacom business and Novell partner to securely manage and optimize cloud services.* Retrieved August 2, 2011, from http://www.prnewswire.com/news-releases/vodacom-business-and-novell-partner-to-securely-manage-and-optimize-cloud-services-94237459.html

Nimbula. (2011a). *Nimbula™ cloud operating system technical white paper.* Retrieved August 6, 2011, from http://nimbula.com/media/nimbula/Nimbula_Technical_White_Paper.pdf

Nimbula. (2011b). *Nimbula™ Director v1.0 datasheet.* Retrieved August 6, 2011, from http://nimbula.com/media/nimbula/Nimbula_Datasheet.pdf

Saurab, H. (n.d.). *Security issues in cloud computing*. Retrieved August 8, 2011, from http://www.serl.iiit.ac.in/cs6600/saurabh.ppt

Signorini, E., & Hochmuth, P. (2010). *Consumerization of the mobile enterprise*. Retrieved July 24, 2010, from http://na.blackberry.com/eng/ataglance/get_the_facts/Yankee_Consumerization_of_the_Mobile_Enterprise.pdf

Solano, P. (2010). *Cloud computing? Concepts and beyond*. Retrieved July 27, 2011, from http://td.revistaitnow.com/bajar.php?a=files/td11/conferencias/93_33-gbm-cloud-computing.pdf

Steele, C. (2011). *Cloud computing business model raises security, maturity concerns*. Retrieved July 27, 2011, from http://searchservervirtualization.techtarget.com/feature/Cloud-computing-business-model-raises-security-maturity-concerns

Thomas, J., & Harden, A. (2008). *Methods for the thematic synthesis of qualitative research in systematic reviews*. Retrieved September 9, 2009, from http://www.biomedcentral.com/content/pdf/1471-2288-8-45.pdf

Virtual Cloud. (2011). *Cloud computing – What does it mean to system administrators?* Retrieved July 27, 2011, from http://virtcloud.blogspot.com/2011/07/cloud-computing-what-does-it-mean-to.html

VMware. (2009). *VMware unveils the industry's first operating system for building the internal cloud — VMware vSphere™ 4*. Retrieved August 2, 2011, from http://www.vmware.com/company/news/releases/vsphere-launch.html

VMware. (2011). *VMware and your cloud - Maximize IT agility to drive business agility*. Retrieved August 2, 2011, from http://www.vmware.com/files/pdf/cloud/VMware-and-Cloud-Computing-BR-EN.pdf

Watters, A. (2010). *Architects of Amazon web services launch Nimbula, promise an OS for the cloud*. Retrieved August 3, 2011, from http://www.readwriteweb.com/cloud/2010/06/former-aws-execs-launch-nimbula.php

Winans, T. B., & Brown, J. S. (2010). *Cloud computing - A collection of working papers*. Retrieved June 6, 2010, from http://www.deloitte.com/assets/Dcom-UnitedStates/Local%20Assets/Documents/us_tmt_ce_CloudPapers_73009.pdf

KEY TERMS AND DEFINITIONS

Autonomic Computing: Autonomic computing is a form of self-regulating computing system capable of handling progressively complex tasks and running diagnostics and checks to compensate for unexpected glitches or irregularities.

Cloud Computing as a Service (CCaaS): This refers to cloud computing being provisioned holistically as a service package to enterprises so as to allow enterprises to choose from the given packaged cloud offerings that meet their business requirements and are tailored to their specific business architectures. It functions in the same way as software as a service (SaaS), infrastructure as a service (IaaS), and hardware as a service (HaaS).

Consumerization: This trend refers to the adoption of electronic devices, first, by general consumers or users and, second, by enterprises or companies. One of its common versions is the consumerization of the IT (information technology).

Cloud Computing: Also regarded as a kind of *cloud-onomics*, cloud computing is a business model or approach in which clients source pay-per-use, on-demand, and shared online services. Other such online services are free and not offered as premium to users. Examples here are Google Apps, Dropbox and SkyDrive.

Platform as a Service (PaaS): PaaS is a platform offering developers tools to build applications on public, private, and hybrid cloud environments or in any virtual computing environment allowing the deployment of such a platform.

Service Oriented Architecture (SOA): This is software architecture for creating and utilizing business processes offered as services.

Virtualization: This refers to creating simulated or an unreal replica of something such as a server, an application, an operating system, a storage device, a network resource, a help desk, or a piece of hardware, thereby obviating the need for its physical deployment.

Chapter 10
Ad-Hoc Parallel Data Processing on Pay-As-You-Go Clouds with Nephele

Daniel Warneke
Technische Universität Berlin, Germany

ABSTRACT

In recent years, so-called Infrastructure as a Service (IaaS) clouds have become increasingly popular as a flexible and inexpensive platform for ad-hoc parallel data processing. Major players in the cloud computing space like Amazon EC2 have already recognized this trend and started to create special offers which bundle their compute platform with existing software frameworks for these kinds of applications. However, the data processing frameworks which are currently used in these offers have been designed for static, homogeneous cluster systems and do not support the new features which distinguish the cloud platform. This chapter examines the characteristics of IaaS clouds with special regard to massively-parallel data processing. The author highlights use cases which are currently poorly supported by existing parallel data processing frameworks and explains how a tighter integration between the processing framework and the underlying cloud system can help to lower the monetary processing cost for the cloud customer. As a proof of concept, the author presents the parallel data processing framework Nephele, and compares its cost efficiency against the one of the well-known software Hadoop.

INTRODUCTION

During the last decade, the number of companies and institutions which have to process huge amounts of data has increased rapidly. While operators of Internet search engines like Google,

Yahoo!, or Microsoft are still prominent examples for these kinds of companies, today we can also constitute a growing demand for large-scale data analysis from scientific institutions (Gray et al., 2005) and companies whose business focus has traditionally been outside of the information management space (Gonzalez, Han, Li, & Klabjan, 2006).

DOI: 10.4018/978-1-4666-2533-4.ch010

Processing data at a scale of several tera- or even petabytes either goes far beyond the scalability of traditional parallel database systems or entails licensing costs which render such solutions prohibitively expensive for most institutions (Chaiken et al, 2008). Instead, recent price developments for commodity hardware and multi-core CPUs have made architectures consisting of large sets of inexpensive commodity servers the preferred choice for large-scale data processing in recent years.

While these new distributed architectures offer tremendous amounts of compute power at an unprecedented price point, they also complicate the development of applications. Developers are suddenly confronted with the difficulties of parallel programming in order to write code which scales well to hundreds or even thousands of CPUs. Moreover, since individual nodes from the large set of compute resources are likely to fail, the programs must also be written in a way to tolerate a certain degree of hardware outages.

In order to simplify the development of distributed applications for these new compute platforms, several operators of Internet search engines, which have also pioneered the new architectural paradigm, have introduced customized data processing frameworks. Examples are Google's MapReduce (Dean & Ghemawat, 2008), Microsoft's Dryad (Isard, Budiu, Yu, Birrell, & Fetterly, 2007), or Yahoo!'s Map-Reduce-Merge (Yang, Dasdan, Hsiao, & Parker, 2007). Although these systems differ in design, their programming models have common goals, namely hiding the hassle of parallel programming, fault tolerance, and execution optimizations from the developer. While developers can typically continue to write sequential programs, the parallel data processing framework takes care of deploying these programs among the commodity servers and executing the parallel instances of them on the appropriate parts of the input data.

Despite the price decline for commodity hardware, a reasonable application of such parallel data processing frameworks has so far been limited to those companies which have specialized in the field of large-scale data analysis and therefore operate their own data centers. However, through eliminating the need for large upfront capital expenses, cloud computing now also enables companies and institutions which only have to process large amounts of data occasionally to gain access to a highly scalable pool of compute resources on a short-term pay-per-usage basis.

Operators of so-called Infrastructure as a Service (IaaS) clouds, like Amazon Web Services (Amazon Web Services, Inc. [AWS], 2011), Rackspace (Rackspace US, Inc. [RS], 2011), or GoGrid (GoGrid, LLC [GG], 2011) let their customers rent compute and storage resources hosted within their data centers. The size of these cloud data centers typically adds up to thousands or ten thousands of servers, creating the impression of virtually unlimited resources to the customer. In order to simplify their deployment, the compute resources are typically offered in form of virtual machines which are available with different hardware properties (such as compute power, amount of main memory, disk space, etc...) and at different costs. The usage of the leased resources is charged on a short-term basis (for example, compute resources by the hour and storage by the day or month), thereby rewarding conservation by releasing machines and storage when they are no longer needed (Armbrust et al., 2010).

Since the virtual machine abstraction of IaaS clouds fits the architectural paradigm assumed by the parallel data processing frameworks described above, first major cloud computing companies have started to combine existing processing frameworks with their IaaS platform and offer these bundles as a separate product. A prominent example is Amazon Elastic MapReduce (EMR) (AWS, 2011b) which runs the parallel data processing framework Hadoop (The Apache Software Foundation [ASF], 2011) on top of Amazon's Elastic Compute Cloud (EC2) (AWS, 2011c).

However, instead of embracing the new features of the underlying cloud platform like on-demand resource allocation or heterogeneous resources with different hardware characteristics, current data processing frameworks rather expect the cloud to imitate the static nature of the cluster environments they were originally designed for. For example, in case of Amazon EMR, all compute nodes the Hadoop job runs on have to be of the same virtual machine type. Moreover, it is difficult to change the number of virtual machines allocated at the beginning of the job in the course of the processing. In sum, once the processing job has been started, it is hard to adapt the underlying cloud setup, although the tasks the job consists of might have completely different demands on the environment. Hence, the rented resources may be inadequate for big parts of the processing job, which may lower the overall processing performance and increase the cost.

This chapter revisits ad-hoc parallel data processing on IaaS platforms and highlights how a tighter integration between the processing framework and the underlying cloud platform can help to improve the cost efficiency of the job processing for the cloud customer. In order to illustrate my case, I present two concrete use cases which currently suffer from the poor interaction between data processing framework and the cloud system. As a proof of concept, the chapter presents our data processing framework Nephele (Warneke & Kao, 2009; Warneke & Kao, 2011). In contrast to previous data processing frameworks, Nephele has been explicitly designed to run on top of IaaS clouds. It supports the automatic allocation or deallocation of cloud resources based on the current processing phase of the job. Moreover, different tasks of the job can be scheduled to run on different types of virtual machines, depending on their individual hardware requirements. In order to illustrate its effectiveness, I demonstrate evaluation results of MapReduce-inspired processing jobs and compare these results to experiments with the popular data processing framework Hadoop.

BACKGROUND

As a result of its current hype, the term cloud computing is used in a variety of contexts. Before I discuss the current shortcomings of parallel data processing on IaaS clouds, it is therefore necessary to establish a common understanding of the services that are typically offered by such a cloud platform. The basis for this discussion will be the Amazon EC2 cloud to a great extent, which is also widely regarded as a de-facto standard for IaaS platforms (Grossman, 2009).

Following the description of the cloud services, I will present two concrete use cases which illustrate how a tighter integration between data processing frameworks and those cloud services can help to improve the resource utilization and therefore also the cost efficiency of parallel data processing in the cloud.

Common Services of IaaS Clouds

In general, IaaS clouds distinguish between compute services, i.e., the provisioning of virtual machines, and storage services. This section will exemplarily describe both service models by means of Amazon EC2. Other IaaS providers like Rackspace (RS, 2011) or GoGrid (GG, 2011) have implemented comparable service models with only minor deviations.

Compute service: The compute service is typically a major cornerstone in an IaaS cloud provider's product portfolio. Amazon Web Services refers to their compute service as the Amazon Elastic Compute Cloud (EC2) (AWS, 2011c). According to the EC2 service model, Amazon's customers can rent compute resources from their data centers on a pay-per-usage basis. In order to facilitate a fast and flexible deployment, Amazon provides the compute resources in the form of virtual machines which can be dynamically allocated or released and fully customized by their users.

In order to start a new virtual machine, the cloud customer must first specify a disk image. The image acts as a template for the virtual machine's initial disk content. Amazon offers a plethora of preconfigured disk images a customer can choose from. However, most disk images only contain the virtual machine's guest operating system and none of the customer's data.

After having specified the disk image, Amazon EC2 asks the customer to select the type of the virtual machine to be started. Amazon EC2 itself refers to a virtual machine as an instance, consequently the type of virtual machine is called an instance type according to Amazon's terminology. The instance type describes the hardware characteristics of the rented virtual machine. Each instance type refers to a distinct combination of processing power, amount of main memory, and disk space. More importantly, the chosen instance type also has a strong influence on the monetary cost of the virtual machine.

Besides the instance type, the price a customer has to pay for a virtual machine on Amazon EC2 depends on two additional aspects: The first aspect is the period of time the machine has been running. Here, Amazon has popularized the per-hour pricing model which is today followed by all major IaaS providers. With the per-hour pricing model, a customer is charged for the machine usage by the hour. Partial hours are typically billed as full hours. After being shutdown, the virtual machine is terminated and incurs no additional charges. The content of the virtual machine's disk is usually discarded upon termination.

The second major cost aspect of a virtual machine is the network traffic it causes. Although parallel data processing frameworks typically depend heavily on the network (Dean & Ghemawat, 2008), they only exchange data among the set of worker nodes. As long as all of these worker nodes run on virtual machines in the same data center, this kind of network traffic is typically free of charge. However, network traffic involving hosts outside of the respective data center is usually billed.

Despite the large amount of compute resources available within their data centers, IaaS providers typically do not guarantee that a customer's request for virtual machines can always be fulfilled. Amazon EC2 addressed this problem by introducing their so-called reserved instances. The basic idea of reserved instances is that customers can reserve the physical resources required to run a virtual machine inside Amazon's data centers for a particular time span, for example one year. Amazon requires a one-time payment for each reservation, however, also allows a discount on the per-hour price when the reserved virtual machine is actually running.

Once the customer has chosen the disk image and the type of the new virtual machine to be started, he issues a create request to the operator of the IaaS cloud. Typically, IaaS providers offer to manage the rented compute resources through a custom RPC API. This API is particularly interesting since it enables the cloud customer to adapt his current setup from external applications or applications running inside the cloud, such as a parallel data processing framework. Amazon EC2 exposes all functions required to manage a deployment on their EC2 cloud through a well-defined Web-Service interface. The authenticity of each RPC request is ensured by a combination of certificates and secret keys which Amazon issues to the respective customer upon registration.

After having received the create request, the IaaS cloud starts instantiating the virtual machine from the selected disk image and boots it on a suitable host inside the operator's data center. Recent evaluations (Dörnemann, Juhnke, & Freisleben, 2009; Marshall, Keahey, & Freeman, 2010) have examined the startup time for virtual machines on Amazon EC2, i.e. the time from issuing the create request until the machines actually becomes accessible. According to their results, the startup time ranges from one to three minutes, depending on the type of virtual machine.

During the boot process, the virtual machine is assigned a network address. The assigned network address is typically also accessible through the cloud's custom RPC API, so external applications, like parallel data processing frameworks, can learn about the new virtual machines' network address and contact them automatically.

Storage service: Since the storage inside the virtual machines is often ephemeral, many IaaS providers have complemented their compute service with an additional storage service. The usage of those storage services is typically billed according to a separate pricing model and therefore not bound to the fine-grained per-hour pricing model of the compute nodes.

Amazon's product portfolio includes two major storage services, Amazon Elastic Block Storage (EBS) (AWS, 2011d) and Amazon Simple Storage Service (AWS, 2011e). While Amazon EBS only works in conjunction with virtual machines hosted on EC2, Amazon S3 can be considered as Amazon's general purpose storage service.

Based on the well-known HTTP protocol, customers can access the S3 storage service using both SOAP- and REST-based protocols from all over the world. The data that is stored inside Amazon S3 is referred to as objects. Objects are organized into one or more so-called buckets. While the size of an object can only range from one byte to five gigabytes, the number of objects that can be stored is unlimited.

The usage of S3 storage is billed on a monthly basis. The exact monthly fee consists of the pure storage cost, cost for outgoing data transfers as well as cost for accessing and modifying objects. In addition, the service prices vary across the different Amazon data centers around the world. In case of very large data sets, as they occur in the domain of parallel data processing, an Internet-based transfer may be prohibitively expensive. For these scenarios Amazon also offers customers to send in physical storage devices like hard disks. This service is particularly interesting for large data volumes since high data transfer cost can be avoided that way. The disk content either copied to the S3 storage, or vice versa, the S3 data is backed up to the storage device and sent back to the customer.

The performance of Amazon S3 has recently been evaluated by Palankar, Iamnitchi, Ripeanu, & Garfinkel (2008). The authors accessed data stored on Amazon S3 from virtual machines hosted on EC2 and measured the read performance. According to the authors, the read performance for small objects suffers significantly from the HTTP transaction overhead. However, for larger objects, as they typically occur in parallel data processing scenarios, the author report throughput rates of approximately 20 to 30 MB/s per object and virtual machine.

Current Issues of Parallel Data Processing on IaaS Clouds

The previous section highlighted that current IaaS clouds represent an interesting platform for ad-hoc parallel data processing, in particular for those customers who only run data analysis tasks on an irregular basis.

The typical separation between compute and storage services allows the cloud customers to store and access the processing job's input and output data independent of the virtual machines' lifetime, so the more expensive compute resource must only be allocated when the processing actually starts. New virtual machines can be allocated at any time through a well-defined interface and become available in a matter of minutes. Due to the per-hour pricing model, machines which are no longer used can be terminated instantly and no longer contribute to the processing cost. Moreover, cloud operators typically offer different types of virtual machines with different hardware properties and usage fees. In sum, an IaaS cloud can be considered a highly flexible and, if desired, heterogeneous compute platform.

However, in contrast to that, the data processing frameworks which are currently used in conjunction with IaaS clouds rather assume a static and homogeneous compute platform. Systems like

Google's MapReduce or Microsoft's Dryad can hardly take advantage of the cloud's new features.

In the following I will discuss two concrete shortcomings of parallel data processing on IaaS platforms today, both leading to an unnecessarily high processing cost for the cloud customer. Both issues could be solved by a tighter integration of the parallel data processing framework with the underlying cloud infrastructure, however, are only poorly supported by the currently existing approaches.

Stragglers: The first very common problem of parallel data processing is stragglers. Stragglers refer to individual tasks of the overall processing job which take exceedingly long to finish, thereby delaying the completion of the entire job. Although stragglers are a nuisance even in static cluster environments, their overall impact on the cluster utilization is negligible here. Since a dedicated cluster for parallel data processing is typically shared between many individual jobs and there are not dependencies between those jobs, the idle machines are simply assigned to another user's job. Given a sufficient number of incoming jobs, the cluster can therefore still be fully utilized.

In an IaaS cloud, the situation is different. As described in the previous section, the billing model of IaaS clouds assumes a set of virtual machines to be assigned to a single customer in the first place. Consequently, the processing jobs of different cloud customers will never . share worker nodes. When processing jobs with Amazon Elastic MapReduce, currently the most prevalent product for parallel data processing in the cloud, each Amazon customer runs its own Hadoop cluster on top of the EC2 compute service. A straggler can therefore result in a vast majority of virtual machine being idle. However, since these machines are paid by the hour and not their actual utilization, they are fully charged and still contribute to the processing cost.

From a cost perspective, an easy solution to this problem would be the deallocation of the idle virtual machines. However, current frameworks

for parallel data processing are not designed to support these kinds of scenarios. They consider the removal of a worker node to be a result of a hardware outage. Although such node failures are tolerated up to a certain degree, they are rather regarded as an exception than a conceptual means to reduce the number of machines in the course of a processing job.

A data processing framework designed with such pay-as-you-go platforms in mind could solve this problem through a tighter integration with the underlying IaaS system. By keeping track of the individual worker nodes' allocation times, the framework could simply terminate virtual machines which are no longer needed for the job processing, yet are about to incur additional processing cost.

Facilitating such a use case imposes some requirements on the design of a processing framework. First of all, the processing framework must be able to communicate with the IaaS cloud in order to control the worker nodes on behalf of the cloud customer. As explained in the previous section, this could be realized using the RPC API most IaaS clouds provide. Moreover, the programming abstraction of the framework must be expressive enough to model the data dependencies between the different tasks a job consists of. The system must be aware of which task's output is required as another task's input in order to decide which virtual machines are no longer needed and can be safely terminated. The MapReduce pattern is a good example of an unsuitable programming abstraction here: Although at the end of a job only few reducer tasks may still be running, it is not possible to shut down the idle virtual machines, since it is unclear if they contain intermediate results which are still required.

Heterogeneous jobs: The second shortcoming of current parallel data processing frameworks that exists in conjunction with IaaS clouds is the lack of support for heterogeneous compute nodes. Although frameworks like Hadoop support to configure individual worker nodes to accept more work than others, it is not possible to assign particular tasks of the overall processing jobs to certain types of worker nodes.

This limitation carries particular weight for processing jobs which consists of several distinct tasks with different demands on the hardware they are executed on. One task might require large amounts of main memory, others could benefit from fast CPUs. Other tasks might also be able to take advantage of special hardware a particular type of worker node is equipped with, for example special graphic adapters.

As explained in the previous subsection, current IaaS clouds offer a variety of different virtual machine types. Each virtual machine type has different hardware properties in order to fit the customers' respective needs as closely as possible and, even more importantly, is charged at a different price per hour. However, without proper support by the data processing framework this resource heterogeneity can currently not be exploited. For example, Amazon Elastic MapReduce requires its users to choose one particular type of virtual machine for the instantiation of his Hadoop cluster. At runtime, all allocated worker nodes are then of this virtual machine type. If possible at all, the customer therefore has to pick the virtual machine type which matches the demand of all tasks of the job. Depending on the task's heterogeneity, this can easily lead to a poor system utilization and impact the overall processing cost adversely.

Again, a tighter integration between the data processing framework and the underlying cloud platform could help to mitigate this problem and increase the cost efficiency. Since the available types of virtual machines usually constitute a well-defined set, the processing framework could provide a programming model which lets the customer explicitly assign particular tasks to particular types of virtual machines. In addition, virtual machines which are only required in a later phase of the processing job must not necessarily be allocated right at the start of the job. Given the quick allocation times outlined in previous section,

the machines could also be allocated on demand, when they are actually required by the job. Both steps help to avoid resource underutilization and therefore improve the processing's cost efficiency.

Facilitating this use case also requires the data processing framework to communicate with the cloud's RPC interface. Moreover, the framework must be aware of which task is required to be scheduled on which type of virtual machine and must allocate the machines accordingly. This information could, for example, be provided through a user annotation to the respective task. In more advanced scenarios, it is also conceivable that the framework itself deduces a preferable virtual machine type for the task, for example through static code analysis or observations of previous task executions.

THE NEPHELE DATA PROCESSING FRAMEWORK

After having sketched two use cases for data processing in the cloud which are only poorly supported by traditional data processing frameworks, we want to present our new data processing framework Nephele in this section. Nephele takes up many ideas of previous processing frameworks but refines them to better match the dynamic and opaque nature of a cloud. In particular, Nephele is the first data processing framework to support the cloud's on-demand resource allocation capabilities and resource heterogeneity.

Architecture

Similar to existing data processing frameworks, Nephele's architecture follows a classic master-worker. As depicted in Figure 1, the master component is called the Job Manager (JM). The Job Manager is responsible for the scheduling of individual tasks and the coordination of their execution. Moreover, it can communicate with the IaaS cloud through the RPC API as described

Figure 1. Nephele's Job Manager (JM) and Task Manager (TM) components running inside an Infrastructure as a Service (IaaS) cloud

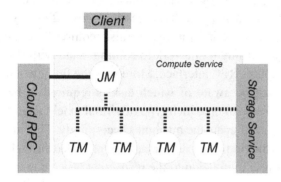

in the previous section. By means of the RPC API, the Job Manager can allocate or release virtual machines and thereby adapt the number of worker nodes according to the job's current execution phase.

Although it is not mandatory from a technical point of view, I assume the Job Manager runs on a distinct compute node. This compute node can either be a virtual machine in the IaaS cloud itself or a node which is connected to the IaaS cloud through the Internet.

The worker component in Nephele's master-worker architecture is represented by one or more so-called Task Managers (TM). A Task Manager receives tasks from the Job Manager, executes them, and sends status updates about the execution back to the Job Manager. Each Task Manager runs on its own virtual machine in the IaaS cloud.

Unless a job is submitted to the Job Manager, I expect the set of virtual machines, and therefore also the set of Task Managers, to be empty. It is not until the reception of the processing job that the Job Manager decides, depending on the concrete tasks of the job, how many of what type of virtual machines the job shall be executed on, and when the respective machines must be allocated/released in order to ensure a continuous but cost-efficient processing. I will discuss our current strategies for these decisions at the end of this section.

The virtual machines which are thereupon started by the Job Manager boot from a preconfigured virtual machine image which automatically load Nephele's Task Manager. In its initialization phase, each Task Manager is responsible for advertising itself to the Job Manager. Depending on the network configuration of the respective IaaS cloud, there are different ways to achieve this. For example, the Task Manager could try to discover the Job Manager through a special IP broadcast mechanism. Some IaaS clouds, such as Amazon EC2, also offer to pass custom parameters to the RPC call which triggers the virtual machines' boot procedure. These parameters can be accessed from within the new virtual machine and used to announce the Job Manager's network address. Once all the necessary Task Managers have successfully registered with the Job Manager, the execution of the processing job is started.

As described in the previous section, the image used to boot up the Task Manager only acts as a template for the virtual machine's initial disk content. As a result, the actual input data the Nephele job is supposed to operate on is not stored inside the virtual machine at first, but must be loaded from an external storage service. We assume the IaaS to offer such an external service (such as Amazon S3) which is accessible both to the Job Manager as well as the different Task Managers.

Job Description

Similar to Microsoft's Dryad (Isard et al., 2007), Nephele lets developers express data processing jobs as a directed acyclic graph (DAG). The tasks the job consists of are modeled as the vertices of the DAG. The graph's edges represent communication channels between the tasks. Our decision to model data processing jobs based on DAGs has been influenced by two major factors:

The first factor has been the DAG's flexibility. In contrast to other programming models, for example MapReduce, a DAG-based programming model allows tasks to have multiple data inputs and outputs. This tremendously simplifies the implementation of classic data combining tasks like, for example, join operations (Yang et al., 2007). In order to benefit from the cloud's new on-demand resource provisioning capabilities, the second factor is even more important though: The edges of a DAG explicitly model the communication paths of the processing job. As long as the individual tasks only exchange data along these designated paths, Nephele can always keep track of outstanding data transmissions and the storage location of intermediate results. This is a crucial prerequisite to decide which virtual machine from the set of worker nodes is no longer needed and can potentially be deallocated.

The definition of a Nephele job encompasses three mandatory steps: First, the program code for each of the processing job's tasks must be implemented or, alternatively, be selected from external libraries. The second step is the mapping of the respective user code fragments to the individual vertices of the DAG. This step determines which task is represented by a vertex in the job schedule at runtime. Finally, as the third step, the vertices must be connected by edges to define the communication paths of the job.

In general, Nephele expects the tasks to be executed to contain sequential code and process so-called records. Being the primary data unit in Nephele, records can be of arbitrary type. Nephele provides default implementations for the most commonly used record types such as strings or integers, however, developers can easily create custom records types. From a technical point of view, records enter and leave a task through so-called input and output gates. The Nephele API offers special classes to access these gates and to either consume incoming or emit outgoing records. Regular tasks, i.e. tasks which are mapped to one of the DAG's inner vertices, are expected to have at least one input and one output gate. In contrast to that, tasks assigned to the remaining vertices either represent data sources or sinks of the overall

data flow. Correspondingly, these tasks must not have input or output gates.

After having specified the code for the job's individual tasks, the developer must assemble the tasks to form a DAG. We call this initial DAG the Job Graph. The Job Graph maps each task to a vertex and defines the communication channels between them. Thereby, the number of a vertex's incoming and outgoing edges must correspond to the number of input and output gates specified inside the tasks. The vertices representing the data sources and sinks can be associated with a URL pointing to the storage location of the input data or the designated storage location of the output data, respectively. Currently, Nephele provides bindings to three different types of storage systems, the local file system, the Hadoop Distributed File System (HDFS) (ASF, 2011) and Amazon's S3. Moreover, developers can implement special data sources which act as general data generators rather than reading data from an existing file. This is particularly valuable for streaming applications.

Figure 2 depicts a simple, but complete Nephele Job Graph. It only consists of one input, one task, and one output vertex. Nephele would accept and execute this Job Graph although the graph only describes the tasks and their relationship on an abstract level. In particular, the graph does not contain any information with respect to the parallelization of the individual tasks or the mapping of the tasks to different (types of) virtual machines. We have intentionally made the specification of these aspects optional in order to provide more degrees of freedom to the Nephele runtime system. However, developers who wish to exert a stronger influence on the actual job execution can augment the Job Graph with a variety of annotations. These annotations are obligatory for the scheduler. They include:

- **Number of subtasks:** Each task of a Job Graph can be executed with an different degree of parallelism at runtime. We will refer to a parallel instance of a task at run-

Figure 2. Example of a simple Nephele Job Graph

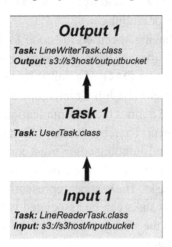

time as a subtask. While subtasks execute the same task code, they typically operate on different fragments of data.

- **Number of subtasks per virtual machine:** By default each subtask is scheduled to run on a separate virtual machine. This annotation can be used to force Nephele to execute several subtasks to run on the same virtual machine.
- **Sharing virtual machines among tasks:** Unless another scheduling restriction prevents it, Nephele schedules subtasks of different tasks to run on different (sets) of virtual machines. This annotation overwrites Nephele's default behavior, causing it to share virtual machines among different tasks during their execution.
- **Channel type:** At runtime, each edge connecting two vertices of the Job Graph is converted into a set of communication channels. Nephele has different types of communication channels to choose from, network, in-memory, and file channels. Each type has different implications on how records are transported from one task to the other. With this annotation, a developer can explicitly advise Nephele to pick a particular channel type for an edge. A more detailed discussion on the character-

istics of the different channel types is provided in the next subsection.

- **Virtual machine type:** As described in the previous section, Nephele aims at exploiting the resource heterogeneity offered by today's IaaS clouds in order to improve the cost efficiency of a processing job. This annotations lets developers specify on which type of virtual machine a particular task is supposed to be executed on. That way the machine type can be explicitly chosen with respect to the respective task's hardware requirements.

All these annotations are optional. If they are omitted, Nephele current applies a set of default strategies which are discussed later on in this section. Once the Job Graph is specified, the developer submits it to Nephele's Job Manager. In case the tasks the job consists of include external libraries, these libraries must be attached to the Job Graph as well. Moreover, the Job Graph must include the credentials the developer has obtained from the cloud provider upon registration. They are mandatory because the Job Manager must allocate/deallocate virtual machines during the job execution on behalf of the developer.

Job Scheduling and Execution

After having received a valid Job Graph, the Job Manager starts to transform the graph into an internal representation which is used for both scheduling and monitoring the execution of the job. This internal representation is called an Execution Graph. It can be considered as a more detailed version of the Job Graph it has been created from, having the same overall structure, but also modeling aspects like task parallelization and the mapping of subtasks to virtual machines. Depending on the level of annotations provided with his Job Graph, Nephele potentially has various degrees of freedom with regard to the construction of the Execution Graph. Figure 3 illustrates

Figure 3. A possible execution graph created from the original Job Graph depicted in Figure 2

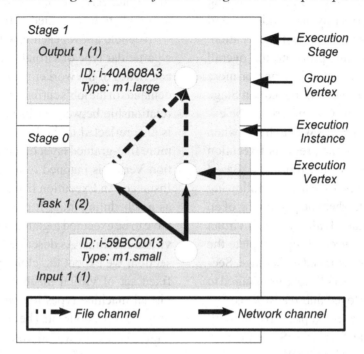

one possible Execution Graph created from the Job Graph depicted in Figure 2. The graph shows Task 1 being split into two parallel subtasks. These two subtasks are connected to a single subtask of task Output 1 through file channels. Moreover, all three subtasks are assigned to the same virtual machine. The concrete structure of an Execution Graph is described in the following.

While the Job Graph is a regular DAG with vertices and directed edges, the structure of the Execution Graph is more complex. In general, the Execution Graph can also be regarded as a DAG, but with two different layers of detail. On the more abstract layer, the Execution Graph models the job on a task level, without parallelization and concrete scheduling information. The more fine-grained layer of the graph, however, explicitly specifies the concrete subtasks of a task, the mapping of subtasks to virtual machines as well as the communication patterns and channels between the subtasks.

The abstract layer of the Execution Graph corresponds to the original Job Graph. For every vertex of the Job Graph the Execution Graph contains a so-called Group Vertex. Group Vertices act as a management abstraction for the individual subtasks Nephele may split a task into at runtime. Therefore, they do not represent executable units. The edges which connect the individual Group Vertices correspond to the edges connecting the respective vertices in the Job Graph. Like for the Job Graph, their main purpose is to capture the data dependency between tasks. Since these edges do not represent any physical communication paths during the job's executing, I omitted them in Figure 3 for the sake of clarity.

In order to improve the cost-efficiency of the job execution on IaaS platforms, Nephele explicitly supports the allocation and deallocation of virtual machines while the job is already being processed. However, this just-in-time allocation of virtual machines also introduces the risk of processing deadlocks. As pointed out in the background section, most IaaS do not provide guarantees in terms of resource availability. As a result, a particular type of virtual machine which is mandatory to enter the job's next processing phase might be temporarily not available and prevents Nephele from continuing the execution. In order to deal with this problem, the overall Execution Graph is separated into one or more so-called Execution Stages. An Execution Stage must contain at least one Group Vertex. The execution of a stage is only allowed to begin when all subtask contained in the previous Execution Stages have been successfully processed. Based on this constraint, Nephele ensures the following three properties: First, when the processing of an Execution Stage is started, all (types of) virtual machines required to successfully complete the stage are available and assigned to the stage. Second, the minimum number of subtasks required to enter the stage is deployed and ready to receive data. Previous versions of Nephele required all subtasks included in an Execution Stage to be set up before processing could begin (Warneke & Kao, 2011). However, for load balancing purposes, we have relaxed this requirement in the most recent version and also allow subtasks in a stage to be executed sequentially. Third, before entering a new Execution Stage, all intermediate results of the preceding stages are stored in a persistent way. Consequently, an Execution Stage can be compared to a checkpoint. In case of temporary resource unavailability, they allow a job to be interrupted in a consistent state and be restored later on when the appropriate types of virtual machines have become available again.

In contrast to the abstract layer of the Execution Graph, which models the overall data dependencies and defines a scope for resource allocation/deallocation, the more fine-grained layer defines the relationship between the subtasks, the parallel instances of the tasks, and their mapping to concrete virtual machines.

Each of those parallel subtask is represented by a so-called Execution Vertex. Execution Vertices can be considered the most fine-grained job unit in the Nephele system. In order to simplify their management, each Execution Vertex is assigned to that Group Vertex which also provides the vertex's user code to be executed at runtime.

Nephele allows each task to be processed on a particular type of virtual machine, so the characteristics of the worker nodes always match the demands of the job's current processing phase. This relationship between tasks and virtual machines is also reflected in the Execution Graph. On the more fine-grained layer of the graph, each Execution Vertex is mapped to a so-called Execution Instance. An Execution Instance can be regarded as a scheduling stub. It defines which subtasks have to be executed together on the same (type of) virtual machine. As described in the background section, we expect the cloud provider to offer a fixed set of virtual machine types. This set of virtual machine types together with the current usage fees per hour must be accessible to Nephele either through a well-defined RPC interface or, in case the cloud provider's machine types and prices have a longer validity period, through a separate configuration file. Moreover, we assume each virtual machine type can be referred by a simple string, such as "m1.small". An additional string like "i-40A608A3" uniquely identifies the machine.

Before entering a new Execution Stage, Nephele collects all Execution Instances from that stage and requests the corresponding virtual machines through the cloud's RPC interface. Once all required virtual machines have successfully completed their boot process and registered with the Job Manager, the subtasks scheduled to run on these machines are deployed and started.

As briefly sketched in the previous subsection, the edges connecting the vertices of the Job Graph have to be converted into concrete communication channels before a job can be executed. In case of task parallelization, when a Group Vertex contains more than one Execution Vertex, the developer of the consuming task can implement an interface which determines how the two different groups of subtasks will be connected at runtime. Nephele provides a library with several default implementations for these connection patterns. For example, it includes bipartite patterns simply creating a communication channel between each subtask of the producer task to each subtask of the consumer task or point-wise patterns connecting the ith subtask of the producer to the ith subtask of the consumer. The actual number of channels connected to a subtask at runtime is hidden behind the task's respective input and output gates. However, the user code can retrieve the number if necessary.

Each communication channel is of a particular type. As indicated in the previous section, the channel type determines how records are actually transported from one subtask to the other. Currently, Nephele supports three different channel types, each putting different constraints on the structure of the Execution Graph:

- **Network channels:** A network channel transports records from one subtask to another via a TCP connection. Network channels support pipelined processing, so a record created by a producing subtask is immediately shipped to the consuming subtask. In order to exploit this pipelining feature, the communicating subtasks must be part of the same Execution Stage, but are allowed to run on different virtual machines.

- **In Memory channels:** In-memory channels also support pipelined processing. However, in contrast to network channels, the records are not transported through a TCP connection, but directly through the virtual machine's main memory. Consequently, the usage of in-memory channels also requires the communicating subtasks to be executed on the same machine. Moreover, since the subtasks also must be running at the same time in order to take advantage of the pipelining, they must be assigned to the same Execution Stage.

- **File channels:** By using a file channel, a producing subtask can send records a to consuming subtask through the local file system. File channels are not suitable for pipelined processing because the records of the producing task are entirely written to an intermediate file before the consuming subtask can start reading them. Nephele requires the two connected subtasks to be assigned to the same virtual machine. Moreover, the consuming vertex must be scheduled to run in a higher Execution Stage than the producing vertex. In general, Nephele only allows subtasks to transmit records across different stages via file channels because they are the only channel type which store the emitted records in a persistent manner.

Parallelization and Scheduling Strategies

Depending on the degree of user annotations, Nephele may have different degrees of freedom in constructing the Execution Graph from the user's original Job Graph. Using this freedom to construct the most efficient Execution Graph (with regard to processing time or monetary cost) entails several research challenges. In this subsection I want to discuss these challenges and present our current strategies to tackle them.

The first challenge pertains to finding an appropriate degree of parallelism for a task. Since renting a thousand CPU cores for a single hour comes at the same price as renting a single CPU core for a thousand hours according to the cloud's pricing model, it might be tempting for cloud customers to strive for shorter completion times of their jobs by splitting the individual tasks into more and more parallel subtasks. Of course, the vast majority of processing jobs cannot be parallelized indefinitely, but will face an I/O bottleneck at some. Parallelization beyond that point will only lead to a worse overall system utilization and therefore decrease the cost efficiency of the job processing.

Unfortunately, predicting the optimal degree of parallelization for a job consisting of arbitrary user code is a very hard task. However, in order to assist the developer in finding a reasonable scale out for his job, we have integrated a profiling subsystem into Nephele. The profiling subsystem monitors the resource utilization of each executed subtask. Based on the obtained data, we have developed special algorithms to detect both CPU and I/O bottlenecks in the job's processing chain. The cloud customer receives immediate feedback about the detected bottlenecks through a special graphical user interface and can use this feedback to continuously improve his job annotations for upcoming job executions. For example, computational bottlenecks suggest a higher degree of parallelization or virtual machine types with faster CPUs. In contrast to that, I/O bottlenecks hint to switch to faster channel types (like in-memory channels) and reconsider the mapping of subtasks to virtual machine (types). Details on the profiling subsystem and the algorithms we use for the bottleneck detection are published in Battré, Hovestadt, Lohrmann, Stanik, & Warneke (2010).

At the current state of Nephele's development, we only exploit the profiling data to detect these bottlenecks and help the user to choose reasonable annotations for his job. However, Nephele is able to compute cryptographic signatures of incoming tasks. Therefore it is also conceivable to recognize recurring tasks and use the previously recorded feedback data to automatically optimize recurring jobs.

Besides finding a reasonable degree of parallelization, proper scheduling strategies for the allocation/deallocation of the individual virtual machines are an important aspect with respect to a processing job's cost efficiency.

As described in the previous subsection, the allocation times for new virtual machines or the termination of machines which are no longer needed are in general determined by the job's Execution Stages. However, further refinements to this general stage-based allocation strategy are possible.

In the background section I pointed out that IaaS clouds typically do not provide guarantees concerning the availability of the requested resources. Nephele addresses this problem by separating the overall processing job in one or more stages, so before new virtual machines are requested the processing job is guaranteed to be in a consistent, recoverable state. However, depending on the job's scale-out as well as the concrete IaaS cloud the virtual machines are requested from, the risk of actually facing a resource unavailability can be negligibly small. Therefore Nephele features an additional lazy initialization mode. In this lazy initialization mode, the individual subtasks of a task are not scheduled until their preceding subtasks actually attempt to send them any records. As a result, the allocation of the respective virtual machines which execute these subtasks can be postponed as well.

The lazy initialization mode especially pays off for jobs that contain one or more tasks which interrupt the processing pipeline. A typical example of such a task is a sort operation because a full sort requires to read the entire input records before any output record can be emitted.

The allocation time of virtual machines is ultimately determined by the latest possible start times of the assigned subtasks. However, for their deallocation, different strategies are conceivable. In order to reflect the fact that most IaaS cloud bill partial hours as full hours, Nephele attempts to reuse virtual machines whenever possible. Therefore, it tracks the virtual machines' allocation times. If a machine of a particular type has finished executing its assigned subtasks, it is not immediately released. Instead, if a virtual machine of the same type is required either later in the same Execution Stage or an upcoming stage, Nephele keeps the machine allocated until the end of its current lease period. In case the machine is again required before the end of that period, it can be reassigned to another subtask. Otherwise, Nephele terminates the virtual machine early enough not to cause any additional cost.

EXPERIMENTAL EVALUATION

After having introduced the Nephele processing framework and highlighted its tight integration with the underlying IaaS cloud, I want to demonstrate the possible benefits of this integration based on an experimental evaluation.

In order to put Nephele's performance on the cloud platform into perspective, I compare it to the performance of the Hadoop data processing framework. The decision to pick Hadoop as our competitor has been influenced by three major aspects: First, Hadoop is open source software easily accessible for experimental evaluations. Second, it currently enjoys a high popularity in the data processing community, and, finally, it is the technical foundation of Amazon's Elastic MapReduce offering, currently the most prevalent commercial product for data-intensive parallel processing in the cloud.

Although I am aware that Hadoop has been designed to run on computing setups with a very large number of nodes (i.e. several thousand nodes), in practice the software is mostly used with considerably fewer machines, in particular in IaaS setups, In fact, Amazon itself limits the number of available virtual machines for their Elastic MapReduce service to 20 unless the respective customer passes an extended registration process (AWS, 2011b).

The evaluation job both Nephele and Hadoop had to process in the scope of these experiments consists of two abstract tasks: Given a set of random integer numbers, the first task is to determine the k smallest of those numbers. Subsequently, the second task has to compute the average those k smallest numbers. I consider the evaluation job to be a classic representative for a variety of data analysis jobs whose individual tasks show large variations in their computational complexity and, thus, their hardware demand. The first task requires to sort the entire input data set. Therefore, it can benefit from virtual machines with large amounts of main memory and a parallel execution. In contrast to that, the second task only has very low demands in terms of main memory and, at least eventually, cannot be parallelized.

Both the sort and the aggregate task of our evaluation job were implemented for three different experiments. For the first experiment, we implemented the two tasks as a series of MapReduce programs and ran them on the Hadoop framework using a fixed set of homogeneous virtual machines. For the second experiment, we reused the MapReduce programs from the first experiment, but replaced Hadoop with Nephele as the parallel processing framework. In order to make the unmodified Hadoop programs run on top of Nephele, we wrote a special wrapper library providing limited interface compatibility with Hadoop and sort/merge functionality. That way, the second experiment emphasizes the advantages of Nephele's dynamic resource allocation/deallocation while still maintaining the MapReduce processing pattern. In contrast to that, the third experiment abandons the MapReduce pattern to additionally illustrate the advantages of exploiting resource heterogeneity.

All three experiments received the same input data with a size of 100 gigabytes. As each integer number had the size of 100 bytes, the data set contained approximately 10^9 integer numbers. We set the cut-off variable k to 2×10^8. As a result, the smallest 20% of the integer numbers from the input data set had to be determined and averaged.

Experimental Setup

We conducted all three experiments on our local Eucalyptus-based (Nurmi et al, 2009) IaaS cloud. Each server of our cloud is equipped with two Intel Xeon 2.66 GHz CPUs, resulting in eight CPU cores per physical server. Moreover, each server has 32 GB of main memory and is connected to the network through a regular 1 GBit/s Ethernet link. The operating system on the physical server was Gentoo Linux with a kernel of version 2.6.30. As the hypervisor we used KVM (Kivity, Kamay, Laor, Lublin, & Ligori, 2007) with virtio (Russel, 2008) to provide virtual I/O access.

In order to facilitate the allocation of heterogeneous resources in the scope of our experiments, we configured the Eucalyptus framework to start different types of virtual machines upon request. Inspired by the virtual machines types available at Amazon EC2, we set up one type of virtual machine with the name "m1.small" which offered one CPU core, one GB of RAM and 128 GB of disk space. The second virtual machine type used in our experiments, "c1.xlarge" had eight CPU cores, 18 GB of main memory and a 512 GB disk. Amazon EC2 offers comparable virtual machine types (except for the capacity of the hard disks) at a price of about 0.10 or 0.78 USD per hour (as of July 2011), respectively.

Similar to Amazon EC2, Eucalyptus also instantiates virtual machines based on predefined virtual machine images. For all three experiments, we used an image based on Ubuntu Linux (kernel version 2.6.28). The image had no additional software installed except for a Java runtime environment (version 1.6.0.13), which is required by both Hadoop and Nephele.

We generated the 100 gigabytes of input data according to the rules of the Jim Gray sort benchmark (O'Malley & Murthy, 2009). In order to make the data accessible to Hadoop and Nephele, we started a so-called data node of the distributed file system HDFS on each allocated virtual machine prior to the processing job and distributed the data evenly among the nodes. Since this initial setup procedure was necessary for both processing frameworks and affected each of our three experiments in the same way, I will ignore it in the following performance discussion.

Description on the Experiments

For the first experiment, we created two different MapReduce programs in order to run the described sort and aggregate tasks on the Hadoop platform. The first MapReduce program was executed once whereas the second one was executed twice. As a result, the first experiment consisted of three consecutive MapReduce jobs.

The first MapReduce program reads the entire 10^9 integer numbers from the distributed file system HDFS, sorts them ascendingly, and writes them back to disk. Since the MapReduce processing pattern requires Hadoop to sort the incoming data between the map and the reduce step anyway, it was not necessary to provide particular user code for the map and reduce function, respectively. Instead, we were able to simply use the existing TeraSort MapReduce program, which has recently been recognized for being well-suited for these kinds of tasks (O'Malley & Murthy, 2009). The output of this first MapReduce job was a set of files storing the sorted integer numbers. If these individual files were concatenated, this would yield the fully sorted sequence of the 10^9 input numbers.

The sorted output of the first MapReduce program was the basis for the second program which ran as the second and third MapReduce job in this experiment. The purpose of this second program was to compute the average of a particular fraction of its input data. Since we chose our cut-off variable k to be 2×10^8, we configured the second MapReduce job to select the first output files of the preceding sort job which, just by their file size, had to contain the smallest 2×10^8 numbers of the initial data set. The program's map function read the selected files and emitted the first 2×10^8 numbers to the reducer. In order to achieve good parallelization properties, we randomly chose the intermediate keys for the reducer from a predefined set. That way each of the n reducers in the system had to compute the average of approximately $(2 \times 10^8)/n$ integer numbers. Finally, the third

MapReduce job reused the second MapReduce program to read the *n* intermediate average values and aggregated them to a single overall average.

As Hadoop is unable to take advantage of heterogeneous compute nodes, the first experiment was conducted using six homogeneous virtual machines of the type "c1.xlarge". All six virtual machines were assigned to Hadoop throughout the entire duration of the experiment.

In order to achieve a fast completion time for the sequence of the three MapReduce jobs, we configured Hadoop to perform best for the first MapReduce program. As this program has to sort the input data, it is the computationally most demanding job in the experiment. In accordance to (O'Malley & Murthy, 2009), we set the number of map tasks per job to 48 (one map task per CPU core) and the number of reducers to 12. Moreover, we increased the memory heap and the in-memory file system of each map task to 1 gigabyte and 512 megabytes, respectively, so spilling transient data to disk was avoided as far as possible.

The second experiment was devised to highlight the impact of dynamic resource allocation/deallocation on the overall processing efficiency while still preserving comparability to the previous Hadoop job. Therefore, we reused the previous two MapReduce programs and executed them in the same sequence as before on top of Nephele. By means of a special wrapper library we were able to run the exact same MapReduce programs with the same data flow characteristics as in the previous Hadoop experiment, however, let Nephele control the allocation and deallocation of the virtual machines as well as the assignment of tasks to virtual machines underneath.

Figure 4 shows the Execution Graph we instructed Nephele to construct so that the communication paths in the graph correspond to the MapReduce processing pattern. Following the overall idea of this experiment, we also ran the first, computationally most complex MapReduce job on six homogeneous virtual machines of type "c1.xlarge", however, after that first job, reduced the number of allocated virtual machines for the remaining two jobs according to the workload we observed during the first experiment. As a result, the sort operation was again carried out on all six virtual machines, but the first and second aggregation operation was only assigned to two and one virtual machine, respectively.

The Execution Graph of the second experiment encompassed three Execution Stages. Each stage contained the tasks required by the corresponding MapReduce jobs. As described in the previous section, Execution Stages can only be crossed by file channels. Hence, all intermediate data which was produced between two consecutive MapReduce jobs was completely written to disk, just like in the first Hadoop experiment.

Execution Stage 0, the first stage, contained four different tasks, split into several different groups of subtasks and assigned to different virtual machines. The first task, BigIntegerReader, was responsible for reading the assigned input files and emitting each integer number within these files as a separate record. The tasks TeraSortMap and TeraSortReduce encapsulated the TeraSort MapReduce code from the previous Hadoop experiment. In correspondence with this previous experiment, we split the TeraSortMap task into 48 and the TeraSortReduce task into 12 subtasks. All of these subtasks were distributed evenly among the six virtual machines of type "c1.xlarge" as illustrated in Figure 4. Moreover, Figure 4 also indicates the network channels we instructed Nephele to construct between each pair of TeraSortMap and TeraSortReduce subtasks. However, in order to improve legibility, only few of the resulting channels are actually depicted.

On a shared-nothing platform like an IaaS cloud the number of TCP connections the operating system can handle efficiently quickly becomes a considerable obstacle. Nephele counteracts this problem by means of a special resource abstraction layer which allows to multiplex multiple network channels going to the same host over a

Figure 4. The execution graph for the second experiment

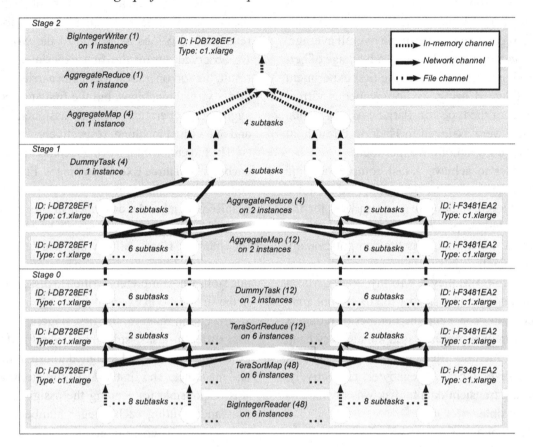

single physical TCP connection. However, we also devised the following optimization: If two subtasks are connected by a network channel, but are assigned to the same virtual machine, Nephele automatically converts the corresponding channel into an in-memory channel. Considering the given MapReduce communication pattern, this optimization reduces the number of network channels by approximately 20% in this experiment.

The records emitted by the BigIntegerReader subtasks were received by those of the TeraSort-Map task. The TeraSortMap task encapsulated the TeraSort partitioning function which determined the distribution of the mappers' records among the TeraSortReduce subtasks. However, before being transferred to the selected reducer, the records were collected in buffers with a size of approximately 44 megabytes and presorted in memory. Given

that each TeraSortMap subtask was connected to 12 TeraSortReduce subtasks, this added up to a total buffer size of 574 megabytes, comparable to the 512 megabytes of in-memory file system we allocated for each Hadoop map task in the first experiment.

In addition to the memory allocated by the TeraSortMap subtasks, each TeraSortReduce also had subtask an in-memory buffer with a size of 512 megabytes at its disposal. The individual reducers used these buffers to store the incoming sets of presorted records from the mappers and thus to avoid unnecessary disk access. Like Hadoop, we started merging the first batches of presorted records using separate background threads while the data transfer from the mapper subtasks was still in progress. The result of the final merge step, i.e. one fully sorted set of records, was directly streamed to the next task in the processing chain in order to improve the overall performance.

The fourth task in the first Execution Stage was the task DummyTask. Simply emitting every record it receives, this task's only purpose was to redirect the output of the preceding tasks to a particular subset of allocated virtual machines. We used the DummyTask task twice in the job, at the end of Execution Stage 0 and Execution Stage 1. In Execution Stage 0 the task forwarded the sorted output of the 12 TeraSortReduce subtasks to only two virtual machines. Following the overall idea of this experiment, i.e. adapting the allocated compute resources to the expected workload of the processing job's individual phases, Nephele would release the remaining four virtual machines before the start of the second Execution Stage because it would be aware that these machines are no longer needed for the upcoming stages. We instructed Nephele to assign one DummyTask subtask to each of the remaining virtual machines. In Execution Stage 0, the output of the preceding 12 TeraSortReduce subtasks was reshuffled in a way, such that each of the remaining two virtual machines would receive a fairly even fraction of the 2×10^8 smallest numbers.

As illustrated in Figure 4, the following Execution Stages 1 and 2 contained the two successive aggregation steps. Like in the previous Hadoop experiment, each aggregation step consisted of two tasks, AggregateMap and AggregateReduce, which encapsulated the respective Hadoop code.

We instructed Nephele to create 12 AggregateMap as well as four AggregateReduce subtasks and to assign those evenly among the two remaining virtual machines of type "c1.xlarge" in Execution Stage 1. At the end of the second stage, we again used the DummyTask to redirect the output of the four AggregateReduce subtasks to the one virtual machine, on which Nephele would execute the final aggregation step. For this final aggregation step, we used four AggregateMap subtasks, all forwarding to a single AggregateReduce subtask. The output of this last

AggregateReduce subtask, which also represents the result of the overall computation, was written back to HDFS.

For the third experiment, we abandoned the MapReduce processing pattern. Instead, we implemented the sort/aggregation problem as a general DAG. As shown in Figure 5, the Execution Graph we instructed Nephele to construct consisted of five distinct Tasks. Similar to the second experiment, we pursued the idea of reducing the number of allocated virtual machines to the expected workload. However, this experiment also involved virtual machines of different types. While we computed the 2×10^8 smallest integer numbers using multiple computationally powerful, but also expensive nodes, the final aggregation was executed on a single, inexpensive virtual machines

As the first task of in this experiment, we reused the BigIntegerReader task from Experiment 2 which was again responsible for loading the initial data from HDFS into Nephele. The BigIntegerReader task forwarded its records to the second task, BigIntegerSorter. The BigIntegerSorter performed a local quick sort of the incoming integer numbers. For performance reasons, task was implemented to sort the entire records in main memory and to only swap data to disk if necessary.

Since the performance of the sort operation was highly dependent on the amount of main memory the BigIntergerTask task could utilize, we assigned to a total of 126 subtasks of it evenly to six virtual machines of type "c1.xlarge". That way, each BigIntegerTask subtask had an in-memory sort buffer of approximately 800 MB.

After having finished the sort, each subtask of the BigIntegerSorter used an in-memory channel to emit its sorted sub-sequence of the 10^9 overall integer numbers to the third task of this experiment, the BigIntegerMerger task. As its name implies, the BigIntegerMerger task was responsible for merging the individually sorted sub-sequence from the different BigIntegerSorter subtasks into a

Figure 5. The execution graph for the third experiment

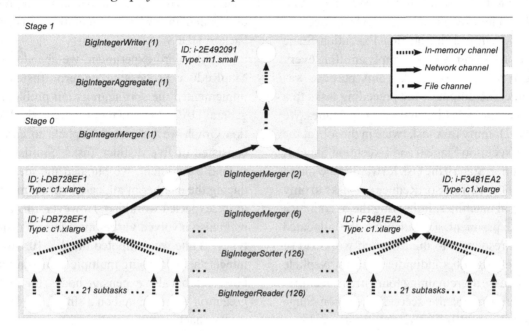

globally sorted sequence. As illustrated in Figure 5, the BigIntegerMerger task occurred three times in a row in the Execution Graph. The first time, we split the task into six subtasks and assigned each subtask to one of the six "c1.xlarge" virtual machines. As a result, each of those BigIntegerMerger subtasks received its input from 21 BigIntegerSorter subtasks. The second time the BigIntegerMerger task occurred in the Execution Graph, it was split into two subtasks. We assigned these two subtasks to two of the previously used virtual machines of type "c1.xlarge". Finally, the third occurrence of the task was scheduled to run on a new virtual machine of type "m1.small".

For the sake of comparability with Hadoop, we wrote all intermediate results back to hard disk in the second experiment. Since this third experiments abandoned the MapReduce processing pattern anyway, we were also able to take advantage of Nephele's pipelining characteristics. Instead of receiving the entire 10^9 integer numbers from the input data set, the final merge subtask was implemented to finish after having forwarded 2×10^8 records. All preceding tasks in the pipeline

thereupon noticed that no further data is required and, in turn, also finished their execution. This feature let Nephele complete the entire first Execution Stage as soon as the final merge subtask emitted the 2×10^8 smallest integer number.

The fourth task in the experiment was BigIntegerAggregater. The BigIntegerAggregater task simply read all incoming records from its input channels and summed them up. It was also assigned to the single "m1.small" virtual machine, following the final BigIntegerMerger subtask. Since the compute power of the six "c1.xlarge" virtual machines was no longer required after the final merge subtask had processed the 2×10^8 records, we connected the final BigIntegerMerger and BigIntegerAggregater through a file channel. As a result, Nephele pushed the aggregation into the next Execution Stage and was able to release the expensive nodes from the previous stage.

Finally, we used the BigIntegerWriter task from the second experiment again in order to write the calculated average of the 2×10^8 smallest integer numbers back to HDFS.

Experimental Results

The performance results of our three experiments are depicted in Figure 6, Figure 7, and Figure 8, respectively. Each plot shows the average CPU utilization of the allocated virtual machines over time, i.e. the average utilization of all CPU cores in all virtual machines assigned to the job at the given point in time. We used the well-known Unix command "top" to record the CPU utilization on each virtual machine. The utilization is subdivided into the categories USR, SYS, HIRQ, SIRQ and WAIT, referring to the time the CPU core spent executing user level code, kernel level code, handling hardware or software interrupts, or the time the CPU core spent waiting for I/O to complete. Moreover, the plots also illustrate the average of amount of network traffic flowing among the different virtual machines over time.

At first, I want to discuss Experiment 1 (MapReduce on Hadoop): As depicted in Figure 6,

the resource utilization for the first MapReduce job, TeraSort, is fairly good. During the map (point (a) to (c)) and reduce phase (point (b) to (d)) the overall CPU utilization ranges from 60 to 80%. This result is reasonable, considering that we configured Hadoop to perform best for this kind of tasks. However, the following two MapReduce jobs cannot take advantage of the available compute power. For the second MapReduce job, which performs the first phase of the aggregation, the resource utilization only ranges between 15 and 40%. The map phase of the job starts at point (d) and finished at point (f) in the plot, while the reduce phase goes from point (e) to (g). The third job, performing the final aggregation and running between point (g) and (h), can only consume about 10% of the overall resources.

The main reason why Hadoop cannot adapt to the changing workload is its assumption to run on a static compute cluster. The removal of machines from a Hadoop setup is considered to

Figure 6. Results of experiment 1 (MapReduce on Hadoop)

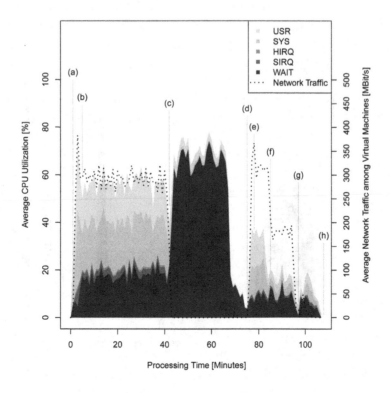

Figure 7. Results of experiment 2 (MapReduce on Nephele)

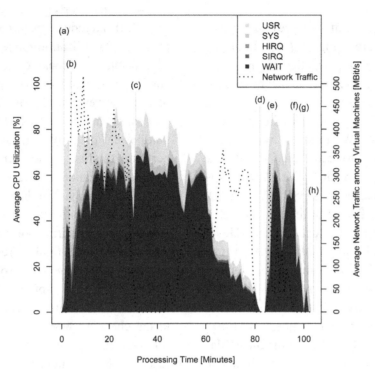

Figure 8. Results of experiment 3 (DAG on Nephele)

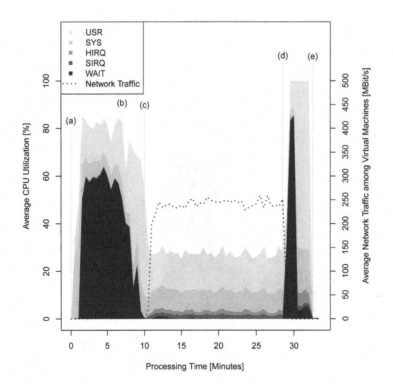

be a consequence of a hardware outage and is only tolerated to a certain degree, depending on replication factor of the underlying distributed file system. Removing machines beyond that point raises the immanent risk of losing important intermediate results, at least for the vast majority of processing tasks which cannot be mapped to a single MapReduce run. As a result, all six expensive virtual machines must be kept allocated throughout the entire experiment and unnecessarily contribute to the processing cost.

The performance results of the second experiment are illustrated in Figure 7. Here we executed the same sequence of MapReduce programs as in the first experiment, but on top of Nephele instead of Hadoop. The system utilization during the first Execution Stage, corresponding to the TeraSort map and reduce tasks, is comparable to the previous Hadoop experiment. During the map (point (a) to (c)) and the reduce phase (point (b) to (d)) all six virtual machines of type "c1.xlarge" show an average CPU utilization of about 80%. After approximately 42 minutes, however, Nephele began to transmit the output of each of the 12 TeraSortReduce subtasks to those two virtual machines which were scheduled to remain allocated in the upcoming Execution Stages. Hence, it was able to deallocate four of the six "c1.xlarge" machines at the end of Execution Stage 0 (point (d)) without running the risk of data loss.

The deallocation of the four virtual machines also reduced the overall number of CPU cores in the second Execution Stage. Consequently, the available compute power again matched the computational demands of the first aggregation step. As shown in Figure 7, the average CPU utilization during the execution of the 12 AggregateMap subtasks (point (d) to (f)) and the four AggregateReduce subtasks (point (e) to (g)) added up to approximately 80%. The same applies to the final aggregation step in Execution Stage 2 (point (g) to (h)) which was performed on only one allocated virtual machine of type "c1.xlarge".

Finally, I want to highlight the results of the third experiment (DAG on Nephele). As shown in Figure 8, the subtasks of the first task, BigIntegerReader, started reading their respective fractions of the input data at point (a). The read records were then forwarded to the connected BigIntegerSorter subtasks via in-memory channels. At point (b), the first BigIntegerSorter subtasks stopped buffering the incoming records and started to sort them. The advantages of Nephele's ability to assign specific tasks of a processing job to specific types of virtual machines are illustrated nicely in this case: Since the entire sort process could be performed in main memory, the corresponding subtasks were able to forward the sorted sub-sequences to the BigIntegerMerger task only three minutes later, at point (c).

Until the end of the compute intensive sort phase, the job processing performance benefits from the large number of available CPU cores. However, for the following merge and aggregation, the six allocated virtual machines of type "c1.xlarge" could no longer be utilized. While, from a cost perspective, it would have been desirable to release the expensive machines as soon as possible, the machines first had to transfer 20 gigabytes of the presorted records to the inexpensive machine of type "m1.small". In our experiment, we found the network to be a major bottleneck, so during the data transfer, ranging from point (c) to (d) in the plot, the actual CPU utilization was low. In general, this transfer penalty clearly must be taken into account when switching between different virtual machine types in the course of a job execution. In order to trade the occurring I/O load against CPU load to a certain extent, we have recently introduced an adaptive online compression scheme (Hovestadt, Kao, Kliem, & Warneke, 2011). The scheme is integrated in Nephele's network channels and can dynamically apply different levels of data compression to the outgoing data stream, depending on the current CPU and IO load as well as the compressibility of the data.

The scheme helps to mitigate the transfer penalty, however, for the sake of an unbiased comparison with regard to the previous two experiments, it was disabled it for this evaluation.

After the final BigIntegerMerger subtask had written the 2×10^8 smallest integer numbers into a file channel (point (d)), it sent a notification to all preceding subtasks in the processing, indicating that no further data is required. Thereupon, Nephele was able to complete the first execution stage and automatically released all of the six expensive "c1.xlarge" virtual machines. The following Execution Stage 1 only contained a single virtual machine of the type "m1.small" which ran one subtask of the tasks BigIntegerAggregater and BigIntegerWriter, respectively. Since the six "c1.xlarge" virtual machines are no longer assigned to the job in that phase, the available processing power again fits the demand of the remaining job. This is reflected in a high resource utilization (point (d) to (e)). After 33 minutes, Nephele was able to complete the entire processing job.

Regarding the relatively short processing time of the presented experiments and the fact that most IaaS providers charge partial hours of virtual machine usage as full hours, I am aware that the savings that Nephele achieved in the presented experiments appear marginal at first glance, both from a time and a cost perspective. However, it is worth to point out that the savings grow by the size of the input data and the number of allocated virtual machines. For this evaluation, the size of our cloud testbed forced us to limit the data set size to 100 GB. Larger data sets increase the need for more complex processing jobs a higher degree of parallelism, therefore they also promise more significant savings.

FUTURE RESEARCH DIRECTIONS

Currently, Nephele is used as the data processing engine for the Stratosphere project (The Stratosphere Project [TSP], 2011). The Stratosphere project aims at facilitating complex and large-scale information management on top of virtualized, massively parallel architecture like IaaS clouds. For this purpose, the project currently develops a rich software stack allowing its users to analyze, aggregate, and query very large collections of either textual or (semi-)structured data. Stratosphere offers different models for formulating those queries, each model is characterized by a different level of abstraction from the actual query execution.

For example, layered on top of Nephele in the Stratosphere software stack is the so-called PACT layer (Alexandrov et al., 2010; Battré et al., 2010). Compared to the Nephele programming abstraction, the programming model of the PACT layer is less flexible, but provides a more declarative way of writing parallel data analysis jobs. Instead of having to implement the entire behavior of a task, users of the PACT programming model can think of their analysis job as a chain of second order functions which already provide certain guarantees in terms of the provided input data, such like the MapReduce programming model. The user only has to develop the corresponding first order functions. A special compiler then translates the PACT jobs into Job Graphs and passes them to Nephele for the actual parallel execution.

In the context of the Stratosphere project, we currently work to improve Nephele's load balancing capabilities while still maintaining its good pipelining properties. In particular, we examine different ways to rearrange the data distribution among different sets of virtual machines without interrupting Nephele's processing pipeline.

Another important aspect of our ongoing research is to enhance Nephele's fault tolerance capabilities beyond the presented stage concept. Current data processing frameworks compensate the risk of resource outages with extensive materializations of intermediate results, even when those intermediate results may be trivial to recompute or the execution of the entire processing jobs only takes several seconds. A more adaptive approach could help to reduce the materialization overhead by only writing those intermediate results to disk which are particularly valuable for a potential recovery.

Finally, we are also interested in extending Nephele's capabilities as a stream processing engine. With the built-in pipeline concept it would be conceivable to write Nephele jobs which operate on a continuous stream of input data. The job could be annotated with an processing deadline for each incoming data unit Nephele then tries to enforce at runtime. In case the processing deadline could not be met, for example because records started to queue at a particular task in the processing chain, Nephele would then automatically allocate additional compute resource from the underlying IaaS cloud and redistribute the load among the available machines.

CONCLUSION

Infrastructure as a Service (IaaS) clouds gain more and more popularity as an inexpensive and highly-scalable platform for ad-hoc parallel data processing. However, despite the unprecedented flexibility of the this new computer platform, the data processing frameworks which are used in conjunction with those clouds still assume to run on a rather static and homogeneous cluster. Therefore, the cloud customer can hardly benefit from the cloud's new features.

In this chapter I described how a tighter integration between a parallel data processing framework and the underlying IaaS cloud can help to avoid resource underutilization and therefore increase the cost efficiency of parallel data processing in such environments. After having highlighted the most common characteristics of today's IaaS clouds, I presented two concrete use cases which are very poorly supported by existing cloud data processing solutions.

As a remedy, I introduced our parallel data processing framework Nephele. Nephele is the first data processing framework explicitly designed to run on IaaS platforms. After having explained its basic architecture, I discussed Nephele's programming abstraction as well as our current strategies for task parallelization and automatic resource allocation.

In general, I think this chapter includes several valuable impulses on how services and applications can take advantage of the still widely unexplored world of cloud computing. For the future, I am confident that cloud computing will continue to attract a growing number of customers and enable new kinds of applications through its flexible cost model.

REFERENCES

Alexandrov, A., Battré, D., Ewen, S., Heimel, M., Hueske, F., & Kao, O. (1625-1628). ... Warneke, D. (2010). Massively parallel data analysis with PACTs on Nephele. *Proceedings of the VLDB Endowment, 3*(2).

Amazon Web Services, Inc. (2011a). *Amazon Web Services*. Retrieved August 26, 2011, from http://aws.amazon.com/

Amazon Web Services, Inc. (2011b). *Amazon elastic MapReduce*. Retrieved August 26, 2011, from http://aws.amazon.com/elasticmapreduce/

Amazon Web Services, Inc. (2011c). *Amazon elastic Compute Cloud (Amazon EC2)*. Retrieved August 26, 2011, from http://aws.amazon.com/ec2/

Amazon Web Services, Inc. (2011d). *Elastic block storage (EBS)*. Retrieved August 26, 2011, from http://aws.amazon.com/ebs/

Amazon Web Services, Inc. (2011e). In *Amazon simple storage service (Amazon S3)*. Retrieved August 26, 2011, from http://aws.amazon.com/s3/

Armbrust, M., Fox, A., Griffith, R., Joseph, A. D., Katz, H. R., & Konwinski, A. (2010). A view of cloud computing. *Communications of the ACM, 53*(4), 50–58. doi:10.1145/1721654.1721672

Battré, D., Ewen, S., Hueske, F., Kao, O., Markl, V., & Warneke, D. (2010). Nephele/PACTs: A programming model and execution framework for web-scale analytical processing. In J. M. Hellerstein, S. Chaudhuri, & M. Rosenblum (Eds.), In *Proceedings of the 1st ACM Symposium on Cloud Computing* (pp. 119-130). ACM.

Battré, D., Hovestadt, M., Lohrmann, B., Stanik, A., & Warneke, D. (2010). Detecting bottlenecks in parallel DAG-based data flow programs. In *Proceedings of the 2010 IEEE Workshop on Many-Task Computing on Grids and Supercomputers* (pp. 1-10). IEEE.

Chaiken, R., Jenkins, B., Larson, P.-Å., Ramsey, B., Shakib, D., Weaver, S., & Zhou, J. (2008). SCOPE: Easy and efficient parallel processing of massive data sets. *Proceedings of the VLDB Endowment, 1*(2), 1265–1276.

Dean, J., & Ghemawat, S. (2008). MapReduce: Simplified data processing on large clusters. *Communications of the ACM, 51*(1), 107–113. doi:10.1145/1327452.1327492

Dörnemann, T., Juhnke, E., & Freisleben, B. (2009). On-demand resource provisioning for bpel workflows using Amazon's elastic compute cloud. In F. Cappello, C.-L. Wang, & R. Buyya (Eds.), In *Proceedings of the 9th IEEE/ACM International Symposium on Cluster Computing and the Grid* (pp. 140-147). IEEE Computer Society.

GoGrid. LLC. (2011). *Cloud Hosting, Cloud Servers, Hybrid Hosting, Cloud Infrastructure from GoGrid*. Retrieved August 26, 2011, from http://www.gogrid.com/

Gonzalez, H., Han, J., Li, X., & Klabjan, D. (2006). Warehousing and analyzing massive {RFID} data Sets. In L. Liu, A. Reuter, K.-Y. Whang, & J. Zhang (Eds.), *Proceedings of the 22nd International Conference on Data Engineering* (pp. 83-93). IEEE Computer Society.

Gray, J., Liu, D. T., Nieto-Santisteban, M., Szalay, A., DeWitt, D. J., & Heber, G. (2005). Scientific data management in the coming decade. *SIGMOD Record, 34*(4), 34–41. doi:10.1145/1107499.1107503

Grossman, R. L. (2009). The case for cloud computing. *IT Professional, 11*(2), 23–27. doi:10.1109/MITP.2009.40

Hovestadt, M., Kao, O., Kliem, A., & Warneke, D. (2011). Evaluating adaptive compression to mitigate the effects of shared I/O in clouds. In *Workshop Proceedings of 25th IEEE International Symposium on Parallel and Distributed Processing* (pp. 1042-1051). IEEE.

Isard, M., Budiu, M., Yu, Y., Birrell, A., & Fetterly, D. (2007). Dryad: Distributed data-parallel programs from sequential building blocks. In P. Ferreira, T. R. Gross, & L. Veiga (Eds.), *Proceedings of the 2007 EuroSys Conference* (pp. 59-72). ACM.

Kivity, A., Kamay, Y., Laor, D., Lublin, U., & Ligori, A. (2007). KVM: The Linux virtual machine monitor. In *Proceedings of the 2007 Ottawa Linux Symposium* (pp. 225-230).

Marshall, P., Keahey, K., & Freeman, T. (2010). Elastic site: Using clouds to elastically extend site resources. In *Proceedings of the 10th IEEE/ACM International Symposium on Cluster Computing and the Grid* (pp. 43-52). IEEE.

Nurmi, D., Wolski, R., Grzegorczyk, C., Obertelli, G., Soman, S., Youseff, L., & Zagorodnov, D. (2009). The Eucalyptus Open-source cloud-computing system. In F. Cappello, C.-L. Wang, & R. Buyya (Eds.), *Proceedings of the 9th IEEE/ACM International Symposium on Cluster Computing and the Grid* (pp. 124-131). IEEE Computer Society.

O'Malley, O., & Murthy, A. C. (2009). *Winning a 60 second dash with a yellow elephant*. Retrieved August 26, 2011, from http://sortbenchmark.org/Yahoo2009.pdf

Palankar, M. R., Iamnitchi, A., Ripeanu, M., & Garfinkel, S. (2008). Amazon S3 for science grids: A viable solution? In *Proceedings of the 2008 International Workshop on Data-aware Distributed Computing* (pp. 55-64). ACM.

Rackspace, U. S. Inc. (2011). *Cloud computing, managed hosting, dedicated server hosting by Rackspace*. Retrieved August 26, 2011, from http://www.rackspace.com/

Russell, R. (2008). Virtio: Towards a de-facto standard for virtual I/O devices. *SIGOPS Operating Systems Review*, *42*(5), 95–103. doi:10.1145/1400097.1400108

The Apache Software Foundation. (2011). *Welcome to Apache™ Hadoop™!* Retrieved August 26, 2011, from http://hadoop.apache.org/

The Stratosphere Project. (2011). Welcome to Stratosphere. In *Stratosphere - Above the Clouds*. Retrieved August 26, 2011, from http://www.stratosphere.eu/

Warneke, D., & Kao, O. (2009). Nephele: Efficient parallel data processing in the cloud. In I. Raicu, I. T. Foster, & Y. Zhou (Eds.), *Proceedings of the 2nd Workshop on Many-Task Computing on Grids and Supercomputers* (pp. 1-10). ACM.

Warneke, D., & Kao, O. (2011). Exploiting dynamic resource allocation for efficient parallel data processing in the cloud. *IEEE Transactions on Parallel and Distributed Systems*, *22*(6), 985–997. doi:10.1109/TPDS.2011.65

Yang, H.-C., Dasdan, A., Hsiao, R.-L., & Parker, D. S. (2007). Map-Reduce-Merge: Simplified relational data processing on large clusters. In C. Y. Chan, B. C. Ooi, & A. Zhou (Eds.), *Proceedings of the ACM SIGMOD International Conference on Management of Data* (pp. 1029-1040). ACM.

ADDITIONAL READING

Borkar, V. R., Carey, M. J., Grover, R., Onose, N., & Vernica, R. (2011). Hyracks: A flexible and extensible foundation for data-intensive computing. In S. Abiteboul, K. Böhm, C. Koch, & K.-L. Tan (Eds.), *Proceedings of the 27th International Conference on Data Engineering* (pp. 1151-1162). IEEE Computer Society.

Condie, T., Conway, N., Alvaro, P., Hellerstein, J. M., Elmeleegy, K., & Sears, R. (2010). MapReduce online. In *Proceedings of the 7th USENIX Symposium on Networked Systems Design and Implementation* (pp. 313-328). USENIX Association.

Deelman, E., Singh, G., Su, M.-H., Blythe, J., Gil, Y., & Kesselman, C. (2005). Pegasus: A framework for mapping complex scientific workflows onto distributed systems. *Journal Scientific Programming*, *13*(3), 219–237.

Foster, I. T., & Kesselman, C. (1997). Globus: A metacomputing infrastructure toolkit. *The International Journal of Supercomputer Applications*, *11*(2), 115–128. doi:10.1177/109434209701100205

Frey, J., Tannenbaum, T., Livny, M., Foster, I. T., & Tuecke, S. (2002). Condor-G: A computation management agent for multi-institutional grids. *Cluster Computing*, *5*(3), 237–246. doi:10.1023/A:1015617019423

Olston, C., Reed, B., Srivastava, U., Kumar, R., & Tomkins, A. (2008). Pig Latin: A not-so-foreign language for data processing. In J. Tsong-Li Wang (Ed.), *Proceedings of the ACM SIGMOD International Conference on Management of Data* (pp. 1099-1110). ACM.

Raicu, I., Zhao, Y., Dumitrescu, C., Foster, I. T., & Wilde, M. (2007). Falkon: A fast and light-weight task execution framework. In B. Verastegui (Ed.), *Proceedings of the ACM/IEEE Conference on High Performance Networking and Computing* (pp. 1-12). ACM.

Ramakrishnan, L., Koelbel, C., Kee, Y.-S., Wolski, R., Nurmi, D., & Gannon, D. … Zagorodnov, D. (2009). VGrADS: Enabling e-science workflows on grids and clouds with fault tolerance. In *Proceedings of the ACM/IEEE Conference on High Performance Computing* (pp. 1–12). ACM.

Wentzlaff, D., Gruenwald, C., III, Beckmann, N., Modzelewski, K., Belay, A., Youseff, L., et al. (2010). An operating system for multicore and clouds: Mechanisms and implementation. In J. M. Hellerstein, S. Chaudhuri, & M. Rosenblum (Eds.), *Proceedings of the 1st ACM Symposium on Cloud Computing* (pp. 3-14). ACM.

Zhao, Y., Hategan, M., Clifford, B., Foster, I. T., von Laszewski, G., & Nefedova, V. … Wilde, M. (2007). Swift: Fast, reliable, loosely coupled parallel computation. In *2007 IEEE International Conference on Services Computing - Workshops* (pp. 199-206). IEEE Computer Society.

KEY TERMS AND DEFINITIONS

Cloud Computing: Cloud computing enables customers to consume possibly large quantities of IT resources as a service over the Internet without any long term commitments. The services are provisioned quickly with no or only little management efforts by the service provider.

Infrastructure as a Service: Infrastructure as a Service refers a particular form of cloud computing in which the resources consumed by the customer mainly consists of fundamental IT services such as operating system-level access to compute nodes or raw storage space rather than predefined platform or software services.

On-Demand Resource Allocation: On-demand resource allocation denotes the ability of a cloud computing customer to gain rapid access to the requested cloud resources without prior announcement.

Pay-As-You-Go: Pay-as-you-go is a popular pricing model in the cloud computing landscape. It enables customers to gain access to the requested cloud resources without any upfront financial investment or long term commitment. The cloud customer can stop consuming the service at any time and will be charged for it no more.

Parallel Data Processing: Parallel Data Processing refers to a particular way of executing an application on a set of data. In contrast to sequential processing, an application is no longer expected to process the entire input data set on its own. Instead, the application is split into several components which run in parallel, so each component only processes a particular fraction of the overall input data set.

Parallel Data Processing Framework: A parallel data processing framework assists software developers in writing applications which are suitable for parallel data processing.

Remote Procedure Call: A remote procedure call refers to a technique which facilitates the communication between different computer programs or components thereof, potentially over a network.

Section 3
Applications of Distributed Computing

Chapter 11
Social Web Services Research Roadmap:
Present and Future

Zakaria Maamar
Zayed University, Dubai, UAE

Jamal Bentahar
Concordia Institute for Information Systems Engineering, Canada

Noura Faci
Université Lyon 1, France

Philippe Thiran
Namur University, Belgium

ABSTRACT

There is a growing interest in the research and industry communities to examine the possible weaving of social elements into Web services-based applications. This interest is backed by the widespread adoption of Web 2.0 technologies and tools developed using various online means such as social networks and blogs. Social Web services incorporate the result of this weaving and are concerned with establishing relationships with their peers like people do daily. This chapter reviews the recent developments in this new topic and identifies new research opportunities and directions that are still unexplored such as security, engineering, reputation, trust, and argumentation.

INTRODUCTION

Web services are among the latest information and communication technologies that people hail for their role in making business processes cross organization boundaries transparently and efficiently. A Web service presents the following properties (Benatallah et al., 2003): independent as much as possible from specific platforms and computing paradigms; primarily developed for inter-organizational situations; and easily composable so that developing complex adapters for the needs of composition is not required. Composition is one of Web services' selling points; it aims at

DOI: 10.4018/978-1-4666-2533-4.ch011

putting several Web services together in response to complex users' requests.

Despite Web services widespread adoption, they have fallen short of their potential as reported in (Maamar et al., 2011a). Web services are isolated: they know about themselves only; they are not aware of the presence of other peers; they cannot reconcile ontologies among each other or with their users; they cannot delegate their invocation requests to other peers when unavailable; they do not instantaneously and voluntarily cooperate with each other or self-organize; limit users' intervention considerably and function as black boxes; and, last but not least, consider only their own internal functional and non-functional details during execution and ignore other external details, such as user past interactions. These limitations simply undermine the capacities of Web services in helping organizations face today's challenges such as agility, competitiveness, and transparency. In this chapter we review some initiatives that inject social elements into Web services operation as an innovative way to address Web services' limitations. These social elements are present in people's daily life like friendship, fairness, and trustworthiness and can be applied to Web services when they engage in compositions. The result of this weaving is referred to as Social Web Services (SWSs) (Maamar et al., 2011a, Maamar et al., 2011b, Maamar et al., 2011c). SWSs are now in a position to establish and maintain networks of contacts; count on their (privileged) contacts when needed; form with other peers strong and long lasting collaborative groups; and, know with whom to partner so that ontology reconciliation is minimized.

SWSs are built upon the results of merging social computing with service-oriented computing. On the one hand social computing is about collective action, content sharing, and information dissemination at large. On the other hand, service-oriented computing is about service offer and request, loose coupling, and cross-organization flow. To support SWSs ``know'' with whom they

transacted in the past and with whom they would like to trade or cooperate in the future, they need to build and maintain their social networks of contacts. Moreover, to empower Web services with social communication capacities, we abstract them as agents that pursue social goals (Bentahar et al., 2007). Different types of networks connecting Web services can be built including collaboration, competition, and substitution. These networks will first, be traversed to identify SWSs' collaborators, competitors, and substitutes, and second be drilled into to assign qualities to SWSs such as selfishness and trustworthy.

This chapter is organized as follows. The next chapter introduces the motivations behind the topic of social Web services and suggests a literature review on this topic. Afterwards existing research initiatives on social Web services are discussed. Prior to concluding, some future research directions are established.

BACKGROUND

Motivations

A good number of today's applications integrate social elements such as collaboration and coordination into their operation to reflect the way people operate. These applications capitalize heavily on the Web as a platform for achieving cross-organization interaction and adopt new tools including weblogs, social networks, and wikis to achieve this integration. Among all these tools social networks are those that have attracted the attention of academia and industry communities. Social networks illustrate the willingness of users to share information, work with others, and recommend services and applications. These various, rich, and yet complex forms of interaction illustrate to a certain extent the principle of "I offer services that somebody else may need" and "I require services that somebody else may offer" upon which Web services are built.

Making applications ``socialize'' requires identifying the relationships that can exist between the components that constitute them. When it comes to Web services, collaboration and competition are the first two relationships to consider but others would definitely rise after addressing the obstacles that would hurdle the leveraging of social computing techniques to Web services. If all these relationships were captured using social networks, a social Web service would recommend the peers with whom it likes to collaborate in case of compositions, recommend the peers that can substitute for it in case of failure, and, be aware of the peers that compete against it in case of selection.

Related Work

SWSs are at the cross-road of two main research streams: social computing (exemplified with Web 2.0) and service-oriented computing (illustrated by Web services). Our literature review revealed two categories of research initiatives; those that adopt Web services to support social networks of users, and those that develop social networks of Web services to satisfy users' needs.

In the category of social networks of users, we cite some research proposals. Maaradji et al. present a Social Composer referred to as SoCo (Maaradji et al., 2010). SoCo advises on the next course of actions to take in response to events such as Web services selection. The advices are built upon the interactions that occur between users and Web services as well as past compositions. SoCo consists of different components including social knowledge extraction and modeling, recommendation manager, connection manager, and service repository. Xie et al. suggest a framework for semantic service composition based on social networks (Xie et al., 2008). Trust between service providers, service consumers, and services themselves, is the social element that is taken into account in this composition. The framework consists of several modules including semantic

extraction and social network construction, social network storage, and trust computing. Wu et al. rank Web services using non-functional properties and invocation requests at run-time (Wu et al., 2009). A Web service's popularity as analyzed by users is the social element that is considered during ranking. Tan et al. apply social networks analysis to mine and analyze a workflow repository, focusing on service usage patterns (Tan et al., 2010). Nam Ko et al. discuss the social Web in which a new type of services called social-networks connect services help third party develop social applications without having to build social networks (Nam Ko et al., 2010). Last but not least, Al-Sharawneh and Williams mix three technologies namely semantic Web, social networks, and recommender systems to assist users select Web services with respect to their functional and non-functional requirements (Al-Sharawneh and Williams, 2009). Besides the market-leader concept that refers to the best Web service, Al-Sharawneh and Williams developed two ontologies called follow-leader to classify users and preferences so that users' preferences are specified.

In the category of social networks of Web services, we recognize the research efforts by Maamar et al. reported in (Maamar et al., 2011d) and (Maamar et al., 2011c). In the first work the authors suggest a method to engineer social Web services. Four steps form this method. In the first step, the objective is to shed the light on the potential relationships between Web services. In the second step, the objective is to associate these relationships, once identified, with social networks. In the third and four steps, the objectives are to build and analyze these networks so that the social behaviors of Web services are established. In the second work the authors develop LinkedWS as a social network-based Web services discovery model. Different social networks permit to describe the situations that Web services engage in for instance collaboration and recommendation. LinkedWS stresses out that Web services should not be treated as isolated components that respond to users' queries, only. Contrarily, Web services compete against other, similar Web services during selection, collaborate with other, different Web services during composition, and may replace other, similar Web services during failure despite the competition. Competition and substitution relationships raise an interesting point, which is Web services competing to take part in compositions and at the same time collaborating to support each other during failure. This kind of "behavior" is referred to as coopetition standing for cooperation and competition (Bengtsson and Kock, 2000).

RESEARCH OPPORTUNITIES

Current Developments

Social Networks for Web Services Discovery

A framework that regulates Web services functioning, in general, and discovery, in particular is discussed in (Maamar et al., 2011b). Current Web services discovery approaches have shown their limitations on many occasions as the literature reports in (Goodwin et al., 2007) and (Juric et al., 2009), for example. In this framework, a Web service is characterized with a set of functional and non-functional properties and can with other peers to build compositions. To discover Web services using social networks, six steps were deemed appropriate in this framework: social network components identification, Web services matching analysis, social networks management, edge weight initial evaluation, social networks navigation, edge weight ongoing evaluation, and social networks ongoing management.

1. Social network components identification: this steps works out the components upon which the future social networks will be built.

These components are known as node and edge and correspond to Web services and relationships between Web services. Three types of relationships exist: collaboration is that Web services recommend other peers to help them satisfy requestors' needs; substitution relationship is that Web services accept that other peers replace them when they fail; and competition relationship is that Web services have the same functional properties and only one can be selected for binding because of its capacity of satisfying the requestors' non-functional requirements.

2. Web services matching analysis: this step establishes the relationships that may exist between Web services. This first, depends on the functional properties that each Web service exhibits and second, calls for a matching analysis of these properties in term of either similarity or complementarity. Existing works on Web services matching analysis can be used (Min et al., 2009; Shua et al., 2007). Regardless of the degree similarity (e.g., strong, weak, average) that might exist between Web services, they will be connected in the future social networks through competition and substitution relationships if their functional properties are declared similar. Otherwise, the Web services will be connected in these networks through collaboration relationship. A degree of complementarity (e.g., yes, no) will be established between them. Not all Web services have to collaborate with each other. Usually this depends on factors such as Web services falling into the same theme for example travelling and data dependencies existing between Web services.

3. Social networks management: this step either initiates the building of a new social network from scratch or extends an existing social network because of node and edge addition to this network. As per the relationships that are now established between the

Web services along with their respective degrees of similarity/complementarity, the management of the social networks in term of either construction and extension can now happen. To this end, the similarity degree is split into strong, average, and weak, and the complementarity degree is split into yes and no. These degrees are later used to assign weights to the edges connecting Web services in the social networks. In the rest of this chapter, we focus on the degree of similarity as the same applies to a certain extent to the degree of complementarity. To simplify the construction of a social network for each Web service, Web services are grouped according to their degrees of similarity to a certain Web service into clusters (Figure 1-(a)). If a Web service has a strong-similarity degree with a peer, then this Web service will be placed into the strong-similarity cluster of this another Web service. It should be noted that a cluster might already be populated with other Web services. The placement of Web services into clusters is a continuous process as long as new Web services are made available and would like to be discovered through

the social-network framework. While the clustering of Web services is in progress, the connection of the Web services together is in progress as well, which leads to social networks extension. In Figure 1-(b), the result of mapping the clusters onto the nodes and edges of a social network is shown. In this part of the figure, the weights of edges are shown. In terms of numbers of edges, all the Web services are of one edge from the Web service root. This latter is in fact the owner of the social network.

4. Edge weight initial evaluation: this step evaluates the weights of edges in a social network. This evaluation takes place either during the construction of the network for the first time or after adding a node to the network. The initial values of the weights correspond to the degrees of similarity between Web services. However these initial values will change as soon as the Web services discovery through the social networks become effective. In Figure 1-(b), the lengths of edges are different per type of cluster and per Web service connected to the Web service root. Although the Web services are in the

Figure 1. Social networks management: (a) Web services clustering; (b) Web services connection

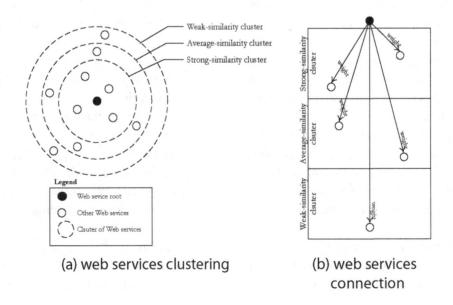

(a) web services clustering

(b) web services connection

same cluster, the lengths of their respective edges to the Web service root are different. By doing this, the value of the degree of similarity is reflected.

5. Social networks navigation: this action develops mechanisms that permit to navigate through the nodes and edges of a social network (Figure 1-(b)). Because of the collaboration, substitution, and competition relationships, two options are planned to deploy a social network with focus on the weights of this network's edges. In the first option, a Web service has three social networks, one per type of relationship. In the second option, a Web service has one social network for the three relationships that it could have with other peers. To differentiate between these relationships in the social network, the weight of an edge is structured as a triple of values corresponding each to a specific relationship. If a value is set to *null* for example, this means that the Web service is not engaged in the relationship associated with this value. Regardless of how a social network is deployed, each Web service constitutes an entry point to its own social network. As a result, the discovery of substitute, collaborative, or competitor peers starts by navigating through the different social networks commencing with the node of this Web service.

6. Edge weight ongoing evaluation: this step reflects the value-added of social networks to Web services discovery. This reflection happens by updating the weights of edges each time a substitute, collaborative, or competitor peer to a Web service is discovered thanks to these social networks. We recall that the initial values of weights of edges are obtained during the first step using the degrees of similarity/complementarity that exist between Web services. In the current action, appropriate functions will be suggested per type of relationship. For example, the

function to evaluate weights in a substitution-centric social network could be given by $w_{similarity(WS\_i,WS\_j)}$ is equal to $|WS_j \text{ selection}|$ over $|WS_i \text{ failure}|$ where $|WS_i \text{ failure}|$ stands for number of times that WS_i has failed and $|WS_j \text{ selection}|$ stands for number of times that WS_j has substituted for WS_i following the use of the substitution-centric social network of WS_i. It is expected that WS_i did not fail as well to complete the update of $w_{similarity(WS\_i,WS\_j)}$.

7. Social networks ongoing management: this step reviews the shape of a social network following the occurrence of different events such as edge's weights dropping below certain thresholds, Web services ceasing to exist, etc. All these events require deleting nodes and edges (incoming and outgoing), which impacts the shape of a social network.

Social Qualities Assignment to Web Services

Social networks of Web services can be subject to mining resulting into assigning social qualities to these Web services such as selfishness, fairness, and trustworthiness. An example of this mining is described in (Maamar et al., 2011e) and looked into the intra- and inter-social relationships existing between Web services that reside in same and separate communities, respectively. We recall that a community as per Maamar et al. is the host of two types of Web services known as slave and master (Maamar et al., 2009). The relationships between the Web services in a community are as follows:

- Supervision relationship between the master Web service and the slave Web services.
- Competition relationship between the slave Web services since they all offer the same functionality and only one slave Web service is selected at a time to satisfy a user's request.

- Substitution relationship between the slave Web services since they all offer the same functionality, so they can replace each other.
- Collaboration relationship between the slave Web services engaged in the same compositions.
- Recommendation relationship between the slave Web services, through their respective master Web services, so that a high compatibility level between the slave Web services is reached when compositions are built. We define the compatibility level between Web services as the efforts to put into addressing semantic and policy conflicts (Mrissa et al., 2007, Sheng et al., 2009).

Five social networks are built upon the aforementioned relationships. For illustration purposes the supervision social network is discussed. Building this network requires two types of nodes to represent the master and slave Web services and one type of edge to represent the supervision relationship. In this social network there is one node for the master Web service and several nodes for the slave Web services. The node of the master Web service constitutes the entry point of the supervision social network. Regarding the rest of nodes they are all connected to this node through supervision edges (Figure 2). These edges are unidirectional from the master Web service to the slave Web services.

To evaluate the weight of a supervision edge, which is referred to Supervision Level (SupL) between the master Web service (mws) of a community and a certain slave Web service (sws$_i$) in this community, three factors are used: Functionality Similarity Level (FSL) between the functionalities of these two Web services (the functionality of a master Web service is the functionality of the community that this master belongs to), Trust Level (TL) that shows how confident the master Web service is in the capac-

ity of the slave Web service to satisfy the user's request, and Responsiveness Level (RL) that shows the acceptance rate of a slave Web service to the demands of the master Web service to satisfy users' requests (SupL$_{(mws,swsi)}$ = FSL$_{(mws,swsi)}$ * TL$_{(mws,swsi)}$ * RL$_{(mws,swsi)}$). It is noted that a slave Web service has the opportunity to turn down these demands. More details on each factor are given in (Maamar et al., 2011e). It is worth noting that the weights of edges change regularly as compositions are executed. The more the supervision level is close to one, the closest a slave Web service is to the master Web service, which makes this slave Web service appropriate for satisfying a user's request. By reassessing the trust and responsiveness levels regularly, it becomes possible to either promote (getting closer to the master Web service) or demote (getting farther from the master Web service) a slave Web service.

As stated earlier the five social networks are subject to mining leading into assigning social qualities to Web services whether master or slave.

- **Selfishness:** a Web service is selfish if it does not show a cooperative attitude towards other Web services while they show a cooperative attitude towards this Web service. By cooperative, it is meant accepting participations in joint compositions or

Figure 2. Supervision social networks

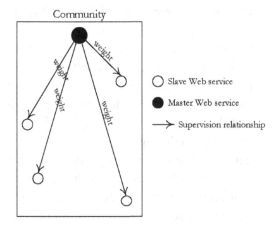

substitutions by responding to the invitations of other Web services. The mining of the recommendation and substitution social networks results in determining whether or not a Web service is selfish. Recommendation social networks reveal the selfishness of a Web service when its requests of recommendation to take part in compositions are accepted by other Web services while it rejects their recommendation requests. Substitution social networks reveal the selfishness of a Web services when it rejects substitution requests.

- **Fairness:** substitutions and compositions reveal the fairness of a Web service towards other Web services. When a Web service fails, it relies on the substitution social network to identify which Web service will replace it. However, the identification can be biased as the failing Web service can decide to exclude the most competitive Web services from being substitutes. In that way, the failing Web service first consults its competitive social network before its substitution social network. In that case, the failing Web service is considered as unfair.

- **Trustworthiness:** composition scenarios reveal the trustworthiness of a Web service in accepting to satisfy the requests it receives. A request is related to either participation in composition or recommendation of participation in composition. Because this Web service is master or slave, trustworthiness needs to be examined from two perspectives namely intra-community and inter-community. The first perspective is explained in this chapter. In a supervision social network, the evaluation of a supervision edge takes into account the Trust Level that shows how confident a master Web service is in the capacity of a slave Web service to satisfy a user's request. TL is calculated based on the total number of

successful participations of a slave Web service in compositions over the total number of participations of this slave Web service in these compositions. Because of the technical nature (success versus failure) that is given to this trust level assessment, an additional metric is required that evaluates the Compliance Level (CmpL) of a slave Web service with the non-functional properties it announces and the effective non-functional properties that are collected at run-time. A slave Web service is declared trustworthy in a community by its master Web service if the combination of trust and compliance levels is higher than a minimal threshold that denotes the acceptable deviation between the announced and effective non-functional properties.

FUTURE RESEARCH DIRECTIONS

To achieve the full potential of SWSs, many challenging issues need to be addressed ranging from better organization, to security and strategic issues in terms of inviting/accepting new members in a social network.

Engineering Social Communities

Recently, many efforts have been put into engineering communities of Web services, which are used as virtual spaces to gather similar Web services (Bentahar et al., 2008) (Maamar et al. 2009). Many advantages of communities have been reported over existing approaches according to which Web services are seen as isolated entities that only engage in interactions if there is need for composition, but they are not grouped together. These advantages include facilitating and speeding-up the discovery of Web services since the respective descriptions are all in the same place, enhancing the composition since Web services can be substituted by peers located in the same community, facilitating task delegation among Web services of the same community, enforcing the security since the community is in charge of checking the credentials of Web services before joining and during their stay in the community, and last but not least maintaining a "healthy" group of members by ejecting from the community those that misbehave or do not perform as expected. Although communities share some similarities with social networks, the two concepts are quite different. For instance, members of the same community might not have social relationships but only be aware of the existence of each other within the same community, and two socially related Web services may not be members of the same community. Membership to communities managed by a special Web service called *master* is also different from membership to social networks. In communities, new members are accepted upon the master's decision if they are expected to bring value to the community, for instance by contributing to raise its reputation, and a Web service decides to join a community if collaborating with other members is expected to bring benefits. An important research direction is the integration of social structures of Web services into communities. This will strengthen both communities and social Web services. This will result in communities where members are part of different social networks. Merging these different social networks deems appropriate based on the similarity among the same community members. Edge weight initial evaluation, edge weight ongoing evaluation, and social networks ongoing management will take place as discussed earlier. Social networks can be easily expanded through communities. On the other hand, new Web services can be identified as potential future members of communities by means of existing social links. This will shift the membership management from master-member regulation to member-member-master relation and regulation as existing members can recommend the hiring of new members. Furthermore, the structure of communities will be shifted from

simple similarity among Web services to social relations, which will even enforce the advantages of communities.

Argumentation and Social Web Services

Another direction for future research is the integration of computational argumentation theory and techniques, used in artificial intelligence, into social Web services. Argumentation is a powerful technique allowing entities having different and probably conflicting beliefs about their environments and polar goals to argue for the sake of supporting their opinions. In the context of communities of Web services, argumentation has been used to model interactions between Web services and the community's master before joining the community, so that the master can persuade these Web services to join by revealing membership benefits, and the Web services can negotiate better joining conditions (Bentahar et al., 2007). In the context of social Web services, establishing new edges (i.e., social relationships) will be made more efficient if two Web services are convinced about the utility of establishing a new relationship. For instance, one Web service can engage in an argumentation process if it is interested in having a tie with another peer based on similarity; this interest would be supported by being recommended as possible substitute in case of failure. Managing social communities can be extended by giving members the chance to convince the master about accepting new members if strong links do exist between the existing and recommended ones. This requires addressing the following issues: 1) how the social Web services generate competing/conflicting hypothesis about, for instance, the utility of an edge, arguments for and against each hypothesis, and analysis (e.g., draw tentative conclusions about the relative likelihood of each hypothesis); and 2) how to combine multiple analyses for providing a collective view. To support argumentation amongst social Web services or social communities deployed on the Web, it would be useful to compare the existing theoretical and computational argumentation models previously developed for studying human as well as artificial agents behaviors in social environments, especially in terms of their potential advantages and disadvantages and evaluate the suitability of these models for different kinds of purposes.

Trust and Reputation for Social Web Services

Reputation and trust are close relatives–but are not one and the same. Organizations and individuals have reputations for a whole range of characteristics other than trust. The role of trust lies in the process by which organizations and individuals build and sustain confidence in those reputations. From economic perspective, four trust principles guide this process: i) the focus on the opponent (e.g., client, partner and subordinate) for the proponent's sake; ii) the collaboration which means a willingness to work together through creating joint goals; iii) the long-term relationships for both parties; and iv) transparency which increases credibility, and lowers self-orientation. Within the context of social Web services, trust is a major concept that Web services consider when deciding about recommending another peer or accepting substitution from another peer. Trust is the degree to which a Web service believes another peer is reliable and possesses integrity where reliability means the belief that the partner will honor its obligations as agreed, while integrity is the belief that the partner is honest and does what is right (Perry, 2004). The presence of trust amongst social Web services establishes an atmosphere of confidence, reliability and integrity, contributes to improving relationships and cooperation, and encouraging the members to accept risk-taking. Trust would constitute an essential criteria used by social Web services to evaluate their interest when deciding whether to participate or not in

collaboration and substitution scenarios. For social Web services, reputation can be propagated through the links, making the identification of malicious peers easier if social Web services are cooperative and have incentives to denounce malicious members. However, this is not always the case because social Web services are deployed by different providers with competing interests. So, several issues have to be addressed such as: how to rate and build trust and reputation amongst social Web services; how to propagate trust and reputation when adding a link between two social Web services in case of contradictory reputation values; and how to detect and weed out malicious social Web services.

Incentives for Social Web Services

Incentive is another major concept that a social Web service needs to evaluate for determining the value of taking part of collaboration or substitution relationships with other Web services. Indeed, as Web services are selfish and strategic, they will only share their experiences if they are incentivized to do so. Incentive mechanisms are systems with designed rules ensuring that the actions of agents honestly reporting their information will produce a better outcome for these agents (Shoham and Leyton-Brown 2009). Designing incentive mechanisms for social Web services to share information with others within the same network needs further research. Game-theoretic mechanism design will help designing such incentives and analyzing their properties as desired equilibrium and in which scenarios they can be applied (Jurca and Falting 2007). An important issue, still open, is the collusion between members. Designing a collusion resistant and incentive-compatible reputation mechanism where honestly sharing past experiences is a Nash equilibrium, will enforce security through social links. Social Web services will accept to recommend or to replace another one only if the generated incentive is at least equal or higher to what it could acquire without any relationships. Incentive mechanisms have been studied using cooperative game theory in the multi-agent context. However, this raises other questions such as: what are the adaptations required for social Web services' incentive analysis; how the incentives influence reasoning about trust and reputation of these social Web services; and what is the link between argumentation and incentives.

CONCLUSION

This chapter discussed the combination of social networks and Web services. Social networks establish relationships between Web services. Different social networks are identified: competition, recommendation and substitution. Web services can capitalize on these networks to identify the social qualities of their peers like selfishness, fairness, and trustworthiness. These social qualities are deemed appropriate for a better management of Web services. For instance, selfish Web services need to be dealt carefully. This chapter also provided some new research opportunities in the domain of social Web services. The different issues range from better management, to security and strategic questions in terms of inviting/accepting new members in the social network.

REFERENCES

Al-Sharawneh, J., & Williams, M.-A. (2009). A social network approach in Semantic Web services selection using follow the leader behavior. In *Proceedings of the 13th Enterprise Distributed Object Computing Conference Workshops* (EDOCW'2009), Auckland, New Zealand, (pp. 310-319).

Benatallah, B., Sheng, Q. Z., & Dumas, M. (2003). The self-serve environment for web services composition. *IEEE Internet Computing*, 7(1), 40–48. doi:10.1109/MIC.2003.1167338

Bengtsson, M., & Kock, S. (2000). Coopetition in business networks to cooperate and compete simultaneously. *Industrial Marketing Management*, 29(5), 411–426. doi:10.1016/S0019-8501(99)00067-X

Bentahar, J., Maamar, Z., Benslimane, D., & Thiran, P. (2007). An argumentation framework for communities of web services. *IEEE Intelligent Systems*, 22(6), 75–83. doi:10.1109/MIS.2007.99

Bentahar, J., Maamar, Z., Benslimane, D., Thiran, P., & Subramanian, S. (2008). Agent-based communities of web services: An argumentation-driven approach. *Service Oriented Computing and Applications*, 2(4), 219–238. doi:10.1007/s11761-008-0033-4

Bui, T., Gacher, A., & Sebastian, H. J. (2006). Web services for negotiation and bargaining in electronic markets: Design requirements, proof-of-concepts, and potential applications to e-procurement. *Group Decision and Negotiation. Special Issue on Hot Topics in Negotiation Support Systems*, 15(5), 469–490.

Goodwin, J. C., Russomanno, D. J., & Qualls, J. (2007). Survey of semantic extensions to UDDI: Implications for sensor services. *Proceedings of the 2007 International Conference on Semantic Web & Web Services* (SWWS'2007), Las Vegas, Nevada, USA, (pp. 16-22).

Ireland, R. D., Hitt, M. A., & Vaidyanath, D. (2002). Alliance management as a source of competitive advantage. *Journal of Management*, 28(3), 413–446. doi:10.1177/014920630202800308

Jurca, R., & Faltings, B. (2007). Obtaining reliable feedback for sanctioning reputation mechanisms. *Journal of Artificial Intelligence Research*, 29, 391–419.

Juric, M. B., Sasa, A., Brumen, B., & Rozman, I. (2009). WSDL and UDDI extensions for version support in web services. *Journal of Systems and Software, 82*(8), 1326–1343. doi:10.1016/j.jss.2009.03.001

Maamar, Z., Faci, N., Krug Wives, L., Badr, Y., Bispo Santos, P., & de Oliveira, J. P. M. (2011). Using social networks for web services discovery. *IEEE Internet Computing, 15*(4), 48–54. doi:10.1109/MIC.2011.27

Maamar, Z., Faci, N., Krug Wives, L., Yahyaoui, H., & Hacid, H. (2011). Towards a method for engineering social web services. In *The Proceedings of the IFIP WG8.1 Working Conference on Method Engineering - Engineering Methods in the Service-Oriented Context* (ME'2011), Paris, France, April, (pp. 153-167).

Maamar, Z., Hacid, H., & Huhns, M. N. (2011). Why web services need social networks. *IEEE Internet Computing, 15*(2), 90–94. doi:10.1109/MIC.2011.49

Maamar, Z., Krug Wives, L., Badr, Y., Elnaffar, S., Boukadi, K., & Faci, N. (2011). LinkedWS: A novel web services discovery model based on the metaphor of social networks. *Simulation Modelling Practice and Theory, 19*(1), 121–132. doi:10.1016/j.simpat.2010.06.018

Maamar, Z., Subramanian, S., Thiran, P., Benslimane, D., & Bentahar, J. (2009). An approach to engineer communities of web services: Concepts, architecture, operation, and deployment. *International Journal of E-Business Research, 5*(4), 1–21. doi:10.4018/jebr.2009040601

Maamar, Z., Yahyaoui, H., Lim, E., & Thiran, P. (2011). Social engineering of communities of web services. In *The Proceedings of the 11th Annual International Symposium on Applications and the Internet* (SAINT'2011), Munich, Germany, (pp. 100-109).

Maaradji, A., Hacid, H., Daigremont, J., & Crespi, N. (2010). Towards a social network based approach for services composition. In *Proceedings of the 2010 IEEE International Conference on Communications* (ICC'2010), Cap Town, South Africa, (pp. 1-5).

Min, L., Weiming, S., Qi, H., & Junwei, Y. (2009). A weighted ontology-based semantic similarity algorithm for web services. *Expert Systems with Applications, 36*(10), 12480–12490. doi:10.1016/j.eswa.2009.04.034

Mrissa, M., Ghedira, C., Benslimane, D., Maamar, Z., Rosenberg, F., & Dustdar, S. (2007). A context-based mediation approach to compose Semantic Web services. *ACM Transactions on Internet Technology, Special Issue on Semantic Web Services: Issues, Solutions, and Applications, 8*(1).

Nam Ko, M., Cheek, G. P., Shehab, M., & Sandhu, R. (2010). Social-networks connect services. *IEEE Computer, 43*(8), 37–43. doi:10.1109/MC.2010.239

Perry, M. L., Sengupta, S., & Krapfel, R. (2004). Effectiveness of horizontal strategic alliances in technologically uncertain environments: Are trust and commitment enough? *Journal of Business Research, 57*(9), 951–956. doi:10.1016/S0148-2963(02)00501-5

Rahwan, T., Ramchurn, S., Jennings, N., & Giovannucci, A. (2009). An anytime algorithm for optimal coalition structure generation. *Journal of Artificial Intelligence Research, 34*(1), 521–567.

Sheng, Q. Z., Yu, J., Maamar, Z., Jiang, W., & Li, X. (2009). Compatibility checking of heterogeneous web service policies using VDM++. In *The Proceedings of the IEEE Workshop on Software and Services Maintenance and Management (SSMM'2009) held in conjunction the 2009 IEEE Congress on Services, Part I* (SERVICES I'2009), Los Angeles, CA, USA, (pp. 821-828).

Shoham, Y., & Leyton-Brown, K. (2009). *MultiAgent systems: Algorithmic, game-theoretic, and logical foundations*. Cambridge University Press.

Shua, G., Rana, O. F., Avisb, N. J., & Dingfang, C. (2007). Ontology-based semantic matchmaking approach. *Advances in Engineering Software*, 38(1), 59–67. doi:10.1016/j.advengsoft.2006.05.004

Tan, W., Zhang, J., & Foster, I. (2010). Network analysis of scientific workflows: A gateway to reuse. *IEEE Computer*, 43(9), 54–61. doi:10.1109/MC.2010.262

Wu, Q., Iyengar, A., Subramanian, R., Rouvellou, I., Silva-Lepe, I., & Mikalsen, T. (2009). Combining quality of service and social information for ranking services. In *Proceedings of ServiceWave 2009 Workshops held in conjunction with the 7th International Conference on Service Service-Oriented Computing* (ICSOC'2009), Stockholm, Sweden, (pp. 561-575).

Xie, X., Du, B., & Zhang, Z. (2008). Semantic service composition based on social network. In *Proceedings of the Demo Session of the 17th International World Wide Web Conference* (WWW'2008), Beijing, China, (pp. 1-5).

KEY TERMS AND DEFINITIONS

Argumentation Theory: Argumentation theory is a computational theory within artificial intelligence discipline that aims to study a particular type of reasoning in which involved entities build arguments from their knowledge bases to support or attack a particular conclusion. It is largely used in agent communication, automated negotiation, conflict resolution, and automated decision making.

Composite Web Service: Composition targets users' requests that cannot be satisfied by any single, available Web service, whereas a composite Web service obtained by combining available Web services may be used. Several specification languages to compose Web services exist for example WS-BPEL (de facto standard), WSCDL, and XLANG. A composite Web service could be built either proactively or reactively. The former is an off-line process that gathers available component Web services in-advance to form a composite Web service. This one is pre-compiled and ready for execution upon users' requests. The latter creates a composite Web service on-the-fly upon users' requests. Because of the on-the fly property, a dedicated module is in charge of identifying the needed component Web services, making them collaborate, tracking their execution, and resolving their conflicts if they arise.

Incentive Compatibility: Incentive compatibility is an integral part of game theory and mechanism design that aims at designing incentives to force the entities to adopt honest behaviors. A process is said to be incentive-compatible if all of the participants fare best when they reveal some private information such as their preferences truthfully. Incentive compatibility is considered as a constraint on the choice of group decision making procedures.

Recommender Systems: They are designed to help users tackle the problem of information overload. They could be built upon three representative techniques namely content-based, collaborative-filtering, and hybrid.

Service-Oriented Architecture (SOA): SOA is an architecture style that builds on loosely coupled, interoperable and composable components or software agents called services. Services have well-defined interfaces based standard protocols (usually web-services but most definitions mention that it is not the only possible implementation) as well as Quality of Service (QoS) attributes (or policies) on how these interfaces can be used by Service Consumers. SOA definitions mentions the basic communication pattern for SOA is request/reply but many definitions also talk about asynchronous communications as well.

Social Computing: Social computing is related to applications that support collaborative work (GroupWare) and techniques for modeling, simulating, studying, and analyzing the society (i.e., study the social behavior). Examples of applications include on-line communities and tools, and interactive entertainment and training. Another definition sees social computing as an emerging paradigm that involves a multi-disciplinary approach for analyzing and modeling social behaviors on different media and platforms to produce intelligent applications. Main characteristics of social computing are connectivity, collaboration, and community.

Universal Description, Discovery, and Integration (UDDI): UDDI specifications define how Web services should be published and discovered by providers and users, respectively. At the conceptual level, information provided in an UDDI registry consists of three components. First, white pages include address, contact, and known identifiers of Web services. Second, yellow pages include industrial categories based on standardized taxonomies. Finally, green pages include the technical information that a provider would like to offer on its Web services. At the business level, an UDDI registry can be used for checking whether a given provider has particular Web services, finding companies in a certain industry with a given type of Web service, and locating information about how a provider has exposed a Web service.

Web Service: It is *"a software application identified by a URI, whose interfaces and binding are capable of being defined, described, and discovered by XML artifacts, and supports direct interactions with other software applications using XML-based messages via Internet-based applica-tions"* (W3C). A Web service implements a functionality (e.g., Book Order and Forecast Weather) that users and other peers invoke by submitting appropriate messages to this Web service. The life cycle of a Web service could be summarized with five stages namely description, publication, discovery, invocation, and composition. Briefly, providers describe their Web services and publish them on dedicated registries. Potential consumers (i.e., requesters) interact with these registries to discover relevant Web services, so they could invoke them. In case the discovery fails, i.e., requests cannot be satisfied by any single Web service, the available Web services may be composed to satisfy the consumer's request.

Web Service Discovery: Discovery is the act of locating a machine-processable description of a Web service-related resource that may have been previously unknown and that meets certain functional criteria. It involves matching a set of functional and other criteria with a set of resource descriptions. The goal is to find an appropriate Web service-related resource. The resources being discovered are usually service descriptions. If a requester entity does not already know what service it wishes to engage, the requester entity must discover one. There are various means by which discovery can be performed. Various things — human end users or agents — may initiate discovery. Requester entities may find service descriptions during development for static binding, or during execution for dynamic binding. For statically bound requester agents, using discovery is optional, as the service description might be obtained in other ways, such as being sent directly from the provider entity to the requester entity, developed collaboratively, or provided by a third party, such as a standards body.

Chapter 12
On the Dissemination of IEEE 802.11p Warning Messages in Distributed Vehicular Urban Networks

Enrique Costa-Montenegro
University of Vigo, Spain

Ana M. Peleteiro
University of Vigo, Spain

Juan C. Burguillo
University of Vigo, Spain

Javier Vales-Alonso
Technical University of Cartagena, Spain

Ana Belén Barragáns-Martínez
Centro Universitario de la Defensa, Escuela Naval Militar de Marín, Spain

ABSTRACT

IEEE 802.11p is a technology used for communication among vehicles, related to security issues, warning of incidents, or mere exchange of different types of information. Future cars will have the ability to communicate among them and with roadside data systems to spread information about congestion, road conditions, and accidents. They will also have access to travel-related Internet services, publicity from business nearby, tourist information, or even to exchange user files. In this chapter, the authors base their work on an ad-hoc highly configurable agent-based simulator that models communication among cars in a distributed vehicular urban network. Using this model, they provide different measurements concerning coverage and dissemination times to describe the behavior of the standard protocol for disseminating warning messages. Based on the results obtained, the chapter presents proposals to enhance the behavior of the protocol, some of them changing the specification, and others with the use of location-based information.

DOI: 10.4018/978-1-4666-2533-4.ch012

INTRODUCTION

Traffic accidents are one of the main causes of human death, being even higher than deadly diseases or natural disasters (Yang et al., 2004). In fact, every year 1.2 million persons die and 50 million get injured in road traffic accidents (Peden et al., 2004). However, there are some studies like (Wang and Thompson, 1997) which show that if the driver was warned with at least one-half second prior to a collision, more than 50% of collisions could be avoided.

The Intelligent Transportation Systems (ITSs) are a set of technical solutions to improve the operation, security and efficiency of transportation systems. The main goals are the reduction of fatalities and financial losses due to traffic accidents, and also the reduction of expenses caused by traffic congestion (in 2007, the extra costs caused by time lost and fuel in 439 urban areas in the US where 87.2 billion dollars, 10600 litters of wasted fuel and a yearly delay for the average peak-period traveler of 36 hours (Texas Transportation Institute, 2009)). Besides the services mentioned above, there is also a motivation to provide private services, as Web access, file sharing, and many others. There is a huge economic interest in this area to improve traffic safety and save lives on road. Besides, vehicle-to-vehicle communication allows the sharing of the wireless channel to improve route planning and traffic congestion (Martinez et al., 2008). Due to this, many communication protocols and methodologies are being developed trying to improve this kind of communications (Wischhof and Ebner, 2005).

Many countries have joined this research field, presenting projects to provide safety in roads, and to be able to detect non-safe situations before they appear. We can mention the Vehicle Safety Communications Consortium in the US, the Internet ITS Consortium (http://www.internetits.org) in Japan, and the Car-to-Car (C2C) Communications Consortium (http://www.car-to-car.org) in Europe.

Besides their main goal of improving safety, they also deal with comfort, transport efficiency and entertainment applications.

In 1999, the US Federal Communications Commission allocated 75 MHz of licensed spectrum of Dedicated Short Range Communications, from 5.8 to 5.925 GHz, to be used in the Intelligent Transportation Systems. This band is used exclusively for vehicle-to-vehicle and vehicle-to-infrastructure communications.

C2C technology, which is akin to Mobile Ad-Hoc networks, provides communications among nearby vehicles and between vehicles and nearby fixed equipment, usually described as roadside equipment. A new family of standards is being developed to ensure these communications. The WAVE (Wireless Access in Vehicular Environments) communications standards, developed for the US Department of Transportation (DOT), describe the architecture and protocols for C2C communications. Also, IEEE is developing a family of standards, IEEE 1609. The IEEE 1609.2 standard deals with methods for securing WAVE messages against eavesdropping, spoofing, and other attacks. The IEEE 1609.1 standard deals with managing multiple simultaneous data streams, memory, and other system resources. The IEEE 1609.4 standard primarily covers how multiple channels -including control and service channels-should operate. Finally, the IEEE 1609.3 standard touches WAVE networking services and protocols. These draft standards cover the five upper layers of the OSI protocol stack.

The two lower layers (data link and physical) are implanted by the Dedicated Short Range Communications (DSCR) at 5.9 GHz. It is standardized in the IEEE 802.11p standard, a variant of 802.11a adjusted for low overhead operations and it uses the extension IEEE 802.11e Enhanced Distributed Channel Access (EDCA) for Quality of Service (QoS). These wireless access standards allow data exchange between high-speed vehicles and between the vehicles and the roadside infrastructure.

The main goal of these technologies is to provide safety and comfort to the passengers. To this end, a special electronic device will be placed inside each vehicle, enabling Ad-Hoc Network connectivity for the passengers. This distributed network will operate without any infrastructure or legacy client-server communication. Each vehicle equipped with this device will be a node in the Ad-Hoc Network, and it will be able to receive and relay messages from others through the wireless network. Collision warning, road sign alarms and in-place traffic view will allow the driver to decide the best path along the way. There will also be multimedia and Internet connectivity facilities for passengers, all within the wireless coverage of each car. However, diverse security issues are relevant in these communications, like confidentiality (information exchanged between cars must be protected against unintended or unauthorized access), integrity (information exchanged must be reliable and should be trusted), availability (information exchange is always possible), and anonymity or privacy (despite of information exchange, car identities should remain anonymous to the rest, and they should not be tracked).

One noticeable characteristic of vehicular networks is that, rather than moving at random, vehicles tend to move in an organized fashion. The interactions with roadside equipment can likewise be characterized fairly accurately. Also, the motion range of most vehicles is restricted, for example to follow a paved highway. These characteristics indicate that connections between cars will last longer than in a typical Ad-Hoc Network situation.

In this chapter, we present a model to analyze and improve the dissemination of warning messages using IEEE 802.11p in urban environments. We consider a simulator that models a city with a car traffic topology typical from a Manhattan-like scenario. During traffic operation, one car randomly chosen will broadcast a warning message to all other cars in the distributed network using the IEEE 802.11p protocol. From this scenario, we present our main contribution: using the results of the simulator, we study the protocol and propose improvements to enhance its behavior.

The chapter is organized as follows: Background section summarizes the advances in C2C technology, IEEE 802.11p dissemination section introduces multi-agent systems and details the way the city is modeled in this chapter, describes the protocol and model used to communicate cars and to exchange information, and simulates and studies the behavior of the standard for disseminating warning messages, analyzes the obtained results, and proposes alternatives to improve the protocol performance, to finally discuss the results, and compare them with other interesting approaches. Future research directions section provides insight about the future of IEEE 802.11p dissemination. The conclusion section ends the chapter.

BACKGROUND

In this section we present some topics related to C2C communications and networks, as well as an overview of the technologies and directions in which research is heading.

VANETs (Vehicular Ad-hoc NETworks) are a class of Mobile Ad-hoc Networks (MANETs), where mobile devices are connected by wireless links in a self-configuring network that does not require any fixed structure (Fiore et al., 2007). VANETs are the application of MANETs to vehicular environment, where elements are mobile vehicles, cars or emergency response vehicles traveling. These networks have a large number of nodes, high node speed, ephemeral topologies, transmissions blocked by buildings, variable density and unrestricted power (Yousefi et al., 2006). The mobile nodes have mobile radio units (On-Board Unit, OBU), and they can share information between them and also with the stations on the roadside (Road-Side Unit, RSU).

Regarding WAVE, firstly, in the US, the ASTM 2313 working group was created to standardize the DSRC radio technology (ASTM 2002). In

2004, this standardization effort was taken by the IEEE 802.11 standard group. Within this group, DSRC is known as IEEE 802.11p Wireless Access Vehicular Environment (WAVE), which intends to serve as an international standard applicable not only in US, but also in other parts of the world (Jiang and Delgrossi, 2008). WAVE consists of IEEE 802.11p for the PHY/MAC layer and IEEE P1609 for higher layers.

Nowadays, IEEE 802.11p is the only standard with support for direct vehicle-to-vehicle communication (Bistrup, 2007). However, it has some problems when trying to ensure real-time constraints and anonymity of the users (Troncoso et al., 2011).

The PHY 802.11p capabilities are treated in several articles (Stibor et al., 2007; Wellens et al., 2007). Apart from the PHY, also the MAC layer is studied. There are several MAC protocols used for VANETs. These protocols have to cope with quickly changing topology, QoS requirements (audio and video applications), and the most important, safety applications, that in turn have to fulfill real-time constraints, since if the information does not arrive on time, it is useless. Besides, we find entertainment applications that are also non-delay tolerant (audio and video) and other that are delay tolerant (search on the Web). MAC layer is usually based on TDMA (Time Division Multiple Access) and CSMA/CA protocols (e.g, EDCA). The second approach is the most used nowadays, but it cannot guarantee deterministic upper bound for the channel access (Bilstrup et al., 2008), thus safety messages are not guaranteed to arrive on time, and this implies serious problems for the traffic safety system.

MAC layer has been evaluated and enhanced in (Bai and Krishnan, 2006), where the authors use real-world data traffic in their investigations. We can also find both analytic and simulated evaluations of 802.11 in (Eichler 2007). The conclusion of this paper is that time-critical message dissemination cannot be ensured. Thus some enhancements as for example better prioritization (Suthaputchakun and Ganz, 2007; Torrent-Moreno et al., 2004) or an evaluation of a different MAC method, the self-organizing time division multiple access (STDMA) (Bilstrup et al., 2008), are studied.

Deploying and testing VANETs involves high costs and an intensive labor. Simulation is a useful alternative prior to actual implementation, and this is why many simulators have been developed, trying to make the simulated model as close to reality as possible.

In (Naumov and Baumann, 2006), the authors review and classify various publicly available simulators (though some proprietary simulators exist, as for example QualNet (Qualnet, 2006) or Carisma (Capra et al., 2003)). The authors divide the simulators into three categories: vehicular mobility generators, network simulators and VANET simulators. In the next paragraphs we provide a short summary of these categories.

Vehicular mobility simulators increase the level of realism in VANET simulations, including road model, scenario parameters, as maximum vehicular speed, reflecting vehicles moves using trace files. Within this category, we find SUMO (Krajzewicz et al., 2002), which is a pure traffic generator, designed to handle large road networks, which includes free vehicle movements, different vehicle types, etc; and CityMob (Martinez et al., 2008), which is a mobility model generator proposed for VANETs with three different models: Simple Model, Manhattan Model and realistic Downtown Model.

The second category includes the network simulators, which allow the study of how the network would behave under different conditions, as for example in our case, the communication among vehicles in an inter-vehicle communication system. As some examples to simulate VANET scenarios, we have ns-2 (Fall and Varadhan, 2000), which is a discrete event simulator and includes node mobility, a realistic physical layer with a radio propagation model, radio network interfaces and IEEE 802.11 MAC. Another example is GloMoSim (Zeng et al., 1998), which is a scalable simulation environment for wireless and wired network.

Finally, we have the VANET simulators, that allow the change of the behavior of vehicles depending on a given application context. Currently, the mobility and the network models are implemented in two separated simulation tools, and it is necessary to integrate them. For example, TranNS (Piórkowski et al., 2008) integrates both a network simulator and a mobility generator, and provides support for realistic 802.11p, automated generation of road networks from TIGER and Shepfile, etc, and also ready-to-use VANET applications, as Road DangerWarning. GrooveNet (Mangharam et al., 2006) is other simulator that integrates those two features. It is a hybrid simulator which enables communication among real and simulated vehicles, using real maps, which eases protocol design and in-vehicle deployment. Its modular architecture incorporates mobility, trip and message broadcasting over a variety of link and physical layer communication models. We can find another example of a VANET simulator in (Burguillo-Rial et al., 2008).

Safety is the main goal of using communication technologies in vehicle environment. Before these systems were developed, there existed other collision warning systems that obtained information of the surrounding vehicles with sensors, being sonar and video camera two possible examples. However, collision avoidance tends towards cooperative systems using wireless communication techniques and GPS systems (Sebastian et al., 2009).

Safety services are delay critical, which means that an upper limit bound must exist in the arrival of this kind of information. Within these safety services, we find assistance, in cooperative collision warning and navigation; information, e.g. speed limit, and finally warning information like road condition warnings. A good example of the utility of these services is in sudden hard braking warning events, where a notification is sent to the other vehicles, preventing from chain vehicle collisions. Besides, these cooperative driver systems permit the extension of the range of perception of the driver. This is done by transmitting data to the cars following on the same road, preventing potential hazardous situations as in a blind corner (Jakubiak and Koucheryavy, 2008).

Broadcast is really important in vehicular communication systems, since if a safety event occurs, the first vehicle noticing it must broadcast this information so that it reaches as many vehicles as possible. However, there must be a tradeoff while broadcasting, because in spite of the fact that we want the information to reach the maximum quantity of vehicles, the network should not be collapsed with this broadcast.

In (Schmidt-Eisenlohr et al., 2007; Torrent-Moreno et al., 2006; Torrent-Moreno and Mittag, 2006), safety-related information dissemination by means of simulation is studied. In (Lyakhov and Poupyrev, 2005; Lyakhov et al., 2005) authors developed analytical methods for broadcasting in IEEE 802.11, where they study the mean notification time.

In (Ma and Chen, 2007; Ma et al., 2007) authors applied broadcasting in IEEE 802.11 in vehicular ad-hoc networks in the saturated and non-saturated case. There are also probabilistic methods, as in (Ibrahim et al., 2009), where a probabilistic function is used to decide if the vehicles should or not rebroadcast to solve the spatial broadcast storm problem.

IEEE 802.11P DISSEMINATION: MODEL, EVALUATION, PROPOSALS, AND DISCUSSION

City Model

We have implemented the city model in NetLogo (Wilensky 2007), a multi-agent modeling environment for simulating natural and social phenomena. Before introducing Multi-agent Systems (MAS), we need to define what we understand by an agent. Unfortunately, there is no general agreement in the research community. Therefore we introduce here a classical definition (Wooldridge and Jennings, 1995): "the term agent is used to denote a hardware or (more usually) software-based computer system that mainly enjoys the following properties":

- **Autonomy:** agents operate without the direct intervention of humans or others, and have some kind of control over their actions and internal state;
- **Social ability:** agents interact with other agents (and possibly humans) via some kind of agent-communication language;
- **Reactivity:** agents perceive their environment, and respond in a timely fashion to its changes;
- **Pro-activeness:** agents do not simply act in response to their environment; they are able to exhibit goal-directed behavior by taking the initiative.

There are some other attributes that can be present, but they are not usually considered as a requisite: mobility, veracity, benevolence, rationality and adaptability (or learning) (Wooldridge and Jennings, 1995).

To simplify, an agent is any entity that can perceive its environment through sensors and change it with actuators (Russell and Norvig, 2003).

Agents coexist and interact with other agents in different ways. A system consisting of an interacting group of agents is called a Multiagent System (MAS). In Software Engineering, MAS technology is viewed as a novel and promising paradigm. A complex software system can be treated as a collection of many agents, each one with its own local functionality and properties, achieving total system functionality. Some of the benefits of MAS technology in large scale software systems are (Sycara 1998):

- Speedup and efficiency, due to asynchronous and parallel computation.
- Robustness and reliability, in the sense that the whole system can undergo a 'graceful degradation' when one or more agents fail.
- Scalability and flexibility, since it is easy to add new agents to the system.
- Cost, assuming that an agent is cheap compared to the whole system.
- Development and reusability, since it is easier to develop and maintain modular than monolithic software.

The use of Multi-agent Systems will simplify the modeling of the traffic in our city scenario, which is done with Netlogo, a multi-agent modeling environment. Netlogo is particularly well suited for modeling complex evolving systems. Modelers can give instructions to hundreds of 'agents', all operating independently. This makes it possible to explore the connection between the micro-level behavior of individuals and the macro-level patterns that emerge from the interaction of many individuals.

In the model in (Gershenson 2004), an extension from the "Gridlock" model (Wilensky and Stroup, 2002) (which is included in the NetLogo distribution), a simple and feasible way in which traffic lights self-organize themselves to improve traffic flow is proposed. It uses a multi-agent simulation to study self-organizing methods, which are able to outperform traditional rigid methods. Using simple rules, traffic lights are able to self-organize and adapt themselves to changing traffic conditions, reducing waiting times, car stops, and increasing average speeds.

We propose a more realistic scenario, and we have added a by-pass road and imposed a four directions approach to the original models. Our model consists of an abstract traffic grid with intersections between single or dual lane bidirectional arteries of two types: vertical or horizontal.

We have also changed the cars' creation/elimination schema. In the original description, cars only appeared at the borders of the scenario, and were only eliminated when reaching a border too. Meanwhile, cars moved in a straight line or randomly. Now, for every car, we have defined a source (a random place at the road map) and a destination (another random place at the road map), such that every car is created at a source, and moves (following the shortest path) to its destination, where it is eliminated. Sources and destinations may be outside the simulated world, leading to some cars appearing/disappearing at the borders of the world.

With these changes, we obtain a scenario with different width of the streets depending on if they are bidirectional, and if they have a single or a dual-lane. Also the traffic lights are distributed on every intersection, and there is a by-pass road surrounding the city.

In this model, each car is modeled as an agent that drives from its current position to its destination, at a maximum speed of 50 km/h, and acting according to the behavior of the rest of the cars and the traffic lights. While moving, it also communicates with other agents (cars), following the IEEE 802.11p standard in order to exchange warning messages.

Communication Model

Given the city model, we let cars move in the scenario. We set as scenario parameters the ratio of cars with wireless capabilities, as well as the characteristics of the wireless technology (communication range, bandwidth, establishment time, etc.).

We model communications among cars by means of IEEE 802.11p technology. The physical layer uses seven different channels of 10 MHz bandwidth each (Figure 1). The channels cannot be used simultaneously; each station should alternate between the Control Channel (CCH) and one of the Service Channels (SCHs) or the safety channels. Only SCHs are designated for extended data transfer, where lower priority communication is conducted after negotiation on the CCH. A period containing one CCH interval and one SCH interval shall last no more than $t_p = 100\ ms$ (Chen et al., 2009). In the case of warning messages, they all use the CCH, so we assume only transmissions in this channel.

The MAC layer uses prioritized Access Classes (ACs) from the Enhanced Distributed Channel Access (EDCA) mechanism originally provided by IEEE 802.11e. It includes *listen before talk* and *random back-off*. The back-off has two components: a fixed and a random waiting time. The fixed waiting time is a number of 'slots' given by the parameter AIFS (Arbitration InterFrame Space), with a slot duration of $16\mu s$. The random waiting time is a number of slots drawn from a Contention Window (CW). The initial size of the CW is given by the factor CW_{min}. Each time a transmission attempt fails, the CW size is doubled $(2 \times (CW + 1) - 1)$ until reaching the size given by the parameter CW_{max}. Retransmission attempts end after seven unsuccessful retries, and prioritization is obtained by using different parameters for each packet priority (Table 1).

Figure 1. IEEE 802.11p channel arrangement

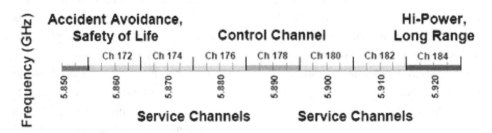

Table 1. EDCA parameters

AC	AIFS	CW_{min}	CW_{max}
AC3 (video)	2	3	7
AC2 (voice)	3	3	7
AC1 (best effort)	6	7	15
AC0 (background)	9	15	1023

In our model, we only use the CCH to simulate the dissemination of warning messages. We randomly choose one of the cars to broadcast a warning message to the rest of the cars in the scenario. The size of the packet is 50 bytes, and it uses a data rate of 6 Mbits/s and a radio range of 250 meters. Due to the distribution of the city, Manhattan-like, we suppose line of sight communications, i.e., the cars cannot communicate if there is a block between them. According to (Xu et al., 2002), the interference distance of a transmission is 1.78 times greater than the transmission range, so in our case we use an interference distance of $250 \times 1.78 = 445$ meters. All the cars within the transmission range of the car sending the warning message will receive it if no other transmission or interference occurs during its reception phase. Once a given car has received the warning message, it will try to broadcast it as well. It will listen to the channel (for transmissions or interferences) before sending the message. If the channel is free, the message is broadcast, if not, it waits the appropriate time to retransmit it (as long as the maximum number of retransmission attempts is not reached). If a car that already has the warning message receives a new copy, it discards it, only the first copy is considered. Finally, all the cars will compete for the channel in order to send their information.

Evaluating the Behavior of 802.11p in the City Model

In order to compare the performance of the dissemination process, which fully follows the standard, with those implementing the proposed

improvements which we will introduce later; we have defined the next five metrics:

- Reachability, i.e., the number of vehicles that got the warning message over the number of vehicles that existed, on our city model, when the message was generated.
- Dissemination Time, i.e., life time of the warning message in the network, since the first car starts to transmit the warning message until the last car finishes transmitting it.
- No-Success Ratio, i.e., number of vehicles unable to transmit the warning message (they wasted all their retransmission attempts) over the total number of cars in the simulation.
- Collisions Ratio, i.e., the number of vehicles that suffer collisions or interferences, when transmitting the warning message, over the total number of cars in the simulation.
- Spreading Time, i.e., average time needed for a particular ratio of cars to receive the warning message. This measure gives, to a certain extent, an idea of the message dissemination speed.

We have implemented the communication model (described previously) in our Netlogo scenario, with a city of size 1 km × 1 km and 100 blocks. Using the four access classes defined in the standard and a different number of cars, from 50 (city almost empty) to 3000 (heavy traffic jam), we calculate the reachability, as seen in Table 2. As we can see in such table, almost all the cars received the warning message if the total number of cars exceeds 500. Using the less priority access classes (AC0 and AC1), this number grows slightly, due to the bigger size of the back-off times. This happens because, as the contention windows grows more in these two access classes, there is less chance of collision, and more chance to send the message. In the cases with less than

Table 2. IEEE 802.11p model results

		Cars									
		50	100	250	500	750	1000	1500	2000	2500	3000
Reachability (%)	AC3	5,2	7,6	49,28	93,14	95,43	97,80	98,84	98,81	98,88	98,88
	AC2	6,6	10,1	34,92	82	97,13	97,75	99,04	99,21	98,54	99,12
	AC1	4,2	13,4	58,48	97,16	98,88	99,17	99,14	99,47	99,76	99,53
	AC0	8,4	4,3	77,24	96,34	99,59	99,86	99,97	99,97	99,96	99,99
Dissemination Time (ms)	AC3	0,92	1,68	8,12	10,68	12,52	13,24	13,64	14,8	15,64	16,8
	AC2	1,08	2	6,56	10,12	11,68	13,48	13,84	15,6	15,28	16,44
	AC1	0,92	3,68	11,2	15,96	14,56	15,6	17,48	18,28	19,04	20,88
	AC0	2,36	2,28	19,8	28,92	39,04	42,76	49,4	50,92	51,48	55,92
No-Success Ratio (%)	AC3	0	0	0,12	3,52	5,65	8,25	13,07	16,74	19,66	21,94
	AC2	0	0	0,24	2,62	6,56	8,72	13,98	16,97	20,20	22,63
	AC1	0	0	1,44	8,8	15,92	21,94	29,66	35,20	39,22	40,92
	AC0	0	0	0	0	0,05	0,23	1,28	2,51	4,12	6,37
Collisions Ratio (%)	AC3	0,8	2,7	29,04	59,92	67,05	69,55	71,85	71,82	70,99	70,44
	AC2	1,2	3,8	20,2	54,94	66,64	69,59	71,40	71,91	70,34	70,18
	AC1	0,4	3,4	22,6	43,94	47,29	48,28	48,61	48,77	47,24	47,80
	AC0	0,4	0,4	15,44	21,12	25,99	28,49	31,51	33,27	35,12	35,97

500 cars, the VANET is not fully connected due to the small number of cars, obtaining worse dissemination results.

Table 2 also shows the dissemination time. Again we observe that AC0, which has the lower priority, needs more time for the whole dissemination as the number of cars increases. This happens because the possibility of collision grows, and being the contention window bigger, the cars have to wait more time to retransmit.

As third parameter in Table 2, we can see the no-success ratio. We observe that AC0 presents good results, considering that it takes more time for transmissions. Fourth parameter in Table 2 presents the collisions ratio. Again, AC0 presents the best results. Finally, in Table 5, we can see the spreading time. In this case, we set the traffic of the city to 2500 cars, and we observe that all the ACs have a similar behavior; but with better results in the access classes with higher priority.

Table 3. First proposal results

	Cars									
	50	100	250	500	750	1000	1500	2000	2500	3000
Reachability (%)	5,8	10,7	49,4	93,4	97,20	98,18	99,37	99,63	99,74	99,79
Dissemination Time (ms)	1,12	2,56	8,92	13,2	14	14,8	14,44	15,12	17,48	17,04
No-Success Ratio (%)	0	0,2	3,12	13,62	19,21	25,52	32,31	37,30	41,36	44,06
Collisions Ratio (%)	1,2	4	22,84	44,64	48,07	47,00	46,61	45,39	43,92	43,22

Table 4. Second proposal results

		Cars									
		50	**100**	**250**	**500**	**750**	**1000**	**1500**	**2000**	**2500**	**3000**
Reachability (%)	AC3	6,2	9	52,36	91,58	96,93	98,29	98,67	98,65	98,83	99,07
	AC2	7,2	8,9	45,2	93,76	96,16	98,02	99,20	98,71	99,18	99,03
	AC1	8,2	8,4	59,92	95,48	98,41	99,26	99,23	99,20	99,59	99,54
	AC0	4,2	17	57,56	97,36	99,72	99,89	99,96	99,99	99,98	99,98
Dissemination Time (ms)	AC3	0,96	1,68	6,64	10,28	10,84	11,48	12,4	13,28	14,76	16,6
	AC2	0,92	1,84	6,6	9,68	11,24	11,72	12,88	14,2	16,16	14,56
	AC1	1,6	2,16	8,32	10,44	11,88	12,56	13,2	14,4	15,68	16,56
	AC0	1,2	4,08	13,08	27,32	35,16	39,64	46	46,92	49,04	49,96
No-Success Ratio (%)	AC3	0	0	0,32	3,46	6,13	9,86	14,62	19,51	21,47	23,47
	AC2	0	0	0,68	4,88	8,39	12,11	18,79	21,88	24,76	28,35
	AC1	0	0	1,48	9,74	17,76	22,63	31,19	36,34	40,08	42,85
	AC0	0	0	0	0,04	0,12	0,27	0,94	2,18	3,47	5,82
Collisions Ratio (%)	AC3	1,8	3,1	28,28	57,76	67,27	68,65	69,90	69,34	69,45	68,75
	AC2	1,4	3,5	24,08	56,58	62,57	65,46	65,78	65,80	65,68	63,22
	AC1	1,6	1,6	18,96	37,3	40,81	43,67	43,88	43,77	43,69	43,42
	AC0	0	2,2	11,04	24,18	28,12	29,77	33,10	34,90	36,62	36,33

Nevertheless, only with AC0 we obtain full dissemination of the warning message.

To summarize, we can see that, in order to obtain the maximum reachability, the best access class is AC0, as shown in Table 2 Reachability and Table 5, due to bigger back-off times, which leads to less collisions (Table 2 Collisions Ratio) and more possibilities to transmit (Table 2 No-Success Ratio). The disadvantages of AC0 are that it needs more dissemination time (Table 2 Dissemination Time) and spreading time (Table 5). On the other hand, access class AC3 completes

Table 5. Spreading time in milliseconds (2500 cars scenario)

		Cars (%)									
		10	**20**	**30**	**40**	**50**	**60**	**70**	**80**	**90**	**100**
802.11p model	AC3	1,39	2,34	3,03	3,70	4,37	5,06	5,84	7,16	8,78	
	AC2	1,27	2,17	2,87	3,63	4,35	5,13	5,98	7,07	8,69	
	AC1	2,12	3,19	3,88	4,55	5,28	6,09	6,94	8,15	9,70	
	AC0	2,39	3,53	4,43	5,01	5,70	6,42	7,21	8,02	9,59	25,27
First proposal		1,95	2,65	3,27	3,91	4,48	5,22	5,84	6,83	8,16	
Second proposal	AC3	1,28	2,04	2,69	3,20	3,93	4,59	5,32	6,56	8,07	
	AC2	1,08	1,95	2,72	3,24	3,87	4,58	5,52	6,69	8,52	
	AC1	1,13	1,53	1,88	2,42	3,02	3,51	4,28	5,48	7,30	
	AC0	1,38	1,89	2,49	2,79	3,15	3,58	4,01	4,83	6,44	25,95
Third proposal		1,44	1,95	2,46	2,96	3,41	3,88	4,46	5,16	6,40	24,15

the dissemination sooner, but with a lower reachability, more no-success and collisions ratio. Classes AC3 and AC2 obtain similar results, as its only difference is one waiting slot in the AIFS. Finally, class AC1 obtains results in between classes AC2 and AC0 as expected.

Proposals to Improve the Dissemination Process

In this section we introduce variations of the protocol for disseminating warning messages, which was described and simulated in the previous section. The main aim is to reduce the dissemination time, and at the same time, to increase the reachability.

First Proposal

Our first attempt to improve the results goes in the direction of trying to reduce the no-success and collisions ratio. This problematic situation happens because the cars use all their possible retransmissions, so we propose to change the use of the access classes. In this first proposal, any car uses in its first transmission attempt the top-priority access class AC3. If it cannot transmit its message in the next attempt, then it uses AC2, later AC1, and finally AC0. With this approach, every car only does 4 transmission attempts, and not 7 as stated in the standard.

Table 3 and 5 show the results of the simulations done for this experiment. Here we only have one value at the table as we are using all the priority classes sequentially (from AC3 to AC0). The simulation results are relatively similar to the ones obtained simulating the standard in the previous section. If we compare these results with the previous ones, we have that, on the one hand, the reachability (Table 3 Reachability) is similar to the previous case with AC0 class. On the other hand, the graphic for the dissemination time (Table 3 Dissemination Time) is slightly better to the one obtained in the standard with

AC1. Moreover, the no-success ratios (Table 3 No-Success Ratio) are more numerous than in the previous case with AC1, because now there are only 4 transmission attempts per car. However, the collisions ratios (Table 3 Collisions Ratio) are similar to the standard case with AC1 and better than AC2 and AC3. Finally, for the spreading time in the scenario with 2500 cars (Table 5), we have obtained a minor improvement with respect to the standard results.

To summarize, the results obtained in this experiment, cycling over the different ACs, provide a minor improvement with respect to the standard.

Second Proposal

As stated in (Ferreira et al., 2008), in the case of warning messages in 802.11p, there should exist a new access class with higher priority than AC3, which was designed to transmit video in 802.11e. In this second experiment, we have created a new access class AC4 with AIFS = 1, $CW_{min} = 3$ and $CW_{max} = 5$. We also assume that cars know their position using a GPS receiver, which is not a hard hypothesis, and it is also assumed in the standard IEEE 1609.4 for time synchronization (Chen et al., 2009). The cars will only use this new AC4 access class if they are located at an intersection. The idea is to maximize the number of cars that receives the warning message, so the car can transmit now at the cross point, reaching the roads that depart in the four directions. Cars that are not in an intersection will use standard access classes for broadcasting.

Table 4 and 5 present the results of this second experiment. We can see an overall improvement. The best results happen when cars that are not in an intersection use AC0, being the bottom-priority access class, as it reduces the contentions with AC4. Nevertheless, in this second experiment, there is an improvement in all the access classes for the reachability and the dissemination time. We point out that for the spreading time in the case with 2500 cars we get an improvement around 24% with respect to the previous cases that do not use the proposed AC4 together with location based information.

Third Proposal

With the second proposal we have obtained better results thanks to the use of a new AC4 with higher priority, which takes advantage of location information to transmit its AC4 messages only at intersections; where a high number of vehicles can be contacted. This experiment involves a change in the standard due to the new AC4 access class. In order to avoid such standard modification, we perform a new experiment where cars at intersections use the highest priority access class AC3, and cars not at intersections use the lowest one, i.e., AC0.

The results obtained with this alternative are similar to the ones described in Table 3 and 5, for the second proposal. Their values are only a little bit worse due to the slightly bigger back-off time that AC3 has with respect to the new created AC4 priority class. This can be seen in Table 5.

Fourth Proposal

In order to improve the results of the third proposal we kept the use of AC3 in intersections and AC0 in the rest, and have increased the number of retransmissions allowed from 7 to 14 and 21. As seen in Table 6, the reachability is improved with small number of cars, while with higher number of cars we already reached almost all the cars. Logically, the no-success ratio is reduced with higher number of retransmissions, although even for just seven retransmissions the no-success ratio is low enough. The rest of the metrics are similar to the third proposal.

Table 6. Fourth proposal results

		Cars									
		50	100	250	500	750	1000	1500	2000	2500	3000
Reachability (%)	7 retx	5,4	13,3	60,56	96,86	99,69	99,98	99,99	99,99	99,98	99,99
	14 retx	8,6	7,8	71,8	98,24	99,88	99,75	99,97	99,98	99,98	99,99
	21 retx	5	14	84,2	98	99,73	99,94	99,97	99,97	100,00	99,98
Dissemination Time (ms)	7 retx	1,56	3,44	12,76	25,28	31,44	40	44,92	46,52	48,44	53,24
	14 retx	1,96	2,68	16,48	26,48	36,2	38,2	46,88	59,88	66,04	72,64
	21 retx	1,16	3,64	17,68	27,64	32,24	40,68	48,24	57,28	67,36	71,72
No-Success Ratio (%)	7 retx	0	0	0	0,12	0,27	0,65	1,46	2,72	4,48	6,07
	14 retx	0	0	0	0	0	0	0,02	0,03	0,11	0,14
	21 retx	0	0	0	0	0	0	0	0,01	0	0,01
Collisions Ratio (%)	7 retx	0,4	1,6	11,84	23,18	26,91	29,53	32,15	33,24	34,97	36,59
	14 retx	1,2	0,8	12,92	23,72	26,93	29,04	32,33	34,12	36,57	37,40
	21 retx	0,8	0,6	15,44	23,04	27,27	30,85	32,43	33,89	36,36	37,12

Discussion of Results

In this section, we compare our proposals with other related works, showing more clearly the contributions of the paper. We also discuss the results obtained by our proposals concerning the dissemination techniques that we have implemented.

Broadcasting Problem

Flooding performs relatively well for a limited small number of cars, but the performance drops quickly as the number of vehicles increases. As each car receives and broadcasts the message almost at the same time, this causes contentions and collisions, broadcast storms and high bandwidth consumption. As we pointed out previously, there must be a trade-off between the spreading time and the bandwidth waste. Besides, there are some other facts that make broadcast in VANETs a difficult task, as the lack of continuous end-to-end connectivity, as well as node density variations.

Many approaches have been developed to try to fix broadcast problems. For example, in (Yu and Cho, 2006; Campelli et al., 2007) the authors propose the use of neighbors' information to take broadcast decisions. However, those methods imply the exchange of salutation messages, increasing the network overload. In this paper, our strategy consists basically in keeping the flooding mechanisms to broadcast the warning messages, but changing the way the access classes are used. We have successfully combined the use of a new access class with location based information, improving the spreading time thanks to the reduction of the collision chance. The obtained improvements with our second, third and fourth proposals were illustrated previously.

Location-Based Information

With respect to the use of location based information in the broadcasting process, the work in (Sun et al., 2000) must be highlighted. It was to the best of our knowledge, the first work in implementing what they called GPS-based broadcasting, i.e., the furthest node is selected as the next one to forward the message.

Other approaches use location information to decide how to broadcast. In (Nekovee and Bogason, 2007), the authors carry out simulations in a highway traffic scenario, and present a protocol to face network partition. In (Korkmaz et al., 2004), the authors present a multi-hop broadcast protocol to address the broadcast storm problem. Finally, in (Chiasserini et al., 2005), vehicles that are about to broadcast again messages access the channel with different priorities depending on their distance to the last vehicle that retransmitted the message. Our proposal just uses the location-based information in order to prioritize the broadcast of messages from cars at intersections, which implies no modification in the standard or the exchange of additional information.

Realistic Model of an Urban Environment

Most of simulations in literature use simple network scenarios, in their vast majority they simulate highways under no very realistic conditions (Sun et al., 2000; Chiasserini et al., 2005; Torrent-Moreno et al., 2004). It should be noticed that our urban model deals with bidirectional arteries with single or dual lanes. It also considers intersections, traffic lights, turns, etc. Some other previous works have also modeled intersections, but with some limitations, for example, authors in (Korkmaz et al., 2004) propose installing repeaters at intersections that forward the packet in all directions; which currently can be done more easily with the location-based features present in the cars, as we do. Moreover, authors in (Korkmaz et al., 2004) consider a road structure of 2.4 km × 2.4 km with only four intersections, while our urban model is a Manhattan-like scenario of 1 km × 1 km with 117 intersections. Aside from that, our simulations were run for a wide range of situations, from those with low density of vehicles (50 cars) to simulations of heavy traffic jam (3000 vehicles), including traffic lights operation. In (Korkmaz et al., 2004), for instance, the maximum number of cars in the simulations was 619.

Warning Message Dissemination

We have presented a performance evaluation of the Warning Message Dissemination (WMD) mechanism using IEEE 802.11p, and we have introduced also new proposals to improve the reachability, the dissemination and the spreading times. Some other studies about message broadcasting performance have been done, for example (Martinez et al., 2009; Torrent-Moreno et al., 2004). The authors in (Torrent-Moreno et al., 2004) study the effects of prioritization in a VANET using a Nakagami radio propagation model, and an 802.11e-based priority access schema. They show how the introduction of priorities reduces the chance of collision. One of the strengths of such work is its realistic propagation model. However, the employed scenarios are quite simple (small number of cars) and not real (a circular highway). In contrast, we use a more realistic model (urban scenario up to 3000 vehicles). Although we have not implemented a Nakagami propagation model, we have fully followed the IEEE 802.11p standard. Other interesting work dealing with warning message dissemination is (Martinez et al., 2009). To the best of our knowledge, such paper carries out the performance evaluation more similar to ours in the literature. They use similar metrics and scenarios to the ones we have employed in this paper with the following limitations and differences:

1. Their warning-mode vehicles, which are in charge of starting the flooding of warning messages, do not move during the entire simulation time, while the normal-mode vehicles can move but can not initiate a warning message dissemination (they can only retransmit). The main drawback of this design is that abnormal situations (e.g., accidents) which happen outside the coverage range of a fixed warning-mode vehicle will never be notified. In our model, given that all vehicles can move and can initiate the dissemination of the warning message, this problem would never take place.

2. In the model proposed in (Martinez et al., 2009), streets are arranged in a Manhattan-like scenario (as in our work). They obtain better reachability results with less number of cars (100 nodes) in bigger scenarios. It is difficult to understand how scenarios with such low density of vehicles do not experience more blind-node problems. In our experiments, we do not obtain a fully connected network until the number of cars reaches 500 vehicles, due to the fact that we suppose line of sight communications, i.e., the cars cannot communicate if there is a block between them.

3. Regarding the spreading time, our results outperforms those obtained in (Martinez et al., 2009) presenting an overall enhancement in one order of magnitude.

Effects of Prioritization

In our second and next proposals, the best results are obtained when we use the bottom-priority access class (AC0), because this approach causes less contention with the top priority access class (AC3 or AC4) used at intersections.

FUTURE RESEARCH DIRECTIONS

Future work will consider the dissemination of different types of warning messages to communicate among groups of vehicles (police, ambulance, fire brigade, normal cars, etc.). It would be also interesting to model the exchange of multiples messages among those groups, i.e., establishing dialogues, for instance, to simulate the communications needed in a rescue operation. Finally, we also plan to consider the dissemination of warning messages from the roadside equipment, which can lead to the dissemination from multiple initial points.

CONCLUSION

In this chapter, we have presented a model to analyze and improve the dissemination of warning messages using IEEE 802.11p in urban environments. We have used a multi-agent model and an ad-hoc Netlogo simulator adapted to the scenario and the communication model we desire to study. This simulator describes a traffic topology typical from a Manhattan-like scenario with horizontal and vertical roads (single direction or bidirectional, and with different number of lanes), and traffic lights. Cars have been modeled as agents that, from a starting point, wish to arrive to a destination point using the shortest path. During this movement, one car randomly chosen will need to broadcast a warning message to the other cars, that once received, it will be broadcast again using the IEEE 802.11p technology.

The main contribution of the paper derives from the results of the simulator of the behavior of IEEE 802.11p technology, we have analyzed those results and introduced improvements to enhance the protocol performance.

The simulation results have shown that the standard IEEE 802.11p is adequate for transmitting hazard messages, and depending on the AC used, the results can vary in the reachability, the dissemination time, the no-success ratio, the collisions ratio and the spreading time. From this starting point, we have presented four proposals in order to obtain better results. The first one consisted in cycling through the ACs, in order to dismiss the number of transmission attempts, and therefore to reduce collisions. The results obtained with this first proposal provided a marginal improvement; but not enough to use it, in our opinion. So it drives us to present a second proposal, using a new access class with the highest priority, AC4, combined with GPS location information. This second proposal provided a significant improvement in the reachability, in the dissemination time and especially in the spreading time. We also have suggested a variation of this second proposal, the third one, which uses AC3 instead of AC4; avoiding the need to change the protocol specification, but providing similar results in terms of reachability, dissemination and spreading time. Finally, our fourth proposal has studied how the number of retransmission affects the results.

Finally, we have compared our approach with some other relevant works, which can be found in the literature, to highlight their similarities and differences with the work presented here.

REFERENCES

ASTM. (2002). *E2313-02: Standard specification for telecommunications and information exchange between roadside and vehicle systems - 5 GHz band dedicated short range communications (DSRC) medium access control (MAC) and physical layer (PHY) specifications*. ASTM.

Bai, F., & Krishnan, H. (2006). Reliability analysis of DSRC wireless communication for vehicle safety applications. *Intelligent Transportation Systems Conference* (pp. 355-362). Washington, DC: IEEE Computer Society. doi: 10.1109/ITSC.2006.1706767

Bilstrup, K. (2007). *A survey regarding wireless communication standards intended for a high-speed vehicle environment*. (Report No. IDE 0712). Retrieved from http://hh.diva-portal.org/smash/get/diva2:239214/FULLTEXT01

Bilstrup, K., Uhlemann, E., Strom, E. G., & Bilstrup, U. (2008). Evaluation of the IEEE 802.11p MAC method for vehicle-to-vehicle communication. *68th Vehicular Technology Conference* (pp. 1-5). Washington, DC: IEEE Computer Society. doi: 10.1109/VETECF.2008.446

Burguillo-Rial, J., Costa-Montenegro, E., Gil-Castiñeira, F., & Rodríguez-Hernández, P. (2008). Performance analysis of IEEE 802.11p in urban environments using a multi-agent model. *19th International Symposium on Personal, Indoor and Mobile Radio Communications* (pp. 1-6). Washington, DC: IEEE Computer Society. doi: 10.1109/PIMRC.2008.4699924

Campelli, L., Cesana, M., & Fracchia, R. (2007). Directional broadcast forwarding of alarm messages in VANETs. *4th Annual Conference on Wireless on Demand Network Systems and Services* (pp. 72-79). Washington, DC: IEEE Computer Society. doi: 10.1109/WONS.2007.340488

Capra, L., Emmerich, W., & Mascolo, C. (2003). Carisma: Context aware reflective middleware system for mobile applications. *IEEE Transactions on Software Engineering, 29*(10), 929–945. doi:10.1109/TSE.2003.1237173

Chen, Q., Jiang, D., & Delgrossi, L. (2009). IEEE 1609.4 DSCR multi-channel operations and its implications on vehicle safety communications. *Vehicular Networking Conference* (pp. 1-8). Washington, DC: IEEE Computer Society. doi: 10.1109/VNC.2009.5416394

Chiasserini, C. F., Fasolo, E., Furiato, R., Gaeta, R., Garetto, M., & Gribaudo, M. ... Zanella, A. (2005). Smart broadcast of warning messages in vehicular ad hoc networks. *Workshop Interno Progetto NEWCOM* (pp. 1-4).

Eichler, S. (2007). Performance evaluation of the IEEE 802.11p WAVE communication standard. *1st International Symposium on Wireless Vehicular Communications* (pp. 2199-2203). Washington, DC: IEEE Computer Society. doi: 10.1109/VETECF.2007.461

Fall, K., & Varadhan, K. (2000). *ns notes and documentation*. Retrieved August 1, 2011, from http://www.isi.edu/nsnam/ns/doc/ns_doc.pdf

Ferreira, N., Fonseca, J. A., & Gomes, J. S. (2008). On the adequacy of 802.11p MAC protocols to support safety services in ITS. *International Conference on Emerging Technologies and Factory Automation* (pp. 1189-1192). Washington, DC: IEEE Computer Society. doi: 10.1109/ETFA.2008.4638552

Fiore, M., Harri, J., Filali, F., & Bonnet, C. (2007). Vehicular mobility simulation for VANETs. *40th Annual Simulation Symposium* (pp. 301-309). Washington, DC: IEEE Computer Society. doi: 10.1109/ANSS.2007.44

Gershenson, C. (2004). Self-organizing traffic lights. *Complex Systems, 16*(1), 29–53.

Ibrahim, K., Weigle, M. C., & Abuelela, M. (2009). p-IVG: Probabilistic inter-vehicle geocast for dense vehicular networks. *69th Vehicular Technology Conference* (pp. 1-5). Washington, DC: IEEE Computer Society. doi: 10.1109/VETECS.2009.5073804

Jakubiak, J., & Koucheryavy, Y. (2008). State of the art and research challenges for VANETs. *5th Consumer Communications and Networking Conference* (pp. 912-916). Washington, DC: IEEE Computer Society. doi: 10.1109/ccnc08.2007.212

Jiang, D., & Delgrossi, L. (2008). IEEE 802.11p: Towards an international standard for wireless access in vehicular environments. *Vehicular Technology Conference* (pp. 2036-2040). Washington, DC: IEEE Computer Society.

Korkmaz, G., Ekici, E., Özgüner, F., & Özgüner, U. (2004). Urban multi-hop broadcast protocol for inter-vehicle communication systems. *1st International Workshop on Vehicular Ad-hoc Networks* (pp. 76-85). New York, NY: ACM. doi: 10.1145/1023875.1023887

Krajzewicz, D., Hertkorn, G., Rössel, C., & Wagner, P. (2002). Sumo (simulation of urban mobility) - An open-source traffic simulation. *4th Middle East Symposium on Simulation and Modeling* (pp. 183-187).

Lyakhov, A., & Poupyrev, P. (2005). Evaluation of broadcasting technologies performance in IEEE 802.11 networks. *International Workshop Distributed Computer and Communication Networks* (pp. 84-94).

Lyakhov, A., Vishnevsky, V., & Poupyrev, P. (2005). Analytical study of broadcasting in 802.11 ad- hoc networks. In J. Filipe & L. Vasiu (ed.), *2nd International Conference on e-Business and Telecommunication Networks* (pp. 86-91). IN-STICC Press.

Ma, X., & Chen, X. (2007). Saturation performance of IEEE 802.11 broadcast networks. *IEEE Communications Letters, 11*(8), 686–688. doi:10.1109/LCOMM.2007.070040

Ma, X., Chen, X., & Refai, H. (2007). Unsaturated performance of IEEE 802.11 broadcast service in vehicle-to-vehicle networks. *66th Vehicular Technology Conference* (pp. 1957-1961). Washington, DC: IEEE Computer Society. doi: 10.1109/VETECF.2007.411

Mangharam, R., Weller, D., Rajkumar, R., Mudalige, P., & Bai, F. (2006). Groovenet: A hybrid simulator for vehicle-to-vehicle networks. *3rd International Conference Mobile and Ubiquitous Systems: Networking Services* (pp. 1-8). Washington, DC: IEEE Computer Society. doi: 10.1109/MOBIQ.2006.340441

Martinez, F., Cano, J.-C., Calafate, C., & Manzoni, P. (2008). Citymob: A mobility model pattern generator for VANETs. *International Conference on Communications* (pp. 370-374). Washington, DC: IEEE Computer Society. doi: 10.1109/ICCW.2008.76

Martinez, F., Cano, J.-C., Calafate, C., & Manzoni, P. (2009). A performance evaluation of warning message dissemination in 802.11p based VANETs. *34th Conference on Local Computer Networks* (pp. 221-224). Washington, DC: IEEE Computer Society. doi: 10.1109/LCN.2009.5355151

Naumov, V., & Baumann, R. (2006). An evaluation of inter-vehicle ad hoc networks based on realistic vehicular traces. *International Symposium on Mobile Ad Hoc Networking and Computing* (pp. 108-119). New York, NY: ACM. doi: 10.1145/1132905.1132918

Nekovee, M., & Bogason, B. (2007). Reliable and efficient information dissemination in intermittently connected vehicular adhoc networks. *65th Vehicular Technology Conference* (pp. 2486-2490). Washington, DC: IEEE Computer Society. doi: 10.1109/VETECS.2007.512

Peden, M., Scurfield, R., Sleet, D., Mohan, D., Hyder, A. A., Jarawan, E., & Mathers, C. (2004). *World report on road traffic injury prevention*. Geneva, Switzerland: OMS.

Piórkowski, M., Raya, M., Lugo, A. L., Papadimitratos, P., Grossglauser, M., & Hubaux, J.-P. (2008). Trans: Realistic joint traffic and network simulator for VANETs. *Mobile Computing and Communications Review, 12*(1), 31-33.

Russell, S. J., & Norvig, P. (2003). *Artificial intelligence: A modern approach* (3rd ed.). Pearson Education.

Scalable Network Technologies Inc. (2006). *Qualnet*. Retrieved August 1, 2011, from http://www.scalablenetworks.com/products/qualnet/

Schmidt-Eisenlohr, F., Torrent-Moreno, M., Mittag, J., & Hartenstein, H. (2007). Simulation platform for inter-vehicle communications and analysis of periodic information exchange. *4th Conference on Wireless On demand Network Systems and Services* (pp. 50-58). IEEE/IFIP. doi: 10.1109/WONS.2007.340475

Sebastian, A., Tang, M., Feng, Y., & Looi, M. (2009). Multi-vehicles interaction graph model for cooperative collision warning system. *Intelligent Vehicles Symposium* (pp. 929-934). Washington, DC: IEEE Computer Society. doi: 10.1109/IVS.2009.5164404

Stibor, L., Zang, Y., & Reumerman, H.-J. (2007). Evaluation of communication distance of broadcast messages in a vehicular ad-hoc network using IEEE 802.11p. *Wireless Communications and Networking Conference* (pp. 254-257). Washington, DC: IEEE Computer Society. doi: 10.1109/WCNC.2007.53

Sun, M.-T., Feng, W.-C., Lai, T.-H., Yamada, K., Okada, H., & Fujimura, K. (2000). GPS-based message broadcasting for inter-vehicle communication. *International Conference on Parallel Processing* (pp. 279-286). doi: 10.1109/ICPP.2000.876143

Suthaputchakun, C., & Ganz, A. (2007). Priority based inter-vehicle communication in vehicular ad-hoc networks using IEEE 802.11e. *65th Vehicular Technology Conference* (pp. 2595-2599). Washington, DC: IEEE Computer Society. doi: 10.1109/VETECS.2007.534

Sycara, K. P. (1998). Multiagent systems. *AI Magazine, 19*(2), 79–92.

Texas Transportation Institute. (2009). *Urban mobility*. (Report). Retrieved from http://americandreamcoalition.org/highways/mobility_report_2009_wappx.pdf

Torrent-Moreno, M., Corroy, S., Schmidt-Eisenlohr, F., & Hartenstein, H. (2006). IEEE 802.11-based one-hop broadcast communications: Understanding transmission success and failure under different radio propagation environments. *9th International Symposium on Modeling Analysis and Simulation of Wireless and Mobile Systems* (pp. 68-77). New York, NY: ACM. doi: 10.1145/1164717.1164731

Torrent-Moreno, M., Jiang, D., & Hartenstein, H. (2004). Broadcast reception rates and effects of priority access in 802.11-based vehicular ad-hoc networks. *1st International Workshop on Vehicular Ad Hoc Networks* (pp. 10-18). New York, NY: ACM. doi: 10.1145/1023875.1023878

Torrent-Moreno, M., & Mittag, J. (2006). Adjusting transmission power and packet generation rate of periodic status information messages in VANETs. *3rd International Workshop on Vehicular Ad Hoc Networks* (pp. 90-91). New York, NY: ACM. doi: 10.1145/1161064.1161081

Troncoso, C., Costa-Montenegro, E., Diaz, C., & Schiffner, S. (2011). On the difficulty of achieving anonymity for vehicle-2-X communication. *Computer Networks, 55*(14), 3199–3210. doi:10.1016/j.comnet.2011.05.004

Wang, C. D., & Thompson, P. J. (1997). *U.S. Patent No. 5,613,039: Apparatus and method for motion detection and tracking of objects in a region for colision avoidance utilizing a real-time adaptive probabilistic neural network*. Washington, DC: U.S. Patent and Trademark Office.

Wellens, M., Westphal, B., & Mahonen, P. (2007). Performance evaluation of IEEE 802.11-based WLANs in vehicular scenarios. *65th Vehicular Technology Conference* (pp. 1167-1171). Washington, DC: IEEE Computer Society. doi: 10.1109/VETECS.2007.247

Wilensky, U. (2007). *NetLogo: Center for connected learning and computer-based modeling.* Evanston, IL: Northwestern University. Retrieved from http://ccl.northwestern.edu/netlogo

Wilensky, U., & Stroup, W. (2002). *NetLogo HubNet gridlock model.* Evanston, IL: NetLogo: Center for connected Learning and Computer-Based Modeling, Northwestern University. Retrieved from http://ccl.northwestern.edu/netlogo/models/HubNetGridlock

Wischhof, L., Ebner, A., & Rohling, H. (2005). Information dissemination in selforganizing intervehicle networks. *IEEE Transactions on Intelligent Transportation Systems, 6*(1), 90–101. doi:10.1109/TITS.2004.842407

Wooldridge, M., & Jennings, N. R. (1995). Intelligent agents: Theory and practice. *The Knowledge Engineering Review, 10*(2), 115–152. doi:10.1017/S0269888900008122

Xu, K., Gerla, M., & Bae, S. (2002). How effective is the IEEE 802.11 RTS/CTS handshake in ad hoc networks? *Global Telecommunications Conference* (pp. 72-76). Washington, DC: IEEE Computer Society. doi: 10.1109/GLOCOM.2002.1188044

Yang, X., Liu, L., Vaidya, N., & Zhao, F. (2004). A vehicle-to-vehicle communication protocol for cooperative collision warning. *1ˢᵗ International Conference on Mobile and Ubiquitous Systems: Networking and Services* (pp. 114-123). doi: 10.1109/MOBIQ.2004.1331717

Yousefi, S., Mousavi, M. S., & Fathy, M. (2006). Vehicular ad hoc networks (VANETs): Challenges and perspectives. *6ᵗʰ International Conference on ITS Telecommunications* (pp. 761-766). doi: 10.1109/ITST.2006.289012

Yu, S., & Cho, G. (2006). A selective flooding method for propagating emergency messages in vehicle safety communications. *International Conference on Hybrid Information Technology* (pp. 556-561). doi: 10.1109/ICHIT.2006.253661

Zeng, X., Bagrodia, R., & Gerla, M. (1998). Glomosim: A library for parallel simulation of large-scale wireless networks. *12ᵗʰ Workshop on Parallel and Distributed Simulation* (pp. 154–161). Washington, DC: IEEE Computer Society. doi: 10.1145/278008.278027

Chapter 13
Adding Personalization and Social Features to a Context–Aware Application for Mobile Tourism

Ana Belén Barragáns-Martínez
Centro Universitario de la Defensa, Escuela Naval Militar de Marín, Spain

Enrique Costa-Montenegro
University of Vigo, Spain

ABSTRACT

The proliferation of location-aware mobile devices, together with the advent of Web 2.0 services, promotes the creation of hybrid applications which can provide innovative personalized context-aware services. Personalized recommendation services aim at suggesting products and services to meet users' preferences and needs, while location-based services focus on providing information based on users' current positions. Due to the fast growing of users' needs in the mobile tourism domain, the provision of personalized location-based recommendation services becomes a critical research and practical issue. In this proposal, the authors present GiveMeAPlan, a mobile service which supplies tourist recommendations taking into account both the user preferences (personalization) and context information (time, location, weather, etc.) enriched with social features and targeted advertisements to support its business model. An application prototype is also being implemented to illustrate and test the system feasibility and effectiveness.

INTRODUCTION

In recent years, the design, development and delivery of mobile services and applications to assist on-the-move users in making mobility-related

decisions is considered a critical research topic, and therefore more research efforts devoted to this area are highly expected. As one of the most important types of mobile services, location-based services focus mainly on providing point of interest information to mobile users based on their current positions.

DOI: 10.4018/978-1-4666-2533-4.ch013

Furthermore, personalized recommendation services aim at suggesting products and services to meet users' needs and preferences. It has been noted that, without proper system support, the integrated process of searching and filtering products, comparing alternatives, and recommending suitable selections for users can be extremely complicated to be carried out; becoming especially hard when taking into account the support of mobile users (because more factors need to be considered).

In the tourist context, nowadays, most people who plan a trip or a day-out initiate a search through the Internet beforehand to locate the main tourist attractions and make the most of their visit. However, travelers usually have a limited knowledge of the city to visit and they are unaware of the local artistic, social or entertainment places. Having static information before traveling is not enough because that kind of activities is not considered and users also want to get on-demand information at any time to make plans depending on their free time, weather conditions, etc. Moreover, tourism is an activity strongly connected to the personal preferences and interests of people which makes the demand for recommender systems in this field to be continuously increased. Therefore, on-the-spot decisions become necessary, as well as real-time recommender systems specialized in the city itself. It is also remarkable the vast penetration of high-end mobile devices equipped with GPS together with the introduction of flat rate data plans from many popular mobile operators which have resulted in larger usage of mobile services.

In this context, we present *GiveMeAPlan*, a system that generates recommendations about local events in the city of Vigo (Spain) to be delivered to a mobile device. It is intended to be a service for foreigners to become deeply familiar with the city (once known the main attractions) and also to locals to plan leisure activities in their free time. *GiveMeAPlan* provides a list of activities (represented in a map) which are recommended by taking into account both the user's preferences and the ratings of other similar users. Aside from that, our service provides details on how and when to perform those offered activities, for example, giving GPS guidance to the points of interest.

The rest of the chapter is organized as follows. Background Section discusses related work in the field of mobile applications for tourism as well as in the recommender systems area. The *GiveMeAPlan* Section constitutes the core of this paper, where a detailed description of the system is provided. This section presents (i) the designed web 2.0 application, (ii) our recommendation system, by describing the implemented algorithms, (iii) the mobile service, (iv) the two business models devised for *GiveMeAPlan* and, finally, (v) implementation details. Future research directions section provides insight about the future of personalization and social features for mobile tourism. The conclusion section ends the chapter.

BACKGROUND

There are two kinds of works related to the contents addressed in this paper: those focused on tourist mobile applications, as well as on recommender systems. Both of them are outlined in the following subsections.

Mobile Tourist Applications

Several mobile tourist information systems have been designed to date and, for most of them, the only context captured is the users' and sights' locations. For example, Guide (Cheverts et al, 2002), Crumpet (Schmidt-Belz et al., 2003), DeepMap (Fink and Kobsa, 2002), and TouristGuide (Simcock et al., 2003) provide facilities to generate a tourist route in a city. Guide and TouristGuide concentrate basically on sight contexts (the latter obtains automatically the location from the GPS sensor without user intervention); and provide no personalization. However, DeepMap and Crumpet offer personalized service since they keep and update the users' profiles (mainly demographic information) during their interaction. In summary, these systems provide information via handheld devices based on the user's location. None of them supports users' feedback about neither visited sights nor information about the interests of similar users. In most cases, a user's history is only used for ranking of sights in order to exclude items that have already been visited.

In the framework presented in (Voulodimos and Patrikakis, 2008), the personalization stage takes place locally in the user's mobile device in order to protect the user data privacy, but however, making unfeasible any kind of collaborative filtering (where information about the remainder of users should be available). In this case, user's feedback is taken into account only for updating or adding missing content which will be only available in future queries to this user in question (not to the remainder of users). More interesting to us is the research carried out in (Hinze and Junmanee, 2006), where more sophisticated recommender techniques are applied in the mobile tourist applications area. However, they do not take advantage of the so-called Web 2.0 which could enrich the application with social features like the addition of user-generated content, collaborative tagging, creation of ad-hoc groups, listing of favorite places or the most popular items, etc. Moreover, none of the previous works provide recommendations about local events including sports activities, exhibitions, live concerts, etc.

We can conclude that the majority of these services carry out a rough process of personalization since they mainly focus on the mobile component and the information delivery. We will address this key limitation by adopting and modifying techniques borrowed from the recommender systems area. That is the reason why the second part of this section is devoted to review the main techniques used in recommender systems.

Recommender Systems

Recommender systems suggest items of interest to users based on their explicit and implicit preferences, the preferences of other users, and user and item attributes. So, based on how recommendations are made, recommenders systems are usually classified into the following two categories (Adomavicius et al., 2005; Adomavicius and Tuzhilin, 2005; Balabanovic and Shoham, 1997):

- Content-based recommendations: Content-based recommendation systems recommend an item to a user based upon a description of the item and a profile of the user's interests. Content-based recommendation systems may be used in a variety of domains ranging from recommending web pages, news articles, restaurants, television programs, and items for sale. Although the details of various systems differ, content-based recommendation systems share in common a means for (i) describing the items that may be recommended, (ii) creating a profile of the user that describes the types of items the user likes, and (iii) comparing items to the user profile to determine what to recommend (Pazzani and Billsus, 2007). Notice that recommendations are made without relying on information provided by other customers, but solely on items' contents and users' profiles. In content-based filtering the features used to describe the content are of primary importance. The more descriptive they are, the more accurate the prediction is.
- Collaborative filtering: These techniques generally involve matching the ratings of a current user for objects (e.g., movies or products) with those of similar users (nearest neighbors) in order to produce recommendations for objects not yet rated or seen by an active user. *User-based* and *item-based*

collaborative filtering are two basic variants of this approach. Within the former category, traditionally, the primary technique used to accomplish this task is the standard memory-based k-Nearest-Neighbor (kNN) classification approach which compares a target user's profile with the profiles of other users in order to find the top k users who have similar tastes (Mobasher 2007).

In order to exploit the advantages of available recommendation methods several hybrid approaches have been proposed, in their vast majority concerning combinations of collaborative filtering and content-based filtering. A good review of hybrid approaches can be found in (Burke 2002; Adomavicius and Tuzhilin, 2005).

GIVEMEAPLAN

System Overview

Next, we present *GiveMeAPlan* by describing each of its three main components:

- **The web 2.0 application:** which has been designed to facilitate user interaction with the system (to fill in her profile, add contents to the website, comment and tag the contents, etc.). This interaction is much more comfortable using a computer than a mobile device.
- **The recommender engine:** accessible from the web application, and,
- **The mobile service:** built on top of the web 2.0 application. It allows the user to receive the recommendations (rate them, tag them, etc.) everywhere.

The overall system is, therefore, implemented as a client-server architecture, supporting desktop clients of the web 2.0 application as well as mobile clients on a handheld device with appropriate interfaces.

The Web 2.0 Application

In the following paragraphs, we give some details about two key aspects of the web 2.0 application related to data management: how information about both events and users is gathered.

Events Information Acquisition

Firstly, the system must gather information (as much as possible) about events which will take place in the city and its surroundings. For this task, we have created a web crawler which collects information from various websites like online city guides, cinemas and theaters websites, local/municipality websites, specialized review sites, information pages about cultural programming in newspapers, etc.

Each event is conveniently tagged with suitable keywords describing its content. Each listing entry in this database includes details such as the event name, location, a short description, the associated tags, and opening hours (if applicable). The events database is automatically constructed and updated on a daily basis by executing a parser which explores the abovementioned websites.

User Information Acquisition

The capture of the users' interests is threefold: the system will use (i) a personal profile, (ii) their history of visited events, and (iii) their explicit feedback about those events. However, the task of entering information should not be too tedious for the user. Hence, the recommender system only requests the user to flag as "like" or "dislike" a list of event types: classic music, live concerts, theater, sports, museums, exhibitions, gastronomic parties (an optimal place to discover and enjoy the local cuisine), cinema, etc. Each of these categories can be, in turn, composed of several sub-categories, for example, music styles for clubs, bars or live concerts (rock, pop, punk, etc.). This way, in a case where a particular music band has a concert in town and this music band seems to match the user's music taste based on past choices, or based on the choices of other users that share many common interests, the system can recommend to the user that concert that would likely interest her.

Another necessary step is to process the user's feedback. Her recent activity is implicitly stored in a transparent way to the user. In addition, when the user logs again into the system, she is asked to rate the activities in the last recommended plan (in case that she had not rated the events after attending them). All this amount of information (user's profile, recent activity and explicit feedback) will be the input to our recommender engine described in the following subsection.

The Recommender Engine

One of the main components of *GiveMeAPlan* is the recommender module, core of the web 2.0 application, which is aimed at gathering the activities that best fit user's preferences. In our previous experience in TV program recommendation domain (Barragáns-Martínez et al., 2010a), the combination of item-based collaborative filtering together with content-based filtering has proved to be very accurate, so this was the starting point to implement our events' recommender. This particu-

lar combination alleviates well-known problems of recommender systems such as *cold-start*, *new user*, and *gray sheep* (that appear in collaborative techniques) as well as *over-specialization*, common in content-based approaches.

Aside from those mentioned above, two of the more severe problems of collaborative filtering systems are *data sparsity* and *scalability*. It is common for the user-item ratings matrix (used in collaborative approaches) to be *sparsely* populated, making it difficult to confidently identify similar users and items, due to a lack of ratings overlap. Another important limitation is their lack of *scalability*: as the number of users and items increases, this approach may lead to unacceptable latency for providing recommendations during user interaction. To solve both problems, our collaborative algorithm utilizes SVD (*Singular Value Decomposition*) (Golub and Loan, 1996) to enhance the recommender system's efficiency and improve the accuracy of the generated predictions (the details will be given later).

Therefore, our system, whose overview is depicted in Figure 1, makes use of a mixed hybridization technique (according to the classification provided by Burke in (Burke 2002)) and gives as output two lists of suggested events: *content-based recommendations* and *collaborative recommenda-*

Figure 1. Overview of our recommender framework

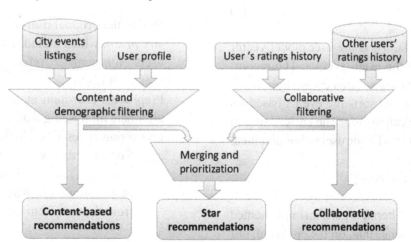

tions. It also offers a set of star recommendations, composed of those events which appear in both lists of recommendations mentioned above.

Content-Based Filtering

The vector space model, used to generate content-based recommendations, has been used to retrieve documents (Lee et al., 1997), and nowadays it is used in TV program recommendation systems (Barragáns-Martínez et al., 2010a). Its basic concept is the selection of an item vector which is the most similar to a retrieval key when there is one retrieval key and several item vectors need to be selected. In an events recommendation system, the item vectors are the number of events and the retrieval key is the user preference. The vector space model selects a desired item by calculating the similarity between each of the item vectors and the retrieval key. Although there are several methods to calculate the similarity, such as the inner product, and the least-square method, we employ a cosine measure to calculate the similarity in our system. Formula 1 shows how the cosine correlation between the event vectors and the user model vectors is calculated.

$$sim(um, ev) = \frac{\sum_i (um(i) \times ev(i))}{\sqrt{\sum_i um(i)^2} \times \sqrt{\sum_i ev(i)^2}}$$

(1)

In this formula, *um* is the user model vector and *ev* is one of the event vectors. The recommendation engine repeats this calculation for all the event vectors and sorts the events based on the results of the calculation. The basic listing of recommended events for the user is thus obtained.

Collaborative Filtering

The collaborative filtering algorithm implemented is twofold in the sense that, on the one hand, our system uses *memory-based item-to-item correlation* to predict the level of interest for each item and calculate the items' neighborhood, and on the other hand, our approach also makes use of *memory-based user-to-user correlation*, as the user neighborhood for a new user has to be computed during runtime of the system.

Next, we describe the algorithm used in *GiveMeAPlan* to implement the item-based collaborative filtering which utilizes the well-known matrix factorization technique called Singular Value Decomposition (SVD) (Golub and Loan, 1996). SVD takes an m x n matrix A, with rank r, and decomposes it into the matrices U, S, and V, whose size is m x m, m x n, and n x n, respectively, as follows:

$$SVD(A) = U \times S \times V^T$$

(2)

An important attribute of SVD, particularly useful in the case of recommender systems, is that it can provide the best low-rank approximation of the original matrix A. Our proposal uses this technique in order to reduce the dimension of the active item's neighborhood, and then it executes the item-based filtering with this low rank representation to generate its predictions. This way, we make the base algorithm more scalable following the proposal in (Vozalis and Margaritis, 2005; Vozalis and Margaritis, 2008).

1. Define the original user-item matrix, R, of size m x n, which includes the ratings of m users on n items. r_{ij} refers to the rating of user u_i on item i_j.
2. Preprocess user-item matrix R in order to eliminate all missing data values. The preprocessing is described in detail here:
   a. Compute the average of all rows, r_i, where $i = 1, 2,..., m$, and the average of all columns, r_j, where $j = 1, 2,..., n$, from the user-item matrix, R.

b. Replace all matrix entries that have no values with the corresponding column average, r_j, which leads to a new filled-in matrix, $R_{filled-in}$.

c. Subtract the corresponding row average, r_i, from all the slots of the new filled-in matrix, $R_{filled-in}$, and obtain the normalized matrix R_{norm}.

3. Compute the SVD of R_{norm} and obtain matrices U, S, and V.

4. Perform the dimensionality reduction step by keeping only k diagonal entries from matrix S to obtain a k x k matrix, S_k. Similarly, matrices U_k and V_k of size m x k and k x n are generated. The "reduced" user-item matrix, R_{red}, is obtained by $R_{red} = U_k$ x S_k x V_k^T, while rr_{ij} denotes the rating by user u_i on item i_j as included in this reduced matrix.

5. Compute $\sqrt{S_k}$ and then calculate two matrix products: $U_k \times \sqrt{S_k}^T$, which represents m users, and $\sqrt{S_k} \times V_k^T$, which represents n items in the k dimensional feature space. We are particularly interested in the latter matrix, of size k x n, whose entries represent the "meta" ratings provided by the k pseudo-users on the n items. A "meta" rating assigned by pseudo-user u_i on item i_j is denoted by mr_{ij}.

6. Then, the neighborhood formation which can be broken into two substeps:

a. Calculate the similarity between items i_j and i_f by computing their adjusted cosine similarity as follows:

$$sim_{jf} = adjcorr_{jf} = \frac{\sum_{i=1}^{k} mr_{ij} \times mr_{if}}{\sqrt{\sum_{i=1}^{k} mr_{ij}^2 \times \sum_{i=1}^{k} mr_{if}^2}}$$ (3)

where k is the number of pseudo-users, selected when performing the dimensionality reduction step. We have to note a change between the adjusted cosine similarity equation utilized in plain item-based filtering and here. In plain item-based filtering the difference in rating scale between distinct users was offset by subtracting the corresponding user average from each co-rated pair of items. In SVD-enhanced item-based filtering, that difference in rating scale was offset during the normalization of the original user-item matrix which yielded matrix R_{norm}.

b. Based on the results from the adjusted cosine similarity calculations for pairs of items including the active item and a random item, isolate the set of items which appear to be the most similar to the active item.

7. The prediction generation is achieved by the following weighted sum:

$$pr_{aj} = \frac{\sum_{k=1}^{l} sim_{jk} \times (rr_{ak} + \overline{r_a})}{\sum_{k=1}^{l} |sim_{jk}|}$$ (4)

which calculates the prediction for user u_a on item i_j. It is similar to the equation utilized by plain item-based filtering in that it bases its predictions on the ratings given by the active user, u_a, on the l items selected as the most similar to active item i_j. Yet, it is different in that the user ratings are taken from the reduced user-item matrix, R_{red}. Also, we have to add the original user average, $\overline{r_a}$, back since it was subtracted during the normalization step of the preprocessing.

As explained in (Vozalis and Margaritis, 2005), a recommender system running item-based filtering with a lower dimensional representation will benefit in the following ways:

- The complexity of item-based filtering, utilizing the original data representation, is $O(mn^2)$. By reducing the dimension to k, where $k << m$, the complexity becomes $O(kn^2)$. We can assume that this reduction in complexity will improve the scalability of the system, while both the processing time and storage requirement should also move down.

- Based on the properties of SVD, any latent relations between users and items should be located when employing the low rank data representation.

- Before the main part of the algorithm is executed, during its preprocessing phase, all the empty entries of the user-item matrix are filled. As a result, once the execution is completed, the n items, taken from the original data array, have now been rated by all, k, pseudo-users. This means that the sparsity problem is solved and the achieved coverage for the recommender system is always equal to 100%.

Merging Algorithm

In order to build the list of star recommendations, *GiveMeAPlan* provides a merging algorithm that combines the results provided by both methods mentioned above. The recommendations are presented to the user according to the prediction generated for each event. When two different items have the same prediction value, the tie is broken by using the averaged rating given by all users in the system to that event in question. However, we have observed the following problem: an item with only one but very high rating appears in the final listing before than other event with much more ratings but whose average is a bit smaller. We believe that this second event should appear always first, according to its popularity which gives more confidence in that recommendation.

To correct this problem (which happens not very often because it is not common at all that two

different items obtain the same prediction value) we resort to the approach presented in (Recuenco and Bueno, 2009). This way, a relevance algorithm is defined where the relationship between the averaged rating of an item and the number of ratings (with respect to the overall number of ratings in the system) received by that item is taken into account. Then, the position of each item in the list of recommendations to be presented to the user will be computed as follows:

$$ranking_i = \frac{\sqrt{\dfrac{total\_ratings}{ratings_i}}}{total\_ratings + 1} \times ratings_i \times Av\_rating_i^2$$

(5)

where $ratings_i$ is the number of ratings received by the element i to be sorted, Av_rating_i is the averaged rating of item i, and

$$total\_ratings = \sum_{\forall i}(ratings_i)$$

is the overall number of ratings received by our recommender system.

The Mobile Application

The mobile application of *GiveMeAPlan* performs in a different way depending on whether the user has previously used our web 2.0 application or not. In the former scenario, the mobile application client requests a nickname and a password to log into the web service; whereas, in the latter, the unregistered user must introduce specific preferences for the current query. Once known the user preferences, the application accesses the mobile application server which, in turn, is connected with the web 2.0 application. In Figure 2 we can see how the overall system works.

For a registered user, the web 2.0 application has a profile with information about her preferred kind of events, her recent activity, her feedback (ratings given to events which she attended in the past), her friends, her neighbors, etc. For a query

Figure 2. How GiveMeAPlan works

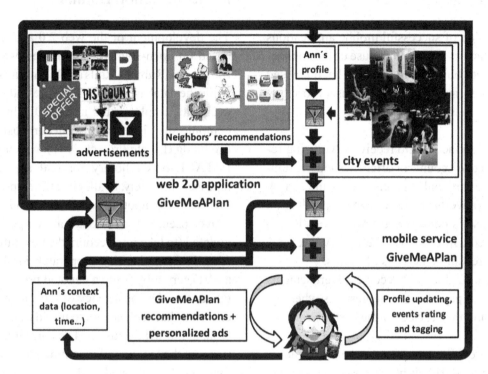

received from the mobile device, the recommender engine computes the list of recommendations suggested for that day, using both content-based and collaborative techniques. This list is modified later according to the user's context (location, time, day of the week, weather, etc.) which is used in a twofold manner: (i) to filter the list of recommendations provided by the web application (for instance, eliminating exhibitions at museums that are closed at that time or on that weekday, or live outdoor concerts when bad weather, etc.) and (ii) to insert, when needed, relevant ads according to the contextual and profile data.

For an unregistered user, the behavior of the application is similar but, as expected, the quality of the recommendations is a bit worse than in the above situation because the personalization process is much simpler. The mobile client submits the user's preferences that are used as input to obtain a set of content-based recommendations. Collaborative recommendations cannot be given because

there is neither previous history nor feedback of the user available in the system. The list of content-based recommendations is adjusted to the context sent by the mobile device as previously explained.

Anyway, the final list of personalized and context-aware recommendations together with the set of relevant ads are sent to the mobile device where they are displayed in the user's mobile phone screen, in a visually attractive way by making use of a Google Maps mashup (Google Maps, 2011).

With respect to the information delivery, the system behavior needs by default that the user explicitly asks for a ranked list of recommendations, following a pull approach (Unni and Harmon, 2007) aiming at bothering the user as little as possible. However, registered users can configure the application to periodically (e.g., every day at the same time) receive a list of suggestions for that day, by following, in this case, an opt-in push approach. Obviously, only these users can rate the suggestions, and, in consequence, they can receive collaborative recommendations.

Business Model

As the design of successful mobile applications involves factors related to the use of the applications and its business model, we have devised two business models that allow users to enjoy our system in two different ways:

- The user accepts to receive advertising related to discounts or offers in shops, restaurants, bars, pubs, hotels, etc. of the nearby area (adverts are customized depending on the user's context and preferences, if registered). In this case, the user will receive free recommendations of events.

- The user does not receive advertisements but she pays for the suggestions when accessing the service for the first time.

In Figure 2, the user employs the first business model, which will likely be the most requested one, taking into account the relevance of the provided advertisements. Considering the chosen business model, and the way of using the application (registered vs. unregistered users) we identify three access modalities as shown in Table 1.

Although we can guess which may be the access modality mostly preferred by the users, it will be necessary a complete study with real users to find it out. This study is also part of our future work in order to assess the recommendations' accuracy and the satisfaction and quality perceived by the users. With respect to the former aspect, the promising results in the evaluation of this hybrid algorithm applied to the TV content recommendation domain (Barragáns-Martínez et al., 2010a) lead us to expect the same success in the tourism domain.

Implementation Details

The development of the web 2.0 application is based on open-source technologies: we use the framework Ruby on Rails (Ruby on Rails, 2011), while the databases of users' profiles, adverts, and events are implemented in MySQL. In order to compute the singular value decomposition, we use linalg (Linalg Project, 2011), which is a fast, LAPACK-based library for real and complex matrices. Precisely, to alleviate the response time invested in computing new recommendations for a given user, the predictions matrix is periodically updated (to take into account the new ratings) offline. To this end, we have separately implemented a SVD server by using a devoted process, which guarantees the consistency of the data matrix by ensuring that each access to modify any value is done in mutual exclusion. The current user location and the location of recommended events are dynamically indicated on the map by making use of a Google Maps mashup (Google Maps, 2011). A first prototype of the mobile client is being developed in Java using Android SDK (Android, 2011) in an Android Dev Phone 1.

We are currently validating the web 2.0 application with undergraduate students. This first version is focused on the city of Vigo but it can be easily extended to any other city or area. A snapshot of the web application showing a list of recommended events can be seen in Figure 3. The user can query recommendations for "today", "tomorrow" or "in two days". For each event, the application shows the name of the event, a brief description and its category. In the example in Figure 3, we can also see that the first event was flagged by the user as "I like it". Finally, the last

Table 1. Access modalities for GiveMeAPlan

	Free access	Pay-per-access
Registered user	The user receives social and content-based recommendations plus relevant ads	The user receives social and content-based recommendations without ads
Unregistered user	The user only receives content-based recommendations and relevant ads	This option does not make sense (the user who pays must be registered)

Figure 3. Snapshot of the web 2.0 application of GiveMeAPlan showing the list of recommended events for user Alberto

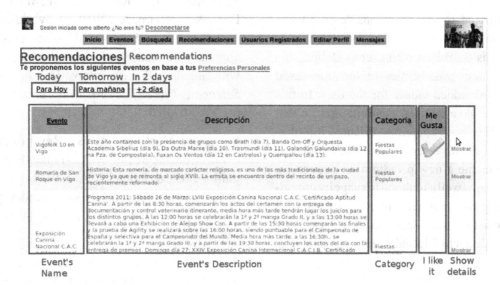

column presents a link when the user can obtain a more detailed description of each event (their location in a map, comments, rating, etc.)

We plan to extend its functionalities adding the possibility of creating users' groups focused on specific events, making easier and enjoyable the communication among users interested, for instance, in attending together a live concert. *GiveMeAPlan* will provide an ad hoc social mobile community for local and foreign people who want to enjoy the city.

FUTURE RESEARCH DIRECTIONS

As future work, the mobile service could combine the recommendations with multimedia contents to complete the information about the events (pictures, videos, etc.). In order to improve the quality of the end-user experience, we propose to generate a multimedia booklet including the events' maps, the abovementioned multimedia contents, and the advertisements. This could be done using LASeR (Lightweight Application Scene Representation) (ISO 2008), also known

as MPEG-4 Part 20. This is the new rich media standard, devoted to the mobile, embedded and consumer electronics industries, which provides easy content creation, optimized rich media data delivery, and enhanced rendering on all devices.

From the service delivery dimension that Grün et al. identify in (Grün et al., 2008), in *GiveMeA-Plan* the user receives information about objects of interest, such as information about restaurants from a gastronomy service. Future work will allow the user to initiate transactional processes such as reservation, booking or ticketing (that is, offer a transaction process). However, we already give a community process where the service is enhanced with features enabling social integration, such as offering possibilities for giving feedback or ratings, tagging or blogging, thus empowering a user to share the tourism experience in a collaborative way.

Moreover, we will emphasize the collaboration of users by defining a new type of recommendation based on the tags that users assign to items, using a twofold algorithm (Barragáns-Martínez et al., 2010b) which performs reasoning over folksonomies and combines collaborative and content-based recommendation techniques.

CONCLUSION

Location-based services are considered a killer application of mobile computing. When location-awareness is combined with user modeling, this opens up new possibilities in location-based services with added values for the user. In this chapter, we have devised a mobile service that provides personalized, tourist-oriented information enriched with relevant advertisements. Our aim is to create a new paradigm for promoting local tourism as well as cultural heritage by providing exciting real-time recommendations of local events near the actual location of the user, and then, to guide her to selected entertainment points.

REFERENCES

Adomavicius, G., Sankaranarayanan, R., Sen, S., & Tuzhilin, A. (2005). Incorporating contextual information in recommender systems using a multidimensional approach. *ACM Transactions on Information Systems, 23*(1), 103–145. doi:10.1145/1055709.1055714

Adomavicius, G., & Tuzhilin, A. (2005). Toward the next generation of recommender systems: A survey of the state-of-the-art and possible extensions. *IEEE Transactions on Knowledge and Data Engineering, 17*(6), 734–749. doi:10.1109/TKDE.2005.99

Android. (2011). *Website*. Retrieved October, 2011, from http://www.android.com

Balabanovic, M., & Shoham, Y. (1997). Fab: Content-based, collaborative recommendation. *Communications of the ACM, 40*(3), 66–72. doi:10.1145/245108.245124

Barragáns-Martínez, A. B., Costa-Montenegro, E., Burguillo, J. C., Rey-López, M., Mikic-Fonte, F. A., & Peleteiro, A. (2010). A hybrid content-based and item-based collaborative filtering approach to recommend TV programs enhanced with singular value decomposition. *Information Sciences, 180*(22), 4290–4311. doi:10.1016/j.ins.2010.07.024

Barragáns-Martínez, A. B., Rey-López, M., Costa-Montenegro, E., Mikic-Fonte, F. A., Burguillo, J. C., & Peleteiro, A. (2010). Exploiting social tagging in a web 2.0 recommender system. *Internet Computing, 14*(6), 23–30. doi:10.1109/MIC.2010.104

Burke, R. (2002). Hybrid recommender systems: Survey and experiments. *User Modeling and User-Adapted Interaction, 12*(4), 331–370. doi:10.1023/A:1021240730564

Cheverst, K., Mitchell, K., & Davies, N. (2002). The role of adaptive hypermedia in a context-aware tourist GUIDE. *Communications of the ACM, 45*(5), 47–51. doi:10.1145/506218.506244

Fink, J., & Kobsa, A. (2002). User modeling for personalized city tours. *Artificial Intelligence Review, 18*(1), 33–74. doi:10.1023/A:1016383418977

Golub, G., & Loan, C. V. (1996). *Matrix computations* (3rd ed.). Baltimore, MD: Johns Hopkins Studies in Mathematical Sciences.

Google Maps. (2011). Retreived October 2011, from http://maps.google.com

Grün, C., Werthner, H., Pröll, B., Retschitzegger, W., & Schwinger, W. (2008). Assisting tourists on the move - An evaluation of mobile tourist guides. *7th International Conference on Mobile Business* (pp. 171-180). doi: 10.1109/ICMB.2008.28

Hinze, A., & Junmanee, S. (2006). Advanced recommendation models for mobile tourist information. *Lecture Notes in Computer Science: Vol. 4275. On the Move to Meaningful Internet Systems 2006: CoopIS, DOA, GADA, and ODBASE* (pp. 643-660). Berlin, Germany: Springer Verlag, doi: doi:10.1007/11914853_38

ISO. (2008). *International Standard ISO/IEC 14496-20:2008*

Lee, D. L., Chuang, H., & Seamons, K. E. (1997). Document ranking and the vector-space model. *IEEE Software*, *14*(2), 67–75. doi:10.1109/52.582976

Linalg Project. (2011). Retrieved October 2011, from http://rubyforge.org/projects/linalg

Mobasher, B. 2007. Data mining for web personalization. *Lecture Notes in Computer Science: Vol. 4321. The Adaptive Web* (pp. 90-135). Berlin, Germany: Springer Verlag, doi: doi:10.1007/978-3-540-72079-9_3

Pazzani, M. J., & Billsus, D. (2007). Content-based recommendation systems. *Lecture Notes in Computer Science: Vol. 4321. The Adaptive Web*. (pp. 325-341). Berlin, Germany: Springer Verlag, doi: doi:10.1007/978-3-540-72079-9_10

Recuenco, J. G., & Bueno, D. (2009). Balanced recommenders: A hybrid approach to improve and extend the functionality of traditional recommenders. *Workshop on Adaptation and Personalization for Web 2.0* (pp. 88-98).

Ruby on Rails. (2011). Retrieved October 2011, from http://rubyonrails.org

Schmidt-Belz, B., Laamanen, H., Poslad, S., & Zipf, A. (2003). *Location-based mobile tourist services - First user experiences.* International Conference on Information and Communication Technologies in Tourism.

Simcock, T., Hillenbrand, S. P., & Thomas, B. H. (2003). Developing a location-based tourist guide application. *Australasian Information Security Workshop* (pp. 177-183).

Unni, R., & Harmon, R. (2007). Perceived effectiveness of push vs. pull mobile location-based advertising. *Journal of Interactive Advertising*, *7*(2).

Voulodimos, A., & Patrikakis, C. (2008). Using personalized mashups for mobile location based services. *International Conference on Wireless Communications and Mobile Computing* (pp. 321-325). doi: 10.1109/IWCMC.2008.56

Vozalis, M. G., & Margaritis, K. G. (2005). Applying SVD on Item-based filtering. *International Conference on Intelligent Systems Design and Applications* (pp. 464-469).

Vozalis, M. G., & Margaritis, K. G. (2008). Identifying the effects of SVD and demographic data use on generalized collaborative filtering. *International Journal of Computer Mathematics*, *85*(12), 1741–1763. doi:10.1080/00207160701598438

Chapter 14
New Directions in Social Question Answering

Mohan John Blooma
RMIT International University, Vietnam

Jayan Chirayath Kurian
RMIT International University, Vietnam

ABSTRACT

Social Question Answering (SQA) services are emerging as a valuable information resource that is rich not only in the expertise of the user community but also their interactions and insights. The next generation SQA services are challenged in many fronts, including but not limited to: massive, heterogeneous, and streaming collections, diverse and challenging users, and the need to be sensitive to context and ambiguity. However, scholarly inquiries have yet to dovetail into a composite research stream where techniques gleaned from various research domains could be used for harnessing the information richness in SQA services to address these challenges. This chapter first explores the SQA domain by understanding the service and its modules, and then investigating previous studies that were conducted in this domain. This chapter then compares SQA services with traditional question answering systems to identify possible research challenges. Finally, new directions in SQA are proposed.

INTRODUCTION

A computer which can calculate the question to the ultimate answer, a computer of such infinite and subtle complexity that organic life itself shall form part of its operational matrix (Adams, 1979). Although Adams's vision of the Earth being transformed into a supercomputer powered by

human intelligence was fictional, today's social computing applications have transformed web towards achieving his vision. Social computing is defined as computational facilitation of social studies and human social dynamics as well as the design and use of ICT technologies that consider social context (Wang et al., 2007). Over the past decade, the Web has been transformed from a repository of largely static content to an interactive information space (Kirsch et al., 2006) where

DOI: 10.4018/978-1-4666-2533-4.ch014

users are able to participate freely in co-creating and sharing various kinds of content (such as text, image, audio and video). This is facilitated by a set of social computing applications such as blogs, social networking services, wikis, vlogs, and social question answering (SQA) services (Iskander et al., 2007).

In particular, a SQA service is defined as a tool for users to respond to other users' questions (Liu et al., 2008b). In recent years, SQA services like Yahoo! Answers, Naver, and AnswerBag have become very popular, attracting a large number of users who seek and contribute answers to a variety of questions on diverse subjects (Wang et al., 2009). While Yahoo! Answers offered by Yahoo! was launched in 2005, Naver is a South Korean search portal that added its SQA service in 2005. Further, AnswerBag, a collaborative online database of FAQs was founded in 2003. Social computing applications such as wikis and blogs provide comments and opinions but may not solicit responses. However, responses from users contributing answers to questions form the backbone of a successful SQA service. These services are dedicated platforms for user-oriented QA and result in building up a community where users share and interactively give ratings and comments to questions and answers. Hence, SQA services are emerging as a valuable information resource that is rich not only in the expertise of a user community but also in the community's interactions and insights. Therefore, the emergence of SQA services raises new research challenges for information systems researchers.

In a typical SQA service, a user can ask a question by posting on the service for other users to contribute answers. These questions are termed open questions. A user who asks a question is referred as an asker, even though the same user is likely to play other roles in a SQA service. Other roles played by the user are as an answerer or a voter. A user who answers a question is termed an answerer while a user who rates an answer is termed a voter. Once a question is posted on a SQA

service, the asker needs to wait until other users contribute their answers to the posted question. After receiving answers to the question asked, the asker selects the best answer and ends the cycle of that question by moving it to the resolved questions section. Users' activities are graded on a point scale system, specific to the SQA service, for identifying top contributors.

SQA services are derived from a branch of Information Retrieval (IR) known as question answering (QA). The goal of QA is to build intelligent systems that can provide succinct answers to questions constructed in a natural language. This approach helps in understanding users' information needs in the form of a question and delivers exactly the required information in the form of an answer (Demner-Fushman, 2006). The development of automatic approaches to QA takes place primarily in the framework of large-scale evaluations, such as QA track at the Text Retrieval Conference (TREC) (Voorhees, 2003). However, QA systems that participate in these evaluations work largely on restricted domains and on closed corpora such as encyclopedia or news articles (Brill et al., 2002). Moreover, these systems focus on fact-based direct questions commonly known as factoid questions, for example: "Who was the US President in 1999?" These questions are involved in finding an exact short string, often representing an entity, such as named entities (person, organization, location), temporal expressions, or numerical expressions. Examples of popular TREC systems are Quanda (Breck et al., 1999), Falcon (Harabagiu et al., 2000), and AskMSR (Brill et al., 2002). Unlike these systems, START (Katz and Levin, 1988), Mulder (Kwok et al., 2001), and AnswerBus (Zheng, 2002) are examples of open-domain QA systems that are scaled to the Web. These systems use the redundancy of information on the Web to answer factoid questions.

A search of the literature suggested that there exist only a limited number of studies that have attempted to consider research gaps in SQA by integrating the QA research (Jeon et al., 2005a; Jeon et al., 2005b; Bian et al., 2008b; Blooma et al., 2009). A research trend analysis of the QA domain revealed that Bian et al. (2008b) was among the first in this field to show that QA is amenable to SQA. They used machine learning methods to automatically answer factoid questions from SQA corpora. This chapter compares previous studies in QA domain and identifies research issues in SQA services for automating these services. Thereafter, this chapter also points out the research directions in SQA that needs to be addressed in future. Furthermore, it was evident that research in SQA needs to evolve to encompass new theories and methodologies that were not addressed in traditional QA research.

AN OVERVIEW OF QA RESEARCH

QA has become a promising research field that aims to provide access to information in a natural form, unlike traditional IR techniques (Lin and Katz, 2003). In contrast to the traditional IR model for formulating queries and browsing results, a QA system accepts user information requests phrased in natural language, and responds with a concise answer. Therefore, QA brings new challenges to the area of IR in both question and answer processing. Enhanced question processing and answer determination are among the new challenges that are continuously evolving (Maybury, 2006). For example, richer semantic analysis of natural-language questions supporting a more conceptual search than simple matching of query keywords, along with user interactions, can significantly enhance question processing. Dealing with partial, incomplete, contradictory or negative (null) answers involved in the selection of most prominent answers form new challenges in answer processing. The following sections give a more detailed description of QA research by presenting processes involved in QA systems, followed by a detailed review of the QA research domain.

Processes in QA Systems

Most QA systems are designed to carry out three distinct sub-tasks: question processing, document processing, and answer processing (Harabagiu et al., 2003). An illustration of the architecture of a typical QA system is shown in Figure 1. The question-processing module accepts a new question from a user and reconstructs the question for further processing (Pasca & Harabagiu, 2001). These processed questions are then fed into a document-processing module. Some methods of QA use keyword-based techniques to locate interesting passages and sentences from the retrieved documents (Salton & McGill, 1983; Jones et al., 2000), while others use more sophisticated syntactic, semantic and contextual processing to extract passages from documents in a corpus (McGuiness, 2004; Guler and Birturk, 2010). The corpus used for question answering depends on its generality, and could contain either simple text documents or Web documents. Once relevant passages are retrieved from documents in a corpus, they are sent to answer processing modules for extracting answers from passages. Answers are then formulated depending on the expected answer type of the questions asked. Finally, the ranked answer is returned to the user. Details of each processing module are described below.

Question Processing

Question processing refers to the process of reconstructing questions, extracting keywords (Pasca & Harabagiu, 2001), and deriving expected answer types (Li & Roth, 2002). Some QA systems also perform question reformulation, where a question is transformed into a number of declarative equivalents to increase the likelihood of finding the correct answer (Harabaigu et al., 2001). Parsing is also done in order to construct some form of structural representation of a question. This process helps in deriving the expected answer type (Pasca, 2004). Expected answer type taxonomies

Figure 1. Processes in a QA system

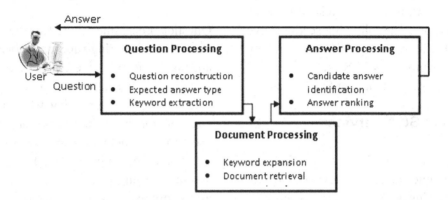

are defined in various studies (Li & Roth, 2002). These taxonomies are used for classifying questions according to a desired answer. Identification of the question type could subsequently be used to locate and verify answers. The extracted keywords from questions are used by retrieval engines to fetch relevant documents (Pasca & Harabagiu, 2001; Hovy et al., 2000).

Document Processing

Document processing includes keyword expansion, document retrieval, and passage identification. Keyword expansion typically involves taking keywords extracted in the question processing stage and adding similar search terms from resources such as WordNet[1] (Fellbaum, 1998) in order to fetch as many relevant documents as possible (Suryanto et al., 2007). Document retrieval uses expanded keywords to retrieve documents with the highest ranks (Page et al., 1999). For passage retrieval, a paragraph or section containing a possible answer is identified within each document (Oh et al., 2007).

Answer Processing

Answer processing consists of candidate answer identification, answer ranking, and answer formulation. Identifying candidate answers involves taking results from the passage identification

phase and further processing it to extract answers from retrieved passages (Berger et al., 2000). This results in a set of candidate answers that is then ranked according to an algorithm or a set of heuristics. Answer extraction aims to retrieve those sentences from passages that contain an explicit answer to a user query (Schwitter et al., 2000).

On reviewing QA research, there is a need to review studies related to SQA services and compare the two domains to identify the new research directions for automating SQA services. The following section gives an introduction to SQA services and an overview of studies related to SQA services.

AN OVERVIEW OF SQA RESEARCH

SQA services have become a popular medium where users share their expertise to answer other users' questions (Bian et al., 2008b). The success of these services has been largely attributed to the fact that users can obtain quick and precise answers to any natural language question (Liu et al., 2008b). A study conducted by Liu et al. (2008b) showed that users approach SQA services for opinions and to answer complex rather than factoid questions. The growth of SQA services has resulted in expanding repositories for opinions and complex questions. Hence, this study proposes an approach that adapts and applies techniques from

QA research and related fields to harness user-generated questions, answers, and related metadata from SQA corpora. The following sections give a more detailed description of SQA research by first presenting processes in SQA services and then discussing major strands of SQA research.

Processes in SQA Services

As illustrated in Figure 2, there are different processing modules in a SQA service. They are question processing, answer processing, and user participation modules. However, the first two modules are distinct from question processing and answer processing modules of a QA system. In a QA system, these processing modules use machine learning techniques and linguistic processing methods. On the other hand, in a SQA service, question processing and answer processing modules rely solely on the voluntary involvement of users. Details of each processing module in a SQA service are described below in Figure 2.

Question Processing

Question processing is initiated when a user posts a question by entering a question subject (i.e. title), and may optionally give details (i.e. description). A question title is referred to as a question in this research. After a short delay, which may include checking for abuse, the question appears open for users to contribute answers. Users may rate the question based on how interesting the subject is and may recommend it to other users. As users are not obligated to rate questions, usually only a small proportion of questions attract ratings (Sun et al., 2009).

An emerging area in SQA research lies in processing the questions asked by users. In particular, SQA research on question processing could be discussed in three strands: identification of similar questions by classification, clustering and retrieval. Hence this section presents a detailed review of the studies related to the identification of similar questions.

Figure 2. Processing modules in a SQA service

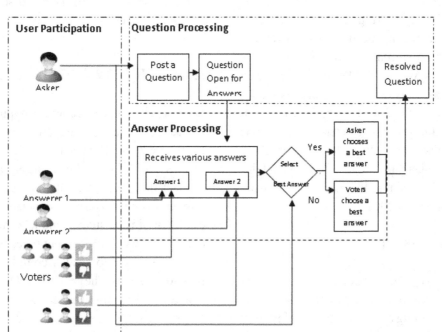

Classification

One of the common question processing methods is to classify similar questions based on the expected answer type (Tamura et al., 2005). Examples of an expected answer type may include a person, location or time. By identifying the type of expected answer, the general category of the question and the nature of its expected answer can be found out. Knowing the expected answer type addresses the "what to find" problem. Since most factoid questions focus on "who, when, where, why, what and how", classification for a factoid question is performed according to the stem of the question. Most answers for these questions are related to named entities (NE). Such answers are classified by different types of NE, such as time, product, organization, and person. The NE identification technique adapted from information extraction research is helpful and is used in the process of identifying the expected answer type (Srihari & Li, 1999). For answer categories that do not belong to NE, a concept hierarchy called Answer-Type Taxonomy was used (Pasca & Harabagiu, 2001). The taxonomy is a tree-like structure constructed off-line which contains all the answer types that can be processed by a system. This method was effective in determining answer types with 90% accuracy in the TREC questions (Sundbald, 2007). These methods are commonly referred to as question classification.

Commonly used categories for answer type taxonomy are named entities (organization, person, and location), temporal expressions (date and time), and number expressions (money and percentage) (Srihari & Li, 1999; Sundblad, 2007). Kim et al. (2000) used WordNet to construct the taxonomy of different semantic categories (Srihari & Li, 1999; Harabagiu et al., 2000). Another approach used was to manually analyse a specific corpus, i.e. a collection of questions, and infer taxonomical relations from it (Li & Roth, 2002).

While question classification is widely accepted for factoid QA (Li & Roth, 2002; Sundbald,

2007), few studies related to SQA corpora adopted this method for identifying similar questions (Tamura et al., 2005; Li et al., 2007). A significant difference between previous studies on the identification of answer type and recent studies on classifying questions from SQA corpora is the nature of questions. The questions asked by users of SQA services are often ill-formatted, ungrammatical, and include online-idioms which lead to poor performance of machine learning methods for classification (Li et al., 2007).

Retrieval

The second type of question processing method reviewed in this section is to identify similar questions by various retrieval techniques. By measuring the semantic similarity between questions, the retrieval of questions could be performed effectively. Measuring the semantic similarity of questions is difficult because of two main factors (Jeon et al., 2005b). First, questions are short and hence the probability of word overlap is low. Second, questions could have the same meaning with very different wording. Hence, traditional sentence distance measures as well as document similarity measures work poorly in the context of questions.

Three different approaches were discussed in the literature to address this word mismatch problem among questions. The first approach (Burke et al., 1997) used knowledge databases such as machine readable dictionaries. However, the quality and structure of current knowledge databases were based on the results of previous experiments and were not good enough for reliable performance. The second approach (Sneiders, 2002) employed manual rules or templates. These methods were expensive and hard to scale for large collections. The third approach (Berger et al., 2000) used statistical machine translation techniques developed for IR and natural language processing research domains. The translation-based retrieval technique used a statistical model to describe how a user translated a pair of similar questions. It was more commonly used in recent studies of SQA corpora for question retrieval because the major focus of identifying similar questions is to address the word mismatch problem.

In the case of SQA corpora, questions are often repeated but might be lexically framed using different words. Jeon et al. (2005a) used the IBM machine translation model 1 (Brown et al., 1993) to identify similar questions. They selected a collection of similar question pairs and considered the collection of similar question pairs as a bilingual corpus. The IBM machine translation model was trained to learn word translation probabilities. Extending their study, Jeon et al. (2005b) used similarity between answers to identify similar questions based on the assumption that if two answers are very similar then corresponding questions should be semantically similar, even though the two questions are lexically different to a greater extent. The translation based retrieval model was used by various other studies to bridge the lexical gap in question retrieval (Lee et al., 2008; Cao et al., 2009). Cao et al. (2009) used a language model with category smoothing, achieved through classification techniques, to obtain better results. Wang et al. (2009a) integrated the retrieval framework with a syntactic tree structure to tackle similar question matching problems.

To conclude, this section on studies related to retrieval of questions, different methods were used to identify similar questions. However, most of the studies required training, and performance of the retrieval depended on training data. Moreover, the above methods required high-level linguistic analysis, both syntactically and semantically, which is computationally intensive.

Clustering

Apart from classification and retrieval, clustering questions helps to identify similar questions. Text document clustering plays an important role in providing better document retrieval while tradi-

tional document clustering approaches aim to find common patterns in a document collection. The algorithm used for clustering could be categorized into partitional, hierarchical and model-based approaches. The partitional clustering approach decomposes a dataset into disjoint clusters through minimization/maximization of a local (or global) criterion based on some measure of dissimilarity/similarity (Steinbach et al., 2000). The hierarchical clustering approach obtains a hierarchy of clusters through an iterative process that merges small clusters into larger ones (agglomerative algorithms) or splits large clusters into smaller ones (divisive algorithms) (Fung et al., 2003; Joo & Lee, 2005). Finally, model-based clustering attempts to learn generative models from documents (Zhong & Ghosh, 2003).

Although clustering of text documents has been well studied (Steinbach et al., 2000; Joo & Lee, 2005), it is not directly applicable to user-generated questions from SQA corpora because of the nature of questions posed in SQA services. As users compose questions in a variety of ways, it is very likely that similar questions are worded in different ways. While one might be asking a question for getting the opinion of other users, another might be expecting a direct answer on the same topic. For example, "What are the best ways and best products to get fresh breath?", "How do you keep your breath always smell fresh and clean?", and "Please tell me what I can do to make my mouth smell go away?" are different ways of asking the same question. Therefore, keywords alone do not provide a reliable basis for clustering user-generated questions from SQA services effectively.

Query clustering is a branch of text clustering that focuses on the length and lexical disagreement problems (Beeferman & Berger, 2000; Wen et al., 2002; Leung et al., 2008). Queries are typically very short and in many cases it is hard to deduce the semantics from the queries themselves. Therefore, keywords alone do not provide a reliable base for clustering queries effectively. To resolve the disadvantages of keyword based query clustering, newer research focused on additional criteria. One criterion is hyperlinks between documents, based on the hypothesis that hyperlinks connect similar documents. Beeferman and Berger (2000) used an agglomerative clustering algorithm (i.e., BB's algorithm) to exploit query-document relationships using click-through data. One disadvantage of their approach was that the algorithm was content-independent, in the sense that it exploited only query-document links to discover similar queries and similar documents, without examining keywords in queries or documents. Another major problem was that the number of common clicks on URLs for different queries was limited. This is because different queries will likely retrieve different result sets in different ranking orders. Due to these disadvantages of using hyperlinks, studies emphasized cross references between documents and queries in query-document clustering (Wen et al., 2002; Leung et al., 2008).

The idea behind this type of clustering is if queries' often lead to similar documents, then those queries are similar, to some extent (Beeferman & Berger, 2000; Wen et al., 2002). However, they do not consider the content. To alleviate this problem, in a more recent study, Leung et al. (2008) introduced the notion of concept-based graphs, by considering concepts extracted from web-snippets, and adapted Beeferman and Berger's (2000) method to this new context. However, their work also neglected word similarity between queries.

The above clustering algorithms can be adapted to questions. However, questions in SQA services are not well formed but are contributed in a free form. Thus, keywords in questions may not be as rich as queries used to search for an information need (Burke et al., 1997). Moreover, recent studies in query clustering have focused on hyperlinks and cross references as keywords and the results showed they are insufficient to perform effective clustering (Leung et al., 2008). Blooma et al., (2011) proposed a quadripartite graph-based clustering by harnessing answers, askers and answerers to identify similar questions.

Answer Processing

In a typical SQA service, once a question is open, other users can answer the question, vote on other users' answers, comment on the question (e.g., to ask for clarification or provide other, non-answer feedback), or provide various metadata for the question (e.g., give stars for quality). When the asker obtains a satisfactory answer, the question is closed by selecting the satisfactory answer as the best answer. The question might have received numerous other answers depending on its popularity. If the best answer is identified, the question is deemed to have been resolved, and will be available for users for future reference. If the asker fails to select a best answer, the question will remain open for a stipulated number of days depending on the SQA service, and would be closed later. In this case, the answer with the highest number of votes would be marked as the best answer. If answers for a question do not have a best answer marked by an asker or voters, the question would remain as undecided. Thus, it is evident that answer processing in a SQA service is driven solely by users' active involvement. Studies on SQA services that focus on user-contributed answers can be divided into two strands of investigation: answer ranking algorithms and answer ranking frameworks.

Answer Ranking Algorithms

This section reviews previous work related to answer processing methods that are used to rank candidate answers for the selection of high-quality answers. The methods reviewed in this section are detailed according to four strands: keyword matching, filtering using heuristic rules, machine learning algorithms, and statistical translation models.

First, in most factoid QA systems, keyword matching algorithms were used to extract a relevant fragment of the answers. Pertinent methods were adopted to expand or shrink keywords to make sure that the required answer fragment was returned (Collins-Thompson & Callan, 2005; Suryanto et al., 2007).

Second, after the fragments were returned further matching was performed and fragments that did not meet strict requirements were filtered out. The filter was used to verify semantic relations or a ranking scheme (Harabagiu et al., 2001). The matching process was enhanced in a few studies by using answer type and answer focus to check in the parse tree of questions and candidate answers (Hovy et al., 2000).

Third, when keyword matching and filtering are not enough for selecting a high-quality answer, ranking candidate answers was performed using machine learning algorithms (Han et al., 2007). The ranking often depends on the heuristics of how candidate answers contain query terms, for example, order of query terms in candidate answers, number of query terms that were matched, and distance from the position of the embedded answer type to the query terms (Riezler et al., 2007). Meanwhile, other systems implemented matching by ranking passages according to weighted features or terms that are chosen off-line (Ferret et al., 1999; Srihari & Li, 1999). Various machine learning and statistical techniques were used for the ranking of answers (Ko et al., 2010; Pasca & Harabagiu, 2001). For example, Ko et al. (2010) used a probabilistic ranking model, Pasca and Harabagiu (2001) used a perceptron model to compare two candidate answers, while Prager et al. (1999) applied logistic regression to score named entities contained in candidate answers for ranking them.

Fourth, questions and their respective answers in a SQA corpus will have more word overlap because the answers in a SQA corpus were created by users according to the question. However, answers in traditional QA were extracted from documents in the QA corpus. Hence, answers to different questions will be easier to distinguish due to the word overlap using translation models. Berger et al. (2000) described several models used to find the connection between question terms and answer terms, such as the support vector model, the mutual information model between query terms and a statistical translation model. They found the statistical translation model to be effective. Statistical machine translation was used to bridge the lexical gap between questions and answers (Brown et al., 1993). Such techniques have also been explored for answering factoid questions by Radev et al. (2002). In this method, questions were translated into answers and the answer finding was based on translations found. In a recent study, Xue et al. (2008) also used a translation model for answer retrieval from SQA corpora, and their work was a follow-up to the studies conducted by Jeon et al. (2005a; 2005b). While the former study used question and answer pairs to train the translation model, the latter used similar question pairs. Noisy channel is a similar approach used for factoid QA, in which the similarity between factoid answers and questions asked were computed using noisy channel transformations (Echihabi & Marcu, 2003).

Answer Quality Frameworks

Retrieval of ranked answers is an important component of a QA system. However, in the case of SQA corpora, many relevant answers could be found because similar questions tend to be asked frequently. Hence, there is a need to investigate the selection of high-quality answers from candidate answers obtained for similar questions. This is because the quality of user-generated answers varies significantly even though they may all be relevant to a question. In addition, user-generated answers could also contain spam (Bian et al., 2009). Hence many related studies have adopted the approach of considering both quality and relevance for the selection of high-quality answers. The studies reviewed in this section use various frameworks consisting of different features that aid the selection of high-quality answers. These frameworks focus on features that are used to judge the quality and relevance of answers and are presented in three strands.

The first strand focuses on Social features. As mentioned earlier, most of the studies used Social features such as user authority and user rating (Jeon et al., 2006; Chen et al., 2006; Bian et al., 2008b). Jeon et al. (2006) considered only Social features such as user rating and authority and ignored content quality for their study. Moreover, in their work they used only the best answer and neglected answers obtained for the same question from other users. However, the best answer is subjective and depends on the asker so considering other answers is important.

In the second strand, both Social and Content features are discussed. In previous studies Content features were limited to Textual Content that was extracted automatically using semantic features such as bag-of-words (Bian et al., 2008b). Agichtein et al. (2008) developed a comprehensive graph based model of contributor relationships and combined it with content and usage features, to classify high-quality answers depending on these features. A similar study by Bian et al. (2008b) presented a general ranking framework for retrieval of factual answers by combining both Textual Content and Social features. However, instead of directly extracting questions and answers from SQA corpora, they used TREC questions and obtained similar questions from SQA services. They found that both Textual Content and Social features were equally important, and user feedback played an important role in relevance judgment.

The third is an emerging but promising strand of SQA research that focuses on Content Appraisal features to identify features that influence high-quality answers. Kim and Oh (2007; 2009) used the asker's open-ended comments to uncover criteria for selecting high-quality answers. Their study pointed to the invariable importance of content-oriented relevance judgment criteria. Though they were unable to capture open-ended comments comprehensively, such a line of inquiry recognizes that high-quality answer selection from SQA corpora involves a measure of subjective judgment. Given the lack of studies in this direction, the theoretical foundation of Content Appraisal features has to be laid by drawing inferences from the information quality literature and was found to be significant predictors of high-quality answers (Blooma et al., 2011).

User Participation

It is evident from the question processing and answer processing modules that user participation forms the backbone of SQA services. Users participate by asking, answering and rating SQA services, which aids in the success of these services. Users are divided into askers, answerers, and voters. Each user is given points based on roles played, activities in which the user participated, and the quality of questions and answers contributed. The point system and scoring vary depending on SQA services, and user participation details are stored as user profiles. Thus the user participation module records user activities and profiles. Studies on SQA services that focus on user participation can be divided into three strands of investigation apart from studies discussed earlier that are related to question processing and answer processing.

User Authority

The first strand of studies analyses knowledge generation characteristics and users' authority as a result of user participation. Nam et al. (2009) found that altruism, learning, and competency are common motivations enticing top answerers to participate, but such participation is often highly intermittent. A major problem with this approach was determining how many users should be chosen as authoritative, from a ranked list. To address this problem, Bouguessa et al. (2008) proposed a method to identify authoritative participants. This method automatically discriminated between authoritative and non-authoritative users.

Social Network Analysis

The second strand of studies investigated user participation and authority using social network analysis. Rodrigues and Frayling (2009) performed an in-depth content analysis using social network analysis techniques to monitor the dynamics of community ecosystems. Their study concluded that SQA services rely on user participation and the quality of users' contributions. Jurczyk and Agichtein (2007) and Suryanto et al. (2009) used link structure to discover the authority of users. Estimating the authority of users has potential applications for answer ranking, spam detection, and incentive mechanism design.

Social Reference Theory

Most research on SQA services has focused on information retrieval and information intermediation. However, there is a new and emerging stream of works that focus on social, technical, and contextual factors. For example, Rosenbaum and Shachaf (2010) describe an approach based on structuration theory and communities of practice. The practice of answering questions is the common social practice for the members of these communities. Shachaf (2010) interprets SQA as an input process output approach to virtual group work and also accounts for the collaborative process of question answering and the interplay between technology and users in their contexts.

On reviewing the state-of-the art research based on SQA services it is evident that there is still an immense potential for the proposed approach on this domain. Gazan (2011) also presents a review and analysis of the research literature in SQA and identifies the major trends of SQA research. The re-use of user-generated questions, answers, and related metadata from a SQA corpus involves finding high-quality answers for a user's question (Blooma and Jayan, 2011). To better illustrate new directions in SQA research there is a need to further compare the differences in the approaches used in QA systems with SQA services as detailed in the next section.

COMPARISON OF QA SYSTEMS WITH SQA SERVICES

A comparison of QA systems and SQA services is detailed in Table 1. The table presents four differences between a QA system and a SQA service. These differences highlight major issues in answering a newly posed question by harnessing user-generated questions, answers, and related metadata collected in a SQA corpus.

The first difference is related to question type. The nature of questions a QA system can handle determines its scope and hence this distinction is important. QA systems handle single-sentence questions that are particularly fact-based. Single-sentence questions are defined as questions composed of one sentence. Since 2006, TREC and other QA systems research groups have started to focus on complex and interactive questions

Table 1. Comparison of QA systems with SQA services

	QA Systems	SQA Services
Question type	Factoid single sentence questions	Multiple sentence questions
Source of answers	Extracted from documents in a corpus	Contributed by users
Quality of answers	High, as answers are extracted from reputed sources	Varying as it depends on answers contributed by users
Availability of metadata	None	Best answer selected by asker and positive and negative ratings given by voters
Time lag	Automatic and immediate	The asker needs to wait for users to post answers

(Dang et al., 2006). However, they are still in the early stages of research. SQA services are rich in multiple-sentence questions, which are defined as questions composed of two or more sentences: For example, "My computer reboots as soon as it gets started. OS is Windows XP. Is there any homepage that tells why it happens?". For conventional QA systems, these questions are not expected and existing techniques are not applicable or barely work in the context of such questions (Tamaru et al., 2005). Therefore, constructing a QA system on SQA corpora that can handle multiple-sentence questions is challenging and desirable to satisfy user needs.

The second difference is related to the source of the answers. This distinction is important as it determines the complexity of processing required to answer questions. Currently, various QA systems have been built on different types of corpora, such as full text news articles or encyclopaedia articles, for closed domain systems (Harabagiu et al., 2000; Brill et al., 2002), and the Web for open domain systems (Katz, 1988; Kwok et al., 2001). However, in a SQA service, questions and answers collected as a SQA corpus are contributed by users, while the producers of content in other types of corpora are professionals, publishers, or journalists (Liu et al., 2008a). Hence they differ in many aspects such as the length of the content, structure and writing style. The noisy nature of the content, probability of spam, and the variance in quality elicits new challenges.

The third difference is related to the quality of answers, which eventually determines the quality of a system. It is evident from the discussion on the source of answers that a QA system extracts answers from a reputed corpus. However, in SQA services, answers are obtained from different kinds of users, with varying reputations (Liu et al., 2008a). Previous studies also showed evidence of variance in the quality of answers in different SQA services. This variance in the quality of answers depends on various factors such as the community that participates, compensation for

answers and whether answers are from experts or casual answerers (Harper et al., 2008). In addition, the quality of answers becomes important when there are many responses to a single question (Jeon et al., 2006).

The fourth difference is related to the availability of metadata. SQA services are abundant in metadata such as comments and positive and negative ratings, together with authorship and attribution information created by an explicit support for social interactions between users. These metadata make the content in SQA services rich. Most of the studies on SQA services harnessed these metadata to sieve high-quality content (Liu et al., 2008b; Bian et al., 2008b). However, this is not the case in traditional QA systems.

The final difference is related to the time lag in obtaining answers to a newly posed question. QA systems generate answers automatically to questions, and hence eliminate any time lag. However, SQA services involve a time lag and askers have to wait for answers to a question from various users (Jeon et al., 2005a).

Hence, the major issues in answering a newly posed question by harnessing a SQA corpus could be summarised with respect to the nature of questions posed, source of answers, variance in the quality of answers, richness of metadata available and the time lag in obtaining answers.

CONCLUSION

Considering the review of SQA research domain and understanding the major challenges in answering a newly posed question by harnessing a SQA corpus, new directions in SQA research is with respect to two major challenges.

The first challenge was to find questions in a corpus that were semantically similar to a users' newly posed question (Jeon et al., 2005b). This facilitates the retrieval of high-quality answers that are associated with similar questions identified in the corpus, reducing the time lag associated with a SQA system. Due to the complex nature of questions posed in SQA services as discussed earlier, it is not an easy task to identify similar questions. Measuring semantic similarities between questions is not a trivial task. In addition, two questions having the same meaning may use entirely different wording. For example, "Is downloading movies illegal?" and "Can I share a copy of a DVD online" have almost identical meanings but they are lexically very different. Similarity measures developed for document retrieval work poorly when there is little word overlap. With respect to previous work in this area that discussed methods for question retrieval, Jeon et al. (2005a) used the similarity between answers in a corpus to estimate probabilities for a translation-based retrieval model. Hence there is a need to work on more comprehensive methods that make use of available metadata to identify similar questions (Bian et al., 2009). Moreover, as there is an increasing amount of data collected in the SQA corpora, identifying semantically similar questions from the corpora for a newly posed question not found in it would be more challenging and rewarding for the ongoing research in this domain. Nevertheless, there is a need to involve users in the role of askers, answers and voters and their interactions in different ways to identify similar questions (Bloom et al., 2011) which eventually leads to a very vast arena of research.

The second challenge was to identify high-quality answers from a set of candidate answers. The quality of user-contributed content in SQA services, in the form of questions, answers and votes, varies drastically from excellent to spam (Agichtein et al., 2008). The open contribution model of the system, the ease of using these services for content creation and sharing, as well as an attraction towards collaboration among like-minded people, have led to significant growth of these services. However, the flipside of growth is that content in SQA services is thematically diverse, lacking a consistent structure together with linguistic style. Moreover, users give poor quality answers for several reasons, including

limited knowledge about a question domain, bad intentions (e.g., spam, making fun of others, etc.) or limited time to prepare good answers. In addition, the absence of any editorial control results in the least relevant answers often being classified as spam (Bian et al., 2008b; Heyman et al., 2007), resulting in poor quality of content (Agichtein et al., 2008). Hence there is a need to work on more comprehensive methods that tap into various features associated with answers that in turn help to recommend high-quality answers for newly posed questions.

REFERENCES

Adamic, L. A., Zhang, J., Bakshy, E., & Ackerman, M. S. (2008). Knowledge sharing and Yahoo Answers: Everybody knows something. In J. Huai, R. Chen, H. W. Hon, Y. Liu, W. Y. Ma, A. Tomkins, & X. Zhang (Eds.), *Proceedings of the 17th International World Wide Web Conference*, Beijing, China, (pp. 665-674). New York, NY: ACM.

Adams, D. (2005). *The hitchhiker's guide to the galaxy*. New York, NY: Del Rey Books.

Agichtein, E., Castillo, C., Donato, D., Gionis, A., & Mishne, G. (2008). Finding high-quality content in social media. In *Proceedings of the International Conference on Web Search and Web Data Mining*, California, (pp. 183-194). New York, NY: ACM.

Agichtein, E., Liu, Y., & Bian, J. (2009). Modeling information seeker satisfaction in community question answering. *Transactions on Knowledge Discovery from Data, 3*(2), 10:1-10:27.

Beeferman, D., & Berger, A. (2000). Agglomerative clustering of a search engine query log. In *Proceedings of the 6th ACM International Conference on Knowledge Discovery and Data Mining*, Massachusetts, United States (pp. 406-416). New York, NY: ACM.

Berger, A., Caruana, R., Cohn, D., Freitag, D., & Mittal, V. (2000). Bridging the lexical chasm: statistical approaches to answer-finding. In N. J. Belkin, P. Ingwersen, & M. K. Leong (Eds.), *Proceedings of the 23rd ACM International Conference on Research and Development in Information Retrieval*, Athens, Greece (pp. 192-199). New York, NY: ACM.

Bian, J., Liu, Y., Agichtein, E., & Zha, H. (2008a). A few bad votes too many? Towards robust ranking in social media. In *Proceedings of the 4th International Workshop on Adversarial Information Retrieval on the Web*, Beijing, China (pp. 53-60). New York, NY: ACM.

Bian, J., Liu, Y., Agichtein, E., & Zha, H. (2008b). Finding the right facts in the crowd: Factoid question answering over social media. In *Proceeding of the 17th International Conference on World Wide Web*, Beijing, China (pp. 467-476). New York, NY: ACM.

Bian, J., Liu, Y., Zhou, D., Agichtein, E., & Zha, H. (2009). Learning to recognize reliable users and content in social media with coupled mutual reinforcement. In *Proceeding of the 18th International Conference on World Wide Web*, Madrid, Spain (pp. 51 – 60). New York, NY: ACM.

Blooma, M. J., Chua, A. Y. K., & Goh, D. H. (2011, January). What makes a high quality user-generated answer? *IEEE Internet Computing, 14*(4), 1–8.

Blooma, M. J., Chua, A. Y. K., & Goh, D. H. (Accepted for Publication). Predictors of high-quality answers in community-driven question answering services. *Online Information Review.*

Blooma, M. J., Chua, A. Y. K., Goh, D. H., & Keong, L. C. (2009). A trend analysis of the question answering domain. In *Proceedings of the 6th International Conference on Information Technology: New Generations 2009*, Nevada, United States (pp. 1522-1527). New York, NY: IEEE Computer Society.

Blooma, M. J., & Jayan, C. K. (July, 2011). Research trends in community question answering. In *Proceedings of Pacific Asia Conference on Information Systems 2011*, Brisbane, Australia.

Breck, E., House, D., Light, M., & Mani, I. (1999). Question answering from large document collections. In *Proceedings of AAAI 1999 Fall Symposium on Question Answering Systems*, Florida, United States (pp. 26-31). AAAI Press.

Brill, E., Dumais, S., & Banko, M. (2002). An analysis of the ASKMSR question-answering system. In *Proceedings of the 2002 Conference on Empirical Methods in Natural Language Processing*, Pennsylvania, (pp. 257-264). Association of Computational Linguistics.

Brown, P. F., Pietra, V. J. D., Pietra, S. A. D., & Mercer, R. L. (1993). The mathematics of statistical machine translation: Parameter estimation. *Computational Linguistics, 19*(2), 263–311.

Burke, R., Hammond, K., Kulyukin, V., Lytinen, S., Tomuro, N., & Schoenberg, S. (1997). Question answering from frequently-asked question files: Experiences with the FAQ finder system. *AI Magazine, 18*(2), 57–66.

Cao, X., Cong, G., Cui, B., Jensen, C. S., & Zhang, C. (2009). The use of categorization information in language models for question retrieval. In D. W. K. Cheung, I. Song, W. W. Chu, X. Hu, & J. Lin (Eds.), *Proceeding of the 18th ACM Conference on Information and Knowledge Management*, Hong Kong, China (pp. 265-274). New York, NY: ACM.

Chen, W., Zeng, Q., & Liu, W. (2006). A user reputation model for a user interactive question answering system. In *Proceedings of the 2nd International Conference on Semantics, Knowledge and Grid*, Guilin, China (pp. 40). New York, NY: IEEE Computer Society.

Collins-Thompson, K., & Callan, J. (2005). Predicting reading difficulty with statistical reading models. *Journal of the American Society for Information Science and Technology, 56*(13), 1448–1462. doi:10.1002/asi.20243

Dang, H. T., Lin, J., & Kelly, D. (2006). Overview of the TREC 2006 question answering track. In *Proceedings of the 15th Text REtrieval Conference (TREC 2006)*, Maryland, United States (pp. 99-116). Gaithersburg, MD: NIST.

Demner-Fushman, D., & Lin, J. (2006). Answer extraction, semantic clustering, and extractive summarization for clinical question answering. In *Proceedings of the 21st International Conference on Computational Linguistics and 44th Annual Meeting of the ACL*, Sydney, Australia (pp. 841–848). Association of Computational Linguistics.

Fellbaum, C. (1998). *WordNet: An electronic lexical database*. Cambridge, MA: MIT Press.

Ferret, F., Grau, B., Illouz, G., Jacquemin, C., & Masson, N. (1999). QALC the question answering program of the language and cognition group at LIMSI-CNRS. In *Proceedings of the 8th Text REtrieval Conference*, Maryland, United States ((pp. 78-85). Gaithersburg, MD: NIST.

Fung, B. C. M., Wang, K., & Ester, M. (2003). Hierarchical document clustering using frequent itemsets. In *Proceedings of the 3rd SIAM International Conference on Data Mining*, California, United States (pp. 59-70). Retrieved from http://www.siam.org/proceedings/datamining/2003/dm03_06FungB.pdf

Gazan, R. (2011). Social Q & A. *Journal of the American Society for Information Science and Technology, 62*(12). doi:10.1002/asi.21562

Guler, F. M., & Birturk, A. (2010). Natural intelligence – Commonsense question answering with conceptual graphs. *Conceptual Structures: From Information to Intelligence. Lecture Notes in Computer Science, 6208*, 97–107.

Han, Y. S., Wang, Y., & Wood, D. (2007). Prefix-free regular languages and pattern matching. *Theoretical Computer Science, 389*(1-2), 307–317. doi:10.1016/j.tcs.2007.10.017

Harabagiu, S., Moldovan, D., Pasca, M., Mihalcea, R., Surdeanu, M., & Bunescu, R. … Morarescu, P. (2000). FALCON: Boosting knowledge for answer engines. In *Proceedings of the 9th Text Retrieval Conference*, Maryland, United States (pp. 479-489). Gaithersburg, MD: NIST.

Harabagiu, S., Moldovan, D., Pasca, M., Surdeanu, M., Mihalcea, R., & Gırju, R. … Bunescu, R. (2001). Answering complex, list and context questions with LCC's question-answering server. *In Proceedings of the 10th Text Retrieval Conference*, Maryland, United States (pp. 355-361). Gaithersburg, MD: NIST.

Harabagiu, S. M., Maiorano, S. J., & Pasca, M. A. (2003). Open-domain textual question answering techniques. *Natural Language Engineering, 9*(3), 231–267. doi:10.1017/S1351324903003176

Harper, F. M., Raban, D., Rafaeli, S., & Konstan, J. (2008). Predictors of answer quality in online Q&A sites. In *Proceedings of the 27th International Conference on Human Factors in Computing Systems*, Florence, Italy (pp. 865-874). New York, NY: ACM.

Hovy, E., Gerber, L., Hermjakob, U., Junk, M., & Lin, C.-Y. (2000). Question answering in Webclopedia. In *Proceedings of the 9th Text Retrieval Conference*, Maryland, United States (pp. 655-532). Gaithersburg, MD: NIST.

Iskandar, D. N. F. A., Pehcevski, J., Thom, J. A., & Tahaghoghi, S. M. M. (2007). Social media retrieval using image features and structured text. In Fuhr, N., Kamps, J., Lalmas, M., & Trotman, A. (Eds.), *Focused Access to XML Documents, INEX 2007, LNCS 4862, Dagstuhl, Germany* (pp. 358–372). Berlin, Germany: Springer.

Jeon, J., Croft, W. B., & Lee, J. H. (2005a). Finding similar questions in large question and answer archives. In *Proceedings of the 14th ACM Conference on Information and Knowledge Management*, Bremen, Germany (pp. 84-90). New York, NY: ACM.

Jeon, J., Croft, W. B., & Lee, J. H. (2005b). Finding semantically similar questions based on their answers. In R. A. Baeza-Yates, N. Ziviani, G. Marchionini, A. Moffat, & J. Tait (Eds.), *Proceedings of the 28th International ACM Conference on Research and Development in Information Retrieval*, Salvador, Brazil (pp. 617-618). New York, NY: ACM.

Jeon, J., Croft, W. B., Lee, J. H., & Park, S. (2006). A framework to predict the quality of answers with non textual features. In E. Efthimiadis, S. Dumais, D. Hawking, & K. Järvelin (Eds.), *Proceedings of the 29th International ACM Conference on Research and Development in Information Retrieval*, Seattle, United States (pp. 228 – 235). New York, NY: ACM.

Jones, K. S., Walker, S., & Robertson, S. E. (2000). A probabilistic model of information retrieval: Development and comparative experiments. *Information Processing & Management, 36*(6), 779–840. doi:10.1016/S0306-4573(00)00015-7

Joo, K. H., & Lee, S. (2005). An incremental document clustering algorithm based on a hierarchical agglomerative approach. In Chakraborty, G. (Ed.), *Distributed Computing and Internet Technology, ICDCIT 2005, LNCS 3816, Bhubaneswar, India* (pp. 321–332). Berlin, Germany: Springer. doi:10.1007/11604655_37

Jurczyk, P., & Agichtein, E. (2007). Discovering authorities in question answer communities by using link analysis. In *Proceedings of the 16th ACM Conference on Conference on Information and Knowledge Management*, Lisbon, Portugal, (pp. 919-922). New York, NY: ACM.

Katz, B., & Levin, B. (1988) Exploiting lexical regularities in designing natural language systems. In *Proceedings of the 12th International Conference on Computational Linguistics*, Budapest, Hungary (pp. 316-323).

Kim, S., Oh, J., & Oh, S. (2007). Best-answer selection criteria in a social Q&A site from the user-centered relevance perspective. In *Proceedings of the 70th annual meeting of the American Society for Information Science and Technology, 44*, (pp. 1–15). Information Today, Inc.

Kim, S., & Oh, S. (2009). User's relevance criteria for evaluating answers in a social Q & A site. *Journal of the American Society for Information Science and Technology, 60*(4), 716–727. doi:10.1002/asi.21026

Kim, S.-M., Baek, D.-H., Kim, S.-B., & Rim, H.-C. (2000). Question answering considering semantic categories and co-occurence density. In *Proceedings of the 9th Text REtrieval Conference,* Maryland, United States (pp. 317-334). Gaithersburg, MD: NIST.

Ko, J., Si, L., Nyberg, E., & Mitamura, T. (2010). Probabilistic models for answer-ranking in multilingual question-answering, *ACM Transactions on Information Systems, 28*(3), 16:1-37.

Krisch, S. M., Gnasa, M., Won, M., & Cremers, A. B. (2006). Beyond the web: Retrieval in social information spaces. In Lalmas, M., MacFarlane, A., Rüger, S. M., Tombros, A., Tsikrika, T., & Yavlinsky, A. (Eds.), *Advances in Information Retrieval, ECIR 2006, LNCS 3936, London, United Kingdom* (pp. 84–95). Berlin, Germany: Springer. doi:10.1007/11735106_9

Kwok, C. C. T., Etzioni, O., & Weld, D. S. (2001). Scaling question answering to the web. *ACM Transactions on Information Systems, 19*(3), 242–262. doi:10.1145/502115.502117

Leung, K. W. T., Ng, W., & Lee, D. L. (2008). Personalized concept-based clustering of search engine queries. *IEEE Transactions on Knowledge and Data Engineering, 20*(11), 1505–1518. doi:10.1109/TKDE.2008.84

Li, X., & Roth, D. (2002). Learning question classifiers. In *Proceedings of the 19th International Conference on Computational Linguistics*, Taipei, Taiwan (pp. 556–562). Association of Computational Linguistics.

Li, X. Y., Yuan, J. S., & Jing, Y. W. (2007). An efficient user access pattern clustering algorithm. In *Proceedings of the 6th International Conference on Machine Learning and Cybernetics*, Hong Kong, China, (pp. 4109-4112). New York, NY: IEEE Computer Society.

Liu, Y., & Agichtein, E. (2008a). On the evolution of the Yahoo! Answers QA community. In S. H. Myaeng, D. W. Oard, F. Sebastiani, T. S. Chua, & M. K. Leong (Eds.), *Proceedings of the 31st Annual International ACM Conference on Research and Development in Information Retrieval*, Singapore, (pp. 737-738). New York, NY: ACM.

Liu, Y., & Agichtein, E. (2008a). On the evolution of the Yahoo! Answers QA community. In S. H. Myaeng, D. W. Oard, F. Sebastiani, T. S. Chua, & M. K. Leong (Eds.), *Proceedings of the 31st Annual International ACM Conference on Research and Development in Information Retrieval*, Singapore, (pp. 737-738). New York, NY: ACM.

Liu, Y., Bian, J., & Agichtein, E. (2008b). Predicting information seeker satisfaction in community question answering. In S. H. Myaeng, D. W. Oard, F. Sebastiani, T. S. Chua, & M. K. Leong (Eds.), *Proceedings of the 31st Annual International ACM Conference on Research and Development in Information Retrieval*, Singapore (pp. 483-490). New York, NY: ACM.

Liu, Y., Bian, J., & Agichtein, E. (2008b). Predicting information seeker satisfaction in community question answering. In S. H. Myaeng, D. W. Oard, F. Sebastiani, T. S. Chua, & M. K. Leong (Eds.), *Proceedings of the 31st Annual International ACM Conference on Research and Development in Information Retrieval*, Singapore (pp. 483-490). New York, NY: ACM.

McGuiness, L. D. (2004). *Question answering on the Semantic Web. The Semantic Web, IEEE Intelligent Systems* (pp. 82–85). New York, NY: IEEE Computer Society.

Nam, K. K., Ackerman, M. S., & Adamic, L. A. (2009). Questions in, knowledge in a study of Naver's question answering community. In D. R. Olsen, R. B. Arthur, K. Hinckley, M. R. Morris, S. E. Hudson, & S. Greenberg (Eds.), *Proceedings of the 27th International Conference on Human Factors in Computing Systems*, Massachusetts, United States (pp. 779-788). New York, NY: ACM.

Oh, H. J., Myaeng, S. H., & Jang, M. G. (2007). Semantic passage segmentation based on sentence topics for question answering. *Information Sciences, 177*(18), 3696–3717. doi:10.1016/j.ins.2007.02.038

Page, L., Brin, S., Motwani, R., & Winograd, T. (November, 1999). *The PageRank citation ranking: Bringing order to the Web*. Technical report, Stanford University. Retrieved from http://dbpubs.stanford.edu:8090/pub/1999-66

Prager, J., Radev, D., Brown, E., Coden, A., & Samn, V. (1999). The use of predictive annotation for question answering in TREC8. In *Proceedings of the 8th Text REtrieval Conference (TREC 8)*, Maryland, United States (pp. 399-410). Gaithersburg, MD: NIST.

Radev, D., Fan, W., Qi, H., Wu, H., & Grewal, A. (2002). Probabilistic question answering on the web. In *Proceedings of the 11th International Conference on World Wide Web*, Honolulu, Hawaii (pp. 408-419). New York, NY: ACM.

Riezler, S., Vasserman, A., Tsochantaridis, I., Mittal, V., & Liu, Y. (2007). Statistical machine translation for query expansion in answer retrieval. In *Proceedings of the 45th Annual Meeting of the Association for Computational Linguistics* (ACL' 07), (pp. 464–471).

Rodrigues, E. M., & Frayling, N. M. (2009). Socializing or knowledge sharing? Characterizing social intent in community question answering. In D. W. K. Cheung, I. Song, W. W. Chu, X. Hu, & J. Lin (Eds.), *Proceeding of the 18th ACM Conference on Information and Knowledge Management*, Hong Kong, China (pp. 1127-1136). New York, NY: ACM.

Rosenbaum, H., & Shachaf, P. (2010). A structuration approach to online communities of practice: The case of Q & A communities. *Journal of the American Society for Information Science and Technology, 61*(9), 1933–1944. doi:10.1002/asi.21340

Salton, G., & McGill, M. J. (1983). *Introduction to modern information retrieval*. New York, NY: McGraw-Hill.

Schwitter, R., Mollá, D., Fournier, R., & Hess, M. (2000). Answer extraction towards better evaluations of NLP systems. In E. Brill, E. Charniak, M. Harper, M. Light, E. Riloff, & E. Voorhees (Eds.), *Proceedings of ANLP/NAACL 2000 Workshop on Reading Comprehension Tests as Evaluation for Computer-Based Language Understanding Systems*, Seattle, WA (pp. 20-27). New York, NY: ACM.

Shachaf, P. (2009). Social reference: Toward a unifying theory. *Library & Information Science Research, 32*, 66–76. doi:10.1016/j.lisr.2009.07.009

Sneiders, E. (2002). Automated question answering using question templates that cover the conceptual model of the database. In B. Andersson, M. Bergholtz, & P. Johannesson (Eds.), *Proceedings of the 6th International Conference on Applications of Natural Language to Information Systems, LNCS 2553,* Stockholm, Sweden (pp. 235–239). Berlin, Germany: Springer.

Srihari, R., & Li, W. (1999). Information extraction supported question answering. In *Proceedings of the 8th Text Retrieval Conference (TREC-8)*, Maryland, United States (pp. 185-196). Gaithersburg, MD: NIST.

Steinbach, M., Karypis, G., & Kumar, V. (2000). A comparison of document clustering techniques. In *Proceedings of the 6th ACM International Conference on Knowledge Discovery and Data Mining*, Boston, United States, (pp. 109-111). New York, NY: ACM.

Sun, K., Cao, Y., Sog, X., Song, Y. I., Wang, X., & Lin, C. Y. (2009). Learning to recommend questions based on user ratings. In D. W. K. Cheung, I. Song, W. W. Chu, X. Hu, & J. Lin (Eds.), *Proceedings of the 18th ACM Conference on Information and Knowledge Management*, Hong Kong, China (pp. 751-758).

Sundbald, H. (2007). A re-examination of question classification. In *Proceedings of the 16th Nordic Conference on Computational Linguistics,* Tartu, Estonia (pp. 394–397). Association of Computational Linguistics.

Tamura, A., Takamura, H., & Okumura, M. (2005). Classification of multiple-sentence questions. In L. P. Kaelbling & A. Saffiotti (Eds.), *Proceedings of the 2nd International Joint Conference on Natural Language Processing, LNAI 3651,* Scotland, UK (pp. 426–437). Berlin, Germany: Springer.

Voorhees, E. M. (2003). Overview of the TREC 2003 question answering track. In *Proceedings of 12th Text Retrieval Conference*, Maryland, United States (pp. 54). Gaithersburg, MD: NIST.

Wang, F. Y., & Carley, K., M., Zeng, D., & Mao, W. (2007). Social computing: From social informatics to social intelligence. *IEEE Intelligent Systems*, *22*(2), 79–83. doi:10.1109/MIS.2007.41

Wang, K., Ming, Z., & Chua, T. S. (2009). A syntactic tree matching approach to finding similar questions in community-based qa services. In J. Allan, J. A. Aslam, M. Sanderson, C. X. Zhai, & J. Zobel (Eds.), *Proceedings of the 32nd International ACM Conference on Research and Development in Information Retrieval*, Massachusetts, United States (pp. 187-194). New York, NY: ACM.

Wen, J., Nie, J., & Zhang, H. (2002). Query clustering using user logs. *ACM Transactions on Information Systems*, *20*(1), 59–81. doi:10.1145/503104.503108

Xue, X., Jeon, J., & Croft, W. B. (2008). Retrieval models for question and answer archives. In S. H. Myaeng, D. W. Oard, F. Sebastiani, T. S. Chua, & M. K. Leong (Eds.), *Proceedings of the 32nd International ACM SIGIR Conference on Research and Development in Information Retrieval*, Singapore (pp. 475-482). New York, NY: ACM.

Zheng, Z. (2002). AnswerBus question answering system. In *Proceedings of the 2nd International Conference on Human Language Technology Research*, California, United States (pp. 399-404). New York, NY: ACM.

Zhong, S., & Ghosh, J. (2003). A unified framework for model-based clustering. *Journal of Machine Learning Research*, *4*, 1001–1037.

KEY TERMS AND DEFINITIONS

Content Appraisal Features: Refer to features that represent different extrinsic dimensions of content such as correctness and comprehensiveness.

Content Features: Are defined as metrics that track intrinsic and extrinsic content quality of answers.

Question Answering (QA): Is defined as intelligent systems that can provide succinct answers to questions constructed in a natural language

Social Features: Are defined as metrics that track users' feedback and interaction in CQA services.

Social Network Analysis: Is defined as a set of methods for the analysis of social structures.

Social Question Answering (SQA) Service: Is defined as a tool for users to respond to other users' questions.

Text Clustering: Is defined as techniques used for grouping text depending on similar content.

ENDNOTES

[1]   http://wordnet.princeton.edu/

Chapter 15
Workflow Validation Framework in Collaborative Engineering Environments

Wikan Danar Sunindyo
CDL-Flex, ISIS, Vienna University of Technology, Austria & STEI-ITB, Indonesia

Thomas Moser
CDL-Flex, ISIS, Vienna University of Technology, Austria

Dietmar Winkler
CDL-Flex, ISIS, Vienna University of Technology, Austria

Richard Mordinyi
CDL-Flex, ISIS, Vienna University of Technology, Austria

Stefan Biffl
CDL-Flex, ISIS, Vienna University of Technology, Austria

ABSTRACT

Automation systems like power plants or industrial production plants usually involve heterogeneous engineering domains, e.g., mechanical, electrical, and software engineering, which are required to work together to deliver good products and/or services to the customers. However, the heterogeneity of workflows used in different engineering domains makes it hard for project managers to integrate and validate such workflows. A workflow modification language can be used to define the workflows and their modifications; however, further formalization is needed to integrate the workflows. The authors of this chapter propose to extend the Engineering Service Bus (EngSB) framework with a mechanism to integrate and validate heterogeneous workflows from different engineering fields and to link connections between different types of signals in broader sense, including process interfaces, electrical signals, and software I/O variables. For evaluation, they perform a feasibility study on a signal change management use case of an industry partner in the hydro power plant engineering domain. Major results show that the framework can support workflow validation and improve the observability of heterogeneous workflows in collaborative engineering environments.

DOI: 10.4018/978-1-4666-2533-4.ch015

INTRODUCTION

Complex automation systems, like power plants or industrial production plants, involve different kinds of engineering fields, e.g., mechanical, electrical, and software engineering, which are required to work together to produce high quality products and/or services. However in collaborative systems, each stakeholder typically works separately in his/her workplace, defining and using his/her own workflow to solve specific tasks. The interactions between different stakeholders are coordinated and monitored by project managers, who have the responsibility to monitor the project progress and take actions or decisions based on the current project status, e.g., adding more personnel or change/improve the overall engineering process.

To be able to monitor the project progress, project managers require an integrated overview of the different workflows used by heterogeneous project stakeholders, such as that project managers can monitor interactions between engineers and that they can validate the designed workflows compared to the actual engineering processes.

The major challenges here are: (a) how to oversee heterogeneous workflows from different stakeholders to support an overview of the project progress and, (b) how to validate the designed workflow model with the actual engineering processes.

Several workflow validation approaches have been introduced, for example by Raedts *et al.* (Raedts, I. et al., 2007), who propose a workflow validation approach for homogeneous and centralized systems. However, heterogeneous notations usually used to represent the workflows (e.g., flowchart, petri net, BPMN notation) make the validation across different workflows in the collaborative systems hard.

For managing workflow validation in collaborative systems, we propose to extend the Engineering Service Bus (EngSB) framework (Biffl, S., Schatten, A., & Zoitl, A., 2009a) with a process

analysis approach. The EngSB is an approach to bridge technical and semantic gaps between engineering models and tools for quality and process improvements of Software Engineering (SE) and other engineering disciplines that interact with SE. The EngSB is based on proven concepts of the Enterprise Service Bus (ESB) (Chappell, D., 2004) approach situated in the business IT context which are adapted to address the needs of software & systems engineering (Biffl, S. & Schatten, A., 2009). By extending the EngSB with a process analysis approach, we aim at advantages as (a) heterogeneous and collaborative systems as the nature of an EngSB context, (b) semantic and technical integration approaches to overcome heterogeneity of collaborative systems, and (c) a process analysis approach to support project monitoring and quality assurance of collaborative systems.

We use the Process Mining[1] (ProM) tool for validating the integrated workflow model with heterogeneous event logs from different engineering fields. We evaluate our proposed approach by implementing the workflow integration and validation method to an industrial use case in the hydro power plant engineering domain, to show the feasibility of the approach for distributed information systems. We compare the efforts required by project managers to integrate and validate the heterogeneous workflows between using a primarily manual approach and using our approach. Major results show that our workflow integration and validation approach can support the work of project managers in monitoring and comparing the designed workflow model and running processes in heterogeneous engineering environments.

The remainder of this chapter is structured as follows. Section 2 presents related work on heterogeneous engineering environments and workflow integration and validation approaches. Section 3 identifies the research questions. Section 4 describes the use case and the solution approach. Section 5 presents a snapshot of a hydro power plant engineering project as a prototypic implementation for workflows integration and validation. Finally, section 6 concludes and identifies future work.

RELATED WORK

This section summarizes background information on automation systems engineering, heterogeneous engineering environments, and the basic concepts of the proposed workflow validation approach.

Automation Systems Engineering

Current automation systems, e.g., complex industrial plants for manufacturing (Biffl, S., Sunindyo, W. D., & Moser, T., 2009b) or power plants (Schindele, A., 2009) involve distributed software to control systems behavior. Software engineering depends on specification data and plans from a wide range of engineering aspects in the whole engineering process, e.g., process planning, mechanical, and electrical engineering artifacts, or physical plan design. This expert knowledge is represented in domain specific terminologies, standards, methods, process, models, tools, and people. Weak semantic integration of expert knowledge across domain boundaries of engineering aspects and weak technical integration of tools within an engineering environment make late changes in the engineering process inefficient, risky, and error-prone.

Other risks originate from the size and complexity of plants and type of projects (Schindele, A., 2009), e.g., customized and large power plants designed according to modernization projects of existing power plants (i.e., extension and maintenance) and individual customer needs (i.e., individual customer-specific solutions). The technical plan documentation often differs from the real solution at the plan site because of last-minute on-site modifications (e.g., during commissioning and/or construction) with limited documentation of changes. Consequently, there is a shortage of feedback of the "as-built" documentation at the plant site to the engineering documentation at the engineering site. Thus, changes are risky (testing of changes), time consuming (research of as-built documentation), and error-prone because of a highly manual activity, e.g., synchronizing engineering documents across disciplines.

Assuming that semantic and technical gaps between different engineering teams can lead to a shortcoming of quality-assured artifacts and inefficient change management approaches across engineering domains (Schäfer, W. & Wehrheim, H., 2007), a major challenge is to address the gap between heterogeneous disciplines on a semantic and technical level to enable data collection and efficient change management for project control and monitoring during development, commissioning, and maintenance. In this chapter, automation systems engineering is the main context of the workflow integration and validation approach.

Heterogeneous Engineering Environments

Research on heterogeneous engineering environments is quite new, while demands on the usage of software as a part of complex systems together with other engineering domains are inevitable (Biffl, S. & Schatten, A., 2009). There are several approaches for technical integration of component-based industrial automation systems. However only little work is available regarding the effective and efficient integration of engineering tools and systems along heterogeneous engineering processes.

Biffl *et al.* (Biffl, S. & Schatten, A., 2009) propose the "Engineering Service Bus" (EngSB) to bridge technical and semantic gaps between engineering processes, models, and tools for quality and process improvements in software and systems engineering. The EngSB applies proven concepts of the "Enterprise Service Bus" from a business IT context to automation systems engineering. The major benefits of the EngSB (see the Open Source prototype implementation OpenEngSB[2]) for heterogeneous engineering environments are as follows. (a) simple aggregation of components and services according to the project needs based on a common abstract infrastructure for communication between tools and systems, (b) improved coordination between tools that were not designed to cooperate by access to data and relevant changes in other tools, (c) legal recording and systematic closing of open loops in engineering team processes. However, further configuration and administration like validation and verification of process models need to be investigated, since the EngSB is only a middleware layer concept and does not provide additional advanced applications out of the box. In this paper, we propose to extend the EngSB approach to include a workflow integration and validation approach.

Workflow Validation

Several works on workflow validation were performed, e.g. by Cook and Wolf (Cook, J. E. & Wolf, A. L., 1999). They suggest for a process validation method based on techniques for detecting and characterizing between a formal model of a process and the actual execution of the process. These techniques are neutral with respect to the correctness of the model and the correctness of the execution. However, this work is more focused on single engineering systems. We need to expand this approach, so that it can handle different processes in heterogeneous engineering environments.

Sadiq *et al.* (Sadiq, S., Orlowska, M., Sadiq, W., & Foulger, C., 2004) propose a data flow and validation approach to address important issues in workflow modeling and specification. They identify and justify the importance of data modeling in workflow specification and verification methods. Their contribution includes an illustration and definition of several potential data flow problems

that, if not detected prior to workflow deployment, may prevent the process from context execution, may execute the process using inconsistent data or even lead to process suspension. However, the focus of their validation approach is more based on data validation, rather than on process validation of the workflow model. But in the context of this chapter, the workflow also consists of processes that are required to be analyzed and validated.

Rozinat *et al.* (Rozinat, A., de Medeiros, A., Günther, C., Weijters, A., & van der Aalst, W., 2008) motivate the need for such a workflow validation mechanism and elements of an evaluation framework that is intended to enable end users to evaluate the validity of their process mining results; and process mining researchers to compare the performance of their algorithms. They focus on providing the means for a comparison of algorithms that discover the control-flow perspective of a process and on validation techniques for these process discovery algorithms. This work supports our work with the vision of validating workflow models in distributed engineering environments. However, more details on applying the common evaluation framework are still needed to be generalized in our context. Our study on several workflow validation approaches leads us to propose our workflow validation approach.

RESEARCH QUESTIONS

Heterogeneous workflow management in distributed engineering environments requires several elements to be considered, namely (a) the ability to deal with heterogeneous workflow notations, e.g., flowchart, petri nets or BPMN, (b) the ability to deal with different goals, purposes and understanding of the workflow design from different types of stakeholders, and (c) the ability to evaluate and validate workflow models with the real process steps running on the systems. Based on these requirements, we identify the following two major research questions.

RQ.1: How to integrate heterogeneous workflows. Heterogeneous engineers from different engineering fields, e.g., mechanical, electrical and software engineering, may have different workflows to manage their work process in a specific field, while project managers need to know the big picture of the whole workflows under their supervision to be able to monitor and control the status of running projects of the systems. Hence, the integration of heterogeneous workflows is an important step to be able to manage heterogeneous workflows in distributed engineering environments. However, this integration is hard due to the complexity of workflow elements that need to be integrated. Current approaches use direct mapping from one workflow to other workflow to create a new workflow that contains information from both workflows. The limitation of this approach is that we have to replicate the efforts each time we want to integrate a new workflow to the old one. We propose a Virtual Common Data Model (VCDM) (Moser, T., Biffl, S., Sunindyo, W. D., & Winkler, D., 2010a) which does not store the information of the workflows physically, but virtually, making the integration of new workflow with old ones more flexible. We discuss further about the VCDM in the use case and solution approach section.

RQ.2: How to validate the integrated workflows with the engineering processes. Validation of workflow models with running engineering processes is a key issue to assess the quality of systems. Project managers want to be able to validate the integrated workflows with engineering processes from different engineering fields, which are usually kept in event logs. An event contains information from a process event that is useful for further analysis, for example the event id, the event type, the event timestamp, the event originator, and other data. Event logs consist of sequences of events from the start to the end of the workflows. The patterns of how the events following the workflow can be analyzed to know the behaviour of the systems comparing to the designed workflow. The results of the validation can be a justification for project managers to improve the engineering processes of systems.

USE CASE AND SOLUTION APPROACH

This section presents: (a) the heterogeneous workflows in hydro power plant engineering as our use case for distributed engineering environments, (b) the framework for integrating and validating heterogeneous workflows from different engineering fields as our proposition of the solution approach to the research questions. The integration process of heterogeneous workflows (RQ.1) and the validation process of the integrated workflows (RQ.2) are parts of the framework.

A Power Plant Workflow Management System

A power plant system, as a case of distributed engineering environments, consists of heterogeneous workflows that are controlled by different stakeholders. One type of such workflows could be a signal change management process, as described by Winkler *et al.* (Winkler, D., Moser, T., Mordinyi, R., Sunindyo, W. D., & Biffl, S., 2011).

In power plant engineering systems integration, signals (Sunindyo, W. D., Moser, T., Winkler, D., & Biffl, S., 2010b) are considered as common concepts in this domain to link information across different engineering fields. Signals include process interfaces (e.g., wiring and piping), electrical signals (e.g., voltage levels), and software I/O variables. We use signals as a vehicle to link domain-specific data between different engineering disciplines and introduce the application field "signal engineering".

Important challenges that should be faced in managing signals change across disciplines are including (a) make signal handling consistent, (b) integrate signals from heterogeneous data models/tools, and (c) manage versions of signal changes across engineering disciplines (Winkler, D. et al., 2011).

For managing these signal changes, several workflows can be used by different stakeholders according to their perspectives on how to accept/reject the signal change requests from other engineering fields.

Figure 1 shows the common workflow for signal change management in the power plan system which is used by the project manager to illustrate how the signal change should be managed. This figure is drawn using the Business Process Model and Notation (BPMN)[3] and consists of three swim lanes, namely *check-in*, *signal comparison* and

termination. The proposed signal is checked-in to the system, and then compared to the other signals which are already in the system. If the signal is similar, then no change is needed, while if the signal different from the other signals, then there are several options whether to update the signal, add the signal as a new signal or do not change the signal. All the actions will be notified and reported to the system. This workflow model is one of models that is used by project managers for monitoring signal changes. Other models can be designed by other stakeholders for different purposes, e.g. the engineer could make the workflow model that represents his/her focus on managing the signals by using other notations.

Figure 1. Signal change management workflow

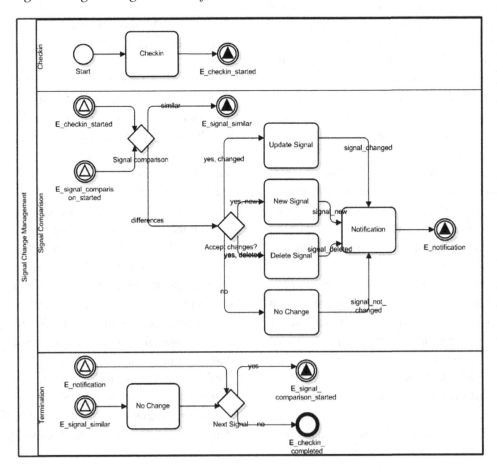

Framework for Integrating and Validating Heterogeneous Workflows

To guide the process of integrating and validating heterogeneous workflows in distributed engineering environments, we propose a framework illustrated in Figure 2. The heterogeneity of the workflows used in distributed engineering environments could come from different stakeholders who participate in the systems (e.g., project managers, mechanical engineers, electrical engineers, software engineers, end users), different notations used (e.g., flowcharts, Petri Nets, BPMN), different formats, different goals and purposes. The framework shows two stakeholders and one project manager as users of the system. We can include more stakeholders to show that our approach can be applied for more stakeholders.

We divide the period of the system into two times, design time and runtime. At design time, the stakeholders can create their own workflow models by using their favorite tools and notations, e.g., BPMN or Petri Net.

Those heterogeneous workflows (e.g., from mechanical engineer, electrical engineer, and software engineer) are then integrated using the EngSB approach (Biffl, S. et al., 2009a). The EngSB approach integrates different workflows by using the concept of the so-called Virtual Common Data Model (VCDM) (Moser, T., Biffl, S., Sunindyo, W. D., & Winkler, D., 2010a) that does not store data from each workflow physically but virtually. It becomes a foundation for mapping proprietary tool-specific engineering knowledge and more generic domain-specific engineering knowledge to support transformation between related engineering tools (Sunindyo, W. D. et al., 2010b).

It is called "virtual" since actually there is no need to provide a separate repository to store the common data model. The common data model is a data model that can accommodate all data structures which are used by different stakeholders from multidisciplinary engineering fields. The management of the common data model with respect to different engineering fields is done via a specified mapping mechanism. The mechanism of

Figure 2. Workflow integration and validation framework

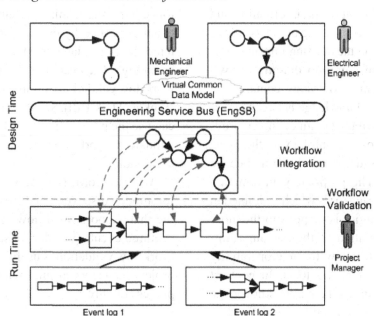

the VCDM approach includes 5 steps (Moser, T., Biffl, S., Sunindyo, W. D., & Winkler, D., 2010b).

a. **Extraction of workflow data from each engineering field:** The data elements which are contained in a particular tool need to be extracted in order to be available to the framework. By now, only a few engineering tools provide APIs for accessing the contained data directly; hence we use the export functionality of the tools. Then the exported data is parsed and transformed into an internal format consisting of key-value pairs for each data attribute.

b. **Storage of extracted workflow data into its own model:** The extracted and transformed key-value pairs of workflow data are stored using a Java Content Repository (JCR)[4] implementation. For data storage, a tree structure is used, and additional functionally like roll-back or versioning is provided.

c. **Description of the knowledge for each engineering field's workflow:** The ontologies of the workflow tool define the engineering-tool-specific, proprietary view on the information exchange (e.g., a list of signals) in an integration scenario. This includes the view on the format of the information and also describes the meaning or the use of the specific view on the existing information.

d. **Description of common domain knowledge:** The domain ontology contains the relevant shared knowledge between stakeholders in distributed engineering environments. The domain ontology is the place to model standardized domain-specific information. The proprietary information of the engineering tools which is defined in the tool ontologies is mapped to the more general information of the domain ontology in order to allow the interoperability with other engineering tools. In contrast to a common data schema, the knowledge stored in the domain ontology is defined on a more general domain level compared to the knowledge stored in the tool ontologies.

e. **Mapping of workflow knowledge to the common domain knowledge:** Each data structure segment in the tool ontology is mapped to one particular corresponding domain concept or domain concept attribute described in the domain ontology. Besides, the granularity of the mapped elements does not need to be the same. This defines the semantic context of the information contained in the segment and allows the detection of semantically similar information produced and consumed by other workflow tools. Furthermore, the format of the information is described, enabling an automated transformation from source to target format. The mapping process can be supported by applying Ontology Alignment methods to provide hints regarding possible mappings (Moser, T. et al., 2010a).

These steps support the information systems interoperability by enabling the stakeholders from different engineering fields to work together in providing engineering process data for workflows integration and validation. During runtime, operators control the running system and capture each event generated by each component of the system. The events later are stored and integrated in event logs. The event logs are the foundation for workflow validation (Sunindyo, W. D., Moser, T., Winkler, D., & Biffl, S., 2010a). Project managers can use the information stored in the event log to validate the workflows that are already integrated in previous steps.

We use ProM, a process mining workbench for model discovery and conformance checking that supports workflow validation based on captured events (van der Aalst, W. M. P., 2005). Workflow validation is useful as justification for project managers in improving the engineering process quality.

PROTOTYPE IMPLEMENTATION

This section presents the scenario and the proto-typic implementation of the change management workflow based on real world-data from a project at our industry partner, a hydro power plant system integrator.

Manual Signal Change Management

To show the improvement, that we have done at our industry partner in the hydro power plant systems integration domain, first we show the manual scenario of signal change management that is usually performed between different engineering fields. In this scenario, there are three different engineering fields, namely mechanical engineering (ME), electrical engineering (EE), and software engineering (SE). The aim of this scenario is to have a consistent signal connection between different engineering fields. Usually, prior

to the signal change, each engineering field, for example from the mechanical engineering, defines its connections to other engineering fields, for example to electrical engineering and software engineering. These connections are useful for cooperation between different engineering fields, for example some mechanical/physical switches are connected to electrical signals that can be controlled or monitored via software variables.

If one signal in the mechanical engineering is changed, other signals in other engineering fields also should be changed as well, to ensure consistent connections. Figure 3 shows two scenarios on how to deal with and disseminate signal changes from one engineering field (ME) to other engineering fields (EE and SE), the first scenario (a) is when the signal is successfully updated, and the second scenario (b) is when the signal updates are not propagated to other engineering fields.

First, the mechanical engineer (ME) checks in the signal changes in his work place. Then the

Figure 3. Signal change management: Manual scenario

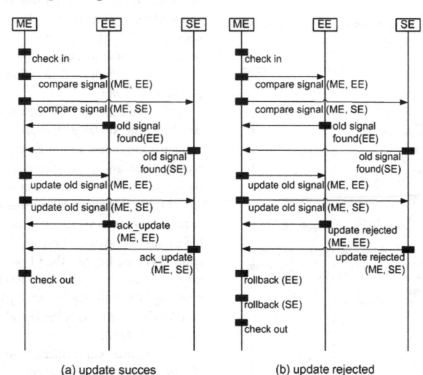

(a) update succes   (b) update rejected

ME will compare the signal to EE and SE. If related signals are found, the EE and SE will return the old related signals to the ME, such that the ME can update the relationships from old signals to EE and SE. If the update succeeds, the EE and SE will send acknowledgments to the ME. After the completion of updates, the ME will check out the scenario. If the update failed, the EE and SE reject the update and this also will be sent to the ME. In this case, the update will be rolled-back from the EE and SE before check out.

Automated Signal Change Management

Automated signal change management, as illustrated in Figure 4, improves the situation described in the manual scenario, by adding the EngSB as a component to integrate and facilitate signal change management. In this case, the EngSB has a mechanism called VCDM to accommodate the signal matching from one engineering field to other engineering fields.

Figure 4. Signal change management: Automated scenarios using EngSB

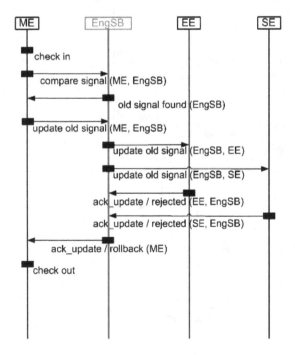

For example, the signal comparison is done only between the ME and EngSB, since all information from the EE and SE are already kept in the EngSB. So the ME only deals with the EngSB for signal comparison and gets feedback from the EngSB that the old signal has been found. The update process is also simpler, since the ME only has to send the update request to the EngSB and gets a notification whether the update is succeed or failed, so the ME should rollback its signal change. The EngSB has the responsibility to propagate the signal change to the other engineering fields, and sends a notification whether the update succeed or failed.

Implementation of Workflows into Petri Net Diagram

In order to validate the heterogeneous workflows of signal change management in hydro power plant engineering, we implement an automated signal change scenario using a Petri Net Diagram, as illustrated in Figure 5. The classical Petri Net is a directed bipartite graph with two node types called places and transitions. The nodes are connected via directed arcs. Connections between two nodes of the same type are not allowed. Places are represented by circles and transitions by rectangles (Murata, T., 1989).

The signal update is started by the ME. He checks in the signal update and sends a signal comparison request to the EngSB. The EngSB receives the signal comparison request, identifies the signal in its VCDM and sends back the old signal to the ME. The ME will send the update request to the EngSB that will be propagated to the EE and SE. After getting replies from the EE and SE via the EngSB, the EE will send his acknowledgement that the signal has been updated or the signal update requests are rejected, in which case he should roll back the signal change in his engineering field.

The workflows implementation using Petri Net diagram well shows the scenario of signal change

Figure 5. Implementation of workflows

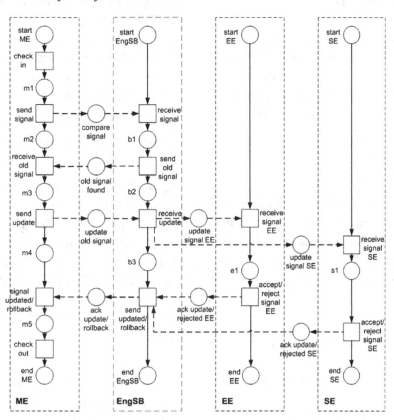

management from mechanical engineer to other engineering fields. This could help project managers to control/overview/manage the big picture of signal change management and the interaction between the engineering fields during the signal change processes.

CONCLUSION AND FUTURE WORK

Integration and validation of heterogeneous workflows from different engineering fields are critical issues in collaborative engineering environments, since individual disciplines apply different tools and workflow notations to represent their activities. This heterogeneity hinders efficient collaboration and interaction between various stakeholders, such as mechanical, electrical, and software engineers. In this chapter, we presented a framework to enable different workflows integration and validation.

The EngSB framework is the core of technical and semantic integration to collect engineering process data from different engineering fields. This framework is important to provide means for validating workflows used in collaborative engineering environments. A virtual common data model (VCDM) can support the workflow integration in the EngSB, while process mining tools such as ProM can be used to analyze and validate the results of the workflow integration. However, we still need to perform more empirical studies to justify the benefit of this approach over related approaches.

Future work will include (a) improvement of process quality based on the workflow validation results, (b) applications of other approaches to validate the workflows, (c) an organizational analysis approach to check the sources of change in the workflows.

ACKNOWLEDGMENT

This work has been supported by the Christian Doppler Forschungsgesellschaft and the BMWFJ, Austria. We want to thank the domain experts at our industry partners for providing their expertise in discussing the processes described in this chapter.

REFERENCES

Biffl, S., & Schatten, A. (2009). *A platform for service-oriented integration of software engineering environments.* Paper presented at the Conference on New Trends in Software Methodologies, Tools and Techniques (SoMeT'09).

Biffl, S., Schatten, A., & Zoitl, A. (2009a, 23-26 June 2009). *Integration of heterogeneous engineering environments for the automation systems lifecycle.* Paper presented at the 7th IEEE International Conference on Industrial Informatics (INDIN 2009).

Biffl, S., Sunindyo, W. D., & Moser, T. (2009b). *Bridging semantic gaps between stakeholders in the production automation domain with ontology areas.* Paper presented at the 21st Int. Conf on SE and Knowledge Engineering (SEKE), Boston, USA.

Chappell, D. (2004). *Enterprise service bus - Theory in practice.* O'Reilly Media.

Cook, J. E., & Wolf, A. L. (1999). Software process validation: quantitatively measuring the correspondence of a process to a model. *ACM Transactions on Software Engineering and Methodology, 8*(2), 147–176. doi:10.1145/304399.304401

Moser, T., Biffl, S., Sunindyo, W. D., & Winkler, D. (2010a). Integrating production automation expert knowledge across engineering domains. *International Journal of Distributed Systems and Technologies, Special Issue: Current Methods in Resource Integration, Allocation and Scheduling, 2011.*

Moser, T., Biffl, S., Sunindyo, W. D., & Winkler, D. (2010b). *Integrating production automation expert knowledge across engineering stakeholder domains.* Paper presented at the 4th International Conference on Complex, Intelligent and Software Intensive Systems (CISIS 2010).

Murata, T. (1989). Petri nets: Properties, analysis and applications. *Proceedings of the IEEE, 77*(4), 541–580. doi:10.1109/5.24143

Raedts, I., Petkovic, M., Usenko, Y. S., van der Werf, J. M. E. M., Groote, J. F., & Somers, L. J. (2007, June 2007). *Transformation of BPMN models for behaviour analysis.* Paper presented at the 5th International Workshop on Modelling, Simulation, Verification and Validation of Enterprise Information Systems (MSVVEIS-2007), in conjunction with ICEIS 2007, Funchal, Madeira, Portugal.

Rozinat, A., de Medeiros, A., Günther, C., Weijters, A., & van der Aalst, W. (2008). The need for a process mining evaluation framework in research and practice. In ter Hofstede, A., Benatallah, B., & Paik, H.-Y. (Eds.), *Business Process Management Workshops* (*Vol. 4928*, pp. 84–89). Berlin, Germany: Springer. doi:10.1007/978-3-540-78238-4_10

Sadiq, S., Orlowska, M., Sadiq, W., & Foulger, C. (2004). *Data flow and validation in workflow modelling.* Paper presented at the 15th Australasian database conference, Dunedin, New Zealand.

Schäfer, W., & Wehrheim, H. (2007). *The challenges of building advanced mechatronic systems.* Paper presented at the ICSE, Future of Software Engineering, Washington DC.

Schindele, A. (2009). *logi.CAD Anwendungen in Wasserkraftanlagen.* Paper presented at the Presentation at logi.cals Powerdays, Monheim, Germany.

Sunindyo, W. D., Moser, T., Winkler, D., & Biffl, S. (2010a, September 1-3). *Foundations for event-based process analysis in heterogeneous software engineering environments*. Paper presented at the Euromicro Conference on Software Engineering and Advanced Applications, Lille, France.

Sunindyo, W. D., Moser, T., Winkler, D., & Biffl, S. (2010b). *A process model discovery approach for enabling model interoperability in signal engineering*. Paper presented at the 1st Workshop on Model Driven Interoperability (MDI), Oslo, Norway.

van der Aalst, W. M. P. (2005). Business alignment: Using process mining as a tool for delta analysis and conformance testing. *RE Journal, 10*(3), 198–211.

Winkler, D., Moser, T., Mordinyi, R., Sunindyo, W. D., & Biffl, S. (2011, 27 - 29 June). *Engineering object change management process observation in distributed automation systems projects*. Paper presented at the 18th European System and Software Process Improvement and Innovation (EuroSPI 2011) Roskilde University, Denmark.

ADDITIONAL READING

Bandinelli, S., Fuggetta, A., & Ghezzi, C. (1993). Software process model evolution in the SPADE environment. *IEEE Transactions on Software Engineering, 19*(12), 1128–1144. doi:10.1109/32.249659

Basili, V., Caldiera, G., & Rombach, D. H. (1994). The goal question metric approach. In Marciniak, J. (Ed.), *Encyclopedia of software engineering*.

Biffl, S., Winkler, D., Höhn, R., & Wetzel, H. (2006). Software process improvement in Europe: Potential of the new V-Model XT and research issues. *Software Process Improvement and Practice, 11*, 229–238. doi:10.1002/spip.266

Brand, A., & Günther, G. (2009). *Collaborative engineering: Centralized engineering environment*. Paper presented at the "Product Life Live" International Conference on Product Lifecycle Management for Automation Systems (PLM), Bochum, Germany.

Chan, K. K., & Spedding, T. A. (2003). An integrated multidimensional process improvement methodology for manufacturing systems. *Computers & Industrial Engineering, 44*, 673–693. doi:10.1016/S0360-8352(03)00002-0

Chinosi, M., & Trombetta, A. (2009, 20-23 July 2009). *Modeling and validating BPMN diagrams*. Paper presented at the IEEE Conference on Commerce and Enterprise Computing (CEC '09).

Cook, J. E., Votta, L. G., & Wolf, A. L. (1998). Cost-effective analysis of in-place software processes. *IEEE Transactions on Software Engineering, 24*(8). doi:10.1109/32.707700

Cook, J. E., & Wolf, A. L. (1994, Oct 1994). *Toward metrics for process validation*. Paper presented at the 3rd International Conference on the Software Process, Los Alamitos, CA.

Farooq, A., & Dumke, R. R. (2007). Research directions in verification & validation process improvement. *SIGSOFT Software Engineering Notes, 32*(4), 3. doi:10.1145/1281421.1281425

Georgakopoulos, D., Hornick, M., & Sheth, A. (1995). An overview of workflow management: From process modeling to workflow automation infrastructure. *Distributed and Parallel Databases, 3*(2), 119–153. doi:10.1007/BF01277643

Gruber, H. (2009, 20-23 July). *Evaluation of workflow management systems*. Paper presented at the IEEE Conference on Commerce and Enterprise Computing, CEC '09.

Harris, I. G. (2006). *A coverage metric for the validation of interacting processes*. Paper presented at the Conference on Design, Automation and Test in Europe, Munich, Germany.

Heinonen, S., & Tanner, H. (2010). *Early validation of requirements in distributed product development: An industrial case study.* Paper presented at the International conference on On the move to meaningful internet systems, Hersonissos, Crete, Greece.

Hill, J. B., Pezzini, M., & Natis, Y. V. (2008). *Findings: Confusion remains regarding BPM terminologies (Vol. ID No. G00155817).* Stamford, CT: Gartner Research.

Johnson, P. (2001). *Project Hackystat: Accelerating adoption of empirically guided software development through non-disruptive, developer-centric, in-process data collection and analysis.* Honolulu, HI: Department of Information and Computer Sciences, University of Hawaii.

Ko, R. K. L., Lee, S. S. G., & Lee, E. W. (2009). Business process management (BPM) standards: A survey. *Business Process Management Journal, 15*(5). doi:10.1108/14637150910987937

LaMarr, Y., & William, E. Fravel, J. (1991). *Software independent verification and validation: A process perspective.* Paper presented at the Conference on TRI-Ada '91: Today's Accomplishments; Tomorrow's Expectations, San Jose, California, United States.

Liang, Z. (2006, 1-3 June 2006). *Research on workflow patterns based on Petri nets.* Paper presented at the IEEE Conference on Robotics, Automation and Mechatronics.

Ouyang, C., Dumas, M., ter Hofstede, A. H. M., & van der Aalst, W. M. P. (2006, 18-22 September). *From BPMN process models to BPEL web services.* Paper presented at the International Conference on Web Services (ICWS '06).

Sargent, R. G. (2008). *Verification and validation of simulation models.* Paper presented at the Proceedings of the 40th Conference on Winter Simulation, Miami, Florida.

Sommerville, I. (2007). *Software engineering* (8th ed.). Addison Wesley.

ter Hofstede, A. H., & van der Aalst, W. M. (2005). YAWL: Yet another workflow language. *Information Systems, 30*(4), 245–275. doi:10.1016/j.is.2004.02.002

Trecka, N., van der Aalst, W., & Sidorova, N. (2009, 22-25 August). *Workflow completion patterns.* Paper presented at the IEEE International Conference on Automation Science and Engineering (CASE 2009).

van der Aalst, W., Weijters, T., & Maruster, L. (2004). Workflow mining: Discovering process models from event logs. *IEEE Transactions on Knowledge and Data Engineering, 16*(9), 1128–1142. doi:10.1109/TKDE.2004.47

van der Aalst, W. M. P. (2005, 24-26 May 2005). *Process mining in CSCW systems.* Paper presented at the Computer Supported Cooperative Work in Design, 2005. Proceedings of the Ninth International Conference on.

Van Solingen, R., & Berghout, E. (1999). *The goal/question/metric method.* McGraw-Hill Education.

Wu, X. (2010, 22-24 Oct. 2010). *A goal-based migrating workflow system model.* Paper presented at the International Conference on Computer Application and System Modeling (ICCASM 2010).

KEY TERMS AND DEFINITIONS

Automation Systems Engineering: The development of industrial automated systems like power plants or production plants which involve heterogeneous engineering domains, e.g., mechanical, electrical, and software engineering.

Collaborative Engineering Environments: Environments which consist of heterogeneous engineering fields, that enable collaboration among engineering groups, supported by workflows, tools and methodologies that allow knowledge sharing and engineering activities in real time, regardless of their locations.

Engineering Service Bus (EngSB): A platform that integrates different tools, systems and steps in the software development lifecycle similar to enterprise service bus (ESB) platform but more in the engineering context.

Process Improvement: A series of actions taken by a process owner to identify, analyze and improve existing processes within an organization to meet new goals and objectives.

Process Mining: A process management technique that allows mine and analyze process data based on collected event logs.

Process Observation: An activity to collect information about running process in the systems.

Signal Change Management: A process to manage signal changes between different engineering domains.

Workflow Integration: A process or activity to integrate some workflows into one workflow.

Workflow Validation: A process of determining the degree to which a workflow model and their associated data are accurate representations of the real world from the perspective of the intended use(s).

ENDNOTES

[1] http://www.processmining.org
[2] http://www.openengsb.org
[3] http://www.bpmn.org/
[4] http://jcp.org/en/jsr/detail?id=283

Chapter 16
Impact Analysis of Web Services Substitution on Configurable Compositions

Salahdine Hachimi
Université Lyon 1, France

Noura Faci
Université Lyon 1, France

Zakaria Maamar
Zayed University, UAE

ABSTRACT

Web services substitution is a promising solution that enables process continuity of SOA-based applications associated with composite Web services (WSs). This chapter proposes an approach that assesses the impact of substitution on the composition and selects the best substitute, from a pool of substitutes, in order to reduce potential conflicts due to different ontologies with other peers in this composition, for example. Two types of impact along with their assessment metrics are defined: local (semantic/policy compatibility matching degree) and global (QoS satisfaction degree). This chapter addresses the selection issue as an optimization problem whose main objective is to minimize the efforts to put into resuming the ongoing composition under some temporal constraints. A set of experiments are conducted as a proof of concept and the findings show that our approach provides the necessary means for achieving Web services substitution with minimal disruption time.

INTRODUCTION

Service-oriented computing promotes Web services as a technology to design and develop loosely-coupled, cross-organization business applications. Depending on users' requests, several Web services are put together to provide the necessary response to these requests. This is usually known as Web services composition. In this paper, we assume ready-to-use compositions, more specifically orchestrations (e.g., (Peltz et al., 2003)), that are configurable in the sense that their Web services can be substituted with semantically

DOI: 10.4018/978-1-4666-2533-4.ch016

similar peers as long as the composition's overall functionality is maintained.

As organizations' needs and requirements change continuously, Web services may be replaced for different reasons such as better competing and reliable Web services are made available, unavailability of some due to failure, withdrawal of some without prior notice, etc. To ensure business process continuity substituting the existing Web services with others seems appealing.

Analyzing the impact of substitution on ongoing compositions (i.e., under execution) permits to determine the scope and complexity of this substitution on these compositions to avoid any major disruption to these compositions. We define impact as the set of efforts to put into resuming an ongoing composition execution due to potential conflicts that arise when substitution happens between the substitute Web service and existing peers at runtime. These conflicts might result in delaying the execution due to additional semantic matching or rejection of these peers to the substitute. The necessary time to resolve conflicts can be significant and may, also, lead into violating the user's non-functional requirements such as response time and total cost.

To the best of our knowledge, none of the existing substitution approaches evaluates this impact (Related work part). The main objective of this chapter is to illustrate how business process continuity is maintained with limited disruption due to replacing the failing Web service and resuming the ongoing composition. For this purpose, we propose the following steps: (i) define the different types of impact of Web services substitution on configurable compositions; (ii) assess each type of impact using criteria we define; (iii) recommend the most suitable substitute based on these criteria; and (iv) assess how this substitute behaves when resuming execution.

This chapter is organized as follows. The next chapter introduces the motivations behind the topic of impact analysis and suggests a literature review on this topic. Afterwards our current research initiatives on substitute recommendations based on substitution impact analysis are discussed. Prior to concluding, some future research directions are established.

BACKGROUND

This part discusses the types of impact on compositions and reviews some research initiatives on change impact analysis and Web services high-availability using replication and diversity.

Impact Identification

To smooth the substitution of Web services, we identify conflicts that can arise between the substitute Web service and existing peers in a composition. For example, there may be a need to adapt the input/output data types of the substitute so that it conforms to the pre- and post-peers' interfaces. Conflicts are due to the nature of relations (execution dependencies) that connect Web services together. Relations between two Web services ws_i and ws_j are as follows (Limthanmaphon & Zhang, 2003): (i) *prerequisite*, ws_i execution should complete before ws_j invocation such as booking service and payment service; (ii) *parallel-prerequisite*, ws_i and ws_j are invoked simultaneously but ws_j needs the results of ws_i to complete its execution such as flight booking service and hotel reservation service that waits for flight confirmation; (iii) *parallel-dependency*, ws_i and ws_j are invoked simultaneously but they may need to exchange some results at some point of the execution time such as flight booking service and hotel reservation service under budget constraints; (iv) *alternative-dependency*, ws_i and ws_j provide functionalities that achieve the same goal such as planning a journey from city x to city y but use different transport modes such as train and flight, respectively; and (v) *overlapping*, ws_i provides results that are included in ws_j such as express delivery service that offers both air and ground delivery and ground delivery service.

We look into substitution impact from two perspectives: local and global. Figure 1 shows the criteria that define substitution impact from these perspectives. These criteria are "semantic and policy matching" and "non-functional properties" that define Quality of Service (QoS). From a local perspective, substitution impact corresponds to the degree of semantic and policy matching between the substitute Web service and its direct (or interdependent) existing peers in a composition. Semantic conflicts may arise due to mismatches between Web services' interfaces (e.g., Input/Output Data). Regarding policy conflicts, they result from internal regulations of organizations that provide Web services, such as security requirements (e.g., different access privileges to resources). Figure 2 shows a set of component Web services in a composition $\{ws_1, ws_2, ws_3, and\ ws_4\}$ connected with prerequisite and/or parallel relations and a set of potential substitutes $\{ws_{31} \ldots ws_{3n}\}$ for ws_3. When ws_3 fails, local impact is calculated through semantic and policy matching analysis between these potential substitutes and w_3's pre- and post- peers before substitution happens.

From a global perspective, substitution impact corresponds to the overall satisfaction level of the user's non-functional requirements (e.g., QoS). A user might insist on some non-functional requirements (e.g., response time and result accuracy) so that some thresholds are not exceeded. Assessing this global impact would help avoid composition reconfiguration such as revisiting the selection of Web services that are already in

Figure 1. Proposed impact types of substitution on configurable compositions

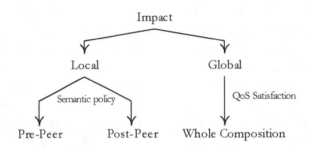

Figure 2. Substitution local impact on a configurable composition

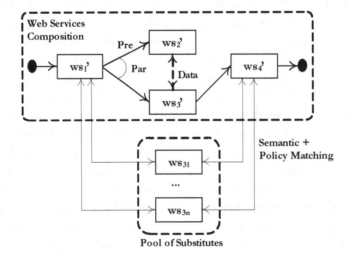

the composition. This might incur costs in terms of the time taken for reconfiguration and the degree of disruption experienced by the component Web services.

Related Work

Software Impact Analysis

Impact analysis techniques determine the potential effect of a proposed software (resp. business process) change on a part or total of a software program (resp. business logic). These techniques, broadly categorized into static and dynamic, can be performed before a modification occurs to estimate the probable costs of the proposed change, which offers some sort of a predictive cost-benefit analysis.

Static techniques rely on data acquired through semantic analysis of the program source code (Xiao et al., 2007) or software development life-cycle (Jashki et al., 2008; Menzies et al., 2011). Xiao et al. perform a cost analysis in terms of source code changes to plan when some business process adaptations will take place (Xiao et al., 2007). They develop a propagation graph for each method that needs to be changed. Dynamic techniques consider information collected from the runtime execution of the software in order to draw relevant conclusions. Such information can be gathered by brute-force execution of the program under all possible circumstances (Boukhebouze et al., 2010) or by test suites with an instrumented code base (Law & Rothermel, 2003; Orso et al., 2003). Boukhebouze et al. propose a rule change cost model to estimate the change impact considering relationships and distances between business rules (Boukhebouze et al., 2010). These rules are expressed in an Event-Condition-Action formalism extended with pre-condition and effect concepts. These concepts enable to enhance business process flexibility when some rule changes occur at runtime.

Web Services High Availability

Our literature review on Web services high-availability indicates a good number of research studies that can be broadly categorized into replication and diversity to ensure operation continuity despite failure. The first category use identical copies of Web services. However, this way of doing suffers from multiple limitations. As all copies have the same implementation code, they are subject to the same undetected design defaults like bugs. To overcome these limitations, the second category stem directly from the competition among software vendors. For the same application type, the vendors propose solutions using different hardware and software technologies.

Keidl et al. propose a flexible architecture, named *Service Globe* that provides automatic service replication (Keidl et al., 2003). When all service instances are running on heavily loaded hosts, a dispatcher generates a new instance on a host having a low workload. If no such service host is available, the dispatcher can either buffer incoming messages or reject them depending on the configuration of the dispatcher instance. Osrael et al. discuss how service replication middleware can benefit from the existing studies and technologies in object replication middleware (Osrael et al., 2007). Various problems limit the existence of these middleware such as stateful service replication that requires synchronization of the replicas' states. The same authors suggest some candidate components that should populate generalized replication architecture, including multi-cast, monitoring, replication manager, and replication protocol.

Laranjeiro and Vieira promote the use of alternative Web services that are grouped by functionality (Laranjeiro & Vieira, 2007). Each group is headed by an adapter that invokes alternative Web services using metrics such as response time and response availability. Dobson proposes a container-based approach for supporting diversity and replication in applications based on service-oriented architecture (Dobson, 2006). The container binds services available in a service marketplace. Salatge and Fabre introduce a connector-based solution for ensuring the dependability of Web Services for clients (Salatge & Fabre, 2007). Clients such as Web service providers and dependability experts specify the connector behaviors in their applications. Gorbenko et al. analyze different dependability-oriented composition models of Web services and also propose solutions guaranteeing that the overall availability and reliability of the composite system can be improved (Gorbenko et al., 2009). These models include various strategies for invoking redundant services and procedures for response adjudication.

IMPACT ANALYSIS APPROACH

Based on the aforementioned research solutions on change impact analysis, we built our approach to analyze impact of Web services substitution on ongoing compositions. Indeed, the proposed approach relies on a predictive cost-benefit analysis through different metrics that are used to assess the substitution impact from local and global perspectives.

The impact analysis approach is defined with three phases (Figure 3): assess the local impact of substitution on an ongoing configurable composition by evaluating the compatibility matching degree D for each potential substitute; assess the global impact of substitution on this composition by computing a QoS satisfaction degree S for each potential substitute; and compute a recommendation degree R based on the outcomes of the previous phases in order to advise on the best substitute.

In the following let us consider $WS'=\{ws_1, ws_2,...\}$ a set of component Web services in a composition and $WS=\{\{ws_{11}, ws_{12},...\}, \emptyset,... \}$ a set of potential substitutes for each ws' in WS', where the mth element $\emptyset$ in WS means the absence of substitutes for ws_m.

Local Impact Assessment Phase

This phase assesses the compatibility matching degree D between a potential substitute (ws) and the pre- and post- direct peers to the failing Web service (ws'). This degree uses the similarity between the semantic meaning of ws's inputs/outputs with those of the pre- and post- direct peers to ws'. D, also, takes into account policy matching to measure the compatibility between

Figure 3. Impact analysis approach overview

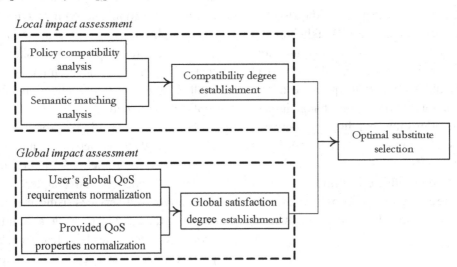

ws's internal regulations and these peers. Thus, we break down this phase in three steps: *semantic matching analysis*, *policy compatibility analysis*, and *compatibility degree establishment*.

Let ws'_i be the failing Web service, R (ws'_i) = {R (ws'_i, ws'_{i-1}), R (ws'_i, ws'_{i+1})} a set of relationships that ws'_i has with its peers, R (ws'_i, ws'_{i-1}) a set of relationships between ws'_i and the pre- direct peer ws'_{i-1}, and R (ws'_i, ws'_{i+1}) with the post- direct peer ws'_{i+1}.

Semantic Matching Analysis Step

This step depends on the functional and non-functional of a Web service (or profile) and calls for a matching analysis of these properties in term of compatibility. A Web service's profile is decomposed into five categories: Preconditions (P), Inputs (I), Outputs (O), Effects (E), and QoS. Many approaches deal with Web services matching using the concepts in their respective profiles. Paolucci et al. define four levels of semantic matching between two concepts c_1 and c_2 described in the same ontology as follows (Paolucci et al., 2002): (i) *exact*, if c_1 and c_2 are the same; (ii) *plug in*, if c_1 is more general than c_2; (iii) *subsume*, if c_1 is more specific than c_2; and (iv) *fail*, if none of the above conditions is satisfied. These levels are ranked as *exact* < *plug in* < *subsume* < *fail* where < is the importance level given to a matching level compared to others.

In our approach, matching degree between two Web services corresponds to the number of *exact* and *plug in* relationships between the concepts of the I/O categories in their profiles. These relationships maintain the functionality semantics of the no longer available Web service by the potential substitute in the ongoing composition and, at the same time, ensure its compatibility with the pre- and post-peers. It, also, is important to note that Web services' I/O refer to concepts in a shared ontology.

To check the semantic compatibility between the potential substitute ws and its pre- (resp. post)

peer ws'_{i-1} (resp. ws'_{i+1}), we look into the relationships that the failing Web service ws'_i has with ws'_{i-1}. In case of *parallel-dependency* relationship, the matching degree is established between the inputs and outputs of ws'_{i-1} (resp. ws'_{i+1}) with those of ws, as proposed by Paolucci et al. (Paolucci et al., 2002). In case of other relationships, this degree is established between the outputs of ws'_{i-1} with the inputs of ws. Based on matching results (i.e., *exact*, *plug in*, *subsumes*, or *fail*), the number of *exact* and *plug in* matchings (resp. $Match_{exact}$ and $Match_{plug}$), and the total number of matching results ($Match_{total}$) are calculated.

Policy Compatibility Analysis Step

Policy compatibility analysis checks the compatibility between the policies of each potential substitute with the pre- and post-peers. It relies on Sheng et al.'s approach (Sheng et al., 2009) to check compatibility between different heterogeneous Web services' policies. Sheng et al. develop an executable formal model of policy languages using the Vienna Development Method (VDM++). For example, let's assume that *FlightBookingWS*, which offers low-cost flights, is part of a composition in which it is composed with a *CarRentalWS*. *FlightBookingWS* has a policy for *CarRentalWS*s (cost<70USD). At some point, *CarRentalWS* fails and should be substituted. There are two potential substitutes: *CarRentalWS$_1$* (cost > 80USD) and *CarRentalWS$_2$* (cost < 50USD). In fact, these policies are most of the time specified in different policy languages. The compatibility checking results show that *CarRentalWS$_2$* is compatible with *FlightBookingWS*. This is relevant to our work as it is important to avoid, as much as possible, potential policy conflicts when substitution happens.

Compatibility Degree Establishment Step

Let *PWS* (ws_i) be the set of potential substitutes of ws_i that has compatible policies with the pre-

and post-direct peers' policies. The compatibility matching degree $D(ws_i)$ for each potential substitute ws_i depends on policy and semantic matching. Two factors (α, β) are also used to specify whether *exact* matching should be privileged over *plug in* matching or *vice-versa*, depending on existing relationships. We define α and β as follows:

- $\alpha \geq \beta$: if there are only *prerequisite, parallel-prerequisite, parallel-dependency* and/or *substitute* relationships, *exact* matching over *plug in* matching is privileged in order to address semantic conflicts.
- $\alpha < \beta$: if there is at least one *overlapping* relationship, *plug in* matching over *exact* matching is privileged in order to ensure that the potential substitute returns a subset of results provided by the post-peer or that the pre-peer returns a subset of results provided by the potential substitute.

To take into consideration whether the policies are compatible or not, $D(ws_i)$ corresponds to the square root of the ratio $(\alpha * \text{Match}_{\text{exact}} + \beta * \text{Match}_{\text{plug}})$ and $\text{Match}_{\text{total}}$ in case of $ws_i \in PWS(ws_{i'})$ in order to enhance the compatibility between $ws_{i'}$ and ws_{ij}; otherwise $D(ws_i)$ corresponds to the square of the ratio $(\alpha * \text{Match}_{\text{exact}} + \beta * \text{Match}_{\text{plug}})$ and $\text{Match}_{\text{total}}$ in order to reduce this compatibility.

Global Impact Assessment Phase

This phase assesses the global satisfaction degree of the user's QoS requirements associated with a whole composition that contains some of potential substitutes. This degree defines the global impact of substitution. We adapt Taher et al.'s approach to compute the global satisfaction degree (Taher et al., 2005). Taher et al. propose a matchmaking algorithm to find the best Web service that meets a user's QoS requirements. We also rely on prediction and planning approaches to evaluate a composition's QoS properties (Limthanmaphon & Zhang, 2003).

We thus break down this phase into three steps: *normalize user's global QoS requirements j* $(\{U_j\})$, *normalize the QoS properties provided by a Web service composition i* (CQ_i), and *establish the global satisfaction degree* (S_i).

Let $\{U_j\}$ be the set of user's global QoS requirements, $\{CQ_i\}$ the set of QoS properties provided by all possible Web service compositions in case of substitution, and $\{S_i\}$ the set of the satisfaction degrees associated with these compositions. U_j is described as a tuple (d_j, v_j, z_j) where d_j and v_j denote the description and value of the jth QoS property respectively, and z_j specifies if v_j should be either minimized $(z_j=0)$ or maximized $(z_j=1)$. A possible composition consists of the ongoing composition in which the failing Web service is replaced by a potential substitute. We also assume that n potential substitutes induce n possible compositions.

User's Global QoS Requirements Normalization Step

We represent $\{U_j\}$ as follows:

$$U = \begin{bmatrix} d_1 & v_1 & z_1 \\ d_2 & v_2 & z_2 \\ \cdots & \cdots & \cdots \\ d_m & v_m & z_m \end{bmatrix},$$

where m corresponds to $|\{U_j\}|$.

Provided QoS Properties Normalization Step

We represent $\{CQ_i\}$ as follows:

$$CQ = \begin{bmatrix} v_{11} & v_{12} & \cdots & v_{1m} \\ v_{21} & v_{22} & \cdots & v_{2m} \\ \cdots & \cdots & \cdots & \cdots \\ v_{n1} & v_{n2} & \cdots & v_{nm} \end{bmatrix},$$

Table 1. Component Web services details

Component Web services	Inputs	Outputs	Policies
FlightBookingWS	departureAirport:City destinationAirport:City departureDate:Date	flightOffer:AirReservation	flightCost≤150 hotelCost≤80
HotelBookingWS	checkInDate:Date checkOutDate:Date location:City	hotelOffer:RoomReservation	hotelCost≤80 rentCost≤60
CarRentalWS	pickUpDate:Date returnDate:Date returnLocation:Address pickUpLocation:Address	rentOffer:CarReservation	rentCost≤60
WeatherForcastWS	zipCode:PostalCode	temperature: Temperature	

where m and n correspond to $|\{U_j\}|$ and $|\{CQ_i\}|$, respectively. We normalize CQ as shown in Box 1.

Global Satisfaction Degree Step

We define $\{S_i\}$ as follows:

$$S = \begin{bmatrix} d(NormU_2, NormCQ_1) \\ \cdots \\ d(NormU_2, NormCQ_n) \end{bmatrix},$$

where n corresponds to $|\{CQ_i\}|$ and d is the distance between the two vectors $NormU_2$ and $NormCQ_j$. We advocate for the Euclidean distance dues to its simplicity and low computational costs as follows:

$$d(NormU_2, NormCQ_i) = \\ \sqrt{\sum_{k=1}^{m} (NormU_{k2} - NormCQ_{ik})^2}$$

Optimal Substitute Selection Phase

This phase establishes a recommendation degree using the Euclidean distance between all potential substitutes and an optimal substitute in order to recommend a substitute that minimizes the disruption time based on the local and global impact analysis.

Let M be the matrix that represents the compatibility matching and global satisfaction degrees along with the composition's execution times (ET) for each potential substitute:

$$M = \begin{bmatrix} D(ws_1) & S_1 & ET_1 \\ D(ws_2) & S_2 & ET_2 \\ \cdots & \cdots & \cdots \\ D(ws_n) & S_n & ET_n \end{bmatrix}$$

We associate the optimal Web service ($OptWS$) with the following characteristics: (i) has the highest compatibility matching degree among a pool of potential substitutes (D_{max}); and (ii) has the lowest satisfaction degree (S_{min}) and execution time among the possible compositions (ET_{min}).

As these three criteria have different measurements, we normalize M and $OptWS$ by using maximization (Equation 2) for D and minimization (Equation 1) for S and ET. We minimize ET since the main objective is to minimize the disruption time as per Equation 1. This minimizes the time needed to resolve the conflicts that may arise at runtime. The next step is to compute a recommendation degree R using the Euclidean distance between the optimal substitute $OptWS$ and other substitutes M as shown in Box 2.

Box 1.

$$NormCQ = \begin{bmatrix} NormCQ_{11} & NormCQ_{12} & \ldots & NormCQ_{1m} \\ \ldots & \ldots & \ldots & \ldots \\ \ldots & \ldots & \ldots & \ldots \\ NormCQ_{n1} & NormCQ_{n2} & \ldots & NormCQ_{nm} \end{bmatrix},$$

where

$$NormCQ_{ij} = \begin{bmatrix} MinNorm\left(v_{ij}\right) & if\, U_{j3} = 0 \\ MaxNorm\left(v_{ij}\right) & otherwise \end{bmatrix}$$

$$MinNorm\left(v_{ij}\right) = \begin{bmatrix} \dfrac{\max_{k=1,n}\left(v_{kj}\right) - v_{ij}}{\max_{k=1,n}\left(v_{kj}\right) - \min_{k=1,n}\left(v_{kj}\right)} & if\, \max_{k=1,n}\left(v_{kj}\right) - \min_{k=1,n}\left(v_{kj}\right) \neq 0 \\ 1 & otherwise \end{bmatrix} \quad (1)$$

$$MaxNorm\left(v_{ij}\right) = \begin{bmatrix} \dfrac{v_{ij} - \min_{k=1,n}\left(v_{kj}\right)}{\max_{k=1,n}\left(v_{kj}\right) - \min_{k=1,n}\left(v_{kj}\right)} & if\, \max_{k=1,n}\left(v_{kj}\right) - \min_{k=1,n}\left(v_{kj}\right) \neq 0 \\ 1 & otherwise \end{bmatrix} \quad (2)$$

The substitute with the minimal distance will be recommended as the one that avoids, as much as possible, conflicts that could arise at runtime. At the same time, it is the one that minimizes disruption time. As a result, designers would be able to smooth Web services substitution by reducing the disruption time in such a way that takes into consideration both the local and global impacts of substitution on configurable compositions.

EXPERIMENTATION

As a proof-of-concept, a set of experiments were carried out. The illustrative scenario is a travel

Table 2. User's QoS requirements

	Availability (%) (A)	Cost(USD) (C)	Response Time(seconds) (RT)	Relevance(%) (R)
Value	90	50	250	90
Choice	maximize	minimize	Minimize	Maximize

Box 2.

$$R\left(ws_i, OptWS\right) = \sqrt{\left(D\left(ws_i\right) - D_{max}\right)^2 + \left(S_i - S_{min}\right)^2 + \left(ET_i - ET_{min}\right)^2}$$

planning system represented as a composition of four Web services (Figure 4): *FlightBookingWS, HotelBookingWS, CarRentalWS,* and *WeatherForcastWS*. Only a *Prerequisite* relationship between the component Web services exists as there is no *Overlapping* relationship between them; i.e., α ≥ β. Let's assume that the execution time of this composition is 150s.

Figure 5 shows a fragment of the travel ontology that represents four domains: hotel, car, flight, and weather. I/O parameters of the component Web services and their substitutes refer to concepts included in this ontology.

Table 1 contains the component Web services' profiles along with their I/O parameters and cost of using a Web service and its successive peer.

Table 2 shows a user's QoS requirements to satisfy whether substitution happens or not.

After failing *HotelBookingWS* a substitute needs to be identified. The pool of potential substitutes is *hb1WS, hb2WS, hb3WS, hb4WS, hb5WS, hb6WS, hb7WS,* and *hb8WS*.

Table 3 contains details on these substitutes' profiles such as I/O parameters, policies, execution time of the ongoing composition using each substitute calculated by the system, and overall QoS properties' values.

Figure 4. Travel planning system composition

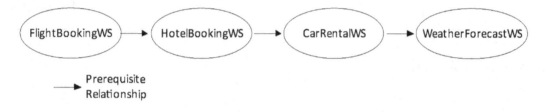

Figure 5. Fragment of the travel ontology

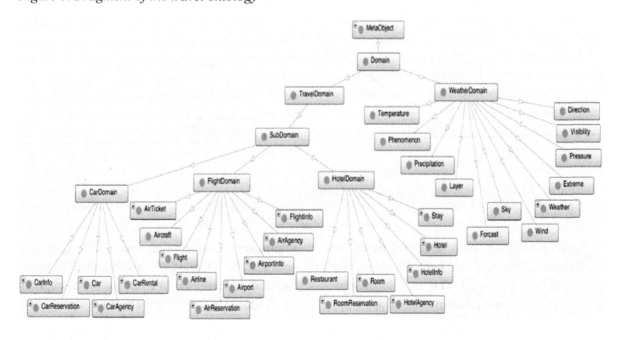

Table 3. Hotel booking potential substitutes details

Substitutes	Inputs	Outputs	ET (seconds)	QoS	Policies
hb1WS	DateRange Location	Reservation	250	A=88;C=47;RT=305(NC);R=80	hotelCost≥85 rentCost≤50
hb2WS	Date Date Country	Stay	205	A=78;C=45;RT=330(C);R=88	hotelCost≤70 rentCost≤50
hb3WS	HolidayDate HolidayDate Address	RoomReservation	180	A=92;C=42; RT=292 (C); R=92	hotelCost≤45 rentCost≤55
hb4WS	DateRange Address	RoomReservation	235	A=0.90;C=35;RT=290(NC); R=86	hotelCost≥85 rentCost≤90
hb5WS	Date Date City	Reservation	220	A=80;C=65;RT=320(C);R=75	hotelCost≤65 rentCost≤45
hb6WS	HolidayDate HolidayDate City	RoomReservation	285	A=0.65;C=32;RT=340(C);R=72	hotelCost≤45 rentCost≤55
hb7WS	DateRange Address	Stay	255	A=85;C=61;RT=288(NC);R=0.89	hotelCost≥90 rentCost≤90
hb8WS	Date Date City	Reservation	197	A=95;C=51; RT=285(C); R=93	hotelCost≤69 rentCost≤59

Figure 6. Experimentation results

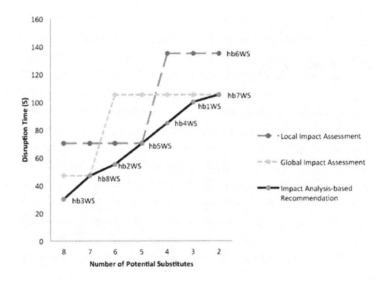

Three recommendation strategies based on local impact analysis, global impact analysis, and both of them are adopted. This experimentation aims to show how our recommendation approach minimizes the disruption time while ensuring semantic, policy, and QoS satisfaction (Figure 6). Simulation permitted to compare the disruption time induced by selecting the best substitute when taking into consideration a certain recommendation strategy.

First, the experiments start with a pool that contains the eight potential substitutes. For each run our impact analysis-based approach recommends the best substitute that is removed from the pool of substitutes. Figure 6 shows that the local impact analysis-based strategy ends-up selecting a substitute that, most of the time, guarantees the semantic and policy compatibilities but does not necessary satisfy the user's QoS requirements. Contrarily the global impact analysis-based strategy ends-up selecting a substitute that satisfies, most of the time, the user's QoS requirements but does not necessarily guarantee the semantic and policy compatibilities. However, the third strategy reveals better results than the previous such as the disruption time is always minimal. Our impact analysis approach thus selects the best substitute as it considers both semantic/policy compatibility and overall QoS satisfaction while minimizing the disruption time.

CONCLUSION

This chapter presented an impact analysis approach when Web services substitution happens in an ongoing composition. This approach addresses the issue of how to select the most appropriate substitute. It is formulated as an optimization problem where the main objective is to minimize the disruption time under some functional and non-functional constraints in term of impact on a Web services composition. We identify two types of impact and define their respective assessment metrics as follows: (i) local impact that corresponds to semantic/policy compatibility matching degree; and (ii) global impact that corresponds to QoS satisfaction degree. Based on these assessments, a recommendation strategy was developed to select the substitute that minimizes disruption time.

In term of future work, we intend to explore the following conceptual issues: (i) how to evaluate substitution impact based on the relationships between pre- and post- direct and indirect peers; and (ii) as the impact analysis might be costly in certain circumstances, how to find a balance between Web service substitution on ongoing compositions and reconfiguration of these compositions.

REFERENCES

Boukhebouze, M., Amghar, Y., Benharkat, N., & Maamar, Z. (2010). A rule-based approach to model and verify flexible business processes. *International Journal of Business Process Integration and Management, 5*(4), 287–307. doi:10.1504/IJBPIM.2011.043389

Dobson, G., Hall, S., & Sommerville, I. (2005). *A container-based approach to fault-tolerance in service-oriented architectures*. In International Conference of Software Engineering, Saint Louis, USA.

Gorbenko, A., Kharchenko, V., & Romanovsky, A. (2009). Using inherent service redundancy and diversity to ensure web services dependability. In *Methods, Models and Tools for Fault Tolerance, Lecture Notes in Computer Science*.

Hua, X., Jin, G., & Ying, Z. (2007). *Supporting change impact analysis for service oriented business applications*. In International Workshop on Systems Development in SOA Environments, Minneapolis, USA.

Jashki, M.-A., Zafarani, R., & Bagheri, E. (2008). Towards a more efficient static software change impact analysis method. In Workshop on Program Analysis for Software Tools and Engineering, Atlanta, USA.

Keidl, M., Seltzsam, S., & Kemper, A. (2003). *Reliable web service execution and deployment in dynamic environments*. In Technologies for E-Services, Berlin, Germany.

Law, J., & Rothermel, G. (2003). *Incremental dynamic impact analysis for evolving software systems*. In International Symposium on Software Reliability Engineering, Washington, DC, USA.

Limthanmaphon, B., & Zhang, Y. (2003). *Web service composition with case-based reasoning*. In Australasian Database Conference, Adelaide, Australia.

Menzies, T., Butcher, A., Marcus, A., Zimmermann, T., & Cok, D. R. (2011). *Local vs. global models for effort estimation and defect prediction*. In International Conference on Automated Software Engineering, Lawrence, USA.

Orso, A., Apiwattanapong, T., & Harrold, M. J. (2003). *Leveraging field data for impact analysis and regression testing*. In European Conference on Software Engineering, Helsinki, Finland.

Osrael, J., Froihofer, L., Weghofer, M., & Göschka, K. M. (2007). *Axis2-based replication middleware for web services*. In International Conference on Web Services, Salt Lake City, USA.

Paolucci, M., Kawamura, T., Payne, T. R., & Sycara, K. P. (2002). *Semantic matching of web services capabilities*. In International Semantic Web Conference, Sardinia, Italy.

Peltz, C. (2003). Web services orchestration and choreography. *The Computer Journal, 36*(10).

Salatge, N., & Fabre, J.-C. (2007). *Fault tolerance connectors for unreliable web services*. In International Conference on Dependable Systems and Networks, Edinburgh, UK.

Sheng, Q. Z., Yu, J., Maamar, Z., Jiang, W., & Li, X. (2009). *Compatibility checking of heterogeneous web service policies using VDM++*. In Congress on Services – I, LA, USA.

Taher, L., El Khatib, H., & Basha, R. (2005). *A framework and QoS matchmaking algorithm for dynamic web services selection*. In International Conference on Innovations in Information Technology, Dubai, UAE.

Vieira, M., & Laranjeiro, N. (2007). *Comparing web services performance and recovery in the presence of faults*. In International Conference on Web Services, Salt Lake City, USA.

KEY TERMS AND DEFINITIONS

Composite Web Service: Composition targets users' requests that cannot be satisfied by any single, available Web service, whereas a composite Web service obtained by combining available Web services may be used. Several specification languages to compose Web services exist for example WS-BPEL (de facto standard), WSCDL, and XLANG. A composite Web service could be built either proactively or reactively. The former is an off-line process that gathers available component Web services in-advance to form a composite Web service. This one is pre-compiled and ready for execution upon users' requests. The latter creates a composite Web service on-the-fly upon users' requests. Because of the on-the fly property, a dedicated module is in charge of identifying the needed component Web services, making them collaborate, tracking their execution, and resolving their conflicts if they arise.

Fault Tolerance: Any type of software application is prone to *failures* due to various types of *faults* such as software bugs and machine crashes that happen unexpectedly. Since it is impractical to predict the potential occurrence of a fault, a widely used strategy consists of duplicating the critical components of the software application. The ability of this application to continue operation despite component failure is referred to as *Fault Tolerance* (FT). Duplication is usually achieved through either replication or diversity. Replication consists of distributing a component's copies over a network. However, this way of doing suffers from multiple limitations. As all copies have the same implementation code, they are all automatically subject to the same undetected design faults like bugs. Moreover, replication is costly in term of resource consumption since all copies need to run or be maintained simultaneously. Diversity stems directly from the competition among software vendors. For the same type of application, vendors develop their own software solution using different hardware and software technologies. Regarding Web services there is a consensus that despite their heterogeneity, their functionalities are sufficiently well defined and homogeneous enough to allow for market competition to happen.

Fault: A *fault* is defined as an abnormal condition or defect at the component, equipment, or sub-system level which may lead to a *failure*. Faults cycle between dormant and active states, and a service failure occurs when a fault becomes active (through the application/use of some input) and is propagated beyond the service interface (Avizienis et al.). For instance, halt failure occurs when the system either stops emitting messages to clients like no more "I'm alive" (heartbeat) messages or fails to respond to requests due to machine crashes or bugs.

Impact Analysis: Impact analysis is the activity of analysing a change in software (e.g., composite Web service) and assessing the consequences it may have, including necessary modifications to make. Thus, it can be used as a very important change control tool such as selecting the most appropriate substitute in case of Web service failure. Furthermore, the consequences may include aspects of time and resources.

Service-Oriented Architecture (SOA): SOA is an architecture style that builds on loosely coupled, interoperable and composable components or software agents called services. Services have well-defined interfaces based standard protocols (usually web-services but most definitions mention that it is not the only possible implementation) as well as Quality of Service (QoS) attributes (or policies) on how these interfaces can be used by Service Consumers. SOA definitions mentions the basic communication pattern for SOA is request/reply but many definitions also talk about asynchronous communications as well.

Web Service Availability: Availability is the probability that a Web service is first, accessible and then, operational to accept users' requests. As Web services are the building blocks for composite Web service, this latter fails in most trivial cases because of the building blocks are unavailable. The availability of a Web service is thus influenced by the server and by the networking media.

Web Service Substitution: Substitution of Web services is closely related with composition and important to fault-tolerance of composite Web services. After a composite Web service assembled from a repository of component Web services has been deployed, one or more constituents of the composite Web service may become unavailable. Hence there arises a need to replace such components with other similar components from the repository while maintaining the overall functionality of the composite service. Among the candidate substitutions that offer the same or similar functionality, the problem is to select the most appropriate ones based functional (e.g., inputs) and/or QoS attributes.

Web Service: It is "*a software application identified by a URI, whose interfaces and binding are capable of being defined, described, and discovered by XML artifacts, and supports direct interactions with other software applications using XML-based messages via Internet-based applications*" (W3C). A Web service implements a functionality (e.g., Book Order and Forecast Weather) that users and other peers invoke by submitting appropriate messages to this Web service. The life cycle of a Web service could be summarized with five stages namely description, publication, discovery, invocation, and composition. Briefly, providers describe their Web services and publish them on dedicated registries. Potential consumers (i.e., requesters) interact with these registries to discover relevant Web services, so they could invoke them. In case the discovery fails, i.e., requests cannot be satisfied by any single Web service, the available Web services may be composed to satisfy the consumer's request.

314

Compilation of References

Adamic, L. A., Zhang, J., Bakshy, E., & Ackerman, M. S. (2008). Knowledge sharing and Yahoo Answers: Everybody knows something. In J. Huai, R. Chen, H. W. Hon, Y. Liu, W. Y. Ma, A. Tomkins, & X. Zhang (Eds.), *Proceedings of the 17th International World Wide Web Conference*, Beijing, China, (pp. 665-674). New York, NY: ACM.

Adams, D. (2005). *The hitchhiker's guide to the galaxy*. New York, NY: Del Rey Books.

Adomavicius, G., Sankaranarayanan, R., Sen, S., & Tuzhilin, A. (2005). Incorporating contextual information in recommender systems using a multidimensional approach. *ACM Transactions on Information Systems*, *23*(1), 103–145. doi:10.1145/1055709.1055714

Adomavicius, G., & Tuzhilin, A. (2005). Toward the next generation of recommender systems: A survey of the state-of-the-art and possible extensions. *IEEE Transactions on Knowledge and Data Engineering*, *17*(6), 734–749. doi:10.1109/TKDE.2005.99

Agarwal, A., Mustafa, M., & Pandya, A. S. (2006, May). *QOS driven network-on-chip design for real time systems* (pp. 1291-1295). Ottawa, Canada: IEEE CCECE/CCGEI.

Agarwal, A., Mustafa, M., Shankar, R., Pandya, A. S., & Lho, Y. (2007, April). A deadlock free Router design for network on chip architecture. *Journal of Korea Institute of Maritime Information and Communication Sciences*, *11*(4), 696–706.

Agichtein, E., Castillo, C., Donato, D., Gionis, A., & Mishne, G. (2008). Finding high-quality content in social media. In *Proceedings of the International Conference on Web Search and Web Data Mining*, California, (pp. 183-194). New York, NY: ACM.

Agichtein, E., Liu, Y., & Bian, J. (2009). Modeling information seeker satisfaction in community question answering. *Transactions on Knowledge Discovery from Data*, *3*(2), 10:1-10:27.

Ahronovitz, M. (2010). *Cloud computing use cases, White Paper Version 4.0*. Retrieved, June 20, 2011, from http://openCloud manifesto.org/Cloud _Computing_Use_Cases_Whitepaper-4_0.pdf

Ajima, Y., Sumimoto, S., & Shimizu, T. (2009, November). Tofu: A 6d Mesh/Torus interconnect for exascale computers. *Computer*, *42*(11), 36–40. doi:10.1109/MC.2009.370

Albrecht, C. C., Dean, D. L., & Hansen, J. V. (2005). Marketplace and technology standards for b2b e-commerce: progress, challenges, and the state of the art. *Information & Management*, *42*(6), 865–875. doi:10.1016/j.im.2004.09.003

Alexandrov, A., Battré, D., Ewen, S., Heimel, M., Hueske, F., & Kao, O. (1625-1628). … Warneke, D. (2010). Massively parallel data analysis with PACTs on Nephele. *Proceedings of the VLDB Endowment*, *3*(2).

Alicherry, M., Bhatia, R., & Li, E. (2006). Joint channel assignment and routing for throughput optimization in multiradio wireless mesh networks. *IEEE Journal on Selected Areas in Communications*, *24*(11), 1960–1971. doi:10.1109/JSAC.2006.881641

Allalouf, M., & Shavitt, Y. (2008). Centralized and distributed algorithms for routing and weighted max-min fair bandwidth allocation. *IEEE/ACM Transactions on Networking*, *16*(5), 1015–1024. doi:10.1109/TNET.2007.905605

Al-Sharawneh, J., & Williams, M.-A. (2009). A social network approach in Semantic Web services selection using follow the leader behavior. In *Proceedings of the 13th Enterprise Distributed Object Computing Conference Workshops* (EDOCW'2009), Auckland, New Zealand, (pp. 310-319).

Amazon Web Services, Inc. (2011a). *Amazon Web Services*. Retrieved August 26, 2011, from http://aws.amazon.com/

Amazon Web Services, Inc. (2011b). *Amazon elastic MapReduce*. Retrieved August 26, 2011, from http://aws.amazon.com/elasticmapreduce/

Amazon Web Services, Inc. (2011c). *Amazon elastic Compute Cloud (Amazon EC2)*. Retrieved August 26, 2011, from http://aws.amazon.com/ec2/

Amazon Web Services, Inc. (2011d). *Elastic block storage (EBS)*. Retrieved August 26, 2011, from http://aws.amazon.com/ebs/

Amazon Web Services, Inc. (2011e). In *Amazon simple storage service (Amazon S3)*. Retrieved August 26, 2011, from http://aws.amazon.com/s3/

Android. (2011). *Website*. Retrieved October, 2011, from http://www.android.com

Armbrust, M., Fox, A., Griffith, R., Joseph, A. D., Katz, H. R., & Konwinski, A. (2010). A view of cloud computing. *Communications of the ACM, 53*(4), 50–58. doi:10.1145/1721654.1721672

ASTM. (2002). *E2313-02: Standard specification for telecommunications and information exchange between roadside and vehicle systems - 5 GHz band dedicated short range communications (DSRC) medium access control (MAC) and physical layer (PHY) specifications*. ASTM.

Athanasiou, G., Korakis, T., Ercetin, O., & Tassiulas, L. (2009). Cross-layer framework for association control in wireless mesh networks. *IEEE Transactions on Mobile Computing, 8*(1), 65–80. doi:10.1109/TMC.2008.75

Athanasopoulos, G., Tsalgatidou, A., & Pantazoglou, M. (2006). Interoperability among heterogeneous services. In *International Conference on Services Computing* (pp. 174-181). IEEE Computer Society Press.

Augonnet, C., Thibault, S., Namyst, R., & Wacrenier, P. A. (2009). Starpu: A unified platform for task scheduling on heterogeneous multicore architectures. In *Euro-Par '09: Proceedings of the 15th International Euro-Par Conference on Parallel Processing* (pp. 863–874).

Ausiello, G., Crescenzi, P., Gambosi, G., Kann, V., Marchetti-Spaccamela, A., & Protasi, M. (2003). *Complexity and approximation*. Berlin, Germany: Springer-Verlag.

Baek Kim, J., & Segev, A. (2005). A web services-enabled marketplace architecture for negotiation process management. *Decision Support Systems, 40*(1), 71–87. doi:10.1016/j.dss.2004.04.005

Bagchi, A., Chaudhary, A., & Kolman, P. (2005). Short length Menger's theorem and reliable optical routing. *Theoretical Computer Science, 339*(2), 315–332. doi:10.1016/j.tcs.2005.03.009

Bai, F., & Krishnan, H. (2006). Reliability analysis of DSRC wireless communication for vehicle safety applications. *Intelligent Transportation Systems Conference* (pp. 355-362). Washington, DC: IEEE Computer Society. doi: 10.1109/ITSC.2006.1706767

Balabanovic, M., & Shoham, Y. (1997). Fab: Content-based, collaborative recommendation. *Communications of the ACM, 40*(3), 66–72. doi:10.1145/245108.245124

Barker, A., Walton, C. D., & Robertson, D. (2009). Choreographing web services. *IEEE Transactions on Services Computing, 2*, 152–166. doi:10.1109/TSC.2009.8

Barragáns-Martínez, A. B., Costa-Montenegro, E., Burguillo, J. C., Rey-López, M., Mikic-Fonte, F. A., & Peleteiro, A. (2010). A hybrid content-based and item-based collaborative filtering approach to recommend TV programs enhanced with singular value decomposition. *Information Sciences, 180*(22), 4290–4311. doi:10.1016/j.ins.2010.07.024

Barragáns-Martínez, A. B., Rey-López, M., Costa-Montenegro, E., Mikic-Fonte, F. A., Burguillo, J. C., & Peleteiro, A. (2010). Exploiting social tagging in a web 2.0 recommender system. *Internet Computing, 14*(6), 23–30. doi:10.1109/MIC.2010.104

Barros, A., Dumas, M., & Oaks, P. (2005). A critical overview of the web services choreography description language (WS-CDL). *BP Trends*.

Barros, A., Dumas, M., & Oaks, P. (2006). Standards for web services choreography and orchestration: Status and perspectives. In *BPM 2005 International Workshops, BPI, BPD, ENEI, BPRM, WSCOBPM, BPS, Revised Selected Papers,* Nancy, France, September 5, 2005 (Vol. 3812, pp. 61–74). Springer.

Basu, S., & Bultan, T. (2011). Choreography conformance via synchronizability. In *Proceedings of the 20th International Conference on World Wide Web* (pp. 795 804). New York, NY: ACM. Retrieved from http://doi.acm.org/10.1145/1963405.1963516

Battré, D., Ewen, S., Hueske, F., Kao, O., Markl, V., & Warneke, D. (2010). Nephele/PACTs: A programming model and execution framework for web-scale analytical processing. In J. M. Hellerstein, S. Chaudhuri, & M. Rosenblum (Eds.), In *Proceedings of the 1st ACM Symposium on Cloud Computing* (pp. 119-130). ACM.

Battré, D., Hovestadt, M., Lohrmann, B., Stanik, A., & Warneke, D. (2010). Detecting bottlenecks in parallel DAG-based data flow programs. In *Proceedings of the 2010 IEEE Workshop on Many-Task Computing on Grids and Supercomputers* (pp. 1-10). IEEE.

Beeferman, D., & Berger, A. (2000). Agglomerative clustering of a search engine query log. In *Proceedings of the 6th ACM International Conference on Knowledge Discovery and Data Mining,* Massachusetts, United States (pp. 406-416). New York, NY: ACM.

Benatallah, B., Sheng, Q. Z., & Dumas, M. (2003). The self-serve environment for web services composition. *IEEE Internet Computing, 7*(1), 40–48. doi:10.1109/MIC.2003.1167338

Bengtsson, M., & Kock, S. (2000). Coopetition in business networks to cooperate and compete simultaneously. *Industrial Marketing Management, 29*(5), 411–426. doi:10.1016/S0019-8501(99)00067-X

Bentahar, J., Maamar, Z., Benslimane, D., & Thiran, P. (2007). An argumentation framework for communities of web services. *IEEE Intelligent Systems, 22*(6), 75–83. doi:10.1109/MIS.2007.99

Bentahar, J., Maamar, Z., Benslimane, D., Thiran, P., & Subramanian, S. (2008). Agent-based communities of web services: An argumentation-driven approach. *Service Oriented Computing and Applications, 2*(4), 219–238. doi:10.1007/s11761-008-0033-4

Berger, A., Caruana, R., Cohn, D., Freitag, D., & Mittal, V. (2000). Bridging the lexical chasm: statistical approaches to answer-finding. In N. J. Belkin, P. Ingwersen, & M. K. Leong (Eds.), *Proceedings of the 23rd ACM International Conference on Research and Development in Information Retrieval*, Athens, Greece (pp. 192-199). New York, NY: ACM.

Berners-Lee, T. (1999). *Weaving the web: The original design and ultimate destiny of the World Wide Web by its inventor.* New York, NY: HarperCollins Publishers.

Bertsekas, D., & Gallagher, R. (1992). *Data networks.* Englewood Cliffs, NJ: Prentice- Hall.

Beynon, M., Ferreira, R., Kurc, T. M., Sussman, A., & Saltz, J. H. (2000). DataCutter: Middleware for filtering very large scientific datasets on archival storage systems. In *IEEE Symposium on Mass Storage Systems* (pp.119–134).

Bhandari, R. (1999). *Survivable networks: Algorithms for diverse routing.* Boston, MA: Kluwer Academic Publishers.

Bian, J., Liu, Y., Agichtein, E., & Zha, H. (2008a). A few bad votes too many? Towards robust ranking in social media. In *Proceedings of the 4th International Workshop on Adversarial Information Retrieval on the Web*, Beijing, China (pp. 53-60). New York, NY: ACM.

Bian, J., Liu, Y., Agichtein, E., & Zha, H. (2008b). Finding the right facts in the crowd: Factoid question answering over social media. In *Proceeding of the 17th International Conference on World Wide Web*, Beijing, China (pp. 467-476). New York, NY: ACM.

Bian, J., Liu, Y., Zhou, D., Agichtein, E., & Zha, H. (2009). Learning to recognize reliable users and content in social media with coupled mutual reinforcement. In *Proceeding of the 18th International Conference on World Wide Web*, Madrid, Spain (pp. 51 – 60). New York, NY: ACM.

Biffl, S., & Schatten, A. (2009). *A platform for service-oriented integration of software engineering environments.* Paper presented at the Conference on New Trends in Software Methodologies, Tools and Techniques (SoMeT'09).

Biffl, S., Schatten, A., & Zoitl, A. (2009a, 23-26 June 2009). *Integration of heterogeneous engineering environments for the automation systems lifecycle.* Paper presented at the 7th IEEE International Conference on Industrial Informatics (INDIN 2009).

Biffl, S., Sunindyo, W. D., & Moser, T. (2009b). *Bridging semantic gaps between stakeholders in the production automation domain with ontology areas.* Paper presented at the 21st Int. Conf on SE and Knowledge Engineering (SEKE), Boston, USA.

Bilstrup, K. (2007). *A survey regarding wireless communication standards intended for a high-speed vehicle environment.* (Report No. IDE 0712). Retrieved from http://hh.diva-portal.org/smash/get/diva2:239214/FULLTEXT01

Bilstrup, K., Uhlemann, E., Strom, E. G., & Bilstrup, U. (2008). Evaluation of the IEEE 802.11p MAC method for vehicle-to-vehicle communication. *68th Vehicular Technology Conference* (pp. 1-5). Washington, DC: IEEE Computer Society. doi: 10.1109/VETECF.2008.446

Black, A. (1987). Distribution and abstract types in Emerald. *IEEE Transactions on Software Engineering, 13*(1), 65–76. doi:10.1109/TSE.1987.232836

Blevins, T., Lounsbury, D., Kirk, M., & Harding, C. (2009). *Cloud computing business scenario workshop.* Retrieved August 8, 2011, from https://www.opengroup.org/cloudcomputing/uploads/40/20362/R091.pdf

Blooma, M. J., & Jayan, C. K. (July, 2011). Research trends in community question answering. In *Proceedings of Pacific Asia Conference on Information Systems 2011,* Brisbane, Australia.

Blooma, M. J., Chua, A. Y. K., Goh, D. H., & Keong, L. C. (2009). A trend analysis of the question answering domain. In *Proceedings of the 6th International Conference on Information Technology: New Generations 2009,* Nevada, United States (pp. 1522-1527). New York, NY: IEEE Computer Society.

Blooma, M. J., Chua, A. Y. K., & Goh, D. H. (2011, January). What makes a high quality user-generated answer? *IEEE Internet Computing, 14*(4), 1–8.

Blooma, M. J., Chua, A. Y. K., & Goh, D. H. (Accepted for Publication). Predictors of high-quality answers in community-driven question answering services. *Online Information Review.*

Bo, Z., & Rentian, C. (2009). *Business model innovations in cloud computing.* Retrieved July 27, 2011, from http://www.huawei.com/en/static/Strategy_New_opportunities--Business_model_innovations_in_cloud_computing-26251-1-087845.pdf

Boden, N. J., Cohen, D., Felderman, R. E., Seitz, C. L., Seizovic, J. N., & Su, W.-K. (1995). Myrinet: A gigabit per second local area network. *IEEE Micro, 15*(1), 29–35. doi:10.1109/40.342015

Boppana, R. V., Chalasani, S., & Raghavendra, C. (1998). Resource deadlocks and performance of wormhole multicast routing algorithms. *IEEE Transactions on Parallel and Distributed Systems, 9*(6), 535–549. doi:10.1109/71.689441

Boppana, R., & Chalasani, S. (1993). A comparison of adaptive wormhole routing algorithms. *Computer Architecture News, 21*(2), 351–360. doi:10.1145/173682.165177

Boukhebouze, M., Amghar, Y., Benharkat, N., & Maamar, Z. (2010). A rule-based approach to model and verify flexible business processes. *International Journal of Business Process Integration and Management, 5*(4), 287–307. doi:10.1504/IJBPIM.2011.043389

Brar, G., Blough, D. M., & Santi, P. (2006). Computationally efficient scheduling with the physical interference model for throughput improvement in wireless mesh networks. In *Proceedings of ACM International Conference on Mobile Computing and Networking (MobiCom),* (pp. 2-13). Los Angeles, CA.

Bravetti, M., & Zavattaro, G. (2009). Contract compliance and choreography conformance in the presence of message queues. In *Web Services and Formal Methods* (Vol. 5387, pp. 37 54). Springer.

Breck, E., House, D., Light, M., & Mani, I. (1999). Question answering from large document collections. In *Proceedings of AAAI 1999 Fall Symposium on Question Answering Systems*, Florida, United States (pp. 26-31). AAAI Press.

Brill, E., Dumais, S., & Banko, M. (2002). An analysis of the ASKMSR question-answering system. In *Proceedings of the 2002 Conference on Empirical Methods in Natural Language Processing*, Pennsylvania, (pp. 257-264). Association of Computational Linguistics.

Brown, P. F., Pietra, V. J. D., Pietra, S. A. D., & Mercer, R. L. (1993). The mathematics of statistical machine translation: Parameter estimation. *Computational Linguistics, 19*(2), 263–311.

Buck, I., Foley, T., Horn, D., Sugerman, J., Fatahalian, K., Houston, M., & Hanrahan, P. (2004). Brook for GPUs: Stream computing on graphics hardware. *ACM Transactions on Graphics, 32*(3).

Bui, T., Gacher, A., & Sebastian, H. J. (2006). Web services for negotiation and bargaining in electronic markets: Design requirements, proof-of-concepts, and potential applications to e-procurement. *Group Decision and Negotiation. Special Issue on Hot Topics in Negotiation Support Systems, 15*(5), 469–490.

Burguillo-Rial, J., Costa-Montenegro, E., Gil-Castiñeira, F., & Rodríguez-Hernández, P. (2008). Performance analysis of IEEE 802.11p in urban environments using a multi-agent model. *19ᵗʰ International Symposium on Personal, Indoor and Mobile Radio Communications* (pp. 1-6). Washington, DC: IEEE Computer Society. doi: 10.1109/PIMRC.2008.4699924

Burke, R. (2002). Hybrid recommender systems: Survey and experiments. *User Modeling and User-Adapted Interaction, 12*(4), 331–370. doi:10.1023/A:1021240730564

Burke, R., Hammond, K., Kulyukin, V., Lytinen, S., Tomuro, N., & Schoenberg, S. (1997). Question answering from frequently-asked question files: Experiences with the FAQ finder system. *AI Magazine, 18*(2), 57–66.

Business Connexion. (2011). *Virtual computing environment.* Retrieved July 27, 2011, from http://www.bcx.co.za/solutions/services/data_centre_solutions/virtual_computing_enviroment/

Cambronero, M. E., D'ıaz, G., Valero, V., & Mart'ınez, E. (2008). A tool for the design and verification of composite web services. In G. J. Pace & G. Schneider (Eds.), *Proceedings of the Second Workshop on Formal Languages and Analysis of Contract-Oriented Software,* November 2008, Malta (pp. 9–16).

Campelli, L., Cesana, M., & Fracchia, R. (2007). Directional broadcast forwarding of alarm messages in VANETs. *4ᵗʰ Annual Conference on Wireless on Demand Network Systems and Services* (pp. 72-79). Washington, DC: IEEE Computer Society. doi: 10.1109/WONS.2007.340488

Cao, X., Cong, G., Cui, B., Jensen, C. S., & Zhang, C. (2009). The use of categorization information in language models for question retrieval. In D. W. K. Cheung, I. Song, W. W. Chu, X. Hu, & J. Lin (Eds.), *Proceeding of the 18th ACM Conference on Information and Knowledge Management,* Hong Kong, China (pp. 265-274). New York, NY: ACM.

Capra, L., Emmerich, W., & Mascolo, C. (2003). Carisma: Context aware reflective middleware system for mobile applications. *IEEE Transactions on Software Engineering, 29*(10), 929–945. doi:10.1109/TSE.2003.1237173

Caytiles, R. D., Lee, S., & Park, B. (2012). *Cloud computing: The next computing paradigm.* Hannam University. Retrieved May 24, 2012, from http://www.oecd.org/document/31/0,3746,en_2649_34223_43912543_1_1_1_1,00.html

Chaiken, R., Jenkins, B., Larson, P.-Å., Ramsey, B., Shakib, D., Weaver, S., & Zhou, J. (2008). SCOPE: Easy and efficient parallel processing of massive data sets. *Proceedings of the VLDB Endowment, 1*(2), 1265–1276.

Chaka, C. (2010). User and enterprise mobility: Mobile social networking and mobile cloud computing. *Cutter IT Journal, 23*(9), 35–39.

Chaka, C. (2011). Social computing: Harnessing enterprise social networking and the relationship economy. In Papadopoulou, P., Kanellis, P., & Martakos, D. (Eds.), *Social computing theory and practice: Interdisciplinary approaches* (pp. 85–100). Hershey, PA: IGI Global.

Chaka, C. (2012). Consumerization of IT, social computing, and mobility as the new desktop. *Cutter IT Journal, 225*(5), 28–33.

Chalasani, S., & Boppana, R. V. (1995). Fault-tolerant wormhole routing algorithms in mesh networks. *IEEE Transactions on Computers*, *44*(7), 848–864. doi:10.1109/12.392844

Chappell, D. (2004). *Enterprise service bus - Theory in practice*. O'Reilly Media.

Chen, Q., Jiang, D., & Delgrossi, L. (2009). IEEE 1609.4 DSCR multi-channel operations and its implications on vehicle safety communications. *Vehicular Networking Conference* (pp. 1-8). Washington, DC: IEEE Computer Society. doi: 10.1109/VNC.2009.5416394

Chen, W., Zeng, Q., & Liu, W. (2006). A user reputation model for a user interactive question answering system. In *Proceedings of the 2nd International Conference on Semantics, Knowledge and Grid,* Guilin, China (pp. 40). New York, NY: IEEE Computer Society.

Cheng, H., & Zhuang, W. (2008). An optimization framework for balancing throughput and fairness in wireless networks with QoS support. *IEEE Transactions on Wireless Communications*, *7*(2), 584–593. doi:10.1109/TWC.2008.060507

Chen, M., Zhang, D., & Zhou, L. (2007). Empowering collaborative commerce with Web services enabled business process management systems. *Decision Support Systems*, *43*(2), 530–546. doi:10.1016/j.dss.2005.05.014

Chen, N. S., Yu, F. P., & Huang, S. T. (1991). A self-stabilizing algorithm for constructing spanning trees. *Information Processing Letters*, *39*, 147–151. doi:10.1016/0020-0190(91)90111-T

Cheverst, K., Mitchell, K., & Davies, N. (2002). The role of adaptive hypermedia in a context-aware tourist GUIDE. *Communications of the ACM*, *45*(5), 47–51. doi:10.1145/506218.506244

Chiasserini, C. F., Fasolo, E., Furiato, R., Gaeta, R., Garetto, M., & Gribaudo, M. … Zanella, A. (2005). Smart broadcast of warning messages in vehicular ad hoc networks. *Workshop Interno Progetto NEWCOM* (pp. 1-4).

Chi, Y., & Lee, H. (2008). A formal modeling platform for composing web services. *Expert Systems with Applications*, *34*(2), 1500–1507. doi:10.1016/j.eswa.2007.01.022

Chou, J., & Lin, B. (2009). Optimal multi-path routing and bandwidth allocation under utility max-min fairness. In *Proceedings of ACM/IEEE International Workshop on Quality of Service (IWQoS)*, (pp. 1-9). Charleston, SC.

Cisco. (2009). *Five virtualised data centres deliver cloud computing*. Retrieved July 27, 2011, from http://www.cisco.com/en/US/solutions/collateral/ns340/ns517/ns224/case_study_itricity.pdf

Cloud Computing User Group. (2011). *Cloud computing use cases,* White Paper, v.4. Retrieved February 20, 2012, from http://openCloudmanifesto.org/Cloud _Computing_Use_Cases_Whitepaper-2_0.pdf

Cloud Computing World. (2011a). *Defining cloud computing virtualization*. Retrieved July 3, 2011, from http://www.cloudcomputingworld.org/cloud-computing/defining-cloud-computing-virtualization.html

Cloud Computing World. (2011b). *What is cloud computing?* Retrieved July 3, 2011, from http://www.cloudcomputingworld.org/cloud-computing/what-is-cloud-computing.html

Cloud Computing World. (2011c). *Cloud computing vs. autonomic computing*. Retrieved July 3, 2011, from http://www.cloudcomputingworld.org/cloud-computing/cloud-computing-vs-autonomic-computing.html

Cloud Security Alliance. (2009). *Security guidance for critical areas of focus in cloud computing* V2.1. Retrieved August 8, 2011, from https://cloudsecurityalliance.org/csaguide.pdf

Collins-Thompson, K., & Callan, J. (2005). Predicting reading difficulty with statistical reading models. *Journal of the American Society for Information Science and Technology*, *56*(13), 1448–1462. doi:10.1002/asi.20243

Cook, J. E., & Wolf, A. L. (1999). Software process validation: quantitatively measuring the correspondence of a process to a model. *ACM Transactions on Software Engineering and Methodology*, *8*(2), 147–176. doi:10.1145/304399.304401

Cormen, T. H., Leiserson, E. C., & Rivest, R. L. (1989). *Introduction to algorithms*. The MIT Press.

Cortes-Cornax, M., Dupuy-Chessa, S., Rieu, D., & Dumas, M. (2011). Evaluating choreographies in BPMN 2.0 using an extended quality framework. *Business Process Model and Notation*, 103-117.

Crane, D., & McCarthy, P. (2008). *Comet and reverse Ajax: The next-generation Ajax 2.0*. Berkely, CA: Apress.

Dally, W. J., & Seitz, C. L. (1986). The torus routing chip. *Journal of Distributed Computing*, *1*(3), 187–196. doi:10.1007/BF01660031

Dally, W. J., & Seitz, C. L. (1987). Deadlock-free message routing in multiprocessor interconnection networks. *IEEE Transactions on Computers*, *36*, 547–553. doi:10.1109/TC.1987.1676939

Dally, W., & Aoki, H. (1997). Deadlock-free adaptive routing in multiprocessor networks using virtual channels. *IEEE Transactions on Parallel and Distributed Systems*, *4*(4), 466–475. doi:10.1109/71.219761

Damodaran, S. (2004). B2B integration over the Internet with XML — RosettaNet successes and challenges. In *Proceedings of WWW 2004.*

Dang, H. T., Lin, J., & Kelly, D. (2006). Overview of the TREC 2006 question answering track. In *Proceedings of the 15th Text REtrieval Conference (TREC 2006)*, Maryland, United States (pp. 99-116). Gaithersburg, MD: NIST.

Dargha, R. (2009). *Cloud computing key considerations for adoption*. Infosys. Retrieved March 3, 2012, from http://www.infosys.com/Cloud /resource-center/documents/Cloud -computing.pdf

De Couto, D. S. J., Aguayo, D., Bicket, J., & Morris, R. (2003). A high throughput path metric for multihop wireless routing. In *Proceedings of ACM International Conference on Mobile Computing and Networking (MobiCom)*, (pp. 134-146). San Diego, CA.

de Mello, A. V., Ost, L. C., Moraes, F. G., & Calazans, N. L. V. (2004, May). *Evaluation of routing algorithms on mesh based NoCs (Tech. Rep. No. 040)*. Rio Grande, Brazil: Faculdade de Informatica PUCRS-Brazil.

Dean, J., & Ghemawat, S. (2008). MapReduce: Simplified data processing on large clusters. *Communications of the ACM*, *51*(1), 107–113. doi:10.1145/1327452.1327492

Decayeux, C., & Seme, D. (2005). 9). 3D hexagonal network: Modeling, topological properties, addressing scheme, and optimal routing algorithm. *IEEE Transactions on Parallel and Distributed Systems*, *16*, 875–884. doi:10.1109/TPDS.2005.100

Delgado, J. (2012). The user as a service. In Vidyarthi, D. (Ed.), *Technologies and protocols for the future of internet design: Reinventing the web* (pp. 37–59). Hershey, PA: IGI Global. doi:10.4018/978-1-4666-0203-8.ch003

Demner-Fushman, D., & Lin, J. (2006). Answer extraction, semantic clustering, and extractive summarization for clinical question answering. In *Proceedings of the 21st International Conference on Computational Linguistics and 44th Annual Meeting of the ACL*, Sydney, Australia (pp. 841–848). Association of Computational Linguistics.

Dıaz, G., & Rodrıguez, I. (2009). Checking the conformance of orchestrations with respect to choreographies in web services: A formal approach. In *Formal techniques for distributed systems* (pp. 231–236). Springer. doi:10.1007/978-3-642-02138-1_17

Dietz, J. (2006). *Enterprise ontology: Theory and methodology*. Berlin, Germany: Springer-Verlag. doi:10.1007/3-540-33149-2

Dijkstra, E. W. (1974). Self stabilizing systems in spite of distributed control. *Communications of the ACM*, *17*, 643–644. doi:10.1145/361179.361202

Dobson, G., Hall, S., & Sommerville, I. (2005). *A container-based approach to fault-tolerance in service-oriented architectures*. In International Conference of Software Engineering, Saint Louis, USA.

Dolter, J. W., Ramanathan, P., & Shin, K. G. (1991). Performance analysis of virtual cut-through switching in HARTS: A hexagonal mesh multicomputer. *IEEE Transactions on Computers*, *40*(6), 669–680. doi:10.1109/12.90246

Dorn, J., Grun, C., Werthner, H., & Zapletal, M. (2009). From business to software: A B2B survey. *Information Systems and e-business Management, 7*(2), 123 142.

Dörnemann, T., Juhnke, E., & Freisleben, B. (2009). On-demand resource provisioning for bpel workflows using Amazon's elastic compute cloud. In F. Cappello, C.-L. Wang, & R. Buyya (Eds.), In *Proceedings of the 9th IEEE/ACM International Symposium on Cluster Computing and the Grid* (pp. 140-147). IEEE Computer Society.

Draves, R., Padhye, J., & Zill, B. (2004). Routing in multi-radio, multi-hop wireless mesh networks. In *Proceedings of ACM MobiCom*, (pp. 114-128). Philadelphia, PA.

Duato, J. (1994). A necessary and sufficient condition for deadlock-free adaptive routing in wormhole networks. *Proceedings of International Conference on Parallel Processing,* (pp. 142-149).

Duato, J. (December 1991). Deadlock-free adaptive routing algorithms for multicomputers: Evaluation of a new algorithm. In *Proceedings of the Third IEEE Symposium Parallel and Distributed Processing* (pp. 840-847). Dallas, TX: IEEE Computer Society.

Duato, J. (1993). A new theory of deadlock-free adaptive routing in wormhole networks. *IEEE Transactions on Parallel and Distributed Systems, 4,* 1320–1331. doi:10.1109/71.250114

Duato, J. (1995, October). A necessary and sufficient condition for deadlock-free adaptive routing in wormhole networks. *IEEE Transactions on Parallel and Distributed Systems, 6*(10), 1055–1067. doi:10.1109/71.473515

Duato, J., Yalamancili, S., & Ni, L. (1997). *Interconnection networks: An engineering approach.* Silver Spring, MD: IEEE Computer Society Press.

Dubuisson, O. (2000). *ASN.1 communication between heterogeneous systems.* San Diego, CA: Academic Press.

Earl, T. (2005). *Service-oriented architecture: Concepts, technology, and design.* Upper Saddle River, NJ: Prentice Hall PTR.

Eichler, S. (2007). Performance evaluation of the IEEE 802.11p WAVE communication standard. *1st International Symposium on Wireless Vehicular Communications* (pp. 2199-2203). Washington, DC: IEEE Computer Society. doi: 10.1109/VETECF.2007.461

Einhoff, G., & Fidler, M. (June 2004). The turnnet concept: Routing in feed-forward networks with prohibited turns. In *2004 IEEE International Conference on Communications,* (Vol. 4, pp. 2009-2013).

Erenkrantz, J., Gorlick, M., Suryanarayana, G., & Taylor, R. (2007). From representations to computations: The evolution of web architectures. In *6th Joint Meeting of the European Software Engineering Conference and the ACM SIGSOFT Symposium on the Foundations of Software Engineering* (pp. 255-264). ACM Press.

Faleh, M. N. M., & Bochmann, G. V. (2011). Transforming dynamic behavior specifications from activity diagrams to BPEL. In *2011 IEEE 6th International Symposium on Service Oriented System Engineering (SOSE),* (pp. 305 311).

Fall, K., & Varadhan, K. (2000). *ns notes and documentation.* Retrieved August 1, 2011, from http://www.isi.edu/nsnam/ns/doc/ns_doc.pdf

Fellbaum, C. (1998). *WordNet: An electronic lexical database.* Cambridge, MA: MIT Press.

Ferreira, N., Fonseca, J. A., & Gomes, J. S. (2008). On the adequacy of 802.11p MAC protocols to support safety services in ITS. *International Conference on Emerging Technologies and Factory Automation* (pp. 1189-1192). Washington, DC: IEEE Computer Society. doi: 10.1109/ETFA.2008.4638552

Ferret, F., Grau, B., Illouz, G., Jacquemin, C., & Masson, N. (1999). QALC the question answering program of the language and cognition group at LIMSI-CNRS. In *Proceedings of the 8th Text REtrieval Conference,* Maryland, United States ((pp. 78-85). Gaithersburg, MD: NIST.

Fielding, R. (2000). *Architectural styles and the design of network-based software architectures.* Unpublished doctoral dissertation, University of California at Irvine, Irvine, California.

Fink, J., & Kobsa, A. (2002). User modeling for personalized city tours. *Artificial Intelligence Review, 18*(1), 33–74. doi:10.1023/A:1016383418977

Fiore, M., Harri, J., Filali, F., & Bonnet, C. (2007). Vehicular mobility simulation for VANETs. *40th Annual Simulation Symposium* (pp. 301-309). Washington, DC: IEEE Computer Society. doi: 10.1109/ANSS.2007.44

Fix, E., & Hodges, J. (1951). *Discriminatory analysis, non-parametric discrimination, consistency properties.* School of Aviation Medicine, Randolph Field, Texas, Computer Science Technical Report.

Fleury, E., & Fraigniaud, P. (1998). A general theory for deadlock avoidance in wormhole-routed networks. *IEEE Transactions on Parallel and Distributed Systems, 9*(7), 626–638. doi:10.1109/71.707539

Foundation for Intelligent Physical Agents. (2002, December). *FIPA contract net interaction protocol specification.* Retrieved from http://www.fipa.org/specs/fipa00029/

Frigo, M., Leiserson, C. E., & Randall, K. H. (1998). *The implementation of the cilk-5 multithreaded language* (pp. 212–223). PLDI.

Fung, B. C. M., Wang, K., & Ester, M. (2003). Hierarchical document clustering using frequent itemsets. In *Proceedings of the 3rd SIAM International Conference on Data Mining*, California, United States (pp. 59-70). Retrieved from http://www.siam.org/proceedings/datamining/2003/dm03_06FungB.pdf

Gabow, H. N., & Kariv, O. (1982). Algorithms for edge coloring bipartite graphs and multigraphs. *SIAM Journal on Computing, 11*(1), 117–129. doi:10.1137/0211009

Gaughan, P., & Yalamanchili, S. (1995). A family of fault tolerant routing protocols for direct multiprocessor networks. *IEEE Transactions on Parallel and Distributed Systems, 6*(5), 482–497. doi:10.1109/71.382317

Gazan, R. (2011). Social Q & A. *Journal of the American Society for Information Science and Technology, 62*(12). doi:10.1002/asi.21562

Gentzsch, W. (2001). *Sun grid engine: Towards creating a compute power grid.* Retrieved September 1, 2011, from http://ieeexplore.ieee.org/xpls/abs all.jsp?arnumber=923173

Gershenson, C. (2004). Self-organizing traffic lights. *Complex Systems, 16*(1), 29–53.

Ghosh, S., & Karaata, M. H. (1993). A self-stabilizing algorithm for coloring planar graph. *Distributed Computing, 7*, 55–59. doi:10.1007/BF02278856

Glass, C., & Ni, L. (1994). The turn model for adaptive routing. *Journal of the ACM, 5*, 874–902. doi:10.1145/185675.185682

GoGrid. LLC. (2011). *Cloud Hosting, Cloud Servers, Hybrid Hosting, Cloud Infrastructure from GoGrid.* Retrieved August 26, 2011, from http://www.gogrid.com/

Golub, G., & Loan, C. V. (1996). *Matrix computations* (3rd ed.). Baltimore, MD: Johns Hopkins Studies in Mathematical Sciences.

Gondaliya, M. (2010). *Virtualization vs cloud computing.* Retrieved July 3, 2011, from http://mayur.gondaliya.com/web-servers/the-difference-between-virtualization-and-cloud-computing-364.html

Gonzalez, H., Han, J., Li, X., & Klabjan, D. (2006). Warehousing and analyzing massive {RFID} data Sets. In L. Liu, A. Reuter, K.-Y. Whang, & J. Zhang (Eds.), *Proceedings of the 22nd International Conference on Data Engineering* (pp. 83-93). IEEE Computer Society.

Goodwin, J. C., Russomanno, D. J., & Qualls, J. (2007). Survey of semantic extensions to UDDI: Implications for sensor services. *Proceedings of the 2007 International Conference on Semantic Web & Web Services (SWWS'2007)*, Las Vegas, Nevada, USA, (pp. 16-22).

Google Maps. (2011). Retreived October 2011, from http://maps.google.com

Gorbenko, A., Kharchenko, V., & Romanovsky, A. (2009). Using inherent service redundancy and diversity to ensure web services dependability. In *Methods, Models and Tools for Fault Tolerance, Lecture Notes in Computer Science.*

Gray, J., Liu, D. T., Nieto-Santisteban, M., Szalay, A., DeWitt, D. J., & Heber, G. (2005). Scientific data management in the coming decade. *SIGMOD Record, 34*(4), 34–41. doi:10.1145/1107499.1107503

Grossman, R. L. (2009). The case for cloud computing. *IT Professional, 11*(2), 23–27. doi:10.1109/MITP.2009.40

Grün, C., Werthner, H., Pröll, B., Retschitzegger, W., & Schwinger, W. (2008). Assisting tourists on the move - An evaluation of mobile tourist guides. *7th International Conference on Mobile Business* (pp. 171-180). doi: 10.1109/ICMB.2008.28

GTSI. (2011). *Cloud computing: Building a framework for successful transition*. GTSI. Retrieved November 3, 2011, from http://www.slideshare.net/jerry0040/Cloud-computing-building-a-framework-for-successful-transition-gtsi

Guedes, D. W. M. Jr, & Ferreira, R. (2006). Anteater: A service-oriented architecture for high-performance data mining. *IEEE Internet Computing*, 36–43. doi:10.1109/MIC.2006.69

Guler, F. M., & Birturk, A. (2010). Natural intelligence – Commonsense question answering with conceptual graphs. *Conceptual Structures: From Information to Intelligence. Lecture Notes in Computer Science, 6208*, 97–107.

Gupta, P., & Kumar, P. R. (2000). The capacity of wireless networks. *IEEE Transactions on Information Theory, 46*(2), 388–404. doi:10.1109/18.825799

Hagel, J., & Brown, J. S. (2010). *Cloud computing storms on the horizon*. Retrieved June 6, 2010, from http://www.deloitte.com/assets/Dcom-UnitedStates/Local%20Assets/Documents/TMT_us_tmt/us_tmt_ce_CloudsStormsonHorizon_042010.pdf

Han, Y. S., Wang, Y., & Wood, D. (2007). Prefix-free regular languages and pattern matching. *Theoretical Computer Science, 389*(1-2), 307–317. doi:10.1016/j.tcs.2007.10.017

Harabagiu, S., Moldovan, D., Pasca, M., Mihalcea, R., Surdeanu, M., & Bunescu, R. … Morarescu, P. (2000). FALCON: Boosting knowledge for answer engines. In *Proceedings of the 9th Text Retrieval Conference*, Maryland, United States (pp. 479-489). Gaithersburg, MD: NIST.

Harabagiu, S., Moldovan, D., Pasca, M., Surdeanu, M., Mihalcea, R., & Gırju, R. … Bunescu, R. (2001). Answering complex, list and context questions with LCC's question-answering server. *In Proceedings of the 10th Text Retrieval Conference*, Maryland, United States (pp. 355-361). Gaithersburg, MD: NIST.

Harabagiu, S. M., Maiorano, S. J., & Pasca, M. A. (2003). Open-domain textual question answering techniques. *Natural Language Engineering, 9*(3), 231–267. doi:10.1017/S1351324903003176

Harary, F. (1998). *Graph theory*. Perseus Books.

Harper, E. (2011). *Vodacom and Novell are changing the rules*. Retrieved July 27, 2011, from http://www.novell.com/connectionmagazine/2011/05/dept2.pdf

Harper, F. M., Raban, D., Rafaeli, S., & Konstan, J. (2008). Predictors of answer quality in online Q&A sites. In *Proceedings of the 27th International Conference on Human Factors in Computing Systems*, Florence, Italy (pp. 865-874). New York, NY: ACM.

He, B., Fang, W., Luo, Q., Govindaraju, N. K., & Wang, T. (2008). Mars: A mapreduce framework on graphics processors. In *Proceedings of the 17th International Conference on Parallel Architectures and Compilation Techniques,* (pp. 260-269).

He, K. (2009). Integration and orchestration of heterogeneous services. In *Joint Conferences on Pervasive Computing* (pp. 467–470). IEEE Computer Society Press.

Henderson, N. (2011). *Telecom provider Vodacom opens Cape Town data center*. Retrieved August 2, 2011, from http://www.thewhir.com/web-hosting-news/072611_Telecommunications_Provider_Vodacom_Opens_Cape_Town_Data_Center

Henkel, M., Zdravkovic, J., & Johannesson, P. (2004). Service-based processes– Design for business and technology. In *International Conference on Service Oriented Computing* (pp. 21-29). ACM Press.

Hewlett-Packard Company. (2002). *Web services conversation language (WSCL) 1.0*. Retrievedc from http://www.w3.org/TR/wscl10/

Higginbotham, S. (2011). *VMware launches open-source cloud*. Retrieved August 3, 2011, from http://gigaom.com/cloud/vmware-open-source-cloud/

Hinze, A., & Junmanee, S. (2006). Advanced recommendation models for mobile tourist information. *Lecture Notes in Computer Science: Vol. 4275. On the Move to Meaningful Internet Systems 2006: CoopIS, DOA, GADA, and ODBASE* (pp. 643-660). Berlin, Germany: Springer Verlag, doi: doi:10.1007/11914853_38

Holdener, A. III. (2008). *Ajax: The definitive guide*. Sebastopol, CA: O'Reilly Media, Inc.

Honkala, I., Karpovsky, M. G., & Levitin, L. B. (2006, February). On robust and dynamic identifying codes. *IEEE Transactions on Information Theory*, *52*(2), 599–613. doi:10.1109/TIT.2005.862097

Hoppe, H. (1997). View-dependent refinement of progressive meshes. In *SIGGRAPH 97 Proceedings* (pp. 189–198).

Horst, R. (1996). ServerNet(TM) deadlock avoidance and fractahedral topologies. *Proceedings of IEEE International Parallel Processing Symposium*, (pp. 274-280).

Hovestadt, M., Kao, O., Kliem, A., & Warneke, D. (2011). Evaluating adaptive compression to mitigate the effects of shared I/O in clouds. In *Workshop Proceedings of 25th IEEE International Symposium on Parallel and Distributed Processing* (pp. 1042-1051). IEEE.

Hovy, E., Gerber, L., Hermjakob, U., Junk, M., & Lin, C.-Y. (2000). Question answering in Webclopedia. In *Proceedings of the 9th Text Retrieval Conference*, Maryland, United States (pp. 655-532). Gaithersburg, MD: NIST.

Hu, J., & Marculescu, R. (2004). DyAD - Smart routing for networks-on-chip. *Proceedings of the 41st annual conference on Design Automation*, (pp. 260-263).

Hua, X., Jin, G., & Ying, Z. (2007). *Supporting change impact analysis for service oriented business applications*. In International Workshop on Systems Development in SOA Environments, Minneapolis, USA.

Huang, X., Feng, S., & Zhuang, H. (2009). Cross-layer fair resource allocation for multi-radio multi-channel wireless mesh networks. In *Proceedings of 5th International Conference on Wireless Communications, Networking and Mobile Computing (WiCom)*, (pp. 2639-2643). Beijing, China.

Huang, S. T. (1993). Leader election in uniform rings. *ACM Transactions on Programming Language and Systems*, *15*(3), 563–573. doi:10.1145/169683.174161

Huang, S. T., Hung, S. S., & Tzeng, C. H. (2005). Self-stabilizing coloration in anonymous planar networks. *Information Processing Letters*, *95*, 307–312. doi:10.1016/j.ipl.2005.03.005

Huang, S. T., & Tzeng, C. H. (2009). Distributed edge coloration for bipartite networks. *Distributed Computing*, *22*(1), 3–14. doi:10.1007/s00446-009-0082-8

Huang, X., & Fang, Y. (2008). Multiconstrained QoS multipath routing in wireless sensor networks. *Wireless Networks*, *14*(4), 465–478. doi:10.1007/s11276-006-0731-9

IBM. (2009). *Your first step to cloud computing - Building a sustainable future*. Retrieved August 3, 2011, from http://www-07.ibm.com/hk/e-business/events/archives/SCCS/pdf/Your_First_Step_to_Cloud_Computing.pdf

IBM. (2010). *Cloud computing insights from 110 implementation projects*. Retrieved August 3, 2011, from http://public.dhe.ibm.com/common/ssi/ecm/en/ciw03074usen/CIW03074USEN.PDF

IBM. (2010). *Review and summary of Cloud service level agreements*. Retrieved April 16, 2012, from http://www.ibm.com/developerworks/Cloud/library/cl-rev2sla.html

Ibrahim, K., Weigle, M. C., & Abuelela, M. (2009). p-IVG: Probabilistic inter-vehicle geocast for dense vehicular networks. *69th Vehicular Technology Conference* (pp. 1-5). Washington, DC: IEEE Computer Society. doi: 10.1109/VETECS.2009.5073804

Inoue, T., Asakura, H., Sato, H., & Takahashi, N. (2010). Key roles of session state: Not against REST architectural style. In *34th Annual Computer Software and Applications Conference* (pp. 171-178). IEEE Computer Society Press.

Ireland, R. D., Hitt, M. A., & Vaidyanath, D. (2002). Alliance management as a source of competitive advantage. *Journal of Management*, *28*(3), 413–446. doi:10.1177/014920630202800308

Isard, M., Budiu, M., Yu, Y., Birrell, A., & Fetterly, D. (2007). Dryad: Distributed data-parallel programs from sequential building blocks. In P. Ferreira, T. R. Gross, & L. Veiga (Eds.), *Proceedings of the 2007 EuroSys Conference* (pp. 59-72). ACM.

Iskandar, D. N. F. A., Pehcevski, J., Thom, J. A., & Tahaghoghi, S. M. M. (2007). Social media retrieval using image features and structured text. In Fuhr, N., Kamps, J., Lalmas, M., & Trotman, A. (Eds.), *Focused Access to XML Documents, INEX 2007, LNCS 4862, Dagstuhl, Germany* (pp. 358–372). Berlin, Germany: Springer.

ISO. (2008). *International Standard ISO/IEC 14496-20:2008*

Iverson, M., Ozguner, F., & Follen, G. (1995). Parallelizing existing applications in a distributed heterogeneous environment. In *4th Heterogeneous Computing Workshop* (pp. 93–100).

Iyer, A., Rosenberg, C., & Karnik, A. (2009). What is the right model for wireless channel interference. *IEEE Transactions on Wireless Communications, 8*(5), 2662–2671. doi:10.1109/TWC.2009.080720

Jäätmaa, J. (2010). *Financial aspects of cloud computing business models*. Retrieved July 27, 2011, from http://hsepubl.lib.hse.fi/FI/ethesis/pdf/12435/hse_ethesis_12435.pdf

Jaekel, M., & Luhn, A. (2009). *Cloud computing – Business models, value creation dynamics and advantages for customers*. Retrieved July 27, 2011, from http://cn.siemens.com/cms/cn/English/it-solutions/Documents/WhitePaper_Cloud%20Computing_EN_200911.pdf

Jain, K., Padhye, J., Padmanabhan, V., & Qiu, L. (2003). Impact of interference on multihop wireless network performance. In *Proceedings of ACM MobiCom*, (pp. 66-80). San Diego, CA.

Jain, L., & Bhardwa, S. (2010). Enterprise cloud computing: Key considerations for adoption. *International Journal of Engineering and IT, 2*(2). Retrieved April 25, 2012, from http://www.techrepublic.com/whitepapers/Cloud-computing-key-considerations-for-adoption/1198637

Jakubiak, J., & Koucheryavy, Y. (2008). State of the art and research challenges for VANETs. *5th Consumer Communications and Networking Conference* (pp. 912-916). Washington, DC: IEEE Computer Society. doi: 10.1109/ccnc08.2007.212

Jashki, M.-A., Zafarani, R., & Bagheri, E. (2008). Towards a more efficient static software change impact analysis method. In Workshop on Program Analysis for Software Tools and Engineering, Atlanta, USA.

Jayasimha, D. N., Schwiebert, L., Manivannan, D., & May, J. A. (2003). A foundation for designing deadlock-free routing algorithms in wormhole networks. *Journal of the ACM, 50*(2), 250–275. doi:10.1145/636865.636869

Jensen, T. R., & Toft, B. (1995). *Graph coloring problems*. New York, NY: John Wiley & Sons.

Jeon, J., Croft, W. B., & Lee, J. H. (2005a). Finding similar questions in large question and answer archives. In *Proceedings of the 14th ACM Conference on Information and Knowledge Management*, Bremen, Germany (pp. 84-90). New York, NY: ACM.

Jeon, J., Croft, W. B., & Lee, J. H. (2005b). Finding semantically similar questions based on their answers. In R. A. Baeza-Yates, N. Ziviani, G. Marchionini, A. Moffat, & J. Tait (Eds.), *Proceedings of the 28th International ACM Conference on Research and Development in Information Retrieval*, Salvador, Brazil (pp. 617-618). New York, NY: ACM.

Jeon, J., Croft, W. B., Lee, J. H., & Park, S. (2006). A framework to predict the quality of answers with non textual features. In E. Efthimiadis, S. Dumais, D. Hawking, & K. Järvelin (Eds.), *Proceedings of the 29th International ACM Conference on Research and Development in Information Retrieval*, Seattle, United States (pp. 228 – 235). New York, NY: ACM.

Jeong, B., Lee, D., Cho, H., & Lee, J. (2008). A novel method for measuring semantic similarity for XML schema matching. *Expert Systems with Applications, 34*, 1651–1658. doi:10.1016/j.eswa.2007.01.025

Jiang, D., & Delgrossi, L. (2008). IEEE 802.11p: Towards an international standard for wireless access in vehicular environments. *Vehicular Technology Conference* (pp. 2036-2040). Washington, DC: IEEE Computer Society.

Jones, K. S., Walker, S., & Robertson, S. E. (2000). A probabilistic model of information retrieval: Development and comparative experiments. *Information Processing & Management, 36*(6), 779–840. doi:10.1016/S0306-4573(00)00015-7

Joo, K. H., & Lee, S. (2005). An incremental document clustering algorithm based on a hierarchical agglomerative approach. In Chakraborty, G. (Ed.), *Distributed Computing and Internet Technology, ICDCIT 2005, LNCS 3816, Bhubaneswar, India* (pp. 321–332). Berlin, Germany: Springer. doi:10.1007/11604655_37

Jouraku, A. (2007). An effective design of deadlock-free routing algorithms based on 2d turn model for irregular networks. *IEEE Transactions on Parallel and Distributed Systems, 18*(3), 320–333. doi:10.1109/TPDS.2007.36

Jurca, R., & Faltings, B. (2007). Obtaining reliable feedback for sanctioning reputation mechanisms. *Journal of Artificial Intelligence Research*, *29*, 391–419.

Jurczyk, P., & Agichtein, E. (2007). Discovering authorities in question answer communities by using link analysis. In *Proceedings of the 16th ACM Conference on Conference on Information and Knowledge Management*, Lisbon, Portugal, (pp. 919-922). New York, NY: ACM.

Juric, M. B., Sasa, A., Brumen, B., & Rozman, I. (2009). WSDL and UDDI extensions for version support in web services. *Journal of Systems and Software*, *82*(8), 1326–1343. doi:10.1016/j.jss.2009.03.001

Kar, K., Kodialam, M., & Lakshman, T. V. (2000). Minimum interference routing of bandwidth guaranteed tunnels with MPLS traffic engineering applications. *IEEE Journal on Selected Areas in Communications*, *18*(12), 2566–2579. doi:10.1109/49.898737

Katz, B., & Levin, B. (1988) Exploiting lexical regularities in designing natural language systems. In *Proceedings of the 12th International Conference on Computational Linguistics*, Budapest, Hungary (pp. 316-323).

Kavantzas, N., et al. (2005). *Web services choreography description language version 1.0.* Retrieved from http://www.w3.org/TR/ws-cdl-10/

Keidl, M., Seltzsam, S., & Kemper, A. (2003). *Reliable web service execution and deployment in dynamic environments.* In Technologies for E-Services, Berlin, Germany.

Khadka, R. (2011). Model-driven development of service compositions for enterprise interoperability. In van Sinderen, M., & Johnson, P. (Eds.), *Lecture Notes in Business Information Processing, 76* (pp. 177–190). Berlin, Germany: Springer. doi:10.1007/978-3-642-19680-5_15

Kim, D., & Shen, W. (2007). An approach to evaluating structural pattern conformance of UML models. In *ACM Symposium on Applied Computing* (pp. 1404-1408). ACM Press.

Kim, S., Oh, J., & Oh, S. (2007). Best-answer selection criteria in a social Q&A site from the user-centered relevance perspective. In *Proceedings of the 70th annual meeting of the American Society for Information Science and Technology, 44*, (pp. 1–15). Information Today, Inc.

Kim, S.-M., Baek, D.-H., Kim, S.-B., & Rim, H.-C. (2000). Question answering considering semantic categories and co-occurence density. In *Proceedings of the 9th Text REtrieval Conference,* Maryland, United States (pp. 317-334). Gaithersburg, MD: NIST.

Kim, J., & Kim, H. (2004). Semantic constraint specification and verification of ebXML business process specifications. *Expert Systems with Applications*, *27*(4), 571–584. doi:10.1016/j.eswa.2004.06.002

Kim, S., & Oh, S. (2009). User's relevance criteria for evaluating answers in a social Q & A site. *Journal of the American Society for Information Science and Technology*, *60*(4), 716–727. doi:10.1002/asi.21026

Kivity, A., Kamay, Y., Laor, D., Lublin, U., & Ligori, A. (2007). KVM: The Linux virtual machine monitor. In *Proceedings of the 2007 Ottawa Linux Symposium* (pp. 225-230).

Kleinberg, J., Rabani, Y., & Tardos, E. (2001). Fairness in routing and load balancing. *Journal of Computer and System Sciences*, *63*(1), 568–578. doi:10.1006/jcss.2001.1752

Klepacki, D. (2003). *Blue gene.* Retrieved from http://lobster.bu.edu/SCV/Archive/IBM/BGL-BU.pdf

Ko, J., Si, L., Nyberg, E., & Mitamura, T. (2010). Probabilistic models for answer-ranking in multilingual question-answering, *ACM Transactions on Information Systems, 28*(3), 16:1-37.

Koibuchi, M., Funahashi, A., Jouraku, A., & Amano, H. (2001, September). L-turn routing: An adaptive routing in irregular networks. In *Proceedings of IEEE International Conference on Parallel Processing* (pp. 383-392).

Kokash, N., & Arbab, F. (2009). Formal behavioral modeling and compliance analysis for service-oriented systems. In Boer, F., Bonsangue, M., & Madelaine, E. (Eds.), *Formal Methods for Components and Objects* (*Vol. 5751*, pp. 21–41). Lecture Notes In Computer ScienceBerlin, Germany: Springer-Verlag. doi:10.1007/978-3-642-04167-9_2

Ko, R. K. L., Lee, S. S. G., & Lee, E. W. (2009). Business process management (BPM) standards: A survey. *Business Process Management Journal*, *15*(5), 744–791. doi:10.1108/14637150910987937

Korkmaz, G., Ekici, E., Özgüner, F., & Özgüner, U. (2004). Urban multi-hop broadcast protocol for inter-vehicle communication systems. *1ˢᵗ International Workshop on Vehicular Ad-hoc Networks* (pp. 76-85). New York, NY: ACM. doi: 10.1145/1023875.1023887

Kortebi, R., Gourhant, Y., & Agoulmine, N. (2007). On the user of SINR for interference-aware routing in wireless multi-hop networks. In *Proceedings of ACM International Workshop Modeling, Analysis, and Simulation of Wireless and Mobile Systems (MSWiM),* (pp. 395-399). Crete Island, Greece.

Kotok, A. (2007, Feb). *Adoption of ebXML: Hiding in Plain Sight.* Retrieved from http://www.ebxmlforum.net/articles/Adoption%20of%20ebXML%20Hiding%20in%20Plain%20Sight.html

Krajzewicz, D., Hertkorn, G., Rössel, C., & Wagner, P. (2002). Sumo (simulation of urban mobility) - An open-source traffic simulation. *4ᵗʰ Middle East Symposium on Simulation and Modeling* (pp. 183-187).

Krisch, S. M., Gnasa, M., Won, M., & Cremers, A. B. (2006). Beyond the web: Retrieval in social information spaces. In Lalmas, M., MacFarlane, A., Rüger, S. M., Tombros, A., Tsikrika, T., & Yavlinsky, A. (Eds.), *Advances in Information Retrieval, ECIR 2006, LNCS 3936, London, United Kingdom* (pp. 84–95). Berlin, Germany: Springer. doi:10.1007/11735106_9

Kumaran, S., et al. (2008). A RESTful architecture for service-oriented business process execution. In *International Conference on e-Business Engineering* (pp. 197-204). IEEE Computer Society Press.

Kundra, V. (2011). *Federal cloud computing strategy.* Washington, DC: White House. Retrieved April 15, 2012, from http://gcn.com/articles/2011/02/14/federal-Cloud-computing-strategy-released.aspx

Kwok, D. (2009). *Cloud computing - "End user deployment and IBM internal experiences."* Retrieved August 3, 2011, from https://www.opengroup.org/conference-live/uploads/40/20793/Kwok.pdf

Kwok, C. C. T., Etzioni, O., & Weld, D. S. (2001). Scaling question answering to the web. *ACM Transactions on Information Systems, 19*(3), 242–262. doi:10.1145/502115.502117

Laitkorpi, M., Selonen, P., & Systa, T. (2009). Towards a model-driven process for designing ReSTful web services. In *IEEE International Conference on Web Services* (pp. 173-180). IEEE Computer Society Press.

Langar, R., Bouabdallah, N., & Boutaba, R. (2009). Mobility-aware clustering algorithms with interference constraints. *Computer Networks, 53*(1), 25–44. doi:10.1016/j.comnet.2008.09.012

Läufer, K., Baumgartner, G., & Russo, V. (2000). Safe structural conformance for Java. *The Computer Journal, 43*(6), 469–481. doi:10.1093/comjnl/43.6.469

Law, J., & Rothermel, G. (2003). *Incremental dynamic impact analysis for evolving software systems.* In International Symposium on Software Reliability Engineering, Washington, DC, USA.

Lee, S., Min, S.-J., & Eigenmann, R. (2009). OpenMP to GPGPU: A compiler framework for automatic translation and optimization. In *PPoPP '09: Proceedings of the 14th ACM SIGPLAN Symposium on Principles and Practice of Parallel Programming* (pp. 101–110).

Lee, D. L., Chuang, H., & Seamons, K. E. (1997). Document ranking and the vector-space model. *IEEE Software, 14*(2), 67–75. doi:10.1109/52.582976

Leung, K. W. T., Ng, W., & Lee, D. L. (2008). Personalized concept-based clustering of search engine queries. *IEEE Transactions on Knowledge and Data Engineering, 20*(11), 1505–1518. doi:10.1109/TKDE.2008.84

Levitin, L., Karpovsky, M., & Mustafa, M. (May, 2009). Deadlock prevention by turn prohibitions in interconnection networks. In *2009 IEEE International Symposium on Parallel & Distributed Processing* (pp. 1-7). Rome, Italy: IEEE Computer Society.

Levitin, L. B., Karpovsky, M. G., Mustafa, M., & Zakrevski, L. (2006). A new algorithm for finding cycle-breaking sets of turns in a graph. *Journal of Graph Algorithms and Applications, 10*(2), 387–420. doi:10.7155/jgaa.00134

Levitin, L., Karpovsky, M., & Mustafa, M. (2010, September). Minimal sets of turns for breaking cycles in graphs modeling networks. *IEEE Transactions on Parallel and Distributed Systems, 21*(9), 1342–1353. doi:10.1109/TPDS.2009.174

Lewis, G. (2010). *Basics about cloud computing*. Carnegie Mellon University.

Li, L., & Chou, W. (2010). Design patterns for RESTful communication. In *International Conference on Web Services* (pp. 512-519). IEEE Computer Society Press.

Li, X. Y., Yuan, J. S., & Jing, Y. W. (2007). An efficient user access pattern clustering algorithm. In *Proceedings of the 6th International Conference on Machine Learning and Cybernetics*, Hong Kong, China, (pp. 4109-4112). New York, NY: IEEE Computer Society.

Li, X., & Roth, D. (2002). Learning question classifiers. In *Proceedings of the 19th International Conference on Computational Linguistics*, Taipei, Taiwan (pp. 556–562). Association of Computational Linguistics.

Libeskind-Hadas, R., Mazzoni, D., & Rajagopalan, R. (1998). Tree-based multicasting in wormhole-routed irregular topologies. *Proceedings of the Merged 12th International Parallel Processing Symposium and the 9th Symposium on Parallel and Distributed Processing*, (pp. 244-249).

Lim, B., & Wen, H. J. (2003, Spring). Web services: An analysis of the technology, its benefits, and implementation difficulties. *Information Systems Management*, 49–57. doi:10.1201/1078/43204.20.2.20030301/41470.8

Limthanmaphon, B., & Zhang, Y. (2003). *Web service composition with case-based reasoning*. In Australasian Database Conference, Adelaide, Australia.

Linalg Project. (2011). Retrieved October 2011, from http://rubyforge.org/projects/linalg

Liu, Y., & Agichtein, E. (2008a). On the evolution of the Yahoo! Answers QA community. In S. H. Myaeng, D. W. Oard, F. Sebastiani, T. S. Chua, & M. K. Leong (Eds.), *Proceedings of the 31st Annual International ACM Conference on Research and Development in Information Retrieval*, Singapore, (pp. 737-738). New York, NY: ACM.

Liu, Y., Bian, J., & Agichtein, E. (2008b). Predicting information seeker satisfaction in community question answering. In S. H. Myaeng, D. W. Oard, F. Sebastiani, T. S. Chua, & M. K. Leong (Eds.), *Proceedings of the 31st Annual International ACM Conference on Research and Development in Information Retrieval*, Singapore (pp. 483-490). New York, NY: ACM.

Loutas, N., Peristeras, V., & Tarabanis, K. (2011). Towards a reference service model for the Web of services. *Data & Knowledge Engineering, 70*, 753–774. doi:10.1016/j.datak.2011.05.001

Lubbers, P., Albers, B., & Salim, F. (2010). *Pro HTML5 programming: Powerful APIs for richer internet application development*. New York, NY: Apress.

Lucchi, R., & Mazzara, M. (2007, January). A Pi-Calculus based semantics for WS-BPEL. *Journal of Logic and Algebraic Programming, 70*(1), 96–118. doi:10.1016/j.jlap.2006.05.007

Luk, C.-K., Hong, S., & Kim, H. (2009). *Qilin: Exploiting parallelism on heterogeneous multiprocessors with adaptive mapping*. In 42nd International Symposium on Microarchitecture (MICRO).

Lyakhov, A., & Poupyrev, P. (2005). Evaluation of broadcasting technologies performance in IEEE 802.11 networks. *International Workshop Distributed Computer and Communication Networks* (pp. 84-94).

Lyakhov, A., Vishnevsky, V., & Poupyrev, P. (2005). Analytical study of broadcasting in 802.11 ad- hoc networks. In J. Filipe & L. Vasiu (ed.), *2nd International Conference on e-Business and Telecommunication Networks* (pp. 86-91). INSTICC Press.

Lysne, O., Skeie, T., Reinemo, S. A., & Theiss, I. (2006). Layered routing in irregular networks. *IEEE Transactions on Parallel and Distributed Systems, 17*(1), 51–56. doi:10.1109/TPDS.2006.12

Ma, X., Chen, X., & Refai, H. (2007). Unsaturated performance of IEEE 802.11 broadcast service in vehicle-to-vehicle networks. *66th Vehicular Technology Conference* (pp. 1957-1961). Washington, DC: IEEE Computer Society. doi: 10.1109/VETECF.2007.411

Maamar, Z., Faci, N., Krug Wives, L., Yahyaoui, H., & Hacid, H. (2011). Towards a method for engineering social web services. In *The Proceedings of the IFIP WG8.1 Working Conference on Method Engineering - Engineering Methods in the Service-Oriented Context* (ME'2011), Paris, France, April, (pp. 153-167).

Maamar, Z., Yahyaoui, H., Lim, E., & Thiran, P. (2011). Social engineering of communities of web services. In *The Proceedings of the 11ʰ Annual International Symposium on Applications and the Internet* (SAINT'2011), Munich, Germany, (pp. 100-109).

Maamar, Z., Faci, N., Krug Wives, L., Badr, Y., Bispo Santos, P., & de Oliveira, J. P. M. (2011). Using social networks for web services discovery. *IEEE Internet Computing, 15*(4), 48–54. doi:10.1109/MIC.2011.27

Maamar, Z., Hacid, H., & Huhns, M. N. (2011). Why web services need social networks. *IEEE Internet Computing, 15*(2), 90–94. doi:10.1109/MIC.2011.49

Maamar, Z., Krug Wives, L., Badr, Y., Elnaffar, S., Boukadi, K., & Faci, N. (2011). LinkedWS: A novel web services discovery model based on the metaphor of social networks. *Simulation Modelling Practice and Theory, 19*(1), 121–132. doi:10.1016/j.simpat.2010.06.018

Maamar, Z., Subramanian, S., Thiran, P., Benslimane, D., & Bentahar, J. (2009). An approach to engineer communities of web services: Concepts, architecture, operation, and deployment. *International Journal of E-Business Research, 5*(4), 1–21. doi:10.4018/jebr.2009040601

Maaradji, A., Hacid, H., Daigremont, J., & Crespi, N. (2010). Towards a social network based approach for services composition. In *Proceedings of the 2010 IEEE International Conference on Communications* (ICC'2010), Cap Town, South Africa, (pp. 1-5).

Maatta, J., & Braysy, T. (2009). A novel approach to fair routing in wireless mesh networks. *EURASIP Journal on Wireless Communications and Networking, Special Issue on Fairness in radio Resource Magement for Wireless Networks*, 1-13.

Maes, F., Vandermeulen, D., & Suetens, P. (1999). Comparative evaluation of multiresolution optimization strategies for multimodality image registration by maximization of mutual information. *Medical Image Analysis, 3*, 373–386. doi:10.1016/S1361-8415(99)80030-9

Mangharam, R., Weller, D., Rajkumar, R., Mudalige, P., & Bai, F. (2006). Groovenet: A hybrid simulator for vehicle-to-vehicle networks. *3ʳᵈ International Conference Mobile and Ubiquitous Systems: Networking Services* (pp. 1-8). Washington, DC: IEEE Computer Society. doi: 10.1109/MOBIQ.2006.340441

Mansouri, V. S., Mohsenian-Rad, A. H., & Wong, V. W. S. (2009). Lexicographically optimal routing for wireless sensor networks with multiple sinks. *IEEE Transactions on Vehicular Technology, 58*(3), 1490–1500. doi:10.1109/TVT.2008.928898

Marshall, P., Keahey, K., & Freeman, T. (2010). Elastic site: Using clouds to elastically extend site resources. In *Proceedings of the 10th IEEE/ACM International Symposium on Cluster Computing and the Grid* (pp. 43-52). IEEE.

Martinez, F., Cano, J.-C., Calafate, C., & Manzoni, P. (2008). Citymob: A mobility model pattern generator for VANETs. *International Conference on Communications* (pp. 370-374). Washington, DC: IEEE Computer Society. doi: 10.1109/ICCW.2008.76

Martinez, F., Cano, J.-C., Calafate, C., & Manzoni, P. (2009). A performance evaluation of warning message dissemination in 802.11p based VANETs. *34ʰ Conference on Local Computer Networks* (pp. 221-224). Washington, DC: IEEE Computer Society. doi: 10.1109/LCN.2009.5355151

Mauve, M., Widmer, J., & Hartenstein, H. (2001). A survey on position based routing in mobile ad hoc networks. *IEEE Network, 15*(6), 30–39. doi:10.1109/65.967595

Ma, X., & Chen, X. (2007). Saturation performance of IEEE 802.11 broadcast networks. *IEEE Communications Letters, 11*(8), 686–688. doi:10.1109/LCOMM.2007.070040

McGuiness, L. D. (2004). *Question answering on the Semantic Web. The Semantic Web, IEEE Intelligent Systems* (pp. 82–85). New York, NY: IEEE Computer Society.

Mejia, A., Flitch, J., Duato, J., Reinemo, S. A., & Skeie, T. (2006). *Segment-based routing: An efficient fault-tolerant routing algorithm for meshes and tori*. In 20th international Parallel and distributed processing symposium, IPDPS 2006. IEEE.

Mell, G., & Mell, P. (2009). *The NIST definition of cloud computing, version 15*. NIST.

Mell, P., & Grance, T. (2011). *The NIST definition of cloud computing (Draft):- Recommendations of the National Institute of Standards and Technology (NIST)*. US Department of Commerce.

Menzies, T., Butcher, A., Marcus, A., Zimmermann, T., & Cok, D. R. (2011). *Local vs. global models for effort estimation and defect prediction.* In International Conference on Automated Software Engineering, Lawrence, USA.

Mesnier, M., Wachs, M., Salmon, B., & Ganger, G. R. (2006). *Relative fitness models for storage* (pp. 23–28). SIGMETRICS Performance Evaluation Review.

Milanovic, N., & Malek, M. (2004, Nov–Dec). Current solutions for web service composition. *IEEE Internet Computing*, 51–59. doi:10.1109/MIC.2004.58

Mili, H., Tremblay, G., & Jaoude, G. B. Lefebvre, E´., Elabed, L., & Boussaidi, G. E. (2010, December). Business process modeling languages: Sorting through the alphabet soup. *ACM Computer Surveys, 43*(1). Retrieved from http://doi.acm.org/10.1145/1824795.1824799

Miller, J., Candler, L., & Wald, H. (2010). *Information security governance: Government considerations for the cloud computing environment.* Booz Allen Hamilton. Retrieved April 20, 2011, from www.boozallen.com/insights/insight-detail/42698843

Min, G., Ould-Khaoua, M., Kouvatsos, D., & Awan, I. (2004, May). A queuing model of dimension-ordered routing under self-similar traffic loads. In *Proceedings of the 18th International Parallel and Distributed Processing Symposium,* (pp. 601-613). Washington, DC: IEEE Computer Society.

Min, L., Weiming, S., Qi, H., & Junwei, Y. (2009). A weighted ontology-based semantic similarity algorithm for web services. *Expert Systems with Applications, 36*(10), 12480–12490. doi:10.1016/j.eswa.2009.04.034

Mobasher, B. 2007. Data mining for web personalization. *Lecture Notes in Computer Science: Vol. 4321. The Adaptive Web* (pp. 90-135). Berlin, Germany: Springer Verlag, doi: doi:10.1007/978-3-540-72079-9_3

Moser, T., Biffl, S., Sunindyo, W. D., & Winkler, D. (2010a). Integrating production automation expert knowledge across engineering domains. *International Journal of Distributed Systems and Technologies, Special Issue: Current Methods in Resource Integration, Allocation and Scheduling, 2011.*

Moser, T., Biffl, S., Sunindyo, W. D., & Winkler, D. (2010b). *Integrating production automation expert knowledge across engineering stakeholder domains.* Paper presented at the 4th International Conference on Complex, Intelligent and Software Intensive Systems (CISIS 2010).

Motal, T., Zapletal, M., & Werthner, H. (2009). The business choreography language (BCL)-A domain-specific language for global choreographies. In *Proceedings of the 5th 2009 World Congress on Services (SERVICES 2009 PART II),* Bangalore, India.

Mrissa, M., Ghedira, C., Benslimane, D., Maamar, Z., Rosenberg, F., & Dustdar, S. (2007). A context-based mediation approach to compose Semantic Web services. *ACM Transactions on Internet Technology, Special Issue on Semantic Web Services: Issues, Solutions, and Applications, 8*(1).

Murata, T. (1989). Petri nets: Properties, analysis and applications. *Proceedings of the IEEE, 77*(4), 541–580. doi:10.1109/5.24143

Mustafa, M., Karpovsky, M., & Levitin, L. (2005, August). *Cycle breaking in wormhole routed computer communication networks.* Washington, DC: Opnet Technologies.

Mustafa, M., Levitin, L., & Karpovsky, M. (August 2006). *Weighted turn prohibition in computer communication networks.* Washington, DC: OPNET Technologies, Inc.

Mykkänen, J., & Tuomainen, M. (2008). An evaluation and selection framework for interoperability standards. *Information and Software Technology, 50,* 176–197. doi:10.1016/j.infsof.2006.12.001

Nace, D. (2002). A linear programming based approach for computing optimal fair splittable routing. In *Proceedings of IEEE Symposium on Computers and Communication (ISCC),* (pp. 468-474). Taormina, Italy.

Nace, D., Doan, L., Klopfenstein, O., & Bashllari, A. (2008). Max-min fairness in multicommodity flows. *Computers & Operations Research, 35*(2), 557–573. doi:10.1016/j.cor.2006.03.020

Nace, D., Doan, N., Gourdin, E., & Liau, B. (2006). Computing optimal max-min fair resource allocation for elastic flows. *IEEE/ACM Transactions on Networking, 14*(6), 1272–1281. doi:10.1109/TNET.2006.886331

Nace, D., & Pioro, M. (2008). Max-min fairness and its applications to routing and load balancing in communications networks: A tutorial. *IEEE Communications Surveys and Tutorials*, *10*(4), 5–17. doi:10.1109/SURV.2008.080403

Nam Ko, M., Cheek, G. P., Shehab, M., & Sandhu, R. (2010). Social-networks connect services. *IEEE Computer*, *43*(8), 37–43. doi:10.1109/MC.2010.239

Nam, K. K., Ackerman, M. S., & Adamic, L. A. (2009). Questions in, knowledge in a study of Naver's question answering community. In D. R. Olsen, R. B. Arthur, K. Hinckley, M. R. Morris, S. E. Hudson, & S. Greenberg (Eds.), *Proceedings of the 27th International Conference on Human Factors in Computing Systems*, Massachusetts, United States (pp. 779-788). New York, NY: ACM.

Naumov, V., & Baumann, R. (2006). An evaluation of inter-vehicle ad hoc networks based on realistic vehicular traces. *International Symposium on Mobile Ad Hoc Networking and Computing* (pp. 108-119). New York, NY: ACM. doi: 10.1145/1132905.1132918

Nekovee, M., & Bogason, B. (2007). Reliable and efficient information dissemination in intermittently connected vehicular adhoc networks. *65th Vehicular Technology Conference* (pp. 2486-2490). Washington, DC: IEEE Computer Society. doi: 10.1109/VETECS.2007.512

Newswire, P. R. (2011). *Vodacom business and Novell partner to securely manage and optimize cloud services*. Retrieved August 2, 2011, from http://www.prnewswire.com/news-releases/vodacom-business-and-novell-partner-to-securely-manage-and-optimize-cloud-services-94237459.html

Ni, L. M., & McKinley, P. K. (1993). A survey of wormhole routing techniques in directed networks. *Computer*, *26*, 62–76. doi:10.1109/2.191995

Nimbula. (2011a). *Nimbula™ cloud operating system technical white paper*. Retrieved August 6, 2011, from http://nimbula.com/media/nimbula/Nimbula_Technical_White_Paper.pdf

Nimbula. (2011b). *Nimbula™ Director v1.0 datasheet*. Retrieved August 6, 2011, from http://nimbula.com/media/nimbula/Nimbula_Datasheet.pdf

Nocetti, F. G., Stojmenovic, I., & Zhang, J. (2002). Addressing and routing in hexagonal networks with applications for tracking mobile users and connection rerouting in cellular networks. *IEEE Transactions on Parallel and Distributed Systems*, *13*(9), 963–971. doi:10.1109/TPDS.2002.1036069

Nurmi, D., Wolski, R., Grzegorczyk, C., Obertelli, G., Soman, S., Youseff, L., & Zagorodnov, D. (2009). The Eucalyptus Open-source cloud-computing system. In F. Cappello, C.-L. Wang, & R. Buyya (Eds.), *Proceedings of the 9th IEEE/ACM International Symposium on Cluster Computing and the Grid* (pp. 124-131). IEEE Computer Society.

NVIDIA. (2007). *NVIDIA CUDA SDK*. Retrieved in September, 10, 2011 from http:// nvidia.com/cuda

O'Malley, O., & Murthy, A. C. (2009). *Winning a 60 second dash with a yellow elephant*. Retrieved August 26, 2011, from http://sortbenchmark.org/Yahoo2009.pdf

OASIS. (2005). *UDDI version 3.0.2*. Retrieved from http://uddi.org/pubs/uddi v3.htm

OASIS. (2006, December). *EbXML business process specification schema 4 technical specification V2.0.4*. Retrieved from http://docs.oasis-open.org/ebxml-bp/2.0.4/OS/spec/ebxmlbp-v2.0.4-Spec-os-en.pdf

OASIS. (2007, April). *Web services business process execution language version 2.0*. Retrieved from http://docs.oasis-open.org/wsbpel/2.0/OS/wsbpel-v2.0OS.html

Object Management Group. (2009, August). *Business process modeling notation (BPMN) version 2 (Beta)*. Retrieved from http://www.omg.org/spec/BPMN/2.0

Object Management Group. (2010, May). *OMG unified modeling language (OMG UML), superstructure, V2.3*. Retrieved from http://www.omg.org/spec/UML/2.3/Infrastructure/PDF

Oh, H. J., Myaeng, S. H., & Jang, M. G. (2007). Semantic passage segmentation based on sentence topics for question answering. *Information Sciences*, *177*(18), 3696–3717. doi:10.1016/j.ins.2007.02.038

Orso, A., Apiwattanapong, T., & Harrold, M. J. (2003). *Leveraging field data for impact analysis and regression testing*. In European Conference on Software Engineering, Helsinki, Finland.

Osrael, J., Froihofer, L., Weghofer, M., & Göschka, K. M. (2007). *Axis2-based replication middleware for web services*. In International Conference on Web Services, Salt Lake City, USA.

Overdick, H. (2007). The resource-oriented architecture. In *IEEE Congress on Services* (pp. 340-347). IEEE Computer Society Press.

Pabst, R., Walke, B. H., Schultz, D., Herhold, P., Yanikomeroglu, H., & Mukherjee, S. (2004). Relay-based deployment concepts for wireless and mobile broadband radio. *IEEE Communications Magazine, 42*(9), 80–89. doi:10.1109/MCOM.2004.1336724

Pacharoen, W., Aoki, T., Surarerks, A., & Bhattarakosol, P. (2011). Conformance verification between web service choreography and implementation using learning and model checking. *IEEE International Conference on Web Services,* (pp. 722-723).

Page, L., Brin, S., Motwani, R., & Winograd, T. (November, 1999). *The PageRank citation ranking: Bringing order to the Web.* Technical report, Stanford University. Retrieved from http://dbpubs.stanford.edu:8090/pub/1999-66

Pal, R. (2008). A lexicographically optimal load balanced routing scheme for wireless mesh networks. In *Proceedings of IEEE International Conference on Communications (ICC)*, (pp. 2393-2397). Beijing, China.

Palankar, M. R., Iamnitchi, A., Ripeanu, M., & Garfinkel, S. (2008). Amazon S3 for science grids: A viable solution? In *Proceedings of the 2008 International Workshop on Data-aware Distributed Computing* (pp. 55-64). ACM.

Paolucci, M., Kawamura, T., Payne, T. R., & Sycara, K. P. (2002). *Semantic matching of web services capabilities.* In International Semantic Web Conference, Sardinia, Italy.

Papazoglou, P., Traverso, P., Dustdar, S., & Leymann, F. (2008). Service-oriented computing: A research roadmap. *International Journal of Cooperative Information Systems, 17*(2), 223–255. doi:10.1142/S0218843008001816

Parhami, B. (1998). *Introduction to parallel processing: Algorithms and architectures.* New York, NY: Plenum Press.

Parhami, B., & Kwai, D.-M. (2001). A unified formulation of honeycomb and diamond networks. *IEEE Transactions on Parallel and Distributed Systems, 12*(1), 74–80. doi:10.1109/71.899940

Park, W., & Bakh, S. (2009). Resource management policies for fixed relays in cellular networks. *Computer Networks, 32*(4), 703–711.

Patterson, D., & Ditzel, D. (1980). The case for the reduced instruction set computer. *ACM SIGARCH Computer Architecture News, 8*(6), 25–33. doi:10.1145/641914.641917

Paurobally, S., & Jennings, N. R. (2005). Protocol engineering for web services conversations. *Engineering Applications of Artificial Intelligence, 18*(2), 237–254. doi:10.1016/j.engappai.2004.12.005

Pautasso, C., Zimmermann, O., & Leymann, F. (2008). Restful web services vs. "big"' web services: Making the right architectural decision. In *International Conference on World Wide Web* (pp. 805-814). ACM Press.

Pautasso, C. (2009). RESTful Web service composition with BPEL for REST. *Data & Knowledge Engineering, 68*(9), 851–866. doi:10.1016/j.datak.2009.02.016

Pazzani, M. J., & Billsus, D. (2007). Content-based recommendation systems. *Lecture Notes in Computer Science: Vol. 4321. The Adaptive Web.* (pp. 325-341). Berlin, Germany: Springer Verlag, doi: doi:10.1007/978-3-540-72079-9_10

Peden, M., Scurfield, R., Sleet, D., Mohan, D., Hyder, A. A., Jarawan, E., & Mathers, C. (2004). *World report on road traffic injury prevention.* Geneva, Switzerland: OMS.

Pellegrini, F. D., Starobinski, D., Karpovsky, M. G., & Levitin, L. B. (2006, February). Scalable, distributed cycle-breaking algorithms for gigabit Ethernet backbones. *Journal of Optical Networks, 5*(2), 122–144. doi:10.1364/JON.5.000122

Pellegrini, F. D., Starobinski, D., Karpovsky, M., & Levitin, L. (2004). Scalable cycle-breaking algorithms for gigabit Ethernet backbones. *Proceedings - IEEE INFOCOM,* 2004.

Peltz, C. (2003). Web services orchestration and choreography. *The Computer Journal, 36*(10), 46–52. doi:10.1109/MC.2003.1236471

Perry, M. L., Sengupta, S., & Krapfel, R. (2004). Effectiveness of horizontal strategic alliances in technologically uncertain environments: Are trust and commitment enough? *Journal of Business Research*, *57*(9), 951–956. doi:10.1016/S0148-2963(02)00501-5

Pifarré, G. D., Gravano, L., Denicolay, G., & Sanz, J. L. C. (1994). Adaptive deadlock-and livelock-free routing in the hypercube network. *IEEE Transactions on Parallel and Distributed Systems*, *5*(11), 1121–1139. doi:10.1109/71.329674

Piórkowski, M., Raya, M., Lugo, A. L., Papadimitratos, P., Grossglauser, M., & Hubaux, J.-P. (2008). Trans: Realistic joint traffic and network simulator for VANETs. *Mobile Computing and Communications Review, 12*(1), 31-33.

Prager, J., Radev, D., Brown, E., Coden, A., & Samn, V. (1999). The use of predictive annotation for question answering in TREC8. In *Proceedings of the 8th Text REtrieval Conference (TREC 8)*, Maryland, United States (pp. 399-410). Gaithersburg, MD: NIST.

Pring, B., Brown, R. H., Frank, A., Hayward, S., & Leong, L. (2009). *Forecast: Sizing the cloud; Understanding the opportunities in cloud services*. Gartner, Inc. Retrieved November 15, 2010, from http://www.lesechos.fr/medias/2009/0519//300350239.pdf

Puhlmann, F. (2006). Why do we actually need the pi-calculus for business process management? In *Proceedings of the International Conference on Business Information Systems* (pp. 77-89).

Qi, B., Biaz, S., Wu, S., & Ji, Y. (2007). An interference-aware routing metric in multi-radio multihop networks. In *Proceedings of the ACM 45th Annual Southeast Regional Conference*, (pp. 549-500). Salem, MA, USA.

Queinnec, C. (2003). Inverting back the inversion of control or, continuations versus page-centric programming. *ACM SIGPLAN Notices*, *38*(2), 57–64. doi:10.1145/772970.772977

Rabanal, P., Mateo, J. A., Rodriguez, I., & Diaz, G. (2011). DIEGO: A tool for deriving choreography-conforming web service systems. *IEEE International Conference on Web Services,* (pp. 187 194).

Rackspace Hosting. (2011). *Planning a move to the cloud tips, tricks and pitfalls*. Diversity. Retrieved April 20, 2011, from http://gcn.com/articles/2011/02/14/federal-Cloud -computing-strategy-released.aspx

Rackspace, U. S. Inc. (2011). *Cloud computing, managed hosting, dedicated server hosting by Rackspace*. Retrieved August 26, 2011, from http://www.rackspace.com/

Radev, D., Fan, W., Qi, H., Wu, H., & Grewal, A. (2002). Probabilistic question answering on the web. In *Proceedings of the 11th International Conference on World Wide Web*, Honolulu, Hawaii (pp. 408-419). New York, NY: ACM.

Raedts, I., Petkovic, M., Usenko, Y. S., van der Werf, J. M. E. M., Groote, J. F., & Somers, L. J. (2007, June 2007). *Transformation of BPMN models for behaviour analysis*. Paper presented at the 5th International Workshop on Modelling, Simulation, Verification and Validation of Enterprise Information Systems (MSVVEIS-2007), in conjunction with ICEIS 2007, Funchal, Madeira, Portugal.

Rahman, S. (2010). *The business of cloud computing*. Retrieved November 15, 2010, from http://www.shibleyrahman.com/business-administration/the-business-of-Cloud -computing.php

Rahwan, T., Ramchurn, S., Jennings, N., & Giovannucci, A. (2009). An anytime algorithm for optimal coalition structure generation. *Journal of Artificial Intelligence Research*, *34*(1), 521–567.

Ramachandran, K., Belding, E. M., Almeroth, K. C., & Buddhikot, M. M. (2006). Interference aware channel assignment in multiradio wireless mesh networks. In *Proceedings of IEEE International Conference on Computer Communications (INFOCOM)*, (pp. 1-12). Barcelona, Spain.

Ramakrishnan, R. (2010). *What is cloud computing? What does it mean to enterprises?* Retrieved June 22, 2011, from http://www.cumulux.com/Cloud %20Computing%20Primer.pdf

Ramanujam, J. (2008). *Toward automatic parallelization and auto-tuning of affine kernels for GPUs*. In Workshop on Automatic Tuning for Petascale Systems.

Rappaport, T. (2002). *Wireless communications: Principles and practice* (2nd ed.). Prentice Hall.

Rebstock, M., Thun, P., & Tafreschi, O. A. (2003). Supporting interactive multi-attribute electronic negotiations with ebXML. *Group Decision and Negotiation, 12*, 269–286. doi:10.1023/A:1024819904305

Recuenco, J. G., & Bueno, D. (2009). Balanced recommenders: A hybrid approach to improve and extend the functionality of traditional recommenders. *Workshop on Adaptation and Personalization for Web 2.0* (pp. 88-98).

Reuther, B., & Henrici, D. (2008). A model for service-oriented communication systems. *Journal of Systems Architecture, 54*, 594–606. doi:10.1016/j.sysarc.2007.12.001

Riezler, S., Vasserman, A., Tsochantaridis, I., Mittal, V., & Liu, Y. (2007). Statistical machine translation for query expansion in answer retrieval. In *Proceedings of the 45th Annual Meeting of the Association for Computational Linguistics* (ACL' 07), (pp. 464–471).

Rocha, B. M., Campos, F. O., Plank, G., dos Santos, R. W., Liebmann, M., & Haase, G. (2009). *Simulations of the electrical activity in the heart with graphic processing units*. In Eighth International Conference on Parallel Processing and Applied Mathematics.

Rodrigues, E. M., & Frayling, N. M. (2009). Socializing or knowledge sharing? Characterizing social intent in community question answering. In D. W. K. Cheung, I. Song, W. W. Chu, X. Hu, & J. Lin (Eds.), *Proceeding of the 18th ACM Conference on Information and Knowledge Management*, Hong Kong, China (pp. 1127-1136). New York, NY: ACM.

Rosenbaum, H., & Shachaf, P. (2010). A structuration approach to online communities of practice: The case of Q & A communities. *Journal of the American Society for Information Science and Technology, 61*(9), 1933–1944. doi:10.1002/asi.21340

Rosenfeld, A. (1984). *Multiresolution image processing and analysis*. Berlin, Germany: Springer. doi:10.1007/978-3-642-51590-3

Rozinat, A., de Medeiros, A., Günther, C., Weijters, A., & van der Aalst, W. (2008). The need for a process mining evaluation framework in research and practice. In ter Hofstede, A., Benatallah, B., & Paik, H.-Y. (Eds.), *Business Process Management Workshops* (*Vol. 4928*, pp. 84–89). Berlin, Germany: Springer. doi:10.1007/978-3-540-78238-4_10

Ruby on Rails. (2011). Retrieved October 2011, from http://rubyonrails.org

Russell, D. (2010). *Weather report: Considerations from migrating to the Cloud*. IBM. Retrieved April 14, 2010, from http://www.ibm.com/developerworks/Cloud/library/cl-wr1migrateappstoCloud /

Russell, R. (2008). Virtio: Towards a de-facto standard for virtual I/O devices. *SIGOPS Operating Systems Review, 42*(5), 95–103. doi:10.1145/1400097.1400108

Russell, S. J., & Norvig, P. (2003). *Artificial intelligence: A modern approach* (3rd ed.). Pearson Education.

Sadiq, S., Orlowska, M., Sadiq, W., & Foulger, C. (2004). *Data flow and validation in workflow modelling*. Paper presented at the 15th Australasian database conference, Dunedin, New Zealand.

Salatge, N., & Fabre, J.-C. (2007). *Fault tolerance connectors for unreliable web services*. In International Conference on Dependable Systems and Networks, Edinburgh, UK.

Salton, G., & McGill, M. J. (1983). *Introduction to modern information retrieval*. New York, NY: McGraw-Hill.

Sancho, J. C., & Robles, A. (2000). *Improving the up*/down* routing scheme for networks of workstations*. European Conference on Parallel Computing (Euro-Par 2000).

Sancho, J. C., Robles, A., Lopez, P., Flich, J., & Duato, J. (2003). Routing in infiniband™ torus network topologies. *International Conference on Parallel Processing*, (p. 509).

Sancho, J. C., Robles, A., & Duato, J. (2004, August). An effective methodology to improve the performance of the up*/down* routing algorithm. *IEEE Transactions on Parallel and Distributed Systems, 15*(8), 740–754. doi:10.1109/TPDS.2004.28

Sancho, J., Robles, A., & Duato, J. (2000). *A flexible routing scheme for networks of workstations* (pp. 260–267). ISHPC. doi:10.1007/3-540-39999-2_23

Saurab, H. (n.d.). *Security issues in cloud computing*. Retrieved August 8, 2011, from http://www.serl.iiit.ac.in/cs6600/saurabh.ppt

Scalable Network Technologies Inc. (2006). *Qualnet*. Retrieved August 1, 2011, from http://www.scalablenetworks.com/products/qualnet/

Schäfer, W., & Wehrheim, H. (2007). *The challenges of building advanced mechatronic systems.* Paper presented at the ICSE, Future of Software Engineering, Washington DC.

Schindele, A. (2009). *logi.CAD Anwendungen in Wasserkraftanlagen.* Paper presented at the Presentation at logi.cals Powerdays, Monheim, Germany.

Schippers, H. (2009). Towards an actor-based concurrent machine model. In *4th Workshop on the Implementation, Compilation, Optimization of Object-Oriented Languages and Programming Systems* (pp. 4-9). ACM Press.

Schmidt-Belz, B., Laamanen, H., Poslad, S., & Zipf, A. (2003). *Location-based mobile tourist services - First user experiences.* International Conference on Information and Communication Technologies in Tourism.

Schmidt-Eisenlohr, F., Torrent-Moreno, M., Mittag, J., & Hartenstein, H. (2007). Simulation platform for inter-vehicle communications and analysis of periodic information exchange. *4th Conference on Wireless On demand Network Systems and Services* (pp. 50-58). IEEE/IFIP. doi: 10.1109/WONS.2007.340475

Schroeder, M. D., Birrell, A. D., Burrows, M., Murray, H., Needham, R. M., Rodeheer, T. L., et al. (1990, April). *Autonet: A high-speed self configuring local area network using point-to-point links* (Tech. Rep. No. SRC Research Report 59). Palo Alto, CA: Digital Equipment Corporation, SRC.

Schwiebert, L. (2001). Deadlock-free oblivious wormhole routing with cyclic dependencies. *IEEE Transactions on Computers, 50*(9), 865–876. doi:10.1109/12.954503

Schwiebert, L., & Jayasimha, D. N. (1996). A necessary and sufficient condition for deadlock-free wormhole routing. *Journal of Parallel and Distributed Computing, 32*(1), 103–117. doi:10.1006/jpdc.1996.0008

Schwitter, R., Mollá, D., Fournier, R., & Hess, M. (2000). Answer extraction towards better evaluations of NLP systems. In E. Brill, E. Charniak, M. Harper, M. Light, E. Riloff, & E. Voorhees (Eds.), *Proceedings of ANLP/NAACL 2000 Workshop on Reading Comprehension Tests as Evaluation for Computer-Based Language Understanding Systems,* Seattle, WA (pp. 20-27). New York, NY: ACM.

Scott, K. (2010). *White paper: The basics of cloud computing.* Retrieved, June 16, 2011, from http://www.akilisystems.com/downloads/BasicsofCloud Computing.pdf

Sebastian, A., Tang, M., Feng, Y., & Looi, M. (2009). Multi-vehicles interaction graph model for cooperative collision warning system. *Intelligent Vehicles Symposium* (pp. 929-934). Washington, DC: IEEE Computer Society. doi: 10.1109/IVS.2009.5164404

Seitz, C. L. (1985, March). *The hypercube communication chip* (Display File 5182:DF:85). California Institute of Technology.

Sertel, O., Kong, J., Shimada, H., Catalyurek, U. V., Saltz, J. H., & Gurcan, M. N. (2009). *Computer-aided prognosis of neuroblastoma on whole-slide images: Classification of stromal development* (pp. 1093–1103). Pattern Recognition, Special Issue on Digital Image Processing and Pattern Recognition Techniques for the Detection of Cancer.

Shachaf, P. (2009). Social reference: Toward a unifying theory. *Library & Information Science Research, 32,* 66–76. doi:10.1016/j.lisr.2009.07.009

Shahrokhi, F., & Matula, D. W. (1990). The maximum concurrent flow problem. *Journal of the ACM, 37*(2), 318–334. doi:10.1145/77600.77620

Sharp, R., Ridgway, R., Iyengar, S., Gulacy, A., Wenzel, P., & de Bruin, A. … Saltz, J. H. (2006). Registration and 3D visualization of large microscopy images. In *Proceedings of the SPIE Annual Medical Imaging Meetings* (pp. 923–934).

Sheng, Q. Z., Yu, J., Maamar, Z., Jiang, W., & Li, X. (2009). Compatibility checking of heterogeneous web service policies using VDM++. In *The Proceedings of the IEEE Workshop on Software and Services Maintenance and Management (SSMM'2009) held in conjunction the 2009 IEEE Congress on Services, Part I* (SERVICES I'2009), Los Angeles, CA, USA, (pp. 821-828).

Shevtekar, A., & Zakrevski, L. (2004). *Hybrid turn-prohibition routing algorithm for the networks of workstations* (pp. 1383–1389). Parallel and Distributed Processing Techniques and Applications.

Shi, Y., Hou, Y. T., Liu, J., & Kompella, S. (2009). How to correctly use the protocol interference model for multihop wireless networks. In *Proceedings of ACM International Symposium on Mobile Ad Hoc Networking and Computing (MobiHoc)*, (pp. 239-248). New Orleans, LA.

Shoham, Y., & Leyton-Brown, K. (2009). *MultiAgent systems: Algorithmic, game-theoretic, and logical foundations*. Cambridge University Press.

Shua, G., Rana, O. F., Avisb, N. J., & Dingfang, C. (2007). Ontology-based semantic matchmaking approach. *Advances in Engineering Software, 38*(1), 59–67. doi:10.1016/j.advengsoft.2006.05.004

Signorini, E., & Hochmuth, P. (2010). *Consumerization of the mobile enterprise*. Retrieved July 24, 2010, from http://na.blackberry.com/eng/ataglance/get_the_facts/Yankee_Consumerization_of_the_Mobile_Enterprise.pdf

Silla, F., Duato, J., Sivasubramaniam, A., & Das, C. R. (1998). Virtual channel multiplexing in networks of workstations with irregular topology. *Proceedings of the International Conference on High Performance Computing*, (pp. 147-154).

Silla, F., & Duato, J. (2000). High-performance routing in networks of workstations with irregular topology. *IEEE Transactions on Parallel and Distributed Systems, 11*(7), 699–719. doi:10.1109/71.877816

Simcock, T., Hillenbrand, S. P., & Thomas, B. H. (2003). Developing a location-based tourist guide application. *Australasian Information Security Workshop* (pp. 177-183).

Sivaram, R., Panda, D., & Stunkel, C. B. (1997). Multicasting in irregular networks with cut-through switches using tree-based multidestination worms. *Proceedings of the 2nd Parallel Computing, Routing and Communication Workshop*, (pp. 35-48).

Skeie, T., Lysne, O., & Theiss, I. (2002). Layered shortest path (LASH) routing in irregular system area networks. In *International Parallel and Distributed Processing Symposium: IPDPS 2002 Workshops* (pp. 162-170). Fort Lauderdale, FL.

Sneiders, E. (2002). Automated question answering using question templates that cover the conceptual model of the database. In B. Andersson, M. Bergholtz, & P. Johannesson (Eds.), *Proceedings of the 6th International Conference on Applications of Natural Language to Information Systems, LNCS 2553,* Stockholm, Sweden (pp. 235–239). Berlin, Germany: Springer.

Solano, P. (2010). *Cloud computing? Concepts and beyond*. Retrieved July 27, 2011, from http://td.revistaitnow.com/bajar.php?a=files/td11/conferencias/93_33-gbm-cloud-computing.pdf

Soldani, D., & Dixit, S. (2008). Wireless relays for broadband access. *IEEE Communications Magazine, 46*(3), 58–66. doi:10.1109/MCOM.2008.4463772

Song, F. YarKhan, A., & Dongarra, J. (2009). Dynamic task scheduling for linear algebra algorithms on distributed-memory multicore systems. In *SC '09: Proceedings of the Conference on High Performance Computing Networking, Storage and Analysis.*

Spínola, M. (2009). *The five characteristics of cloud computing*. Retrieved October 24, 2010, from http://ornot.files.wordpress.com/2009/08/Cloud-computing-paradigm-chart1.jpg

Srihari, R., & Li, W. (1999). Information extraction supported question answering. In *Proceedings of the 8th Text Retrieval Conference (TREC-8)*, Maryland, United States (pp. 185-196). Gaithersburg, MD: NIST.

Staples, G. (2006). Torque resource manager. In *SC '06: Proceedings of the 2006 ACM/IEEE Conference on Supercomputing.*

Starobinski, D., Karpovsky, M., & Zakrevski, L. (2003). Application of network calculus to general topologies using turn prohibition. *IEEE/ACM Transactions on Networking, 11*(3), 411–421. doi:10.1109/TNET.2003.813040

Staten, J. (2008). *Is cloud computing ready for the enterprise?* Forrester Research, Inc. Retrieved November 27, 2010, from http://ceria.dauphine.fr/cours98/CoursBD/doc/Forrester-Cloud-computing-report080307%5B1%5D.pdf

Steele, C. (2011). *Cloud computing business model raises security, maturity concerns.* Retrieved July 27, 2011, from http://searchservervirtualization.techtarget.com/feature/Cloud-computing-business-model-raises-security-maturity-concerns

Steinbach, M., Karypis, G., & Kumar, V. (2000). A comparison of document clustering techniques. In *Proceedings of the 6th ACM International Conference on Knowledge Discovery and Data Mining*, Boston, United States, (pp. 109-111). New York, NY: ACM.

Stibor, L., Zang, Y., & Reumerman, H.-J. (2007). Evaluation of communication distance of broadcast messages in a vehicular ad-hoc network using IEEE 802.11p. *Wireless Communications and Networking Conference* (pp. 254-257). Washington, DC: IEEE Computer Society. doi: 10.1109/WCNC.2007.53

Stojmenovic, I. (1997). Honeycomb networks: Topological properties and communication algorithms. *IEEE Transactions on Parallel and Distributed Systems, 8*(10), 1036–1042. doi:10.1109/71.629486

Subramanian, A. P., Buddhikot, M. M., & Miller, S. (2006). Interference aware routing in multi-radio wireless mesh networks. In *Proceedings of IEEE Workshop in Wireless Mesh Networks (WiMesh)*, (pp. 55-63). Reston, VA.

Sun Microsystems, Inc. (2009). *Introduction to cloud computing architecture*, White Paper, 1st ed.

Sun, K., Cao, Y., Sog, X., Song, Y. I., Wang, X., & Lin, C. Y. (2009). Learning to recommend questions based on user ratings. In D. W. K. Cheung, I. Song, W. W. Chu, X. Hu, & J. Lin (Eds.), *Proceedings of the 18th ACM Conference on Information and Knowledge Management*, Hong Kong, China (pp. 751-758).

Sun, M.-T., Feng, W.-C., Lai, T.-H., Yamada, K., Okada, H., & Fujimura, K. (2000). GPS-based message broadcasting for inter-vehicle communication. *International Conference on Parallel Processing* (pp. 279-286). doi: 10.1109/ICPP.2000.876143

Sun, Y.-M., Yang, C.-H., Chung, Y.-C., & Huang, T.-Y. (2004). An efficient deadlock-free tree-based routing algorithm for irregular wormhole-routed networks based on the turn model. In *ICPP '04: Proceedings of the 2004 International Conference on Parallel Processing* (pp. 343–352). Washington, DC: IEEE Computer Society.

Sundaram, N., Raghunathan, A., & Chakradhar, S. T. (2009). A framework for efficient and scalable execution of domain- specific templates on GPUs. In *IPDPS '09: Proceedings of the 2009 IEEE International Symposium on Parallel & Distributed Processing* (pp. 1–12).

Sundbald, H. (2007). A re-examination of question classification. In *Proceedings of the 16th Nordic Conference on Computational Linguistics,* Tartu, Estonia (pp. 394–397). Association of Computational Linguistics.

Sunindyo, W. D., Moser, T., Winkler, D., & Biffl, S. (2010a, September 1-3). *Foundations for event-based process analysis in heterogeneous software engineering environments.* Paper presented at the Euromicro Conference on Software Engineering and Advanced Applications, Lille, France.

Sunindyo, W. D., Moser, T., Winkler, D., & Biffl, S. (2010b). *A process model discovery approach for enabling model interoperability in signal engineering.* Paper presented at the 1st Workshop on Model Driven Interoperability (MDI), Oslo, Norway.

Suthaputchakun, C., & Ganz, A. (2007). Priority based inter-vehicle communication in vehicular ad-hoc networks using IEEE 802.11e. *65th Vehicular Technology Conference* (pp. 2595-2599). Washington, DC: IEEE Computer Society. doi: 10.1109/VETECS.2007.534

Sycara, K. P. (1998). Multiagent systems. *AI Magazine, 19*(2), 79–92.

Taher, L., El Khatib, H., & Basha, R. (2005). *A framework and QoS matchmaking algorithm for dynamic web services selection.* In International Conference on Innovations in Information Technology, Dubai, UAE.

Takai, M., Martin, J., & Bragodia, R. (2001). Effects of wireless physical layer modeling in mobile ad hoc networks. In *Proceedings of ACM International Symposium on Mobile Ad Hoc Networking and Computing (MobiHoc)*, (pp. 87-94). Long Beach, CA.

Tamura, A., Takamura, H., & Okumura, M. (2005). Classification of multiple-sentence questions. In L. P. Kaelbling & A. Saffiotti (Eds.), *Proceedings of the 2nd International Joint Conference on Natural Language Processing, LNAI 3651,* Scotland, UK (pp. 426–437). Berlin, Germany: Springer.

Tang, J., Xue, G., Chandler, C., & Zhang, W. (2005). Interference-aware routing in multihop wireless networks using directional antennas. *Proceedings of IEEE International Conference on Computer Communications (INFOCOM)*, (pp. 751-760). Miami, FL.

Tang, J., Hincapie, R., Xue, G., Zhang, W., & Bustamente, R. (2010). Fair bandwidth allocation in wireless mesh networks with cognitive radios. *IEEE Transactions on Vehicular Technology*, 59(3), 1487–1496. doi:10.1109/TVT.2009.2038478

Tan, W., Zhang, J., & Foster, I. (2010). Network analysis of scientific workflows: A gateway to reuse. *IEEE Computer*, 43(9), 54–61. doi:10.1109/MC.2010.262

Tassiulas, L., & Sarkar, S. (2005). Maxmin fair scheduling in wireless ad hoc networks. *IEEE Journal on Selected Areas in Communications*, 23(1), 163–173. doi:10.1109/JSAC.2004.837365

TATA. (2011). *Moving from legacy systems to cloud computing*. Tata Communication. Retrieved March 23, 2012, from http://www.tatacommunications.com/downloads/whitepapers/Tata_Communications_Cloud Compuing_WhitePaper_v2.0-web.pdf

Teodoro, G., Fireman, D., Guedes, D., Jr, W. M., & Ferreira, R. (2008). *Achieving multi-level parallelism in filter-labeled stream programming model*. In The 37th International Conference on Parallel Processing (ICPP).

Teodoro, G., Hartley, T. D. R., Catalyurek, U. V., & Ferreira, R. (2010). Run-time optimizations for replicated dataflows on heterogeneous environments. In *Proceedings of the 19th ACM International Symposium on High Performance Distributed Computing* (HPDC).

Teodoro, G., Sachetto, R., Sertel, O., Gurcan, M., & Jr, W. M. Catalyurek, U., & Ferreira, R. (2009). *Coordinating the use of GPU and CPU for improving performance of compute intensive applications*. In IEEE Cluster.

Teo, J.-Y., Ha, Y., & Tham, C.-K. (2008). Interference minimized multipath routing with congestion control in wireless sensor network with high rate streaming. *IEEE Transactions on Mobile Computing*, 7(9), 1124–1137. doi:10.1109/TMC.2008.24

Texas Transportation Institute. (2009). *Urban mobility*. (Report). Retrieved from http://americandreamcoalition.org/highways/mobility_report_2009_wappx.pdf

The Apache Software Foundation. (2011). *Welcome to Apache™ Hadoop™!* Retrieved August 26, 2011, from http://hadoop.apache.org/

The Stratosphere Project. (2011). Welcome to Stratosphere. In *Stratosphere - Above the Clouds*. Retrieved August 26, 2011, from http://www.stratosphere.eu/

Thomas, J., & Harden, A. (2008). *Methods for the thematic synthesis of qualitative research in systematic reviews.* Retrieved September 9, 2009, from http://www.biomedcentral.com/content/pdf/1471-2288-8-45.pdf

Thulasiraman, P., & Shen, X. (2010). Disjoint multipath routing and QoS provisioning under physical interference constraints. In *Proceedings of IEEE Wireless Communications and Networking Conference (WCNC)*, (pp. 1-6). Sydney, Australia.

Thulasiraman, P., Chen, J., & Shen, X. (2010). Max-min fair multipath routing with physical interference constraints for multihop wireless networks. In *Proceedings of IEEE International Conference on Communications (ICC)*, (pp. 1-6). Cape Town, South Africa.

Thulasiraman, P., Ramasubramanian, S., & Krunz, M. (2006). Disjoint multipath routing in dual homing networks using colored trees. In *Proceedings of IEEE Global Communications Conference (GLOBECOM)*, (pp. 1-5). San Francisco, CA.

Thulasiraman, P., Ramasubramanian, S., & Krunz, M. (2007). Disjoint multipath routing to two distinct drains in a multi-drain sensor network. In *Proceedings of IEEE International Conference on Computer Communications (INFOCOM)*, (pp. 643-651). Anchorage, AK.

Thulasiraman, P., Chen, J., & Shen, X. (2011). Multipath routing and max-min fair QoS provisioning under interference constraints in wireless multihop networks. *IEEE Transactions on Parallel and Distributed Systems*, 22(5), 716–728. doi:10.1109/TPDS.2010.145

Tolk, A. (2006). What comes after the Semantic Web - PADS implications for the dynamic web. In *20th Workshop on Principles of Advanced and Distributed Simulation* (pp. 55-62). IEEE Computer Society Press.

Torrent-Moreno, M., & Mittag, J. (2006). Adjusting transmission power and packet generation rate of periodic status information messages in VANETs. *3rd International Workshop on Vehicular Ad Hoc Networks* (pp. 90-91). New York, NY: ACM. doi: 10.1145/1161064.1161081

Torrent-Moreno, M., Corroy, S., Schmidt-Eisenlohr, F., & Hartenstein, H. (2006). IEEE 802.11-based one-hop broadcast communications: Understanding transmission success and failure under different radio propagation environments. *9th International Symposium on Modeling Analysis and Simulation of Wireless and Mobile Systems* (pp. 68-77). New York, NY: ACM. doi: 10.1145/1164717.1164731

Torrent-Moreno, M., Jiang, D., & Hartenstein, H. (2004). Broadcast reception rates and effects of priority access in 802.11-based vehicular ad-hoc networks. *1st International Workshop on Vehicular Ad Hoc Networks* (pp. 10-18). New York, NY: ACM. doi: 10.1145/1023875.1023878

Toshniwal, R., & Agrawal, D. (2004). Tracing the roots of markup languages. *Communications of the ACM, 47*(5), 95–98. doi:10.1145/986213.986218

Troncoso, C., Costa-Montenegro, E., Diaz, C., & Schiffner, S. (2011). On the difficulty of achieving anonymity for vehicle-2-X communication. *Computer Networks, 55*(14), 3199–3210. doi:10.1016/j.comnet.2011.05.004

Tzeng, C. H., Jiang, J. R., & Huang, S. T. (2007). A self-stabilizing (Δ + 4)-edge-coloring algorithm for planar graphs in anonymous uniform systems. *Information Processing Letters, 101*(4), 168–173. doi:10.1016/j.ipl.2006.09.004

Unni, R., & Harmon, R. (2007). Perceived effectiveness of push vs. pull mobile location-based advertising. *Journal of Interactive Advertising, 7*(2).

Valero, V., Cambronero, M. E., Diaz, G., & Macia, H. (2008, May-June). A Petri net approach for the design and analysis of Web Services Choreographies. *Journal of Logic and Algebraic Programming, 78*(5), 9–16.

van der Aalst, W. (1999). Process-oriented architectures for electronic commerce and interorganizational workflow. *Information Systems, 24*(8), 639–671. doi:10.1016/S0306-4379(00)00003-X

van der Aalst, W. M. P. (2005). Business alignment: Using process mining as a tool for delta analysis and conformance testing. *RE Journal, 10*(3), 198–211.

Varia, J. (2010). *Migrating your existing applications to the AWS cloud: - A phase-driven approach to cloud migration.* Amazon Web Service. Retrieved June 26, 2012, from http://media.amazonwebservices.com/CloudMigration-main.pdf

Vieira, M., & Laranjeiro, N. (2007). *Comparing web services performance and recovery in the presence of faults.* In International Conference on Web Services, Salt Lake City, USA.

Virtual Cloud. (2011). *Cloud computing – What does it mean to system administrators?* Retrieved July 27, 2011, from http://virtcloud.blogspot.com/2011/07/cloud-computing-what-does-it-mean-to.html

VMware. (2009). *VMware unveils the industry's first operating system for building the internal cloud — VMware vSphere™4.* Retrieved August 2, 2011, from http://www.vmware.com/company/news/releases/vsphere-launch.html

VMware. (2011). *VMware and your cloud - Maximize IT agility to drive business agility.* Retrieved August 2, 2011, from http://www.vmware.com/files/pdf/cloud/VMware-and-Cloud-Computing-BR-EN.pdf

Voorhees, E. M. (2003). Overview of the TREC 2003 question answering track. In *Proceedings of 12th Text Retrieval Conference,* Maryland, United States (pp. 54). Gaithersburg, MD: NIST.

Voulodimos, A., & Patrikakis, C. (2008). Using personalized mashups for mobile location based services. *International Conference on Wireless Communications and Mobile Computing* (pp. 321-325). doi: 10.1109/IWCMC.2008.56

Vozalis, M. G., & Margaritis, K. G. (2005). Applying SVD on Item-based filtering. *International Conference on Intelligent Systems Design and Applications* (pp. 464-469).

Vozalis, M. G., & Margaritis, K. G. (2008). Identifying the effects of SVD and demographic data use on generalized collaborative filtering. *International Journal of Computer Mathematics, 85*(12), 1741–1763. doi:10.1080/00207160701598438

W3C. (2001, March). *Web services description language (WSDL) 1.1.* Retrieved from http://www.w3.org/TR/wsdl

W3C. (2007, April). *SOAP version 1.2 part 1: Messaging framework* (2nd ed.). Retrieved from http://www.w3.org/TR/soap12-part1/

Walke, B. H., Mangold, S., & Berlemann, L. (2006). *IEEE 802 Wireless systems: Protocols, multi-hop mesh/relaying, performance and spectrum coexistence.* West Sussex, UK: John Wiley. doi:10.1002/9780470058800

Wang, C. D., & Thompson, P. J. (1997). *U.S. Patent No. 5,613,039: Apparatus and method for motion detection and tracking of objects in a region for colision avoidance utilizing a real-time adaptive probabilistic neural network.* Washington, DC: U.S. Patent and Trademark Office.

Wang, K., Ming, Z., & Chua, T. S. (2009). A syntactic tree matching approach to finding similar questions in community-based qa services. In J. Allan, J. A. Aslam, M. Sanderson, C. X. Zhai, & J. Zobel (Eds.), *Proceedings of the 32nd International ACM Conference on Research and Development in Information Retrieval,* Massachusetts, United States (pp. 187-194). New York, NY: ACM.

Wang, F. Y., & Carley, K., M., Zeng, D., & Mao, W. (2007). Social computing: From social informatics to social intelligence. *IEEE Intelligent Systems, 22*(2), 79–83. doi:10.1109/MIS.2007.41

Wang, P., Jiang, H., Zhuang, W., & Poor, H. V. (2008). Redefinition of max-min fairness in multi-hop wireless networks. *IEEE Transactions on Wireless Communications, 7*(12), 4786–4791. doi:10.1109/T-WC.2008.070804

Warneke, D., & Kao, O. (2009). Nephele: Efficient parallel data processing in the cloud. In I. Raicu, I. T. Foster, & Y. Zhou (Eds.), *Proceedings of the 2nd Workshop on Many-Task Computing on Grids and Supercomputers* (pp. 1-10). ACM.

Warneke, D., & Kao, O. (2011). Exploiting dynamic resource allocation for efficient parallel data processing in the cloud. *IEEE Transactions on Parallel and Distributed Systems, 22*(6), 985–997. doi:10.1109/TPDS.2011.65

Watters, A. (2010). *Architects of Amazon web services launch Nimbula, promise an OS for the cloud.* Retrieved August 3, 2011, from http://www.readwriteweb.com/cloud/2010/06/former-aws-execs-launch-nimbula.php

Weigand, H., de Moor, A., Schoop, M., & Dignum, F. (2003). B2B negotiation support: The need for a communication perspective. *Group Decision and Negotiation, 12,* 3–29. doi:10.1023/A:1022294708789

Wellens, M., Westphal, B., & Mahonen, P. (2007). Performance evaluation of IEEE 802.11-based WLANs in vehicular scenarios. *65th Vehicular Technology Conference* (pp. 1167-1171). Washington, DC: IEEE Computer Society. doi: 10.1109/VETECS.2007.247

Wen, J., Nie, J., & Zhang, H. (2002). Query clustering using user logs. *ACM Transactions on Information Systems, 20*(1), 59–81. doi:10.1145/503104.503108

Wen, Y.-F., & Lin, Y.-S. (2007). Fair bandwidth allocation and end to end delay routing algorithms for wireless mesh networks. *IEICE Transactions on Communications, 90-B*(5), 1042–1051. doi:10.1093/ietcom/e90-b.5.1042

Wilensky, U. (2007). *NetLogo: Center for connected learning and computer-based modeling.* Evanston, IL: Northwestern University. Retrieved from http://ccl.northwestern.edu/netlogo

Wilensky, U., & Stroup, W. (2002). *NetLogo HubNet gridlock model.* Evanston, IL: NetLogo: Center for connected Learning and Computer-Based Modeling, Northwestern University. Retrieved from http://ccl.northwestern.edu/netlogo/models/HubNetGridlock

Winans, T. B., & Brown, J. S. (2010). *Cloud computing - A collection of working papers.* Retrieved June 6, 2010, from http://www.deloitte.com/assets/Dcom-UnitedStates/Local%20Assets/Documents/us_tmt_ce_CloudPapers_73009.pdf

Winkler, D., Moser, T., Mordinyi, R., Sunindyo, W. D., & Biffl, S. (2011, 27 - 29 June). *Engineering object change management process observation in distributed automation systems projects.* Paper presented at the 18th European System and Software Process Improvement and Innovation (EuroSPI 2011) Roskilde University, Denmark.

Wischhof, L., Ebner, A., & Rohling, H. (2005). Information dissemination in selforganizing intervehicle networks. *IEEE Transactions on Intelligent Transportation Systems, 6*(1), 90–101. doi:10.1109/TITS.2004.842407

Wooldridge, M., & Jennings, N. R. (1995). Intelligent agents: Theory and practice. *The Knowledge Engineering Review, 10*(2), 115–152. doi:10.1017/S0269888900008122

Wu, Q., Iyengar, A., Subramanian, R., Rouvellou, I., Silva-Lepe, I., & Mikalsen, T. (2009). Combining quality of service and social information for ranking services. In *Proceedings of ServiceWave 2009 Workshops held in conjunction with the 7th International Conference on Service Service-Oriented Computing* (ICSOC'2009), Stockholm, Sweden, (pp. 561-575).

Wuu, L. C., & Huang, S. T. (1995). Distributed self-stabilizing systems. *Journal of Information Science and Engineering, 11*, 307–319.

Xie, X., Du, B., & Zhang, Z. (2008). Semantic service composition based on social network. In *Proceedings of the Demo Session of the 17th International World Wide Web Conference* (WWW'2008), Beijing, China, (pp. 1-5).

Xu, K., Gerla, M., & Bae, S. (2002). How effective is the IEEE 802.11 RTS/CTS handshake in ad hoc networks? *Global Telecommunications Conference* (pp. 72-76). Washington, DC: IEEE Computer Society. doi: 10.1109/GLOCOM.2002.1188044

Xu, X., Zhu, L., Liu, Y., & Staples, M. (2008). Resource-oriented architecture for business processes. In *Software Engineering Conference* (pp. 395-402). IEEE Computer Society Press.

Xu, Z., Huang, C., & Cheng, Y. (2008). Interference-aware QoS routing in wireless mesh networks. In *Proceedings of 4th International Conference on Mobile Ad-Hoc and Sensor Networks*, (pp. 95-98). Wuhan, China.

Xue, X., Jeon, J., & Croft, W. B. (2008). Retrieval models for question and answer archives. In S. H. Myaeng, D. W. Oard, F. Sebastiani, T. S. Chua, & M. K. Leong (Eds.), *Proceedings of the 32nd International ACM SIGIR Conference on Research and Development in Information Retrieval*, Singapore (pp. 475-482). New York, NY: ACM.

Xu, X., Zhu, L., Kannengiesser, U., & Liu, Y. (2010). An architectural style for process-intensive web information systems. In *Web Information Systems Engineering* (Vol. 6488, pp. 534–547). Lecture Notes in Computer Science-Berlin, Germany: Springer-Verlag. doi:10.1007/978-3-642-17616-6_47

Yang, H., Zhao, X., Qiu, Z., Pu, G., & Wang, S. (2006). A formal model for web service choreography description language (WS-CDL). In *ICWS '06: Proceedings of the IEEE International Conference on Web Services* (pp. 893–894). Washington, DC: IEEE Computer Society.

Yang, H.-C., Dasdan, A., Hsiao, R.-L., & Parker, D. S. (2007). Map-Reduce-Merge: Simplified relational data processing on large clusters. In C. Y. Chan, B. C. Ooi, & A. Zhou (Eds.), *Proceedings of the ACM SIGMOD International Conference on Management of Data* (pp. 1029-1040). ACM.

Yang, X., Liu, L., Vaidya, N., & Zhao, F. (2004). A vehicle-to-vehicle communication protocol for cooperative collision warning. *1st International Conference on Mobile and Ubiquitous Systems: Networking and Services* (pp. 114-123). doi: 10.1109/MOBIQ.2004.1331717

Yang, Y., Wang, J., & Kravets, R. (2005). Designing routing metrics for mesh networks. In *Proceedings of IEEE Workshop in Wireless Mesh Networks (WiMesh).* Santa Clara, CA.

Yeung, W. L. (2008). A formal basis for cross-checking EbXML BPSS choreography and web service orchestration. In *Proceedings of the Third Asia Pacific Services Computing Conference,* December 2008, Yilan, Taiwan.

Yoo, T., Jeong, B., & Cho, H. (2010). A Petri nets based functional validation for services composition. *Expert Systems with Applications, 37*(5), 3768–3776. doi:10.1016/j.eswa.2009.11.046

Yousefi, S., Mousavi, M. S., & Fathy, M. (2006). Vehicular ad hoc networks (VANETs): Challenges and perspectives. *6th International Conference on ITS Telecommunications* (pp. 761-766). doi: 10.1109/ITST.2006.289012

Yu, S., & Cho, G. (2006). A selective flooding method for propagating emergency messages in vehicle safety communications. *International Conference on Hybrid Information Technology* (pp. 556-561). doi: 10.1109/ICHIT.2006.253661

Zaki, M. J., Parthasarathy, S., Ogihara, M., & Li, W. (1997). New algorithms for fast discovery of association rules. In *3rd International Conference on Knowledge Discovery and Data Mining* (pp. 283– 296).

Zakrevski, L. (2000). *Fault-tolerant wormhole message routing in computer communication networks*. Doctoral dissertation, Boston University, College of Electrical Engineering.

Zakrevski, L., Jaiswal, S., & Karpovsky, M. (1999). Unicast message routing in communication networks with irregular topologies. *Proceeding of Computer Aided Design* (CAD-99).

Zakrevski, L., Jaiswal, S., Levitin, L., & Karpovsky, M. (1999). A new method for deadlock elimination in computer networks with irregular topologies. *Proceedings of the International Association of Science and Technology for Development (IASTED) Conference, Parallel and Distributed Computing Systems* (PDCS-99), Vol. 1, (pp. 396-402).

Zakrevski, L., Mustafa, M., & Karpovsky, M. (2000). Turn prohibition based routing in irregular computer networks. *Proceedings of the IASTED International Conference on Parallel and Distributed Computing and Systems,* (pp. 175-179).

Zeng, X., Bagrodia, R., & Gerla, M. (1998). Glomosim: A library for parallel simulation of large-scale wireless networks. *12ᵗʰ Workshop on Parallel and Distributed Simulation* (pp. 154–161). Washington, DC: IEEE Computer Society. doi: 10.1145/278008.278027

Zhang, J., Li, F., & Chi, C. (2008). On web service construction based on representation state transfer. In *International Conference on e-Business Engineering* (pp. 665-668). IEEE Computer Society Press.

Zhao, J. L., & Cheng, H. K. (2005). Web services and process management: A union of convenience or a new area of research? *Decision Support Systems, 40,* 1–8. doi:10.1016/j.dss.2004.04.002

Zheng, Z. (2002). AnswerBus question answering system. In *Proceedings of the 2nd International Conference on Human Language Technology Research*, California, United States (pp. 399-404). New York, NY: ACM.

Zhong, S., & Ghosh, J. (2003). A unified framework for model-based clustering. *Journal of Machine Learning Research, 4,* 1001–1037.

Zhou, J., Lin, X.-Y., & Chung, Y.-C. (2006). A tree-turn model for irregular networks. In *NCA '06: Proceedings of the Fifth IEEE International Symposium on Network Computing and Applications* (pp. 11–18). Washington, DC: IEEE Computer Society.

Zhou, J., & Mitchell, K. (2010). A scalable delay based analytical framework for CSMA/CA wireless mesh networks. *Computer Networks, 54*(2), 304–318. doi:10.1016/j.comnet.2009.05.013

Zou, J., Mei, J., & Wang, Y. (2010). From representational state transfer to accountable state transfer architecture. In *International Conference on Web Services* (pp. 299-306). IEEE Computer Society Press.

Zyp, K. (Ed.). (2010). *A JSON media type for describing the structure and meaning of JSON documents*. Internet Engineering Task Force. Retrieved August 26, 2011, from http://tools.ietf.org/html/draft-zyp-json-schema-03

About the Contributors

Alfred Loo is at the Department of Computing and Decision Sciences, Lingnan University in Hong Kong. Before he became an academic, Alfred had more than 10 years working experience in developing, maintaining and managing computer systems for shipping companies, factories, banks, and various commercial firms. He is the author of 29 books and has published over a hundred articles in journals, proceedings, book chapters, newspapers, and trade magazines. He is a Chartered Scientist (CSci), Chartered Engineer (CEng), Chartered Mathematician (CMath) and Chartered Information Technology Professional (CITP) of the United Kingdom. His research interests are in the areas of distributed computing, wireless security, and peer-to-peer systems.

* * *

Jamal Bentahar is an Associate Professor at Concordia Institute for Information Systems Engineering, Concordia University, Canada and Adjunct Professor at the Department of Computer Science and Software Engineering, Laval University, Canada. Before joining Concordia University in 2006, he was postdoctoral fellow at the School of Computing Science, Simon Fraser University, Canada. His research interests include multi-agent systems, service computing, computational logics, model checking, and digital trust and reputation. He received his Ph.D. in Computer Science and Software Engineering from Laval University, Canada and he is a Professional Engineer in Ontario, Canada. He has received many research grants and graduated many Master and Ph.D. students.

Stefan Biffl is an Associate Professor of Software Engineering at the Institute of Software Technology and Interactive Systems, TU Vienna (http://qse.ifs.tuwien.ac.at/~biffl). He received MS and PhD degrees in computer science from TU Vienna and an MS degree in social and economic sciences from the University of Vienna in 2001. He received an Erwin-Schrödinger research scholarship and spent one year as researcher at the Fraunhofer IESE, focusing on quality management and empirical software engineering. Also, in 2001 he received the Habilitation degree Venia Docendi for his work on empirical software engineering in project management and quality management. In 2006 he worked as guest researcher at Czech Technical University, Department of Cybernetics. Since 2010 Stefan Biffl is the head of the Christian Doppler research laboratory "CDL-Flex" (http://cdl.ifs.tuwien.ac.at).

Juan C. Burguillo is an Associate Professor in the Department of Telematic Engineering at the University of Vigo (Spain). His research interests include intelligent agents, multi-agent systems, evolutionary algorithms, game theory, and telematic services. Burguillo has a PhD in Telematics Engineering from the University of Vigo.

Chaka Chaka is a Senior Lecturer in the Department of Applied Languages at Tshwane University of Technology (Gauteng, South Africa). His research interests include: computer mediated communication (CMC); electronic learning (e-learning); computer assisted language learning (CALL); mobile learning (m-learning); mobile assisted language learning (MALL); online genre and discourse analysis; Web 2.0 learning/Mobile Web 2.0 learning; Web 3.0/Mobile Web 3.0; Semantic Web/Mobile Semantic Web; social computing; cloud and virtual computing; knowledge management (KM); and learning organization (LO). His latest book chapter and journal article in the field of social computing are social computing: harnessing enterprise social networking and the relationship economy and Consumerization of IT, social computing, and mobility as the new desktop (Cutter IT Journal, 225(5), 2012), respectively.

José C. Delgado is an Associate Professor at the Computer Science and Engineering Department of the Instituto Superior Técnico (Lisbon Technical University), in Lisbon, Portugal, where he earned the Ph.D. degree in 1988. He lectures courses in the areas of Computer Architecture, Information Technology, and Service Engineering. He has performed several management roles in his faculty, namely Director of the Taguspark campus, near Lisbon, and Coordinator of the B.Sc. and M.Sc. in Computer Science and Engineering at that campus. He has been the coordinator of and researcher in several research projects, both national and European. As an author, his publications include one book, several book chapters and more than 40 papers in international refereed conferences and journals.

Noura Faci is an Associate Professor at the University Lyon 1, France since October 2008. Her research interests or themes are fault tolerance in multi-agent systems, dependable e-business systems, and service computing. Prior Noura was a Research Associate at King's College London in Agents and Intelligent Systems Group where she led a work package as part of a European IT Research Project entitled "CONTRACT". She graduated for her PhD in Computer Sciences from Reims University in France in 2007. She contributes in the review process of several international conferences (e.g., ICSOC, AAMAS) and journals (e.g., ACM TOIT, IEEE TSC).

Salahdine Hachimi is an Information Systems Consultant at Capgemini in Lyon. He has had the opportunity to participate in a variety of workshops and seminars throughout his academic and professional career. Mr. Hachimi has both a Master of Science in Information Technology and Web, and an International Master in Information Systems from INSA Lyon. He also graduated from Al Akhawayn University in Ifrane with an Honors Bachelor of Science in Computer Science. Through his experience and education, Mr. Hachimi has oriented his research interests towards service-oriented computing during his Master's thesis, and policy based management and ubiquitous computing during his Bachelor.

Rosiah Ho has had over 25 years of working experience in both industry and higher education sector of HKSAR. Dr. Ho is now working in the Lingnan University (LU) as the Associate Director since 1994. He has taken up responsibility and leadership in overseeing the technical support, system and networking support, AV/multimedia support, PC support, and user services support teams during his employment in the university to render timely, quality, and cost-effective professional IT services and trainings to both academic, administrative, students, and researchers of the university. He has been the main architect to plan, design, and implement the first phase of the University IT/IS communication & application infrastructure. He was also the representative of University in various internal and external committees and task forces. Prior to his academic career in Lingnan, Dr. Ho worked in the industrial sector as a professional IT Consultant and Project Manager in HK Telecom and Datacraft (HK) Ltd. specialized in the field of multi-dimensional and multi-national large scale systems integration for many famous worldwide projects like:- The corporate network for Motorola (Beijing & Tianjin), American Express (New Deli & Bombay), Hang Seng Bank, ShunTak Shipping, Mass Transit Railway Corporation, China Light & Power, Universities of HK, and the Pamela Youde Hospital, et cetera.

Shing-Tsaan Huang received his Ph. D. degree in Computer Science in 1985 from University of Maryland at College Park. He joined National Tsing-Hua University at Taiwan in 1985 and then National Central University at Taiwan in 1998. He was serving as Vice President at National Central University from May 2003 to January 2006. Dr. Huang was elected as a Fellow of IEEE in 2002 for contributions to parallel and distributed computing. His research interests are mainly in parallel and distributed computing and self-stabilizing systems.

Jehn-Ruey Jiang received his Ph. D. degree in Computer Science in 1995 from National Tsing-Hua University, Taiwan, R.O.C. He joined Chung-Yuan Christian University as an Associate Professor in 1995. He joined Hsuan-Chuang University in 1998 and became a full Professor in 2004. He is currently with the Department of Computer Science and Information Engineering, National Central University. He was Guest Editors of *International Journal of Ad Hoc and Ubiquitous Computing* (IJAHUC) and *Journal of Information Science and Engineering* (JISE). His research interests include distributed algorithms, self-stabilizing algorithms, mobile ad hoc networks, and wireless sensor networks.

Blooma Mohan John is a Lecturer at RMIT International University, Vietnam. She completed her PhD from Nanyang Technological University (NTU), Singapore in 2011. Her research interest is in the area of social media, text mining, and digital libraries. She completed her Master of Science in Information Studies from NTU, Singapore and Bachelor of Engineering in Electronics and Communication Engineering from Bharathiyar University, India. She is serving as the Treasurer of Vietnam Association of Information Systems. Blooma participated in the Google Summer of Code 2008 program.

M. Karpovsky has been Professor of Computer Engineering and Director of Reliable Computing Laboratory at the Department of Electrical and Computer Engineering, Boston University, Boston since 1983. He has been conducting research in the areas of design, testing and diagnosis of computer communication networks, combining on-line and off-line techniques for error detection and location, and fault-tolerant message routing for multiprocessors and networks of workstations. His current research interests are in error detecting codes for reliable and secure communications and computations and in design of computer hardware, smart cards, and cryptographic devices resistant to attacks. He teaches graduate courses on testing of computer hardware, fault-tolerant computing, error correcting codes, computer networks, and design of reliable and secure digital devices. He was consultant for IBM, Digital Corporation, Honeywell Corporation, AT&T, Raytheon, and several companies in Europe. He has published more than 200 papers and several books. Dr. Karpovsky is a Fellow of IEEE.

Jayan Chirayath Kurian is a Lecture at RMIT International University, Vietnam. He is also pursuing his PhD at the Royal Melbourne Institute of Technology, Australia. He has worked at National University of Singapore, Nanyang Technological University, Singapore, Modern College of Business and Science, Oman, and Ngee Ann Polytechnic, Singapore. He holds several professional certifications from Microsoft, Sun Microsystems, Oracle, CompTIA, and Prosoft. He holds a Master's in Computer Application from Madurai Kamaraj University, India and his recent Mphil is from The University of Nottingham. His current research interest is on emerging web technologies and social media.

Lev B. Levitin received the M.S. degree in physics from Moscow University, USSR, in 1960 and the Ph.D. degree from the USSR Academy of Sciences in 1969. He worked at the Institute of Information Transmission Problems from 1961 to 1973, and taught at Tel Aviv University, Israel, from 1974 to 1980. During 1980-1982, he was with the Heinrich-Hertz Institute, Berlin, at Bielefeld University, Germany, and at Syracuse University, NY. Since 1982, he has been with the College of Engineering, Boston University, and since 1986 has been Distinguished Professor of Engineering Science. He has published over 180 papers and patents. His research areas include physical information theory, quantum communication systems; physics of computation; quantum computing; mathematical linguistics; theory of complex systems; coding theory; computer hardware testing; reliable computer networks; and bioinformatics. He is a Life Fellow of IEEE, a member of the International Academy of Informatics and other professional societies.

Zakaria Maamar is a Professor in the College of Information Technology at Zayed University in Dubai. His research interests are primarily related to service computing and enterprise application interoperability. He graduated with his M.Sc. and Ph.D. in Computer Sciences from Laval University in Canada in 1995 and 1998, respectively. In 2009, he received an IBM Faculty Award to conduct research on social networks.

Ana Belén Barragáns-Martínez is an Associate Professor at the Centro Universitario de la Defensa en la Escuela Naval Militar de Marín (Pontevedra. Spain). Her research interests include recommendation algorithms, using social networks, and Web 2.0 technologies. She has a PhD in Computer Science from the University of Vigo. She's a member of IEEE, the IEEE Consumer Electronics Society, the ACM, and ACM SIGSOFT.

Enrique Costa-Montenegro is an Associate Professor in the Department of Telematic Engineering at the University of Vigo (Spain). His research interests include wireless networks, car-to-car communication technologies, multi-agent systems, and recommendation technologies. Costa-Montenegro received a PhD in telecommunication engineering from the University of Vigo.

Richard Mordinyi received his Master's and PhD degrees in Computer Science at the Vienna University of Technology and works as a post-doctoral researcher in the research area "technical integration & security" in the Christian Doppler Laboratory Software Engineering Integration for Flexible Automation Systems since 2010. His main research areas are secure coordination strategies in complex distributed systems, agile software architectures, and model-driven configuration of technical platforms.

Thomas Moser is a post-doctoral researcher at the Institute of Software Technology and Interactive Systems, Vienna University of Technology. He received his MSc and PhD degrees in business informatics from the Vienna University of Technology in 2006 and 2010, respectively, and works in the research area "semantic integration" in the CDL-Flex since 2010. His main research areas are data and knowledge modeling, as well as practical and business applications of Semantic Web technologies.

Mehmet Mustafa received the BS degree in Physics from the Middle East Technical University (METU), Ankara, Turkey, in 1972; the MS degree in Electrical and Systems Engineering from Rensselaer Polytechnic Institute (RPI), Troy, New York, in 1978; and the MS degree in Computer Science and the PhD degree in Computer Engineering from Boston University in 1997 and 2006, respectively. He was employed at GTE Laboratories, Inc., in 1979 as a member of Technical Staff and became a senior principal member of Technical Staff in 1999. He has worked at Verizon Laboratories till his retirement in 2006. He has taken up some consulting activities until he joined MIT Lincoln Laboratory in Lexington, Massachusetts, in 2008. He has been a visiting scholar at Boston University, participating in research in computer communication networks and conducting research at MIT Lincoln Laboratory. He has a handful of published papers and six patents. He is a member of the IEEE.

Ana M. Peleteiro is a PhD student in the Department of Telematics at the University of Vigo (Spain). Her research interests include intelligent agents, multi-agent systems, self-organization, evolutionary algorithms, and game theory. Peleteiro has an MSc in Telecommunications Engineering and an MSc in Telematics Engineering from the University of Vigo.

Wikan Danar Sunindyo is an associated researcher at the Christian Doppler Laboratory for "Software Engineering Integration for Flexible Automation Systems" (CDL-Flex). He received his Master's degree in computational logic at the Dresden University of Technology, Germany in 2007. Since 2008 he works as a PhD researcher at TU Vienna, Austria in the research area "Complex Systems". His main research areas include Open Source Software, automation systems, process observation and analysis, and Semantic Web technologies to better integrate heterogeneous engineering environments.

George Teodoro is currently a Postdoc at Emory University in the Center for Comprehensive Informatics. His research interests include runtime systems for data-intensive computing, execution dataflow computing in modern parallel environments, efficient execution of dataflows under online variable demands, and auto-tuning for scientific applications. He received his PhD, MS, and BS in Computer Science from Universidade Federal de Minas Gerais, Brazil, in 2010, 2006, and 2004, respectively.

Philippe Thiran is Senior Cloud Architect and Project Manager at Sirris, the collective centre of the Belgian technology industry. He is also a part-time full Professor of Computer Science at the University of Namur, Belgium. His interests cover Web technologies, SOA and SaaS. He has co-authored over 70 peer-reviewed scientific papers. Previously, Philippe studied Geography (University of Louvain - Belgium and University of Rennes - France), Computer Science (University of Namur), got his Ph.D. in Computer Science with a thesis on autonomous database interoperability. In 2003, he was a guest Professor at the University of Lyon, France. From 2003 to 2005, he was an Assistant Professor at the Mathematics & Computer Science Department of the Eindhoven University of Technology, The Netherlands.

Preetha Thulasiraman has been an Assistant Professor in the Department of Electrical and Computer Engineering at the Naval Postgraduate School, Monterey, California, USA since January 2011. She received her PhD degree from the Electrical and Computer Engineering Department at the University of Waterloo, Waterloo, Ontario, Canada in September 2010, the M.Sc. degree in Computer Engineering from the University of Arizona, USA in 2006 and the B.Sc. degree in Electrical Engineering from the University of Illinois, Urbana-Champaign, USA in 2004. Since 2005 she has been involved in wireless networking research, studying various algorithmic and protocol design issues for wireless mobile ad hoc networks, mesh, and sensor networks. Her current research interests include cross layer design of resource allocation algorithms, interference management, routing and fault tolerance, and general applications of graph theory/network science. She is currently pursuing interests in network management of unmanned ground systems and cyber security of cyber physical systems with an emphasis on quality of service provisioning, mobility management and performance evaluation. She has been an active IEEE and ACM member since 2006, being on the technical program committees of several IEEE and ACM sponsored conferences as well as an editorial board member of the *International Journal on Wireless Sensor Networks*. She is the prime author of several journal and conference publications.

Chi-Hung Tzeng received his M. S. and Ph. D. degrees in Computer Science from National Tsing-Hua University, Hsinchu, Taiwan, in 2009. He is currently a Research Engineer at MStar Semiconductor, Inc. He is responsible for designing high-performance yet resource-constraint embedded systems by using combinatorial optimization and compiler technologies. His research interests are in graph theory, distributed computing, and performance analysis and improvement on embedded systems.

Javier Vales-Alonso holds an Engineer degree in Telecommunications, Telematics speciality (Universidade de Vigo, Spain 2000) and a PhD in Telecommunications (Universidad Polítecnica de Cartagena-UPCT, Spain 2005). Since 2003 he is an Associate Professor at the Technical School of Telecommunications of the UPCT. Since 2008 he has tenure at the UPCT. His main research interests are wireless communications systems, including cellular communications, wireless sensor networks (WSN), RFID, and development of services and contextual applications in the field of ambient intelligence. He has authored over 25 publications in prestigious journals and over 40 international conference papers.

Daniel Warneke is a Postdoctoral Researcher at the Complex and Distributed IT Systems Group of Technische Universität Berlin in Berlin, Germany. In 2011, he received his Ph.D. for this work on massively-parallel data processing on infrastructure as a service platform. Before that, he earned his Diploma and BS degrees in Computer Science from the University of Paderborn in 2008 and 2006, respectively. Daniel's research interests center around large-scale data processing on shared-nothing architectures, cloud computing, and resource management. In addition, he has also conducted research in the area of (wireless) computer networks. Currently, Daniel is working in the DFG-funded research project Stratosphere.

Dietmar Winkler is working as Researcher and Lecturer at the Christian Doppler Laboratory for "Software Engineering Integration for Flexible Automation Systems" (CDL-Flex) and the Institute of Software Technology and Interactive Systems at the TU Vienna. In 2003 he received an MS in Computer Science from TU Vienna, Austria. He worked as a guest Researcher at the Czech Technical University, Department of Cybernetics in 2007 and received a PhD research scholarship at Fraunhofer IESE in Kaiserslautern, Germany, in 2008. Since 2010 he is researcher for quality management and software process improvement at the CDL-Flex at TU Vienna. Moreover, he is working as software engineering and process and quality management consultant in software and systems engineering industry. His research interests include software engineering, engineering processes, quality management, and empirical software engineering.

W L Yeung is an Assistant Professor in the Department of Computing and Decision Sciences at Lingnan University, Hong Kong. He received his MSc and PhD in Computer Science in the United Kingdom. His research interests include business processing modelling, web services, and multi-agent systems. He has published research articles in *Information & Management, Journal of Systems and Software, Science of Computer Programming, Information Software & Technology, Expert Systems and Applications,* and *International Journal of Production Research.* He is a member of the British Computer Society, Association of Computing Machinery, and the IEEE Computer Society.

Index

W

Warning Message Dissemination (WMD) 246
Web 2.0 application 253, 255-256, 259, 261-262
Web of Documents 111, 113-114, 122
Web of Services 110-114, 122, 129, 131
Web Service Business Process Execution Language
    (WSBPEL) 136, 150

Web Services Conversations Language (WSCL)
    136, 138, 150
Weighted Cumulative ETT (WCETT) 24
Wireless Access Vehicular Environment (WAVE)
    236
wireless multihop networks 18-19, 43
workflow validation 284-287, 291, 294, 298